Tourism
and Economic
Development

Tourism and Economic Development

European Experiences

Third Edition

Edited by
Allan M. Williams and Gareth Shaw
University of Exeter, UK

JOHN WILEY & SONS
Chichester • New York • Weinheim • Brisbane • Singapore • Toronto

Other Wiley Editorial Offices

John Wiley & Sons, Inc., 605 Third Avenue,
New York, NY 10158-0012, USA

WILEY-VCH Verlag GmbH, Pappelallee 3,
D-69469 Weinheim, Germany

Jacaranda Wiley Ltd, 33 Park Road, Milton,
Queensland 4064, Australia

John Wiley & Sons (Canada) Ltd, 22 Worcester Road,
Rexdale, Ontario M9W 1L1, Canada

John Wiley & Sons (Asia) Pte Ltd, 2 Clementi Loop #02-01,
Jin Xing Distripark, Singapore 129809

Library of Congress Cataloging-in-Publication Data

Tourism and economic development : European experiences / Allan M.
  Williams and Gareth Shaw [editors]. — 3rd ed.
      p. cm.
  Includes bibliographical references and index.
  ISBN 0-471-98316-0 (cloth)
    1. Tourist trade—Europe. I. Williams, Allan M.   II. Shaw,
  Gareth.
  G155.E8T675 1998
  338.4'7914—dc21   98–22511
                                                             CIP

British Library Cataloguing in Publication Data

A catalogue record for this book is available from the British Library

ISBN 0-471-98316-0

Typeset in 10½/11pt Bembo by Mayhew Typesetting, Rhayader, Powys.
Printed and bound in Great Britain by Biddles Ltd, Guildford and King's Lynn.
This book is printed on acid-free paper responsibly manufactured from sustainable forestry, in which at least two trees are planted for each one used for paper production.

Contents

List of contributors

Tommy Andersson	Bodo Graduate School of Business, Norway
Andrew Gilg	Department of Geography, University of Exeter, UK
Desmond A. Gillmor	Department of Geography, Trinity College Dublin, Ireland
Derek R. Hall	Leisure and Tourism Management Department, The Scottish Agricultural College, UK
Morten Huse	Scandinavian Institute for Research on Entrepreneurship, Norway
Russell King	School of European Studies, University of Sussex, UK
Lila Leontidou	Department of Geography, University of Aegean, Greece
Jim Lewis	Department of Geography, University of Durham, UK
Armando Montanari	Department of Geo-economics, Statistics, and Regional Analysis, University of Rome 'La Sapienza', Italy
David Pinder	Department of Geographical Sciences, University of Plymouth, UK
Peter Schnell	Institut für Geographie, Westfälische Wilhelms University, Germany
Gareth Shaw	Department of Geography, University of Exeter, UK
Paul Thornton	Department of Geography, University of Exeter, UK
John Tuppen	Institut de Géographie Alpine, University of Grenoble, France
Manuel Valenzuela	Department of Geography, Universidad Autonoma de Madrid, Spain
Allan M. Williams	Department of Geography, University of Exeter, UK
Friedrich M. Zimmermann	Department of Geography, University of Graz, Austria

List of figures

List of tables

Preface to the third edition

When we were invited by the publishers to produce the third edition of this book, we took the opportunity to review the aims and contents of the earlier volumes. Although there have been many changes in the European tourism scene since work started on the first volume in 1987, we found more continuity than change in the issues relating to tourism and economic development. Then, as now, the two main themes shaping the demand for and provisions of tourism services have been the impact of globalisation, understood in terms of the growing interrelationships between different geographical scales of analysis, and the response to this by the state, in all its manifestations. In the course of the last decade, the pressure brought about by the globalisation of trade, capital and the media have increased the interdependencies between places, while intensifying the speed of change. This has brightened the spotlight on the public/ private divide in the production and reproduction of the tourism economies of Europe. To some extent there has been a 'hollowing out' of the role of the national state as power has drifted upwards and downwards to the EU and to regional/local bodies. There has also been a redistribution of power and responsibilities between the state and civil society, particularly through the increasing emphasis on partnerships. However, neither the tendencies to globalisation nor to hollowing out of the state should blind us to the simple fact that the national level, and the nation state, remain key actors influencing the development of tourism in Europe. That is why this edition of the volume, in common with the first two, remains firmly focused on national case studies.

While continuity rather than change is the dominant theme in the issues that we seek to address, there has been one profound shift in the European tourism scene in the last decade, namely the post-1989 collapse of the political regimes in the centrally planned economies of Central and Eastern Europe. The resulting and continuing transformation of these societies has already led to major changes in the international flows of tourists to such destinations as Prague and the former Yugoslavia. However, the incomplete nature of these transformations, particularly in respect of the creation of new forms of regulation and of capital accumulation, means that many of their implications for the production and consumption of tourism services within and beyond Central and Eastern Europe have not yet been fully worked out. But it is already clear that in the post-1989 era we can no longer talk or write about Western and Eastern European tourism but instead have to embrace the notion of an increasingly interlinked European tourism space. For this reason, an entirely new chapter has been added to this volume which addresses some of the changes which have been shaping tourism and economic development in Central and Eastern Europe. At the same time, in the continuing extension of the geographical coverage of the volume, we have also added a chapter on Ireland. This recognises both an earlier lacuna in our coverage, and the remarkable and distinctive expansion of international tourism in this country.

As ever, we are pleased to acknowledge the support and encouragement of a number of people who have helped to produce this book. First and foremost are the contributors, who have been given, and mostly have adhered to, tight deadlines. In addition, Wiley—especially Iain Stevenson, who at one time was their Geography Editor—have been enthusiastic supporters of the project. Finally, we have received very considerable support from Terry Bacon, who produced the final versions of the diagrams in this book, and from Jan Thatcher, who helped to disentangle the early electronic versions of the individual chapters which arrived in Exeter in a variety of challenging formats!

As always, any errors or misinterpretations in the volume remain the sole responsibility of the editors and the authors.

Allan M. Williams
Gareth Shaw
Exeter, December 1997

1 Introduction: tourism and uneven economic development

Allan M. Williams and Gareth Shaw

1.1 Introduction: economic development and tourism

The speed and extent of the economic transformations associated with tourism development, together with the social and territorial changes consequent upon this, are by now familiar subjects in tourism. Such transformations are epitomised by the sequence of changes in the social construction of the Costa del Sol as a tourism destination, and the territorial reorganisation associated with this (Barke and France 1996; Marchena 1987). The Costa del Sol was little more than a scatter of fishing villages in the 1950s, but by the 1960s it had become a fashionable international destination, and by the 1970s a mass tourism destination. The changing social construction was accompanied by a new geography of development, as construction spread along the coast and new territories were assigned tourism functions. Some more individualistic tourists sought out less developed locales in the interior, thereby diffusing the impacts of international tourism. The Costa del Sol also illustrates the role of migration systems in the development of tourism. Early tourism development generated intra-regional labour migration from the interior of Andalusia which, through a system of remittances, spatially diffused some of the income gains. Subsequently, Third World migrants (King 1995) and Northern European entrepreneurs (Eaton 1995) provided new social components of the regional labour market, generating particular flows of remittances and capital. Finally, inward international retirement migration has added another dimension to the region's economic transformation through the creation of new layers of consumption (Williams et al. 1997).

The Costa del Sol is only one, if a rather extreme, example of the economic and territorial changes which accompany tourism development. Many other examples are considered in this volume. Scandinavia illustrates the role of mega tourism events in the case of the Lillehammer Olympics, whilst Eastern Europe presents both the positive and negative economic consequences of the opening of international tourism markets after 1989, as well as the disastrous affects for tourism of ethnic and territorial conflicts in the Balkans during the course of economic and political transition. The UK presents a range of examples of how the commodification of heritage and culture can provide a base for economic development, while Austria illustrates the challenges of economic restructuring experienced by some resorts, such as its summer lake destinations, which

Tourism and Economic Development: European Experiences, 3rd Edition. Edited by A.M. Williams and G. Shaw.
© 1998 John Wiley & Sons Ltd.

face declining or static markets. In the introduction to the second edition of this volume (Williams and Shaw 1991, p. 2) we wrote that:

> As tourism emerges from the shadows of economic policy to a centre-stage position, it has become imperative to evaluate its role in economic development. The industry is shrouded in myths and stereotypes, and there is a need to examine critically recent trends in tourism, its economic organisation and its contribution to economic development.

The above brief examples emphasise that this clarion call to research is even more apposite in the late 1990s.

While tourism is increasingly becoming a globalised industry, the focus of this book is on Europe. Although it is impossible to analyse developments in Europe in isolation from wider trends, such as the globalisation of destinations in the 1980s/90s and the transnationalisation of capital and labour flows (see Williams and Montanari 1995), this is a coherent unit of analysis. There are of course substantial international tourist flows between Europe and other world regions, but it still accounts for more than half of all international tourist arrivals in the late 1990s. Even though these data exaggerate the importance of Europe in terms of all tourism flows (given the high levels of long-distance domestic tourism in the USA), they underline its dominance of international markets. The growing role of the EU in tourism regulation (Chapter 16) also increases the significance of this macro-regional focus. This applies as much to the existing members as to the aspirant ones in Central and Eastern Europe which, given their adoption of EU regulation, are already becoming *de facto* members of the Union. In fact, the opening of the ex-communist bloc countries to trade and population movements after 1989 have reinforced the importance of Europe as a unit of analysis. Finally, elements of shared histories and cultures, particularly in relation to urban form and the reification of nature, have meant that there is a degree of commonality in European tourism experiences.

While Europe is the overall concern of the book, and the principal focus in Chapters 2 and 16, the main unit of analysis is the nation state. Most but not all European countries are included, either singly, or—as in the case of Scandinavia and Central/Eastern Europe—as groups of countries. Central and Eastern Europe are considered in further detail elsewhere (Hall 1991b) and the aim here is to bring this case study within the analytical framework that had previously been applied to Western Europe in the first two editions of this book.

Each case study has two main levels of analysis—the national and the regional—and the relationships between these. In this volume, the regional takes precedence over the local, if only because of the constraints of space, but it should not and is not ignored, as is evident in the presentation of a range of case studies. Whether the focus is the tourism product, tourist movements or economic impacts, the national and the regional levels are inextricably bound together. For example, the effectiveness of national marketing programmes, of state investment in capital projects and of international currency management influence the ability of regions to attract tourists and to restructure in the face of changing market conditions. However, these relationships are not unidirectional; for example, the tourism product 'France' or 'Germany' is in large part a sum of its differentially weighted regional components. Furthermore, the national and regional levels are also linked by flows of capital and labour.

Finally, while most of the chapters do not engage with the ideas of globalisation *per se*, global–national–regional relationships cannot be ignored in any study of the economic impacts of tourism in Europe. Held (1995, p. 20) argues that globalisation:

... can be taken to denote the stretching and deepening of social relations and institutions across space and time such that, on the one hand, day-to-day activities are increasingly influenced by events happening on the other side of the globe and, on the other hand, the practices and decisions of local groups can have significant global reverberations.

This is important because it takes us away form territorial conceptualisations of the local, regional, national and global. Instead, each of these is at the centre of a large number of uneven interrelationships. In this view, localities are not just entities seeking to resist global changes. Rather, there is a need to analyse the evolution of the global, the national and the regional in terms of the changing relationships between them. This approach is very much at the heart of this volume, albeit most of the country and regional analyses have an empirical rather than a theoretical focus; tourist flows to any particular locality, and their economic implications, are shaped by tourism flows to other competing localities, the organisation of capital and labour, and global shifts in tourism as a positional good, in transport technologies and in the internationalisation of markets.

1.2 Changing forms of production and consumption

There have been major shifts in the production and the consumption of tourism over time. While we do not consider the long history of tourism here, Claval (1995) identifies four distinctive phases in the modern period, each characterised by particular transport technologies, forms of social access and social construction of tourism. In the first of these, the Grand Tour, access to tourism was highly socially constrained, and there were distinctive spatial flows from the more prosperous parts of Northern Europe to Italy and Greece. In the second phase, in the nineteenth century, there was a broadening of the social base of tourism to the middle classes; the objects of their visits were romanticised landscapes in non-industrialised Europe, including large swathes of the coastline. In the late nineteenth and early twentieth centuries, the Mediterranean was socially reconstructed as the world's leading winter pleasure play-ground (Reynolds-Ball 1914). The third phase, modern mass tourism, embraced most social classes in Northern Europe: the principal destinations were the Mediterranean coast and, for winter activities, the Alps. Holidays changed from being '. . . an annual ritual of considerable cultural significance into just one element within a more universally market-orientated society' (Soane 1992, p. 23). Finally, the rise of 'green tourism', rooted in more individualistic tourism and environmentalism, saw a renewal of interest in many of the less industrialised regions of Northern and Central Europe.

Here we focus on mass tourism in the post-1945 period and the challenges from new forms of tourism in the late twentieth century. Mass tourism is a form of mass consumption and is characterised by standardisation, by the dominance of producers over consumers, and the domination of markets by individual producers (Urry 1990, p. 14). The growth of mass tourism can be traced from the late nineteenth century but the golden era (in terms of volumes and growth rates) of domestic mass tourism was the 1950s and of international mass tourism was the 1960s and 1970s (Shaw and Williams 1994). Standardisation was most evident in domestic-market North Sea resorts and international-market Mediterranean, Black Sea and Alpine destinations.

The growth of demand was linked to the emergence of mass consumption in Western Europe in the 1950s and the 1960s, as a component of Fordist expansion in the first two decades after World War II. Tourism benefited from a one-off redistribution of income, expanded public expenditure, and the success of organised labour in enhancing entitlements to paid annual leave. In addition, workplace and work–time constraints were relaxed, so that not only did the majority of workers in Northern Europe have more free time but they were able to spend more time away from their home areas (Shaw and Williams 1994, pp. 175–6).

The demand for mass tourism was rooted in a diverse set of motivations, including a desire for relaxation, for 'escape' and for stimulation. Demand was reinforced by the social reconstruction of Mediterranean tourism as an icon of consumption by the travel industry and the media. This is what Krippendorf (1987a, p. 10) terms 'the promise of the paradise seekers'. Tourism is a positional good, which Lury (1996, p. 46) defines as commodities which '. . . are actively used as markers of social position and cultural style by consumers who seek to define their position *vis-à-vis* other consumers'. Foreign holidays became positional goods for major segments of the population during the 1960s and the 1970s. Urry (1990, p. 138) also contends that mass tourism rests upon the collective gaze which requires the presence of 'others' to give atmosphere to a place, and to indicate that '. . . this is the place to be and that one should not be elsewhere'. Additionally, mass tourism generates the critical level of demand to sustain the types of accommodation, entertainment and other services required by mass tourists. The general consumption of mass tourism was translated into demand for a specific set of resorts or destinations by the interplay between the tourist gaze and the image makers who direct that gaze to particular tourist 'signs', associated with particular places.

There were also a number of critical supply-side changes, notably reductions in air travel costs (technology-related) and development of air-inclusive package tours; the phenomenal growth of the latter is denoted by the fact that, since 1970, the volume of passengers carried by charters has exceeded that on scheduled flights (Pearce 1987). International tour companies benefited from scale economies in purchasing, marketing and their oligopsonistic relationships with sub-contracting enterprises in the resorts; these have facilitated cost and price reductions, thereby broadening the social base of mass international tourism by extending it to lower income market segments (Williams 1995, 1996). Inclusive air holidays also allowed tour companies to internalise market transactions (Dunning 1977) and maximise total profits across the different components of the total holiday package.

Not all forms of mass tourism were dominated by international tour companies (ITCs), but these were particularly strong in the short- and medium–haul air travel-inclusive holiday sector, which represents the quintessential European package holiday market. The extent of standardisation should not be exaggerated; while mass tourism (unlike some other forms) minimised place differences, the social relationships that constitute local and national differences remained important in the organisation of tourism and its economic impacts. There were also differences in the form and timing of the insertion of particular localities, and even countries, into the mass tourism market. They were not simply passive recipients of their designation as sites of mass tourism: some were in a position to actively seek or reject such a role, while all were able to at least modify the ensuing reshaping of social relationships.

While the growth of mass tourism was the dominant European trend in the 1960s and 1970s, this has been challenged (although rarely supplanted) in recent decades.

Lury (1996, p. 94) argues that consumption has been reshaped by three broad sets of changes: greater flexible specialisation in production; availability of a wider range of commodities, with shorter life cycles given more rapid changes in fashion and greater differentiation by market segments; and more individualised and hybrid consumption patterns. Consumer preferences have also become more volatile, and consumption is more fluid. Whilst such changes have occurred, mass tourism still persists as, of course, do considerable variations in life styles.

These changes in consumption have, of course, also embraced (and partly been led by changes in) the production and delivery of tourism services. On the one hand, there is some evidence of a crisis in the mass production of tourism (see Pollard and Rodriguez 1993) as well as a 'general weariness' with the mass coastal tourism product (Marchena and Rebollo 1995, p. 114), even if it remains the dominant form. This mirrors the product cycle that is observable in other economic sectors. On the other hand, there is relatively more rapid expansion of more individualised and flexible forms of tourism, sometimes termed post-modernist or post-Fordist (Urry 1990, 1995). There has, for example, been growing interest in mega events, in cultural tourism, in heritage tourism and in rural tourism. To some extent these developments involve the exploitation of place differences rather than similarities, as in mass tourism. There are also shifts away from the mass production of tourism services, and conceptually this can be understood in terms of Lash and Urry's (1987) 'disorganised capitalism'. Compared to mass tourism, these 'new' forms of tourism usually involve more flexible production, and smaller-scale and more spatially diffused consumption. In addition, tourism destinations are less different from other leisure spaces. Urry (1997, p. 104) argues that there is now a consumption spaces hierarchy—which includes resorts, shopping centres, theme parks and the like: 'These consumption spaces are distinguished from each other in more diverse and complex ways than was the case with the former hierarchy of coastal resorts'. Such hierarchies are neither rigid nor intransmutable in space and time, but rather vary considerably even at the inter-regional scale.

There have been shifts in the production and consumption of tourism services, but these are only tendencies and, inevitably, the detailed picture is more complex. First, as Williams and Montanari (1995, p. 4) argue, 'There was no simple linear and universal shift from Fordism to post-Fordism'. Even at its peak in the 1970s and early 1980s, mass tourism in Europe co-existed with other forms of more individualised tourism. Second, mass tourism areas are differentiated in terms of their labour markets and capital structures (Shaw and Williams 1994, pp 186–196). Third, although the growth of mass tourism markets has abated somewhat, and perhaps even stagnated in much of Northern Europe, there is still strong absolute and relative growth in markets in Southern and Eastern Europe. Fourth, many of the demands for more individualised holidays, for greater quality and for more environmentally-sustainable tourism, are leading to modifications to mass tourism rather than to entirely new forms (and locations) of tourism.

Tourism in the late twentieth century is characterised by a variety of tourism products and by the co-existence of different forms of production. There are global-isation tendencies, and these operate at the material and cultural levels, but, as has been noted, globalisation does not diminish the importance of the local and the regional (Held 1995) any more than it heralds the demise of the role of the nation state (Anderson 1995). Instead, there is a need to consider how these different levels are interrelated. In the next two sections of this chapter, we consider one aspect of these relationships—the economic impacts of tourism for national states and regions.

1.3   Tourism and uneven development: national perspectives

There are two pressing reasons why the role of tourism in national economic development is of concern to policy makers: its contribution to the current account/ national income, and to employment. In neither case is it possible to make definitive pronouncements about the role of tourism in development, as this is contingent. Even though there is a tendency to greater harmonisation of the regulation of tourism (Chapters 2 and 16), its economic impacts are mediated by company structures, the embeddedness of firms in national and regional economies, and the particular productive, labour market and capital features of national economies.

Tourism plays a clear and relatively transparent role in the current account, not least because this is one of the more easily quantifiable dimensions of international tourism. The contribution of tourism to the net balance of payments surplus has long been recognised in the economic strategies of European governments, particularly in the late industrialising Southern European economies in the early post-war decades. Since the late 1970s, the economic potential of tourism has also been recognised in the more mature economies that have faced crises of deindustrialisation. Tourism earnings can help balance the overall current account and finance imports, whether of consumer, intermediate or capital goods.

The overall contribution of tourism to the current account is dependent on a number of contingent features. The first of these is the overall balance between the outflow and the inflow of tourists and tourist expenditures. Second, there are leakages of expenditures from the national economies, which is partly a function of the structure and ownership of the tourism and related industries. Third, there is the scale and complexity of the economy: not surprisingly, tourism tends to be relatively most important in small open economies such as Cyprus and Malta, but it also accounts for a significant share of the current account balance, even in relatively large and complex economies such as Spain (see Chapter 2). Fourth, there is the question of whether tourism has a demonstration effect, leading to some induced multiplier effects (the use made of incomes from tourism) being 'lost' via expenditure on imported foreign goods and services.

One of the most important mediators of the income impacts of tourism is company structures. Tourism, generally, tends to have highly polarised firm structures, although there are significant sectoral differences (Chapter 2). While large companies dominate air transport, small firms are prevalent in accommodation and catering. Ownership tends to be *very* small scale in Europe compared to, say, the USA. In Europe, for example, an estimated 70 per cent of hotels are independents, while 19 per cent are in domestic chains and 11 per cent are in foreign chains (Pizam and Knowles 1994, p. 284). In contrast, 85 per cent of North American hotels belong to chains. There are considerable national differences, with chains and quoted hotel companies having stronger market positions in the UK, The Netherlands and France than in the rest of Europe. In addition, there are differences in business culture, with the 'innkeeping' tradition of Switzerland contrasting with the 'management and business' orientation to be found in larger groups in the UK (Pizam and Knowles 1994, p. 285). Not all sectors of the hotel industry are similarly affected by differences in ownership structures. The leisure tourism hotel section is largely dominated by independent enterprises, and surprisingly this applies almost to the same extent to mass tourism as to, say, rural tourism (Williams 1995). In contrast, large hotel chains are strongest in major cities and play a significant role in urban tourism, particularly in the business segment (Go and Pine 1995). Ownership differences are important because operating scale is linked to the degree of insertion in international markets (Beattie 1991) which, in turn, affects the distribution of tourism income between countries. Size and ownership structure also has labour market implications because smaller enterprises are sometimes only able to survive via self- or family-exploitation (Shaw and Williams 1994, p. 148). The tourism sector in Central and Eastern Europe is markedly different, having largely been in state ownership for most of the post-war period. It is now subject to change due to two linked processes: privatisation of property rights, and inward investment (see Chapter 15 and Hall 1995).

The role of tour companies is another important feature of how industrial structure mediates the economic impact of international tourism and, to a limited extent, domestic tourism. Even within the international segment, their role is variable and is strongest in the mass tourism segment, particularly for Northern European flows to the Mediterranean region. Most European tour companies have little direct investment in the destination countries, even though they may belong to larger complexes owning travel agencies or airlines. In the destination countries, they tend to operate mainly through short-term sub-contractual relationships with locally-owned hotels, restaurants, bus companies and other service providers. The size and market power of the larger tour companies are a source of oligopsonistic power (see Storper 1985 for a general discussion of this concept), allowing them to depress the prices paid to local firms and hence reducing the overall price of the inclusive tour. This, in turn, facilitates market widening so that inclusive air tours have come within the budgets of most Northern Europeans; one consequence of this is that the tour companies remain under immense pressure to continue to hold down costs and prices (Williams 1995). In addition, the lack of fixed capital investments in the destinations means that the tour companies are relatively free to shift the sites of their package holidays to new destinations when either following or shaping new demand trends. In a sense, therefore, there is an element of the hypermobility of capital in the way that they can rapidly restructure the geographical composition of their portfolio of holiday packages, to the economic detriment and benefit of particular destinations.

To some extent these arguments are over-stated. The international tour companies (ITCs) are not in equally dominant positions in all the main European markets; they are strongest in Northern Europe, particularly in Germany, the UK and Scandinavia. Seven of the 10 largest, and 22 of the 50 largest international tour companies in Europe are German or British (Bywater 1992; see Chapter 2). There are important differences in the structures and linkages of international tour companies, even in the UK and Germany (Williams 1995). German companies have the advantage of serving the largest market in the world, but they have also extended their market reach by extensive investment abroad; some 30 per cent of the sales of TUI and more than 50 per cent of the sales of ITS are located outside of Germany. They have also developed strong vertical linkages, particularly with the hotel sector. In contrast, the three largest UK tour companies have concentrated almost exclusively on air travel and on the UK market. They are strongly vertically integrated and own or have strategic alliances with travel agencies and with airlines, but less so with hotels. Taken together with the fact that, in both countries, the top three companies control more than half of the air-inclusive holiday industry, the tour companies have strongly influenced the evolution of mass tourism.

Empirical evidence on the operations of the tour operators, and especially on their sub-contracting practices and costs, are notoriously difficult to obtain. In one of the most comprehensive comparative studies to date, Edwards (1993) has surveyed the brochures of companies operating in France, Italy, Germany and the UK. In the UK, inclusive tours dominate leisure travel and, while their market share has declined in recent years, they still account for 50 per cent of all leisure travel abroad. In Germany, inclusive tours account for 40 per cent of the market, while in France and Italy they are less significant. The products on offer were more highly standardised and more focused on beach holidays in the UK and Germany than in the other two countries. In France and Italy there are more diverse destinations within a much smaller overall market, with particular stress on 'off-beat' destinations and touring holidays. As a result:

> The way in which inclusive tours are sold to German and British travellers emphasises price in particular, and great efforts are made by tour operators to minimise prices and maximise value for money. For French and Italian inclusive tour customers this is not the case. In Italy, and especially in France, tour operators are selling mainly an image in which price is not the primary concern (Edwards 1993, p. xii).

In broad terms, inclusive tours are cheaper in the UK and Germany than in France and Italy, reflecting both lower purchasing power due to lower volumes, and higher tour operator margins in the latter two countries. For short-haul, that is for European, destinations the French and Italians pay about 25 per cent more than the British and 20 per cent more than the Germans for the same products.

Theoretical insights into transnationalisation are provided by Dunning's (1977) eclectic theory of multinationals. Dunning and McQueen (1982) have applied the eclectic theory of multinationals to the hotel sector: they found that there were ownership, internalisation and locational advantages for firms to transnationalise their activities. However, this applies mainly to the international business tourism segment (Williams 1995) because of cost-minimising conditions in mass tourism, the role of tour companies in internalisation, and the capacity of small firms to survive either via niche markets or self-exploitation. In addition, the eclectic theory is of limited value in explaining transnationalisation of tour companies (Williams 1995): tour operators secure the benefits of internalisation via a system of subcontracting rather than direct ownership of assets abroad.

The question of internalisation of inter-firm linkages leads to the issue of embeddedness. Research on the economic impact of inward investment in manufacturing (see Turok 1993) highlights the importance of whether a firm is deeply embedded in the local economy; this is a question of whether it has created a network of sophisticated, interdependent linkages which facilitates growth in endogenous firms, and therefore self-sustaining growth in the local economy. At first sight, mass tourism seems to fit the description because of the high degree of reliance by tour companies on subcontracting. This does support growth in local firms (in hotels, restaurants, etc.) but it is highly selective and excludes the more sophisticated links to producer services. These latter are localised in the home countries of the tour operators, so that combined with their oligopsonistic powers, there are severe doubts as to the ability of tour operators to generate embedded structures which support self-sustaining growth. Whether large hotel and catering companies are able to do so is also questionable; the available evidence suggests that many of their linkages are initially external to the region, but that links to local suppliers may develop during the product life-cycle. Another aspect of the embeddedness of firms in mass tourism destinations, such as the Costa del Sol, relates to the presence in particular markets of expatriates serving foreign tourists (Eaton 1995). In short, it is not possible to generalise about the embeddedness of tourism firms; this is a matter of contingent relationships. The country case studies in this volume provide some insights into the issues but it remains an area long on speculation and short on research (Shaw and Williams 1997a).

One issue that is linked to the question of embeddedness concerns the impact of tourism on local artisanal production (Sharpley 1994). Does tourism stimulate demand for products that were otherwise in danger of disappearing due to a lack of local demand, or does tourism inevitably lead to more intensified commodification and the displacement of artisanal production by mass production techniques? The answer to this is, once again, contingent, and depends on the type and the scale of the tourism development. A balanced summary is provided by de Kadt (1979, pp. 14–15):

> Even though curio production, 'airport art' and performances of fake folklore are of course stimulated by tourist demand . . . frequently arts, crafts and local culture have been revitalised as a direct result of tourism. A transformation of traditional forms often accompanies this development but does not necessarily lead to degeneration. To be authentic, arts and crafts must be rooted both in historical tradition and in present-day life; true authenticity cannot be achieved by conservation alone, since that leads to stultification.

The other key aspect of the economic impact of tourism concerns employment, and some of the issues here are similar to those discussed in relation to the current account/income. The evidence on employment is possibly even less clear, not least because of the classic problem of defining what constitutes a job in tourism. Much of the debate has centred on the more visible jobs in hotels and catering, leading to the conclusion that tourism jobs are of low quality in terms of pay, security and skills. This is necessarily an oversimplification, given the range of jobs which tourism supports in, say, public administration, manufacturing and producer service suppliers, retailing and in transport (Shaw and Williams 1987).

One of the key aspects of tourism employment is the extent to which it is characterised by flexibility, and whether the shift from Fordist to post-Fordist production is leading to an increase in flexibility. Starting from the ideas of Atkinson (1984) on core and peripheral workers, Shaw and Williams (1994, pp. 145–7) have shown that the small scale of tourism establishments, combined with temporal fluctuations in demand, have encouraged the development of a range of numerical and functional flexibility strategies. The empirical evidence for this thesis is by no means unequivocal and, for example, Lockwood and Guerrier's (1989) study of major hotel groups found very limited evidence of functional flexibility. There was, however, evidence of numerical flexibility being pursued though part-time and casual employment. Yet, the key role of these part-time and casual workers was recognised by management who rewarded them with the same benefits as full-time workers; 'no longer are they seen as 'peripheral'' (p. 14). It is likely, however, that an analysis of smaller and independent establishments would have found stronger evidence of informalisation and flexibility in employment and working practices.

One of the most significant dimensions of tourism employment is the existence of sharp social divisions of labour, linked to social constructions of the nature of tourism employment. This can be seen in respect of gender and migration. Turning first to gender, despite some progress in women's participation in waged labour, there are still stark gender inequalities in incomes, power and influence (Kinnaird and Hall 1994). In addition, some of society's most powerful regulatory mechanisms are grounded in the relations of civil society and the family. Socially constructed expectations as to the roles of mothers and wives still largely determine the domestic division of labour in many, perhaps most, households. This socially constructed gender division of labour has important implications for women's participation in the waged labour market, especially in having to combine domestic responsibilities with paid work in 'dual careers'. It is not by accident that women, compared with men, employed in tourism, tend to be peripheral rather than core workers, to be in part-time jobs and to receive lower wages.

> Women workers carry into the workplace their subordinate status in society at large. The work of women is often regarded as inferior or unskilled, simply because it is undertaken by women. The definitions of skills may be no more than a social classification based on gender (Shaw and Williams 1994, p. 150).

This is most obvious in the way that women often perform tasks such as cooking, bed-making and cleaning in small hotels and farm tourism establishments, thereby replicating the tasks they perform in, and the subordinate status that they may hold within, the domestic division of labour (see Leontidou 1994).

There are also strong links between tourism development and international labour migration. The 1960s, in particular, were years of mass labour migration from Northern to Southern Europe (King 1984). With rising unemployment in Northern Europe and economic growth in the South, this migration flow was substantially reduced in the 1980s. It has, however, been replaced by new labour migration flows from the Third World (particularly Northern Africa) into Southern Europe (King 1995). Venturini (1992) has estimated that more than half and perhaps as many as 80 per cent of immigrants in Italy are employed in the informal sector. They are often employed in hotels and catering or self-employed as peddlers in tourist resorts (King 1995; Montanari and Cortese 1993, p. 184). Street hawkers, who are highly visible in the street scene and beach life of Mediterranean tourist resorts, are mainly from Senegal and other West African countries. Despite these recent trends in international migration, most immigrant workers are not to be found in Southern Europe. King (1995) reports that international migrants are particularly important in the tourism industries in Switzerland and Luxembourg, are of lesser importance in France, Belgium and Germany, and are of least importance in the UK and The Netherlands. There are, in turn, gender and national differences within those labour market segments occupied by international migrants. For example, in Spain and Italy, chambermaids and cleaners tend to be from The Philippines and Latin America (King 1995, p. 184).

What is the role of international labour migration in the tourism industry? First, along with intranational migration, it helps to meet the need—particularly in mass tourism—to assemble large pools of labour at the points of tourism consumption. Second, it helps to meet some of the numerical flexibility needs of the tourism industry in terms of temporal, especially seasonal, variations in demand. Third, and no less important, it helps to depress general wages in the tourist industry, thereby reducing costs, but making such jobs even more unattractive to locals although helping to maintain competitiveness.

1.4   Tourism and uneven development: local and regional perspectives

Localities are not simply subject to forces of globalisation; instead there are a series of interrelationships between the local and the global. This is recognised in the work of Bull and Church (1994) on the territorial changes in employment in hotel and catering in the UK in the 1980s. They conclude that:

> In order to understand this spatial variety it is necessary to consider not only how the industry interacts with external processes, such as the changing nature of international tourism, but also how it relates to local economic, social and cultural structures (p. 267).

In the case of tourism, which is highly localised in some respects (many tourism services have to be produced and delivered at the point of consumption), there is particular interest in its role in local economic development. Many aspects of tourism that are of relevance to local development are similar to those already considered in respect of national economic development. Not only is tourism an important generator of incomes and jobs, but it is one of the few sectors which has experienced increases in employment opportunities in the late twentieth century. Tourism products can also be created (e.g. via theme parks) even where the natural and cultural attractions for tourism are relatively weak, such as devastated industrial zones or little-valued areas of landscape; in a sense, therefore, it is potentially ubiquitous. Furthermore, as tourism can be developed in a short time-span, and requires only moderate levels of investment, its local and regional impacts can be realised relatively quickly. For example, in the Val d'Anniviers in Switzerland a number of investments linked to a Club Méditeranée project resulted in a dramatic turnaround in the local economy in little more than a decade (Diem 1980).

Tourism is also important in local economic development because of its role in reshaping place images. This is evident in the way that tourism has often been used as a key element in the restructuring of cities such as Manchester, Bradford and Wigan in the UK, which had experienced substantial closures and job losses in their traditional economic bases (see Law 1994; Page 1995). Place imaging, often based on cultural activities and/or heritage, is prominent in such restructuring strategies. Shachar (1995, p. 156) stresses that cultural tourism is particularly important in helping to determine the emerging ranking of world cities: the '. . . geographical patterning of the performing arts in the culture industries gives urban tourism a strong metropolitan character, with an emphasis on the world cities which occupy the highest level of the global urban hierarchy'. Barcelona has been particularly successful in marketing its cultural and heritage attractions, and has been aided in this by skilful exploitation of the promotional opportunities provided by the 1992 Olympic Games (Carreras i Verdaguer 1995).

Thus far, this discussion has focused on the role of tourism in economic growth. However, tourism is a product and is subject to the product cycle, as conceptualised in Butler's (1980) resort cycle model. Gordon and Goodall (1992, p. 48) provide an useful insight into the nature of the tourism product:

> In essence, they involve an experience produced from a combination of activities, resort and accommodation characteristics, together with some resources supplied by the tourists themselves. Resorts may produce a number of distinguishable products, with each being to some degree differentiated from those offered by rival resorts.

Not only are there phases of growth and decline in particular tourism products, but localities have different degrees of success in resisting or supporting these (see Chapter 16).

In practice then, the map of tourism products (and of the employment and income related to these) is constantly shifting. One of the most intriguing aspects of these shifts is the question of whether they contribute to the processes of regional convergence or divergence. There are at least two key questions here: whether tourism development is spatially polarised, and whether tourism contributes to overall regional economic convergence or divergence. In other words, how does it contribute to the generation and redistribution of capital, income and employment between rich and poor regions?

This is an intriguing and again under-researched topic, particularly at the European level. The classic view expounded by Peters (1969, p. 11) is that '. . . tourism, by its nature, tends to distribute development away from the industrial centres towards those regions in a country which have not been developed'. Montanari and Williams (1995, p. 6) conclude in their discussion of tourism and restructuring in Europe:

> The social construction of tourism—with an emphasis especially in mass tourism on the 'flight' from the pressures of working and urban life—have meant that 'peripheral' areas (in contrast to dominant and prosperous 'cores') have been important tourist destinations.

However, they qualify this argument to stress that even international mass tourism does not inevitably privilege the peripheral regions, as is shown by the experiences of Mediterranean coastal tourism in relatively prosperous Catalonia, and of mass urban tourism to Paris or London. The evidence from Hungary and the Czech Republic, where tourism is massively concentrated in the capital cities, also shows that tourism may reinforce the advantages of the richer regions (Hall 1995).

The late twentieth century relative shift from mass tourism to new forms of tourism has had significant territorial implications for the question of regional convergence–divergence. Mass tourism was highly polarised, and tended to favour the European periphery (at least for the beach product) if not necessarily the least developed parts within this. In contrast, new forms of tourism are more evenly distributed spatially and touch almost all urban and rural areas. The post-modernist tourism product, by its very nature—emphasising individualistic or flexible holidays—is small-scale and geographically dispersed. Hence there is less need to assemble large pools of migrant labour and instead there is greater reliance on local labour. We can also note that the emergence of new forms of tourism has made for an increasingly complex map of tourism economic impacts, not least because localities in both rich and poor regions have pursued tourism development strategies in the face of rising unemployment in the 1980s and the 1990s. It would therefore be more accurate to argue that, at present:

> . . . there are many different forms of tourism and that each has distinctive regional implications which do not necessarily conform to any simplistic periphery–centre or centre–periphery model (Williams and Shaw 1994, p. 308).

Some of the different regional outcomes of tourism development are illustrated by the examples of the UK, Austria and Greece. In the UK, mass tourism has traditionally favoured poorer regions, but recent changes in tourism markets and investments have favoured richer regions (Williams and Shaw 1995). This is partly related to the continuing internationalisation of UK tourism markets, which have tended to privilege London and the southern regions, in terms of both gains from incoming tourism and relative losses to outgoing tourism. In addition, compared to mass tourism, the rapid expansion of new, less spatially polarised, forms of tourism has also favoured these regions. The fact that many of these new forms of tourism—such as urban tourism, cultural tourism, theme parks, heritage tourism and sporting activities—depend more on short break markets than on the traditional long summer holiday also favours those destinations which are relatively accessible to major metropolitan areas.

A similar regional pattern is evident in Austria (Zimmermann 1995, p. 38). Tourism income has contributed to reducing regional disparities, and this has been particularly marked in the take-off phase of tourism development. In particular, the expansion of gross domestic product (GDP) was greater between 1970 and 1992 in the winter tourism-dominated areas of Tyrol, Salzburg and Voralberg than in most other Austrian provinces, especially Carinthia, where the summer tourism industry had peaked in the 1960s and early 1970s. However, there has been an important shift in recent years and the richer regions, such as Vienna and Lower Austria, have experienced more rapid tourism growth due to the increasing importance of international tourism, drawn to the capital, and to the short break markets provided by the recreational needs of the Viennese population.

Komilis (1994, p. 67) presents another example, this time relating to Greece. In the 1960s, the spatial growth of tourism in Greece could be characterised in terms of a 'centre–periphery' dichotomy. Tourism was concentrated in a dominant centre (Greater Athens), and two types of peripheral area: small holiday-resort areas, usually small islands, dependent upon the centre for their tourist transport links and logistics; and a few areas—such as Rhodes and Corfu—which are emerging as 'independent' destinations. Over time this pattern has changed, with some peripheral areas experiencing higher growth rates. The apparent decentralisation of activity, inter-regionally, is, however, highly polarised spatially at the intraregional level. In addition, the economic impacts of tourism are significantly affected by multiplier and leakage effects, so that the economic impacts are more dispersed than is suggested by the initial review of spatial polarisation of tourism activity.

Regional convergence–divergence is not only a question of which regions have and have not attracted tourists. There are a number of contingencies to be taken into account. One of the more important of these is the composition of the demand for any particular region. For example, the Algarve (Chapter 6) is highly dependent on the UK market, which is a relatively large-volume, low-spending market. There are major variations in market profiles across Europe, reflecting in part the distribution of potential local markets (that is, concentrations of populations and incomes), and Jansen-Verbeke and Spee (1995) provide a useful analysis of the most basic of these, the level of dependency on intra- as opposed to inter-regional tourism flows. They found that in the UK in 1990, the proportion accounted for by intraregional flows varied from 37 per cent in the North of England to 17 per cent in Wales; in Germany the range was from 36 per cent in West Germany to 12 per cent in Middle Germany, while in France it was from 34 per cent in Normandy/Nord to 5 per cent in Ile de France. Such statistics on visitor numbers are indicative of important differences in expenditures and incomes.

The importance of markets can also be see in the differential regional impacts of the crisis in mass tourism in Spain during the late 1980s and early 1990s. Priestley (1995, p. 191) writes that:

The crisis has not affected the country in a uniform fashion. Its repercussions have depended on the structure of tourism in each region, or even at resort level. The regions or resorts that depend most heavily on air charter or coach travel package clients staying at low category rated hotels have suffered the effects of the crisis most seriously. These include many of the resorts on the island of Mallorca, the Catalan resorts of Lloret de Mar, Platja d'Aro, Calella de la Costa and Salou and the Andalusian resorts of Torremolinos and Benalmadena. The higher-quality tourism of the Canary Islands and parts of the Andalusian coast has been less adversely affected.

The actual economic impacts of tourism on a region or locality cannot, of course, simply be read off from the scale or even the origins of tourism flows. Many of the questions raised in relation to national economic development apply equally well to the regional and local scales. There are, for example, the issues related to labour migration, and Cavaco (1980) has shown that the Algarve has a geographically dispersed catchment area for labour migration; it can be assumed that these flows of workers will be matched by reverse economic flows, constituted of emigrants' remittances.

There is also the key question of how firms are embedded into local economies, a subject already touched upon in relation to national economic development. Once more, there are contingent relationships here, for embeddedness is linked to the scale and structure of the local economy. One of the key issues is whether tourism development is integrated into existing sites of production and population concentration or is on greenfield sites. Barker (1982) provides some insights into the embeddedness of tourism development in the Alps. Low-altitude resorts in the east tend to be more integrated with existing settlements than are high-altitude resorts further west, and there are clear differences in their embeddedness as measured in terms of labour and capital flows. Embeddedness also raises questions about the nature of local entrepreneurship and its ability to respond to new tourism opportunities and linkages, or more generally to be innovative. The available evidence from tourism destinations as diverse as Cornwall (Williams *et al.* 1989; Shaw and Williams 1997a) and Sardinia (Zuddas 1997) highlights the role of informal capital and lack of professionalism amongst tourism entrepreneurs.

The importance of regional economic structures in the utilisation of local resources in highlighted by Loukissas's (1982) comparative study of Greek islands. The economic impact of tourism is most beneficial in the larger islands because these have more diversified economic structures, leakage effects are limited and the pressures on the local population are reduced because tourism tends to be concentrated in specialised villages. In contrast, tourism tends to dominate the economies of the smaller islands but may lead to unstable short-term and dualistic development.

There are a number of other contingent features of local economic development that need to be considered. One of the most important of these is the way tourism employment, characteristically in the early stages of development, may be a source of intergenerational conflict. There are studies in such diverse settings as Southern Spain (Fraser 1974) and the Alps (Kariel and Kariel 1982), which highlight how the lure—in both material and cultural terms—of tourism can draw young workers away, functionally and sometimes spatially, from the traditional farm-based local economy. Employment in tourism may provide economic independence and new cultural values, with the outcome being the rejection not only of working on the family farm, but also of the parents' way of life. While we have to be careful not to subscribe to tourism the only, or even the leading, role in such changes, the effects are palpable and highlight the links between tourism and other sectors of the local economy. The same point can be made in respect of land markets. Low land prices in previously largely agricultural regions can facilitate tourism development. In turn, the income transfers from tourism to the agricultural sector, following such land transfers, can provide an important stimulus to local farming; it can contribute to household survival strategies, or provide the capital for investments which allow the farms to respond more effectively to the new market opportunities stemming from tourism. Vincent (1980), in the Alps, and Andronicou (1979) in Cyprus provide detailed case studies of such processes although they also identify a number of negative effects as some local people are excluded from farming and from housing markets by rising land prices.

Given that many of these tourism changes are generated by the internationalisation of leisure practices, investments and population movements, this serves to underline Held's (1995, p. 20) view that '. . . globalisation can be taken to denote the stretching and deepening of social relations and institutions across space and time'. It is not a case of dominance of the local by the global but of a series of interconnections between the two levels, so that neither can be considered in isolation.

1.5 A note on data sources

In the second edition of this book (Williams and Shaw 1991, p. 2) we wrote that 'the definition of tourism is a particularly arid pursuit'. We do not deviate from that view in this, the third edition. In broad terms, tourism is understood to constitute travelling away from home for periods of more than 24 hours; the principal purposes are recreation or business activities, but may also include visiting family, educational motives or health reasons. However, while we do not wish to dwell on definitions, it is important to draw attention to some of the data limitations faced in the study of tourism and economic development, particularly where comparisons are drawn between countries (Chapter 2) and even regions with differing data collection, classi-fication and presentation systems. There are four points that need to be stressed at this juncture.

First, tourism is statistically invisible, whether we consider it as a process, a product or an economic system. There are major statistical lacunae even in the most essential of data, the numbers of tourists. Historically, there have been more complete data sources for international than for domestic tourism, because the former involved the crossing of frontiers and therefore offered particular conditions for monitoring flows and movements. However, even international comparisons are fraught with difficulties because of differences in recording procedures, while not all countries (e.g. the UK) record tourism movements at their frontiers. Other countries have preferred to record international tourism at the accommodation bases rather than at frontiers. Not surprisingly then, many commentators have argued the need for more reliable, robust and comparable statistics (e.g. Baron 1983). In practice, with the deregulation of frontier crossings in Europe, especially within the EU and Scandinavia, the collection of comparable data on international movements has become even more fraught with difficulty.

A second problem relates to data collected at accommodation establishments, which is the main source of data on national, and sometimes for international, tourism flows. Not only are there differences in the registration requirements of different countries (e.g. the UK has no such requirement) but also in their comprehensiveness. Such data are usually far more reliable and more available for the hotel sector than for the various forms of self-catering, including camping, caravaning and rented apartments. In addition, such data are unable to record the often substantial numbers of tourists housed in the informal sector or staying with friends and relatives (Chapter 2).

A third set of problems relates to differences in the spatial and temporal desegrega-tion of these data series. As can be seen in the country case studies in this volume, there are significant differences between countries in the extent to which tourism data are disaggregated by regions and types of tourism environments. There are also discontinuities in particular time series due to changes in how tourism data are collected in particular countries, or to border changes (as in the former Yugoslavia, or Germany).

Fourth, there are even greater obstacles to the economic evaluation of tourism. While foreign exchange transactions provide some indication of the economic role of international tourism, there is not even this data possibility for domestic tourism. The only data available are from national tourism surveys, which do not take into account the particular structures of local tourism economies, or specially-commissioned local economic impact studies. As the latter are relatively expensive, such data are scarce and comparisons between localities are problematic given their methodological differences.

To some extent these problems of comparability are recognised in the structure of this volume, which is organised around national case studies. However, as the individual authors indicate, there are considerable difficulties of interpretation, even within this framework. The development of robust and comparable statistical data series for European tourism therefore remains a major challenge, and it can not be ignored for long given the increasingly important role of tourism economically, as well as culturally and environmentally.

2 Western European tourism in perspective

Gareth Shaw and Allan M. Williams

2.1 Introduction: the emergence of mass tourism

The history of tourism can be traced via the 'Grand Tour', the spa towns of the eighteenth century and the railway-borne day-trippers of the late nineteenth century to the emergence of mass tourism during the second part of the twentieth century (Towner 1985). As Krippendorf (1986. p. 131) states:

> Travel has become one of the most curious phenomena of our industrialised society. Travel occupies 40 per cent of our available free time, made up of 30 per cent for excursions and other short trips—note the weekend exodus from the cities—and 10 per cent for longer holidays. Human society, once so static, has gained true mobility.

This has partly been based on the requirements of business and, in a world of increased geographical mobility, the need to visit friends and relatives. However, holidays and leisure activities have been the primary motive and Europe accounted for 58.6 per cent of international tourist arrivals in 1996 (World Tourism Organisation Website, 1998). Indeed, Urry (1995, p. 164) believes that the democratisation of travel and its social organisation are distinctive characteristics of modernity. Both domestic and international tourism have been based on rising standards of living (for most groups in many developed countries) and greater leisure time. In general, there have been reductions in the working week, increased entitlement to paid leave, and increased numbers of retired or early-retired people. For example, in the European Union (EU) there was a 10 per cent cut in working hours for manual workers in the 1970s, while annual paid holidays increased to about four weeks (Edwards 1981). At the global scale, it has been estimated that about 1,700 million people had the right to paid holidays during the mid-1980s (World Tourism Organisation 1984, p. 45).

The combination of increases in real incomes and holiday leave need not automatically result in increased tourism. Instead, the preferences of individuals, and the social construction of tourism consumption (Urry 1990) determine this. At its most basic, Murphy (1982) argues that the goals of leisure time can be classified as physical (relaxation), cultural (learning), social (visiting friends and relatives) and fantasy. The last of these stems from the fact that, increasingly, people 'do not feel at ease where

Tourism and Economic Development: European Experiences, 3rd Edition. Edited by A.M. Williams and G. Shaw.
© 1998 John Wiley & Sons Ltd.

Table 2.1   Europe's major package holiday companies: top ten ranked by turnover, 1992

Company	Location of company	(Turnover in ECU, millions)
TUI	Germany	2590
Thomson	UK	1623
NUR	Germany	1220
LTU	Germany	1206
Kuoni	Switzerland	1190
Club Méditerranée	France	1122
DER	Germany	1056
NRT Nordisk	Sweden	1019
ITS	Germany	963
First Choice	UK	916

Source: modified from Economist Intelligence Unit 1993.

they are, where they work and where they live. They need to escape from the burdens of their normal life' (Krippendorf 1986, p. 131). Where people choose to go depends on their locational and activity preferences, their past experiences of tourism and, possibly, the desire to use tourism as a 'positional' good which implies being seen to patronise the 'right' resorts (Shaw and Williams 1994, Chapter 4). Whereas in the past these had been defined by the holiday activities of royalty and the aristocracy, they are increasingly dependent on the opinions of travel writers and the images projected by the advertising industry.

However, the growth of tourism depends on much more than just the expansion of demand, for it is partly supply-led. The costs of travel have declined especially because of the expansion of car-ownership and reductions in the real costs of air transport. For example, in 1949 it took 18 hours to fly from London to New York, but by 1979 technological change had reduced this to a minimum of 4 hours (Kahn 1979). Changes in transport technology have not only accelerated travel but also reduced costs. In this context, the organisation of the tourism industry is significant in that changing cost structures have stimulated increases in demand. This in turn has led to scale economies and further cost reductions, especially in the package tour market (Yale 1995). Of particular importance is the role played by tour operators, who have keenly promoted packaged holidays, which have allowed tour companies to reduce their margins on particular elements of the holiday whilst maintaining acceptable levels of overall profit. The majority of European tour operators are small-scale, and it has been estimated that in 1992–1993 such tour companies took some 51.3 million tourists on holiday (Gratton and Richards 1995). The same survey also identified concentration tendencies, and highlighted the fact that the eight largest operators accounted for an estimated 38 per cent of all holidaymakers (Table 2.1). Indeed, Gratton and Richards (1995) found that the average number of tourists carried by the 50 largest European tour operators increased from 400,000 in 1988 to 600,000 by 1993. Intense competition amongst tour companies has also reinforced the downward pressure on costs, as did the shift from serviced accommodation to self-catering during the 1980s.

There is, then, a strong positive demand for tourism and this is an especially 'deeply-rooted social custom in European countries, which have benefited from the good transport networks and a variety of facilities, especially in the non-hotel category, which facilitate tourism for a broad range of social groups' (World Tourism Organisation 1984, p. 32).

Tourism is characterised by a positive income elasticity of demand, whereby demand rises proportionately greater than an increase in income levels. This is based on its status, at least in economic terms, as a luxury rather than a basic needs good. Tourism figures prominently in the aspirations to, and expectations of, improvements in standards of living (Sharpley 1994, Chapter 4). The nature of the product is also important for there is an almost infinite variety of places to visit, each of which is unique in some way. As Waters' (1967, p. 59) early, and gendered, work pointed out: 'the travel industry is not made up of people taking a once-in-a lifetime trip. The average tourist is a collector of places, and his appetite increases as his collection grows'. Furthermore, the supply of tourism products is not fixed in any absolute sense, for investment can and does create new tourist attractions, the scale of which is tending to increase. For example, the European theme park industry had investments totalling an estimated £36m in 1994 (Tourism Research and Marketing 1994) and this was effectively reshaping the map of the European leisure industry.

There is little quantitative evidence on the elasticity of demand. However, in the mid-1960s Waters (1967) considered that in the USA, $10,000 was a critical threshold in terms of household incomes and that, beyond this, there was a sharp rise in the taking of holidays. More recent figures from the EU from a Europe wide survey highlight the effect of income on holiday taking, showing that upper-income groups are, in most cases, at least twice as likely to participate in a foreign holiday as are lower-income groups (Commission of European Communities 1993, p. 56). It was estimated that, during the mid-1980s, households in the EU spent about 7 per cent of their budgets on holidays (Commission of the European Communities 1985). This average figure has only risen slightly during the 1990s and, in any case, masks wide national variations. These range from a low of 5.37 per cent of household budgets spent on leisure and tourism in Portugal, through averages of over 10 per cent in most northern European countries (Euromonitor 1995).

The numbers participating in tourism provides one indication of demand and, while deficient in some ways, these data do emphasise that strong growth has accrued. The most reliable statistics are those for international tourists, which increased from 25 million in 1950, through to 69 million in 1960, and 160 million in 1970 to 429 million in 1990, and 500 million by 1993. By the year 2000 it is estimated that there will be well over 637 million travellers. In comparison, comprehensive statistics are not available on domestic tourists but these are considered to account for around 90 per cent of the total, which places the international numbers in perspective. Growth in tourism demand has not been constant throughout the post-war period and can be disaggregated into three distinctive elements. These are long-term growth trends, cyclical movements and short-term erratics.

Long-term growth trends show that a major expansion of international mass tourism occurred during the 1950s, with increases of 10.6 per cent per annum, and the 1960s, but there has subsequently been a slowdown. Growth in the period 1975–1982, for example, was only 3.8 per cent per annum but this recovered to 5–7 per cent per year during 1984–1988. Cyclical movements average 6 or 7 years (World Tourism Organisation 1984) while, as would be expected, erratic events such as oil price increases or bombings are largely unpredictable in their occurrence and in the duration of their impact. In the case of Greece, for example, the major erratics—all of which led to a downturn in foreign tourist arrivals—have been political instability in 1964, the

Table 2.2   International tourism: arrivals by region, 1950–2000 (per cent)

Region	1950	1971	1975	1984	1995	2000[1]
Europe	66	75	71	67	57	53
Americas	30	19	20	19	20	20
Africa[2]	3	3	4	6	4	5
Asia/Pacific	1	3	5	9	19	22
Total	100	100	100	100	100	100

Sources: Young 1973; World Tourism Organisation 1984, 1994, 1996; Commission of European Communities 1993.

Notes: 1. Estimated figure.
2. Includes the Middle East.

coup d'etat in 1967, the oil crisis and the invasion of Cyprus in 1974, oil price increases in 1980, the sharp world recession in 1982–1983 (Buckley and Papadopoulos 1986, p. 87), and a number of events in the 1980s and 1990s linked to Middle East conflicts, including the Gulf War.

Not all the world's major regions have shared equally in the expansion of tourism (Table 2.2). The relative position of the Americas has slipped since 1950, although absolute numbers have risen, while the share of Australia and Asia has increased sharply. This partly reflects the emergence of the Japanese as an important group of tourists, but also indicates the steady growth of countries such as Australia and India as tourist attractions. However, Europe dominates international movements of tourists, which is not surprising given the large numbers of relatively prosperous people living in close proximity to other countries. Between 1950 and 1990 the number of international tourists in Europe increased 16 times. Its share of tourists increased up to 1971, largely as a result of the growth of mass tourism particularly in the Mediterranean region, but it has subsequently fallen from 71 per cent in 1975 to just under 60 per cent by 1994. It is significant that the erosion of the European share occurred at a much faster rate in the period 1990–1994 than in the preceding decade. Thus, during the 1980s its market share diminished at 0.3 per cent per annum, compared with 0.75 per cent during the 1990s (European Commission 1995, p. 13).

2.2   Tourism in Western Europe

2.2.1   *Access to tourism and patterns of holiday taking*

There are many ways of measuring tourism demand, and these often vary from country to country. Furthermore, such national surveys are based on different sample sizes and available time series. Surveys undertaken by the EU have attempted to overcome such variations by applying uniform measures. One such measure is that based on 'length of stay' and estimates put the total number of holidays of four nights or more by EU residents between 250 and 300 million in 1992. Moreover, holiday participation, which is defined as the proportion of the population that takes at least one holiday of four overnight stays per year, is between 55 and 60 per cent of the population. Surveys also suggest that approximately 65 per cent of all holidays generated by EU residents are domestic ones, with 22 per cent associated with 'foreign' tourism within the EU region, and 13 per cent in areas outside the EU (Commission of the European Communities 1993, p. 52).

There are, however, wide variations in the pattern and scale of holiday taking across Europe. For example, it was estimated in 1985 that some 56 per cent of EU residents took a holiday, whilst 21 per cent habitually stayed at home, and 23 per cent only sometimes take a holiday (Commission of the European Communities 1987, p. 16). By 1990 the proportion of non-travellers had declined to an estimated 40 per cent. Significantly (in terms of future demand changes), in some Central and Eastern European countries the proportions were well over 60 per cent (Commission of European Communities 1993, p. 112). Tourism is, therefore, a relatively widely shared experience within the EU, although a large proportion of its residents—by choice or constraint—do not participate. The ability to take holidays away from home is, of course, dependent on household income. The 1985 survey found that 46 per cent of those who did not take holidays were constrained by income, although this average masked higher proportions in Portugal, Ireland and Greece. Socio-demographic features also influence holiday taking, and these include age, the presence of children in the household, and location: older persons, those with large families, and those living in rural areas were less likely to take holidays away from home.

There are important signs of change in the travel and holiday patterns of some older people. Studies in Germany, for example, have shown that the travel behaviour of retired Germans is strongly influenced by their travel habits earlier in life. The survey estimated that between 1990 and 2010 the level of trip taking by people in the 65–75 year age group would increase from 53 per cent to 74 per cent, an increase of around 5.3 million travellers (Commission of the European Communities 1993, p. 170). There is also evidence that holiday taking may shade into various forms of peripatetic residence, with retired Northern Europeans living parts of the year in the Mediterranean countries (Williams *et al.* 1997).

While there is clear evidence of the spread of tourism across social boundaries, there are important exceptions to this tendency, including those on low incomes, those with some disabilities, and those with particular occupational ties or social caring roles. The differences between socio-economic groups appear to be greater in the less prosperous societies, such as parts of Central and Eastern Europe, Greece and Portugal, than in the wealthier Northern European societies such as Sweden (Travis 1982). The rich–poor gap in tourism access can partly be closed through state and voluntary sector social tourism programmes. A number of European countries have initiated such programmes to help the disadvantaged gain access to holidays: they include the 'workers home' scheme (Greece); 'Villages Vacances Familles' (France); 'Loisirs et Vacances' (Belgium); 'Familienferienwerk' (Germany); and 'REKA' (Switzerland). Moreover, with particular support from the French government, there are also attempts to promote social tourism at the EU level.

2.2.2   *Changes in tourist flows*

There have been important shifts in the origins and destinations of tourist flow during the post-war period. These affect both domestic and international tourism but reliable comparative data are only available for the latter. This section, therefore, focuses on foreign tourism, while domestic tourism is discussed in the individual case elsewhere in the book.

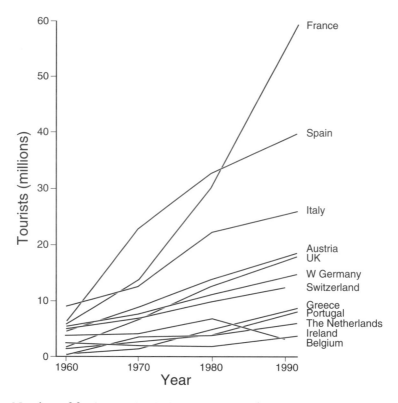

Fig. 2.1 Number of foreign tourists in Western Europe by country, 1966–1995

Source: OECD reports

Figure 2.1 summarises changes in the major destinations of tourist flows during the period 1960–1992. Almost all the major European countries have experienced important increases in foreign tourist arrivals since 1960. The earliest and most significant growth was in the Mediterranean countries, with Spain, Italy and Greece experiencing large absolute and percentage increases. Portugal, however, had a mixed experience, with rapid growth in the 1960s being followed by stagnation in the 1970s because of recession and the political aftermath of the 1974 military coup. Spain's growth was so rapid that it overtook France as the main tourist destination until the early 1990s, when France attained primary spot again. These Mediterranean countries benefited from the development of inclusive, low-cost package holidays, and from the social construction of mass tourism as a sea and sunshine product.

The growing importance of winter holidays in Switzerland and Austria is also evident, especially in the latter, which experienced rapid growth based on successful marketing of lower-cost skiing holidays. Elsewhere, the UK and France experienced rapid increases in foreign tourist arrivals. In the case of France this can be explained by a variety of attractions (Paris, the Riviera, the Alps, touring and self-catering, and theme parks, including Euro-Disney; indeed, France had the highest attendance at theme parks within Europe). In the UK, London still acts as the gateway and the dominant attraction for many visitors to Europe.

Table 2.3 Nights spent by foreign and domestic tourists in all means of accommodation, 1994

	Nights spent by foreign tourists	Nights spent by domestic tourists	Proportion spent by foreign tourists (%)
Austria	92,216.4	30,143.4	75.4
Belgium	14,261.8	21,293.6	40.1
Denmark	26,126.5	15,950.9	62.1
Finland	3,377.0	10,090.2	25.1
France	94,976.2	156,648.5	37.7
Germany	34,777.0	279,357.5	11.1
Greece	41,424.9	12,782.3	76.4
Italy	102,355.3	172,950.9	37.2
The Netherlands	17,991.8	38,189.3	32.0
Norway	7,243.8	12,155.6	37.3
Portugal	20,660.1	13,795.6	60.0
Spain	104,156.4	70,676.9	59.6
Sweden	6,780.4	28,118.5	19.4
Switzerland	36,290.9	37,917.4	48.9

Source: OECD 1996.

Not all countries benefited equally from international tourism movements; for example, in Belgium and The Netherlands there has been more limited expansion and even decline in some time periods. This is hardly surprising as they lacked the resources around which international mass tourism was constructed—sea and sunshine, or ski conditions. In addition, most countries experienced a downturn in international tourism in the mid-1980s, especially in 1986 due to the threat of terrorism, although there has been a strong recovery since the late 1980s.

Another important trend is the increasing flows of tourists between the EU and Central and Eastern Europe. In the early 1990s, Western Europeans made almost 19 million trips to Eastern Europe, generating some 186 million nights. The main points of origin for such trips are Germany (46 per cent share of market), Italy (13 per cent), Austria (8 per cent) and the UK (7 per cent). The main destinations, excluding the once popular former Yugoslavia, are Poland, the Czech Republic and Hungary (Commission of European Communities 1993, p. 87; Euromonitor 1995). Table 2.3 provides some idea of the relative importance of foreign and domestic tourism. While not providing comprehensive coverage across Europe, it does indicate major international differences. In particular, there is a group of countries where foreign tourists greatly outnumber domestic ones; this includes Turkey, Greece, Austria, Spain and Portugal. One surprising omission from this list is Italy, where international tourism is balanced by strong domestic tourism in both the summer and winter seasons.

2.2.3 Types of tourism demand

The market for tourism is highly segmented and, in part, the relative success of particular countries in attracting tourists depends on their ability to provide particular tourism products. This, of course, is partly dependent on their resource base, which includes both climatic and topographic features, although cost structures, state policies and marketing strategies all contribute to the ability of particular countries to realise their comparative advantages. These tourism resources are heterogeneous and are not fixed, with the social construction of 'the popular' changing over time. During the 1980s the major forms included beach holidays, alpine tourism, urban/cultural tourism, rural tourism and business/conference tourism. In terms of domestic tourism, seaside holidays accounted for 52 per cent of all main holidays within the EU in 1993. By comparison, the rural-based holidays accounted for 25 per cent and urban tourism 19 per cent (Euromonitor 1995).

As the figures suggest, the mainstay of holidays in the late twentieth century remains beach-orientated tourism. This still dominates the domestic tourism industry throughout Europe, although a major change occurred with the expansion of international tourism along the coastline of Southern Europe (Claval 1995). Mediterranean holiday packages have become the model of mass tourism since the initiation of the first charter holiday flight to Corsica in 1950 (Sharpley 1994, p. 58). These are based on low-cost charter airfares or (excluding Ireland, the UK and Scandinavia) self-drive to Mediterranean destinations. The basic attractions are sun, sea, cheap wine and food, presented in a non-challenging, standardised international format. In recent years, additional recreational facilities, such as golf courses and tennis courts, have been added in the face of subtle changes in demand. Spain represents the most highly developed example of Mediterranean mass tourism, at least in terms of dependence on foreign visitors (Chapter 3), but this model is also characteristic of substantial parts of the international tourism market in Greece, Portugal, Italy and, to a lesser extent, France. The tourism resorts which are developed within this model tend to be little differentiated and Holloway (1994) terms them 'identikit destinations'. That such resorts remain attractive to large numbers of tourists is shown by the fact that Montanari (1995) estimates that some 160 million international tourists visited the Mediterranean in 1994 and it is forecast that this figure will at least double by 2025 (Croall 1995, p. 9). Set against this view is the suggestion that the traditional 'sun, sea and sand' holiday has reached a mature phase in its life-cycle, and that many resorts will have difficulties in coping with changing conditions (Commission of the European Communities 1993).

Similarly, Alpine holidays are another location for mass tourism, attracting around 50 million tourists per year who spend 300 million overnight stays, together with 150 million day visitors (Williams and Shaw 1996). The major international ski destinations within Europe are Austria and Switzerland which, in 1994, accounted for 5.4 million trips and some 54 per cent of the European ski market (Economist Intelligence Unit 1994). The roots of this lie in the nineteenth century when the Alps were visited for summer relaxation by Europe's wealthy élites (Barker 1982). By the mid-nineteenth century, development of the international railway network and the emergence of the first modern tour company, Thomas Cook, was leading to increased tourism; although this was still restricted to the middle classes and to exclusive resorts such as Montreux and Merano (Brendon 1991). Early in the twentieth century, winter tourism increased in importance, boosted by the first Winter Olympics which were held at Chamonix in 1924. By 1933, winter tourism accounted for 44 per cent of the Alpine total. Finally, since the late 1950s there has been growth of mass tourism based on inclusive package holidays (see also Chapters 7 and 8). This has been stimulated by rising standards of living which have allowed more families to enjoy second holidays, which is often the priority allocated to skiing as opposed to sunshine holidays. There are many different forms of resort, as illustrated by Préau (1970), who differentiates between resorts based on existing settlements, such as Chamonix, and greenfield development of resorts, such as Les Bellevilles. The latter are often situated at very high altitudes, as at La Plagne in France, with more reliable snow conditions. Of course, not all tourism in the Alps or Mediterranean is mass, package tourism. Large numbers of visitors make their own travel and accommodation arrangements in both these macro-regions, and may deliberately seek out more individualistic sites of consumption.

Urban tourism encompasses two distinctive strands: cultural tourism and business/conference tourism. Estimates suggest that some 48 per cent of trips are associated with business/professional reasons, compared with 27 per cent for leisure and recreation (Grabler *et al.* 1997). Reliable statistics are scarce, but some surveys exist. First, data collected by the Federation of European Cities' Tourism Offices estimated that 59 European cities accounted for up to 270 million tourist bednights (Grabler *et al.* 1997, p. 44). Second, a detailed survey conducted in 1993 (van den Berg *et al.* 1995) highlighted differences in tourist demand at the city level, with London having some 82 million bednights compared with just 28 million for Paris. London's lead over Paris is, however, much reduced when tourist arrivals are considered, the explanation being that the average length of stay in London is 5.62 days compared with just over two days for Paris. The opening of the Channel Tunnel along with Euro-Disney, has helped to increase tourism arrivals in Paris. Indeed, two days marked the average for most city visits, with the exceptions of Antwerp, Budapest and Rome, where they averaged more than four nights. Urban and cultural tourism is continuing to expand, as many urban communities have sought to develop tourism for economic and social gains (van den Berg *et al.* 1995). In addition to these newer markets, the traditional centres for cultural tourism are based on diverse attractions, ranging from archaeological remains through to outstanding architecture, museums and art galleries. This is a continuing tradition associated with Europe's extraordinary rich heritage, although quantifying the demand is difficult given data inadequacies. However, the World Tourism Organisation has estimated that 37 per cent of all trips have a cultural element and the growth rate for such trips to the year 2000 will be around 15 per cent per annum (Economist Intelligence Unit 1993).

Urban tourism is also strongly supported by business and conference travel. This market segment has shown strong increases both globally and regionally at the European level because of the need for increasing international personal contacts in the face of globalisation of economy and society. The EU captures one of the largest shares of the business travel market, accounting for some $129 billion dollars in 1995 compared with $135 billion for North America (World Travel and Tourism Council 1995, p. 15). However, Central and Eastern Europe's share has increased very rapidly, and between 1995 and 2005 it is estimated that business travel will increase by almost 274 per cent. In addition to business travel for purely economic reasons, many companies are using incentive travel to reward their staff, a feature strongly associated with UK-based companies. Within European countries, 27 per cent of employees travel on business at some time during an average year. The largest market is Germany, which spent over $38 billion, or 28 per cent of the European total, in 1992, although the UK and France also have significant expenditure levels. Indeed, it is estimated that European countries spend, on average, 2.5 per cent of their GDP on business travel, although there are strong variations around this figure (Davidson 1994). Conference travel is also an important part of business travel to urban areas. According to van den Berg *et al.* (1995), the leading venue for conventions was Paris, with 407 international meetings in 1992, followed by London and Brussels.

2.2.4   *European tourists*

Successive studies of tourist demand within the EU have highlighted variations in travel between different nationals (see, for example, Commission of the European Communities 1987 and 1993). However, at a different level, increasing interest has been shown in differentiating tourist behaviour based on patterns of consumption (Gratton 1993). For example, Mazanec and Zin (1994) have argued that it is possible to identify at least 16 different life-styles within Europe, ranging from the 'wealthy, spendthrift young' through to 'prudent retired people seeking security'. Such work, as both Mazanec and Zin (1994) together with Horner and Swarbrooke (1996) show, can be used to identify, at least in marketing terms, broad segments of European travel motives and activities. Other research has strongly suggested that there is a high degree of customer convergence within Europe, such that buying habits—including leisure and tourism behaviour—are becoming increasingly similar across different countries (Halliburton and Hünerberg 1993). These studies identify cross-national processes in leisure behaviour with a strong element of market segmentation based on socio–economic and demographic factors. Such trends are leading to a more coherent European travel and leisure market that has strong implications for both domestic and EU based tourism.

Whilst it may be premature to accept the details of these marketing-based studies, it is possible to discuss some broader-based groupings of European tourists. There is, for example, a small but significant trend away from mass, packaged holidays, particularly amongst middle income groups. Increasing numbers of tourists are seeking very different holiday experiences, often informed by concerns for the environment. In this context, we can recognise increasing interest in 'green' or sustainable tourism, starting in German-speaking countries during the 1970s (Becker 1995). By the mid-1980s, surveys of German tourists found that 85 per cent stated that they wanted holidays that were 'environmentally correct' (Williams and Shaw 1996, p. 126). Lack of hard evidence makes it very difficult to be precise about the scale of such geographical variations in such tourist attitudes. However, it does appear that at least one-fifth of tourists from Austria, Germany and Switzerland, and possibly also Scandinavia, could be classified as 'ecologically critical' tourists who would demand certain types of holidays. In contrast, while there is little hard evidence, there is a commonly held view that British tourists tend to be more traditionalist. Croall (1995), for example, takes this view based on the sentiments of Brackenburg, the Chairman of the Federation of Tour Operators. However, it is important that set against these trends is the fact that around 44 per cent of all holidays booked by EU residents are inclusive tours.

2.2.5   *Seasonality*

Seasonality is not exclusive to tourism—for example, it also occurs in fishing and agriculture—neither is it typical of all branches of tourism. However, it is a feature often associated with the tourist industry. It arises both from the timing of holidays (traditionally in the summer, at Christmas and Easter) and from the seasonal nature of some forms of tourist environments—summer sun, winter snow. According to the World Tourism Organisation (1984, p. 43):

> The most specialised destinations (some beach or fishing destinations at certain times of the year, etc.) are usually the most seasonal because of the seasonal factor associated with

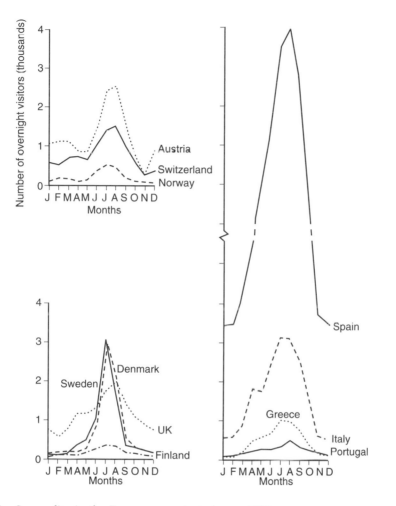

Fig. 2.2   Seasonality in the European tourist industry, 1983

Source. OECD (1985)

tourist utilisation of their basic resources. Tourist destinations supported by large urban centres, while having high points of activity, have more continuous operation throughout the year because they depend upon a more diversified demand.

The pattern of seasonality in parts of the European tourist industry is shown in Figure 2.2. In spite of the fact that important regional differences are averaged out in the national data, these indicate the significance of seasonality in almost every country. The figures only cover foreign tourism, but domestic tourism usually has a similar, if sometimes less sharply peaked, pattern; there has been little or no change in such seasonality patterns over recent decades (see Economist Intelligence Unit 1995). There is a small group of countries which have double peaks in tourist arrivals, as represented by Austria, Switzerland and, to a lesser degree, Norway, all countries with strong winter and summer tourist seasons. A second group of countries, the Mediterranean destinations, display the classic pattern of peak summer tourism. The third group, consisting of most of the Northern European countries, also has single-season tourism peaks.

As the graphs in Figure 2.2 are drawn on absolute scales, it is difficult to assess the degree of seasonality. However, the proportion of tourist arrivals which occurs in the two peaks of the year gives a relative index of seasonality. In Sweden, Denmark, Italy and Greece, over 35 per cent of tourists arrive in two months. This is climatically determined, in part. Given their double peaks, Switzerland and Austria occupy intermediate positions on this index. The countries with the lowest degree of seasonal peaking—between 24 and 27 per cent—are The Netherlands, Germany and the UK. In all three cases, cultural and business tourism are relatively important and these are less affected by climatic conditions. This pattern is borne out by general surveys at a European level, which show that 64 per cent of holidays occurred in summer (Commission of the European Communities 1993). Finally, it is interesting to note that Spain has a relatively low index (29 per cent), indicating a measure of success in attracting tourists out of season to enjoy the relatively mild winters in the far South, especially in Andalusia (see Chapter 3) and its islands.

2.3   Tourism: economic structures

The tourist industry is especially heterogeneous and combines large numbers of small businesses or self-employed alongside large companies. Over time the industry has been subject to two major trends: internationalisation and concentration (Shaw and Williams 1998). There are several reasons for this, including the possibilities of selling a package of services rather than an individual product, economies of scale in purchasing and advertising, the internationalisation of travel and tourism, and the need to reduce costs in the face of intense price-orientated competition (McQueen 1989; Cleverdon 1992). In this section, three interrelated features of the economic structure of tourism are considered: the international environment for tourism services; patterns of ownership; and the structure of the accommodation sector.

2.3.1   The internationalisation of tourism

The increasing growth of international tourism has made it inevitable that there has been internationalisation of tourism services. This takes many forms, including direct ownership, long-term subcontracting, or short-term agreements for the provision of transport, accommodation, tourist attractions and supporting services such as car rentals, catering and leisure retailing. The importance of such international groups as Holiday Inns, Avis car rental, the Centre Parc holiday centres, fast food chains like McDonalds, and tour companies such as Thomson and Kuoni, bear testimony to the importance of internationalisation. Despite the limited research on such organisations, it seems clear that they influence the distribution of employment, international profit flows, and the relationship between local and international expenditure on inputs of goods and services.

Undoubtedly there has been an internationalisation of tourism and the tourist industry. During the early 1970s and 1980s such expansion did not occur in an environment of unfettered competition (World Tourism Organisation 1984, pp. 10 11). However, since the early 1990s a number of factors have combined within Europe to facilitate internationalisation (Thomas 1996). These include:

1. The move towards a Single Market, including fiscal, regulatory harmonisation and air travel liberalisation.
2. The promotional activities of directorate DG XXIII, which is charged with developing tourism within the EU.
3. EU tourism marketing campaigns involving organisations such as the European Travel Commission, along with attempts to attract more non-Europeans to visit Europe.
4. Rapidly developing tourism markets, such as those in Southern Europe where there is growing demand for international travel.
5. The widening of intra-regional travel flows, especially between western and Central/Eastern Europe.

In response to such factors, Go and Pine (1995, p. 133) argue that most large corporations are orientating 'towards greater internationalisation, cooperation and concentration'. Within individual domestic markets, such trends are creating intense competition and forcing many small companies to become more specialised. As Thomas (1996, p. 10) points out, the concern of the European Commission is that the Single Market will disproportionately benefit larger firms and, as a consequence, there are initiatives to support small- and medium-sized enterprises. The two major approaches are the reduction of regulatory costs and the encouragement of cross-border co-operation between enterprises, especially through the provision of business support. There has also been increasing awareness of the need for an EU tourism policy, especially since the European Year of Tourism in 1990 (see Chapter 16).

2.3.2   Patterns of ownership

Two major trends in the ownership patterns of tourism businesses are concentration and polarisation. One of the most impressive features of ownership patterns since 1945 has been increased concentration. This has involved both horizontal (the take-over of similar/competing businesses) and vertical (the take-over of linked or related businesses) expansion. Examples of the latter include airlines buying hotels and tour companies buying travel agencies. Linkages between these elements of the industry already exist, and vertical expansion is one strategic response to formalise and control them through ownership changes. This is particularly important in the face of intense competition in a multiproduct, multinational industry.

One of the most impressive features of the European tourism industry has been the growth of major tour operators (see Table 2.1). Although these companies have international activities, their markets are largely national. There are, however, differences in the organisation of the sector even within those countries where large tour operators are most important, that is the UK, Scandinavia and Germany. For example, Thomson of the UK has its own travel-agency chain and transport subsidiaries, whilst Touristik Union International (TUI) in Germany has important investments in travel agencies and accommodation. Equally, diverse types of products are offered. Some, for example Club Méditerranée, offer highly structured, all-inclusive packages providing virtually all services for the holidaymaker.

There is intense competition in this market segment and large companies have considerable cost advantages: first, because they sell 'bundles' of services—flights, accommodation, holiday insurance, car hire, supplementary tours and activities—they can reduce margins on single items while maintaining overall profits; second, because of the scale of their operations, they are able to negotiate large-scale, low-unit cost contracts with transport and accommodation providers (Williams 1995). For example, in the early 1970s large tour companies were reputed to be paying hoteliers in Spain no more than £0.40 per capita per day for full board.

The keen competition amongst tour companies was particularly evident in the UK in 1985 when, following a sharp downturn in the holiday business by around 6 per cent, Thomson, the market leader, reacted with price cuts of up to 20 per cent: 'Thomson was able to take this step because a massive investment in new technology had enabled it to cut operating margins and cope with a large increase in volume of business' (*Financial Times*, 4 November 1986). As a result, Thomson increased its market share from 20 per cent to 30 per cent, and other tour operators had to cut prices and profit margins in the ensuing price war.

Large tour operators have focused on three main strategies for expansion, namely vertical and horizontal integration, buying established companies to open up new markets, and expanding into new geographical markets. The latter holds potential within Europe but has not been adopted as a strategy by many companies. In contrast, Thomson have used both of the first two strategies by, first, developing its own airline and travel agency chain and, second, purchasing brand leaders in the self-catering market, as well as rivals such as Horizon. Similarly, the Airtours company has followed an expansionist development policy by adding hotels, airlines and retail travel outlets to its overall portfolio between 1990 and 1994.

In contrast to these large operations, there are also many smaller tour operators. A number of these are also members of consortia, such as the Association of Independent Tour Operators in the UK (Horner and Swarbrooke 1996). In 1995 this organisation had some 229 small operators who sought to collaborate so as to counter the economies of scale of the large tour operators.

Internationalisation or concentration can also be seen in the hotel sector (Go and Pine, 1995) A league table of the largest hotel groups shows that American companies (Table 2.4) dominate these. There are, for example, only three European-based organisations within the top ten. Of these, Forte has developed an extensive range of hotels throughout Europe and in the early 1990s completed a re-branding exercise, together with the acquisition of Meridien hotels from Air France in 1995. Significantly, Forte themselves were taken over by Granada plc in 1996, thereby highlighting the complex and dynamic nature of this sector (Mogendorff 1996, p. 39). Similarly, the Paris-based Accor organisation has been a major developer in so-called 'multi-tier branding', being especially active in the budget hotel market. In this context, Accor has developed a range of accommodation products to satisfy a number of specific markets. This is typical of the strategies adopted by most large, international hotel groups who sell to more than a single market or brand image. Some of the groups are truly global in scale, as in the case of Sheraton hotels owned by ITT. One of the most potent indicators of global shift in recent years was the decision by ITT to disinvest from its traditional telecommunications interests in order to concentrate on more lucrative investments in other services, such as tourism.

Table 2.4 Leading multinational hotel chains, 1993

Company	Nationality	Number of rooms
Holiday Inn	USA	340,881
Accor	France	250,319
Choice Hotels International	USA	299,784
Marriott International	USA	173,048
ITT Sheraton Group	USA	129,714
Hilton Hotels Corporation	USA	94,952
Forte Hotels (Granada Group)	UK	78,691
Hyatt International	USA	76,057
Club Méditerranée	France	65,128
New World/Ramada	Hong Kong	55,591

There are a number of significant factors that, in combination, yield competitive advantages to transnational hotel groups. According to Go and Pine (1995, p. 8) these include:

- The provision of high quality services under a brand clearly recognised by customers.
- The ability of such groups to respond quickly to new or changed market conditions.
- Considerable organisational and managerial economies that enable good standards of service to be provided.
- Availability of global travel reservation systems.

There are several different types of transnational hotel groups, as identified by the United Nations Centre on Transnational Corporations (UNCTC 1982, 1988). One group involves ownership by airline companies, whilst a second consists of large transnationals which are not directly associated with airlines such as Club Méditerranée and Forte. There is a third group consisting of specialist hotel development and management companies, although these are of minor importance. Finally, there is a fourth group, hotel chains which are part of a larger enterprise, and a fifth cluster characterised by hotels owned by tour operators. The latter is especially important within Europe, as represented by companies such as Vingreson of Sweden and Hotelplan of Switzerland. Each of these types of hotel groups has different interests and varying strategies but, together, they increasingly dominate hotel provision. However, their market capacity is nationally differentiated. Concentrations are highest in the UK, The Netherlands and France (Table 2.5). However, the position of larger companies is likely to strengthen in most markets: for example, the French-based ACCOR group operated well over 2,000 hotels in 1995 and is very active outside France (Table 2.6).

Travel agencies are also subject to concentration and internationalisation although, again, most companies operate almost exclusively within national markets. There are three main types of ownership. First, there are agencies that are part of larger companies with multi-sectoral interests in tourism; examples include Lunn Poly and Going Places in the UK, which are owned by tour operators (Horner and Swarbrooke 1996, p. 336). Second, there are those travel agencies which belong to groups with

Table 2.5   Concentration of hotel rooms in company hotels, 1992

	Total room capacity	Percentage in hotel companies
UK	490,000	25.3
France	518,000	22.4
Germany	335,000	11.1
Italy	300,000	6.5
Spain	359,000	3.5
The Netherlands	50,200	22.2
Belgium	60,000	15.2
Luxembourg	10,000	9.5
Portugal	30,400	12.7
Ireland	20,700	11.2
Denmark	36,500	2.2
Greece	191,000	1.2

Source: modified from Slattery and Jonston 1993, p. 67.

Table 2.6   Distribution of hotels owned
by ACCOR, 1993

	Number of hotels
France	668
Germany	63
Belgium	25
UK	24
The Netherlands	17
Portugal	6
Italy	5

Source: Euromonitor 1994.

significant non-tourism interests; for example, the Havas Voyages agency of France has strong media interests. Third are the many privately-owned independent agencies that vary in size from medium-sized companies to small owner-operated firms. The UK market is dominated by a few large companies, such as Thomas Cook, Lunn Poly and Going Places, which, in turn, belong to larger groups. A similar pattern exists in other countries, such as Germany, where TUI is a leading travel agency and tour operator. There is also growing evidence of the internationalisation of ownership. In the mid-1980s the Spanish travel agency, Melia, was taken over by SASEA, a Swiss holiday company, and Interpart Holding of Luxembourg. More recently, Thomas Cook of the UK has been taken over by American Express Travel and the German tour operator LTU. This is a sector where there is growing competition from two sources. First, there is a move by airlines and other companies to bypass travel agencies, through such measures as walk-on flights and direct ticket sales. Second, there is competition from other high street retailers attempting to diversify into the travel agency business. The former is the most important and it is significant that the three largest agencies in the UK are either controlled by or associated with the main tour operators (see Horner and Swarbrooke 1996, p. 340).

Other sectors associated with tourism and leisure, such as restaurants, also display internationalisation tendencies. As with hotels, there is a strong American influence through the activities of fast food chains such as McDonald's and Kentucky Fried Chicken. McDonald's has franchised some 2,000 outlets, with a turnover estimated at 4 billion ECU throughout Europe (Mogendorff 1996, p. 43). At present these large chains tend to be focused in the UK, Germany, France and, to a much lesser extent, Spain. Within the most competitive environment, the UK, companies like Burger King have expanded by purchasing other chains, such as Wimpy. Such take-overs are likely to increase and become more transnational as companies expand into newer European markets.

2.3.3 The accommodation sector: polarisation tendencies

The accommodation sector, more than any other component, 'dictates the sort of tourism industry a country can expect' (Young 1973, p. 88). The supply of accommodation is, of course, both determined by and helps to influence demand. Whether accommodation is in second homes, rented villas, private homes, camping or large hotels has a major influence on the types of tourists attracted, the duration of their visits, and the types and quantities of employment created, as well as income generated. These differences are underlined by considering, for example, the differences between tourism in many parts of the Costa del Sol (based on large hotels and apartment blocks) and in Denmark, where second homes are relatively important. Europe dominates the world hotel industry, accounting in 1993 for an estimated 43.5 per cent of the world-wide hotel capacity (World Tourism Organisation 1995). Significantly, its share is declining relative to other world regions and Europe's increase in hotel rooms between 1985 and 1993 was only 8.8 per cent, well below the global average (Mogendorff 1996, p. 36). Non-hotel accommodation (self-catering) is also important in Europe, especially in the Mediterranean and Alpine regions, because, according to the World Tourism Organisation (1984, p. 64):

> In these countries the quantitatively high demand, also very diversified with regard to socio-economic origin, available income, motivation, etc., has made it necessary to diversify supply, which exceeded the possibilities of the hotel business in this regard. This has given rise to inns, company sites, apartments, holiday towns, houses, spas, etc., which have basically met the desires and economic possibilities of each segment of demand!

This may be so but there is also growing demand for flexible holidays, and prices are also critically important, especially in package holidays. Moreover, the emphasis on hotels versus supplementary accommodation is misleading, for there are strong polarisation tendencies within both sectors. The major expansion of large hotels and hotel chains has already been noted. However, as Viceriat (1993) points out, independently owned hotels represent some 90 per cent of establishments within the EU, and an estimated 80 per cent of bed capacity. Increasingly, many small hotels are finding it difficult to compete, especially if they lack facilities such as private bathrooms, bars and swimming pools, which are becoming standard expectations. These smaller establishments have to compete, instead, in terms of price by cutting their margins to the minimum, often through exploitation of unpaid family labour, or offering a distinctive product. This may be highly personalised service, exceptional food or, as in farm holidays, participating in establishment activities.

Some medium-sized, independent hotels have attempted to improve their competitive position by affiliating to voluntary hotel chains. These give advantages in purchasing, marketing and reservation systems, permitting scale economies (HOTREC 1995). Europe contains more than half of the world's 20 largest voluntary chains, with Utell International being the largest, followed by Best Western. Viceriat (1993) argues that these voluntary chains will continue to expand within Europe by integrating their members' products into a common distributional system.

There has been similar polarisation in the self-catering sector. Until fairly recently, rented houses and apartments were dominated by small-scale operators who owned one or two properties. While this pattern is still characteristic of some areas, especially parts of Central and Eastern Europe, there has been increased professionalisation and commercialisation from the mid-1970s. This has involved both greater reliance on large commercial booking agencies and the emergence of large companies. Lower-quality and individually-owned self-catering accommodation is likely to find it increasingly difficult to compete in this market. One of the fastest growing elements in the self-catering sector is that of timeshare, and in the mid-1990s some 2.5 million households worldwide owned timeshare property (Haylock 1994). The concept started in Switzerland during the late 1950s, spreading rapidly throughout Europe and North America. Indeed, Europe is now the second largest market and the European timeshare business is centred in the UK, with UK holidaymakers being the main owners, followed by Germany, France and Spain. There is evidence that the market is becoming more segmented, with such developments as the creation of short breaks in timeshare accommodation. Supporters of this system claim that timeshare supports a more environmentally sound approach and has a longer season than other forms of holiday taking, that is, 20–50 weeks compared with 10–20 for some other forms of holiday homes (Haylock 1994).

2.4   The economic role of tourism

The structure of tourism, and its economic development, have long fascinated analysts. The challenge is summarised most succinctly in the questions posed in the titles of two books: *Tourism: Passport to Development?* (de Kadt 1979) and *Tourism: Blessing or Blight* (Young 1973). The answer obviously has to be conditional, depending on the evaluation criteria (for example, growth versus equity), the structure of the industry and the characteristics of the local economy. In this broad review, therefore, it is only possible to outline some salient international comparisons of the economic impact of tourism in terms of income, balance of payments and selected broader economic relationships. More detailed evaluations are provided in the country case studies elsewhere in this volume. As with other international comparisons, data constraints make it easier to comment on international than domestic tourism.

2.4.1   *Gross domestic product and national income*

Measuring the contribution to GDP of tourism receipts is difficult because the major component of the latter—domestic tourism receipts—is not known for some

Table 2.7   International tourism and the national economy in Western Europe, 1994

	Tourism receipts to the GDP (%)	Tourism receipts as a percentage of export goods and services	Tourism expenditure as a percentage of imports of goods and services
Austria	6.6	16.0	11.2
Belgium–Luxembourg	2.2	2.1	3.3
Denmark	2.2	4.1	4.9
Finland	1.4	3.7	4.6
France	1.9	5.5	3.2
Germany	0.5	1.9	7.5
Greece	4.1	25.0	4.9
Ireland	2.3	4.5	4.1
Italy	2.3	8.6	4.7
The Netherlands	1.4	2.3	4.9
Norway	1.8	4.3	9.4
Portugal	4.7	15.0	5.1
Spain	4.5	18.4	3.3
Sweden	1.4	3.4	6.0
Switzerland	3.2	6.8	6.4
UK	1.5	3.9	5.8

Source: OECD 1996, pp. 139–140.

countries. Estimates in the 1980s suggested that domestic tourism expenditure was five to ten times greater than international tourism expenditure in many countries (World Tourism Organisation 1984, p. 2). Subsequently, both the OECD Tourism Committee and the World Travel and Tourism Council have improved the statistical basis for assessing the economic contribution of tourism to GDP (OECD 1995, p. 31; World Travel and Tourism Council 1995). It has been estimated that international tourism contributed around 2.0 per cent to GDP in Europe but, taking into account domestic tourism, this figure rises to just over 13 per cent. Within individual economies, tourism can account for a significant share of income generation, as Table 2.7 shows. Tourism makes its greatest contribution to GDP in those countries involved in the various forms of mass tourism, that is in the Mediterranean and the Alps. Thus, Austria is strongly dependent on tourism, with 6.6 per cent of GDP being attributed to this source in 1992 and a similar figure in 1994 (Table 2.7). By comparison, tourism in Switzerland is of lesser importance because of the smaller number of tourists and, more importantly, the role of multinational manufacturing and financial activities within the national economy. Amongst the Mediterranean destinations, tourism is significant in Spain, accounting for 4.5 per cent of GDP in 1994. In other countries, such as Germany, whilst international tourism is less significant, in combination with domestic tourism it does make an important contributions to GDP.

Other than employment, income is the major benefit of tourism to local communities. Tourist expenditure provides direct income which, via the multiplier effect, is amplified by indirect income. The total income effects can be considerable. For example, Law (1985) reported that annual tourist expenditure in the early 1980s amounted to £16 million in Nottingham, £58 million in Merseyside and £54.6 million in Glasgow. The multiplier effects in these examples are unquantified. However, earlier, more reliable estimates provided by Archer (1977) calculated that the local tourism income multiplier was between 1.68 and 1.78 in the UK. Arguably, the local multiplier effects are greatest in the larger and/or specialist tourist economies, because these are more able to support linked specialist services and manufacturing. In contrast, a tourist economy dominated by 'branch plants' is more likely than one characterised by indigenous firms to be dependent on external services or products purchased by company headquarters (Shaw and Williams 1998). The income leakage can be considerable, especially if the tourist projects are large-scale and exceed the capacity of the local economy. For example, very little of the capital invested in developing resorts such as Playa de los Americanos (Tenerife) originated locally.

Finally, with regard to income, the effects of tourism can be very considerable in particular sectors/locations, such as farmhouse tourism. In regions of small-scale farming, income from tourism may be critical in farm survival strategies, in the face of limited returns from agriculture. This varies in importance within Europe, and the largest proportions of farms offering tourist accommodation tend to be in Scandinavia and the Alps. For example, agritourism is growing in importance in parts of the Alps, with farms providing some 109,000 guest rooms and one-sixth of all tourist beds (Williams and Shaw 1996, p. 20). Similarly, one survey in England and Wales found that in 1991 some 24 per cent of farms were involved in tourism (Croall 1995, p. 138). In contrast, the role of farm tourism is usually limited in the Mediterranean countries of mass tourism: for example, only 0.4 per cent of Spanish farms participated in tourism enterprises.

2.4.2 International tourism and the current account

Tourism is a major source of income for many countries and in 1995 accounted for approximately 11 per cent of GDP. Moreover, during the 1970s international tourism income grew considerably faster than international merchandise trade (Ascher 1983). Not surprisingly, therefore, tourism has been actively promoted in a number of countries, specifically so as to increase foreign earnings and improve the 'invisibles' component of the current account. The overall position in Western Europe is summarised in Table 2.7, which shows a clear North–South pattern (Burton 1994). Tourism expenditure by nationals accounted for between 3 and 10 per cent of all imports of goods and services in most northern European states, compared with 5.1 per cent or less in the Mediterranean countries. In contrast, the pattern is reversed when considering tourism receipts relative to exports and services. Over 25 per cent of all exports derive from tourism in the Mediterranean countries (except Italy, which has a diversified economy), compared with less than 6 per cent in most northern European countries. Foreign exchange earnings from tourism have been significant in the industrialisation of southern Europe since 1960, effectively financing the imports of raw material and technology for the manufacturing sector. They were particularly important in Spain in the 1960s, accounting for almost half of export earnings (UNCTC 1982). The Alpine countries occupy a special role in these international flows, being significant sources and recipients of foreign tourists' expenditure. In general, while the growth of tourism receipts in Europe has been considerable (almost 4 per cent per annum during the early 1990s) this has been less than in the global tourism economy (OECD 1996, p. 11).

A measure of the magnitude of the receipts and expenditure involved in international tourism is given in Table 2.8. In absolute terms, the largest net earners are

Table 2.8 Receipts from and expenditures on international tourism in Western Europe, 1994 ($ millions)

	Receipts	Expenditure	Balance
Austria	13,151	9,399	3,752
Belgium–Luxembourg	4,666	7,130	−2,464
Denmark	3,175	3,582	−407
Finland	1,400	1,664	−264
France	24,844	13,736	11,108
Germany	10,816	42,348	−31,532
Greece	3,857	1,128	2,729
Ireland	1,794	1,599	195
Italy	23,754	12,084	11,670
The Netherlands	4,743	9,239	−4,496
Norway	2,168	3,942	−1,774
Portugal	3,825	1,696	229
Spain	21,490	4,118	17,372
Sweden	2,838	4,890	−2,052
Switzerland	7,629	6,375	1,254
UK	15,185	22,196	−7,011

Source: OECD 1996.

Italy and Spain, while Germany and The Netherlands have the largest net deficits. Countries such as the UK and Switzerland have relatively small net balances which conceal large flows of receipts and expenditures. These data confirm the argument of the Commission of the European Communities (1985), that tourism generates a net distribution of wealth from the North to the South of Europe, and from the richer to the poorer states. The obvious exceptions to this tendency are the Alpine states, which are geographically and economically in the centre of these financial exchanges. With the expansion of mass tourism, there is evidence that the relative and absolute gap between the net financial revenues of the recipient and donor countries has increased over time.

Finally, a note of caution is required in interpreting these estimates, for foreign 'leakage' effects can reduce the balance-of-payments surplus. These are particularly significant for those economies which have weakly developed service and manufacturing activities to supply the needs of foreign tourists. Amongst the most important leakage effects are:

- Imported goods, particularly food and drink.
- The foreign exchange costs of foreign imports for the development of tourist facilities.
- Remittances of profits abroad by transnational companies.
- Remittances of wages by expatriate workers.
- Management fees and royalties for franchised businesses.
- Payments to overseas airlines, tour companies and travel agents.
- Overseas promotion costs.
- Extra expenditures on imports by nationals resulting from earnings from and the demonstration effect of tourism.

Table 2.9   Tourism employment (direct and indirect) in selected Western
European countries, 1994

	Direct and indirect employment (thousands)	Percentage share of tourism employment in labour force
Austria	586	13.9
Belgium	74	2.0
Denmark	97	2.6
France	1,200	4.8
Germany	1,800	6.5
Greece	360	10.0
Luxembourg	11.5	6.4
The Netherlands	199.8	2.8
Norway	53.7	3.4
Portugal	250.0	5.6
Spain	1,400	9.1
Sweden	153	3.4
Switzerland	293.2	8.2
UK[1]	1,489.4	N.K.

Source: OECD 1995, p. 33.

[1] *Note*: Covers only staff employed in hotels and restaurants, and other tourism sectors.

It is difficult to obtain precise estimates of these income leakages, especially of extra expenditures on imports by nationals. Mathieson and Wall (1982) report one such estimate for Italy in 1975: whereas receipts were $2,578 million, leakages reduced net earnings to $1,528 million.

2.4.3   International tourism and employment creation

Estimating tourism employment is a difficult task, made more complex by different national data collection methods. But the importance of tourism as a source of employment is unquestioned, and in many European countries it has recorded above-average growth rates since the 1980s and the early 1990s. The hotel and catering sector has contributed most to employment, whilst in percentage terms the travel agency sector has seen some of the highest growth rates (OECD 1995, p. 37). Indeed, information for the UK suggests that employment in travel agencies and other sectors exceeds that in hotels and catering.

New calculation methods on the significance of tourism employment by the OECD (1995) give a more detailed picture of both direct and indirect employment levels (Table 2.9). The figures of tourism employment are impressive, with Germany having 1.6 million jobs, Spain 1.4 million and France 1.2 million. Even in those countries where the total number of tourism jobs is relatively small, the proportion of the labour force occupied in tourism is high: 10 per cent in Greece and almost 13 per cent in Austria.

Employment in tourism is also important because, in the face of global recession, it has been one of the most consistent sources of job growth. There is, however, the question of whether the jobs are filled by nationals or by immigrants, and this largely depends on the scale of tourism, the types of jobs available, and the labour-market alternatives. Few countries keep accurate records on this aspect but the proportion of immigrant labour employed in hotels and catering can be considerable. For example, in Austria 33 per cent of tourism jobs are occupied by foreigners compared with just 6.5 per cent in other economic sectors. In Switzerland the proportion of foreign nationals is even higher, rising to 45 per cent in 1994 (OECD 1995, p. 41).

The actual quality of jobs in the tourist industry is a matter of debate. Most jobs are classified as being semi- or unskilled; according to Swiss employment statistics, 74.2 per cent of jobs in the hotel and catering sector are unskilled, as compared with 60.6 per cent in the economy as a whole. However, while direct employment in tourism (in bars, hotels and restaurants, etc.) may be mostly unskilled, indirect employment (in supply industries, producer services, etc) may be highly skilled and well rewarded.

The same distinction between direct and indirect employment is necessary in considering the gendered distribution of jobs. Employment in some tourism sectors is clearly dominated by women, especially in serviced accommodation. Most bed-makers and cleaners in small and large hotels seem to be women. The same tendency is even more marked in small-scale, rooms-to-let accommodation. For example, Hadjimi-chalis and Vaiou (1986, p. 71) writing about tourism on the Greek island of Naxos, state that:

> rooms-to-let is a household operation run almost entirely by women. They are rooms within or near the family house which are rented during the summer. Cleaning rooms and serving guests is regarded as an extension of daily housework, 'naturally' women's work. Negotiating prices and making contracts with the authorities is usually left to men.

Bouquet (1982) reports similar gendered divisions of labour in the farmhouse bed-and-breakfast trade in the South West of England. In all these instances, women carry over into the formal labour market their socially constructed and subordinated role in the domestic division of labour.

Skill-levels and gendered relationships are only two of the characteristics of the labour force. Other important features include full-time/part-time ratios, seasonality, wages, and the geographical origins of the work force. All of these clearly depend on the nature of the local economy, and the scale and ownership of tourism enterprises. For example, Barker (1982, p. 407) writing about high-level, specialised ski resorts in Alpine France, states that the 'combination of corporate capital, distant investors and a state-planning mechanism has limited the participation of the valley populations chiefly to unskilled, seasonal occupations'. There is some evidence available on the inter- and intraregional migration of labour. For example, Cavaco (1980) reports that only 58 per cent of the labour force in the town of Faro (Algarve) has been drawn from the surrounding districts; this reflects the large scale of tourism developments relative to the size of local labour markets. Nevertheless, such data as are available are fragmented and often unsuitable for comparative purposes.

2.5   Tourism: some broader economic considerations

The review of the economic role of tourism presented in this chapter is limited to brief comparisons of simple economic indicators. These are sufficient to indicate important differences in terms of the absolute and relative economic importance of tourism in various European countries. However, the relationship between development and tourism is more complex than this, as we suggested in Chapter 1. The contingencies of the relationships are such that they are best investigated in the context of particular case studies. This is the focus of the following chapters, and here it is only possible to indicate some major themes.

First, tourism has been criticised as a strategy for economic development because it is associated with *dependency* upon external—and often fickle—sources of growth (de Kadt 1979). The choice of tourist destination may fluctuate from year to year, either because recession in northern Europe reduces overall demand, or because of changes in the competitiveness of individual countries. The latter may stem from political uncertainty as, for example, in Portugal, where the number of foreign tourists was halved between 1974 and 1976, following the coup of 1974. Demand fluctuations may also result from price changes in tourism in particular countries. This is partly because the products of mass tourism—whether Alpine skiing or Mediterranean sea and sun— are characterised by uniformity rather than place differentiation. Instead, competition is centred on prices, so that even small price changes following, say, a currency devaluation or revaluation, can affect tourist numbers. Spain provides an example of the positive and negative aspects of this process. While devaluation of the peseta in 1959 was a key in the development of Spanish mass tourism, occasional price 'leaps', such as that in hotel prices in the mid-1980s and the early 1990s, have a detrimental effect on competitiveness.

The development of tourist facilities tends to be *spatially and temporally polarised* (Shaw and Williams 1994, Chapter 1). Tourism is particularly spatially concentrated in Spain; in the Balearics, one-fifth of all jobs are in hotels and restaurants and, allowing for a multiplier of about 1.5, this takes the proportion nearer to one-third. Such mass tourism brings about intense local pressures in terms of congestion, the need for new infrastructure and pollution, to the point that the attractions of an area are eroded. These features are not immutable, for there is no simple linear relationship between the growth of tourism and economic benefits for local communities. Initially, tourism may create more jobs for locals while increased demand for food leads to intensi- fication of agriculture. Later, with further development, negative consequences may become more apparent.

Tourist developments can also generate *land-use conflicts* with industrial, agricultural and other users competing for the same 'optimum' sites, limited water supplies and, possibly, limited labour reserves. Tourism may provide jobs but it can attract labour away from agriculture, leading to abandonment of some marginal farming areas, which has both social and landscape consequences. In Portugal's Algarve, for example, the coastal growth of hotels in the 1960s and 1970s was matched by population losses of about 30 per cent or more in municipalities located only 50–65 km inland (Cavaco 1980). At the same time, good agricultural land, near tourist resorts, may be left uncultivated, being held speculatively in expectation of future development gains.

Inter-sectoral links can be complementary, as is evident in the case of agriculture. Tourism provides markets for agricultural products, while farms can establish accom- modation enterprises as well as tourist attractions such as farm visits and horse-riding. Such diversification represents a form of risk-spreading, but can also generate signifi- cant income streams which, in some instances, equal or surpass the returns from agriculture. Tourism activities may become essential components in household survival strategies: the additional income may enable a family to maintain an otherwise unprofitable farm, with tourism income being invested in farm modernisation or simply subsidising farming activities. Access to supplementary income need not involve farm tourism for members of the family may take up jobs in tourism outside the farm. The overall balance between benefits and disadvantages is complex; it also depends on whether the seasonality of tourist and family work is complementary, and on whether tourism significantly increases the price of farm land and labour.

In summary, the relationship between tourism and development is contingent. Above all, it depends on the structure of the tourist industry itself and the nature of the local, regional or national economy. There is, therefore, enormous diversity of economic experiences, as the following national case studies illustrate.

3

Spain: from the phenomenon of mass tourism to the search for a more diversified model

Manuel Valenzuela

3.1   Mass tourism and the Spanish economy: a positive balance

The outstanding feature of Spanish tourism after World War II has been a rapid growth in the number of visitors, which has been linked to the incorporation of domestic and foreign middle- and lower-class social groups into the market for its tourism products. This expansion has been based on external factors such as generalisation of paid holidays, rising living standards and increases in air travel—but social and economic conditions in Spain (lower price levels, absence of labour conflicts, etc.), as well as state policies for the promotion of tourism through the provision of financial credit and international publicity campaigns, have also been important. The dictatorial regime of General Franco prioritised tourism, regarding it not only as a valuable economic sector but also as a means of legitimisation in respect of other European states, or at least of large elements of their populations (Cals 1983, p. 15).

On the eve of the 1936–1939 Civil War, foreign tourism to Spain was still relatively small-scale, involving barely 200,000 tourists. The major expansion in volume came after the 1950s, with an increase from 2.5 million visitors in 1955 to 43.2 million in 1985, to 52.0 million in 1990 and 63.2 in 1995. Of the latter, only around 71 per cent were tourists as opposed to excursionists or travellers in transit (especially Portuguese and North Africans).

The increase in the number of visitors continued until 1973, with a reduction between 1973 and 1976 (Table 3.1), reflecting the economic crisis in a sector which was particularly sensitive to rising prices (a high elasticity of demand). After 1983 there was a further increase in arrivals which has made Spain the second-ranked country in world tourism, accounting for 8.8 per cent of all tourists and 10.5 per cent of all foreign exchange earnings. Another significant indicator of the position occupied by Spain in world tourist flows is the fact that it is included in the brochures of approximately 50 per cent of foreign tour operators. More recently, between 1989 and 1992, there was a fall in visitor numbers, related to both a loss of quality and the strong competitiveness of other Mediterranean destinations, such as Yugoslavia, Tunisia and Greece; in the same time period, income from tourism fell by 28 per cent, the mean length of stay declined and daily expenditure decreased (Pearce 1996, p. 126).

Tourism and Economic Development: European Experiences, 3rd Edition. Edited by A.M. Williams and G. Shaw.
© 1998 John Wiley & Sons Ltd.

Table 3.1   Foreign visitors to Spain, 1955–1995

	Number of visitors	Index
1955	2,522,402	100
1960	6,113,255	242
1965	14,251,428	565
1970	24,105,312	956
1975	30,122,478	1194
1980	38,022,816	1507
1985	43,235,362	1714
1986	47,388,793	1879
1987	50,484,996	2001
1988	54,178,150	2148
1989	54,057,562	2143
1990	52,044,056	2063
1991	53,494,964	2121
1992	55,330,716	2194
1993	57,263,351	2270
1994	61,428,034	2435
1995	63,255,000	2508

Sources: Secretaría General de Turismo (various), *Anuario de Estadísticas de Turismo*; Secretaría General de Turismo (various) *Nota de Coyuntura Turística.*

However, by the mid-1990s Spanish tourism had regained its world position and accounted for 8.2 per cent of tourist arrivals (second after France), but was only ranked fourth in terms of foreign exchange earnings, with 6.7 per cent of world total.

Domestic Spanish tourism, expanding as a result of higher standards of living and increased car-ownership after the mid-1970s, has also contributed—and in no small part—to the growth of mass tourism. Indeed, in the 1980s 40 per cent of Spaniards already participated in tourism; of this number, 90 per cent took their holidays in Spain in 1985. A decade later (summer 1995), 45.3 million trips were made by the Spanish population, with 93.1 per cent of these taking place within the country.

The fact that Spanish tourism has experienced largely uninterrupted growth reflects the intrinsic strength of the industry, as much as that of the economy as a whole. It is not surprising, therefore, that tourism has been favoured by successive policy-makers. The role of tourism in balancing some of the structural deficiencies of the Spanish economy in the 1960s (such as lack of industrial investment, the commercial deficit, and low consumption capacity) is well known. Even the advent of democracy in the mid-1970s, at the height of a global economic crisis, did not substantially change attitudes within successive Spanish regimes and governments. Ideology seems to have little influence on the prioritisation of tourism and the policies developed for the industry before and after the fall of Franco's dictatorship.

In the last four decades, tourism has made a substantial contribution to the Spanish economy, and this is underlined by the fact that it accounts for 10 per cent of GDP. Equally important is its contribution to the accumulation of foreign exchange reserves, in the absence of which Spanish development in the 1960s would have been far more problematic. Tourism has stimulated value added in several sectors of production, but especially in accommodation and catering (hotels and restaurants have secured about

Table 3.2   Tourism foreign exchange earnings in Spain, 1975–1994

	Earnings (US$ millions)	Index (1975 = 100)	Percentage of value of exports
1975	3,404.20	100	25.1
1980	6,967.70	205	20.5
1985	8,150.80	239	35.8
1986	12,058.00	354	35.8
1987	14,759.90	434	44.6
1988	16,542.80	486	40.9
1989	16,174.20	475	36.3
1990	18,593.00	546	33.3
1991	19,004.30	558	30.4
1992	22,180.80	652	38.4
1993	20,445.90	601	32.5
1994	21,410.30	629	39.0

Sources: Secretaría General de Turismo (various), *Anuario de Estadísticas de Turismo*; Secretaría General de Turismo (1994) *Notas de Coyuntura Turística.*

half of the economic growth generated by tourism), followed by transport, travel agencies, recreation and commerce (Alcaide 1984, p. 34). Since 1970, official input–output tables for tourism (produced every four years) have made it possible to trace the impact of tourism on the national economic system as well as providing estimates of the multiplier effect of tourist spending. Tourism provides a stimulus to virtually the entire economy through the mechanisms of secondary expenditure effects. As a result, the input–output analysis indicates that tourism accounted for a global weight of 8.84 per cent of total Spanish production in 1992 (Instituto de Estudios Turisticos 1996, p. 293). It has also contributed to capital development, accumulated from the savings of residents as much as from foreign investment; this has mostly been channelled into real estate. In some periods, tourism investments have accounted for approximately 10 per cent of the gross formation of fixed capital (Figuerola 1983, p. 24).

The most important economic effect of tourism at present is its contribution to employment generation, whether directly or indirectly. Partly due to tourism, the outflow of emigrants to Europe, which was characteristic of the 1960s, has been stemmed. However, poor working conditions, seasonality and low skill levels are widespread in the tourism industry (Cals 1974, p. 121). Tourism activities directly employed 500,000 persons in the mid-1960s; this increased to 1 million in 1975, and it is usually accepted that tourism accounted for 9.5 per cent of the economically active population by 1994. In absolute terms, tourism in 1994 was responsible for 1,116,000 jobs; of these, 664,000 were directly dependent, and 452,000 were indirect). Nevertheless, of all the economic changes brought about by tourism, the most spectacular is the generation of foreign exchange earnings; these have been a critical element in the balance of payments (Table 3.2).

Following the stagnation of growth in the mid-1970s, the position of tourism in the Spanish economy strengthened after 1983, and it had become the principal economic sector from the mid-1980s and this continued after the short critical period 1989–1992. A number of economic indicators corroborate this statement; tourism is a prolific source of foreign currency (21,410 million pesetas in 1996), surpassing Italy

Table 3.3   Arrivals of visitors in Spain by country or macro-region of origin, 1955–1993

	Percentage of all visitors										
	1955	1960	1965	1970	1975	1980	1985	1990	1991	1992	1993
Benelux	2.8	2.9	4.0	6.2	7.9	6.3	5.9	6.3	6.7	6.5	4.6
France	36.8	41.8	45.2	36.6	31.1	26.5	25.4	22.3	22.5	21.3	21.1
Germany	4.6	5.4	7.3	8.6	14.1	12.3	13.1	13.2	14.3	14.0	15.2
Portugal	6.9	5.7	7.0	10.9	11.8	24.0	17.9	19.4	19.7	20.9	19.8
Scandinavian countries	1.0	1.6	2.0	3.6	4.0	2.6	3.7	3.0	2.8	2.4	2.1
UK	13.2	10.2	9.5	11.3	11.3	9.5	11.6	12.1	11.5	11.8	13.1
USA and Canada	8.8	8.5	5.1	4.8	3.7	2.5	2.7	1.9	1.2	1.7	1.6
Other countries	25.9	23.9	19.9	18.0	16.1	16.3	19.7	21.7	21.2	21.3	22.5

Sources: Secretaría General de Turismo (various), *Anuario de Estadísticas de Turismo*; Secretaría General de Turismo (various), *Nota de Coyuntura Turística*.

and France in this respect, and contributes 9 per cent of GDP. The beneficial effects on the commercial balance have increased further, with tourism earnings providing 39 per cent of all exports, and being almost double the commercial deficit (144 per cent in 1996).

3.2   Intense geographical concentration: a major and traditional feature of Spanish tourism

Three countries together contribute more than 50 per cent of Spain's foreign tourists in most years: France, the UK and Germany (Table 3.3). Over time there have been changes in the geographical origins of the visitors: Germany and Belgium have increased in relative weight while, on the contrary, the UK and Scandinavia have declined. Despite their minor numerical importance at present, non-European tourists (mostly North American or Japanese) are being encouraged because of their higher spending capacity compared to Europeans; they also have a greater propensity to participate in inland and quality tourism (cultural tourism, hunting, golf, etc.); the results of this effort are evident in the case of USA tourists. In contrast, the 'average' profile of European tourists is more modest: they visit Spain in the peak season, and generate relatively low expenditures, compared to the world average. This is largely due to the manner in which tour operators control tourism demand and contribute to strong geographical concentration of both demand and supply, even if their oligopolistic hold has weakened somewhat in recent years; thus, by 1996 only 56 per cent of foreign tourists had booked their holidays through a tour operator, with the precise level depending on the countries of origin. Until the present, the coastal regions and the Spanish archipelagos (the Balearic and Canary Islands) have provided very attractive environments to northern European tourists: a dry and sunny climate, picturesque landscapes and low cost levels. Promotional campaigns, emphasising the bright and pleasant climatic conditions, have contributed to creating and sustaining this image. This was stressed in the current official slogan of Spanish tourism ('Everything under the sun'), while place names with climatic resonance (for example, the Costa del Sol, and the Costa de la Luz) have been used to market many coastal regions (Figure 3.1).

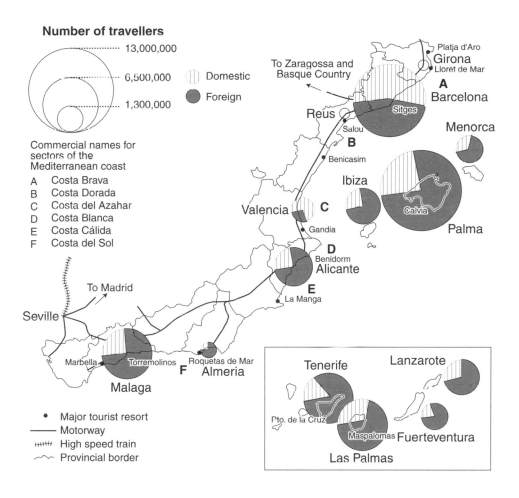

Fig. 3.1 Arrivals by air in Spain's leading tourism Mediterranean regions and islands, 1995

Source: Aeropuertos Españoles (AENA)

Efforts to break the dominance of the 'sunshine' regions have not been very successful, as is evident in surveys of the motivations of foreign tourists. In 1985, 82.1 per cent of tourists still admitted that their principal reason for coming to Spain on holiday was to enjoy the climate, even though there are differences according to countries of origin; this reason was most important for the British, Scandinavian and Germans and least important for the Italians. However, tourist perceptions are starting to change, with culture, sports and leisure retailing becoming more important tourism attractions; by the summer of 1996 some 80 per cent of tourists had participated in some kind of cultural activity during their holidays (Instituto de Estudios Turísticos 1997, p. 26).

Apart from the coastal regions, the foremost tourism destination is Madrid, which combines the attractions of a major city (museums, palaces, first-class hotels, luxury

Table 3.4   Regional distribution of tourists using hotels in Spain, 1994

	Total	Foreign tourists		Domestic tourists	
		Total	(%)	Total	(%)
Andalusia	6,285,922	2,597,591	17.0	3,688,331	18.3
Aragón	1,050,083	112,693	0.7	937,390	4.7
Asturias	453,606	30,730	0.2	422,876	2.1
Balearics	4,916,747	3,961,702	25.9	955,045	4.8
Canaries	2,952,059	2,040,786	13.3	911,273	4.5
Cantabria	526,416	73,059	0.5	453,357	2.3
Castille-La Mancha	1,027,154	179,648	1.2	847,506	4.2
Castille-León	2,023,156	334,114	2.2	1,689,042	8.4
Catalonia	5,576,948	2,985,419	19.5	2,591,529	12.9
Extremadura	599,843	67,247	0.4	532,596	2.6
Galicia	1,353,542	160,241	1.0	1,193,301	5.9
Madrid	4,094,739	1,640,197	10.7	2,454,542	12.2
Murcia	414,572	46,053	0.3	368,519	1.8
Navarra	328,413	40,405	0.3	288,008	1.4
Basque country	942,183	208,912	1.4	733,271	3.6
La Rioja	240,779	29,583	0.2	211,196	1.1
C. Valenciana	2,580,782	787,451	5.1	1,793,331	8.9
Ceuta y Melilla	83,384	14,646	0.0	68,738	0.3
Total	35,450,328	15,310,477	100.0	20,139,851	100.0

Source: Instituto Nacional de Estadística (1995), *Movimiento de viajeros en establecimientos turísticos.*

retailing, etc.) with good accessibility by air travel from rest of Europe. It is also the 'door to Europe' for most North and South American tourists. The historic cities of the interior are also widely visited by excursionists, either from the nearby coasts (Córdoba, Seville, Granada) or Madrid (Toledo, Segovia). Many small and medium-sized historic towns of the interior (Ciudad Rodrigo, Alcalá de Henares, Sigüenza, and Lorca, among many others) are promoting their images as tourism destinations, either via individual publicity campaigns or as parts of networks of historic routes. An example of the latter can be found in the case of Spain's World Heritage Cities, which have created a consortium, chaired by Avila, for promoting themselves with the assistance of Turespaña (Vera Rebollo and Dávila Linares 1995).

The regional distribution of tourists—whether foreign or Spanish—is far from homogeneous, as is evident for hotel users at the level of the autonomous regions in 1994 (Table 3.4 and Figure 3.2a,b). Andalusia, with 6.2 million visitors, is the leader, followed by Catalonia (5.5 million), the Balearics (4.9 million), Madrid (4.1 million), the Canary Islands (2.9 million) and Valencia (2.6 million). There is a rough balance between Spanish and foreign travellers in all regions, except the Balearics and the Canary Islands where foreign tourism dominates.

Data on overnight stays provide another measure of geographical concentration (Table 3.5). The importance of the Balearic Islands for foreigners is evident, accounting for 40.4 per cent of overnights, a figure which has been virtually static since the mid-1980s. However, in Catalonia and Valencia there is a more stable relationship between foreign and domestic overnights. The distribution of domestic tourists—73.4 per cent of whom in 1995 preferred seaside holidays—is more evenly spread amongst

(a)

Fig. 3.2   Distribution of tourists and accommodation, by type, in Spain's autonomous regions
in 1994: (a) Autonomous regions; (b) number of tourists staying in hotels, 1994;
(c) registered accommodation, 1994

Source: Secretaría General de Turismo

the tourist regions, except the archipelagos. However, there is some preference in the
domestic market for the classic 'sun and sea' product provided by the leading tourism
destinations: Andalusia (17.5 per cent), Catalonia (14.6 per cent), the region of
Valencia (13.8 per cent) and the Balearics (10.2 per cent). Domestic tourists also have a
stronger preference than foreign ones for other Spanish destinations, including the
mountains and rural areas of the interior.

There are important variations in the geographical preferences of tourists, according
to their country of origin (Table 3.6). Germany and the UK are the major foreign
sources of tourists; the British are in a majority on the Costa Blanca (Alicante), the
Balearics and the Costa del Sol, while Germans predominate on the Costa Brava and
the Canary Islands. The French continue to be important on the Costa Brava and the
Costa Blanca. North American tourism is increasing in volume and is already significant in inland areas (Madrid, Seville and Granada), but is also important in Alicante
and Málaga, seaside resorts which attract elderly tourists. Other urban destinations such
as Barcelona, La Coruña (Galicia) or San Sebastián (Basque Country) are also

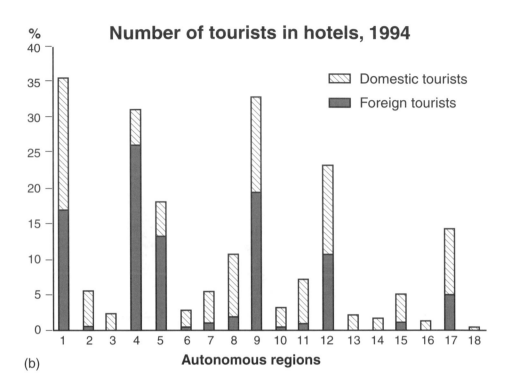

Fig. 3.2 (*continued*)

becoming more attractive for American tourists. Even European tourists have been adapting over a number of years to a more balanced distribution, and this is especially true of the French, Italians and British (Table 3.6); to some extent, there appears to be a return a much earlier period of tourism, when it seemed to be imperative for tourists to visit Granada, Seville or Toledo.

3.3   Tourism and a new territorial model of development

The Spanish regime realised in the 1960s that development of coastal tourism offered considerable economic advantages, and for this reason a number of promotional measures were introduced. There was even a special law to facilitate the creation of new tourist settlements in the zones favoured by spontaneous tourism development, the so-called 'Centros y Zonas de Interés Turistico Nacional' Act of 1963 (Valenzuela 1985). Nevertheless, state intervention was limited to sectoral actions (for coasts, marinas, natural spaces, etc.). Furthermore, no regional planning mechanisms existed, even in those areas where the pressures of congestion were strongest (for example, the Balearic Islands), so that there was no overall spatial planning framework. A high price has been paid for this lack of foresight because valuable and valued natural and tourism spaces have been lost, such as forests and fertile agricultural land. As a result, many sensitive ecological spaces have been seriously damaged or destroyed; this is the case in

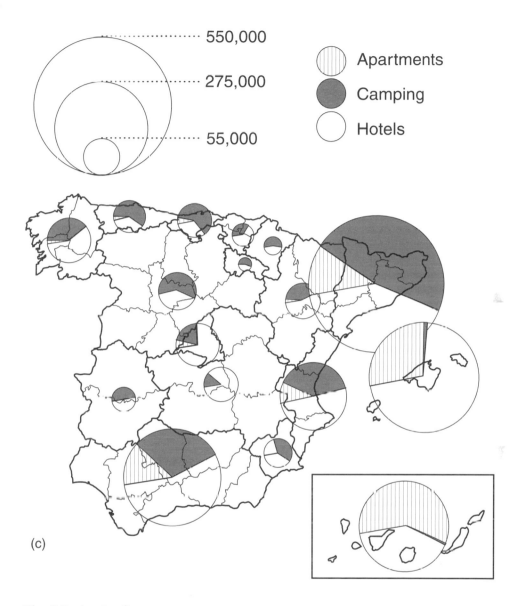

(c)

Fig. 3.2   *(continued)*

some marshland areas along the Mediterranean coasts such as the Delta del Ebro and the Valencia coast (Valenzuela 1993). For the same reason, tourism development has been accompanied by negative environmental impacts and serious shortfalls in collective infrastructure.

One of the priorities for state intervention has been the transport infrastructure so as to ensure adequate accessibility to the tourism zones. This was one of the objectives of the *Planes de Desarrollo* (1960s and mid-1970s). Although the planned coastal motorway

Table 3.5   Foreign and domestic overnights by Autonomous Regions in Spain, 1995

	Foreign tourists		Domestic tourists		Average stay (days)
	Total	(%)	Total	(%)	
Andalusia	12,669,544	12.5	10,206,393	17.5	3.4
Aragón	245,751	0.2	2,080,731	3.6	2.0
Asturias	53,188	0.1	1,031,992	1.8	2.3
Balearics	40,922,785	40.4	5,960,605	10.2	9.5
Canaries	20,676,780	20.4	4,562,007	7.8	8.3
Cantabria	137,481	0.1	999,726	1.7	2.1
Castille-La Mancha	242,499	0.2	1,391,034	2.4	1.5
Castille-León	452,066	0.4	2,956,606	5.1	1.6
Catalonia	15,091,233	14.9	8,520,446	14.6	3.9
Extremadura	98,248	0.1	940,789	1.6	1.6
Galicia	308,231	0.3	3,086,354	5.3	2.2
Madrid	3,779,852	3.7	4,630,716	7.9	2.0
Murcia	191,357	0.2	1,437,425	2.5	3.7
Navarra	74,009	0.1	523,694	0.9	1.8
Basque country	409,844	0.4	1,352,120	2.3	1.9
La Rioja	42,662	0.04	404,457	0.7	1.9
C. Valenciana	5,764,472	5.7	8,039,591	13.8	5.0
Ceuta y Melilla	21,742	0.02	156,678	0.3	2.0
Total	101,181,744	100.0	58,281,364	100.0	4.3

Source: Turespaña: Instituto Español de Turismo; unpublished data.

axis has not been yet completed (see Figure 3.1), this has directly linked the Mediterranean coast, as far as Almería, with the European motorway network. A lack of investment in motorways in north-western and interior regions has been an obstacle to tourism expansion, given that 54.5 per cent of tourists entered the country by road in 1995, even though a state-owned system of express ways has been expanded across the country. There has also been investment to upgrade and expand airports in response to the increased numbers of air-borne inward tourists (39.7 per cent of total arrivals in 1995), although the regional distribution is uneven with the Costa del Sol and the archipelagos being most dependent on air transport. New airports have been opened (Tenerife Sur) and others expanded and refurbished, as at Malaga and Son San Joan (Mallorca); in the latter case, an airport that received 12.3 million passengers in 1995 will have the handling capacity for 24 million by 2010. However, the supply of other essential infrastructures (water supply and sewers, for instance) has tended to lag behind demand. An inadequate water supply is a particular problem in the Canary Islands, where it has been necessary to rely upon sea-water desalination, especially in the case of Lanzarote.

The accommodation supply is a critical element in the organisation of tourism and is also usually the principal component of the built environment of tourism areas. In practice, the accommodation supply tends to be heterogeneous, and different forms often coexist within the same tourism zones (Morales Folguera 1982) (Table 3.7). In Spain as a whole, the official supply of tourist beds numbered 2,182,560 in 1996, representing the outcome of a long cumulative period of growth; 137,036 beds were in hotels and similar establishments (51.8 per cent), 640,829 on camping sites (29.4 per

Table 3.6 Regional distribution of foreign hotel visitors in the main tourist provinces in Spain, 1995

	Germany	Belgium	France	The Netherlands	Italy	UK	USA	Others
Alicante (C. Valenciana)	1.8	12.7	5.0	7.4	2.7	61.7	0.4	8.1
Balearic (Balearic Islands)	46.4	2.2	4.2	1.5	3.5	33.2	0.2	8.7
Barcelona (Catalonia)	19.9	2.6	6.9	11.1	8.2	15.3	4.5	31.4
La Coruña (Galicia)	18.7	2.2	10.1	2.9	8.9	9.9	6.4	41.0
Girona (Catalonia)	23.6	10.1	18.5	8.5	6.3	13.2	0.6	19.3
Granada (Andalusia)	14.5	5.9	12.8	3.6	9.1	15.3	10.7	28.0
Guipúzcoa (Basque Country)	10.8	2.9	16.3	3.6	11.2	19.0	9.6	26.6
Huelva (Andalusia)	75.2	8.2	4.6	1.2	0.5	1.9	0.3	8.1
Madrid	6.8	1.3	6.6	1.9	9.8	7.6	15.7	50.3
Malaga (Andalusia)	10.2	5.7	10.4	6.9	7.4	40.4	3.0	15.9
Murcia	25.9	6.5	8.9	4.6	4.3	22.7	2.7	24.4
Las Palmas (Canary Islands)	61.9	2.3	1.2	4.2	4.1	11.4	0.1	14.8
St. Cruz (Canary Islands)	35.8	6.6	6.1	2.6	7.9	30.2	0.3	10.7
Sevilla (Andalusia)	13.6	2.1	13.7	2.7	12.4	10.5	14.2	30.7
Tarragona (Catalonia)	19.1	13.4	9.8	15.6	2.7	27.4	0.2	11.8
Toledo (Castille–La Mancha)	10.0	3.2	19.9	3.2	9.0	9.0	15.4	30.3
Valencia (C. Valenciana)	13.6	3.4	18.4	2.6	12.9	11.9	5.0	32.1
Zaragoza (Aragón)	15.0	2.2	21.0	2.0	8.9	9.2	9.0	32.7

Source: Instituto Nacional de Estadística (1996), *Movimiento de viajeros en establecimientos turísticos.*

Table 3.7   Regional distribution of tourist accommodation (registered beds) in Spain, 1995

	Percentage of total			
	Hotels	Apartments	Camping	Tourism rate[1]
Andalusia	14.3	10.2	14.4	18,078.0
Aragón	2.4	0.3	3.3	2,352.2
Asturias	1.4	0.2	4.2	1,306.0
Balearics	23.8	25.9	0.6	16,489.6
Canaries	9.8	40.03	0.2	12,676.2
Cantabria	1.4	0.1	4.5	1,441.8
Castille–La Mancha	3.9	0.1	1.0	1,204.3
Castille–León	2	0.1	5.4	2,838.8
Catalonia	19.8	15.2	40.6	18,060.8
Extremadura	1.3	0.04	2.3	8,24.2
Galicia	3.9	0.5	4.8	3,150.6
Madrid	4.9	1.2	2.7	9,981.3
Murcia	1.3	2.1	2.1	1,141.0
Navarra	0.7	0.1	1.3	1,033.9
Basque country	1.4	0.02	1.4	1,985.5
La Rioja	0.4	0.01	0.8	346.6
C. Valenciana	7.3	3.5	10.3	6,966.4
Total	100.0	100.0	100.0	100,000.0

Source: Secretaría General de Turismo; Federación Española de Hoteles; Banco Español de Crédito (1993), *Annuario del Mercado Español* (Tourism rate).

[1] Calculated as the number of places in hotels and camping × prices × months opened during the year (Spain = 100.000)

cent), and 404,695 in registered apartments (18.5 per cent) (Figure 3.2c). In addition, there was a significant informal sector, with substantial numbers of unregistered beds; although difficult to quantify, there may be as many as 10 million lodgings, consisting of apartments and villas for rent, including some second homes. The demand for second homes by German and British purchasers is particularly strong in the Canaries, especially in south Gran Canaria (Maspalomas-Playa del Inglés). There are also concerns that Mallorca, following extensive advertising in German newspapers, will become a German 'colony' as a result of real estate transactions. In addition, an estimated 65 per cent of second home buyers in Marbella are foreigners. This highlights the fact that housing market mechanisms tend to exclude large segments of potential Spanish buyers from many resorts, who in consequence are constrained to investments in resorts such as Benidorm, Torrevieja or Gardía (Comunidad Valenciana), where property prices are lower.

One of the problems in studying the unregistered sector is that, even where ownership is known, functions remain ambiguous; for example, it is difficult to distinguish between tourism accommodation which is rented out seasonally and homes which are used by the owner and his family throughout the year. Owning a house or an apartment in a coastal resort is a widely held aspiration in all social classes. It can even be argued that ownership of a weekend home constitutes part of the mythology of what constitutes general social progress, and this partly explains recent expansion of second homes, especially in those areas which are easily accessible from the larger cities (Valenzuela 1976; Canto 1983) and in the major tourism regions (Miranda 1985; Valenzuela 1988). However, there are also issues of distorted or 'unfair' competition here, between the undeclared used of second homes for renting to tourists and the formal, registered sector.

Strong growth of foreign investment in the second-home market means that there are already more than 1.5 million foreign-owned dwellings in the Spanish coastal areas. In the period January–August 1996 alone, foreign investments in real estate and housing totalled 136 billion pesetas, and 80 per cent of these belonged to tourists. It is estimated that foreigners purchase approximately 50,000 dwellings a year in Spain. The preferred destination of foreign real estate investment is the Costa del Sol, which accounts for around one-quarter of the total, followed by the Balearic and Canary islands; 'off shore' financial bodies play an important role in channelling this investment, particularly to the Costa del Sol and above all to Marbella.

The large-scale settlement of retired foreigners on the Mediterranean coast and in the Canary Islands started in the 1970s, especially in the Costa Blanca (Gaviria 1977b) and in parts of the Costa del Sol, such as Marbella and Mijas (Jurdao 1979); it has subsequently spread over a wider geographical arena, as the ageing of the European population feeds demand. In total, there are more than 500,000 foreign-owned second homes on the Costa del Sol and the Costa Blanca; the remainder are divided amongst the Costa Brava, the Balearics and the Canary Islands. The majority of owners are British (30 per cent) or German (25 per cent) nationals. One indicator of the recent hectic round of foreign purchasing is the emergence of new types of property acquisition, such as lease-back and time-share. Both these forms of property ownership are largely controlled and organised from abroad and the lack of a clear regulatory framework in Spain is now being discussed in the Spanish parliament following an EU initiative in this sphere. Time-share is of particular concern to the hotel sector, as it competes head-on in the short-holiday market segment (one or two weeks). In the mid-1990s more than 50,000 families made use of this type of tourism accommodation, and there were an estimated 400 tourism time-share complexes.

In places, permanent foreign residents threaten to overrun the capacity of municipal services, which were designed for smaller local populations, and they are also set to become the strongest political force in future local elections, under EU franchisement regulations. This reflects more than speculation, for in Mijas (Costa del Sol) more than 40 per cent of the registered inhabitants are foreigners (see Williams *et al.* 1997). Nevertheless, the growth of second homes can help reduce the acute seasonality experienced in coastal tourism areas, as it is a major factor in determining whether tourists eventually become permanent settlers (Bosch 1987, pp. 133–6).

Tourism has contributed to urbanisation ever since the middle of the nineteenth century, when summer holidays became fashionable among the middle and upper classes. The first tourism towns, such as San Sebastián and Santander on the north coast, and Málaga, Alicante and Palma de Mallorca on the Mediterranean, developed on the basis of their climatic resources, their environmental surroundings and the role of human agency in the form of astute promotion. Alicante, for example, became known as the 'Playa de Madrid' when, after the inauguration of a direct railway link in 1858, it became fashionable with the middle classes of Madrid, not least because seabathing supposedly had healing properties (Vera Rebollo 1985). There were similar reasons for the take-off tourism in Málaga and Palma de Mallorca, whose fame as winter resorts spread across Europe at the turn of the nineteenth century.

In contrast to these older resorts, the specialised 'leisure towns' of the 1960s tourism boom are very different, for their spatial and economic organisation tend to be subordinate to tourism. Many are based on small, existing farming or fishing settlements, as in the case of Torremolinos, Benidorm or Lloret de Mar. However, some developed on new 'greenfield' sites, spatially discrete from existing municipal centres, and can be regarded as new settlements: examples include Platja d'Aro (Costa Brava) and Playa de San Juan (Alicante). Benidorm is the archtypical leisure town, its tourism development having been planned from the 1960s (Gaviria 1977a, pp. 24–31), while its enterprises—in the hotel sector, transport, retailing and other services—are totally dependent, directly or indirectly, on tourism. Benidorm, with 125,000 registered bedspaces (33,000 in hotels), receives more than 3 million tourists annually, while its permanent population is only about 47,715 (1995). In the peak season it has accommodation for 300,000 tourists but it is also one of the leisure towns which suffers least from seasonality because of its effectiveness in attracting elderly tourists out of season.

Other forms of tourism settlement also line the coast, ranging from 'marinas' linked to new sports harbours to exclusively residential urbanisations. There are extensive urban areas covering hundreds of hectares and many involve high-quality urban projects, with some even having been designated *Centro de Interés Turístico Nacional* (for example, La Manga, Sotogrande or Matalascañas). They boast high-quality residential accommodation and a variety of select sporting opportunities (golf, riding, sailing, etc.). In contrast, some urbanisations involve illegal construction on land in non-zoned areas and have critical infrastructure deficits (Diputación Provincial de Valencia 1983).

In some municipalities, new tourism settlements already occupy a major part of the total land available for development, as in Calviá (Balearics), Calpe (Alicante) or Mijas (Málaga). Not surprisingly, such areas tend to be widespread along the coastal fringes but, from the 1980s, a second group of municipalities has been incorporated into the tourism-oriented real estate market (Vera Rebollo, 1987, Navalón 1995). There is a high level of foreign capital involvement in such developments which, for this reason, have been labelled 'neo-colonialist'. Frequently, they have poorly-defined residential landscapes and this constitutes one of the major challenges to planning in these regions. Studies exist of tourist settlements on the Mediterranean coast as a whole (Zahn 1973) and of particular regions such as the Costa Brava (Barbaza 1966, pp. 618–24), and Valencia (Miranda 1985), as well as the Canary Islands (Gaviria 1974, pp. 9, 75, 383) and the Costa de la Luz (Fourneau 1979, pp. 145–61).

3.4   Economic impacts on uneven regional development of tourism specialisation

Tourism has traditionally been considered to be a means of reducing regional economic disparities, even though it exhibits extreme coastal concentration (Pearce 1981, pp. 59–60). In Spain, the economic effects of tourism have mostly been evaluated on a national scale, and there has been comparative neglect of regional perspectives until the 1980s, when the autonomous regional governments were made the competent bodies for tourism policies.

Table 3.8 Tourism and regional economic structures in Spain, 1991

| | Economic impact of hotels and restaurants | | | |
| | Production (GVA)[1] | | Employment | |
	Million Pesetas	(%)	Number	(%)
Andalusia	446,942	6.4	115,102	6.1
Aragón	86,943	4.8	20,624	4.7
Asturias	59,113	4.4	14,723	4.1
Balearics	401,801	28.1	98,120	29.4
Canaries	277,582	13.7	67,213	13.8
Cantabria	39,988	5.9	9,458	5.7
Castille-La Mancha	64,754	3.3	19,967	3.8
Castille-León	124,298	4.0	36,838	4.4
Catalonia	602,606	5.6	131,586	5.6
Extremadura	38,812	3.8	12,528	4.3
Galicia	159,792	5.1	41,678	4.3
Madrid	539,823	6.0	106,495	5.8
Murcia	50,097	4.1	12,385	3.8
Navarra	35,547	4.2	8,825	4.5
Basque country	121,035	3.7	28,016	4.0
La Rioja	15,085	3.8	3,855	3.8
C. Valenciana	312,578	5.6	74,548	5.4
Ceuta and Melilla	5,678	3.7	1,590	4.2
Total	3,382,474	6.2	803,551	6.1

Source: Banco Bilbao-Vizcaya (1993); Instituto Español de Turismo, unpublished data.

[1] Gross value added.

3.4.1 Tourism as an instrument of change in regional economic structures

Tourism may benefit production and employment creation in a region by means of three multiplier effects—direct, indirect and induced linkages (Lecordier 1979). However, econometric techniques have not yet captured the full extent of the structural change which occurs in the productive structures of tourism regions. Input–output tables for tourism regions, such as Andalusia or the Canary Islands, do serve to underline the importance of tourism. Nevertheless, it has not been possible to assess fully the impact of activities such as air transport, which are closely connected with mass tourism. Similarly, the full impact of tourist expenditures is not known except for the direct contracts between tour operators and hoteliers. Furthermore, it is difficult to estimate the multiplier effect of tourist expenditure because of the high import propensity in consumption (Rodríguez Marín 1985, pp. 253–61). However, it can be stated that the regional economic effects of tourism broadly reflect contrasts in tourism supply and demand, and this is confirmed by the contribution of the regions to Spain's total gross value added (GVA) from more easily identifiable tourism sectors such as hotels and restaurants (Table 3.8).

The sector of tourism which has been most thoroughly researched is hotels and restaurants, not least because of data availability. The Balearics (28.1 per cent) and the Canary Islands (13.7 per cent) stand out for their contribution to regional production, measured in terms of GVA. The impact of tourism is less clear in larger regions, such as Andalusia, or in diversified economies, such as Catalonia or Valencia, where the weight of the hotels and restaurant sector in the regional economy hardly differs from the national average. Yet, at the provincial level, tourism contributes 9 per cent of GVA in Gerona (Costa Brava) and 10.5 per cent in Málaga (Costa del Sol).

Hotels and restaurants have considerable intersectoral links. In Andalusia, for example, input–output analysis has shown that they impact strongly on the regional economy, not only in terms of GVA (61.2 per cent of production) but also because of a low level of import propensity from outside the region (Cuadrado and Aurioles 1986, pp, 57–8). In Valencia, input–output analysis has shown that hotels and restaurants are the branch of the service sector which possesses the greatest propulsive power for the regional economy (Denia and Pedreño 1986, pp. 394–5).

The effects of tourism on real-estate activity are of particular geographical interest, even if the economic benefits are more questionable owing to partial leakage of the income generated by land and property sales. Among 'local' agents, large landowners have captured a large share of gross benefits, either from agricultural land sales to developers or by becoming promoters themselves. However, the resulting value added hardly benefits the economy of the tourism region, as the landowners are mostly absentees (Mignon 1979, pp. 69–72). There have been even greater benefits for the developers, who have commercialised either rural land in the expectation of development or land already subdivided into plots for development, or who have converted existing buildings for tourism-related businesses. All these various forms of real estate transactions have attracted investment from the wealthiest regions (Madrid, Catalonia and the Basque country) and from abroad.

In the Canary Islands, German investment has been responsible for the development of one of the most distinctive leisure towns in Spain (Maspalomas-Playa del Inglés, in Gran Canaria). The initial stimulus for this was the fiscal advantages provided for West German investment in 'underdeveloped countries' by the 1968 Strauss Act (Rodríguez Marín 1985, p. 265). More recently, German capital has diffused throughout the archipelago, although it is currently most active on Lanzarote, developing leisure towns such as Costa Teguise and Puerto del Carmen. The potential for realising profits from tourism-related real-estate business has provided a strong stimulus for the building trade, especially on Tenerife, where it has been responsible for most construction. The origin of investment in real estate on the Costa del Sol is more diversified but German, Belgian, British and French capital have secured a larger share of the benefits than has Spanish capital, not least because of the national priority accorded to foreign exchange earnings in the face of an endemic current account deficit.

Tourism does not always have net positive regional economic effects. There is intense conflict along the Mediterranean coast between tourism and traditional economic activities such as fishing, salt mining and, above all, agriculture. Tourism competes for land, water and labour, usually to the detriment of these other activities. Another consequence has been the farm labour shortages in the hinterlands of the tourism zones and this has hindered agricultural commercialisation (Mignon 1979, pp. 127–9). The implications are even graver if account is taken of the way that these other activities have, over the centuries, shaped a cultural space which is valued, fragile and of great scenic importance. Furthermore, the imprudent exploitation of water resources threatens the survival of intensive agriculture (fruit trees, early vegetables, sub-tropical products, etc.) on the Costa del Sol, in Almeria and on the Canary Islands.

Agrarian structures have literally been torn apart as residential settlements have invaded fields and vineyards, as, for example, at Marina Alta in Alicante.

Prior to the 1990s no overall framework was available for tourism development in the form of a plan which was informed by the principles of environmental preservation and complementing traditional economic activities. There is an economic logic for such plans, for many complementary activities are profit-yielding and are competitive in EU markets. Agricultural activities can also be viewed positively from a tourism perspective, for they create valued landscapes and supply consumer products which help to reduce the propensity to import; the latter is a particularly acute problem in the archipelagos (Salvá 1984, p. 227). All of this highlights the urgent need for the regional authorities (the competent bodies, at present, for regional planning) to establish clear criteria for the spatial zoning of tourism and other activities in the coastal areas, following the principle of complementarity. The production of White Papers on tourism in some regions in the 1980s (Catalonia, the Balearics and Andalusia) has indicated a shift in this direction, although they have not been very effective. At the same time, many coastal municipalities have modified their urban planning practices in order to avoid further losses of fertile agricultural land (Valenzuela, 1986a). On the other hand, there are concerns that stricter territorial controls may deter tourism investment.

In response to changing market conditions in the 1990s, which include more environmentally-sensitive tourism demand, there has been a revision of the institutional framework for tourism and for enhancing the tourism product, in order to improve competitiveness. The lead was taken by the Central Government through the FUTURES Programme (1992), which had the goal of increasing competitiveness by prioritising quality; this implies a commitment to reducing over-dependence on mass low-price coastal tourism, which has paid scant attention to environmental issues and plant obsolescence. This programme was formally agreed by all the Autonomous Communities (AA.CCs), that is the regions, and their responsible tourism bodies have been putting into effect sectoral plans with a long-term quality orientation. Examples of such operational plans are provided by the Andalusian Plan DIA and the Balearic *Plan de Ordenación de la Oferta Turística* (1995), the aim of both of which was to enhance environmental quality in the tourism zones and the quality of the tourism product (Pearce 1996, p. 130).

3.4.2 Tourism and regional labour markets

There have been considerable demographic changes in the provinces of mass tourism, which have had above-average population growth rates between 1960 and 1991 (the date of the last census) (Table 3.9). Girona is an exceptional case, with the population multiplying almost threefold in this period. Demographic growth has mainly been a consequence of in-migration, and by 1991 in-migrants already accounted for 25–30 per cent of the resident populations of the single-province tourism areas (Costa Brava, Costa Blanca and the Balearics). There is a distinctive regional patterning of labour migration flows; migrants from Murcia have a preference for neighbouring Alicante, which has also attracted in-migrants from the eastern provinces of Andalusia (Granada and Jaen) and from Castille-La Mancha (Albacete, Ciudad Real, etc.). Andalusia and Murcia are also the dominant sources of migration to the Balearics, while the most underdeveloped provinces of Andalusia (Granada and Jaen) provide the less-qualified

Table 3.9 Demographic evolution in the main tourism provinces of Spain, 1960–1991

	Number of inhabitants		Increase	
	1960	1991	Absolute	1960 = 100
Alicante	711,942	1,292,563	580,621	181.6
Balearics	443,327	709,138	265,811	160.0
Gerona	177,539	509,628	332,089	287.1
Málaga	775,167	1,160,843	385,676	149.8
Santa Cruz de Tenerife	490,655	725,815	235,160	147.9
Spain	30,430,698	38,872,279	8,441,581	127.7

Source: Instituto Nacional de Estadística (1960, 1991).

labour working in hotels and catering on the Costa Brava. The three provinces mentioned above are among the first ten ranked with respect to volume of in-migration, 1961–1982, although the largest contingent arrived between 1962 and 1973 (Santillana 1984, p. 29).

Migration to the tourism zones in the less-developed regions (Andalusia and the Canary Islands) has a different pattern. The coastal regions of Málaga province (the Costa del Sol) have received a major part (40 per cent) of their inmigrants from the province itself, with most (33 per cent) of the remainder originating elsewhere in Andalusia. Marbella and Fuengirola have probably experienced the greatest demographic increases as a result of this migratory process (López Cano 1984, p. 74). To some extent the impact of tourism development on regional labour markets can be deduced from the increasing weight of the tertiary sector in the economies of the tourism provinces. Hotels provide the most obvious examples of direct tourism employment, although this type of accommodation is now in decline. Table 3.10 shows the distribution of hotel jobs by region, differentiating maximum (more than 50 per cent of which is seasonal) from permanent employment. These figures highlight the extent of seasonality in hotel employment which, in the low season, can fall to only one-fifth of that in the peak season in the Costa del Sol and the Balearics, and to 30 per cent in Alicante. Only the Canary Islands have no pronounced seasonality in tourism labour markets.

The regional distribution of hotel and restaurant employment is indicated in Table 3.10 (see also Figure 3.3). This type of employment is dominant only in the smaller regions and in specialised tourism areas, attaining 29.4 per cent in the Balearics. In Alicante, hotel and restaurant jobs represent only 6.0 per cent of the total, in Málaga 11.5 per cent and in the Canary Islands 13.8 per cent. However, these relatively modest figures do not reflect the real extent of labour market dependence on tourism, given the extensive multiplier linkage effects of this sector. This is exemplified by construction; in the more tourism-orientated provinces (indicated in Table 3.11), with the exception of Alicante, the share of total employment in construction is 1.5 points above the national mean, reaching a maximum in Málaga (12.0 per cent).

It is also possible to assess the overall contribution of tourism to improving standards of living and family income. Tourism is directly responsible for the Balearics and Gerona occupying, respectively, first and second place in the ranking of the 50 Spanish provinces in terms of per-capita incomes, according to the latest issue (1993) of the *Renta Nacional de España*. The situation in Alicante is less clear but family income is still 6 per cent higher than the national average. Traditionally, Tenerife and Las Palmas

Table 3.10   Regional distribution of hotel employment in Spain, 1994

	Permanent employment		High season employment	
	(No.)	(%)	(No.)	(%)
Andalusia	9,073	17.5	8,134	15.3
Aragón	1,492	2.9	1,133	2.1
Asturias	772	1.5	342	0.6
Balearics	4,554	8.8	13,778	25.8
Canaries	8,265	16.0	7,679	14.4
Cantabria	524	1.0	440	0.8
Castille-La Mancha	1,357	2.6	902	1.7
Castille-León	2,799	5.4	1,547	2.9
Catalonia	6,061	11.7	8,126	15.2
Extremadura	832	1.6	747	1.4
Galicia	1,785	3.4	1,487	2.8
Madrid	7,774	15.0	2,189	4.1
Murcia	705	1.4	778	1.5
Navarra	550	1.1	354	0.7
Basque country	1,555	3.0	750	1.4
La Rioja	290	0.6	245	0.5
C. Valenciana	3,333	6.4	4,596	8.6
Ceuta and Melilla	147	0.3	89	0.17
Total	51,868	100	53,334	100

Source: Secretaría General de Turismo (1995), *El empleo en el sector hotelero, 1994.*

(Canary Islands) were considered to be economically disadvantaged provinces, but tourism has contributed to an improvement in their positions to 23rd and 29th place, respectively. The effects of tourism on standards of living in particular communities is more difficult to assess; however, in Valencia the most tourism-orientated municipalities tend to occupy leading positions in ranking of municipalities in terms of per capita incomes (Esteban and Pedreño 1985).

3.5   New directions for Spanish tourism: seeking quality and diversity

The excellent outcomes of the tourism seasons in the mid-1990s, as shown earlier, have not eliminated the structural problems which have traditionally characterised the Spanish tourism sector: the seasonality of demand and spatial concentration, as well as the loss of competitiveness compared to its direct Mediterranean and Caribbean competitors. Different measures and policies have been, and are being, adopted to ameliorate these structural problems and the loss of quality, obsolescence in some sectors and rising prices, but these have had uneven results. Spanish tourism faces a dilemma for there is a strategic choice to be made between, on the one hand, further growth of low–middle market hotels and apartments concentrated along in the coastal areas, or quality improvements and greater spatial diffusion with enhanced economic benefits.

As already indicated, the upgrading of the tourism industry requires more far-reaching developments both inside and outside the hotel and apartment sector. Many

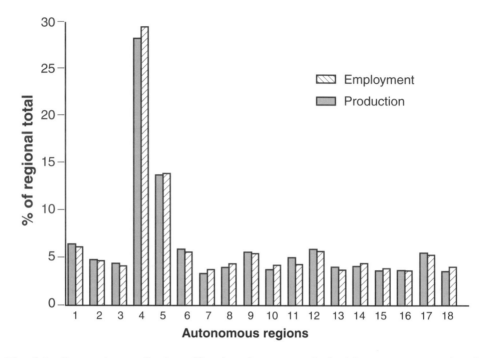

Fig. 3.3 Economic contribution of hotels and restaurants in Spain's autonomous regions in 1991

Source: Instituto Nacional de Estatística (1995), *Movimento de viajeros en establecimientos turísticos*; Banco Bilbao-Vizcaya (1993)

Table 3.11 Employment linkages of tourism in specialised tourism areas in Spain, 1991

	Tertiary sector		Building industry		Hotels and restaurants	
	Employment	(%)	Employment	(%)	Employment	(%)
Alicante	235,669	54.5	42,115	9.7	26,102	6.0
Balearics	251,693	75.4	33,980	10.2	98,120	29.4
Gerona	140,052	59.0	24,639	10.4	29,551	12.5
Málaga	216,983	69.0	37,820	12.0	36,220	11.5
Santa Cruz de Tenerife	175,552	73.4	25,770	10.8	27,180	11.4
Total	7,774,193	58.7	1,284,142	9.7	544,337	4.1

Source: Banco Bilbao-Vizcaya (1993).

interest groups are now demanding such changes. Rediscovering the traditional quality of service is an example of such changes and this has to be linked to improved professional training, which has become part of the responsibilities of the AA.CCs. It is also important not to neglect the quality of the complementary supply in aspects such as infrastructure (roads, telephones, sewage, etc.) and services, as well as the environment and landscape of the tourism resort. Supply-side improvements also require diversification, with the development of sport and leisure facilities in and around the tourism resorts, so as to make golf, riding or sailing more widely accessible rather than being the preserve of a small élite of wealthy customers. In the same way it is assumed that traditional seaside tourism should be linked to inland tourism, based on the attractions of a rich cultural and natural landscape. The extent to which these changes have been effected will be considered in the following pages.

Some progress has been made in the upgrading of coastal tourism in Spain. Preservation of unspoilt coastal landscapes and restoration of less seriously damaged ones were major aims of the *Ley de Costas*, approved in 1988. This established free public access to all the beaches, dunes, cliffs and marshes adjacent to the sea and prohibited any new construction within 100 metres of the shore. An important role has also been played by the former *Ministerio de Obras Públicas y Urbanismo* (*Ministerio de Fomento* from 1996) in the restoration of beaches on some coasts where the sand had almost disappeared (e.g. the Maresme coast in Catalonia). In this region the sea-front of Barcelona was designated for tourism and leisure uses, as part of an urban restructuring plan to improve urban tourism facilities for the 1992 Olympic Games. Similarly, in Andalusia, the decision to hold a World Exhibition at Seville in 1992 has been the catalyst for improvement of the entire Huelva Coast (Costa de la Luz), situated an hour from Seville. Since 1993 there has been a *Plan Director de Infraestructuras* (1993–2007); one of its major aims is to promote integrated coastal management, orientated to sustainable use of these areas. In addition to this rather idealised goal (which is very difficult to attain given the current starting point), the plan foresees the realisation of new infrastructures, mainly for transport. Linked to this, a new *Plan de Actuaciones en la Costa 1993–1997* has been approved. Thanks to these measures, and those adopted by the AA.CC, municipalities and *mancomunides* (associations of municipalities for cooperation in specialised areas, such as tourism promotion), Spain has been able to achieve Blue Flag status for a large number of its beaches: 329 in 1996 as against 168 in 1991.

3.5.1 New institutional forms of tourism organisation: the protagonism of regional power

An important political shift took place in Spain during the 1980s: the establishment of the regional autonomous governments which became responsible for tourism policy within their own territories. Consequently, the role of Central Government has been reduced and its main responsibility has been the international promotion of Spain as a tourist destination, although even in this it acts in cooperation with the regional and local institutions and the entrepreneurial sector. The State also has responsibility for overviewing the evolution of the tourism sector, and for evaluating its main weaknesses and strengths, with a view to establishing an overall strategy (Secretaría General de Turismo 1990). In addition, it is charged with management of some singular nationwide tourism facilities, such as the network of *parador* hotels and some congress and convention palaces (Madrid, Torremolinos, etc.). While tourism had a specific ministry during Franco's regime, it now has a different administrative status; since 1996 the central body responsible for promoting tourism is the Instituto de Turismo de España (TURESPAÑA), which is located within the Ministry of Economy and Finances.

In the 1990s every AA.CC has the right to pursue its own promotion and regulation of tourism but is not always empowered to solve all the specific problems related to this, such as the provision of infrastructure and the quality of beaches and sea water. These exclusive regional rights in respect of tourism carry the risk of creating confusion amongst customers and tour operators. Consequently, the regional approach may give rise to a lack of uniformity and compatibility that potentially could limit the development of tourism in Spain and weaken the country's image as a tourism destination. Furthermore, the regional rivalry in what is essentially the same international market may also be an obstacle to tourism development. This situation becomes even more complicated when local scale or locally-based political organisations (*Diputaciones Provinciales, mancomunidades,* etc.) also compete in the promotion and development of tourism.

While all the AA.CCs agree on the need to upgrade and diversify the tourism supply in order to enhance competitiveness, each region has chosen its own way to pursue these goals. After drawing up White Papers in the early 1990s, many regions (Catalonia, Andalusia, Valencia, Balearic Islands) have progressed to issuing specific plans and programmes and even to enacting tourism laws: examples range across the many different forms of tourism areas, including the Mediterranean (Plan DIA in Andalusia), the northern region (Galicia) and inland (Junta de Castilla y Leon, 1996). Promotion and planning of tourism has been incorporated within the new regional governments as a part of larger departments (*consejerías*), usually as a General Direc-torates, except in the Balearics where a separate department for tourism has been created. Specialised agencies to channel and market the growth of tourism have also been created, such as the Balearic IBATUR (*Instituto Balear de Turismo*), the Andalusian *Empresa Andaluza de Turismo* and the Valencian *Institut Turistic Valencià* (ITVA). The extent to which all the AA.CCs agree on the need to enhance the quality of the tourism product and to discover new tourism strategies is exemplified by the fact that they have all signed the FUTURES Programme for the upgrading of the Spanish tourism supply. This incorporates five specialized plans, dealing with different targets, ranging from coordination and modernisation of the tourism supply to developing new products (Leno Cerro, 1997). Of particular note is the specialised plan devoted to improving the tourism environment in order to regain standards of excellence which are more in harmony with the growth of more responsible tourism, both in foreign and domestic markets. One of the most outstanding results of this policy has been an extensive collection of *Planes de Excelencia Turística*, understood as a set of measures for the regeneration of mature tourist resorts, which expanded rapidly during the period of 'hard' mass tourism in the 1970s and which are located both on the Mediterranean coasts (Torremolinos, Gandía, etc.) and the islands (Calviá, Puerto de la Cruz, etc). The municipality of Calviá (Mallorca) has been engaged for some years in a wide programme of actions (reducing densities, eliminating obsolescent buildings and opening up new green areas and services) tightly linked to the idea of sustainable development, as formulated by Agenda 21 of the Rio Conference (1992).

At a lower political level, many provinces, through their own institutions (*Diputa-ciones Provinciales*) and the municipalities, singly or integrated into intermunicipal organizations (*mancomunidades*), have made tourism the main instrument of their strategies for economic restructuring and especially for generating employment. This is particularly acute in the case of some northern regions such as Asturias and Cantabria, which are striving to establish their position in the tourism market (mainly the domestic segment), offering new kinds of alternative tourism based on their landscape, culture and gastronomy and even their recent industrial and mining heritage (for example, Museo de la Minería at El Entrego, Asturias). Tourism development is therefore seen as a means of counterbalancing the process of decay suffered in their traditional economic bases (heavy industry, mining, fishing or shipbuilding). The rural interior regions are converging in the promotion of their enormous cultural and rural heritages, even if their tourism images lack efficacious marketing. Exceptional efforts have been made to promote them as tourism destinations in both Castilles, that is to the north and south of Madrid. Castilla-León has its own tourism development plan. For many areas in the interior, with the obvious exception of Madrid Metropolitan Region, with a population of more than five million, tourism is seen as the only possible strategy for combating depopulation and maintaining economic activity at a level sufficient for their territorial survival.

3.5.2   *New tourism products for a new tourism industry*

The strengthening of the tourism products has been one of the principal concerns of Spanish tourism policy in the 1990s, and this has mainly involved the implementation of the FUTURES Programme (Figure 3.4), whose major objectives are:

- To mitigate the strong seasonality of tourism.
- To diversify the tourism product, which has been excessively dependent on the 'sun and beach' attractions.
- To respond to the emergence of more qualified demand requirements, in both the interior and the coastal regions.
- To create new economic development opportunities and social welfare in depressed interior urban areas.

The various tourism initiatives can be considered under three headings: the restructuring of mature tourism destinations; developing the potential for new forms of urban tourism; and innovations in rural tourism.

3.5.2.1   The restructuring of mature tourism destinations

There is consensus amongst expert commentators that the policy priorities should be to broaden out the base of seasonal demand, and secure higher-spending customers though improvements to the quality of supply. During the 1980s some improvements in seasonality were secured though the retirement boom to Alicante and the Costa del Sol. More recently (1985), a national specialized state social services agency (INSERSO) has been established, which has a responsibility for channelling the social (out of season) travel organised for elderly, low-income people to those areas with the most marked tourism seasonality. This policy serves the twin goals of enhancing the quality of life of older people, and helping to maintain tourism employment during the low season. The Third Age Holidays Programme has offered 360,000 beds for the 1995–1996 season alone. Between October and April, those aged over 65 can travel to and stay for 14 days, at very low prices, in any one of a designated list of seaside resorts. In addition, since 1989–1990, INSERSO has had a programme of spa tourism, which offers pensioners access to two weeks' holidays at some 30 spa resorts located thoughout Spain.

There has been greater progress in improving availability in the mature tourist destinations of complementary recreational activities which are essential for attracting

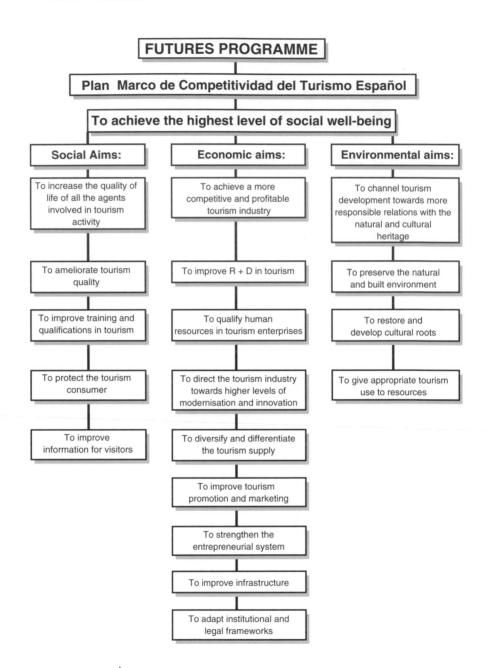

Fig. 3.4   Basic aims of Spain's FUTURES programme, 1992

Source: Secretaría General de Turismo

higher-income and more activity-orientated tourism. In the hotel sector, there have been programmes to develop provision of integrated services, including sport and organised leisure activities. Moreover, specialised tourism is being increased through the promotion of particular interests (for example, painting and computing); Club Méditerranée has been a pioneer in this, and the approach has been imitated elsewhere, with the mushrooming of club resorts (Gutiérrez 1985, pp. 157–67). The same motivation underlies the opening of a large number of amusement parks, such as the aquaparks which are widely scattered along the Mediterranean coast. Of particular note is the Disney-like theme park Port Aventura (near Salou in Tarragona province), which has been a major commercial success, not only during the high season but also as an instrument to combat seasonality. Seville is destined to become the location of a second major theme park, the Isla Mágica, devoted to historic relationships between Seville and America; this has been open in 1997. With a budget of 13,356 million pesetas, it is expected to generate 1,000 jobs and to attract some 2 million visits annually, 15 per cent of whom will be tourists. Isla Mágica (Magic Island) will introduce the visitor to the same historic background (the age of discoveries) that was used as a theme in the 1992 World Exhibition in Seville, and is often held to have been the first urban theme park in the world.

The provision of selective sports facilities is an important component of any strategy to attract middle- and high-income tourists (Esteve 1986, pp. 237–66). One response has been a tendency to link golf courses to luxury hotels (for example, the Parador de 'El Saler' near Valencia) or to large residential-tourism developments such as Nueva Andalucía (Málaga) and Almerimar or La Manga Club in Murcia (Ortega Martínez 1986, pp. 44–5). In the same way, marinas have been a critical promotional attraction for many residential complexes, sometimes incorporating traditional Mediterranean architecture (for example, Marina de Benalmádena in Costa del Sol). Without doubt, the Costa del Sol has the finest and largest number of sports facilities, linked to the development of residential areas and high-quality tourism (Valenzuela 1982); for this reason, it has been called the 'Costa del Golf', a promotional slogan which was acknowledged by the Rider Cup organisers when the region hosted the event in 1997, the first time it had been held outside of the USA and the UK. In any case, golf resorts have become widely spread throughout almost every tourism area, including the inner and northern regions of Spain. Conceived of as a luxurious and exclusive small residential estate, strategically situated around a golf course with the complementary facilities (hotel, club, restaurant, etc.), the golf resort has been taken up by developers as an ideal response in the search for high-quality tourism, irrespective of associated social (exclusion) and environmental problems (lack of water).

Another element in the expansion of quality tourism is 'talasotherapy', which has a long-established tradition in a number of internationally famous coastal tourist centres (Estoril, Knokke, etc.). In Spain 'talasotherapy' has been practised since the late nineteenth century at a number of coastal resorts (Cadiz, Málaga, Alicante, etc.) and even for low-income consumers (as at Mar Menor). At present, the wealthiest tourist have access to specialised luxury facilities, as at the Biblos Hotel (Mijas), but there is also provision for middle-income clients at hotels such as the Meliá Costa del Sol (Torremolinos). There will probably be increased demand for cure-bathing in the future as the European population ages and third-age tourism continues to expand. A similar trend can also be observed in the case of inland balneotherapy. After many years of decay, spa tourism now constitutes a dynamic element of tourism supply in the interior of Spain, and is especially attractive to middle-class, educated tourists who are seeking a quiet, peaceful and healthy atmosphere. Some historic spa resorts (such as La Toja, Galicia) have opened a new page in their market acceptance but the majority survive only by virtue of social tourism, having become destinations for the third-age holiday programmes financed by INSERSO, which performs a similar function in respect of sea-side resorts, as previously mentioned.

3.5.2.2   The potential for new forms of urban tourism

Since the 1960s the Spanish central administration has also invested in the construction of exhibition and conference halls in order to diversify the tourist industry. This has been supported by many hotel-owners who are able to offer high quality facilities for conferences and conventions, or benefit more indirectly from the high-spending propensity of conference tourists; this type of tourism also responds to the double challenge of improving quality and reducing seasonality. In the 1990s there is a real problem of the oversupply of exhibition and congress facilities, which may cause new problems for their current owners. Nevertheless, congress and exhibition tourism do have considerable potential in many inland and urban destinations. The new regional and municipal authorities have become very active as promoters of conference centres; many of these have been designed by famous architects, such as Siza (Santiago), Moneo (San Sebastián) and Bofill (Madrid). However, in some instances they have been highly politically contested, as has happened in Cantabria. In some regions, such investments have been used as instruments to counterbalance the over-concentration of economic and political power in the regional capital; this is the case in Castilla-León, where Salamanca has been chosen as the location for a conference centre, so as to balance the power of the regional seat of government, Valladolid. However, in general, conference tourism tends to be concentrated in the larger cities and capitals, which have a high density of institutions and other decision-making centres, which generate specialised information flows and demands for meeting places. This partly accounts for the strong competition amongst cities and the promoters of particular facilities, both public and private, to attract this type of quality tourism. The potential conflicts have partly been resolved through a partnership arrangement, the creation of the Spanish Convention Bureau, involving 27 local convention bureaus in 1995. The dominant conference cities are Madrid, Barcelona, Seville and Valencia, and most of the others probably lack sufficient demand to become economically viable. By far the most important centre is Madrid, which accounts for one-third of all events held in Spain, and was ranked fifth, at the international level in 1995, as seat of international conferences, with a 3 per cent market share. The Madrid Congress Palace, managed by Turespaña, hosted 139 events in 1996 with a global participation of 130,000 visitors (Turespaña: Instituto de Turismo de España 1997).

The major cities are also the only ones with the capacity for hosting major fairs and exhibition complexes (with more than 100,000 m² of sheltered surface area). In Spain as a whole, there are 20 fair institutions which are organised under the umbrella of the *Asociación de Ferias Españolas* (AFE), founded in 1964. Four fair and exhibition complexes (Madrid, Barcelona, Valencia and Bilbao) alone account for 800,000 m² of covered surface area, which gives them effective control of the fairs and exhibitions market. The attractions of such centres are clear; not only does business tourism have a far higher level of spending than leisure tourism, but its benefits are widely distributed

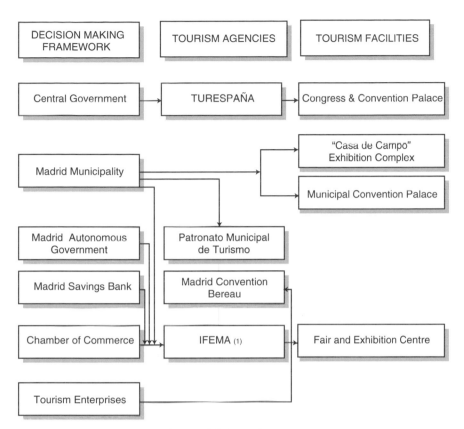

| DECISION MAKING FRAMEWORK | TOURISM AGENCIES | TOURISM FACILITIES |

Central Government → TURESPAÑA → Congress & Convention Palace

"Casa de Campo" Exhibition Complex

Madrid Municipality → Municipal Convention Palace

Madrid Autonomous Government — Patronato Municipal de Turismo

Madrid Savings Bank — Madrid Convention Bereau

Chamber of Commerce → IFEMA (1) → Fair and Exhibition Centre

Tourism Enterprises

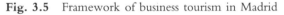

(1)   Institución Ferial de Madrid (Madrid Fair Agency)

Fig. 3.5   Framework of business tourism in Madrid

Source: Adapted by the author from various sources

throughout the urban economy, including commerce, leisure and culture. This is why the ideal business organisation needs to be a partnership involving all these different elements; Madrid provides a model of such a partnership (Figure 3.5), where IFEMA (*Institución Ferial de Madrid*) is the owner of 130,000 m² of exhibition facilities which are located in a large tertiary estate which also houses supporting services for business tourism, including hotels, a congress palace (owned by Madrid municipality and managed by the public enterprise Campo de las Naciones) and a golf course (Valenzuela 1992).

Events and mega events tourism supposedly have similar effects on urban economic development and employment creation, the assumption being that this kind of tourist normally has a high level of spending power. 1992 can be considered to be the starting point for a sequence of mega urban events in Spain, which have had considerable significance in terms of both economic and urban development; in that year three important events took place—the World Exhibition (Seville), the Olympic Games (Barcelona) and designation as European Cultural Capital (Madrid). The event which generated the largest tourism flows was Seville Expo 92; according to official data sources, there were 41.8 million visitors in total, which implies a daily mean of 237,582 in the period 20 April–12 October. In reality, the impacts of mega events in terms of economic benefits and stable employment creation are not always so clear because of the temporary nature of the activities. Their effects tend to be intense but short-lived and they therefore need to be complemented by programmes of other activities and spectacles in future, as is intended in Seville's case through the Isla Mágica project. In other instances, the mega events have opened the door to attracting other congresses and meetings to the organising city, with the complementary benefit of improvements to their physical and functional environment (Barke and Towner 1996). The strategies adopted in other cities has taken into account the experiences of these three mega events, whether at the local (Sefarad 92 at Toledo) or regional (Xacobeo 93 in Galicia) scale. The organisation of specialised cultural events is becoming increasingly frequent, given the search of tourism dynamism; this is exemplified by the exhibitions of the works of monographic famous painters (Velázquez in 1989; Goya in 1996) and of religious masterpieces from church and cathedral collections, as well as occasional exhibitions (such as Edades del Hombre), which have been presented in several Castillian cities (Valladolid in 1988; Burgos in 1990; León in 1991; Salamanca in 1993; and Burgo de Osma in 1997).

3.5.2.3   Major innovations in tourism in the interior

Historically, the first measure to encourage tourism in the interior was the construction of *paradores* (state-owned hotels); this policy dates from the 1920s but was intensified in the 1960s, marking an outstanding chapter in the activities of the *Ministerio de Información y Turismo*. Its contribution, although significant, was muted because it lacked clear aims and criteria, and was essentially a prestige operation. This is why some of the *paradores* have poor profitability, which makes their retention in state ownership problematic. In the 1990s, regional and local institutions are particularly keen to promote tourism in the interior, but the central government has also understood that this is one of the key elements for Spanish tourism as a whole; this was demonstrated in its 1997 marketing campaign, which was orientated basically to promoting all the specific tourism products in its 17 targeted international markets. One of the slogans in this campaign was 'Spain by greenery', which attracts the support of those with a passion for the green side of the life, and marks a major change from the former slogan of 'Everything under the sun'.

The autonomous regions have emphasised the promotion of 'green and nature' tourism, through creating and widening their networks of parks and nature reserves, while marketing new tourism products (excursions on foot, on horseback, boating, etc.). The northern regions have been pioneers in this field, relying on the fact that they contain the most attractive and well-preserved natural parks and a number of beautiful rural resorts (in Asturias, Cantabria and northern Aragón, for example). Meanwhile, Andalusia has undertaken a pilot study of the recreational potential of the Sierra de Cazorla natural park (Marchena 1991). All these projects aim to increase foreign and domestic demand, while showing a high level of environmental and cultural awareness (Fuentes Garcia, 1995; Robinson 1996, p. 412). As a result, many small-scale developments have emerged, whose attractions are based on local and regional history, culture, gastronomy and landscape attractiveness. As previously remarked, the promotion of tourism of the interior is encouraged at all political levels, from the EU to the local, including the provincial and the regional, with decision-making capacity mainly being located in the lower levels. There are already many local and provincial agencies devoted to tourism development and these are normally supported by the regional tourist organisations. They usually focus on the domestic markets through promotion campaigns, having in mind the weekend and short breaks segments. The common problem of all these promotional programmes is the need to differentiate their tourism products; consequently, it causes difficulties in commer-cialisation in the face of international visitor demand. Therefore, a minimum level of coordination and specialisation is urgently required at least amongst similar destinations in the interior (Valenzuela 1997).

The wide range of new tourism products in the interior of the country are normally marketed as rural tourism, which also reflects their entrepreneurial back-ground. The Navarre Foral Community and Cantabria are two of the more active regions in terms of providing organisational support for rural tourism initiatives (for accommodation, restaurants, traditional activities such as horse-riding or hunting, and new adventure sports including rafting and canoeing). The refurbishing of country houses and rural settlements has provided new forms of accommodation—both as rented houses and small family hotels—and these have been successful amongst urban tourists (Mulero Mendigorri, 1990). The process of bringing new tourist accom-modation into the market has been supported by various forms of public sector subsidies; the EU's LEADER initiative is particularly important, having provided 52,000 million pesetas for rural tourism projects in its first phase. Some regional governments have even become involved as hotel promoters for tourism in the interior; for example, the Andalusian regional government has opened four medium-quality tourism complexes (*villas turísticas*) in mountainous areas such as the Alpujarras, in the heart of Sierra Nevada and little more than 100 kilometres from the Costa del Sol (Calatrava 1984, pp. 310–12); another of these complexes has been developed in the Sierra de Cazorla.

The regional government in Castille-La Mancha has invested in and is managing directly a small hotel chain (Red de Hosterías de Castilla-La Mancha) based on the restoration of historic building, mainly of religious origin (Pastrana, Villanueva de los Infantes, etc.). Asturias, in the far north, provides one of the most ambitious pro-grammes of rurally-based tourism, and this is part of a larger development project for its eastern sub-region, Oscos-Eo; essentially the aims are to restructure the economy of Taramundi municipality through tourism, including the restoration of traditional crafts. In addition, the intensification of the real estate market in this area has been the outcome of a previous round of public investment in one of the most original, high quality new hostelries in the interior of the country (*La Rectoral*). This has provided a demonstration model, with more than a dozen private, large mansions—*casonas*—formerly owned by wealthy American return migrants from Spain (the *indianos*) have been refurbished as small, charming family-owned and managed hotels. Some of these are marketed through a shared trademark. Rural tourism has also provided oppor-tunities for privately-owned hotel chains to diversify their activities; recently-established chains, such as Confort, which has hotels in small touristic towns (Baeza, Almagro, etc.) are entering this market. Even the strongest of all the Spanish hotel chains, such as Sol-Meliá, is awakening to these new market opportunities in the interior and has invested in new high-quality hotels in medium-sized touristic towns (for example, Cáceres and Avila).

The heterogeneity of rural accommodation is demonstrated by the many different denominations used for marketing by the AA.CC; in fact, there does not exist any quality control such as is found in the traditional hostelry sector. This is one reason why tourism agencies have tended not to accept this as a worthwhile commercial proposition. Nevertheless, it has been very successful amongst the urban middle class. While rural tourism officially began in Spain in the late 1960s, with the support of the Ministry of Agriculture and with around 1,000 beds, by the 1990s there were 27,516 beds, with 51 per cent being in small hotels, mostly concentrated in the interior and northern regions (Turespaña: Instituto de Turismo de España, 1996).

More than 50 per cent of demand originates in only two AA.CCs (Madrid and Catalonia), with Madrid providing the major rural tourism market both for tourists (30.2 per cent) and travel (33.9 per cent). Motivations are relatively predictable, and in Spain as a whole the principal interest of 56 per cent of those travelling in the interior is to seek out a quiet place, accommodated in a rural building which has been made comfortable for tourist use. Nevertheless, the major part of rural accommodation (65 per cent) is provided outside of the commercial sector, by relatives, friends or second homes (Bote 1995). There are half a dozen AA.CCs where 15–20 per cent of tourists are accommodated in their own second homes, but even more remarkably, in three AA.CCs (Asturias, Castille-León and Extremadura), between 24 and 30 per cent of tourists stay in accommodation owned by a relative or friend (Instituto de Estudios Turísticos, 1996). Most of these second homes in rural areas in the interior (Castille-León, Extremadura, Galicia) are owned by people who migrated to the cities in the 1960s and 1970s; frequently, these country houses have been refurbished for use as weekend and family homes, by themselves, their families and their friends. In time, on the retirement of the owners, they may again become permanent homes. In the Mediterranean regions, such as Catalonia and the Balearic Islands, large country houses have often been bought by wealthy urban (both Spanish and foreign) artists and professionals as positional goods, indicating prestige.

There is even greater potential for promoting tourism related to game-hunting, for which excellent conditions exist in the south and centre of Spain (López Ontiveros 1981). Hunting could become a useful tool for economic regeneration in many depressed, and virtually unpopulated, areas in the interior. The autonomous government of Castille-La Mancha, a region which has one of the best-endowed hunting-grounds in Europe (Montes de Toledo), has already realised this.

Traditionally, cultural and historic-artistic attractions have drawn excursionists to the historic cities in the interior of the country, especially where they are also easily accessible from the coastal tourism centres (Granada, Cordoba), or Madrid (Toledo, Segovia) or areas situated along the main transport routes (Burgos, Trujillo). Historic and virtually forgotten routes are also being opened up to tourism, such as the medieval Camino de Santiago (Figure 3.4) or the Roman Ruta de la Plata, thereby developing a new model of cultural tourism. Examples of the adaptation of ancient trails for tourism are to be found in all parts of Spain, ranging from Gran Canaria's *caminos reales* (the king's trails) to the Castillian *cañadas* (historic routes for shepherding flocks of sheep over long distances). Old train routes also provide possibilities for alternative walking tourism: many 'green ways' for walking or cycling have been opened along out-of-service railway lines all over Spain, or have been adapted for tourism transport as at the old mining railway at Riotinto (Huelva) or old narrow gauge lines (Limón Express in Alicante or Ferrocarril de Sóller in Mallorca). Historic waterways which have lost their previous economic functions, such as the Canal de

Fig. 3.6 Selected features of cultural tourism in the interior of Spain

Source: Adapted by the author from various sources

Castilla, are being also reorientated to tourism. Many other comprehensive cultural itineraries have been developed by tourism promotion agencies, at all levels; one of the most ambitious is the El Legado Andalusí, based on andalusian moorish heritage (Figure 3.6).

3.6 Conclusions for the twenty-first century: the challenge of quality and coordination

It is generally accepted that the shift in Spanish mass tourism from a tendency to crisis and under-occupation in the 1980s to very high levels of occupancy in the 1990s, should not be allowed to obscure the structural weaknesses of tourism. The reasons for these weaknesses are very complex and need to be addressed by both the private sector and by the various levels of tourism administration (national, regional and local). The most visible effect has been the loss of competitiveness in relation to both traditional Mediterranean and Caribbean competitors and more recent and emergent destinations (such as Portugal and Russia), with a resultant decline in tourism earnings per visitor, which are far lower than in other countries: 1,035 US$ in the USA and 928 US$ in Italy, against 555 US$ in Spain. Even if it is not always obvious, the most accurate diagnosis of this problem is that beneath the surface of the current tourism prosperity there exists a loss of quality, a point that has frequently been emphasised by both professional and academic critics. Strong concentrations of tourists in some places during the high season have had serious adverse effects on the environment and landscape, but especially on the quality of life in these areas in such matters as transport and personal services. The excessively low prices of holiday packages have also contributed to the pressure on the natural and built environment.

There are now signs of change, as can be seen in the central government's FUTURES Programme, and the re-qualification programmes of the AA.CCs and the municipalities (*Planes de Excelencia*). Recent policies of promotion abroad of the 'new' tourism resources of the interior (culture, greenery, etc.) also serve to channel higher tourism revenue to Spain, even though the AA.CCs campaigns tend not to be coordinated, and consequently result in competition amongst them so that the product 'Spain' is losing a clear image amongst potential customers.

The tour-operator system exercises considerable power in negotiation with hotel chains and sometimes they are able to control the entire tourist cycle from transport (using their own aircraft) to accommodation (in their own hotels); consequently, an estimated 50–60 per cent of all tourist spending accrues to the tourists' country of origin. Domestic tourism, which accounts for more than half of global tourist expenditure in Spain, provides the basis for the successful development of some new initiatives in the interior; nevertheless, even this domestic market is becoming weaker because of the increasing tourism flows to emergent destinations in the Caribbean and the Maghreb. But, above all it is imperative that Spain regains its traditional warm welcome for visitors. Only in this way will come about the situation foreseen some years ago by the UNO Economic Commission for Europe, whereby tourism will be the major sector of the service economy by the year 2000, or at least, alongside leisure, will be a source of rapid employment creation in Spain.

Acknowledgements

D. Barrado has collaborated in the statistical updating of this chapter and J. Espada has assisted in production of the figures.

4 Italy: diversified tourism

Russell King and Armando Montanari

4.1 Introduction: diversity and change

Italy has one of the oldest, largest and most diversified tourist economies in the world. The country has strong claims to be the first home of tourism, for it was the patrician families of Ancient Rome who built the first second homes, inventing the idea of the holiday at their coastal and country resorts. Later, Italy's widely-recognised cultural and historical attractions brought the first impetus to European leisure travel as élite visitors started to arrive in the eighteenth century; extended visits to Venice, Florence, Rome and the temples of Paestum near Naples were highlights of the 'Grand Tour'. During the present century, and especially since World War II, Italy has seen dramatic expansion away from the aristocratic and cultural bases of tourism to embrace the mass markets of beach and ski tourism. Nevertheless, the artistic and architectural heritage of many cities remains an important feature on the itineraries of many tourists and visitors. Overall, then, Italy possesses a tourist industry that is more diversified than that of any other European country.

Despite the more recent and rapid development of mass tourism in countries like Spain and Thailand, Italy retains its place as one of the most important tourism countries in the world. By the mid-1990s, it was listed by the World Tourism Organisation as fourth in terms of tourist arrivals (after France, the USA and Spain) and in second place (alongside France and after the USA) as regards earnings. In fact the early mid-1990s was a phase of significant recovery for the Italian tourist industry, following a period of crisis and restructuring over the previous 15 years. In 1995 more than 29 million foreigners arrived in Italy, an increase of 9 million over the 1992 figure, whilst the financial surplus on the tourism balance of payments was 24,500 billion lire in 1995 compared to just 6,000 billion lire in 1992.

4.2 Italy's tourism resources

Italy has particularly diverse resources to attract tourists. The two major ones are its climate and its cultural heritage; these bring in the bulk of the foreign tourists. Other attractions include beaches, lakes, spa resorts, centres of religious pilgrimage and

Tourism and Economic Development: European Experiences, 3rd Edition. Edited by A.M. Williams and G. Shaw.
© 1998 John Wiley & Sons Ltd.

beautiful mountain and hill scenery; some of these are of key importance for the substantial currents of internal tourism. Also not to be overlooked is the more nebulous concept of the 'Italian way of life' which, despite modern changes in Italian society, remains a symbolic attraction for visitors from abroad.

The climatic resource is essentially twofold: the mountain areas are frequented for their snow in winter and for their fresh climate in summer; the coastal areas are tourist magnets because of their heat and reliable sun in summer. The Italian Alpine region has a well-established international market for skiing, whereas the high Apennine slopes have more local markets. The most popular tourist coasts are the Ligurian Riviera, stretching from the French border to Viareggio in Tuscany, and the Adriatic coast where several mass tourism resorts are strung out in a continuous belt south of Rimini (see Figure 4.1). Also of importance are the Neapolitan and Amalfitan coasts, the north-east corner of Sicily (especially Taormina) and the high-status Costa Smeralda in Sardinia.

With regard to historic sites, Italy's resources are incomparable. According to Quilici (1984), Tuscany alone has more classified ancient monuments and artistic treasures than any other European country. The peninsula and the islands of Sicily and Sardinia are rich in archaeological ruins, whereas most of the finest medieval towns are in the north, either in the Po Plain or in the northern third of the peninsula. Here, within the triangle defined by Turin, Venice and Perugia, there are not less than 30 cities which in any other country would be classified as outstanding. Pride of place goes to Venice, Florence and, further south, Rome; but there are also gems like Mantua, Pavia, Verona, Padua, Pisa, Lucca, Siena and many more.

Of more recent importance in the geography of Italian tourism is the development of rural tourism, typified above all by the popularity of Tuscany and Umbria for residential holidays in converted farmhouses and castles. As discussed later, rural tourism is itself a multi-faceted phenomenon, with many variants and overlapping terminologies. Although it is part of the international circuit of tourism to Italy, it also has complex links to the widespread ownership of second homes, which complicates the statistical measurement of rural holiday-making.

Figure 4.1 shows some of the main places and areas of tourism of importance in Italy. The major feature of this map is the concentration of tourism attractions and facilities in the northern half of the country. In the south the incidence of tourism is much more scattered. Thus, tourism reinforces the persistent spatial dualism in the economic geography of Italy, adding another layer to the economic pre-eminence of the north in the fields of agriculture, industry and advanced producer services (King 1987).

4.3   Sources of data on Italian tourism

In its *Annuario Statistico Italiano*, the national statistical agency ISTAT every year publishes quite detailed statistics on the tourism industry. These data are continuous since 1949 and cover two broad areas: the supply of hotel and other tourism accommodation; and the movement of the tourists themselves. The figures are published at national level and for each of Italy's 20 administrative regions. Since 1988 a more detailed array of statistics has been presented in an annual volume of tourism statistics, also published by ISTAT. Amongst other elaborations, this source includes data by month and at the level of Italy's 90 provinces.

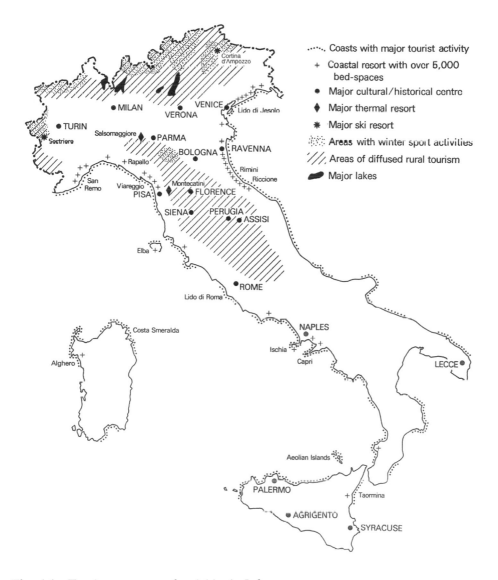

Fig. 4.1 Tourist resources and activities in Italy

Sources: After Cole (1968, p. 159); White (1987, p. 556)

Italy's supply of tourism accommodation is classified into two broad categories: the hotel sector (*esercizi alberghieri*), and the non-hotel sector (*esercizi complementari*). Each of these is further subdivided. Since 1985 hotels have been categorised by star-rating; before this there was a more complex classification which also comprised *pensioni* and *locande* (guest houses). The non-hotel sector contains a wide variety of accommodation types including camping-grounds, youth hostels and privately-rented units. Here, too, the precise categories and definitions have tended to fluctuate, so that long-term statistical trends are difficult to monitor. A major problem surrounds the existence of unregistered accommodation, which is thought to account for a significant fraction of total tourist overnights.

The movement of tourists and visitors into officially registered accommodation is recorded according to the following parameters: number of arrivals, number of over-nights spent, average length of stay, month of arrival and departure, and nationality. Most of these data are available by region, some also by province. Data on domestic tourism tend to be more limited than for international arrivals, whilst figures on Italians holidaying abroad are restricted to special surveys (for example, ISTAT 1997a).

4.4   Supply of accommodation: structure and regional diversity

In 1994 Italy offered nearly 3.25 million bed-spaces for tourists and visitors in various kinds of officially recognised accommodation; 1.72 million in hotels and 1.52 million in the non-hotel sector. These numbers appear to have fluctuated quite widely over recent decades (for instance total bed-spaces numbered 3.20 million in 1970 and 4.63 million in 1980), but this is partly explained by shifting definitions of the non-hotel sector. If we take a relatively long-term view of the more statistically stable hotel sector, then three trends are clear: first, a decline in the number of enterprises; second, an increase in the number of beds (Table 4.1); and third, an increase in the number of high quality hotels (5-, 4- and 3-star) coupled with a decrease in the inferior categories (Table 4.2). Table 4.1, especially, shows how, during the 'restructuring decade' of the 1980s, many uneconomic and substandard *pensioni* and *locande* were either closed down or upgraded to hotel status.

Outside the hotel sector the evidence, albeit fragmentary, points to a faster rate of increase in the supply of accommodation. For instance, the number of campsites (with bed-space capacities) increased from 1,138 (476,922) in 1970 to 1,902 (853,002) in 1980, 2,149 (1,094,574) in 1986, and 2,279 (1,224,791) in 1993. Beds in privately-owned accommodation (holiday flats, private lodgings, second homes rented to tourists, etc.) are more difficult to monitor. The most recent data show that 19,977 private lodgings were registered with the *Registro degli Esercenti per il Commercio* for tourist accommodation in 1994, but other estimates suggest that there is a much larger quantity of 'submerged accommodation' which is marketed through informal channels to both foreign and domestic clients (Montanari 1996).

Figure 4.2 shows the regional distribution of the main types of tourist accom-modation in 1994. The map shows that the total stock of bed-spaces is highest (over 300,000) in a group of four regions—Trentino-Alto Adige, Veneto, Emilia-Romagna and Tuscany—which lie adjacent to the main centres of population located in the highly urbanised and industrialised North-West of Italy. As Figure 4.1 indicates, these four regions are by no means uniform as regards their tourist resources: Trentino-Alto Adige is a land-locked mountain region where skiing and summer rural tourism are popular; Veneto also has a share of the eastern Alps, plus Venice and some seaside resorts; Emilia-Romagna's tourist attractions are mainly coastal but also include Bologna and other historic towns; whilst Tuscany has beautiful terraced landscapes, dozens of historic centres ranging from Florence to smaller towns like Arezzo and San Gimignano, and some coastal resorts and islands. The north-western regions of Lombardy and Liguria are themselves important for tourism, the former because of its mountains, lake and ski resorts, the latter because of its attractive Riviera coast. In

Table 4.1   The supply of hotel accommodation in Italy, 1970–1994

	1970	1980	1990	1994
No. of enterprises	41,290	41,697	36,166	34,549
No. of beds	1,332,530	1,569,733	1,703,542	1,724,333
Beds per enterprise	32.3	37.7	47.1	49.9

Source: ISTAT, *Annuario di Statistico Italiano* (1971, pp. 261–3; 1981, p. 230; 1996, p. 430).

Table 4.2   The supply of hotel accommodation in Italy by category of hotel, 1986–1993

	1986		1993	
Category of hotel	No.	Beds	No.	Beds
5-Star and de luxe	87	17,738	94	14,971
4-Star	1,222	168,845	2,193	287,323
3-Star	6,702	517,990	9,508	660,815
2-Star	11,409	488,130	11,289	419,681
1-Star	18,687	412,902	10,656	244,237
Residential hotels	610	40,908	1,149	97,969
Total	38,717	1,646,513	34,889	1,724,996

Source: ISTAT, *Statistiche del Turismo* (1988, Vol. 1, p. 53; 1995, Vol. 8, p. 33).

central Italy, Marche, Latium and Abruzzi are significant tourist regions. Latium contains the great tourist honeypot of Rome, whilst Abruzzi has the highest mountains of the Apennine chain, with ski resorts and a national park. Both Abruzzi and Marche have a virtually continuous alignment of coastal resorts patronised by both domestic and foreign tourists. Italy's southern regions also capitalise mainly on seaside tourism.

The pattern of growth in the supply of tourist accommodation over recent decades has also varied regionally. Since 1970 growth has been strongest in Trentino-Alto Adige and the south. Particularly dramatic has been the growth of campsite accommodation on the southern mainland and of hotels in Sardinia. Nevertheless, most of the southern regions remain under-provided with tourist accommodation compared with the rest of the country. Although the 'Mezzogiorno' (Abruzzi and Molise southwards, including Sicily and Sardinia) comprises two-fifths of Italy's surface area, three-quarters of its coastline and nearly two-fifths of its population, it accounted in 1994 for one-quarter of national bed-spaces and only 17.5 per cent of tourist arrivals. Nevertheless, the situation is changing, for the Mezzogiorno's share of bed-spaces was 19 per cent in 1984, and of arrivals only 11 per cent (King 1991, p. 65).

The single biggest problem of the Italian hotel industry is its generally low utilisation rate, below that for most other European countries. This lack of balance between the supply and consumption of tourism facilities is largely, but not entirely, a function of the seasonality of demand. This, in turn, is related to two broad controlling factors: seasonal variations in climate and the institutionalised availability of free time linked to holiday leave, factory closures, school holidays and so on.

At the national level the *crude* utilisation index, obtained by dividing the total potential overnights (number of bed-spaces × 365) in hotel enterprises by the number

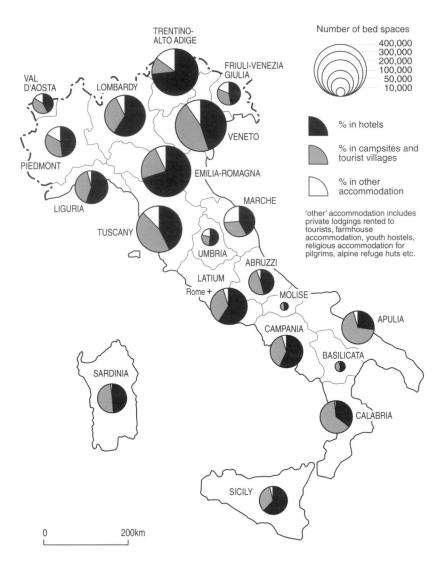

Fig. 4.2 Regional supply of tourist accommodation in Italy, 1994

Source: ISTAT, *Annuario Statistico Italiano*, Rome (1996, p. 430)

of nights the beds were actually occupied, was 29.7 per cent in 1994. The *net* utilisation index, which takes into account the seasonal closure of some establishments, was 38.5 per cent. These indices have shown only a slight tendency to increase over recent decades (in 1970 they were 26.3 and 34.9 per cent, respectively, but in 1982 they stood at 30.0 and 40.6 per cent). Moreover, the indices vary by hotel category, by region and, of course, by month (Table 4.3). Crude occupancy rates are five times higher in August (65.5 per cent) than in November (13.3 per cent); only in July and August are hotels more than half-full. Regarding hotel type, high-quality hotels have

Table 4.3   Italian hotel sector, 1994: utilisation indices by month, class of hotel and region

	Crude	Net		Crude	Net
Month			*Region*		
January	17.2	27.6	Piedmont	24.2	27.6
February	19.9	27.4	Val d'Aosta	27.6	38.2
March	19.7	29.5	Lombardy	30.3	35.1
April	24.8	33.2	Trentino-Alto Adige	31.1	32.3
May	25.7	32.1	Veneto	34.8	41.9
June	37.7	41.5	Friuli-Venezia Giulia	25.5	34.3
July	53.4	56.7	Liguria	36.4	44.0
August	65.5	68.1	Emilia-Romagna	28.9	56.2
September	41.1	45.1	Tuscany	34.0	36.9
October	22.4	31.5	Umbria	33.8	39.2
November	13.3	21.7	Marche	22.2	37.2
December	14.4	22.5	Latium	38.6	44.3
Year	29.7	38.5	Abruzzi	20.9	28.0
Hotel class			Molise	17.0	18.9
5-Star and de luxe	37.6	39.5	Campania	31.6	45.4
4-Star	34.4	42.7	Apulia	23.1	48.0
3-Star	30.4	40.1	Basilicata	14.7	25.2
2-Star	27.8	35.0	Calabria	12.4	21.7
1-Star	24.5	29.6	Sicily	25.9	32.8
All hotels	29.7	38.5	Sardinia	20.2	30.0
			Italy	29.7	38.5

Source: ISTAT, *Statistiche del Turismo* (1995, Vol. 8, p. 49).

Note: for explanation of 'crude' and 'net' utilisation indices, see text.

the highest occupancy rates, although the difference between crude and net utilisation is greatest for the middle-ranking 2-, 3- and 4-star establishments, probably reflecting the closure of a number of these hotels (many of which are in seaside resorts) for the off-season (Vaccaro and Perez 1986). Regionally, too, there are wide variations in utilisation rates. The highest rates are in the major tourist regions of the north: Emilia-Romagna, Veneto and Liguria. Much lower rates are recorded in the south, especially in Molise, Basilicata and Calabria. The poor southern rates are partly a reflection of the lower efficiency of the tourism industry in this part of Italy, and the related fact that hotel owners are more willing to survive on lower incomes (given the lack of alternative business outlets); and partly due to the South's greater reliance on summer beach tourism. Northern regions, by contrast, not only have a more efficiently managed coastal holiday industry, but also contain a large number of cities which attract year-round cultural tourists.

In addition to the fundamental problem of seasonality, there are other reasons why Italy's supply of hotel accommodation remains relatively under-utilised. More and more people, especially Italians themselves, are holidaying outside the traditional hotel networks in privately-owned flats, holiday villages and campsites. Many hotels are old and in need of upgrading and repair. But Italy remains a country of medium-sized and small family-run hotels where investment capital for modernisation is scarce. National hotel chains such as Jolly Hotels or the state-owned Agip Motels have emerged only relatively recently. The type of mass tourism with foreign investment in big hotels, bringing in tourists by cheap charter flights and package deals, has never been so important in Italy as in Spain. Although it is true that the standard of hotel accommodation has steadily improved, Italy still has a legacy of mostly family-owned establishments with low occupancy rates.

4.5   Tourist flows: sustained but uneven growth

ISTAT data enable tourist flows and trends to be measured and displayed in several ways: arrivals versus overnights, domestic versus foreign tourists, type of accommodation used, month of arrival, destination region, etc. These data can be further disaggregated (for example, by nationality) and cross-tabulated to produce an almost infinite variety of analyses. The following account must therefore be selective and will concentrate first on the long-term evolution of aggregate flows, then on foreign tourists, then on domestic tourism, and conclude with a summary of a recent survey of Italians' holiday habits. Throughout the account, emphasis will be placed on the differential regional impact of tourist flows as a major source of spatial disequilibrium.

Figure 4.3 graphs the evolution of tourist flows to the hotel sector over the period 1956–1994. A similar graph for the non-hotel sector cannot be constructed because of reclassification problems and the unknown quantity of tourist overnights in unregistered accommodation. Figure 4.3 shows a pattern of more or less uninterrupted tourist growth until the first oil crisis in 1973–1974; thereafter, growth in both arrivals and overnights continued until the end of the decade, when the second oil crisis and a major period of uncertainty and restructuring in the Italian tourist industry ensued, lasting through the first half of the 1980s. Subsequent recovery was initially uneven, related to a sequence of factors (Chernobyl, devaluation of the American dollar, appearance of algae in the Adriatic, the Gulf War, the Yugoslav crisis), but became more evident, even spectacular, by the mid-1990s, due partly to the weakening of the lira exchange rate. After the strong recovery of the early–mid-1990s, a period of consolidation is predicted for the late 1990s (Montanari 1996, p. 193).

Tourism in Italy is unevenly distributed in both time and space. The seasonal pattern of overnights reveals a marked concentration in the summer months and is, of course, responsible for the uneven occupation of hotel beds noted earlier. More than two-fifths (42 per cent) of total overnights are recorded in the two months of July and August, and 63 per cent in the four months between June and September. Overall the number of overnights in the peak month of August (64.7 million in 1994) is eight times the number spent in the trough month of November (8.1 million). This temporal unevenness does, however, show some signs of improvement: 10–15 years ago the figures were over 50 and over 70 per cent for the two-month and four-month peak periods, respectively.

Figure 4.4 shows that domestic tourism is much more seasonally concentrated than foreign tourism. Foreign tourists are keener to holiday in Italy outside of the summer months, especially for trips to cities of art and culture. Seasonality is more marked in the non-hotel sector, which for Italians sees 67 per cent of overnights registered in July and August alone, reflecting the tradition—also widespread in other countries like France and Spain—of taking a month by the sea. In fact Becheri (1993) has advanced the hypothesis that the concentration of overnight stays would be even sharper if it was possible to define statistically the period 20 July–20 August. Only business tourism and, of course, winter sports, decline during the high summer.

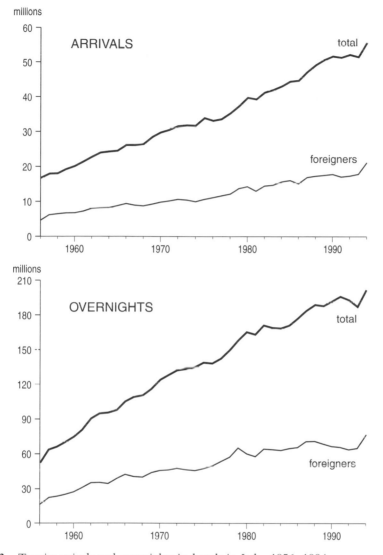

Fig. 4.3   Tourist arrivals and overnights in hotels in Italy, 1956–1994

Sources: ISTAT, *Sommario di Statistiche Storiche 1926–1985*, Rome (1986, p. 253); *Annuario Statistico Italiano*, Rome (various years)

Table 4.4 presents selected features of the tourist flow to Italy in 1994. Six of Italy's 20 regions (Lombardy, Trentino-Alto Adige, Veneto, Emilia-Romagna, Tuscany and Latium) account for two-thirds of tourist arrivals. However, this does not take into consideration the varying size of Italian regions. When tourist arrivals are indexed by the area and population of the regions, a more sensitive measure of tourist impact is achieved. This calculation shows that the 'demographic impact' of tourism is more than five times the national average in the mountain regions of Val d'Aosta and

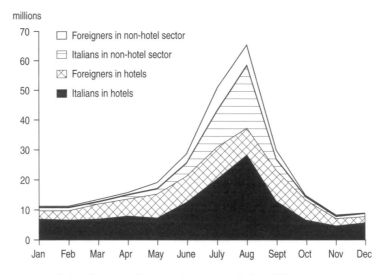

Fig. 4.4 Seasonal distribution of overnight stays in Italy, 1994

Source: Plotted from data in ISTAT, *Annuario di Statistico Italiano*, Rome (1996, pp. 436–7)

Table 4.4 Regional impact of tourist arrivals in Italy, 1994

Region	Total arrivals (thousands)	Foreigners' share (%)	Arrivals (per 100 population)	Arrivals (per km²)
Piedmont	2,203	34.5	48	81
Val d'Aosta	772	19.0	718	261
Lombardy	6,997	37.7	84	313
Trentino–Alto Adige	5,718	50.0	648	435
Veneto	8,774	57.4	210	507
Friuli-Venezia Giulia	1,398	42.1	131	198
Liguria	3,057	27.7	193	591
Emilia-Romagna	6,221	22.3	163	289
Tuscany	7,717	46.2	232	356
Umbria	1,725	24.1	204	199
Marche	1,555	15.4	114	170
Latium	7,066	50.1	138	417
Abruzzi	1,007	8.9	79	93
Molise	151	6.6	41	31
Campania	3,538	33.6	64	273
Apulia	1,521	10.7	37	78
Basilicata	217	8.3	37	23
Calabria	763	5.8	40	54
Sicily	2,750	32.2	57	114
Sardinia	1,324	18.3	83	57
Italy	64,474	38.3	117	223

Sources: ISTAT, *Annuario di Statistico Italiano* (1996, p. 430); ISTAT, *Rapporto sull' Italia* (1997, p. 100).

Table 4.5   Trends in overnights spent in different types of
destination in Italy, 1990–1994

	1990 (thousands)	1994 (thousands)	Change (%)
Seaside areas	76,724	93,133	+21.4
Historic and artistic cities	43,077	50,548	+17.3
Lakeside locations	14,950	15,807	+5.7
Spa resorts	13,573	12,525	−7.7
Mountains	25,454	29,894	+17.4
Localities in hill areas	6,631	8,759	+32.1
Provincial towns	17,401	14,524	−16.5
Other localities	54,407	49,563	−8.9
Total	252,216	274,753	+8.9

Source: ISTAT (1996, p. 264).

Trentino-Alto Adige, and approximately twice the national average in Veneto, Liguria, Tuscany and Umbria (Table 4.4). The territorial density of tourist arrivals is seen to be highest in Trentino Alto Adige, Veneto, Liguria, Tuscany and Latium. On both area and population criteria, tourist impact is low in most southern regions. These calculations of tourist intensity reveal, on the one hand, those regions where environmental pressure from tourists (water, energy, waste products, traffic congestion, etc.) is highest, and on the other hand those regions—mainly in the south of Italy— where further scope for tourist development would appear to exist (ISTAT 1997b, pp 99–100).

The 20 Italian regions listed in Table 4.4 and used in other tables and maps in this chapter are not the ideal framework for exploring the geography of tourism in Italy, not least because of the strong polarisation of tourism activities within the regions— along the coastal strip in Emilia-Romagna and Marche for instance, or in Rome in the Latium region. Several other regional typologies have been suggested (see Montanari 1996) but most lack the data to feed into any analysis. Probably more useful for an analysis of recent trends are the categories of holiday destination listed in Table 4.5. This shows that the tourism boom registered by Italy in the early 1990s has mainly affected seaside resorts, historic and artistic cities, and destinations in mountain and hill regions. Visits to other types of destinations, such as lakes, spas and provincial towns, have not kept pace with the overall rate of increase.

One final but important caveat regarding tourist flows in Italy concerns the extent to which the ISTAT data, based on recognised accommodation, capture the real movements taking place. Despite the apparent detail and clarity of the official statistics, they have been defined by Becheri (1993) as 'dim'. Becheri goes on to suggest that unrecorded overnights by Italian and foreign visitors staying in private dwellings and other 'unofficial' accommodation actually exceed the total overnights in registered accommodation. He also estimates that around a quarter of Italy's 30,000 estate agents carry out 'tourist intermediation', allowing massive access of holiday-makers and visitors to Italy's 'submerged sector' of holiday and leisure accom- modation. Indeed, for 1994, Becheri *et al.* (1995, p. 36) estimated that, as against an official total of 275 million tourist and visitor overnights, the real total may have exceeded 800 million!

4.5.1   Foreign tourists: faithful to a mature tourism destination

Returning to the official data, the number of tourist arrivals from abroad recorded via registered accommodation returns grew steadily until 1980, stagnated for a decade or more, and then increased sharply in the period 1993–1995. Foreign tourist arrivals totalled 8.5 million in 1960, 12.7 million in 1970, 17.9 million in 1980, and reached 29 million in 1995. However, from 1982 until 1992 the figure hovered around 20 million. The foreign proportions of total arrivals and total overnights have generally oscillated around 35–38 per cent in recent years, showing a slight tendency to increase since the early 1990s. As regards types of accommodation, foreign tourists opt mainly for hotels, while domestic holiday-makers prefer rented accommodation and camp-sites. Foreigners are over-represented in de luxe and 5-star hotels and, at the other end of the price and quality spectrum, in youth hostels. The Dutch and the Danes are exceptional in that they are the only foreign groups to spend more overnights in the non-hotel sector (Table 4.6).

Table 4.6 lists all countries sending at least 50,000 tourists to Italy in 1994. The list is long, reflecting Italy's status as a 'mature' tourist destination, able to attract visitors from all of Western Europe as well as from North America, Japan, Australia and elsewhere. Recently there have been new tourist flows from the former Soviet Union and other East European countries. Some of these visitors enter with tourist visas but their real objective is to find work in the informal economy; hence for many Poles, Romanians, Albanians, etc., coming to Italy involves a blend of travel, tourist and work experiences. However, one country dominates all others in Table 4.6: Germany accounts for 30 per cent of total foreign arrivals and 40 per cent of foreign overnights.

Length of stay varies significantly from one group of supply countries to another (Table 4.6). Generally, northern European tourists have the longest stays, due to their participation in one-week (or longer) package holidays, whereas southern European and non-European visitors have much shorter stays (2–3 nights), reflecting tendencies either to come on weekend visits or to spend a short time in Italy as part of the European tour. This latter pattern is especially true of the important Japanese and North American markets.

The proportion of foreign to Italian tourists varies greatly from region to region within Italy, with a general trend to diminish from north to south, as would be expected given increasing distance from Italy's continental neighbours (the main source areas for foreign tourists) and the generally less publicised nature of the South as an international tourist destination. Reference back to Table 4.4 shows that four regions (Trentino-Alto Adige, Veneto, Tuscany and Latium) receive around half of their visitors from abroad. The first of these regions contains the German-speaking province of Bolzano (Bözen) which is extremely popular with German tourists; the others have the 'big three' tourist cities of Venice, Florence and Rome. In most southern Italian regions, less than one-tenth of tourist arrivals are foreigners. The two main exceptions—Campania and Sicily—contain some well-known international resorts (Amalfi, Positano, Sorrento, Capri, Taormina) and world-famous archaeological sites (Pompeii, Herculaneum, Paestum, Syracuse, Agrigento, etc.).

Another way of measuring the regional impact of foreign tourism is to calculate the balance of overnights between foreign visitors to each region and that region's out-going tourists who take foreign holidays. This is done in Figure 4.5a, which shows a strongly positive balance of at least 3 million net overnights in Trentino-Alto Adige,

Table 4.6   Foreign tourists in Italy: by nationality, 1994

	Arrivals (thousands)	Overnights (thousands)	Average length of stay (nights)	Overnights in	
				Hotels (%)	Other accommodation (%)
France	2,115	6,505	3.1	84.2	15.8
Germany	7,275	40,501	5.6	70.1	29.9
The Netherlands	678	3,685	5.4	48.2	51.8
Belgium	550	2,714	4.9	78.5	21.5
UK	1,537	6,768	4.4	85.6	14.4
Ireland	76	274	3.6	86.1	13.9
Denmark	213	1,218	5.7	47.7	52.3
Norway	84	369	4.4	76.1	23.9
Sweden	241	1,059	4.4	71.0	29.0
Finland	73	339	4.6	84.5	15.5
Switzerland	1,161	5,402	4.6	74.8	25.2
Austria	1,331	6,236	4.7	70.4	29.6
Spain	895	2,062	2.3	91.9	8.1
Portugal	138	339	2.5	89.4	10.6
Greece	205	538	2.6	89.6	10.4
ex-Yugoslavia	246	970	3.9	85.5	14.5
ex-Soviet Union	198	874	4.4	92.3	7.7
USA	2,369	6,435	2.7	92.4	7.6
Canada	247	722	2.9	78.6	21.4
Mexico	122	316	2.6	92.5	7.5
Brazil	266	690	2.6	90.6	9.4
Argentina	201	527	2.6	90.9	9.1
Israel	169	410	2.4	92.4	7.6
Japan	1,287	2,576	2.0	97.3	2.7
Australia	329	776	2.4	82.8	17.2
EU (1994)	13,714	64,810	4.7	72.9	27.1
All countries	24,664	101,005	4.1	75.4	24.6

Source: ISTAT, *Annuario di Statistico Italiano* (1996, p. 433).

Veneto and Tuscany, and positive balances of 0.5–3 million overnights in Friuli–Venezia Giulia, Latium and Campania. The largest deficits, indicating a net 'loss' of tourist overnights abroad, are in the industrial regions of Lombardy and Piedmont, and the southern region of Calabria. The first two are major sources of Italians holidaying abroad, whilst Calabria registers a negative score simply because it fails to attract many foreign tourists (Table 4.4).

The monitoring of foreign tourists through statistics supplied by overnights recorded in officially-recognised tourist accommodation has shortcomings; as noted previously, it fails to record foreigners who stay in private houses or in other kinds of clandestine accommodation; and it misses out day visitors who flock over Italy's northern frontier for picnics, hiking, skiing, shopping and sightseeing. Also relevant here are the large numbers of Italian emigrants, some of whom have taken foreign nationality, who return to their native land for holidays but stay with relatives.

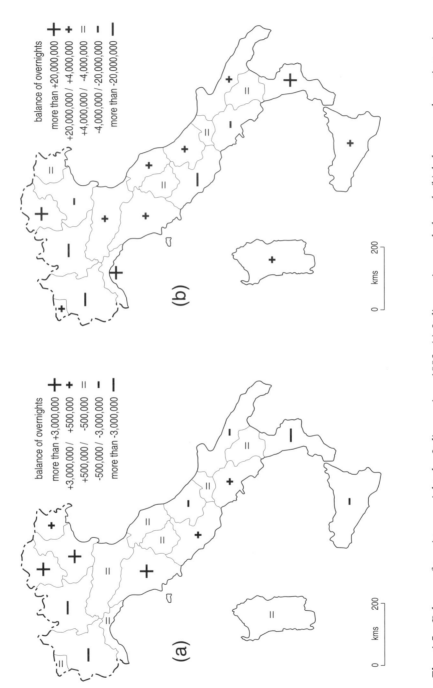

Fig. 4.5 Balance of tourist overnights by Italian region, 1993: (a) Italian regions and abroad; (b) balance on domestic tourism

Source: Montanari (1996, pp. 203–4), based on ISTAT data for 1993, reproduced with permission

4.5.2   *Domestic tourists: regional differences*

Internal tourism accounted for 63 per cent of overnights and 62 per cent of arrivals recorded in registered tourist accommodation in 1994. Figure 4.5b gives an idea of the regional expression of domestic tourism, dividing regions into three broad categories: deficit regions, inflow regions and regions in approximate balance. 'Deficit regions' are those whose outflow of tourists significantly exceeds the inflow of tourists from other regions: Piedmont, Lombardy, Latium, Campania and Veneto. All of these are regions of important tourist attraction, but the key feature is that they are densely populated and highly urbanised regions from which people seek to escape for holidays elsewhere in Italy. These regions contain Italy's major metropolitan areas—respectively Turin, Milan, Rome, Naples and the Po Plain linear conurbation of Verona–Vicenza–Padua–Venice. Net tourist inflow regions are those which attract more Italian visitors than they send out. These regions have one or more of the following tourism resources: mountains, seaside resorts, cultural and pilgrimage sites, or attractive hill country for rural tourism. They also tend to lack industrial agglomerations or big cities. In the southern regions, in this category, the net inflow is basically a product of the low propensity of residents to holiday elsewhere, combined with the attraction of the South to visitors from the North and Centre of Italy. In the case of northern regions like Liguria, Tuscany, Emilia-Romagna and Trentino-Alto Adige, the net inflow reflects significant outflows being outweighed by more massive inflows. Finally, four regions are in approximate balance. Molise and Basilicata are small, rural regions which do not generate many tourist flows in either direction. Umbria, a land-locked region, loses many of its own holidaymakers to coastal resorts, but this is balanced by visitors who appreciate the region's fine hill scenery and cultural and pilgrimage sites, including Assisi. Friuli-Venezia Giulia is a peripheral but relatively prosperous region whose departing tourists are counterbalanced by modest inflows to seaside and mountain resorts.

   In reality most Italian domestic tourism is fairly local, and thus intraregional or to adjacent regions. Much is to second homes, or to holiday flats rented via informal channels; neither is recorded in the tourism statistics. There are relatively few long hauls and little to match the French 'rush to the Mediterranean', partly of course because northern Italy, unlike northern France, enjoys a good summer climate. The main patterns of internal tourist movement are diverse but well established: residents of inland districts travel to take their holidays by the sea; residents of the coast and lowland regions move to the fresher air of the mountains to spend time in holiday villages, farmhouses or second homes; and residents of the northern industrial belt take short-stay winter skiing holidays in the nearby Alps. Few Italians are 'culture-lust' tourists, unlike foreign visitors, especially the Americans and Japanese. On the other hand, there is a growing attraction to *agriturismo* and to the pleasures of the countryside. Intra-regional tourism is particularly characteristic of Sardinia, Sicily, Apulia and Calabria, four large, isolated southern regions with a sufficient range of beach resorts and other holiday attractions to keep most of their holidaymakers relatively close to home.

4.5.3   *Italians as tourists*

Further information on Italians' holiday habits—both at home and abroad—is provided by a 1993 ISTAT survey (ISTAT 1997a, pp. 87–120). This survey, one of a

Table 4.7 Proportion of Italians taking a holiday, 1965–1993

	Number (thousands)	(%)	Average no. of days per year	Average no. of holidays per person
1965	11,007	21.2	20.9	1.06
1968	14,025	26.3	20.5	1.07
1972	16,855	31.2	20.5	1.08
1975	19,621	35.4	20.5	1.08
1978	21,263	37.8	20.4	1.09
1982	23,994	42.8	21.4	1.11
1985	26,085	46.0	21.5	1.14
1993	25,897	45.8	21.3	1.24

Source: ISTAT (1997a, p. 102).

series stretching back to 1965, interviewed 23,376 respondents, distributed throughout Italy, and asked about holiday and travel experiences over the previous 12 months.

First, the holiday behaviour of the 1993 survey respondents can be compared with the results of previous surveys, which were carried out using the same methodologies. This comparison (Table 4.7) shows a steady increase in the proportion of Italians taking holidays (of at least four consecutive nights' duration), although there was little or no change since the previous survey in 1985. Also evident is the gradual tendency for Italians to take more than one holiday, and the length of holiday period taken—an average of three weeks.

Table 4.8 shows regional variations in the propensity to take holidays. Two-thirds of the inhabitants of Lombardy took a holiday in 1993, at least half the population in several other northern regions, but barely a quarter in the southern regions of Calabria, Sicily and Sardinia. This North–South divide has been persistent throughout the period of the ISTAT surveys. It is partly explained by variations in disposable income, but also partly reflects customs—taking a holiday is less a part of the more traditional South Italian way of life than it is in the more 'European' North of Italy.

Table 4.9 presents the characteristics of Italians' holidays, the salient features being: a relatively stable pattern of types of destination with an enduring preference for seaside holidays; a trend towards spreading the timing of holidays away from the peak months of July and August; and a tendency to stay less in hotels and holiday flats, and more in properties owned by the holidaymakers themselves. Broadly speaking, in 1993 around one-fifth of holidays were spent in each of the four main accommodation types (hotels, officially-rented flats, second homes, and properties owned by relatives and friends). A preference for travel by car has remained dominant, accounting for over 70 per cent of all holiday journeys. Journeys by train have sharply diminished, whilst those by air have risen.

Finally, the destination data (Table 4.10) show a steady increase in the number of foreign holidays taken by Italians over the past 20 years, particularly to the USA and other non-European destinations. For many Italians, an exotic foreign holiday has become a fashion statement and a number of tropical destinations such as Cuba, the Dominican Republic and Mauritius have become incorporated as important niches in the overseas holiday market. Within Europe, Ireland has recently become the 'in' place

Table 4.8 Proportion of Italians (%) taking a holiday by
region, 1975–1993

	1975	1982	1993
Piedmont	48.1	53.2	55.9
Val d'Aosta	34.5	43.4	51.7
Lombardy	53.8	59.5	67.4
Trentino–Alto Adige	37.6	49.6	51.9
Veneto	36.0	41.4	48.6
Friuli–Venezia Giulia	33.9	42.3	44.4
Liguria	36.5	39.5	45.1
Emilia–Romagna	44.3	47.2	52.1
Tuscany	42.1	47.3	53.2
Umbria	26.6	41.8	45.4
Marche	18.8	23.2	28.6
Latium	43.6	56.7	48.3
Abruzzi	16.8	27.2	27.6
Molise	19.2	21.0	28.3
Campania	21.8	38.2	43.4
Apulia	24.5	27.8	32.3
Basilicata	22.5	26.2	28.6
Calabria	20.8	22.3	24.5
Sicily	17.5	27.6	25.4
Sardinia	18.6	28.9	25.6
Italy	35.4	42.8	45.8

Source: ISTAT (1997a, p. 103).

for Italians to go on holiday. However, France (17.6 per cent of foreign overnights) and Spain (13.5 per cent) are pre-eminent, whilst holidays to the former Yugoslavia are only slowly picking up after a complete collapse in the early 1990s.

Within Italy, the traditional seaside holiday regions of Liguria, Emilia–Romagna and Tuscany retain their popularity but there has been, to some extent, a regional evening out process with a growth in visits to Trentino–Alto Adige in the Alps and to regions in the 'deep south' (Calabria, Apulia, Sicily and Sardinia). These data on internal tourism reinforce in large measure those discussed earlier with reference to Table 4.4 and Figures 4.2 and 4.5b.

4.6 The economic importance of Italian tourism

Tourism has long been a major income earner for Italy. Over the last 50 years its importance as a source of foreign exchange has grown more or less continuously. The consistency of this rate of growth has been interrupted by a variety of internal and external factors, some of which have been mentioned already. Broadly speaking, the rapid growth of tourism receipts enjoyed during the 1950s and early 1960s was checked by domestic inflationary problems in 1963, then by the West German recession of 1966–1967, and then by the effects of the two oil crises and subsequent restructuring.

The competitiveness of Italian tourism in the international market rests essentially on two variables (Manente 1986): the disposable income of potential visitors to Italy

Table 4.9 Characteristics of holidays taken by Italians, 1975–1993
(all data are percentages of total overnights spent on
holiday)

	1975	1982	1993
Holiday type			
Seaside	57.7	63.6	59.1
Mountains	19.9	17.5	18.9
Hill location	11.1	7.8	7.9
Spa or health cure	1.9	1.9	1.5
Tour or cruise	4.8	4.8	6.2
Other: not identified	4.6	4.4	6.4
Accommodation			
Hotel, pension	26.6	22.2	17.4
Privately-rented lodging	22.0	21.6	18.8
Camping, tourist village	6.2	9.2	7.0
Own property (second home)	14.8	17.7	22.9
Property of friends, relatives	25.5	25.2	23.8
Other: not identified	4.9	4.1	10.0
Month			
January–May	1.8	3.5	6.0
June	5.4	5.7	9.0
July	33.1	28.6	30.6
August	51.4	55.3	45.6
September	6.3	4.5	4.3
October–December	2.0	2.4	4.5
Transport			
Car	73.7	75.9	71.7
Train	17.2	13.0	8.6
Air	1.7	2.3	8.6
Sea	1.7	2.5	3.7
Other: not indicated	5.7	6.3	7.4

Source: ISTAT (1997a, pp. 107–8).

Note: Total number of overnights: 1975, 402,771; 1982, 514,322; 1993, 551,031.

from the major sending countries (Manente calculated a positive income elasticity of
1.44); and the price of the Italian 'tourism product' measured against those of its main
competitors (negative elasticity of 1.28). The interaction of these two factors shows
that Italy was generally attractive as a tourist destination until the late 1970s, but after
1980 the rising value of the Italian lira (tied to the European Monetary System), the
increasing cost of living in Italy, as well as a range of other events (strikes, urban
terrorism, the 1980 earthquake), caused a loss of competitive edge. All this has changed
in the last few years. The recovery in Italian tourism started in 1990 but at first
stuttered because of the Gulf War, which caused a collapse in flights and hotel
reservations. The Yugoslav War probably had a more marginal effect. Overall, during
the period 1989–1992, the stagnation of foreign tourist arrivals in Italy at 20 million
per year contrasted with a 6 per cent rise in Europe as a whole and 18 per cent in
France. Over the same period, whilst the lire/ECU exchange rate was constant, both

Table 4.10 Destinations of Italians taking holidays, 1975–1993 (all data are percentages of total overnights spent on holiday)

	1975	1982	1993
Abroad	4.7	5.5	12.3
Within Italy	95.3	94.5	87.8
Main foreign destinations			
Austria	3.4	3.5	5.0
France	18.0	17.7	17.6
Germany	6.6	8.1	2.5
Greece	5.2	8.6	8.7
Spain	9.6	9.6	13.5
Switzerland	11.9	7.0	2.5
UK	7.2	5.1	5.9
ex-Yugoslavia	13.7	10.8	2.9
Other European countries	11.5	9.4	10.4
USA	4.4	5.9	8.1
Other overseas countries	8.5	14.3	22.8
Total	100.0	100.0	100.0
Italy			
Piedmont	5.0	3.6	3.6
Val d'Aosta	1.6	1.4	1.3
Lombardy	6.2	5.6	5.5
Trentino-Alto-Adige	3.7	4.4	6.6
Veneto	8.0	6.8	5.8
Friuli-Venezia Giulia	2.1	1.7	2.0
Liguria	9.9	7.6	7.3
Emilia-Romagna	13.2	11.4	9.6
Tuscany	9.1	7.8	7.7
Umbria	0.9	0.8	0.8
Marche	3.3	3.4	3.3
Latium	7.4	7.8	5.0
Abruzzi	3.2	3.6	3.7
Molise	0.4	0.6	0.5
Campania	6.4	7.7	6.0
Apulia	5.6	5.9	8.6
Basilicata	0.8	0.7	0.9
Calabria	5.3	8.0	9.0
Sicily	5.1	7.0	7.6
Sardinia	2.8	4.2	5.2
Italy (total)	100.0	100.0	100.0

Source: ISTAT (1997a, p. 109).

the dollar (by 20 per cent) and the yen (by 13 per cent) lost ground to the lira, putting a squeeze on Italy's two high-spending groups of foreign tourists. At the same time, inflation, consumption and the public debt in Italy were rather higher than in other European countries. In 1992, in order to reduce such divergences with EU partners, the Italian government blocked automatic salary rises and increased tax burdens; then it left the EMS. The conditions of the previous three years were inverted: spending was

Table 4.11   Italy's foreign exchange earnings from tourism, 1972–1995 (lire, billions)

Year	Earnings	Losses	Balance	Main countries	Earnings	Losses	Balance
1972	1,466	520	946	France	2,625	2,336	289
1973	1,628	667	961	Germany	10,474	1,964	8,510
1974	1,815	626	1,189	The Netherlands	296	178	118
1975	2,216	676	1,540	Belgium	328	116	212
1976	2,728	735	1,993	UK	1,071	856	215
1977	4,310	986	3,324	Ireland	35	115	−80
1978	5,440	1,229	4,211	Denmark	60	43	17
1979	6,961	1,446	5,515	Norway	30	30	0
1980	7,828	1,501	6,327	Sweden	66	37	29
1981	8,773	2,336	6,437	Finland	15	14	1
1982	11,343	2,857	8,486	Switzerland	1,939	552	1,387
1983	13,784	3,202	10,582	Austria	1,224	584	640
1984	15,099	3,686	11,413	Spain	508	982	−474
1985	16,722	4,360	12,362	Portugal	71	87	−16
1986	14,691	4,112	10,579	Greece	74	223	−149
1987	15,783	5,880	9,903	USA	7,576	6,621	955
1988	16,139	7,879	8,760	Canada	248	88	160
1989	16,443	9,291	7,152	Australia	48	51	−3
1990	23,654	16,569	7,085	Japan	499	74	425
1991	22,853	14,451	8,402	ECU	40	11	29
1992	26,447	20,380	6,067	Lire from ext. accounts	17,478	5,090	12,388
1993	34,625	22,070	12,555				
1994	38,308	19,489	18,819				
1995	44,718	20,232	24,486	Total	44,718	20,232	24,486

Sources: Barucci (1984, p. 233); ISTAT, *Annuario di Statistico Italiano* (1985, p. 446; 1986, p. 457; 1991, p. 428; 1996, p. 439).

reduced for Italians and increased for foreign tourists in Italy as the lira depreciated against major currencies. The results were dramatic: foreign arrivals exceeded 21 million in 1993, leapt to 24.7 million in 1994 and surpassed 29 million in 1995 (Montanari 1996, p. 193).

4.6.1   Macro-economic impact of tourism

The first part of Table 4.11 shows Italy's annual foreign exchange earnings and losses from tourism since 1972. Earnings broadly represent the expenditures of foreign tourists in Italy; losses what Italians spend abroad. The figures given are at current prices and the real increases, for all three columns (earnings, losses, balance), will have been less; indeed, in some years (1974, 1981, 1986, 1988, 1989, 1991) the real gross earnings fell with respect to the preceding year. Nevertheless, the overall importance of tourism to the Italian economy remains critical, as is shown by the adjusted figures plotted for 1982–1995 (Figure 4.6). The chief features of this graph are the gradually diminishing positive balance on the tourism account during the 1980s, the fluctuating recovery in the early 1990s, and the remarkable increase in both gross and net receipts after 1992. By 1994 the net balance of earnings from foreign tourism had regained the real levels of the early–mid-1980s, and by 1995 had surpassed them.

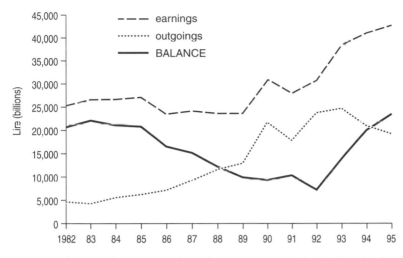

Fig. 4.6 Contribution of tourism to the Italian economy, 1982–1995 (real value adjusted to 1995 level)

Source: Montanari (1996, p. 194), based on data from ISTAT and Ufficio Italiano Cambi, reproduced with permission

The second half of Table 4.11 gives the latest data on net foreign earnings (or losses) from tourism by country of origin (or destination). Germany heads the list as the main market for Italian tourism, followed in turn by Switzerland, USA, Austria and Japan. Significant negative balances are recorded with regard to other southern European countries that have become popular with Italian holidaymakers (especially Spain and Greece), and also with Ireland.

Economically tourism is a phenomenon with complex links and relationships with many other sectors of activity. The closest relationships are obviously to the hotel and accommodation sector, considered already (see Section 4.1 and Tables 4.1 and 4.2), and to complementary catering and leisure services. In 1994 there were, in round figures, 93,000 restaurants, 139,000 bars, 8,000 clubs and discotheques, and 4,000 swimming establishments and pools. Of course, not all of these enterprises cater exclusively for tourists, but visitors constitute a major, if seasonally fluctuating, part of the clientele. Sustained both by tourism and by Italians' generally increasing standards of well-being and orientation to leisure, all of these service activities are increasing in number. A sub-sector more directly linked to tourism is travel agents. These grew from 2,400 in 1981 to 4,800 in 1991 and 5,600 in 1993 (ISTAT 1997a, p. 17; Montanari 1996, p. 195).

According to ISTAT (1997b, p. 99), tourism accounts for the employment of 972,000 persons (1995), an increase of 23 per cent over the 790,000 recorded in 1984. These figures are problematic for two sets of reasons. First, the tourist industry and its allied services (restaurants, pizzerias, etc.) is heavily reliant on a flexible and seasonal labour supply. This means that advantage is taken of unregistered and clandestine labour obtained in the informal labour market which, by definition, escapes official statistics. Such unregistered employment would include undocumented immigrants, mainly from the Third World, who work on a variety of mostly illegal and part-time or seasonal 'contracts'—for example, washing dishes or changing beds in hotels—as well as unregistered and perhaps unpaid family helpers in small businesses. In addition, there are tens of thousands of immigrant street-vendors who hawk their wares (leather belts, bags, fake Lacoste tee-shirts, sunglasses, cheap jewellery, etc.) to tourists in big cities, cultural centres and seaside resorts the length and breadth of the country (King 1995).

Second, the boundary between direct and indirect employment in tourism is hard to define, not only because many enterprises (shops, restaurants, taxis, etc.) cater to both tourists and non-tourists, but also because much employment in seemingly unconnected sectors of the economy (agriculture, fishing, craft industries and transport, to name but a few) is dependent on a tourism segment of aggregate demand. Using data for the mid-1980s, Manente (1986) calculated that indirect employment (including an estimated 163,000 in farming and 90,000 in manufacturing) raises total employment in tourism by over 400,000, leading to a total tourist employment figure (for 1984) of 1.2 million, or 5.8 per cent of the total national labour force. Adding the unregistered employment of part-time, casual and seasonal workers—mostly immigrants, women, family members and students—could raise the total employment impact of tourism to 2 million, nearly one-tenth of the Italian workforce.

4.6.2   Tourism and local and regional development

The contribution of tourism and recreational activities to local economies and regional development has only recently received attention in Italy, probably because of the surviving orthodoxy that regional economic growth is driven by production rather than consumption. The emergence since the 1970s of particular economic dynamism down the eastern coast arguably owes a good deal to the growth of a succession of tourist resorts from the Po Delta to Molise. Yet the abundant literature on the remarkable economic growth of the 'Third Italy'—that large diagonal region interposed between the deindustralised North-West and the economically troubled South—pays scant attention to the role of tourism, preferring instead discussions of 'productive decentralisation' and 'diffuse industrialisation' (see King 1989). Surely it is no accident that the 'Emilian model'—the showpiece of Third Italy success—is also where the Italian mass tourism industry has its most intensive presence?

As we have seen, tourism can be the source both of regional development and of geographical disequilibrium in Italy. In the course of their past tourism development, Italy's coastal areas have attracted migrants from other parts of the country, mainly from the hilly interior of the peninsula and the South. Often the migrations have been relatively short-range and intraregional, such as the movement from the interior uplands of Emilia-Romagna, Marche and Abruzzi down to the Adriatic coastal strip, where 'the action is'—not only in terms of resort development but also with regards to new industry, transport axes and other service activities. Over the entire country, the map of population change since the 1950s shows the coastal strip to be a virtually unbroken ribbon of continuous growth and net in-migration (Dematteis 1979). Within the setting of seaside resort development, the subdivision of the tourist market by price and locality enables clear contrasts to be drawn between the density and character of the built environment of different stretches of Italian coastline. For example, the tightly-packed mass tourism developments of the Rimini area contrast with the longer-established upper- and middle-status resorts of the steep Ligurian

Riviera, now patronised by many elderly visitors and retired residents (Tinacci 1969). Capri has its own cachet, where land and property prices rival those of central Rome. Different again is the carefully managed development of the Sardinian Costa Smeralda; here low-density development in traditional building styles attempts to minimise impact on the stunning natural environment of pink granite headlands and white-sanded bays. This too is a holiday playground for an international élite. Meanwhile, much of the littoral of the mainland South, especially the long coastlines of Apulia and Calabria, has been encased in a concrete wall of speculative second-home development which has little aesthetic appeal and flouts local planning regulations (Montanari 1991).

Given the diverse nature of Italian tourism, its economic and demographic impact is not restricted to coastal areas. Towns and cities famous for their cultural attractions have often gained dynamism and prosperity from tourist revenues. The same is true of those rural areas which have been affected by tourism. Since the 1960s the ski boom has transformed dozens of small mountain villages in the Alps and a few localities in the high Apennines into winter sports centres, joining the older-established ski resorts of Cortina, Sestriere and Courmayeur. Not only has skiing transformed the landscapes of many mountain districts, it has also altered the seasonal regimes and life-styles of both local inhabitants and the holidaymakers—winter and early spring being the periods of peak activity (Bonapace 1968).

Aside from skiing, rural tourism has made the greatest impact on the Sylvan landscapes of Tuscany and Umbria, where there are well-rooted, if scattered, colonies of British and German residents and second-home owners. Here, too, Italian second-home ownership has burgeoned, to the obvious disadvantage of locals seeking to buy houses. The phenomenon has involved both the renovation of old, abandoned dwellings, either in villages or in the open countryside, and the construction of new housing and holiday complexes, not always in a carefully planned way (Pedrini 1984).

According to Innocenti (1990, p. 128), rural Italy is the 'third touristic space' after the earlier discovery and colonisation of the coast and the mountains. Although Innocenti foresees an antagonistic relationship between tourism and agriculture, as urban capitalist interests colonise and ultimately destroy this 'last frontier', there are several examples of a more mutually supportive relationship. In these lively Italian debates on the merits of *agriturismo*, which also draw on concepts of eco-tourism, 'soft tourism' and the like, tourism is seen to provide sustainable rural development (Bellencin Meneghel 1991). Farm holidays, gastronomy, wine-tasting, trekking, cycling, horse-riding, study-tours of architecture and folklore, painting holidays and naturism are just some of the activities that are now promoted in the Italian countryside (Velluti Zatti 1992). Of all the Italian regions, Tuscany is the leading example of a relatively harmonious partnership between, on the one hand, large numbers of visitors who holiday in scattered locations throughout the region and, on the other hand, a productive agriculture of vineyards and olive groves, the products of which are also bought by visitors to enhance the symbiosis between a well-preserved yet 'working' rural landscape and a relatively high holiday absorption capacity (Telleschi 1992).

The fragmented structure of the Italian tourist industry, with its reliance on small enterprises and self-employment and its wide diffusion in coastal, urban, rural and mountain settings, means that tourism is quite well integrated with local economies. Family effort has often been the guiding principle behind many enterprises related to tourism—the small hotel, the pizzeria, the beach-side bar. In other cases, the solidarity of the family as both an economic and a social unit enables the dovetailing of tourism with other activities, different members working on a full- or part-time basis in different sectors, perhaps from a residential base on a farm in the agricultural hinterland. Especially in the south, injections of remittances or migrant savings accrued from a period of foreign work by one or more members of the family have often enabled the establishment of tourist enterprises on the coast. King *et al.* (1984) studied the small Calabrian resort of Amantea, where returned emigrants from Venezuela have played a leading role in investing in small hotels, tourist apartments, restaurants and the like.

4.6.3   Tourism and the development of the Mezzogiorno

Over the period since the 1960s, tourism has become increasingly championed as an economic policy to develop the South. The tendency has been to argue that the labour-intensive tourist industry, with its spin-offs into private accommodation, cafés, restaurants, shops, local transport and so on, is better suited to the needs of the underdeveloped and labour-rich South than the capital-intensive industrial policy pursued in the Mezzogiorno during the 1960s and 1970s (King 1987).

Unfortunately, hopes that tourism might function as a 'leading sector' in the South's development have largely been misplaced. Results have been modest despite some financial and planning support from the Cassa per il Mezzogiorno, the government's southern development agency, which operated between 1950 and 1984. As early as 1957, the Cassa had recognised the potential for tourism, and loans were offered for building, enlarging and modernising hotels and holiday villages (Gambino 1978). General tourist infrastructure—roads, water, beach facilities, etc.—were also improved. By the early 1980s, Cassa funds had contributed to the construction and modernisation of 14,000 hotels, resulting in a net addition of 65,000 rooms. Such improvements have undoubtedly had some impact. Since the 1960s, the south has, on the whole, become greatly 'modernised', and tourist arrivals have tended to grow faster in the south than the national average in recent years. But tourism, like the region's economy as a whole, has yet to 'take off' in the Mezzogiorno. In spite of fast, and mostly free, motorways, the South of Italy is still considered too far for car-bound tourists arriving from central and northern Europe, especially when areas like the Italian lakes, Venice and Tuscany offer such attractive intervening opportunities, and Spain, Greece and Turkey compete favourably on price.

In 1994 the Mezzogiorno absorbed only 19 per cent of all tourist overnights in Italy, a proportion barely half the South's share of the national population. For foreign tourists, the share was even lower—13 per cent. Cultural tourism is particularly weakly developed. The Pompeii excavations are in first place with 1.8 million visitors per year; this compares to the 3 million visiting the Vatican Museum in Rome. Next come the temples at Paestum and the Naples Archaeological Museum, with 316,000 and 215,000 annual visitors respectively. All these attractions are in Campania, the south's foremost tourist region (Table 4.4). Yet the problems of the city of Naples have tended to ward off many tourists. In the case of the major attractions of Campania, many tourists follow a Naples–Sorrento–Capri–Pompeii 'package' which brings them in for a day or two and does not maximise benefits to the region in terms of hotel trade or spin-offs into other sectors of the local economy. Once outside Campania, the museums of the rest of the Mezzogiorno account for only 5 per cent of national museum visits, a measly proportion given the South's immensely rich archaeological, historic and artistic heritage (Montanari 1996, pp. 201–2).

Several diagnoses can be offered for why the hoped-for tourist bonanza in the South has not so far happened. First and foremost is the lack of a coherent national policy for tourism within which tourism planning for the Mezzogiorno might be set. Second, tourism loans have been distributed not according to the criteria of carefully considered spatial economic planning, but on the basis of political favouritism and clientelism—following, in other words, the well-established patterns of agricultural and industrial loan and grant allocation of earlier phases of southern development policy (King 1987). A reflection of the minimum attention paid to proper planning controls is the untidiness of much of the South's coastal landscape and the failure to provide good, clean tourist facilities to all visitors. Another aspect of the generally poor quality of the planning environment has been the lack of attention paid to effective publicity and to the proper training of local personnel in tourist industry activities. Generally, the character of southern Italian tourism has become polarised between, on the one hand, big hotels built for an élite clientele and, on the other, the mushrooming of second homes around the coast, many stretches of which have been effectively ruined. Locally-run hotels, often poor in quality and inefficient, have been squeezed out; yet this is the sector which needs assistance and improvement if the long-term benefits of tourism to the region are to be promoted.

4.7   Conclusion: tourism, planning and the future

In spite of 'tourist saturation' in Venice and Florence, and in spite of 'wall to wall people' shochorned into regimented beaches in the summer in places like Rimini and the Lido di Roma, the future of Italian tourism is likely to be one of consolidation and stability rather than dramatic growth or decline. The major changes in the future of Italian tourism are likely to be in organisation and marketing (Becheri and Manente 1997). During the 1970s, powers in the fields of tourism planning and administration of the industry at local level passed to the regions. After some delay, a *legge quadro* or 'framework law' for tourism was passed in 1983 and, at least theoretically, regional administrations have the scope to introduce innovations such as attractive off-season packages or holiday arrangements for special categories such as pensioners. Regions also have the responsibility for identifying areas to be developed for, or protected from, tourism; for the preservation and rehabilitation of historic town centres and specific monuments and artistic treasures; for the classification of hotels (within the national framework described earlier); and for the co-ordination of the activities of their various provincial and local tourist boards. All the signs are that most regional authorities are working hard to promote tourism, with the northern Italian regions being most effective (Lazzeretti 1986). At the local level, the election of many imaginative mayors in important tourism cities and resorts has led to the development of a number of tourist-friendly plans, such as pedestrianisation schemes and promotion of local festivals.

At a national level, the two critical structural tasks to confront are the 'deseasonalisation' of tourist flows and the diversion of more tourists to the South and to relatively 'undiscovered' rural areas, which are losing population. These objectives are slowly being achieved, but they are not being achieved in harmony. In other words, visitors holidaying outside the summer peak months are going on skiing or city holidays to northern Italy or to Rome, whilst most of the South's increasing share of tourism is concentrated into the summer months. The ironic situation thus arises that hotel occupancy rates remain lowest, due to the high seasonality factor, in the region which climatically has most to offer in terms of Spring and Autumn holidays.

5 Greece: hesitant policy and uneven tourism development in the 1990s

Lila Leontidou

5.1 Introduction

As the map of the Balkans is radically transformed during the 1990s, former tourist resorts become theatres of war and destruction, and a new type of tourism is promoted by tour operators: war tourism, visits to sites destroyed or war zones. The only Balkan EU member, Greece, located near war zones, has lost not only its Yugoslavian visitors, but also a substantial proportion of its already poorly developed cultural tourism. Tourism waves shift, opportunities and hopes (such as the 1996 Golden Olympics) are betrayed and then revived, and stagnation has been the main feature since the last edition of this volume appeared in 1991. This chapter is capturing Greek tourism at a low point, especially from the viewpoint of regional development. However, this is because quantitative data can not go beyond 1993; being written in 1997, the chapter will also highlight more optimistic prospects linked with the emergence of inter-national residential tourism. In fact, this chapter is being written at the turning point from a period of disappointment to a seven-year period of reconstruction, leading to the 2004 Olympic games.

The cultural landscape of Greece has a density of memory which is rarely found in other places, despite the scattering of its archaeological treasures to foreign museums all over Europe and the world: the Parthenon marbles in the British Museum, Venus de Milo and the Victory of Samothrace in the Louvre, and the Afaia marbles in Munich, are but three of the best-known examples of exported treasures which impoverish Greece and profit urban tourism in other countries. The country's archaeological excavations are still carried out predominantly by foreigners, to the exclusion of Greek archaeologists, with pitifully few exceptions. Meanwhile, cultural tourism is still sinking: the homeland of these treasures is still used as a sun and beach destination, rather than for cultural exploration. Tourist flows increase only seasonally, during the months when the country's mild climate (ranging from continental in the North to Mediterranean in the South) is at its hottest. Tourists flock to the islands, attracted by the clear sea and the beaches that are blessed by the charm of small attractive bays rather than large sandy stretches, as in Indonesia or California. Tourists also follow the natural beauty and the charm of whitewashed villages, although the latter are gradually corrupted by petty speculators and sold to foreigners. Greece is thus still a predomi-

Tourism and Economic Development: European Experiences, 3rd Edition. Edited by A.M. Williams and G. Shaw.
© 1998 John Wiley & Sons Ltd.

nantly sun-and-beach tourism destination in the mid-1990s. Its role as the cradle of European civilisation and the gateway to three worlds, to Europe (East and West) and the Middle East, is hardly evident in the types of tourism development. In fact, the deeply seasonal, sun-and-beach type of tourism seems to have been reinforced in the years up to 1993, when tourists abandoned the cities and flocked to the Aegean islands, as shown in Section 5.4. The following analysis inevitably draws on incomplete documentation about what continues to be a 'statistically invisible' industry, in order to highlight its development, nature, rhythm, regional polarisation and informalisation trends.

5.2   Greece in international tourism

5.2.1   *Types of tourism and travelling*

As the Italian and Iberian peninsulas tend to become congested during the summer months, the Balkan coast, and especially Greece, has a claim to a major role in the future of European tourism—at least according to the Greek Five-Year Plans (see, for example, Doxiadis Association 1974; CPER 1976; Greek Parliament 1984; Komilis 1995).[1] Its 15,000 km coastline, of which 3,000 km of sandy beaches and attractive bays are suitable for swimming, has an estimated capacity of 6–9 million swimmers a day during the peak season, while it accommodated only about 1.5 million in the 1970s (CPER 1976, pp. 47–8, 136). Major attractions include the 337 inhabited Greek islands scattered in the Aegean and Ionian seas of the Mediterranean (with 1.5 million of the 10.26 million Greek population in 1991); many traditional villages; areas of physical beauty and ecological importance; and, of course, a wealth of ancient and Byzantine monuments. Some developed areas already present signs of congestion and environmental deterioration, particularly due to a lack of planning control. Greater Athens, in particular, is rapidly losing its popularity among tourists (Koncouris and Skouras 1991).

Visitors to Greece usually combine sightseeing with relaxation, but rest and recreation rather than exploration and cultural tourism seem to be their priorities. The nature of Greek tourism is thus rather specialised; its seasonality is among the most extreme in Europe and, moreover, is increasing with time. Extreme peaks occur during the summer months for both the arrivals and overnight stays of foreign tourists (Figure 5.1). In 1981, 61.6 per cent of arrivals and 66.7 per cent of overnight stays were concentrated between June and September, and the rates had increased by 1993 to 66 per cent and 68.5 per cent, respectively.

The number of Greeks travelling abroad is currently half of the number of foreign tourists visiting Greece, so that the country is one of tourist destination rather than of origin. The population has actually been discouraged from travelling abroad by the imposition of strict foreign exchange controls. Before 1981, the annual foreign exchange allowance was only $250; in the 1980s, this increased gradually, and is currently unlimited for travel within the EU. Emigration and repatriation complicate the study of actual vacation or short-term travel, especially after 1977, when customs authorities no longer collected emigration statistics. There are students abroad visited by their families, people working who host friends, and in general travelling on an individual rather than package-holiday basis. Overall, it seems that the number of

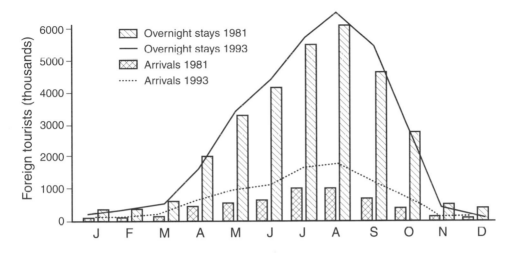

Fig. 5.1 Arrivals and overnight stays of foreign tourists in Greece, 1981 and 1993

Source: Adapted form NSSG (1985, 1995)

Greek travellers is rapidly rising and trebled from 1.54 million in 1985 to 4.73 million in 1993 (Figure 5.2). Their proportion in the total population increased sharply during the years of economic development, the early 1960s, and of EU integration, the mid-1980s. In the 1980s the proportion of travellers was only 14.5 per cent of the total population, but by 1993 it had risen to 45.7 per cent (adapted from EOT–The National Tourist Organisation–and National Statistical Service of Greece (NSSG) data, which are doubtful because the same person might travel several times in one year).

5.2.2   Foreign visitors

International tourist flows, as evidenced in arrivals and receipts, expanded consistently until the late 1970s. Two major exceptions were during the world recession in 1974 and in 1967–1968, the first years of dictatorial rule in Greece. After every decline, however, the country has recovered remarkably (Figure 5.2). The number of foreign tourists almost doubled every five years, and now every 10 years, and rose from 58,238 in 1951 through 471,983 in 1961 and 2,103,281 in 1971, to 5,577,109 in 1981. By 1993 arrivals had risen to 9,913,267 (equivalent to 97 per cent of the Greek population). There are some differences if cruise passengers and Greeks residing abroad are excluded from the definition of foreign tourist. Among tourists in 1993, 500,444 were cruise passengers visiting the islands (NSSG data). The growth of package-holiday mass tourism is indirectly indicated by the increase of charter passengers from 16 per cent of the total in 1970 to 46 per cent in 1985 and 58 per cent in 1993 (Figure 5.2).

These numbers are still low in comparison with some other northern Mediterranean countries, and the share of Greece in total arrivals in all Mediterranean countries was until recently only 3 per cent. However, whereas in the latter group arrivals grew by

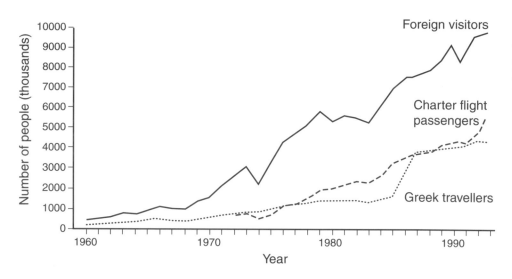

Fig. 5.2   Foreign visitors, domestic travellers and charter-flight passengers in Greece, 1960–1993

Source: Adapted from *Statistical Yearbooks of Greece* (1960–1995)

8.4 per cent annually, the rate for Greece was almost double this (16.4 per cent in 1960–1975 and 8.3 per cent in 1975–1987). Consequently, the country increased its share of total arrivals in the European countries from 2.2 per cent in 1970 to 3.5 per cent in 1982 (CPER 1987, p. 83).

Foreign and domestic tourist nights spent in all types of registered accommodation (including camping) grew by 19.8 per cent per annum in 1970–1978, and by 2.3 per cent in 1981–1986; they were estimated at 49,604,625 in 1993 (provisional EOT data). Nights spent by foreigners also increased as a proportion of total nights from 44 per cent in 1970 to 70 per cent in 1978 (Singh 1984, pp. 64–6), and 72 per cent in 1993 (see Table 5.4). Furthermore, a series of surveys by EOT, covering the 1966–1985 period, found that the average length of stay varied by nationality, but had grown from 11.4 days in 1967 to 12.6 in 1977–1978 and 14 in 1984–1985 (Fragakis 1987).

The national origins of foreign tourists are shown in Table 5.1. The largest numbers originate in Europe, which increased its share from 63.4 per cent in 1971, through 74.5 per cent in 1978 to 89.9 per cent in 1987, and 90 per cent in 1993, of which 86 per cent were from the EU (post-1995 definition). In the 1970s this was especially due to tourists from Scandinavia and Yugoslavia and, in the 1980s, to visitors from the UK, the Federal Republic of Germany, France and Austria. Whereas in 1963–1973 Greece was dependent on the USA for the inflow of tourists and on Italy for their outflow (Komilis 1986, pp. 52–4), this is no longer so. If the flow from the USA in 1970 was 13 times higher than in 1953 (Alexandrakis 1973, p. 154), thereafter its share in arrivals dropped from 27 per cent in 1970 to one-tenth of this, a mere 2.7 per cent in 1993. The share of US citizens in nights spent was considerably lower—about half these percentages each year. This seems to reflect the changing leisure preferences of American tourists, from the Woodstock to the yuppie generation. It also relates, to a surprisingly high degree, to political conjuncture (see Section 5.5.1).

Table 5.1   The origin of foreign tourists to Greece, 1971–1993

	Arrivals (%)					
	1971	1975	1981	1984	1987	1993
UK	13.85	12.10	19.12	18.90	20.00[1]	
FR Germany	11.52	15.05	12.39	15.65	24.00[1]	
France	7.88	8.47	5.88	7.35		
Italy	6.19	5.22	4.47	5.95	8.00[1]	
Denmark	2.07	1.90	2.62	2.25		
The Netherlands	2.64	2.25	3.37	3.49		
Spain, Portugal	0.57	0.76	0.74	0.78		
Belgium, Luxembourg, Ireland	1.98	1.71	2.03	1.94		
Austria	2.20	3.11	2.91	4.31	3.30	3.07
Sweden	2.62	4.15	5.00	3.52	3.21	3.37
Finland	1.14	1.70	1.92	2.43	2.36	1.24
EU	54.17	58.34	64.40	63.46	80.96	78.13
Yugoslavia	5.36	9.84	12.47	4.77	5.06	2.04
Switzerland	2.50	2.53	2.85	2.84	1.55	1.75
Norway	0.27	0.74	1.90	1.93	1.66	1.09
Rest of Europe	2.60	2.48	3.46	3.63	3.30	6.98
NON-EU EUROPE	9.23	13.68	16.73	16.29	8.97	11.86
Former USSR	0.04	0.07	0.10	0.13	0.10	1.24
USA	24.66	17.37	6.37	8.60	2.84	2.73
Canada, Latin America	3.64	2.42	2.30	2.27	1.37	0.92
Asia	3.90	4.16	6.06	5.41	3.38	3.93
Africa	2.15	1.88	1.82	1.83	1.06	0.52
Oceania	2.21	2.07	2.22	2.00	1.38	0.67
REST OF WORLD	36.60	27.98	18.87	20.25	10.07	10.01
Total (%)	100.00	100.00	100.00	100.00	100.00	100.00
Total number (millions)	1.78	2.64	5.04	5.52	7.64	9.4

Source: Adapted from NSSG, *Statistical Yearbooks of Greece* (1976, 1987, 1995) (excluding cruise passengers).

[1] 1989 percentages from Eurostat (1991, p. 12).

5.3   Political change and tourism policy

5.3.1   *The emergence of tourism as a public policy concern, 1950–1967*

Tourism played only a minor role as Greece was emerging from under-development in the mid-1960s. Regional policy was not promoted at the time. Indeed, for a long period, developed and even congested areas received incentives for tourist development. Although tourist flows increased in the 1950s after the war, when the country's infrastructure was partially restored, tourism expanded rapidly only in the 1970s. The Greek government has actively developed infrastructure after World War II, but tourism began to feature in policies and programmes only in the early 1960s, when its potential for economic development was realised. Legislation permitting incentives for tourist developments began with LDs (legislative decrees) 3213/1953, 3430/1955, 4171/1961 and 276/1969 (TCG 1981, pp. 74–5; Singh 1984, p. 131).

During the 1960s state assistance to tourism enterprises particularly centred on loans for the construction of accommodation. Direct investment in infrastructure to facilitate communications and create opportunities for the private sector also helped tourism development.

The main executive public institution for the development and promotion of tourism and for the formulation and implementation of policy has been EOT. It became an autonomous agency in 1950, but its origins can be traced back to 1929. Its role was both supervisory and developmental, involving planning, promotion, education (for example, the School of Tourism Professions), construction and management of accommodation and infrastructure, and financial assistance for private tourism businesses. Promotion was undertaken by a network of offices in Greece and abroad, as well as through the organisation of summer festivals and increasingly through advertisement.

The policies of EOT were only marginally influenced by other agents until 1983, when EOT came under the direct surveillance of the Ministry of National Economy and Planning. The Ministry of the Environment influences tourism through land policy and building controls. The Ministry of the Interior controls the tourism police, collects data, and co-ordinates local services. The Ministry of Culture is responsible for the maintenance of museums and monuments. Finally, the School of Tourism Professions is supervised by the Prime Minister's Office. Consequently there has been highly diversified and fragmented administration for tourism, and policy has tended to lack co-ordination until recently.

5.3.2   Policy during the dictatorship, 1967–1974

In 1951–1964 the largest share of public investment in tourism (56 per cent) was allocated to construction of accommodation and its management. By contrast, infrastructural work predominated in 1965–1974 (Komilis 1986, p. 165), reflecting a major change of policy during the late 1960s. Greater emphasis on tourist development followed the imposition of dictatorial rule in Greece in 1967, involving construction, financing and promotion. A simultaneous emphasis on the construction sector was not incidental: house building, as well as tourism, was used as an instrument of macro-economic management (heating up the economy). Such objectives were incorporated into the 1968–1972 Five-Year Plan more explicitly than in its predecessor. All former legislation on tourism was consolidated into a single LD, 1738/ 1973, providing special concessions for hotels in the form of tax and depreciation allowances (Singh 1984, p. 131).

The initiative for tourism development shifted to private enterprises, and state activity was limited to the provision of infrastructure to facilitate their operation (Alexandrakis 1973, p. 180). Meanwhile, the banking system and government incentives were mobilised to boost private investment. The average annual rate of growth of tourism loans rose from 11.3 per cent in 1960–1966 to 26.7 per cent in 1967–1973 (Komilis 1986, p. 166). Private investment in tourism rose sharply during the dictatorship, while public investment declined during the first years, as indicated in Table 5.2. Foreign investment hit a peak in 1968, when it rose to 66.1 per cent of all investment in tourism (from 4 per cent during 1962–1967) and 37 per cent of total foreign capital investment in all sectors of the Greek economy. This was mostly US capital (51.8 per cent of the total in 1968–1970), although West German, Swiss and French sources were also important (Alexandrakis 1973, p. 181). Foreign investment

Table 5.2 Public and private investment in tourism in Greece, 1957–1970
($ thousands)

	Public[1]	Private[2] domestic	Private, foreign[3]	(%)	Total
1957	1,100	300	134	8.74	1,534
1958	6,600	5,100	889	7.06	12,589
1959	8,500	8,400	635	13.62	17,535
1960	8,500	8,400	47	0.28	16,947
1961	10,400	7,900	407	2.18	18,707
1962	6,900	15,100	1,208	5.21	23,208
1963	7,300	10,300	229	1.28	17,829
1964	4,000	8,100	1,391	10.31	13,491
1965	7,800	9,100	844	4.76	17,744
1966	9,700	10,700	1,151	5.34	21,551
1967	6,800	17,600	0	0.00	24,400
1968	8,100	35,100	84,430	66.15	127,630
1969	13,100	57,400	13,468	16.04	83,968
1970	14,100	65,900	6,100	7.08	86,100
1957–61	35,100	30,100	2,112	3.14	67,312
1962–67	42,500	70,900	4,823	4.08	118,223
1968–70	35,300	158,400	103,998	34.93	297,698

Source: Alexandrakis (1973, p. 179).

Notes: 1. Financed by government budget and EOT, including infrastructure.
2. Financed by banks only.
3. Foreign: projects approved by Ministry of Co-ordination.

was mostly concentrated in hotel businesses, especially in coastal locations. Consequently, it is possible to talk of a speculative upsurge and the 'sell-out' of several Greek coastal areas to foreigners during the dictatorship.

Regional imbalance was blatantly reinforced by government policy at this time. Public investment in tourism tripled during the early 1970s, in relation to the previous period, but the share of Greater Athens increased from 49 per cent to 52 per cent. Investment was also directed to other cities and to already developed tourism areas such as Salonica, Crete and Khalkidiki (Komilis 1986, p. 166). Mass, large-scale tourism was promoted, and a goal of attracting 13 million foreign tourists was set for 1982 (CPER 1972).

A peculiar type of domestic tourism also appeared during the dictatorship: summer vacations in 'mobile homes'. This came about following legislation allowing for prefabricated construction on plots smaller than those specified in existing by-laws. It has been estimated that by 1973 about 100,000 such houses had been erected, especially by low-income groups in areas around Greater Athens, notably in the island of Salamina (Polychroniadis and Hadjimichalis 1974).

5.3.3 Policy trends, 1974–1989

After the fall of the dictatorship (1974), tourism increasingly featured in successive Five-Year Plans as a means of dealing with foreign exchange problems and the chronic trade deficit, and as an appropriate strategy for economic development. Public sector participation in investment increased especially after the effective nationalisation of Olympic Airways on 1 January 1975. Domestic interests were also given greater priority at this time. The 1976–1980 Plan emphasised the role of local capital and of small non-hotel tourism as a means to local development. Subsequently, the 1983–1987 Plan carried through the same policy of discouraging large units and foreign capital. It also set goals for public involvement, where 56 per cent of investment would be public and 44 per cent would be private (Greek Parliament 1984, p. 62). Legislation also emphasised the development of small lodgings with less than 80 beds (TCG 1981, p. 78). This policy was reversed recently, as outlined below.

There had been an emerging concern with regional policy and an emphasis on underdeveloped regions by the 1980s. Further development in Greater Athens was already to be discouraged (Leontidou 1983). New legislation, especially LDs 1116/1981 and 1262/1982, treated tourism investments in the same manner as industrial ones. The former law introduced grants in place of tax exemptions, as well as regional criteria, subdividing the country into four zones (TCG 1981, pp. 75–6). Both laws, however, continued to stress the criteria of investment viability rather than reduction of congestion, and often encouraged financing of traditional buildings in all areas. Although congested areas were delimited by ministerial decision in 1983, the 1983–1987 Five-Year Plan for Economic Development and investment realised under LD1262/1982 (see Table 5.6 and analysis below) did not promote regional development. Locality considerations were also not mentioned in 'social tourism' programmes, which annually have assisted about 100,000 less affluent citizens to take low-cost vacations since 1983 (TCG 1981, p. 6; CPER 1987, pp. 95–100).

Tourism policy and institutions changed in 1987.[2] The gradual decentralisation of EOT and management of its property by local authorities and mixed 'popular-base' companies was being considered, and EC policy also started to have some impact alongside national policy. The Integrated Mediterranean Programmes, as well as the new Five-Year Plan for Economic Development 1988–1992, tended to promote more selective tourism in large hotels with additional services.[3] This policy to attract higher-income tourism was combined with a reorientation toward decentralisation and creeping 'privatisation' of the tourism sector.[4] Areas for tourism development were also delimited by LD 1650/1986 on the environment. Overseas promotion (advertising campaigns, pamphlets and posters) was being intensified, with the aim of attracting off-season and higher-income tourists. However, only 18 per cent of tourists surveyed in 1986 claimed to have been influenced by advertising campaigns, while 34 per cent had been influenced by friends and relatives (EOT, cited in Papachristou 1987). This stresses the importance of return visits and the need to improve the quality of tourism services in Greece. Tourism agents and tour operators influenced 24 per cent of choices, and their impact is evident in the regional/local concentration of national groups of visitors (see next section).

5.3.4   *Residential tourism and place marketing*

Many of the localities preferred by foreigners have now been purchased by them. A new type of tourism, residential tourism, is surfacing as European integration intensifies the movement across countries and retirement tourism increases. Since 1 January 1993, EU law permits European citizens to buy property anywhere within the Union.

Greece is affected less than Spain or Southern France, but it is nevertheless a place for second homes bought by foreigners (Leontidou and Marmaras 1998). The profile of these foreigners differs amongst countries. In Spain, they are typically retired persons mainly from the UK, Germany, Scandinavia and The Netherlands. In Greece, the phenomenon has more of an intellectual rather than a mass character; there is a preponderance of middle-aged, educated, self-employed people from the UK, The Netherlands and Germany and they have usually bought on the recommendation of friends rather than real estate agents, as in Spain (Leontidou and Marmaras 1998). Their use of space is not regulated and often becomes arbitrary: many Greek beaches are, at present, 'private', sold off, and inaccessible to Greek and foreign visitors. At the same time, illegal Greek homes and tavernas on other beaches are being demolished by local authorities, in a show of combating illegality in tourist regions.

The trend of foreign second home purchases is one face of the impact of European integration on Greek tourism development. The other face relates to urban tourism, where the trends are disheartening. The lack of Greek urban cultural tourism is particularly regressive in a Europe of place marketing, during the present period of neo-liberal urban boosterism and the creation of post-modern environments of leisure and tourism (Bailly *et al.* 1996; Leontidou 1995, 1997). The turn of Greece has yet to come: Athens is now modernising its infrastructure with major transport works, a metro and an international airport, in order to host the 2004 Olympics; and Salonica has been revitalised as the European Cultural Capital of 1997, although many difficulties and speculation were reported.

National tourism policy is still very weak and hesitant. Planning strategies and tourism education therefore remain at a very low level. Greece has not succeeded in developing a quality, diversified tourism product based on its comparative advantages. The inert bureaucracy which formulates tourism policy tends to come up with fragmentary measures and peculiar ideas about planning. The tourism law LD 2160/1993 focused on casinos and marine tourism. The new developmental law LD 2234/1994 has invented a peculiar notion of zoning of Greek space in order to attract high-income tourism: the concept of Areas of Integrated Tourist Development (POTA, see Komilis 1995), modelled on technoparks, treats tourism as if it were a form of manufacturing industry. This type of linkage re-emerges in recent Greek planning history, as has also been the case during and after the period of dictatorial rule (Section 5.3 above).

5.4 Regions and localities

5.4.1 *The uneven regional distribution of demand*

Tourism has tended to abandon mainland Greece, as Figure 5.3 clearly demonstrates. Until 1986, only metropolitan regions were losing visitors (Leontidou 1991,1993, 1996). By 1993, however, decline had spread throughout Greece excepting the islands. Only the Aegean and the Ionian islands attracted more visitors in 1993 than in 1981. Figure 5.3 and Table 5.3 are based on primary material analysed within standard administrative boundaries. Sub-regions are delimited in relation to tourism attractions. Mainland Greece is treated separately from the islands and from the two largest cities— Greater Athens and Salonica. A qualitative stepwise investigation has been adopted, so as to avoid the traps of data and information 'intransparencies', especially with respect

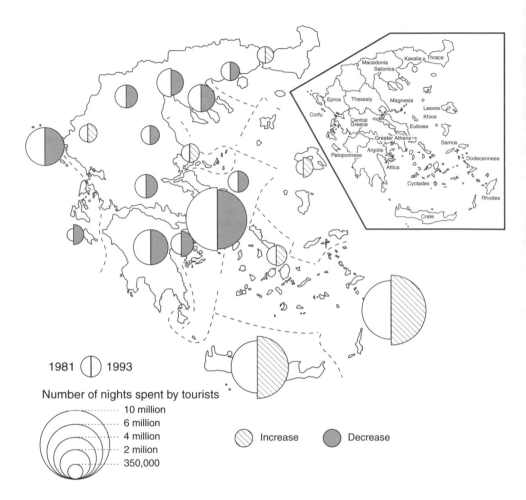

Fig. 5.3   The regional distribution of demand (overnight stays) in Greece, 1981–1993
Source: Adapted from NSSG (1985, 1995)

to unrecorded accommodation. In any case, it should be emphasised that domestic tourist demand is not adequately reflected in overnight stays—the main unit of the following analysis—as Greeks have access to additional accommodation outlets. Relative preferences rather than absolute numbers of domestic tourists can be concluded from such spatial analysis. In addition, as residential tourism, camping and cruise tourism increase in importance, so foreigners are also abandoning the hotel sector (Leontidou and Marmaras 1998).

A first approach to the regional concentration of demand (overnight stays) by nationality has shown that in the 1980s visitors from northern Europe flocked to certain localities, while Mediterranean nationalities had a more dispersed pattern of preferences, or opted for cultural tourism (Leontidou 1991). The most dispersed pattern of preferences was to be found in the case of Germans and Italians. Italian and French citizens seemed to opt for exploration as much as for vacation tourism: they

Table 5.3 Regional distribution of demand (overnight stays) in Greece, 1981–1993[1]

	1981		1993		
	(%)	Foreigners as percentage of total	(%)	Foreigners as percentage of total	1981–93 difference
Greater Athens	23.73	77.00	15.89	61.90	−2,962,700
Salonica (Nomos)	4.62	44.54	3.05	36.20	−597,897
Rest of mainland Greece					
Central Greece[2]	3.05	41.16	2.55	26.00	−164,019
Argolis	2.68	80.12	1.77	65.50	−345,281
Rest of Peloponnese	5.73	54.63	5.47	46.45	−21,792
Epiros	1.61	33.09	1.84	29.47	+124,625
Thessaly[3]	1.40	26.38	1.22	20.41	−56,750
Khalkidiki	3.04	80.13	2.85	73.56	−32,184
Rest of Macedonia[4]	2.74	36.31	2.17	27.95	−196,728
Thrace	1.14	17.22	1.35	10.23	+108,779
Aegean islands					
Dodecanese	17.37	95.97	23.66	93.85	+2,960,576
Cyclades	1.82	73.32	2.20	64.34	+187,404
Lesvos, Samos, Chios	1.41	66.23	2.18	73.55	+351,921
Rest of eastern islands					
Euboea	2.16	44.99	1.44	40.89	−271,035
Magnesia (Sporades)	1.46	42.25	1.75	41.69	+146,140
Kavala (Thasos)	1.45	50.19	1.29	37.91	−47,797
Crete	14.73	91.90	19.51	92.41	+2,277,448
Ionian islands					
Corfu	8.93	93.59	7.46	84.90	−487,457
Zante, Kephalonia, Lefkada	0.91	55.23	2.36	74.73	+634,529
Total	100.00	74.63	100.00	72.09	1,607,782

Sources: Adapted from NSSG (1993, p. 48).

Notes: 1. Includes camping.
   2. Excluding Attica and Euboea.
   3. Excluding Magnesia.
   4. Excluding Salonica, Kavala and Khalkidiki.

mostly used individual forms of travel, and moved between two and four times during their visit (EOT 1979). The Spanish tended to prefer cultural tourism, concentrating in Greater Athens. Other Mediterranean and US visitors also displayed a preference for the city. In contrast, northerners, such as Finnish and Swedish tourists, tended to congregate in a few areas, especially the island of Rhodes, which was actually developed as an area for mass tourism by Swedish tour operators (TCG 1981, p. 106).

During the 1970s there was remarkable stability in the regional pattern of tourist demand, which poses questions about the control exercised by tourism agents, charter flights and package holidays. Certain flows were entrenched, and their direction was not easily modified for long periods, at either the regional or the international level (Komilis 1986, pp. 51, 104–6). Demand was concentrated in Greater Athens and three tourism islands: Rhodes, Crete (northern coast), and Corfu (Table 5.3 and Figure 5.3). Domestic tourism did not compete with foreign tourism, either in regional terms or by type of accommodation. By 1986 foreigners were over-represented in the Dodecanese (Rhodes), Crete, Corfu, Attica and Khalkidiki, while Greeks were more represented in the largest cities, the mainland, and islands near the coast such as Sporades and Euboea (Table 5.3).

Changes since the 1980s only benefited the islands and involved a fall in the popularity of Attica and a shift of foreign tourists' preferences from the larger towns towards Corfu, northern Crete and Khaldikiki (Komilis 1986, pp. 136–7). Nights spent in Greater Athens declined dramatically by 2 million in 1981–1986 and another 1 million in the period 1987–1993, and the popularity of Attica has continued to fall: 40 per cent of tourists preferred it in 1983, and only 25 per cent in 1986 (unofficial estimate, Papachristou 1987). Islands near Athens (in Attica, Euboea) and the city of Salonica also lost popularity. Capacity in Attica declined proportionately in the late 1970s and, in the 1980s, three luxury hotels closed down and a central historical hotel began to rent out rooms to Greeks as residences. Tourist flows are now directed to islands, especially to the Dodecanese, which gained nearly 3 million overnight stays in 1981–1986, and Crete, which gained 2 million, but destinations remained stable thereafter (Table 5.3). Corfu, by contrast, gradually lost its attraction after 1987.

5.4.2   Capacity and types of accommodation

Infrastructure and accommodation facilities improved rapidly in the post-war period throughout Greece, but especially in the largest cities and in the islands. The composition of tourist accommodation changed as follows: until the mid-1960s, standard types of lodgings predominated; yachting appeared from the late 1960s; bungalows and apartment hotels emerged in the early 1970s and from the mid-1970s, organised cruises and summer villas appeared, along with a strong tendency for foreigners to purchase private homes (Zacharatos 1986, p. 84). Capacity in 1993 included 7,510 hotel units with 499,606 beds, 145,704 rented rooms with 315,313 beds, and a large number of unauthorised rooms (adapted from NSSG 1995). The number of small cruise ships hired by better-off tourists grew slowly, from 1,200 in 1975 to 1,700 in 1987 and 6,654 in 1993. About 600 cruise ships changed to the Turkish flag in the 1980s, due to the more favourable conditions offered for tourist development (Papachristou 1987). The number of yachts which called at Greek ports increased from 1,737 in 1960 (38 per cent under the Greek flag), through 16,249 in 1970 (only 9 per cent Greek), to 29,098 in 1977 (30 per cent Greek).

As with demand, hotel capacity was sharply concentrated in Greater Athens (17.2 per cent of beds in 1985 but 14.2 per cent in 1993), Rhodes (14.8 per cent in 1985 rising to 17.4 per cent in 1993) and Crete (13.9 per cent in 1985 rising to 18.5 per cent in 1993) and, to a lesser extent, Corfu (6.6 per cent; Table 5.4). This concentration has changed little since 1963 (Komilis 1986, pp. 102–3) except in Athens. Auxiliary accommodation facilities, such as camping and rented rooms (officially registered) also increased rapidly: in 1985 they provided 59 per cent of total beds in Kavala-Thasos, rising to 63.4 per cent in 1993, 49 per cent in the Ionian Islands excluding Corfu rising to 60.7 per cent in 1993, 54 per cent in the Cyclades rising to 62.6 per cent, and 48 per cent in the Magnesia-Sporades area rising to 60.7 per cent. They were less important in the main tourist areas (Greater Athens, the Dodecannese,

Table 5.4   The structure of tourist capacity in Greece by region, 1993

Hotel[1] beds (HB), camping (C), rented rooms (RR, beds)	Total capacity		Regional distribution (%)	
	Bed	(%)	HB only	C+RR (% of total)
Greater Athens	87,572	9.64	14.19	19.06
Salonica (Nomos)	17,989	1.98	1.72	52.19
Rest of Mainland Greece				
Central Greece[2]	27,469	3.03	3.55	35.37
Peloponnese	73,261	8.07	8.28	43.53
Epiros	19,922	2.19	1.54	61.40
Thessaly[3]	12,113	1.33	1.14	53.01
Macedonia[4]	75,242	8.29	5.44	63.27
Thrace	16,801	1.85	2.60	22.59
Aegean islands				
Dodecanese	113,958	12.53	17.36	23.90
Cyclades	72,539	7.99	5.43	62.62
Lesvos, Samos, Chios	40,145	4.42	3.49	56.52
Rest of eastern islands				
Euboea	23,244	2.56	2.59	44.30
Magnesia (Sporades)	37,051	4.08	2.91	60.74
Kavala (Thasos)	23,253	2.56	1.70	63.42
Crete	141,684	15.60	18.47	34.88
Ionian islands				
Corfu	84,113	9.26	6.52	61.28
Zante, Kephalonia, Lefkada	41,689	4.59	3.06	63.30
Total (%)		100.00	100.00	37.07
Absolute number	908,045		499,606	

Source: Adapted from NSSG (1995, pp. 32–7).

Notes: 1. Includes: hotels, bungalows, motels, furnished suites, guest rooms, boarding-houses, inns. Excludes: 2. Attica, Euboea; 3. Magnisia; 4. Salonica, Kavala.

and Crete) but their important role increased there, too (see Table 5.4). This correlates with the regional preferences of native and foreign tourists: the latter tended to prefer hotel accommodation, especially luxury and Class A hotels (Singh 1984, pp. 76–7).

A large concentration of auxiliary accommodation in some regions, by contrast, is indicative of the predominance of domestic tourism. Approximately 90 per cent of the clients of rented rooms are Greek. Domestic tourism is difficult to measure, because it is far less dependent on overnight stays in hotels and related accommodation. Greeks usually prefer rooms to let, the houses of relatives and, of course, second homes. The regional distribution of second homes can be deduced indirectly from the distribution of houses found empty during the population censuses.[5] Such an analysis for 1981 (Leontidou 1991) found a spectacular increase everywhere, in both absolute and relative terms. As domestic tourism originates mainly in Greater Athens and Salonica, second homes predominate on the fringes of the metropolitan areas (especially Attica), and in the nearby eastern islands (Cyclades).

5.4.3　Regional polarisation, seasonality and informalisation

The spatial polarisation and concentration of different nationalities and types of accommodation in specific localities is a feature of mass tourism. In fact Greeks are increasingly excluded from some well-known regions by inaccessible hotel prices: these cater for organised tourism and are far more expensive for individual (domestic) visitors. Concentration of mass tourism in seaside resorts and underutilisation of the mainland is evident in both capacity and demand. Beaches and recreation spots rather than ancient and historical sites are preferred. In the mid-1970s, 50–60 per cent of foreigners' hotel nights were spent in coastal summer resorts and only 6–7 per cent near archaeological sites, while another 25–30 per cent were spent in Greater Athens (CPER 1976, p. 184).

This type of demand intensifies seasonality. Auxiliary accommodation in standard lodgings is withdrawn from the market during the winter, and some hotels close down. Many islands are deserted for long periods during the winter. Of 82,346 hotel beds in 1970, 34.4 per cent operated on a seasonal basis (for 3–9 months). Of these, about two-thirds were located on the islands and one-third in the rest of Greece, except Athens, Piraeus and Salonica, where hotels operate all year round (Alexandrakis 1973, p. 174). National estimates in 1984[6] indicated that hotel occupancy rates were unsatisfactory, even during the peak period, reaching 82.1 per cent in July and 91.4 per cent in August. By 1993 these had fallen to 78.7 per cent and 90.2 per cent, respectively. The highest average annual rates by 1993 were in Northern Crete (88 per cent) and Kos (88 per cent), and the lowest in Athens (31 per cent; NSSG 1995).

Hotel occupancy rates appear low, especially in those regions where cheaper beds are offered in the market. The relationship between hotel and auxiliary lodging facilities in Greece is apparently 1:0.76 compared to 1:2–1:3 in other European tourist countries (CPER 1976, pp. 30–32; 1989). This is deceptive, however, since it ignores the large sector of unrecorded rooms for rent. The registration of rented rooms forming part of private houses started in 1972, but only a small percentage of owners have complied thus far. Undeclared rooms in private homes—whether empty or inhabited in the winter—exist in all tourism regions. There are also larger undeclared units of 80–100 beds, known as 'para-hotel' businesses (*paraxenodokhia*). According to various estimates, the ratio of official to unofficial beds ranges from 1:3 to 1:1.[7] In 1975 it was officially admitted that, due to undeclared rooms, overnight stays were underestimated by at least a quarter (CPER 1976, p. 28). In the mid-1980s, in addition to the 406,000 beds in hotels and officially declared rooms, there were at least 450,000 beds in 230,000 undeclared rooms, with a further 100,000 added yearly.

Such inconsistencies between official data and actual capacity abound in areas where illegal building occurs. Real-estate accumulation and building without a permit outside authorised settlement plans have been widespread processes in Greek cities and villages, involving a variety of social classes (Leontidou 1990). In tourist localities, as opposed to metropolitan housing areas, property accumulation and illegal building are petty speculative rather than popular activities. After the mid-1970s, property accumulation underwent a form of decentralisation, as real-estate investment was diverted from Greater Athens, the rest of Attica, and Salonica to peripheral regions. As it became profitable to be a seasonal landlord in the islands and other tourist resorts, investors turned from urban apartments to small furnished houses in provincial Greece, which were often unauthorised. These forces were triggered during the period of dictatorial rule, but the practice continued in the following decade. Residents built in unauthorised areas, and pressurised the authorities for post-legalisation. The Land Laws, especially LD 1337/1983, which taxed land according to the size of properties, became a counter-incentive for large organised development, and led to an increase in small units. Auxiliary but sub-standard rooms were built illegally and later 'legalised', although some remained undeclared and uncontrolled.

The main tangible negative environmental effect of informalisation is unplanned development and overburdening of infrastructure and the environment, since small as well as large units require a share of the coastline, parking and facilities (Briassoulis and Van der Straaten 1992). Therefore, although small inns and houses are not necessarily sub-standard, they can lead to sub-standard tourism. Competition between land uses is usually resolved to the detriment of agricultural activities, with the abandonment of land and the fragmentation of farming in tourism areas. In most cases the agricultural sector has declined where tourism has developed, and the case of Rhodes is typical in this respect (TCG 1981, p. 67; see also Komilis 1986, p. 38). In a few localities, however, the tourist diet and demand did lead to the intensification of agriculture. But even where the produce is summer fruit and vegetables, as in Crete, imported food-stuffs are the norm.

The conflict between tourism and industrial development, on the other hand, usually sparks off political debate and local social movements. It is interesting that both in Pylos in 1975 (Vaiou-Hadjimichalis and Hadjimichalis 1979, pp. 181–96) and in the debate in Delphi in June 1987 on the location of an aluminium factory, part of the local population mobilised against the Ministry of Culture. They opted for industrial development rather than protection of the archaeological and cultural heritage and the environment, implying an indifference to tourism. Such an attitude was especially surprising in Mykonos, the island which has three-quarters of the total nights spent in the Cyclades. In 1975 the local population mobilised against a proposed regional plan (Kalligas *et al.* 1972), protesting that protection of traditional housing was an obstacle to 'economic development', and demanding greater permissiveness in building permits (Romanos 1975, p. 201). The alternative posed to protection was not industrialisation, but speculative building.

5.5 A note on income and employment

5.5.1 *Research difficulties and 'intransparencies'*

Given intense segmentation and illegality, tourism has been underestimated in Greek economic and geographical research. Undeclared activities confuse data matrices and there is a hidden economy in tourism, which is far more pronounced than in other consumption or production sectors. The Five-Year plan, 1983–1987, recognised the need to obstruct the action of intermediaries and the tourism 'black economy' (Greek Parliament 1984, p. 59), but this is a formidable task. Besides evading taxation and controls, non-registrations in tourism also have an impact on research and policy formulation. Additional difficulties in assessing the economic impact of tourism stem from the complicated nature of the industry. It has been conceptualised as an export industry, where the purchaser consumes the product on the spot (Singh 1984, p. 26). Elsewhere it has been argued effectively that it should be treated as a specific form of

Table 5.5 Foreign tourists' expenditures in Greece, 1983–1993

	1983	1986	1993
Arrivals	4,778,477	7,339,015	9,913,267
Expenditures, total ($ million)	1,175	1,833	3,335
Average per-capita expenditure ($)	246	250	336
Nights spent in hotels	32,429,206	33,740,110	33,146,540

Sources: Adapted from NSSG (1995) and Parachristou (1987).

private consumption or final demand, rather than as an industry or sector of the economy (Zacharatos 1986).[8]

If tourism is generally criticised as an uncertain developmental strategy (de Kadt 1979), in Greece it is particularly dependent on external economic fluctuations and socio-political conjunctures. This was evident in President Reagan's 'travel proclamation', issued in June 1985 after a TWA highjacking, which curbed US tourism in Greece (Table 5.1). The Chernobyl accident in early 1986 had the same effect throughout Europe. The impact of tourism on localities is especially evident where seasonality is acute. By contrast, the devaluation of the drachma in 1998 to 86 per cent of its value, related to policies for the Single European Currency, had boosted reservations for vacations by foreigners by an estimated 15 per cent by May 1998. Positive impacts which have been stressed by analysts include economic revitalisation, the development of cultural contacts and increased communication between previously isolated localities and the outside world. This is relativised by the contradictions of the demonstration effect, influencing the propensity of Greeks to consume non-essential, luxury goods, and their desire to travel. In general, however, the external effects of tourism have been considered positive in Greece (Alexandrakis 1973, pp. 183–97; Singh 1984).

5.5.2   On the economic impact of tourism at the national level

The lack of any specific study of patterns of tourism expenditure complicates evaluation of economic impact. Available figures underestimate foreign exchange receipts, as they only refer to foreign exchange transactions recorded by the Bank of Greece. These are much lower than actual tourism consumption, which includes unofficial transactions (Zacharatos 1986, pp. 65–6, 89; Singh 1984, p. 85). Even so, the available information shows that tourism receipts maintained a high rate of growth in 1960–1978—21.4 per cent per annum—while exports, invisible receipts and current account receipts grew by only 16 per cent (Singh 1984, pp. 86–9). Tourism receipts grew from $49.3 to $1,326.3 million between 1960 and 1978, while receipts per arrival doubled in the same year from $140 to $282 (Singh 1984, pp. 92–3), and grew slowly after that (Table 5.5).

Average tourist expenditures have always been low in Greece by international standards. In 1970 they were $13 daily (compared with $16.80 in Portugal, $15.70 in Spain, and $13.70 in Turkey; Alexandrakis 1973, p. 156). Expenditures per visit were $120 in 1968 (compared with $130 in Italy and $170 in Spain; Alexandrakis 1973,

p. 157). This can be attributed to cheap services, especially in the informal sector, as well as to the type of tourism. It seems that medium- or even low-income tourists do continue to visit Greece. In the early 1980s per-capita expenditure fell consistently, and the number of nights spent in hotels remained stable. However, per capita expenditure started to grow later (Table 5.5). In general, foreign tourists tend to consider Greece a place for cheap vacations: in a 1985 survey (EOT 1985) 66 per cent of respondents found the cost accessible, 29 per cent low, and only 5 per cent high. Tourism expenditure abroad by Greek nationals was also low, and only constituted 3.4 per cent of all imports of goods and services (OECD 1985).

Studies of the economic effects of tourism in Greece estimated the net impact of tourism in the 1970s by subtracting the negative impact (foreign exchange expenditure) from the positive one (total receipts from foreign tourism); the balance was positive and had grown from $170 million in 1970 to $1,186 million in 1978 (Singh 1984, pp. 177–8). Other analyses have shown that the share of tourism receipts in GDP increased from 1.6 per cent in 1960 to 2.4 per cent in 1970, and 4.9 per cent in 1978 (Singh 1984, p. 98). Later estimates indicate that tourist receipts have decreased to 3.4 per cent of GDP (OECD 1985). By contrast, as much as 16.4 per cent of all exports came from tourism. According to the same source, international tourism financial flows (receipts minus expenditures) gave a positive balance of $1,006 million in 1984. The positive impact of tourism on the balance of payments is manifested in its contribution to total invisible receipts, which increased from 18 per cent to 32 per cent in 1970–1978 (OEDC 1985, pp. 95–6). Tourism earnings have covered about one-fifth of the balance of current transactions in many years, and this rose to 24 per cent ($492 million) in 1986 (Papachristou 1987).

By 1994, tourism produced 10 per cent of the Greek GDP, supported 11–18 per cent of employment (280,000–380,000 people employed directly and another 110,000 indirectly) and generated 35 per cent of invisible exchange receipts and 6.4 per cent of capital investment (CPER 1994), which underlines its importance for the Greek economy. However, Greece fared worst among European countries in 1992 (with the exception of Germany) in terms of the annual rates of increase of tourist receipts (5.5 per cent compared to 8 per cent in Europe as an average, topped by Spain and Italy with over 12 per cent each; Komilis 1995, p. 77). In 1994, the country's share of tourism was 2.3 per cent of the world market, 4.3 per cent of the European one and 5.2 per cent in the Mediterranean one (CPER 1994).

5.5.3   Employment, gender and family work strategies

There is a growing literature on the gender dimensions of tourism, especially with respect to employment and culture, with particular references to the case of Greece (Kousis 1989; Castelberg-Koulma 1991; Leontidou and Ammer 1992; Leontidou 1994). Gender in tourism employment is an extreme case of 'statistical invisibility', since women extend their domestic work into the informal sector as assistants in an industry which, during peak months, will absorb all available labour in each community at an exhausting pace of work. The stark contrast with visitors' leisurely lifestyles creates cultural tension.

Employment in tourism is difficult to measure on the basis of official statistics. Even direct employment (hotels, restaurants, and transport including travel agencies) is difficult to track, let alone indirect employment. One of the sectors which expanded most rapidly during the last two decades is that of 'renting goods and property': average annual rates of employment growth in this sector were a phenomenal 18.34 per cent in Greece as a whole, 17.6 per cent in the Aegean and 14.2 per cent in Athens (Leontidou 1994, pp. 86–91). Other sectors related to tourism are recreational and cultural services, which stagnated or declined, and national and local tourism administration, which is difficult to separate from the rest of the public services. Greek tourist enterprises are small-scale, with an average size of about 2.5 employees per hotel and restaurant establishment and 3.4 per recreational and cultural establishment. Only transport establishments have grown in size, reaching an average of 17 employees per establishment at present (adapted from NSSG data).

It is difficult to construct an accurate indicator of direct employment in tourism, as all sectors, except hotels, serve local residents as well as visitors. The labour force recorded in hotels and restaurants, recreational and cultural services and transport increased by 59,679 persons over the period 1961–1971, and by 88,460 over the period 1971–1981, and grew from 6.1 per cent to 10.5 per cent of total employment in Greece. Two more detailed studies during the late 1960s, although difficult to compare because of their different methods, give compatible estimates. Direct employment in tourism was estimated at 23,500 in 1966 (Spartidis 1969) and this was corroborated by a 1970 study by the Ministry of Co-ordination (1971), which found 26,100 working in the sector. Thereafter, employment grew considerably and, by 1984, employment in hotels alone had risen to 50,000 (OECD 1985). The Five-Year Development Plan 1988–1992 estimated employment in all types of accommodation in 1987 to be 118,000 at the peak period, rising to 180,000 if indirect employment is added (CPER 1987, pp. 135–6). Amongst these, about 25,000 qualified and 50,000 less skilled labourers were employed in hotel businesses (Greek Parliament 1984, p. 61).

Official employment censuses do not show a particularly marked seasonality. Monthly fluctuations in 1978 showed 12 per cent of the labour force in restaurants and 54 per cent in hotels to be temporary. According to the Hotel Employees' Insurance Fund, seasonality was higher during the 1970s and has not improved over time (Komilis 1986, pp. 127–35). In the larger cities (Athens, Salonica, Patras, Volos, Larisa) monthly fluctuations were almost negligible, as these centres cater for domestic and commercial movements as well as tourism. By contrast, some tourist towns (Heraklion, Rhodes, Ayios Nicolaos, and Corfu) have experienced considerable peaks in employment from May to November, especially in July and August. Even more acute peaks occurred in small seaside settlements.

High seasonality in hotels and restaurants particularly affects the female labour force. While female participation in the labour force decreased in the country as a whole over the period 1961–1981, it doubled in sectors associated with tourism but is very low in transport. The increase would be even greater if unrecorded employment were included. Jobs in accommodation are dominated by women (bed-makers, cleaners, servants, etc.) especially in unrecorded rooms and the informal sector, where such jobs come 'naturally' as an extension of housework. Indeed, the attraction of 'housewives' into tourist employment has been a government proposal since the mid-1970s (CPER 1976, pp. 51–2). In the Greek islands the gender division of labour involves women taking care of the guests and rooms (usually parts of family houses), and men collecting the clients at the port (usually accompanied by their sons), negotiating prices and, where the rooms are declared, contacting the authorities (Leontidou 1994).

Seasonality is both an economic and a socio-cultural problem. In fact, the cultural impact of tourism should be discussed in this context, but only a brief reference can be made to what seems to be one of the most crucial issues for a country such as Greece. Tourism breaks up certain long-entrenched traditions and introduces cultural innovation, having both negative and positive impacts on localities. The changing role of women in areas incorporated into the tourist market, influences family strategies and creates new conflicts on the societal and cultural level (Castelberg-Koulma 1991; Leontidou 1994).

5.5.4 *Economic aspects of regional polarisation*

The importance of tourism in Greek economic development has been considerable. This was less evident until the mid-1960s, but later emphasis on tourism added a certain dynamism in the 1980s. As the bulk of expenditure occurred in the countryside and the islands, moreover, tourism affected previously isolated areas more than developed urban centres. Most of the Greek islands were inaccessible in the 1950s, and their economies were characterised as a mixed monetary and bartering system (Alexandrakis 1973, pp. 196–7). They were then connected with Piraeus and Athens by sea and air transport, and later a few of them were interconnected (although the communication systems still remain radial and centralised on Athens). Finally, several islands have been directly connected with European cities by charter flights. By the late 1970s, more than 50 per cent of charter arrivals already occurred at island airports such as Rhodes, Kos, Corfu and Heraklion (Singh 1981; NSSG).

Uneven development is pronounced in tourism, as has already been shown. At a deeper level of analysis, the apparent decentralisation of activity is highly polarised spatially, being concentrated in a few localities (with resulting congestion) and absent in other areas with remarkable natural and cultural resources. In the former type of localities tourism can be advantageous from the residents' viewpoint, or it can disrupt labour markets and overload social infrastructure and the environment as, for example, has occurred in Rhodes (TCG 1981, pp. 67–72). Spatial polarisation, however, is not of the urban-rural type of development as it is related to trends of diffuse urbanisation in the 1980s (Leontidou 1990) and the decline of urban tourism. Mass tourism, if highly seasonal, disrupts rural communities and labour markets, and there are examples (such as Rhodes) where social segregation between tourists and inhabitants has been observed (Loukissas 1977).

Polarisation is apparently intensifying through investment in already congested areas which, ironically, is still going on during a period when decentralisation goals have been explicitly set. Table 5.6 underlines the impact of LD 1262/1982 on tourism development by region. The law specifies non-assisted areas according to certain criteria, and excludes large cities from incentives policy. With the exception of Attica and Salonica, however, new investment in 1982–1988 was directed towards areas which already had considerable tourism capacity: the Dodecanese (especially Rhodes, 19 per cent of investment) and Corfu (10 per cent). The correlation coefficient between existing (1983) and new (1983–1993) hotel beds by region (including cities) in Greece is as high of 0.90, and even if total existing capacity (including camping, rented rooms, etc.) is compared with new beds, the coefficient remains at 0.85. This analysis indicates that new investment is attracted to already developed areas and its

Table 5.6   Hotel capacity, 1983, and new investment by region in Greece, 1983–1993

	Hotel[1] beds 1983		New investment 1983–1998		Hotel[1] beds 1993	
	(Abs.no.)	(%)	(Abs.no., drs)	(%)	(Abs.no.)	(%)
Attica and Piraeus	71,125	22.33	94,998,890	0.76	70,880	14.19
Salonica (Nomos)	8,903	2.80	0	0.00	8,600	1.72
Rest of Mainland Greece						
Central Greece[2]	16,169	5.08	141,524,263	1.13	29,493	5.90
Peloponnese	36,037	11.31	590,303,389	4.70	29,631	5.93
Epiros	5,614	1.76	356,699,718	2.84	7,690	1.54
Thessaly[3]	4,977	1.56	68,043,621	0.54	5,692	1.14
Macedonia[4]	19,108	6.00	1,352,310,780	10.78	35,694	7.14
Thrace	2,915	0.92	406,357,344	3.24	4,499	0.90
Aegean islands						
Dodecanese	43,896	13.78	2,372,449,007	18.91	86,718	17.36
Cyclades	12,550	3.94	634,293,635	5.05	27,115	5.43
Lesvos, Samos, Chios	6,754	2.12	1,182,152,190	9.42	17,457	3.49
Rest of eastern islands						
Euboea	10,810	3.39	29,451,021	2.35	12,946	2.59
Magnesia (Sporades)	7,668	2.41	675,096,342	5.38	14,548	2.91
Kavala (Thasos)	5,301	1.66	173,932,977	1.39	8,507	1.70
Crete	39,760	12.48	2,675,012,604	21.32	92,267	18.47
Ionian islands						
Corfu	20,713	6.50	1,264,162,164	10.07	32,570	6.52
Zante, Kephalonia, Lefkada	6,125	1.95	266,646,844	2.12	15,299	3.06
Total	318,515	100.00	12,548,554,789	100.00	499,606	100.00

Source: Adapted from NSSG (1985/1995) and MNE (unpublished series of investments realised on the basis of LD 1962/1982 until April 1988).

Notes 1. Includes: hotels, bungalows, motels, furnished suites, guest rooms, boarding-houses, inns.
        Excludes: 2. Attica, Euboea: 3. Magnisia: 4. Salonica, Kavala.

impact by 1993 on the increase of hotel beds especially in the islands, is evident on Table 5.6.

Greek Five-Year Plans from the mid-1970s have considered small-scale tourism development to be advantageous from the viewpoint of the local population, while large-scale developments were found to drain local income. According to the Khalkidiki Regional Plan, only 19 million out of 126 million drachmas (15 per cent of the total) gained in hotel tourism remained in the locality, and only 27.5 per cent of employees were recruited from the local population (OAOM and Associates 1976, Vol. 1, pp. 335–48). Small-scale local tourist developments and inns were generally promoted by the government after the mid-1970s in order to assist regional development by channelling additional income to the local population, family units and small businesses. In retrospect, the economic impact of the growth of small-scale tourism was positive, as the amount of income remaining within localities increased. However, the environmental impact was rather negative, as the quality of services and of the environment deteriorated, segmentation intensified, and illegal building and unrecorded activities mushroomed.

The regional developmental effect of tourism, however, is complex and contradictory and has yet to be adequately studied. Congestion and environmental deterioration have diverted tourists from Athens, but have not dispersed them: they still flock to Rhodes, Crete and other islands. In these as well as other peripheral localities, contradictions emerge from seasonality, regional polarisation and segmentation on several levels: most importantly, domestic versus foreign tourist resorts (approximately the mainland versus the islands), and formal versus informal activities in tourism.

5.6   Conclusion

The above analysis has shown that uneven tourism development was consolidated rather than superseded in the 1990s: seasonality became more acute, cultural tourism never surfaced over sun and beach tourism, hotel capacity was under-used, and tourism waves abandoned many resorts. The mid-1980s were structurally not very different from the mid-1990s: they were just more hopeful and vivacious. The present crisis of Greek tourism is considered to be structural rather than conjunctural, and is usually attributed to fragmentary and often absurd policies (CPER 1994; Komilis 1995); and yet, as during the late 1990s, Greece is consistently re-evaluating its position in a vulnerable world region of Europe, and changes envisaged bear profoundly on tourism policy. The latter is not systematically re-thought in the context of the neo-liberal Europe of urban boosterism and post-modern place marketing (Bailly *et al.* 1996; Leontidou 1993, 1995). However, as new strategies are linked up with the attraction of international events, an air of recovery is already blowing through urban tourism.

The negativities of stagnation and the loss of urban tourism are not really assessed in public policy, but strategies to supersede them are already under way. Policies are definitely contradictory: the effort to recall Greek archaeological treasures from London (and not Paris or Munich, unfortunately), goes hand-in-hand with permissiveness over building on attractive isolated beaches. However, the seeds for new directions in tourism development are planted. Problems related to uneven development have not obstructed tourism from being one of the main motors of regional revitalisation in Greece. There are other sectors which figure in relevant studies but, in fact, flexible production does not play the role usually attributed to it. Banks, services, peripheral universities and technological development in the tertiary and quaternary sector are important in diverse regions in incorporating previously isolated areas. However, tourism seems to have taken the lead in evening out some regional inequalities in post-war Greece.

The late 1990s were particularly good years for urban tourism: this has been given a boost by Salonica's designation as the Cultural Capital of Europe and Athens being host to the Sixth World Athletics Championships. But enthusiasm culminated in September, with the selection of Athens to host the 2004 Olympics after having lost the Golden Olympics of 1996 to Atlanta. The Olympics are not unanimously welcome in Greek society, of course. With the prospective attraction of investment and the revitalisation of urban tourism, there is a risk of losing the sector's equilibrating regional impact in the years to follow. Yet Athens has suffered considerable losses for a long period, as shown above, and tourism in the rest of Greece is already picking up in 1998, which has been another pivotal year because of the devaluation of the drachma.

The interplay of stagnation and low performance until 1993 and restructuring in the midst of encouraging prospects from 1997 onwards, has been evident throughout this Chapter. It underlines the ephemeral and elusive nature of the tourism industry, especially for a country such as Greece, in one of the most vulnerable world regions today.

Notes

1. Main abbreviations used in this chapter: CPER, Centre of Planning and Economic Research; EOT, National Tourist Organisation of Greece; LD, Legislative Decree; NSSG, National Statistical Service of Greece; RD, Royal Decree; TCG, Technical Chamber of Greece; YPEHODE, Ministry of the Environment, Regional Planning and Public Works.
2. The Ministry of Tourism, established in 1987, for a short period supervised EOT, the Xenia Hotels, the Summer Festivals and the casinos, but not Olympic Airways. The role of EOT was reviewed recently, and its modernisation is being sought, with the introduction of tourism higher education courses and the review of its entrepreneurial role, with the creation of limited liability companies in certain areas, and the combination of central with local intervention in tourism development.
3. Additional services include conference rooms, recreation and sporting grounds, etc. Information about the provisions of the 1988–1992 Development Plan, which has not been published except for a brief document, was kindly provided by Panagiotis Komilis (CPER). Information about the Ministry of Tourism and its policy, especially the Integrated Mediterranean Programmes, was kindly provided by Dimitris Kavadias (EOT).
4. The Integrated Mediterranean Programmes encouraged large investments (over 300 million drachmas) in hotels of range 'A' or above, with additional services, in under-developed areas (earmarked as 'D' areas). About 29 per cent of the expenditures of the Programmes approved by EOT were directed towards infrastructure, especially marine tourism and sailing. As for the 1988–1992 Development Plan, it explicitly referred to the attraction of higher-income tourism and to the dominant role of private investment in the creation of large tourism complexes, including those with recreational and sports facilities. To this effect, some of the limits set by LD 1262/1982 were relaxed. Its impact on regional structure is studied in the final part of this chapter (Table 5.4).
5. A word of caution is required here. The large numbers of empty residences on the islands also reflect the existence of abandoned dwellings, and the building boom in 1976–1979 created excess empty houses all over Greece, especially in the cities.
6. The NSSG and EOT calculate the ratio of bednights occupied to bednights available on the basis of the number of beds actually available each month.
7. The 1:3 estimate by the Greek Chamber of Hotels is calculated on the basis of hotel beds (excluding auxiliary accommodation). It may be an exaggeration, given their vested interest in the control of this flourishing para-hotel business. In Corfu, 20,000 hotel beds are thought to correspond to 60,000 additional undeclared beds. This is an average which rises in undeveloped areas: for example, Casiopi in Corfu is believed to have 60 official and 4,000 unofficial beds. They are not only offered on the spot: undeclared rooms have even appeared in British brochures advertising summer vacations in Greece! The cost is considerably lower, being no more than one-third that of hotels at the most, especially after the latter suddenly increased their prices by 32 per cent in the summer of 1987.
8. This suggests a new treatment in place of earlier approaches to tourism as an industry with intersectoral linkages in the Greek economy: tourism should be treated as a separate column of final demand in input–output tables (Zacharatos 1986, pp. 47–55). Earlier approaches, using 1960 data (Alexandrakis 1973, pp. 183–8), showed that backward linkages were weaker in tourism than in manufacturing. However, tourism created stronger linkages than had been

suggested, including, for example, dynamic effects such as the appearance of industries producing basic metal products for hotel construction, leading to a decrease of such imports. Tourism was also considered significant because linkages were created by exogenous money brought into the economy with a relatively small promotional cost. It was calculated through regression equations that each $1 of promotion would foster approximately $16 of tourism receipts. In 1975 the percentage of intermediate inputs created by tourism was calculated at 20 per cent compared to 13 per cent in services, 40 per cent in transport, and over 68 per cent in manufacturing (CPER 1976, p. 34).

6 Portugal: market segmentation and economic development

Jim Lewis and Allan M. Williams

6.1 Introduction: the late emergence of international mass tourism

Portugal was a relatively undiscovered part of Europe before the 1960s, with the exception of the capital, Lisbon, and Madeira, which had long been favoured by the British upper middle classes. Thereafter, Portuguese tourism gradually internationalised, although this remained a very uneven process in both time and space. The temporal irregularities relate not only to the periodic economic crises in leading markets such as the UK and Germany, but also to the political instability which followed the 1974 coup that overthrew the Salazar/Caetano regime, and to changing relationships with Spain following accession to the EU in 1986. In addition, there is a high degree of spatial polarisation related to the territorial requirements of different tourism markets. Despite these irregularities, Portugal as a destination has passed from relative obscurity to being the twelfth-ranked destination in Europe, in terms of international arrivals, by the mid-1990s. There is clear evidence of international and domestic tourism growth in most regions, ranging from the increasingly continuous development of the coastal strip in the Algarve, to major investments in Lisbon, linked to EXPO 1998, to the more modest, but significant, spread of rural tourism in the interior.

Despite the importance of the industry, it remains relatively little researched, even in Portugal, although Cavaco's (1979, 1980, 1981) pioneering work is now being added to (for example, the special theme issue of *Inforgeo*, 1993). Yet there are many features of Portuguese tourism which merit further investigation:

- First, there is the economic importance of the industry; by 1994 international visitors generated a net inward balance of $2,100 million for the economy, receipts were equivalent to some 5 per cent of GDP and covered 44 per cent of the net current account deficit. Tourism also accounted for approximately 4.8 per cent of GDP.
- Second, the industry exhibits a high degree of regional polarisation in terms of capacity and types of employment, reflecting well-developed market segmentation, and making a significant contribution to the economies of regions such as Madeira and the Algarve.

Tourism and Economic Development: European Experiences, 3rd Edition. Edited by A.M. Williams and G. Shaw.
© 1998 John Wiley & Sons Ltd.

- Third, official Portuguese tourist policy initially favoured the development of luxury tourism (Cavaco 1979). Consequently, tourism in Portugal developed in a different manner from that in neighbouring Spain. This is highlighted by the simple fact that there are more hotel beds in Spain's Costa del Sol than there are in the whole of Portugal. However, there have been broad shifts in governance since the 1970s, partly reflecting the end of dictatorship and also the increasing power of tourism capital, so that the emphasis has shifted from luxury to mass tourism, especially in the Algarve but also, increasingly, in Madeira. This pattern has been further compounded by complex shifts in the markets for Portuguese tourism.
- Finally, the development of tourism in Portugal has been marked by a very uneven rhythm, with a disastrous decline in the mid-1970s being followed by slow recovery and then, from the mid-1980s, rapid expansion.

This chapter aims to provide a broad introduction to the Portuguese tourist industry. First, there is a review of its national-level evolution, followed by an analysis of the changing regional pattern of tourist arrivals and provision. This leads to an analysis of the national and regional economic features of tourism. Particular attention is paid to the relationship between market segmentation and the types of employment provided by tourism. Finally, current developments in policy are reviewed in relation to the future of tourism in Portugal.

6.2   The making of a mass tourism industry

The first significant development of tourism in Portugal was based around the thermal spas of the interior, such as Vizela, Vidago, Curia and Luso. These became popular with both foreign visitors and the emerging Portuguese middle class after the mid-nineteenth century. Even by the early twentieth century, beach tourism was little developed, and was mostly limited to daily visits from large urban centres, such as Oporto, Coimbra and Lisbon to nearby beaches at Foz do Douro, Figueira de Foz and Belem, respectively (Cavaco 1979). One significant initiative in the early twentieth century was the development of Portugal's first planned resort, Estoril, in the environs of Lisbon, in 1914 (Pina 1988). By 1932 Estoril already attracted 2,500 international tourists. But Portuguese tourism remained mainly based on domestic markets during most of the first half of the twentieth century, and there were only about 36,000 foreign visitors annually in the 1930s.

In contrast, tourism in the Algarve barely existed before the middle of the twentieth century. In the early twentieth century, a handful of tourists stayed in the hill town of Monchique, and at the beaches of Monte Gordo and Praia de Rocha (Pina 1988). The first hotel was opened in 1918, the Hotel Grande do Faro, but of greater significance was the opening of the elegant Hotel Bela Vista at Praia da Rocha in 1936, which signified the leading role that this coastal resort was to assume. However, there was little other accommodation available in this period except for some *pensões*. Foreign tourists, notably the British, started to arrive in the 1920s and the 1930s, but most tourists were wealthy families from Lisbon and the Alentejo.

World War II retarded tourism development in Portugal, but growth was renewed subsequently. During the 1950s the number of foreign tourists increased from 70,700 in 1950 to 353,000 by 1960, and between 1955 and 1963 alone, foreign exchange

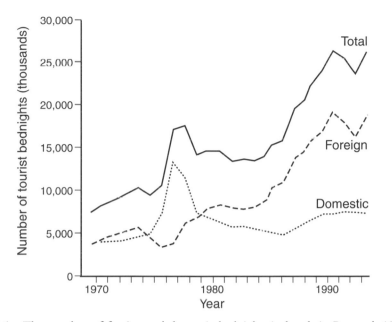

Fig. 6.1 The number of foreign and domestic bednights in hotels in Portugal, 1970–1994

Source: Direcção Geral do Turismo (1986, 1996)

receipts quadrupled. This was actively encouraged by state aid, after 1952, to promote foreign tourism (Cunha 1986). Despite the difficulties caused by the major devaluation of the Spanish peseta in 1958—a move designed to promote Spanish tourism but which also inhibited the movement of Spanish tourists abroad—Portuguese state policy seems to have been moderately successful in the 1950s and early 1960s.

The most significant phase in the expansion of Portugal's international tourist trade was the period 1963–1974, when its growth comfortably exceeded the average for the OECD countries. Portugal benefited from the general expansion of demand for tourism in Western Europe, combined with falling costs—especially as a result of the expansion of package holidays (Williams 1995). Expansion was brought to a halt by the 1973 devaluation of the dollar, a rise in transport costs and the recession that followed the 1973–1974 oil crisis. While all European tourist destinations suffered from these events, Portugal also experienced considerable political instability following the 1974 military coup, which ended almost 50 years of dictatorship and led to the reintroduction of democracy. In 1973 there had been over 4 million foreign visitors, and this number was not again exceeded until 1977. The 41 per cent fall in tourist bednights in hotels and guesthouses (see Figure 6.1) which occurred in 1975 constituted a major setback for the economy as a whole. This was only partly compensated for by a sharp rise in domestic tourist bednights in 1974–1976, generated by a temporary increase in real purchasing power and the use of vacant hotel rooms to house some of the thousands of *retornados*—refugees from the decolonisation of Angola and Mozambique.

International tourism began to revive from the late 1970s, and then to expand rapidly in the mid-1980s and early 1990s, putting Portugal at the head of the European tourism growth league. Total foreign arrivals increased from about 4 million in the 1970s to some 8 million in 1985, and then more than doubled in just five years to 19 million in 1991. Numbers then declined to a little over 16 million in 1993, before rebounding to almost 19 million in 1994. The pattern was different in domestic tourism. The boom in the mid-1970s was short-lived, and—given the recurrent problems of the Portuguese economy in the early 1980s—numbers declined gradually until 1986. Thereafter, there has been steady if unspectacular growth from around 5 million in 1986 to 7.3 million in 1994, reflecting national economic expansion and a major domestic consumer boom.

The structure of the tourist industry also changed during these years, with there being a pronounced shift to higher quality provision, related to an increase in hotels and apartments, matched by an absolute decline in *pensões* (Table 6.1a). The temporal rhythm of these structural shifts in the accommodation sector reflects the growth and selective targeting of international tourism. While there was a sharp increase in the number of hotels in the late 1960s, numbers were static through the relatively depressed 1970s, before growth took off again in the 1980s. There have also been changes within these broad categories, with the highest growth and decline rates being, respectively, in the more luxurious hotels/apartments and in the poorest quality hotels. There was a 25 per cent expansion in the number of hotels in the period 1965–1980, mostly in higher-quality hotels (that is in 3-, 4- or 5-star units), so that 78 per cent of hotel bedrooms had their own bathrooms by the mid-1980s. This was followed by an even sharper increase in the number of hotels, by 52 per cent in the period 1980–1994. This has been supplemented by marked increases in other types of higher quality accommodation, including tourist apartments, motels and *pousadas* (state-owned hotels).

To some extent, different forms of accommodation have evolved to cater for very different markets segments. *Pensões* were mostly developed in response to domestic demand, while international demand stimulated investment in the more up-market forms of accommodation, especially in the leisure as opposed to the business tourism sector. By 1988 over 47 per cent of foreign tourists stayed in 3-star (or superior) hotels, compared to only 33 per cent of domestic tourists (Table 6.1b). This proportion had fallen to 42 per cent by 1994, but this does not reflect a shift to lower quality accommodation because the share of the international market accounted for by the *pensões* fell from 8 to 6 per cent during this period. Instead, there was a shift to self-provisioning (Urry 1987) in the international market, with marked growth in the shares of hotel apartments, and other non-hotel apartments. In contrast, hotels (although not the 5- and 4-star ones) became more important for national tourists, while the domestic market share of the *pensões* fell sharply from 37 to 28 per cent in this period. Portuguese tourists also shared foreign tourists' preference for self-provisioning. In fact, these figures understate the importance of self-provisioning, given the poor quality or absence of data on second homes, the unregistered letting of apartments, and camping.

These developments are firmly associated with the shift to beach tourism and rapid expansion of the Algarve: only 10 per cent of *pensões* are in the Algarve, compared to 25 per cent of 5-star establishments, and 64 per cent of hotel apartments. There has also been expansion of other forms of tourism–related accommodation in the Algarve, such as time-sharing or co-ownership schemes. In addition, the Algarve has become an important focus of international in-migration from northern Europe, especially from the UK and Germany, related to the process of international retirement (Williams *et al.*

Table 6.1 Development and domestic/foreign utilisation of tourist accommodation in Portugal

(a) Development of hotels and other forms of tourist accommodation, 1965–1994

	1965	1970	1975	1980	1987	1994	Percentage change 1965–1980	1980–1994
Hotels	212	263	258	266	320	404	+25.5	+51.9
Hotel apartments	–	–	24	33	47	92	–	+178.8
Motels	–	–	17	13	15	16	–	–
Pousadas	–	17	22	26	32	36	–	+12.5
Inns	–	76	75	68	62	65	–	+4.8
Pensões	1,029	1,019	1,003	988	988	947	–4.0	–4.2
Total	(1,320)	1,375	1,429	1,456	1,464	1,560	18.2	–7.1

(b) Portuguese and foreign visitors' use of hotels and other forms of accommodation, 1988–1992

Type of accommodation	Foreign			Domestic		
	1988	1994		1988	1994	
	(%)	(%)	thousands	(%)	(%)	thousands
Hotels (total)	50.9	45.6	8,565	40.6	42.0	3,092
Five-star	14.7	10.2	1,903	5.4	5.2	385
Four-star	19.4	18.9	3,558	11.5	11.3	831
Three-star	13.2	13.3	2,495	15.7	18.2	1,337
One and two-star	3.5	3.2	607	7.9	7.3	539
Hotel apartments	13.8	18.4	3,845	6.4	13.3	980
Motels	0.4	0.4	66	1.2	0.7	54
Pousadas	1.4	1.0	193	0.8	1.2	87
Inns	1.4	1.4	271	1.7	1.4	105
Pensões	8.0	6.3	1,186	37.4	28.4	2,089
Tourist villages	11.1	9.3	1,753	4.6	4.5	335
Apartments	13.1	15.5	2,906	7.2	8.4	618
Total	100.0	100.0	18,785	100.0	100.0	7,361

Source: (a) Instituto Nacional de Estatística (1985a, 1985b) Direcção Geral do Turismo (1996); (b) Direcção Geral do Turismo (1996).

1997). There is a lack of reliable data on this phenomenon, but according to the 1991 Population Census there were 3,080 British residents in the Algarve; this is probably a considerable underestimate, for the British Honorary Consul has estimated there were at least 10,000 British people living in the Algarve (Williams *et al.* 1997). There are very strong links between previous knowledge of the Algarve, obtained through tourism, and the decision to retire there (Williams and Patterson 1998). While the British are probably still the largest group of international retired migrants in the Algarve, this is changing, with increasing numbers of German developers and German purchasers becoming active in the housing market.

Despite the changing nature of the Portuguese tourist industry, it has remained highly seasonal. In 1972, 44 per cent of all tourists arrived in the three peak months of July, August and September, and this had risen to 47 per cent by 1980 (see Figure 6.2a). Increased seasonal peaking has occurred despite the winter sunshine product in the Algarve and Madeira, proving attractive to British and Scandinavian tourists. Not least, the increased seasonal polarisation is due to the increasing importance of Portugal, especially the Algarve (Lewis and Williams 1988), as a mass tourism summer destination. By the mid-1980s the lower per-capita expenditure, and the environmental pollution problems, associated with mass tourism had become matters of serious concern. The extreme seasonal peaking has subsequently abated and arrivals in the three peak months had fallen to 36 per cent by 1994, reflecting the attraction of these two regions, but especially Madeira, as all-seasons destinations. Seasonal peaking has also been eased by the expansion of business tourism (in line with general economic recovery since the mid-1980s) and Lisbon-based cultural tourism. In contrast, the growth of rural tourism (Cavaco 1995) has mostly tended to reinforce seasonal peaking of demand, but the effects are limited because, in absolute terms, this remains a modest market.

6.2.1   Market segmentation: domestic and international sources

While foreign tourists are pre-eminent in terms of both visitor numbers and income generation in Portugal, domestic tourism represents a significant market segment. In terms of bednights (in hotels and similar accommodation), there were periods in the 1970s when domestic visitors (including rehoused *retornados*) in Portugal outnumbered foreigners (see Figure 6.1). Even after the boom in foreign tourism in the 1980s, domestic tourists still accounted for 28 per cent of all recorded nights in 1994, and they were dominant in some holiday market segments; for example, the Portuguese accounted for two-thirds of all overnights in *pensões*, and 75 per cent of nights on camp sites in 1994 (Direcção Geral do Turismo 1996). However, there is very low participation in tourism within Portugal in general. In 1978 only 19 per cent of the Portuguese took holidays away from home, and the proportion had only risen to 29 per cent in 1993, which is still substantially below northern European averages. The low participation rate is a consequence not only of low per-capita incomes but also of highly polarised incomes and access to leisure. While only 34 per cent of the population had any paid holidays at all, 45 per cent of these in 1994 had 23 days or more (Direcção Geral do Turismo 1996).

The most reliable evidence on where the Portuguese take holidays comes from a household survey undertaken in 1987. This suggested that only 7 per cent went abroad for holidays; 2 per cent went to neighbouring Spain, a further 2 per cent to France and 2 per cent to the rest of Europe. Given the weakness of the escudo on international exchange markets, the preference for adjacent countries is hardly surprising. More recent data for 1994 suggest that only 4.6 per cent of *all* Portuguese adults took holidays abroad in that year, and in 62 per cent of cases the reasons for not doing so were financial. Given the striking rise in per capita incomes, and in most forms of consumption since the mid 1980s, as well as generally low rates of unemployment, the persistence of such low rates of foreign holiday-taking is surprising. Within Portugal, the major change in domestic tourism, in line with foreign tourism, has been the shift from thermal resorts since World War II. Aged hotels, a lack of modern sporting

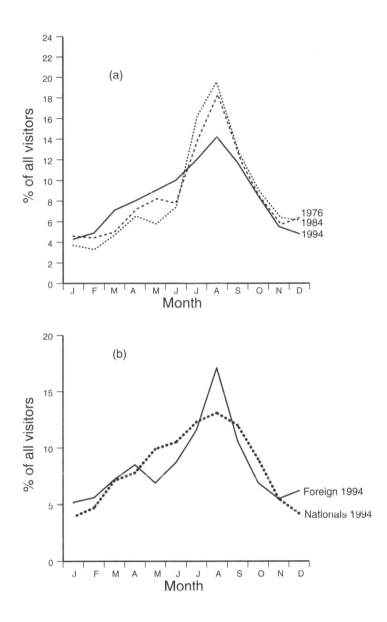

Fig. 6.2   Seasonality trends in Portuguese tourism: (a) changing patterns of seasonality, 1972–1994; (b) seasonality patterns for national and foreign tourists, 1994

Source: Direcção Geral do Turismo (1986, 1996)

facilities, the isolation of many spas and a growing preference for beach holidays have all led to a preference for coastal resorts. Although thermal spas are now dependent on Portuguese nationals for over 90 per cent of their trade, few visitors stay for more than a few nights and the spas have continued to decline in importance (Cunha 1986). In coastal resorts, the Portuguese tend to rely more than foreign tourists on camping and lower-quality hotel and boarding-house accommodation: 28 per cent of domestic tourists, compared to only 6 per cent of foreign tourists, stay in *pensões* (Table 6.1b). The Algarve is the single most important destination, accounting for 26 per cent of all domestic overnights (Direcção Geral do Turismo 1996). There is also considerable reliance on second homes, especially in the Algarve and around Lisbon (see Cavaco 1981; Williams 1981) and on unregistered accommodation.

Another feature of domestic tourism is that seasonality is much less marked than in foreign tourism. Accurate data are only available for bednights spent in hotels, apartments and *pensões* (see Figure 6.2b), but it is clear that in 1994 domestic tourism was distributed more evenly throughout the year. There are relatively more domestic tourist nights in winter and more foreign tourists in summer; the one exception is August which accounts for 17.1 per cent of all domestic tourist overnights, reflecting the highly institutionalised tradition of taking holidays in that month.

Turning to the international tourism market, this is highly segmented. There is a fundamental division between excursionists and tourists, which reflects international accessibility. In 1994 excursionists outnumbered tourists by 12.4 million to 9.2 million. As would be expected, most (day) excursionists (97 per cent) are from Spain, the inevitable outcome of Portugal's location. Historically, the balance between tourists and excursionists has changed. In 1973, for example, tourists considerably outnumbered excursionists, which was in keeping with the high degree of isolation between the countries in terms of trade and other interchanges. In the 1980s, however, there was a sharp increase in excursionism from Spain to Portugal, and this can be accounted for by rising real incomes in the former, changes in the relationship between the Iberian neighbours after their accession to the EU, and price differentials for some commodities leading to cross-border shopping trips. Some Portuguese border towns, such as Miranda do Douro and Vilar Formoso, have prospered as a result of this trade. Consequently, excursionists have outnumbered tourists since the 1970s. However, the Spanish market for day visits to Portugal appears satiated, so that the flows of excursionists and tourists are moving back into balance; between 1987 and 1994, there was a 51 per cent increase in the number of tourists compared to only 23 per cent increase in the number of excursionists.

While excursionists usually outnumber tourists, the latter are clearly more economically important, as their average stay was for 6.9 days in 1994; this is still a relatively long duration, compared to other European countries, despite a decline in the average stay from 10.4 days in 1980. Between 1940 and 1984, the total number of nights spent by foreign tourists in Portugal increased from 500,000 to 36 million, and by 1994 had increased again to an estimated 63 million. One of the keys to understanding the economic contribution of tourism is market segmentation, because different nationalities have very different activity and expenditure patterns. The composition of the international tourist trade has changed significantly over the years (see Table 6.2). The dominant group in terms of bednights is the UK, which has accounted for at least one-fifth of all tourist nights for most of the post-1945 period. There was a long, if fluctuating, increase in the UK market share from 22 per cent in 1960 to between 35 and 40 per cent in the mid 1980s. The absolute number of tourists

Table 6.2   Tourist bednights spent by selected foreign nationals in hotels, apartments and tourist villages in Portugal, 1960–1994

	1960		1980	1988	1994	
	Thousands	(%)	(%)	(%)	Thousands	(%)
FRG/Germany	86	6.9	16.2	13.8	4,273	22.7
Spain	110	8.8	10.1	8.4	1,628	8.7
UK	278	22.3	28.0	34.9	5,523	29.4
The Netherlands	39	3.1	10.3	8.0	1,488	7.9
USA	150	12.0	4.8	4.3	541	2.9
France	220	17.6	5.4	5.0	886	4.7
Sweden	29	2.3	4.7	3.8	452	2.4
Total (including others)	1,246	100.0	100.0	100.0	18,785	100.0

Sources: Direcção Geral do Turismo (1986, 1996).

from the UK then stabilised at approximately five and a half million, which meant that the market share declined to 29 per cent by 1994. The other leading market is Germany, whose share has increased from 7 per cent in 1960 to 23 per cent in 1994. In contrast, there been sharp declines in the market shares of both France and the USA. It is no coincidence that tour companies dominated the tourism industry in the two market leaders, the UK and Germany, for inclusive holidays play a key role in Mediterranean tourism (Williams 1997). A number of implications stem from this market segmentation.

National groups of foreign tourists have very distinctive holiday patterns in terms of length of stay, type of accommodation, reliance on commercial travel agencies, and seasonality (Table 6.3). The Spanish and the Italians have relatively short stays, relatively peaked seasonality, especially in the case of the Italians, and both tend to organise their holidays independently. For the Italians, this is likely to be in hotels or *pensões* but the Spanish are more likely to rely on camping and—not revealed in these official data—the informal sector. The French have relatively similar characteristics because although they have a longer average stay, their vacations are highly peaked seasonally, their use of hotels is relatively low and their use of camping relatively high, and they are more inclined to organise their holidays independently. Another group is made up of tourists from Belgium, The Netherlands, and the Federal Republic of Germany. Their average stay is 10–14 days, their visits are highly peaked in mid summer and they have a relatively high propensity (excepting the Belgians) for self-provisioning, while about half to three-quarters arrange their holidays through travel agencies. The Brazilians are superficially similar to this group but, given their emigration ties, are heavily reliant on friends and family for accommodation. The Swedes (and other Scandinavians) and the British form another distinctive group. They also have relatively long stays but, partly reflecting their severe domestic winters, their seasonality is less peaked. They rely mainly on hotels or apartments, and on inclusive tours. Finally, American tourists have relatively low seasonal peaking, and a heavy reliance on hotels. Such segmentation is of fundamental importance for each group makes a different contribution to economic development, as can be judged from their reliance on inclusive tours, accommodation type and average length of stay.

Table 6.3 Market segmentation: major features of the holidays of selected groups of international tourists in Portugal, 1994

Country of origin	Average length of stay (days)	Percentage of holidays taken in three peak months	Percentage nights in			Percentage using travel agencies to organise their holiday (1984)
			Hotels, etc.	Camping	Apartments	
Spain	3.0	39	76.5	17.8	5.8	39
Italy	6.2	48	NA	NA	NA	53
Brazil	9.5	38	NA	NA	NA	71
Belgium	10.8	45	75.2	14.8	10.0	70
The Netherlands	15.2	42	47.9	15.5	36.6	79
France	8.9	46	64.1	30.0	5.9	71
FRG/Germany	12.4	42	72.0	8.0	20.0	56
USA	8.6	38	94.5	0.9	4.4	75
UK	11.4	38	58.7	2.1	39.2	92
Sweden	12.7	38	NA	NA	NA	93

Sources: Direcção Geral do Turismo (1988, 1996).

6.3   Regional differentiation in the Portuguese tourism industry

Between 1974 and 1988 the main feature of the regional growth of tourism has been an impressive increase in numbers going to the main centres: that is the Algarve (Faro *distrito*), Lisbon and Madeira. The number of foreign visitor bednights spent in Faro quadrupled to 7 million while the numbers in Lisbon and Funchal both increased by almost 1 million to 3.1 and 2.5 million, respectively. Most of this expansion occurred in the 1970s and visitor numbers were relatively static in the early 1980s. Absolute increases in the other regions have been much smaller, although in percentage terms they have been broadly similar. Consequently, the overall share of the foreign tourist market held by the three main centres remained static at a level of 84 per cent (Direcção Geral do Turismo 1988). Changes in the reporting practices of the Direcção Geral do Turismo invalidate direct comparisons between 1994 and earlier dates. However, the data provided for tourism regions (Table 6.4a) allow some comparisons due to the co-terminous definitions in the cases of the Algarve, Madeira and the Azores, although these data exclude some sectors of accommodation. Nevertheless, the pattern is very striking, with the Algarve alone accounting for 54 per cent of all foreign tourist overnights, which reflects the remarkably high level of development in this region. Together with Madeira and the Costa de Lisboa (a larger area than the district of Lisbon), these regions account for 89 per cent of market share, indicating a high level of concentration. No other region accounts for more than 5 per cent of market share. Disaggregation by national market segments reveals an even more polarised distribution, for 74 per cent of the UK and 63 per cent of the German market segments were captured by the Algarve.

The regional distribution of domestic tourists is different from that of foreigners; there is a greater geographical spread and the Algarve is less prominent. Absolute numbers of visitors to most *distritos* remained static or actually decreased between 1974 and 1988. The one region which avoided this fate was Madeira, where the number of domestic tourists remained stable in the 1980s. The influence of falling living standards in Portugal in the 1980s was also evident in changes in the accommodation used. While the number of hotel and *pensão* holidays declined, there was an increase in the bednights spent on campsites from 1.4 million in 1974 to 4.9 million in 1987. The renewal of growth in the domestic market since the mid-1980s has not been evenly distributed regionally, and again the Algarve has the largest gains. By 1994 it accounted for 26 per cent of all domestic tourists, followed by the Costa de Lisboa with 22 per cent. The share of the Algarve in the leisure tourism market is even greater due to the large element of business tourism in the Costa de Lisboa. The other regional feature to note is the much more even spread of domestic rather than foreign tourism amongst the other regions of Portugal, especially the Mountains and the Azores. It can be surmised that most Portuguese regions are strongly reliant on the domestic market, despite attempts in recent years to attract international visitors to the interior of the country.

Distinctive regional markets have developed and their major characteristics, in 1994, at the *distrito* scale are shown in Table 6.4b. The Algarve, followed by Lisbon, and at some distance by Madeira, have the largest stocks of accommodation (58 per cent of the total). There are, however, important differences in their accommodation stocks. The Algarve has a large stock of self-catering accommodation, and relatively small shares of hotels and *pensões* compared to its share of all accommodation. It does, however, account for one quarter of all 5-star hotel rooms. In contrast, Lisbon—as

Table 6.4   Regional features of Portuguese tourism

(a) Market shares of tourism promotion regions, 1994

	Percentage of all domestic overnights	Percentage of all foreign overnights	Percentage of British overnights	Percentage of German overnights
Costa Verde	15.3	5.0	1.7	2.8
Costa Prata	11.4	3.9	0.8	2.1
Costa de Lisboa	21.8	19.8	6.5	9.9
Mountains	9.4	0.6	0.2	0.3
Plains	5.8	1.0	0.2	0.8
Algarve	26.0	53.5	74.1	63.2
Azores	3.7	0.5	0.2	0.8
Madeira	6.0	15.7	16.2	20.0
Total	100.00	100.00		

(b) *Ditritos* 1994

District/region	Percentage of all apartment, hotel and *pensões* beds	Percentage of all hotel beds	Percentage of all 5-star hotel beds	Percentage of all *pensões* beds	Percentage of all *distrito* employment in hotels, apartments and *pensões*
Aveiro	4	3	1	5	3
Beja	1	0	0	2	0
Braga	3	3	0	5	3
Bragança	1	0	0	3	1
Castelo Branco	1	1	0	2	1
Coimbra	4	3	0	5	2
Evora	1	1	0	1	1
Faro	27	22	25	11	31
Guarda	1	1	0	1	1
Leiria	4	3	0	7	3
Lisbon	21	29	40	19	23
Pontalegre	1	1	0	1	1
Oporto	8	9	12	10	7
Santarém	4	3	0	7	2
Setúbal	4	3	0	4	3
Viana do Castelo	2	1	0	3	1
Vila Real	1	1	0	3	1
Viseu	2	2	0	4	2
Azores	2	2	0	4	3
Madeira	10	11	23	4	13
Total	100	100	100	100	100

Source: Direcção Geral do Turismo (1996).

would be expected—has little self-catering and has a larger share of hotel beds than of all beds, and these are of decidedly higher quality, with the capital accounting for 40 per cent of all 5-star beds. Madeira also has an up-market profile for it accounts for 23 per cent of all 5-star as opposed to 11 per cent of all hotel beds. Elsewhere in Portugal—with the exception of the second city, Oporto—there is relatively little accommodation capacity, and *pensões* are relatively important. The remainder of this section considers further the three leading Portuguese tourism regions.

The relatively late development of the Algarve has already been commented upon. However, in the 1950s and the 1960s there was a deliberate attempt in both marketing and product development (high-quality hotels, especially golf hotels as at Penina and Val do Lobo), not only to stimulate growth but also to target relatively high-income market segments. Of particular note was the opening of Faro airport in 1965, which also heralded future rapid growth and popularisation. Tourism overnights in the Algarve increased from a mere 232 in 1950 to 1.1 million in 1970, 7.3 million in 1988, and 12.0 million in 1994 (Direcção Geral do Turismo 1996). There has been growing concern that the pursuit of higher volumes has led to a lowering of the socio-economic profile of tourism, and some slippage in the status of a holiday in the Algarve as a positional good (Lewis and Williams 1988).

With the acceleration of growth, the Algarve became the largest tourism region in Portugal with more than one quarter of all bed-spaces. It has a relatively broad spread of accommodation provision, ranging from camping sites to luxury hotels, and caters—in socio-economic terms—for a relatively broad market. While it attracts one-quarter of all domestic tourists, its primary appeal is to foreign tourists and it accounts for more than half of this market segment. Domestic tourists stay for relatively short periods (only 2.7 days in 1987; Direcção Geral do Turismo 1988), reflecting not only good accessibility but also the large numbers of second homes available for weekend breaks (Williams 1981). Foreign tourists, many of whom were package tourists, stayed an average of seven days. The high degree of dependence on foreign tourists (84 per cent of the total), and especially on the UK market (41 per cent of all foreign bednights), makes the Algarve particularly vulnerable to market fluctuations.

The island of Madeira represents the elite end of the Portuguese tourist market. While it has one-tenth of all bed-spaces, it has almost one-quarter of 5-star hotels and very few *pensões*. It relies heavily on foreign tourists, and its share of these is three times greater than of the domestic market. Given the high costs of flights, average stays are relatively long—9 days for foreigners. The equable year-round climate means that it attracts large numbers of tourists throughout the year and monthly overnight totals in 1994 ranged only between 23,000 and 37,000. The industry was relatively static in the late 1970s and the 1980s, but growth has since been renewed with a 21 per cent increase in bed-space capacity between 1991 and 1994 alone. The island is even more dependent on foreign tourists (86 per cent of the total) than is the Algarve, and while dependence on the British market is less extreme than in the latter, the UK and Germany account for almost 60 per cent of all foreign bednights.

Lisbon has a very different character as a tourism region. Most of its accommodation is in the serviced sector, especially hotels. Given its high volumes of business tourism, it has attracted substantial interest from major hotel groups and in 1994 accounted for 40 per cent of all Portugal's stock of 5-star hotel beds. In the Costa de Lisboa, which includes surrounding leisure resorts such as Troia and Estoril, as well as Lisbon itself, foreign tourists account for 70 per cent of all overnights. Unlike the other leading tourism regions, no single nationality accounts for more than 11 per cent of all foreign overnights, reflecting Lisbon's business functions. In the 1990s the city experienced an increase in short-break leisure visits, related to its cultural attractions, as well as a strengthening of business and conference tourism.

The rest of Portugal has only a small-scale tourist industry. Domestic visitors outnumber foreign ones, average stays are short, and occupancy rates are extremely low, being around one-fifth of capacity. Within this group, the coastal distritos of central and northern Portugal, such as Aveiro, Coimbra, Leiria, Setúbal and Viana do Castelo, are popular summer resorts for the Portuguese, and this is reflected in their relatively large shares of camping places. Their resorts mainly serve their immediate hinterland; for example, three-quarters of the residents of the district of Oporto who took holidays away from home in 1994 did so in the surrounding region (Direcção Geral do Turismo 1995). Other important centres of tourism in the interior are spa towns such as Luso and Geres, which have faced a vicious downward spiral of lack of investment and falling demand in most of the post-1945 period.

6.4   Tourism and the national economy

It is notoriously difficult to estimate the importance of tourism in the national economy. However, Cunha's (1986) estimate that tourism accounted for some 5–7 per cent of GDP in the mid-1980s does not seem unreasonable, and is comparable to the Secretaria de Estado do Turismo's (1986) estimate of 5.9 per cent of GDP in 1982 and to da Silva's (1986) estimate of 7 per cent of value added. This approaches the share accounted for by agriculture. By 1993 the impact of tourism on GDP was estimated to be 4.8 per cent (OECD 1995), which is greater than in both Greece and Spain. The importance of tourism to the Portuguese economy is considered here in terms of its role in the balance of payments, investment and employment.

6.4.1   The balance of payments

Receipts from international tourism have grown steadily (in terms of current prices) throughout the 1970s and 1980s (except for 1975–1976), and Portugal has higher earnings per tourist than most other Southern European destination countries (Williams 1993). International tourist expenditures (by the Portuguese) have grown more slowly, being depressed by the weakness of the escudo and the recurrent economic crises of the 1970s and early 1980s; consequently, the gap between receipts and expenditure has widened (Table 6.5). Between 1980 and 1985 the net balance, expressed as a proportion of receipts, increased from 75 to 79 per cent. Subsequently, improved standards of living and reductions in unemployment have led to a sevenfold increase in Portuguese foreign expenditures between 1985 and 1994, a period in which receipts increased some three-and-a-half-fold. Consequently, the net balance, although increasing in absolute terms, has been reduced to 54 per cent of receipts. There are also a number of 'leakage' effects which reduce the net economic contribution of tourism, such as expenditure on imported consumer and capital goods, profit remittances from foreign-owned hotels and other tourist businesses, payments to foreign tour companies and promotion costs. According to da Silva's (1986) estimates,

Table 6.5 International receipts and expenditure (billions of escudos): Portugal, 1980, 1985 and 1994

	Receipts	Expenditure	Balance	Balance as percentage of receipts
1980	57.5	14.6	42.9	74.6
1985	191.8	40.1	151.7	79.1
1994	634.4	290.1	344.3	54.3

Source: Direcção Geral do Turismo (1996).

imports accounted for approximately a quarter of all expenditure by national and foreign tourists—a not inconsiderable leakage. If the same proportion holds true for the mid-1990s, then the net balance may actually be only 29 per cent. To some extent earnings from international tourism are constrained by the mass nature of the industry; for example, there is a 168 per cent difference in receipts per tourist bednight between the high point in February and the low point in August, when mass tourism is assumed to be relatively most important (da Costa 1996, p. 25).

The positive balance on international tourism has helps to cover at least a part of Portugal's enormous visible trade gap. This coverage has varied over time but has generally increased since 1975, being 21 per cent in 1983 and 51 per cent in 1987. The rate of coverage of the trade gap had fallen to 41 per cent by 1993 (OECD 1995), reflecting more widespread economic growth and recovery in this period. Different segments of the international market make varying contributions to the foreign exchange balance. Detailed expenditure data for particular market segments are no longer available. However, data for 1984 show that while UK visitors accounted for 35 per cent of bednights in that year, their spending power was relatively low and they contributed only 20 per cent of receipts. In contrast, French and West German visitors have relatively high per-capita spending, while the Spanish contributed only 3 per cent of receipts; this may be a considerable underestimate because of unregistered currency exchanges. The largest contributors, however, were US visitors, who provided a staggering 33 per cent of receipts, although only accounting for 6 per cent of bednights (Instituto Nacional de Estatística 1985a). Exchange rate movement and shifts within particular national market segments make it difficult to project these ratios to the mid-1990s with any confidence. However, they underline the importance of distinguishing changes in market volumes from expenditure volumes.

6.4.2 Investment

While the Portuguese tourist industry is firmly based on foreign markets, direct foreign investment has played a relatively minor role in developing tourist facilities. Over time this role has diminished and there was a particularly sharp reduction in foreign investment in 1975, following the 1974 coup (Table 6.6). Indeed, pre-coup levels of foreign investment were only surpassed in current price terms as late as 1984. This pattern changed in the mid-1980s with foreign investment being attracted into new forms of facilities, especially in the Algarve. A number of examples

Table 6.6 Sources of investment (millions of escudos) in tourism in Portugal, 1973–1986

	1973	1977	1981	1986
1. National capital	2,440	844	4,910	23,553
(a) Personal	1,357	358	2,077	13,330
(b) Credit	1,061	474	2,631	10,205
(i) Fundo do Turismo	158	26	260	756
(ii) Caixa N. Crédito	70	12	1	–
(iii) Caixa G. Depositos	183	168	747	3,021
(iv) Banks	459	189	1,355	4,534
(v) Particular sources	192	79	269	1,894
(c) General state budget	23	12	202	18
2. Foreign capital	507	152	244	3,392
(a) Personal	112	152	244	3,076
(b) Credit	395	–	–	316
Total	2,947	997	5,154	26,945

Source: Direcção Geral do Turismo (1986, 1988).

illustrate the size and nature of some of these recent investments. For example, Shell Oil invested $26.6 million in a 700-bed holiday village extension to the Vilar do Golf complex at Quinta do Lago; whilst Elliot Property and Leisure Group (UK) opened a new water park at Porches. The Algarve accounted for more than half of all foreign investment in the hotels sector in Portugal in the period 1986–1992 (Duarte 1996). However, hotels (and similar accommodation) generally have not been particularly attractive to foreign investors; foreign investment peaked at about one-sixth of the total in 1973, fell sharply after 1974 and, although it recovered somewhat in the 1980s, only accounted for between 3 and 13 per cent a year in this sector during the decade (Duarte 1996). Even in the 1990s, hotels and restaurants accounted for less than 4 per cent of all authorised foreign direct investment in any one year. Consequently, the vast majority of hotels are in Portuguese ownership and these subcontract to international tour companies. The economic weaknesses associated with the resultant system of oligopsonistic relationships between foreign tour companies and relatively weak and fragmented endogenous capital are discussed elsewhere (Williams 1995).

While foreign investment was static in the late 1970s, domestic investment recovered rapidly from a low point in 1977, increasing by some 300 per cent per annum. This involved both personal capital and credit from the banks or other financial institutions. In some cases the investors have been industrial companies seeking to diversify their activities—such as the investment by the Petrogal oil group in the Meriden Hotel in Lisbon. Given the small scale of most tourism businesses, they offer considerable opportunities for small business formation relying on personal or family savings. This may include emigrant remittances, as Mendonsa (1983a,b) shows in Nazaré (in central Portugal). Almost one-quarter of returned migrants had invested in commercial establishments related to tourism, thereby widening the range of 'coping strategies' traditionally adopted in this small fishing town, and contributing to the general trend towards increasing economic and social polarisation in the community.

6.4.3   Employment

Perhaps the greatest contribution of tourism to the Portuguese economy is in terms of employment. According to the Plano Nacional de Turismo 1986–1989 there were some 145,000 jobs in tourism in 1985. Of these, 26 per cent were in hotels, *pensões* and camping sites, 70 per cent were in restaurants, 3 per cent were in travel agencies and 1 per cent were in public sector administration. These data are not entirely reliable for they underestimate employment in car-hire firms, sporting and other tourist attractions, while the figure for restaurants is, at best, a crude approximation. Only the data for accommodation can be considered with any confidence. These show that in 1984, 67 per cent of accommodation-related jobs were in hotels, 19 per cent in *pensões*, and 8 per cent in hotel apartments. Clearly, hotels are the most important source of jobs in this subsector of the tourist industry. By 1994 tourism was estimated to account for 300,000 jobs, equivalent to about 6 per cent of the total labour force (Instituto Nacional de Estatística 1994).

With the expansion of the industry, employment numbers in the accommodation sector increased by almost one half in the period 1969–1986. There was also a small shift from male to female employment, which were almost in balance by 1984. At the same time—and a clear indicator of the changing structure of the industry—the proportion of non-paid labour diminished from 13 per cent to only 5 per cent by 1984. However, formalisation did not necessarily mean increased professionalisation. While no accurate data are available on this, Cavaco's (1981) study of the hotels in the Costa do Estoril showed that only 16.5 per cent of male and 8.2 per cent of female employees had more than a basic primary school education. Only the larger hotels recruit from the hotel schools.

While employment has increased over time, it has fallen relative to the number of guests. For example, in the 1970s employment per bed in higher-quality hotels fell by some 20 per cent (Cavaco 1981); and the overall number of jobs per bed-space also fell from 0.28 in 1984 to 0.19 in 1994 (Table 6.7). This reflects two processes: a shift to self-catering holidays, and increased self-provisioning in hotels, together with a general substitution of capital for labour in such diverse activities as catering and cleaning. These changes are influenced by the demand for more flexible holidays and the pressure to reduce costs. To some extent, the up-market shift in accommodation has ameliorated the negative employment implications, for employment 'densities' (that is, relative to the number of beds) vary by subsector (Table 6.7). The employment ratio for hotels is almost double that for *pensões* with, not surprisingly, the largely self-serviced motels and hotel-apartments and tourist apartments providing fewest jobs. However, there are also considerable variations within each of these types, especially in that 5-star hotels provide two-and-a-half times as many jobs as 1-star hotels and twice as many as 3-star hotels. Portugal's strategy of favouring up-market tourism may, therefore, have beneficial employment effects, although an alternative strategy of mass tourism may have produced a larger global employment figure—at least in the short term. Over time, employment densities have declined in all forms of accommodation but especially in the more up-market hotels.

Employment in tourism represents different degrees of formalisation, ranging from full-time work for professionally trained personnel to the family who combine running a small guesthouse with other activities. Such pluriactivity is relatively widespread in Portugal (see Lewis and Williams 1986b, for the example of industrial employees). Savings are transferred from waged employment in tourism into other activities, as

Table 6.7   Employment ratios and tourism as a secondary economic activity by accommodation type in Portugal, 1984–1994

| | Number of jobs per bed | | Percentage of those employed in tourism for whom this is a secondary economic activity (1984) |
	1984	1994	
Hotels	0.38	0.26	0.30
5-star	0.64	0.41	–
4-star	0.39	0.27	–
3-star	0.30	0.20	–
2-star	0.21	0.15	–
1-star	0.15	0.16	–
Hotel apartments	0.23	0.13	0.24
Tourist apartments	N/A	0.09	3.88
Motels	0.23	0.19	5.96
Holiday villages	N/A	N/A	0.88
Pousadas	0.76	0.58	2.96
Inns	0.35	0.31	–
Pensões	0.15	0.14	17.77
4-star	0.20	0.20	–
3-star	0.14	0.13	–
2-star	0.14	0.14	–
1-star	0.13	0.13	–
Total	0.28	0.19	3.80

Sources: Direcção do Turismo (1996); Instituto Nacional de Estatísticas (1985a).

Bennett (1986) shows in the case of land and agriculture in the Algarve, and vice versa. Furthermore, Lewis and Williams (1986a) have shown that returned migrants in central Portugal favour investments in cafes, bars and *pensões* as one productive use of their savings. Tourism-related work therefore needs to be seen as one element of wider household strategies.

6.5   Tourism and regional development

Portugal has long had a highly polarised regional economic structure (Lewis and Williams 1981). The two main nodes of industrial development are the Lisbon and Oporto metropolitan regions, although there is also a substantial spread of small and medium-sized firms throughout the coastal region, between Braga and Setúbal. Agriculture is poorly developed, especially in the interior, and the introduction of more intensified and commercialised farming geared to exports has been limited and relatively late. Tertiary activities are probably the most polarised economic sector, and both private and public services are highly centralised in Lisbon and, to a lesser extent, Oporto. Tourism development partly reinforces this broad pattern of uneven regional development, in that it is heavily concentrated in the littoral region, and the Costa do Estoril is effectively part of the larger Lisbon metropolitan region.

However, tourism also serves to modify the general regional pattern, especially in the case of Madeira and the Algarve which have not been prominent centres of industrial production. These two districts have obtained, relative to their economic weight, a relatively large share of tourism investment (Sirgado 1990), as well as for more than 60 per cent of all foreign investment in the hotel sector, 1986–1992 (Duarte 1996). While precise data are not available on the contribution of tourism to these regional economies, there is fragmented information on the regional features of the industry.

6.5.1 Tourism and regional income

Estimates of the income generated by tourism are not available at *distrito* level. However, the regional government in semi-autonomous Madeira does provide historical estimates of the receipts earned by tourism from both national and foreign visitors (Madeira 1982). These show that receipts increased from 288 million escudos in 1967 to 898 million in 1974 and 4,140 million in 1982 (de Freitas 1984). In the 1970s and 1980s tourism earnings almost equalled Madeira's visible trade gap and exceeded emigrant remittances. Tourism is of exceptional importance to the Madeiran economy, but is also highly significant in some parts of mainland Portugal. The distribution of visitors (especially of foreigners) and of higher-quality tourist facilities clearly suggest that tourism is of greatest absolute economic importance in Lisbon and Faro *distritos*. While the relative importance of tourism in Lisbon *distrito* is likely to be limited, it is of considerable importance in the Costa do Estoril sub-region. However, it is undoubtedly of enormous relative importance in the Algarve, where manufacturing industry is little developed (Sirgado 1990). Tourism can also be of considerable importance in particular communities. For example, in Nazaré in the early 1980s, other than formal tourist businesses, about one-half of all households had rooms to let. These provided, on average, an extra $500 in income at a time when mean annual household income was only $3,160 (Mendonsa 1983b, p. 228). In this instance, the ownership of housing is crucial in the ability to benefit from tourism, and serves to exclude many lower income households.

The importance of ownership is further underlined in Cavaco's (1996) study of the development of Quarteira (Algarve). In the early twentieth century the Quinta de Quarteira estate belonged to the Santos Lima family, who sold it in 1929—before the tourism destiny of the Algarve could be foreseen—to the Casa Júdice Fialho, a newly rich bourgeoisie family who derived their wealth from fish processing and trading. In turn, the latter sold on the estate to the Lusotur tourism development company in 1965; this was financed by American capital and the Banco Português do Atlântico. Each of these sales represented a transfer of wealth and of wealth-generating opportunities to different social strata. This example is not untypical of tourism development in the Algarve in the twentieth century, and illustrates how land ownership and property rights have been one of the keys to understanding the distribution of tourism-related income.

6.5.2 Regional employment in tourism

The employment data for hotels and similar accommodation confirm that the economic benefits of tourism are highly concentrated. While national employment in the sector was only 37,700 in 1994, there were only four *distritos* with more than 2,000

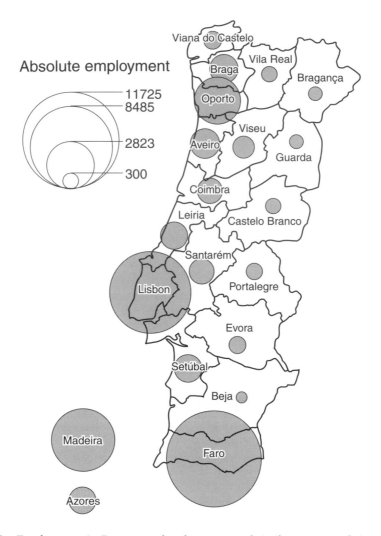

Fig. 6.3   Employment in Portuguese hotels, *pensões* and similar accommodation, July 1994

Source: Instituto Nacional de Estatísticas (1995)

jobs and together these account for 74 per cent of the total: the Algarve has 31 per cent, Lisbon has 23 per cent and Madeira has 13 per cent. In contrast, most interior *distritos* have less than 400 persons employed in this sector, with Beja having the exceptionally small number of only 162 (Figure 6.3).

This broad pattern of regional employment can be further disaggregated, although only at the level of the tourism regions (Instituto Nacional de Estatísticas 1995), to take into account employment in higher-quality accommodation establishments (defined as 3-star or above) and seasonality (Figure 6.4). The highest proportions of employment in higher-quality establishments are in Madeira and the Costa de Lisboa, reflecting both the size of the units in these regions, and their respectively up-market leisure and

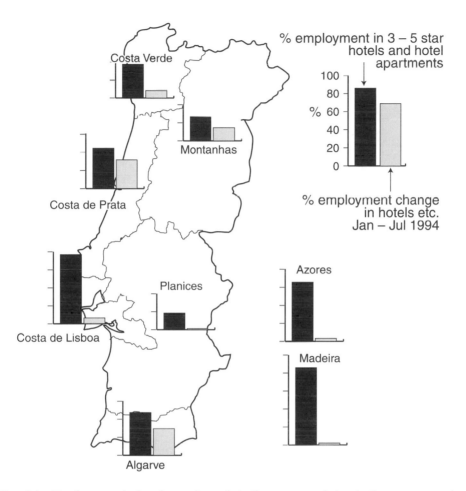

Fig. 6.4 Employment in hotels, *pensões* and similar accommodation in Portuguese tourism regions, 1994

Source: Instituto Nacional de Estatísticas (1995)

business tourism market segments. In contrast, the Algarve has a lower proportion of employment in such establishments because of the existence of a large stock of tourist apartments, holiday villages and *pensões*, which reflects its increasingly diverse holiday markets. The lowest proportions of jobs in high quality establishments are in the Mountains and Plains regions; here the limited economic role of tourism is further reinforced by the preponderance of lower quality provision, with lower employee/ bed-space ratios. The data on seasonality have a very complex pattern. Madeira and the Azores have a notable lack of seasonality, with only a 2.2 per cent difference in employment levels between January and July in the former, reflecting their year-round tourism markets. Lisbon (Costa de Lisboa) also has a year-round tourist industry and has a seasonal employment shift of only 6.4 per cent, which is to be expected given its business and cultural tourism markets. In contrast, Faro has more peaked seasonality and has an employment gain of 29.6 per cent in the summer. This is exceeded only by the Costa de Prata (central coastal Portugal), where the climate makes for an even more sharply seasonal peaking of demand. Other aspects of the regional distribution of employment are discussed in Lewis and Williams (1988).

The available statistical data only allow for limited analysis of the regional economic effects of tourism in Portugal. Sirgado (1990, p. 236) provides a fuller analysis of the key issues, and concludes that tourism:

- Leads to unbalanced age structures in tourism locales.
- Accelerates the concentration of population in the littoral regions (especially in the Algarve).
- Intensifies patterns of commuting.
- Changes the capacity for traditional forms of social regulation.
- Changes local economic structures.
- Increases employment, although a part of this is part-time and/or seasonal.
- Increases the feminisation of the labour force.
- Increases income levels.

While agreeing with the broad thrust of these conclusions, the previous discussion indicates that the economic effects are highly contingent, depending on the particular structures of the regional economies and their tourism industries.

6.6   Tourism and governance in Portugal

There have been sharp shifts over time in the governance framework for tourism development in Portugal. These reflect both the working out of internal political changes, with the rise and fall of Western Europe's longest twentieth century dictatorship (1926–1974), and external pressures related to globalisation of trade and tourism markets, EU membership and, most recently, the tide of neo-liberal economic policies. This section examines the evolution of policies and planning for tourism during the course of the twentieth century.

The organisational starting point for the management of tourism development in Portugal was probably the establishment of the Sociedade de Propaganda in 1906 (Pina 1988). This state-supported body was responsible for overseas promotion and for bringing about improvements in the basic tourism infrastructure, especially in the quality of hotels. This was followed by the creation of the first official state agency for tourism, the Repartição de Turismo in 1911, which assumed the responsibilities of the Sociedade de Propaganda. This formal institutionalisation of tourism management within the state did not herald a significant state commitment to the sector; rather, tourism remained a bridesmaid of economic policy for the first half of the twentieth century. This was particularly so after the installation of the military dictatorship in 1926, for the resultant Salazarist regime was more interested in controlling population movements (including tourism) as part of its inward-looking strategy of autarky, than in developing the potential of tourism (Pina 1988). Similarly, the creation of the Comissões de Iniciativa in 1921, to establish local governance agents for tourism, was stillborn because after 1926 the centralising Salazarist regime was preoccupied with limiting the competencies and financial autonomy of the municipalities.

Against this background of conscious neglect, the policy framework for tourism remained weak and fragmented. Not surprisingly, in 1952, one traveller commented that:

> The Portuguese government has little time to spare for encouraging tourists. I say this because their official Tourist Office, under the control of the Secretary of Information, is a distinct contrast with the offices of most other Western European countries. Outside of Lisbon, in fact, with the exception of Tomar and Estoril, the visitor would, I suggest, do better to seek independently for advice rather than at the local information office (Cooper 1952, pp. 193–4).

Within a decade this had changed markedly, as was evident in the emphasis given to tourism development in the Intermediate Development Plan and the Fourth Development Plan in the late 1960s and early 1970s. The leading priorities were to attract foreign tourists and to develop higher-quality tourism. These plans were largely indicative but there were some changes in policies. From the 1960s the National Institute of Tourism Training and the first hotel training schools, and the first Regional Tourist Boards, were established, while new regulations were introduced for private sector operations in sectors such as hotels and car rentals. Perhaps of greater importance was the creation of the Tourism Fund, which channelled credit to the tourism sector, and this was to be particularly influential in the development of the Algarve. However, the most important change in governance was the relaxation of government controls over the sector, allowing private capital to take the lead in development. da Costa (1996, p. 209) writes that '. . . the expansion of tourism in Portugal was based on action implemented by private sector organisations, to which some scattered government strategies were added'. If the state had any priority in this period, then it was to avoid conflict with the private sector.

After the restoration of democracy, 1974–1976, there was a further shift in governance. A succession of governments recognised the economic importance of the sector and—except for a few years—tourism was represented by its own ministry at the centre of national government. This culminated in 1995 in the creation of a new super-ministry, the Ministry for Industry, Trade and Tourism, which served to enhance the overall priority given to the sector. In line with the commitment in the new constitution to regionalisation of administration and planning, the Regional Tourist Boards were reorganised and were given, for the first time, a significant measure of administrative and economic autonomy. Local authorities—acting individually, or through the Comissões Municipais de Turismo—also assumed stronger roles in the development of tourism in this period (see Syrett 1997 for a general review of local governance and partnerships in Portugal). At the same time, however, the Cavaco e Silva governments of the late 1980s and early 1990s wholeheartedly embraced neo-liberalism, and private capital retained a dominant role in tourism development.

Over time, a comprehensive organisation has been created within the Secretaria de Estado do Turismo (now located within the super-Ministry) to develop Portugal's tourist industry. In the mid-1990s this had six divisions:

- The Direcção Geral do Turismo, responsible for international relations, for tourist information and with administering (licensing, etc.) the supply side of the industry.

- The Empresa Nacional de Turismo, responsible, amongst other things, for managing the state-owned hotels and restaurants, the *pousadas*.
- The Fundo do Turismo, responsible for financial assistance.
- The Instituto Nacional de Formação Profissional, responsible for professional training, including the tourism schools.
- The Instituto de Promoção Turistica, responsible for promotion abroad.
- The Gaming Inspectorate, responsible for licensing and regulation.

In addition, the Secretaria is advised by the Conselho Nacional de Turismo, which is constituted of representatives of most of the public and private sector agents with an interest in the management of the tourism sector. In practice, however, the powers of the Secretaria tend to be limited to co-ordination, promotion, training and intelligence gathering. Other than this, its most important role is the provision of financial assistance. The Fundo do Turismo has both financial and fiscal measures at its disposal. There are four main financial aids: direct loans at low rates of interest (these favour less-developed areas such as the Douro Valley); subsidised bank loans for development projects; outright grants (not used in practice); and, since 1987, acting as a channel for European Regional Development Fund (ERDF) grants. The main fiscal measures are designed to provide tax relief on investment. When first introduced in 1957, the relief could extend over 25 years, but since 1983 it has been limited to total tax exemption for 7 years, followed by 50 per cent exemption over a further 7 years. This fiscal instrument was particularly important in the development of new hotels during the 1960s boom. Together, these measures constitute a considerable level of financial aid. In contrast, government investment in essential infrastructure—such as water, waste treatment and roads—has tended to lag behind demand, especially in the Algarve. This has been ameliorated recently, especially with the availability of European Investment Bank and ERDF assistance to build new roads, extend airports and provide improved water treatment plants in Madeira and the Algarve.

In recent years there has been a reassessment of policy and the overwhelming emphasis on increased volumes of foreign tourists has been qualified in the light of growing concerns about sustainability, despoliation of much of the landscape of the Algarve, and increased emphasis on diversification. The Plano Nacional de Turismo, 1986–1989 (Secretaria de Estado do Turísmo, 1986), set out four major objectives for the industry:

1. To increase tourism so as to contribute to the balance of payments by:
   (a)   Increasing external receipts
   (b)   Increasing earnings
   (c)   Increasing foreign investment.
2. To contribute to regional development by:
   (a)   Creating priority zones for tourist development
   (b)   Developing spa towns
   (c)   Implementing measures that favour regional development.
3. To contribute to the quality of life in Portugal by:
   (a)   Increasing domestic tourism
   (b)   Increasing agritourism
   (c)   Increasing *turismo de habitação*
   (d)   Supporting social tourism.

4.   To contribute to conservation of the national and cultural heritage by:
     (a)   Organising a more balanced use of space between tourism and other needs
     (b)   Protecting the natural environment, especially flora, in the littoral
     (c)   Defining the optimum numbers of tourists in particular areas
     (d)   Protecting regional and urban traditional architecture
     (e)   Preserving monuments
     (f)   Developing artisanal crafts and supporting folklore.

This is a wide-ranging set of objectives but the failure of the plan to prioritise them, and indeed the failure to update the plan, have created conditions for potential conflicts. It is difficult not to believe that the greatest weight will tend to be given to the first objective—if only because of national economic necessity. However, other developments can also be expected, especially in terms of tourism in rural areas. The *turismo de habitação* programme (involving rural houses of great character) already had 1,500 bed-spaces available in the mid-1990s, while there are also specific projects to develop rural tourism, as in the north-east Algarve, a zone of sustained population losses. Rural tourism is being promoted in this isolated area as a means to encourage artisanal crafts, and upgrade social and physical infra-structure, as much for the benefit of the local inhabitants as for the potential tourists.

6.7   Conclusions

The rapid development of Portuguese tourism in the 1960s and early 1970s also saw a transformation in the nature of the industry. Domestic tourism and spa tourism gave way to foreign tourism and beach tourism, which, moreover, attracted a higher-income market segment than did the neighbouring Costa del Sol. While there were reforms in the governance of tourism in this period, the leading role in development was taken by individual, mostly endogenous, private capitals. Demand slumped badly in the mid-1970s following political instability, and thereafter recovery was hampered by recessionary economic conditions in major markets such as the UK. Nevertheless, by the mid-1980s Portugal was experiencing rapid tourism expansion, outstripping most other countries in Western Europe (Williams 1997). Tourism currently accounts for about 5 per cent of GDP, employs over 300,000 and is a vital element in international trade.

Tourism development has been regionally uneven and the leading regions have very different structures and markets. In terms of numbers of foreign overnights, the first place has passed from Lisbon to the Algarve. While the key role of Lisbon serves to reinforce existing structures of regional inequality in Portugal, the considerable absolute and relative importance of tourism in Madeira and the Algarve partly ameliorates the low level of overall development in these regions. However, even in these cases, the tourist industry adds on new layers of inter-regional (that is, most of the interior is still excluded) and intraregional (development is highly concentrated in coastal areas) polarisation, rather than contributing to a generally more spatially equitable distribution of growth.

Not surprisingly, the current major policy concerns are to secure a more even 'spread' of the industry, in terms of market segmentation, as well as temporally and territorially. The high degree of dependency on the UK market, especially in the case of the Algarve, is a concern because of its volatility, relatively low propensity to spend, and the ability of highly organised tour companies to minimise the prices paid to local subcontractors (Edwards 1993). This is recognised in the Plano Nacional de Turismo, which seeks to maximise tourists' expenditures through policies of product and market diversification. The temporal spreading of demand is also a priority, especially for the Algarve, particularly in the 'shoulder' months. In this respect, UK visitors—with a distinct preference for winter holidays—make a welcome contribution to a more even distribution of visitors between seasons. Seasonality is far less of a problem in Madeira and Lisbon. Finally, an attempt is being made to attract foreign visitors to lesser-known regions, such as the Costa Verde of the North, the mountains of the northern interior and the plains of the Alentejo. Rural tourism, *turismo de habitação* and agritourism are also being promoted, including high-spending hunting tourism, so as to encourage the spread of tourism to the interior (Cavaco 1995).

Each of the regions has different resources as well as different challenges to face in future. Madeira currently faces the greatest problems. Climatic and topographical conditions make it difficult to expand the tourist industry either in situ or intra-regionally, without destroying those precious environmental qualities that constitute its prime tourist attraction. In contrast, the challenge for the Algarve is how to alleviate the many traffic and environmental problems which have resulted from its exceptionally rapid development in recent years. New regional plans for tourism and the environment have been approved, but the real challenge is their effective implementation. If successful, they will effectively contain tourism development within the existing tourism zones, and protect the still relatively unspoilt interior and far west from tourism pressures. Lisbon offers opportunities for further development of cultural and urban tourism. There is scope for expansion of business and conference tourism, and the acute lack of specialised conference facilities has partly been remedied by the construction of new conference centres in the city and at Estoril. Expo 1998 will further boost tourism in Lisbon, and the challenge is to secure long-term benefits from this macro-event. Finally, there is a flowering of local and regional tourism initiatives in much of the interior of Portugal, and these are also benefiting from the modernisation of the country's transport infrastructure. These are likely to become even more important in future as changes in the agricultural sector reinforce the need for rural economic diversification.

Finally, while this chapter has focused mainly on international tourism, some of the more significant future changes are likely to concern the domestic market. Despite a decade of sustained economic growth, Portugal still has one of the lowest holiday participation rates in Europe. In part, this reflects the highly polarised distribution of income, but there are probably also cultural reasons for this. Domestic demand is likely to rise as standards of living continue to converge—albeit slowly—towards Western European levels. This may provide the basis for product innovation and for further development of cultural and nature tourism in many parts of the interior, but it may equally well presage an increase in the net outflow of tourists as the Portuguese tourist gaze changes to incorporate more 'exotic' foreign destinations.

7 Switzerland: structural change within stability

Andrew Gilg

7.1 An environmentally based and long-established tourism product

The tourism product in Switzerland is fundamentally founded in its landscape and either its passive enjoyment in the form of 'lakes and mountains' tourism or its active enjoyment in the form of 'winter sports' tourism. Both these types of tourism were pioneered in Switzerland. Because the Swiss tourism product was developed at such an early date, and has been in a period of mature stability since the 1970s, it is essential to review its history as a forerunner to understanding its current nature.

7.1.1 The developmental phase: brief history of tourism before the 1970s

Even though Hannibal dented the myth of the Alps as an inhospitable barrier full of trolls and fearsome weather, it was not until the days of the 'Grand Tour' that Switzerland began to be seen as a desirable place to visit in its own right. Even then the Alps were but a scenic backdrop on the journey between the great cities of Europe. Gradually, however, more and more travellers and—more importantly—writers, poets and artists began to appreciate the scenic beauty of the Alps and the pre-Alpine lakes. Visits specifically to Switzerland began to be popular from around 1850 onwards, with Thomas Cook leading the first package tour in 1863 (Gilg 1983). At the same time, climbers began to extol the Victorian virtues of climbing the hitherto unscaleable peaks of the Alps. At the end of the nineteenth century, another dimension to Swiss tourism was added with the growth of specific resorts devoted to health cures, notably tuberculosis. By the early twentieth century, therefore, the Swiss tourist industry had been created, based on three types of tourism: first, genteel tourism in the grand hotels to be found along the shores of lakes like Geneva and Thun, as for example in the resorts of Montreux and Interlaken; second, mountaineering centred in Alpine valley resorts like Grindelwald and Zermatt at the foot of the picturesque peaks of the Eiger and Matterhorn, respectively; and third, health-based tourism in resorts like Leysin and Davos, which were normally placed on sunny Alpine terraces above the foggy lowlands.

Until this time tourism, apart from mountaineering, had been a mainly passive activity, but gradually the delights of winter sports became apparent, often to the

Tourism and Economic Development: European Experiences, 3rd Edition. Edited by A.M. Williams and G. Shaw.
© 1998 John Wiley & Sons Ltd.

younger, healthier members of family parties taking health cures. To fill the empty hours, they invented competitive skiing and ice-skating as new types of recreation. However, in spite of the development of new ways of scaling the mountains in the inter-war years, for example *telepheriques* (ski-lifts), winter sports remained the preserve of the wealthy. In the post-war years, however, increasing affluence and mobility allowed millions rather than thousands of people to participate in winter sports, and this development, above all, was to change the nature of Swiss tourism (Schilling *et al.* 1974).

Between 1955 and 1975 the overall number of hotel beds doubled (Office Fédéral de la Statistique Suisse, 1986a and 1997) but the real expansion came with the creation of large self-catering apartment blocks, often with 30–40 apartments per block. The number of beds in such developments grew by more than tenfold in this period of massive expansion, notably in existing resorts like Crans-Montana or in new resorts like Anzere, where self-catering came to dominate tourism provision. However, demand in this period grew by only about 50 per cent, creating a structural problem of over-capacity.

7.1.2   *Stabilisation of tourist numbers accompanied by structural change: trends from the 1970s to 1990s*

Swiss tourism has thus had a long and successful history, based on its natural environment but also within a framework which values a 'genteel and civilised' consumption of its product. At first this was a passive experience and 'lakes and mountains' holidays are still a significant if declining sector, albeit a lucrative one, mainly based on older people with high disposable incomes, who can afford levels of service reminiscent of the early twentieth century. In the 1950s, 1960s and 1970s the explosive growth in winter sports more than compensated for a relative decline in the traditional product area. However, from the 1970s onwards, Swiss winter sports began to be perceived as expensive, with rather outdated equipment, non-purpose built resorts and low altitude compared to France. In the 1990s, new destinations, either low-cost as in Bulgaria or offering high quality skiing, e.g. the USA, also provided competition. Nonetheless, Switzerland retains the lead in resorts that offer the type of facilities demanded by the 'jet set', like Gstaad and St Moritz, although it has ceded first place in terms of size of skiing terrain and facilities to resorts such as Val d'Isere.

In summary, the 25 post-war years of massive expansion set the scene for modern Swiss tourism, for since 1970 the overall number of nights spent in Switzerland has remained static. However, within the overall pattern of static demand, two main changes have occurred: first, a trend towards self-catering; and second, a reduction in seasonality.

7.2   The changing structure of the tourism industry since the 1970s

7.2.1   *A trend towards self-provisioning*

The gradually changing nature of Swiss tourism is shown in Figure 7.1a, which demonstrates a slow but steady rise in the supply of beds from 1976 to 1986 but a

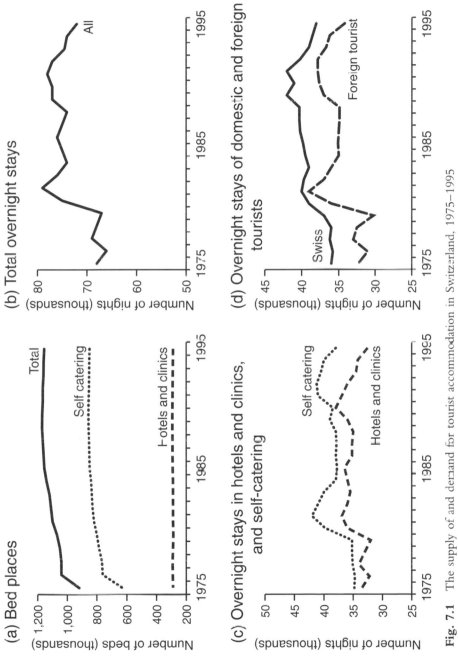

Fig. 7.1 The supply of and demand for tourist accommodation in Switzerland, 1975–1995

Source: Swiss Tourism Federation (1996)

Table 7.1 Capacity and demand in Swiss tourism, 1985–1995

Type of accommodation	Total capacity (thousands of beds)			Swiss demand (thousands of nights)			Foreign demand (thousands of nights)		
	1985	1995	(%)	1985	1995	(%)	1985	1995	(%)
Hotels	275.3	265.1	−4	14.0	12.8	−9	20.3	18.7	−8
Clinics	6.7	6.1	−9	1.3	1.2[1]	−8	0.3	0.3[1]	0
Apartments	375.0	360.0	−4	13.9	12.9	−7	10.0	10.3	+3
Camping/caravanning	270.0	237.6	−12	4.9	5.6	+14	2.0	2.2	+10
Group lodgings	214.1	226.3	+5	5.0	4.9	−2	1.9	2.3	+21
Youth hostels	7.9	7.3	−8	0.3	0.3	0	0.4	0.4	0
Total	1,149	1,102	−5	39.4	37.6	−5	35.1	34.0	−3

Sources: Schweizerischer Fremdenverkehrsverband (1986); Swiss Tourism Federation (1996) and Office Fédéral de la Statistique Suisse (1994, 1996a).

[1] 1993 data.

gradual decline to 1993. The increase was accounted for by a growth in the self-catering sector, mainly due to a rise in bed spaces in chalets and apartments constructed as second homes with letting potential, rather than purpose-built self-catering units as in France. The demand for all beds (Figure 7.1b) has fluctuated, with a rapid increase in the early 1980s being followed by a fall to a plateau in the mid-1980s, before a brief recovery in the early 1990s was followed by a steep decline in the mid-1990s as Switzerland experienced an economic crisis. The overall result was long-term stability around 75 million bednights. Much of the change in the 1980s can be accounted for by rises and falls in the number of foreigners (Figure 7.1d) but in the 1990s the numbers of both Swiss and foreign tourists have risen and fallen roughly in tandem. In terms of overnight stays (Figure 7.1c) self-catering and hotels were broadly in tandem in the 1980s, but in the 1990s the number of hotel bednights has fallen sharply as the Swiss franc rose making Swiss hotels less competitive.

In general, the major problem of the last three decades has been that expansion of supply in the first part of this period has left a structural surplus in excess of demand. For example, there is a restaurant for every 260 Swiss, and half of the resident population could sit down for a meal at the same time (Swiss Tourism Federation, 1996). In the period 1985–1995 (Table 7.1) there has been some readjustment. For example, the total number of beds fell by 4 per cent in both the main sectors of hotels and apartments, and only group lodgings increased in capacity. It is important to remember that these figures refer to total capacity and not the actual beds available, which are usually considerably fewer as operators do not offer all their beds all the time. Domestic demand fell in every sector except camping/caravanning as foreign destinations were made more attractive by the strong Swiss franc. Meanwhile foreign demand fell less but, crucially for the economy, it shifted from the lucrative hotel trade to the much lower income-generating sectors of self-catering, camping/caravanning and group lodgings.

In more detail (Table 7.2), hotel demand fell from 34 to 31 million nights, but self-catering demand grew from 40 to nearly 41 million nights between 1985 and the mid-1990s. Foreigners remain the mainstay of the Swiss hotel industry accounting for nearly 60 per cent of customers. Visitors from countries who prefer hotels have either

Table 7.2 Changing pattern of demand for hotel and self-catering accommodation usage in Switzerland in the 1980s and 1990s

Overnight stays (millions)	Hotels		Self-catering		Hotel/self-catering ratio
	1985	1995	1982–1983	1992–1993	
Total	34.3	31.2	40.1	40.8	46/54
Swiss	14.0	12.8	24.4	24.2	38/62
Foreign	20.3	18.4	15.7	16.6	55/45
Germany	6.0	6.6	9.0	9.3	44/56
USA	3.3	1.7	0.2	0.3	88/12
UK	1.9	1.3	0.8	0.7	70/30
France	1.6	1.2	0.9	0.9	61/39
Italy	0.9	0.8	0.3	0.6	65/35
The Netherlands	0.8	0.8	2.4	2.5	27/73
Belgium	0.8	0.9	1.1	1.1	47/53

Sources: Swiss Tourism Federation (1996) and Office Fédéral de la Statistique Suisse (1994).

Note: Only those countries which accounted for more than 1 million visitors in either category are shown.

declined or remained static or, where growth has been recorded, as for example from Japan, the numbers are not as yet sufficiently economically important. Unfortunately, the only main growth of foreign visitors in recent years has come from Germans, who prefer self-catering.

7.2.2 Changes to seasonal patterns

Seasonally, summer is still the peak season, with July and August accounting for nearly 21 million of the 75 million annual bednights, while the two peak winter-sports months—February and March—only account for 15 million nights (Office Fédéral de la Statistique Siusse 1996a). Within the accommodation sectors, hotels have a fairly even seasonal rhythm, with 10 of the 12 months being near to the monthly average of 3 million bednights. In contrast, self-catering shows much greater swings around the mean of 3.3 million bednights, with peaks of 6.6 million and 4.8 million in August and February, yet with two months—November and December—only just registering over 1 million nights.

Both sectors have seen a move away from the bimodal peaks of the past, with falls in both peak seasons, but rises in the early summer and early winter seasons. This is welcome news for tourism, an industry often plagued by seasonality. Unfortunately, most of the growth in the extended seasons has come from self-catering, notably in the early summer and in December, and its economic impact may not be sufficient to offset the decline in hotel tourism in all but 3 months of the year.

Vacation apartments account for 54 per cent of all overnight stays in self-catering accommodation (Swiss Tourism Federation 1996). However, this pattern varies markedly between summer and winter, with camping more than accounting for the higher summer usage, further weakening the economic impact of this sector. In more detail, vacation apartments account for 14 million nights in the winter, but only

11 million in the summer, while camping and caravanning account for only 1 million nights in the winter, but over 7 million in the summer.

7.3   The contribution of tourism to Swiss economic development

7.3.1   *Overall economic impact*

Tourism is very important to the Swiss economy. In 1995 it contributed 5.6 per cent to Swiss GNP, albeit down from 6.6 per cent in 1984 (Swiss Tourism Federation 1996). Total revenue, however, was up from 14.0 billion Swiss francs in 1984 to 20.3 billion in 1995, of which foreign tourists accounted for 11.2 billion. Tourism is Switzerland's third most important export, accounting for 9 per cent of all export revenues. However, the revenue of 11.2 billion Swiss francs is well behind the 40.8 billion accounted for by the metal and machine industry, and the 24.0 billion accounted for the by the chemical industry. Furthermore, the net revenues from tourism fell to only 2.1 billion in 1995 from 2.8 billion in 1985, when the expenditure of Swiss tourists abroad is taken into account. Nonetheless, this still represents a surplus of around 350 Swiss francs for each Swiss national, albeit less than the 435 francs recorded in 1984 (Office Fédéral de la Statistique Suisse 1986b). The balance of trade has largely fallen because expenditure by the Swiss abroad has trebled while expenditure by visitors to Switzerland has only doubled, largely because of the high value of the franc.

Internationally, Switzerland accounts for 3 per cent of world tourism revenue. Within Europe it ranks tenth in terms of arrivals but seventh in terms of revenue, reflecting its high-value 'lakes and mountains' and winter sports holiday products. It ranks eighth country in the world in terms of its share of GDP dependent on international tourism, at 2.6 per cent, compared to its neighbour Austria, which is the most dependent at 6.6 per cent (Swiss Tourism Federation 1996).

The Federal Statistical Office of Switzerland, with the OECD, has played a role in developing a model for the macro-economic analysis of tourism within a General System of National Accounts (SNA). Table 7.3 shows how the model has been used to compare Switzerland and Austria. In particular, it shows the advantage employed by Austria as a lower-cost, lower-income country in attracting foreign visitors, although over-dependent on Germany, a country with which it has close cultural links and, of course, a common language.

7.3.2   *Employment impact and international labour migration*

It has been estimated, from a variety of data sources, that one in eleven of the Swiss population works in tourism (Swiss Tourism Federation 1996) with 208,000 being employed directly and 92,000 indirectly. However, other estimates based on narrower employment data reveal that accommodation and restaurants alone employed 220,000 people in 1995, but that only 112,000 of these were Swiss nationals (Office Fédéral de la Statistique Suisse 1996a).

In 1995 the restaurant and hotel sector registered the largest fall of any Swiss employment sector, with 5,500 jobs lost (*Le Matin*, 21.2.96), but overall the number of jobs had grown from 175,000 in 1984 to 220,000 in 1995, even though virtually all

Table 7.3   Economic impact of tourism: a model for analysis

1990	Switzerland	Austria
Population (thousands)	6,673.9	7,660.3
GDP per capita (EC PPS)	24,308.0	18,615.0
Nights spent in all accommodation establishments	77,026,685	123,629,478
Domestic tourists	40,137,929	28,841,188
Foreign tourists	36,888,756	94,788,290
Germany	14,728,798	56,819,027
The Netherlands	3,343,389	9,112,348
UK	2,802,762	4,931,102
Tourism share of GDP (%)	7.7%	9.2%
Restaurants	40%	40%
Transportation	40%	35%
Air traffic	11%	3.6%
Share of foreign tourists of total private consumption (%)	7	12
Share of tourism of total employment (%)	10.6	11.1

Source: Swiss Tourism Federation (1996).

Note: EC PPS = value expressed in constant purchasing power based on the ECU in 1975 and annually updated in line with the average EC price indices for GDP.

this growth had come from foreign workers. Foreign workers now account for nearly one worker in two in the hotel and restaurant sectors. This is largely because few Swiss want to work in jobs which are seen as poorly paid and offering poor career opportunities, and because Switzerland until recently had a very low unemployment rate, until this rose to around 6 per cent in the mid-1990s. Foreigners are a major component of Swiss society, with 19 per cent of the population of just over 7 million being non-Swiss, up from 14 per cent in 1979 (*Le Matin*, 10.2.96), and to some extent these workers could be seen as semi-permanent residents.

7.3.3   Income generating capacity of different forms of tourism

Receipts from tourism vary dramatically by the type of tourism (Office Fédéral de la Statistique Suisse 1996b). In 1995 foreign tourists spent 8,048 million Swiss francs, of which 5,485 were spent in hotels. This can be disaggregated into: 2,836 on rooms; 1,214 on meals; and 1,434 on other hotel services. Self-catering only accounted for 1,234 million francs. The remainder was accounted for by students (528 million) and hospital stays (799 million).

The economic impact of different types of tourism has also been changing. Not only do hotel-based tourists spend four times more than those in vacation apartments and nearly six times more than campers and caravanners, but their expenditure has also risen fastest. Since expenditure by foreign hotel-based tourists is so important financially, the eight per cent decline shown in Table 7.1 represents a real blow to the Swiss tourism industry as a major foreign exchange earner for the Swiss economy (Office Fédéral de la Statistique Suisse 1986a, 1996a). The disregard now shown to the self-catering sector is demonstrated by the decision in the 1990s to reclassify self-catering accommodation as 'supplementary accommodation'.

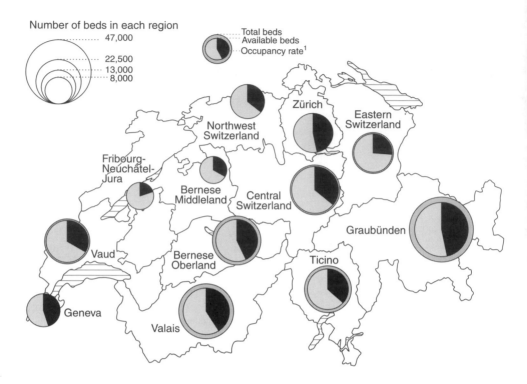

Fig. 7.2   The potential and actual supply of tourist beds and the rate of occupation by cantons or groups of cantons in Switzerland, 1995

[1] *Note*: actual occupancy indicated by dark portions of circles

Source: Office Fédéral de la Statistique Suisse (1996a)

7.4   Tourism's contribution to regional economic development

7.4.1   *Regional variations in supply and demand*

There are significant regional variations in the supply of all hotel beds for tourism (Figure 7.2), which account for nearly 70 per cent of expenditure. First, the most important areas are the two winter sports cantons of Valais and Graubünden, closely followed by the lakeside/mountain regions of the Bernese Oberland and central Switzerland, and then by the lakeside cantons of Vaud and Ticino. Second, occupancy rates are highest in the main city areas and in a few mountain areas, notably Graubünden, but occupancy rates are generally low (around 40 per cent) in the main mountainous areas, and very low elsewhere, with rates of between 19 and 33 per cent (Swiss Tourism Federation 1996).

Another important feature is that many beds are not actually available. In 1995, of the 264,000 beds that existed, only 222,000 were available all the time, or 84 per cent of the total (Swiss Tourism Federation 1996) The regional distribution of available beds is difficult to estimate, since the number in apartments and other forms of self-catering tend to be available only on an adventitious basis, since most of these double-up as second homes or putative retirement homes. For example, two surveys of tourist accommodation in Switzerland in 1978–1979 and 1986 (Office Fédéral de la Statistique Suisse 1986a) showed two major concentrations of apartments in Graubünden and Valais. In Valais, out of the 178,000 second homes surveyed, only 87,000 were available to be let. This represents a major under-use of fixed capital and a positive misuse of the resources of land and public services in these areas.

In terms of demand, four features stand out (Swiss Tourism Federation 1996). First, the pattern of demand is dominated by the winter sports canton of Graubünden, with Valais some way behind. The other major areas of demand centre on a combination of winter sports and 'lakes and mountains' tourism. Second, the percentage of Swiss amongst the tourists varies widely but without any simple pattern: they dominate in the less spectacular but pleasant landscapes of the Jura and north-east Switzerland, but account for a tiny share in Zurich and Geneva. Third, winter sports areas have increased their share of both supply and demand, mainly at the expense of the cities. Fourth, foreign tourists are the majority of visitors in all types of area, but only just so in the mountains.

In the mid-1990s occupancy rates varied from 45 per cent in the large cities, to 42 per cent in mountain resorts, to 38 per cent in the lakeside zones, and down to 29 per cent in the other areas, with a national mean of 38 per cent (Swiss Tourism Federation 1996). In more detail, Zurich and Geneva led the way in tandem with Graubünden. Elsewhere, the north-western cantons fared very badly. In terms of hotel beds, Grubünden and Valais—the two high alpine cantons—dominate, followed by the lower alpine areas of Central Switzerland and the Bernese Oberland. In terms of bednights, Graubünden and the Bernese Oberland have more than their pro rata share of bednights to hotel beds, while Valais and Central Switzerland have less than their pro rata share. Foreigners are attracted to the higher and lower Alps and to the large cities, notably Geneva. The Swiss, however, are more attracted in terms of relative numbers to the Ticino, although numerically the high Alps remains popular. The Alps also experience much longer stays (Figure 7.3).

Hannss and Schröder (1985) have visibly demonstrated a regional shift to the south-east and south-west by mapping out the capacity of ski-lifts in each resort. On their map, Crans-Montana, Verbier and Zermatt in the south-west stand out as larger resorts than the traditional Oberland resorts, as do Laax, Lenzerheide, Davos and St Moritz in the south-east. Of these large resorts, Crans-Montana, Verbier, Laax and Lenzerheide are relatively new resorts, reflecting the regional shift of winter tourism away from the Oberland. In terms of major regions, Graubünden leads with 29.6 per cent of capacity. Valais follows close behind with 28.7 per cent and the Oberland is next with only 14.7 per cent.

7.4.2 Regional studies of the impact of tourism

Regional studies have tended to concentrate on those areas where tourism has expanded to the extent that there have been growing doubts about its overbearing importance and the dangers of a monostructural economy (Boesch 1983), notably in cantons like Graubünden, where some commentators consider it has reached saturation point (Frosch 1992). For example, Elsasser and Leibundgut (1982) have identified 10 regions centred on Crans-Montana, Zermatt, Saas Fee and Grindelwald that are 'dangerously'

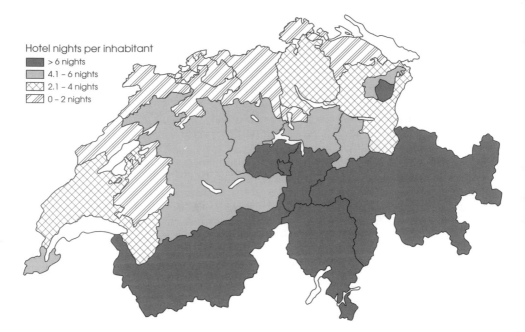

Hotel nights per inhabitant
■ > 6 nights
▨ 4.1 – 6 nights
▧ 2.1 – 4 nights
▨ 0 – 2 nights

Fig. 7.3 The average number of nights spent by tourists in different regions of Switzerland, 1994

Source: Conseil Fédéral Suisse (1996)

dependent on tourism. One measure they use to identify over-dependence is the ratio of annual tourist nights to local people, as shown below:

Tourist Cantons		*Tourist resorts (type of tourism)*		
Switzerland	12:1	Ascona	157:1	(lakeside resort)
Ticino	28:1	St Moritz	210:1	(winter sports)
Valais	58:1	Grindelwald	267:1	(all-year round)
Graubünden	85:1	Arosa	347:1	(winter sports)
		Saas Fee	800:1	(winter sports)

Canton Valais and Grindelwald in canton Berne provide specific examples. In canton Valais, Bertrisey (1981) found that industry employed 15,096 people, while tourism employed 9,976 directly, 15,738 indirectly, and 6,053 partially. This gave a figure of 31 per cent of the working population of Valais being totally dependent on tourism, even when the 6,053 who are partially dependent on tourism were excluded.

In Grindelwald it has been calculated that the resort as a whole is 57 per cent totally dependent on tourism, 35 per cent indirectly dependent, and only 8 per cent independent of tourism (Krippendorf 1987b). Services provided the largest source of income for the resort, at just over 55 million francs, and about 40 per cent of this came directly from tourism. Hotels provided over 50 million francs in income, with nearly 100 per cent being derived from tourism. The next largest earner was construction, with nearly 30 million francs, of which 20 million francs was indirectly dependent on tourism. Transport, self-catering, and administration each brought in between 11 million and 18 million francs, most of which was directly or indirectly dependent on tourism. Agriculture brought in less than 5 million francs, but this was mostly independent of tourism.

A study of Crans-Montana, a major resort in canton Valais (Darbellay 1979), has shown that it grew rapidly via the medium of self-catering apartments, with a twelvefold increase in self-catering beds between 1950 and 1974, compared to a mere doubling of hotel beds. Crans-Montana thus became totally dependent on tourism for probably three-quarters of its income, when direct and indirect effects are taken into account. Darbellay also found major age differences amongst employment sectors. Young people have been the main employment beneficiaries of the tourist boom, although he notes that many farmers have cashed in by selling land at very high prices (for example, at 400 francs/m^2 in the resort centre, compared to 3.5 francs/m^2 for good meadowland).

The experience of the high Alpine regions contrasts starkly with the experience of one of Switzerland's neglected tourist areas, the Jura, which has suffered recently from poor snow seasons. In this region, Rumley (1983) has found very low winter occupancy rates of between 8.9 and 28.4 per cent, a low length of stay (between 2.4 and 3.5 days), and a high percentage of Swiss tourists (between 63.2 and 86.4 per cent). The summer figures are only marginally and not consistently better, with occupation rates ranging from 12.5 to 40.3 per cent, and a lower length of stay (from 1.8 to 2.7 days), reflecting the transit nature of tourism in the area.

A recent study in the Bernese Jura (Muller *et al.* 1996) found that tourists spending the day in the area accounted for 79 per cent of visits, but only 69 per cent of expenditure, with the bulk of their spending being made in restaurants. In contrast, overnight visitors who accounted for 21 per cent of expenditure spent only 37 per cent of their money in restaurants. Overall, restaurant spending was 62 per cent of the total, followed by shopping (11 per cent), accommodation (9 per cent) and ski-lifts (9 per cent). Even in such an area, however, tourism accommodation was the most important value added sector (13 per cent) of the regional economy, while also contributing 9.7 per cent of employment, 8.3 per cent of cantonal GDP and having a multiplier of 1.89.

7.5 The political economy of Swiss tourism: limited responses to a growing sense of crisis

7.5.1 The reluctant growth of state aid for tourism until 1979

Switzerland has always been a country reluctant to adopt state, especially central government, measures, to guide let alone direct its economy. Such measures are anathema to the Swiss view of federalism, local political power and free enterprise. The development of measures to shape the pattern of Swiss tourism has therefore been slow (Commission Consultative Fédérale pour le Tourisme (CCFT) 1979).

The first measures, in 1915, were attempts to protect hotels from the effects of World War I. These led quickly to a vote to allow the Confédération to use state finances to publicise Swiss tourism, and the Swiss National Tourist Office was set up for this purpose in 1917. In 1922 the Confédération voted to help pay for the repair of hotels, and in 1933 it took over the collection of tourism statistics from the private sector. Faced with a dramatic drop in visitor numbers during World War II, the Confédération gave itself powers to assist sectors of the economy, including tourism, mainly through loans. These economic aids were increased in the 1970s. This principle is central to the first of the modern measures for aiding tourism, the introduction in 1974 of LIM regional aid (the Loi Fédérale sur L'Aide en Matiere d'Investissements dans les Regions de Montagne). Under this measure, regions throughout the Alps and the Jura (Gilg 1985; Grafton 1984) can qualify for a regional development investment loan to develop their infrastructure. Such a loan can cover a new road to a ski resort, or a new ski-lift, and thus can benefit tourism indirectly. By the end of 1985, 52 regional development programmes had been approved, and within this framework 2,209 individual community projects had been financed with funds totalling 612 million francs (OECD 1987). The 80.6 million francs spent in 1985 were allocated as follows: tourist transport 20.6 million; sports facilities 42.4 million; swimming pools 9.2 million; museums 7.5 million; and conference centres 0.9 million. Tourism was clearly the main beneficiary of the aid.

The LIM measure was the first official response to a growing crisis in Swiss tourism in the mid-1970s, as the number of bednights became static as a result of the oil crisis, competition from Mediterranean tourism, modern and often cheaper ski resorts in France and Italy, and the strength of the Swiss franc. In response to this crisis, the Confédération set up a Federal Consultative Commission on Tourism in 1973 (CCFT 1979), doubled Federal funds for aiding tourism between 1969 and 1977, and admitted that the encouragement of tourism was a Federal task which served the interests of the whole country and not just the tourist regions; this was an essential move in a country where intercantonal jealousies can wreck attempts to introduce new national policies.

7.5.2   The 1979 'Concepts' report

One of the main tasks of the Commission was to produce a report for the Confédération on the role of tourism and to propose policy measures, the so-called 'Concepts' report (CCFT 1979). The report began by setting out the reasons for the growth in tourism, which included increased income, more cars, more urbanisation (and thus a need to escape stress) and a growing passion for skiing. However, in the early to mid-1970s the first falls in demand were noted, especially in the number of foreigners. The Commission attributed Switzerland's success up to the mid-1970s crisis to five factors: (a) the slogan of the Swiss Tourist Office, 'Switzerland works'; (b) a safe, liberal and stable country; (c) Switzerland's position at the crossroads of Europe; (d) tradition; and (e) Switzerland's beauty. The Commission also noted some adverse factors, notably the decreasing amount of land remaining for development, the strong franc, a moderate climate, and a reluctance amongst Swiss people to work in tourism.

In spite of these adverse factors, the Commission found that most experts still forecast a doubling of tourism between 1975 and 2000, with self-catering leading the way. However, the growing pressure of such rapid development on the environment was also recognised, and it was forecast that some resorts would have to stop expanding by 1990, while new areas would have to be developed. Another problem was said to be the declining attraction of older resorts in terms of their facilities.

Concerning the other current problems, the Commission pointed to the issues of seasonality, the high rate of spare capacity, the role of foreign workers, and structural problems within the industry. For example, they pointed out that hotel employment had fluctuated between 71,000 and 45,000 in 1977, and that out of the 90,000 foreign workers in the country in 1977, no less than 41,000 were employed in tourism. In terms of capacity use, the report noted that while industry was running at 80 per cent, hotels only used 40 per cent, and telepheriques a miserable 23 per cent. The report highlighted the poor social image of tourist work for the Swiss, and also that skiing was degrading some mountain pastures, while there were many conflicts between agriculture and tourism. Finally, the report noted the large number of small hotels (80 per cent had fewer than 50 beds) and, conversely, a geographical over-concentration in a few large resorts (60 per cent of hotel nights were in the 20 largest resorts).

On the basis of these introductory findings, the report offered guiding principles and objectives. The overriding principle was that tourism is an attribute of a healthy and sane society. Within this overall principle, the importance of tourism was justified under the headings of overall, social, economic and environmental factors:

Overall	(a)	Without relaxation and tourism a healthy society cannot exist.
Social	(a)	Recreation makes the daily round more productive.
	(b)	Tourism integrates society and nations.
	(c)	Tourism improves quality of life in the tourist area.
Economic	(a)	Tourism provides an economic motive to preserve the countryside.
	(b)	Tourism is an integral part of the Swiss economy.
	(c)	Tourism is important to the balance of payments.
	(d)	Tourism has 170,000 direct employees (5.6 per cent of work force), 240,000 indirect employees, and when combined this makes 15 per cent of the work force.
	(e)	Tourism is the only alternative to agriculture in the mountains.
Environment	(a)	Tourism depends on a good environment.
	(b)	Tourism depends on beauty and spiritual value of monuments.
	(c)	So tourism must in the end respect the environment.

(Commission Consultative Fédérale pour le Tourisme 1979)

Three linked objectives were then broken down into 29 intermediate and partial objectives, some of which are shown in Table 7.4, and into 40 possible detailed strategies and 114 recommendations for the future of Swiss tourism.

Finally, the report outlined the existing powers of the Confédération and the measures already in force. Although there is no specific legal basis for tourism aid or development in Switzerland, tourism can be encouraged by the Confédération under Article 31 of the Constitution, which allows encouragement of certain economic activities and the assistance of areas whose economy is threatened. Using this Article, the Confédération spent 59 million francs on tourism development in 1977: the most important expenditures were on repayable grants to develop tourist facilities (19.6 million francs) and publicity in Switzerland and abroad (17 million francs). In addition to direct economic aid, the Confédération also promoted tourism through a range of social, economic and environmental measures (Table 7.5), which are seen as overlapping and complementary. Indeed, the Confédération tends to see its role as coordinating the policies of the cantons and the communes, and the policies of individual ministries. This is important for certain parts of the tourism industry, where responsibility lies with several sub-departments in various ministries.

Table 7.4   Objectives for Swiss tourism

Global objective
   To guarantee optimal satisfaction of the needs of tourists and individuals from all walks of life in effectively grouped facilities and keeping the environment healthy

Partial objectives
   Social: Create the best possible social conditions for both tourists and locals
   Economic: Encourage a tourist industry that is both competetive and efficient
   Environmental: To ensure the relaxing quality of both natural and man-made countryside

Intermediate and partial objectives
   Social: 10 more objectives, e.g. more participation from all walks of life; create better conditions for people to take holidays
   Economic: 11 more objectives, e.g. optimise the structure and operation of the industry; improve the quality of tourist transport
   Environmental: 8 more objectives, e.g. develop facilities in harmony with the environment; observe ecological constraints

---

Source: Commission Consultative Fédérale pour le Tourisme (1979).

Table 7.5   Summary of the overlapping measures taken by the Swiss Confédération with regard to tourism

---

Social
   Infrastructure, e.g. aid for rail, post, roads and other infrastructure
   International, e.g. relaxation of boundary formalities
   Promoting the image of Switzerland

Direct
   Publicity
   Advice, finance and approval of regional development programmes
   Aid for regional infrastructure for tourism (LIM)
   Renovation, construction and aid for the purchase of hotels and village facilities
   Collection of tourism statistics
   Encouragement of tourism planning and research
   Concessions for foreigners to buy land

Environmental
   Encouraging good land use planning
   Protecting the environment

Economic
   Labour market, e.g. maintaining supply of seasonal workers; encouraging the retraining of workers; encouraging professional associations
   Encourage regional economy
   Campaigns
   Limitation of excessive growth

Source: Commission Consultative Fédérale pour le Tourisme (1979).

The result of the Commission's report was a list of 30 measures, of which three were urgent, two were supplementary measures in the field of planning, and the remaining 25 were measures for the medium term.

7.5.2 *Events in the 1980s following the 1979 'Concepts' report*

In 1981 the Confédération asked government departments and ministries to take due account of the recommendations when dealing with tourism (OECD 1982) and in June 1981 they invited the cantons to cooperate in a similar fashion, especially in the preparation of their detailed plans, the *Plans Directeurs* or Cantonal Land Use Plans (Gilg 1985).

Elsewhere, as part of long-term research on Swiss tourism, a survey of over 10,000 tourists in 1982–1983 discovered considerable loyalty to Switzerland amongst tourists, with 60 per cent of those surveyed being on at least their fourth visit. Many visitors cited the consistently high quality:price ratio as the main appeal of Switzerland (OECD 1984). Furthermore, in 1984 the development fund for mountain infra-structure was increased to 300 million Swiss francs, after 73.4 million francs had been spent specifically on tourism projects between 1975 and 1984 (OECD 1985).

The main change in 1984, however, was the relocation of the Tourism Service into the Federal Economic Department, so that measures directly linked with tourism could be concentrated in the single office of the Federal Office of Industry, Arts and Crafts and Labour within that Department (OECD 1985). The new organisation was given the following responsibilities:

1. To formulate tourism policy for the Confédération.
2. To promote tourism via the Swiss National Tourist Office.
3. To supervise and fund hotel loans via the Societe Suisse de Credit Hotelier (SSCH, Swiss Hotel Credit Society).
4. To give financial aid to tourism projects.
5. To contribute to tourism planning.
6. To fund vocational training.
7. To act on the tourism labour market.
8. To service the CCFT (the authors of the 'Concepts' report) and the 100-strong parliamentary group on tourism in administrative matters.

Finally, with regard to measure No. 7 of the 1979 'Concepts' report, the Con-fédération voted to increase the annual funding of the Swiss National Tourist Office from 21 million to 27 million francs between 1988 and 1990, and to 31 million francs for the years 1991 and 1992 (Conseil Fédéral Suisse 1986). This recognised the need to expand the work of the office in four key areas: (a) researching potential supply; (b) attracting foreigners to Switzerland; (c) publicising Switzerland; and (d) coordinating the supply of tourist facilities. Swiss tourism was also promoted to the tune of some 200 million Swiss francs in 1985 by the cantons, communes and businesses, and by a further 60 million by local tourist offices. Combined with the 10 million francs spent on promotion by the Swiss National Tourist Office, this brought total spending on tourism promotion in Switzerland to 270 million francs against receipts of 16,500 million francs (Conseil Fédéral Suisse 1986).

Another organisation, the SSCH, makes loans for modernising hotels and resorts, constructing new hotels and purchasing hotels; 16.5 million francs were loaned for these purposes in 1985 (OECD 1986). The SSCH also guarantees loans for these purposes, amounting to another 16.3 million francs in 1985; in turn, 75 per cent of this amount was guaranteed by the Confédération.

Swiss tourism is promoted by a variety of organisations and, in addition to those already mentioned, the tourism section in the Office Fédéral de la Statistique publishes monthly, seasonal, annual and occasional reports on all aspects of tourism, often in detail and sometimes down to the commune level. Swiss tourism is thus well-served by accurate, up-to-date and highly disaggregated tourism data (Office Fédéral de la Statistique Suisse 1997). Other important sources of information are the Swiss Travel Service, the Swiss Federation of Tourism, the Institute of Tourism and Travel in the University at St Gallen, and the Institute for Tourism and Leisure at the University of Berne.

7.5.4   *The Krippendorf report*

The Krippendorf report (Krippendorf, 1987b) is a summary of a series of research projects conducted on behalf of the Man and Biosphere programme of UNESCO and is based on the Pays d'Enhaut, Aletsch, Grindelwald and Davos. It identified seven possible benefits of tourism:

1.   Tourism can stop the exodus of people from the mountains.
2.   Tourism can create employment, which in 1985 was estimated at 350,000 jobs.
3.   Tourism can create revenue.
4.   Tourism can finance infrastructure through a positive chain reaction.
5.   Tourism can improve an area's facilities.
6.   Tourism can help to support agriculture and the management of the countryside.
7.   Tourism maintains the character and customs of mountain areas and people.

These possible benefits are countered by seven possible dangers of tourism:

1.   Tourism can lead to a fragile mono-structural economy.
2.   Tourism can develop in an uncoordinated way, can undermine the real economy, may only use 20 per cent of its capacity, and is a poor economic use of land compared to industry.
3.   Tourism can take over valuable cultivable land. The growth in self-catering is problematic, since a hotel bed requires five times less land and is used three times as often as an apartment bed.
4.   Tourism can spoil the countryside—for example, ski pistes reduce forage yields by 4–18 per cent, floral diversity by 15–18 per cent—and can lead to avalanches.
5.   Tourism can lead to over-dependence on foreign investment, with decisions being taken abroad. This is anathema to the Swiss with their fierce local pride in their commune.
6.   Tourism can undermine the authenticity of local culture, and replaces it with 'commercial folklore'. There is also a growing problem of alcoholism among young people, with nothing to do between seasons in tourist resorts.

7. Tourism can generate social tensions and accentuate disparities of wealth, both locally and regionally.

The report then tried to produce a balance sheet of the benefits and the dangers. It emphasised that it is not a case of all or nothing. Instead, the choice is one of adjusting the costs and benefits to produce a balanced tourism, and to stop growth at the point at which tourism yields diminishing returns. In a devolved political economy it is, of course, difficult for small communal councils to prevent the goose from laying one too many golden eggs, but Krippendorf noted that there were signs that local populations were beginning to think in terms of a self-sustaining rather than continuously developing tourism.

Krippendorf then addressed the future pattern of tourism and, following one of the themes of the 1979 'Concepts' report, advocated that tourism be based on the growth of quality rather than quantity. In this scenario tourism is increased by: extending the season; offering new types of tourist experiences; limiting tourist traffic, notably low-spending day-trippers; aiding local suppliers of self-catering apartments and hotel rooms; stressing the quality of life in the resort; introducing new services for conferences; offering training schemes for tourists in rural skills and crafts; widening employment opportunities through the use of electronics, and by combining jobs between sectors; and finally by aiding agriculture.

7.5.5 The 1996 Federal Council Report on the political economy of Swiss tourism

In 1996 the Swiss Federal Council produced a report (Conseil Fédéral 1996) which described the increasingly difficult problems faced by the Swiss tourist industry arising from the strong Swiss franc, and strong social and environmental regulations imposed in the 1980s. They concluded that a new political economy, including an action plan, was needed to redynamise the industry which had failed either to grow quantitatively or to provide the extra quality of provision which had been seen as the solution in the 1980s by the Krippendorf report.

The report began by reviewing the 1981 conception of Swiss tourism adopted by the Federal Council following the 1979 Concepts report. 1981 was a record year for Swiss tourism but since then, as the report notes, tourism has stagnated in the 1980s and declined in the 1990s, leading to the question of whether Swiss tourism had become uncompetitive, since the index of competitiveness had declined from 0.95 in 1981 to 0.06 in 1993, according to an econometric study cited by the report. Concern in the 1980s was expressed by a number of Federal Councillors and organisations and by a report by the Federal Office for Industry (Office Fédéral de l'Industrie, des Arts et Metiers et du Travail 1990) on 'Future Perspectives for Swiss Tourism'.

The 1996 report responded to these concerns by listing the advantages of tourism. First, tourism contributes to the quality of life by providing facilities and infrastructure that would not otherwise exist, and these benefits outweigh the environmental damage. Second, tourism is the fourth most important sector in the Swiss economy in terms of value added, creating 26,000 million francs. Using other indices, tourism also comes out strongly, being the second biggest employer (with 300,000 or 9 per cent employed directly or indirectly), the third most important earner of foreign exchange, and contributing 8 per cent to GDP. Third, tourism is the principle component of economic and social life in the mountainous areas, where it accounts for at least half of

GDP, and is the only realistic economic option for these areas. Fourth, tourism makes Swiss people more aware of their cultural identity and has made them more sensitive to the need to protect their environment in response to visitor demands for a high quality environment.

The report then examines the growth of international tourism. In the 1950s Switzerland had few competitors in a small global market of 25 million tourists. By 1995, however, the market had grown to 567 million tourists, and Switzerland was faced with competition from a multitude of world-wide destinations. In addition, Swiss industry has remained small-scale and locally-run, compared to the economies of scale enjoyed by global companies which have invested in large tourism complexes around the world, linked by major transportation and booking systems. Prices are also high in Switzerland, due to the strong Swiss franc, high hotel wages (30 per cent higher than in France) and high land prices, and this was exacerbated in the early 1990s by the imposition of VAT. This is important, since the millions of new tourists are more price-conscious than their predecessors, and less likely to be loyal to traditional destinations like Switzerland which are not perceived to offer modern or cheap facilities. Even visitors from traditional origins, like the UK and USA, have been affected by the high prices of Switzerland, with visits falling by 15 and 12 per cent, respectively, after a 10 per cent rise in the Swiss franc between 1972 and 1993.

The report then turns to structural problems. These include a lack of professionally trained Swiss managers, an over-dependence on foreign labour for manual work, an infrastructure in need of modernisation, a lack of innovation, a poor image of tourism as an employer and industry by Swiss people, and a lack of cooperation between all the organisations involved in tourism. In addition, the Swiss environment has come to be very protected compared to elsewhere. For example, the power of the Confédération to control all new ski-lifts since the introduction of an Ordinance in 1978 has cut construction to one-third of the former rate (Krebs 1995), and the need for environmental impact assessments, although well-accepted, has prevented economically desirable tourism developments, according to a study by Messerli cited by the report. However, agriculture is rapidly becoming greener and more environmentally friendly and sustainable (Curry and Stucki 1996) and, combined with the high quality of developments that are allowed, this means that the Swiss environment can compare favourably with other less well-planned environments.

In spite of these areas of concern, the report notes that Switzerland was the eleventh most important tourist country in terms of receipts in 1995, and in 1991 produced the highest value added per person involved at 92,000 Swiss francs compared with its rival, seventh-placed Austria, at 67,000 francs. Forecasting that tourism will grow to become the principal world industry in the next century, the report argues that Switzerland has an opportunity to take advantage of this trend and grow too alongside a forecast doubling of tourist numbers from 457 million in 1990 to 937 million in 2010, at an annual rate of 3.7 per cent.

Without appropriate action, however, the report forecast that the outlook for Swiss tourism was not good, referring to a study by the Research Institute of Basle, which forecast that the value added by tourism would decline by 1.2 per cent a year, against a general rise of 1.6 per cent in the overall Swiss economy between 1995 and 2000. However, Switzerland does offer a unique tourist destination and the report argues that a new political economy for tourism could improve the future. For example, the development of new products, activities and concepts, like snow boards, snow-boarding and 'le wellness'. In addition, 75 per cent of visitors come from Germany and there is thus great potential to attract customers from other countries, by stressing the advantages of having the highest density of tourist establishments in the world linked by an attractive public transport system. They can also be attracted by a high-quality rural environment and by a quality assurance based on the fact that Swiss customers are amongst the most critical and discerning in the world.

Turning to what can be done, the report begins by stressing that only the private sector can revive tourism in Switzerland, but also that those countries where the state has played an active role in the tourist industry have produced the best results. In this respect Switzerland has suffered from the lack of promotion by its government and is ranked only twenty-second in terms of expenditure on tourism promotion, with such spending accounting for only 0.1 per cent of federal, cantonal or communal expenditure. Even the very tourist-dependent canton of Graubünden, where more than 50 per cent of GDP derives from tourism only spends 0.5 per cent of its budget on tourism.

Switzerland does though have an organisational structure for dealing with tourism, as shown in Figure 7.4. In addition, Switzerland was the first country to set up a professorial Chair of Tourism in 1981 and there are now three research institutions at the University of Berne, St Gall and Lausanne. Turning to how this structure could be used to advantage, the report restresses the nature of the Swiss free market economy, which limits the role of the State to ameliorating general conditions and integrating activities. In particular, the predominance of small and medium-sized enterprises in Switzerland requires that the State plays a role that provides promotion and encourages innovation and integration, not only within tourism but also in other related sectors of the economy. The resultant strategies are shown in Table 7.6.

Turning to the future, the report sets out a new type of promotion strategy based on relaunching Swiss tourism. It likens Switzerland to a multinational company that needs to make the world aware of a new product, but one based on the high quality reputation of its previous products. The report believes that this will allow the Swiss to recapture lost market share by the twin strategy of a reinforced image of proven quality and international marketing. This is not the formula, for example, adopted by the watch industry, which responded to a severe decline in its fortunes by inventing the 'Swatch' image. Instead it is a formula designed to make Swiss tourism competitive again in its own market segment, based on high-quality service but offering value for money. In particular, the image should be based on: an idyllic countryside; an efficient infrastructure; a well-protected environment; and a well-trained workforce.

The report concludes with an action plan which requires neither new laws nor increased (albeit reorganised) expenditure. The action plan proposes action in five broad areas, and these are now considered in turn:

1. *Research and development* The plan proposes developing existing data collection and inaugurating new studies into Swiss tourism, with a particular emphasis on providing better information on the role of tourism in the economy and how small operators can benefit from research findings.
2. *International collaboration* There should be further liberalisation of border controls, in line with the EU Schengen agreement and recent GATT agreements on world trade. In addition, the Swiss will build on the 'Protocol on Alpine Tourism' which it has already signed.
3. *Promotion of demand* There is a need to build on changes to 'Swiss Tourism', formerly the 'Swiss National Tourist Office', which in 1992–1993 cut its fixed costs but doubled its marketing expenditure. The first main task of 'Swiss

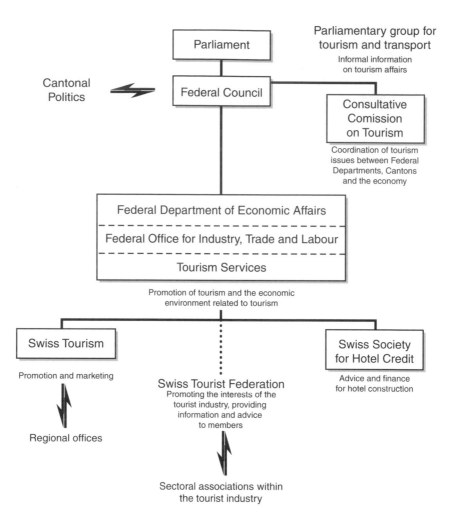

Fig. 7.4   National-level tourism institutions in Switzerland

Source: Conseil Fédéral Suisse (1996)

Tourism' has been to create an '*image de marque Suisse*' or '*un label Suisse*' and to market this world-wide. In addition, it is encouraging the development of an integrated information and booking service.

4. *Measures to renovate resorts and provide a better-trained workforce*   Here the plan proposes building on existing measures designed to help entrepreneurs through all the stages of renovation. In addition, aid to the regions via LIM is being revised to better target infrastructure developments based on tourism, a new series of measures to encourage structural changes in rural areas are available under the REGIO PLUS scheme, and the EU INTERREG programme can aid cross-border tourism developments. Finally, the plan proposes re-establishing well-known Swiss hotel schools in order to offer training which will make a career in tourism a more

Table 7.6   Strategies for creating favourable conditions for Swiss tourism

Improving the context in which Swiss tourism operates
   (a) By creating more favourable public attitudes to tourism both as an industry and as a career
   (b) By developing better research and development and better dissemination of the findings
   (c) By opening up Swiss tourism to global flows of capital, especially with regard to recent GATT liberalisation of trade

Reinforcing the market economy
   (a) By appealing to new clients in the world market by creating a long-term brand image which can sell a small country
   (b) Creating niche products and services unique to Switzerland or certain regions within Switzerland
   (c) Stressing that high prices in Switzerland are matched by excellent quality of provision
   (d) Using the Internet to link demand and supply better

Improving the attraction of places
   (a) By replacing the vertical integration of professional tourism organisations with an integrated horizontal system which is based on professionally-trained staff in all areas of the tourist industry
   (b) By making a career in tourism more attractive so that Swiss replace foreign workers and provide a more indigenous experience for tourists
   (c) By demonstrating to tourism enterprises how they can improve their services to meet the demands of the new global market
   (d) By improving infrastructure, notably in terms of sporting, cultural and congress facilities to meet the demands of the twenty-first century
   (e) The high quality of the environment must be maintained by keeping the consumption of land and energy to a minimum and by respecting the landscape

Source: Conseil Fédéral Suisse (1996).

attractive option for young Swiss nationals so that they can compete with foreign labour, particularly as these will have easier access as the European labour market opens up.

5. *Integration*   It is proposed to integrate a number of Swiss and international initiatives, such as a special rate of VAT for tourist accommodation. In addition, the plan proposes the better integration of land use and countryside plans across the country, so that tourism development does not spoil its environment and can actually benefit from the promotion of preserved or enhanced historic and ecological sites. In the longer term, the measures taken to reduce carbon dioxide emissions as a result of the UN Rio conference in 1992 should reduce the greenhouse effect and reverse the retreat of snowlines, which has been threatening the future of winter sports. Thus, finally, the plan reinforces the need to take a holistic view of the environment in all economic developments and that tourism policies must be related to policies for energy, transport and agriculture. In this regard the plan concludes by stressing the value of Switzerland's dense network of public transport which, under the label of the 'Swiss Travel System', offers tourists environmentally acceptable access; for example, the proposed extension of Eurostar and TGV services to all the main winter resorts by the turn of the century.

The report concludes that if the industry is to come out of crisis it must take new initiatives and reinforce existing strengths. The Confédération, the Cantons and the communes can help this process by providing a favourable political and legal climate, by financial aid, by helping to market the revised product globally, and by integrating the activities of other sectors with tourism.

Much of the doom and gloom of the report was, however, based on the Swiss franc remaining strong while uncertainties remained around EMU. However, in 1996–1997 the Swiss franc fell heavily, for example by 25 per cent against the UK pound, and though it remained overvalued one of the main causes of the crisis of the 1990s had been removed.

7.5.6   Comparisons of key points in the major reports on Swiss tourism

Table 7.7 outlines the key points in the three major points. The current problems were first perceived in the 1979 report, but initially it was not believed that these would curtail growth; indeed, the 1979 'Concepts' report forecast a doubling of tourism between 1975 and 2000. The Krippendorf Report (1987) and the Federal Council Report (1996) then largely endorsed the problems identified in 1979. However, both these reports reject tourism growth as either a likely or a desirable option and they both focus on improving the current industry. All three reports, however, claim that tourism is a net social, economic and environmental benefit to Switzerland and thus feel the need to propose solutions to the identified problems. Given the nature of Swiss political economy, however, the range of policy options is limited, since direct state interference and financial grants and subsidies are virtually ruled out. Thus, the 1979 report limits itself to repayable loans and to promotional budgets, Krippendorf advocates a host of measures mainly aimed at enhancing tourism in local environments, and the 1996 Report reiterates many of the proposals of the 1979 report. In conclusion, the Swiss State can help the tourist industry to help itself, but will not indulge in the sort of entrepreneurial activity used by other countries to boost their tourist industries.

7.6   Concluding remarks

In the 1990s the Swiss economy experienced a crisis and for the first time confidence in its economy has been weakened. The 1992 referendum decision, by a narrow majority, not to join the EEA, began a process which combined a fear of political isolation and economic uncompetitiveness related to tariff barriers and an overvalued Swiss franc, which created a sense of crisis among the Swiss. Even worse, the twin horrors of inflation and unemployment afflicted Switzerland for the first time in living memory, and although the inflation rate fell to 0.8 per cent in 1996 (*Le Matin*, 1.1.97), unemployment in Switzerland rose to over 5 per cent. At the same time, existing and future access became more problematic with green-inspired moves to restrict traffic access to the Alps and to encourage rail access only, notably in trans-Alpine routes, thus reducing the income created by traffic in transit.

For the first time the Swiss really had to sell their tourism product, not only because its own market share was falling but also because the Swiss economy needed its income more than ever. The temptation to relax controls and go for mass-market tourism was, however, rejected and instead the cautious response of both the Krippendorf and 1996 reports has been to repackage the existing product in a quest for quality.

Table 7.7   Comparison of key points in major reports on Swiss tourism

The 1979 'Concepts' Report	The 1987 Krippendorf Report	The 1996 Federal Council Report
Identification of problems		
First falls in demand noted, and problems of strong franc, seasonality, pressures on the environment and reluctance of Swiss to work in tourism	Tourism can lead to an unbalanced fragile economy overdependent on foreign investment, can spoil the environment and destroy local culture	Problems of first static and then falling demand, strong franc and environmental controls, and a poorly-structured tourism industry with too many small units and an overdependence on foreign labour
Conceptual vision		
Nonetheless, tourism forecast to double 1975–2000	Tourism growth should be based on quality not quantity	Need to redynamise tourism by an action plan
Benefits of tourism to build on		
Tourism provides social, economic and environmental benefits	Tourism provides work, income, better infrastructures and can support farming environmental management	Tourism improves the quality of life, is a key sector of the Swiss economy and is the key factor in sustaining mountain communities
Proposed solutions		
Limited solutions suggested mainly based on repayable grants/loans available to all sectors of the economy and to promotional budgets of Swiss Tourist Office	Solutions suggested included extending the season, limiting day visitors, increasing supply of local foods and services, and enhancing resort quality	Only the private sector can revive tourism, the State can support however by promoting the product, providing research and development, finance, training and organisation

In light of tough internal and external competition, guests are now being sought after and pampered and regulations are being relaxed, e.g. dress codes. However, any drop in traditional standards would be fatal, since Swiss tourists are very loyal (55 per cent of summer visitors are on at least their fourth visit as are a massive 65 per cent of winter visitors) to the Swiss product of orderliness and changelessness. Swiss tourists are also very independent and less than 10 per cent are with an organised group (Swiss Tourism Federation), and around 70 per cent make their own reservations. Switzerland must, therefore, continue to offer to these discriminating customers the level of service in its hotels and restaurants that used to be *de rigeur* elsewhere, but are now only to be found in small enclaves throughout Europe. In addition, the wider environment of each resort must also be kept free of the McDonalds sub-culture of fast food typified by the proletarianisation of Oxford Street in London, if traditional high-spending tourists are not to be driven away. At the same time, the Swiss need to attract a new generation of young skiers and other tourists who might prefer a leisurely lunch at a table with a tablecloth, with cutlery and glasses, served by bow-tied waiters, to grabbing fast food from a self-service scrummage, if they are to avoid the trap of the Butler (1980) model of the resort life-cycle, which sees maturity inevitably followed by decline as loyal clients die never to be replaced. The challenge for Swiss tourism is to extend the Saas Fee slogan of 'Q for Quality' to every resort, and to revalue the customer as a precious asset to be cosseted at all costs, without pandering to the lowest common denominator. For as the 1996 Federal Council report observed, sometimes the client needs to be told that it is the hotelier or restaurateur who is right.

Future developments will be crucial, not only for the local communes who have a stake in the future of Swiss tourism, but also for the population of the world, since the Alps are a world-wide resource. In this respect, their future use is of widespread concern, not least to those—like the author—who are addicted to the high-quality Swiss skiing experience. However, the future for economic development looks bleak, for although the potential for the further expansion of winter sports is enormous, both in terms of potential demand and the extent of areas yet undeveloped, the environmental arguments have become so powerful in Switzerland that it is difficult to see any further major developments. For example, a recent geography of the country (Racine and Raffestin, 1990) not only largely ignored tourism, but when it did mention this in passing, it was very critical of both its harmful effect on the environment and its low occupancy rates, notably in the huge areas of apartments built in resorts like Crans-Montana and Verbier and its satellites.

This negative attitude has meant that there has been a virtual moratorium on further ski resort development, the construction of second homes and the installation of snow-making machinery, since the late 1980s. For example, the three-year moving average of new ski-lifts fell from 40 per year in 1980–1982 to 11 in 1991–1992 (Krebs 1995). This has meant that the pursuit of 'Q for Quality' has been undermined for some resorts which are now overcrowded at peak times, lift queues are long, and rarely does the skier find the 800 m^2 of space around him/her which, according to psychologists, are necessary to create the feeling of well-being from skiing (Sinnhuber 1978). Nonetheless, the route proposed by Krippendorf, namely a further move to high value/quality at the expense of quantity, appears to be the only sensible route open to the Swiss if it is not to undermine its prime resource, a unique cultural and physical environment, which remains on the margin of despoliation. If Switzerland has reached the point where its tourism product can only be maintained and renovated when necessary, then it can teach the world how to cope with stability via modest structural change at the end of the twentieth century, just as it once taught the world how to develop a tourist industry at the beginning of the century.

8 Austria: contrasting tourist seasons and contrasting regions

Friedrich M. Zimmermann

8.1 Austria in an international context

8.1.1 Europe and the international tourism market

Despite very positive international perspectives for tourism, some traditional tourism areas in Europe—such as Austria—are facing problems because of increasing pressures from international competition. Tourist arrivals in Europe have more or less stagnated since the beginning of the 1990s, and receipts registered a first drop since the mid-1980s. Europe has lost 10 per cent of its international market share since 1975, while East Asia and the Pacific have made the most significant gains (11 per cent). Future projections suggest that Europe's share of international arrivals will further decrease to close to 50 per cent by 2010, while Asia's share will increase to more than 25 per cent (World Tourism Organisation 1996b).

The main tourist flows in Europe are intraregional, accounting for more than 75 per cent of total international tourist arrivals. But Europeans are increasingly preferring more distant, fashionable, relatively cheap and easily accessible (by air) destinations; Europe's traditional tourism regions have become less able to satisfy the demand generated by such preferences. Additionally, tourist arrivals from North America (almost 20 per cent of market share) to Europe are declining, largely due to high price levels and exchange rate movements. Asia (with a market share of 18 per cent) is increasing in importance as a future market for Europe, especially for city tours, business and incentive trips, but—excepting Vienna and Salzburg—without affecting other Austrian tourism regions.

8.1.2 Internationalisation and Europeanisation of tourism

Tourism can be characterised by a dualistic structure, polarised between a small number of large companies and a large number of small enterprises. The internationalisation of tourism, as part of the process of globalisation of international investment, and the growth of mass leisure tourism, has largely influenced and changed these structures.

Tourism and Economic Development: European Experiences, 3rd Edition. Edited by A.M. Williams and G. Shaw.
© 1998 John Wiley & Sons Ltd.

1. There is an *internationalisation* of tourism activities and investments, based on competitive strategies such as product differentiation, cost leadership and niche-market policies, which is affecting international airlines, hotels and tour operators. This dynamism has negative effects upon the small- and medium-scale Austrian tourism industry.
2. There is a kind of *'Europeanisation'* of mass leisure tourism activities, based on consumerism, changing social and demographic factors and cultural values in Europe, as well as the European Union's integration tendencies, and the effects of the opening of Eastern Europe (Shaw and Williams 1994).

8.1.3   Competitive and comparative advantages of destinations

With the exception of well known cities like London, Paris, Rome and Vienna which figure in tours such as 'Europe in a week', and certain flight destinations like Turkey, which are part of the international mass tourism business, the development opportunities for traditional tourism areas in Europe, such as Austria, are negatively influenced by the following considerations (cf. also Zimmerman 1997):

- The small scale of Europe promotes car-based, individually organised tourism.
- Single-seasonal peaks, which are essential characteristics of several regions in Western Europe, lead to reduced economic efficiency.
- Economic problems are caused by a decreasing demand for certain forms of traditional provision; the domination of some multinational tourism businesses exerts enormous pressure on small- and medium-scale tourism structures.
- Existence of a large number of small-scale enterprises with low marketing efficiency, indebtedness and capital shortage.
- Capital shortage and structural problems lead to lack of investment and innovations, so that the market share of outmoded products is increasing.
- Image problems and the effects of inertia contribute to the failure of the emergence of new products.
- Local concentration effects favour regions with entrepreneurs with initiative.
- Tourism enterprises offer high quality but have to raise high prices (caused by high taxes and high labour costs).
- Organisational problems in commercial businesses and at the regional and federal level remain unresolved.
- High ecological standards characterise many European destinations; they are associated with higher costs and strict development limits.
- Social changes are leading to more critical attitudes towards tourism among guests as well as the local population, for saturation level seems to have been reached.
- A high level of dependency on European tourists.

All these problems lead to a lack of the innovations that would be necessary for traditional European tourism regions to regain competitiveness. It is doubtful whether the support of tourism through policy initiatives is sufficiently effective, considering the competitive advantages of international tourism.

In contrast to this perspective, dynamic international trends indicate that:

- 70 per cent of international tourists use air transport, so that airlines effectively can structure the tourism market.

- 90 per cent of international tourists use tour operators, so that tour operators dominate the market.
- Tour operators shape the international supply of tourism and create place images and tourism fashions.
- Moreover international capital is creating new destinations and is enlarging the tourism over-supply.
- Business concentration offers organisational and marketing advantages.
- Economies of scale and low-cost labour offer price advantages.
- International tourism investors take advantage of comparable lower ecological standards and legal restrictions in less developed countries.
- Travel-experienced and curious guests are looking for new excitements and new tourism regions.
- There are diversified source areas of tourists (e.g. for Asia: 40 per cent Europe, 40 per cent Asia, 20 per cent America)

These international shifts lead to an increasing shift of guests away from traditional destinations such as Austria towards newly developed destinations.

8.2 National tourist trends

8.2.1 Foreign demand as a dynamic component?

Among international destination countries, Austria has a very distinctive market profile in terms of tourist origins.[1] Austria's special position in the international market stems from two particular features. First, there is the extremely high share—75 per cent—of foreigners in total demand. By comparison, the proportion in Spain is 66 per cent, in Switzerland 46 per cent and in Italy 29 per cent. Second, there is a very high level of dependency on guests from a single country of origin, that is Germany, which traditionally accounts for two thirds of all foreign overnight stays in Austria. The comparable values are 29 per cent in Greece, 35 per cent in Spain, and 40 per cent in Italy.

The very large foreign market segment, which has a positive effect on both the tourist trade and the national budget, is not a problem as long as there are no major difficulties in the world economy, such as the sectoral or the regional incidence of recession and employment. In other words, as long as the values, standards, incentives, and so on, of this very significant element of the market do not change, there are few difficulties for the Austrian industry. However, any developments of this nature considerably affect Austrian tourism, such as has occurred with respect to the extreme losses of summer overnights between 1991 and 1996: there was a total loss of 13 per cent, and a 16 per cent loss in the foreign market segment.

During the early 1970s, foreigners in Austria were referred to as the 'dynamic variable in the system of mass tourism' (Figure 8.1) (Lichtenberger 1976). Nowadays, this assertion is only partly true. Total foreign demand has not only declined more in Austria than in the rest of Western Europe, but the losses have also been discernible at an earlier stage than in other countries (mid-1980s), temporarily interrupted by the effects of the opening of Eastern Europe at the beginning of the 1990s, and a remarkable recent decline.

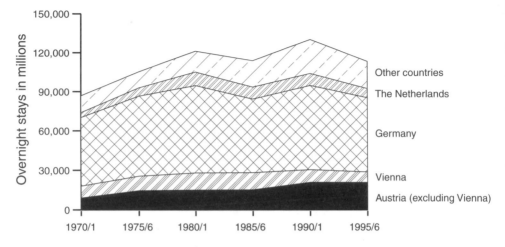

Fig. 8.1   The foreign dependency of Austrian tourism, 1970/1–1995/96

The central problem of the structural changes in demand has been a shift to shorter stays—and therefore an essential loss of overnight stays—by visitors from Germany. Although this group overcame the effects of the 1973–1974 oil shock relatively well, they were adversely affected by the general economic and social changes outlined earlier. Until the mid-1980s, there were considerable losses of demand emanating from this group; between 1981 and 1985, the number of overnight stays of tourists from Germany fell by more than 10 million. Above all, there were fewer tourists from the large urban centres of northern and central Germany (Hamburg, Berlin, etc.) and less summer tourism. The increase (by 9 million) to 1993 was the effect of new dynamism, following the opening of Eastern Europe and the unification of Germany. Yet, by 1996 (that is, within only three years) the previous gains had already been lost.

The net balance of change has been particularly disadvantageous for the summer season, but the figures are somewhat improved by winter tourism, whilst growing numbers of tourists from southern Germany are visiting Austria for short-stay holidays.

There is a similar situation with tourists from the Benelux countries. Whereas Austrian marketing strategies initially proved successful in these countries, the effects of recession on the traditional branches of manufacturing have resulted in labour market problems, as well as falling real incomes, with a resulting reduction in travel intensity. This has especially affected the lower-income social groups, which are important to Austria's summer tourism, a fact that is mirrored by a decline of 25 per cent in the number of overnights between 1991 and 1996.

The percentages of tourists from the UK and France more than doubled in the 1980s but were affected by heavy losses in the 1990s (by 45 and 36 per cent respectively). The American share of the tourist market increased mainly after the dollar rose in value in the early 1980s. However, the fall in the dollar exchange rate at the end of 1985 (engineered so as to reduce the current account deficit), together with the effects of economic recession, as well as fear of terrorism and the impact of Chernobyl, resulted in a considerable decline in American demand all over Europe in the late 1980s. However, mirroring the recent economic dynamism in the USA, the

American demand for Austrian tourism has increased by almost 20 per cent over the last five years.

Domestic demand cannot be ignored in this analysis. In view of the fact that Austria is a small country with a population of only 7.5 million, there is only limited endogenous demand potential. Furthermore, this is characterised by a very low travel intensity of less than 50 per cent, compared with Switzerland (76 per cent), the Scandinavian countries (more than 70 per cent), the UK and The Netherlands (about 60 per cent) and Germany with close to 60 per cent. Moreover, Austrian nationals also have a very strong propensity to travel to foreign countries (involving more than half of all Austrian travellers annually). Summing up, it can be said that domestic demand, originating mainly from Vienna, dominates the east of Austria. The share of Austrian guests in the eastern provinces is more than 60 per cent, but in the western regions is less than 10 per cent. With a total share of 25 per cent, domestic visitors are not capable of contributing significantly to tourism and certainly cannot compensate for the fluctuations arising from the loss of foreign tourists, although domestic demand seems to be a more stable component of the overall demand for Austrian tourism (during 1991–1996 it declined by 5 per cent).

8.2.2   *The seasonal rhythm of tourist demand*

The Alpine regions have virtually no real competition for winter tourist activities. Together with a growing number of second and third holidays, as well as short trips, and the expansion of the middle class (the key social component of the market), this has resulted in continuous growth of demand in winter, with increases of almost 12 per cent per annum between 1966 and 1981. The winter season seemed to have its own development dynamism. In the 1980s, the increases slowed to a rate of 8 per cent, and in the 1990s to less than 2 per cent per annum. This tendency to stagnation, as well as two years of declining demand in winter (1994–1995, 4.1 per cent; 1996–1997, 3 per cent) despite the dynamic development of a sub-product (snowboarding), suggests that winter sports tourism seems to have reached maturity in the early 1990s, suffering from a decline in younger visitors and the competition of overseas destinations during winter time.

In contrast to winter tourism, the summer season, with all its long traditions, has been characterised by strong fluctuations since the beginning of the 1970s. During recent years there have been dramatic recessions (Table 8.1). While up to 1972 there were annual rates of increase of around 7 per cent, subsequently there were losses up to 1978, followed by a short but vigorous phase of recovery. A peak of overnight stays of more than 78 million was attained in the summer of 1981. Thereafter, the following years were characterised by substantial decline, with a resulting decrease in income.

Serious problems followed for the summer tourist industry in Austria. In 1986 overnight summer stays reached only 67 million and they have dropped to a level comparable to 1970. The next peak was reached in summer 1991—as a consequence of the political changes in Europe and less restricted travelling for Eastern Europeans, new marketing ideas and positive environmental effects—with more than 78 million overnights, followed by another dramatic decline until 1996 with just 62 million overnights.

This reversal has had a number of consequences. The tourist product 'Summer in the Alps', in its traditional form, no longer seems to be sufficiently attractive given

Table 8.1 The seasonal development of tourism in Austria, 1950/1–1995/6

Year	Overnights in total	Percentage share		Revenues (billion ATS)	Percentage share	
		Summer	Winter		Summer	Winter
1950–51	19.22	75	25			
1955–56	31.65	78	22			
1960–61	50.77	78	22			
1965–66	70.15	78	22			
1970–71	96.49	76	24			
1975–76	105.00	69	31			
1980–81	121.30	64	36	97.48	56	44
1985–86	113.34	59	41	123.60	54	46
1990–91	122.56	59	41	182.39	53	47
1995–96	112.38	55	45	178.50	48	52

Source: Österreichisches Statistisches Zentralamt (various years).

prevailing socio-economic, demographic and social changes; moreover, it is subject to considerable international competition. Special attention must be paid to the problems of these structural seasonal differences because summer season losses are not just restricted to the single-season regions (the lakeside destinations) which lost between 40 and 50 per cent of their overnights between 1991 and 1996. The losses also increasingly involve the so-called 'mountain summer' areas in the western provinces. Beside the factors already mentioned, there are other reasons for the negative developments in summer tourism. For example, there has been a loss of attractive countryside for summer activities due to the building of large hotels, cableways, ski slopes, second homes, roads and so on. All kinds of resources (investment, subsidies, marketing, etc.) have been reallocated to the winter season. Since 1993 the receipts from winter tourism have exceeded summer receipts: in 1996 the receipts per overnight in summer were ATS 1,380, compared to ATS 1,850 in winter (Table 8.1).

8.2.3 Modern recreational trends and short-term tourism

In addition to the seasonal rhythm of the demand peaks of long-term tourism, there are also short-term tourism rhythms. This is linked to the growth of day trips and short-term tourism. While this offers some advantages for the winter season, it requires more flexibility in the provision of accommodation and some regions are increasingly faced with utilisation conflicts.

There is a definite stagnation of travel intensity in the case of main holidays, not least because main summer holidays are being spent at more distant destinations (mostly on package tours). However, there is also a strong tendency to make several shorter journeys, and short holidays—especially in winter— are frequently spent in the Alps.

It is expected that the future development of short-term tourism in Austria will involve a quantitative increase in the number of day trips and short holidays. Of greatest interest is the development of demand from Germany (see Ruppert and Maier 1970; Ruppert *et al.* 1986; Zimmermann 1985b, 1986a). The industry needs to pay special attention to this, especially where there is a danger of utilisation conflicts with long-term tourism. The most significant negative aspect of the overlap between short- and long-term tourism are summarised below (cf. Röck 1977; Haimayer 1984):

1. High traffic intensity at week-ends, with considerable noise and exhaust pollution, and lack of parking-spaces for long-term tourists.
2. Environmental damage caused by visitors who do no identify with the region.
3. On days when tourist numbers reach a maximum, the basic and tourism infrastructures are overloaded (with, for example, long queues at cableways, overcrowded restaurants, and problems with garbage).
4. Trying to extend the infrastructure to cope with maximum tourist demand causes economic problems because of the enormous maintenance costs involved and the long periods during which the facilities are not fully utilised.
5. Excessive exploitation of the landscape for sports activities, and for construction.
6. Special problems due to second homes and their pressure on local real estate markets.

In spite of some positive aspects, such as better use of recreational facilities and thus higher profitability, it seems to be advantageous to plan for a development which would separate long-term and short-term tourism. This would reduce the problems for both the people and the landscape, and would help to preserve the quality of recreation experiences for guests, and of the environment for the resident population.

8.3 Regional trends

8.3.1   A lop-sided distribution

The distribution of tourism in Austria is extremely lop-sided (Figure 8.2a). The majority of guests visit the western provinces; thus the Tyrol, Salzburg and Vorarlberg have 65 per cent of all overnight stays. This concentration has been increasing constantly, from 50 per cent in 1962, and 60 per cent in 1982. There has been a correspondingly large reduction in the importance of the eastern provinces; they registered half of all overnight stays in 1952, but now have barely 25 per cent. The main areas of demand can be classified into five major types.

The first are the *cities*, which include not only those specially favoured by business or congress tourism, but also those which offer either important cultural activities and sights (Vienna, Salzburg, etc.) or have been able to enhance their image by hosting international sporting events (Innsbruck). These cities, despite the aggregate decline in demand, show very large rates of increase. Vienna ranks fourth in the league table of European city tourism after London, Paris and Rome; it registered about 7 million overnight stays in 1995, which represented an increase from more than 5 per cent per annum since 1981. These rates of increase are due to a poly-structured demand and worldwide expansion of congress tourism and city tours.

The second main area of demand is the *spas*, which have survived the different phases of tourism development by adapting their specialist facilities to modern circumstances. They include communities in northern and eastern Austria which are monofunctional spas, visited mainly for health reasons and mainly by Austrians (Bad Schallerbach, Bad Hall, Bad Tatzmannsdorf, Bad Gleichenberg). In the Salzkammergut, the Gastein Valley and Carinthia there is a very strong overlap between, on the

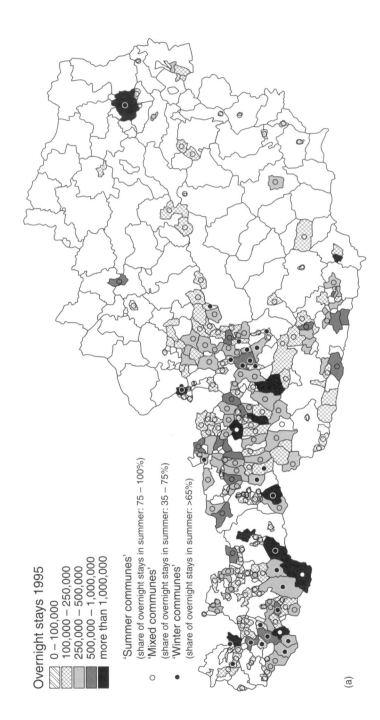

Overnight stays 1995

	0 – 100,000
	100,000 – 250,000
	250,000 – 500,000
	500,000 – 1,000,000
	more than 1,000,000

'Summer communes'
(share of overnight stays in summer: 75 – 100%)
'Mixed communes'
(share of overnight stays in summer: 35 – 75%)
'Winter communes'
(share of overnight stays in summer: >65%)

(a)

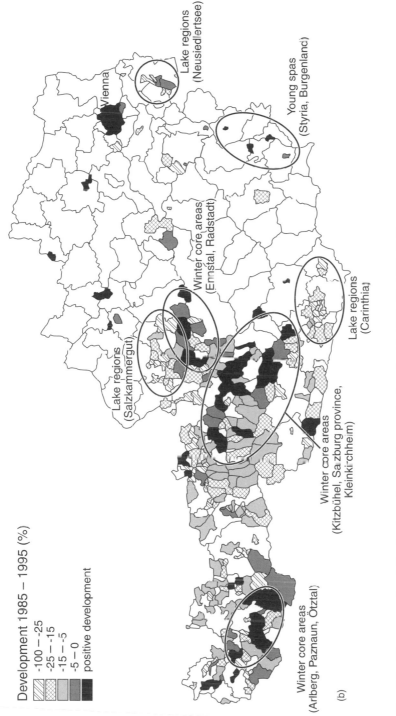

Fig. 8.2 The county-level distribution of overnight stays in Austria: (a) 1995; (b) 1985–1995

one hand, the curative function (with recreation in summer) and, on the other hand, winter sports, and there is a considerably higher proportion of foreign visitors. Examples include Bad Ischl, Bad Aussee, Bad Mitterndorf, Bad Gastein, Bad Hofgastein and Bad Kleinkirchheim. In these places short-term tourism is also more important. Additionally there is a very recent development with spas in the provinces of Styria and Burgenland, where new sites of tourism were built up, supported heavily by the provinces in order to improve the economic situation in these peripheral areas.

Lake communities, located in the areas of the Carinthian Lakes and the Salzkammergut, constitute the third main area. They have long-established traditions, which makes it difficult to respond to the new structures of demand because of the effects of inertia. The region around the Neusiedler See is a rather special case due to the scenic attraction of the Pannonic-Continental lowland; this is unique in Austria and is suitable for further development.

The fourth main area of demand is the *mountain communities*, which represent the favoured places in western Austria, characterised by a combination of summer and winter tourism, by a preponderance of foreign tourists, and significant demand from short-term tourism. Monofunctional winter regions can be found in the area of Arlberg, the Paznaun and the Radstätter Tauern.

The fifth and final main area of demand is the *recreational communities*, which mostly lie either close to the major tourist centres, and take advantage of their infrastructure, or offer alternative, 'small scale', additional supplies. The product of *rural tourism*, as an indigenous development in peripheral areas, is playing an increasingly important and diversified role in local development (see Cavaco 1995). Rural tourism, based upon sustainable development strategies, offers opportunities to revalue the cultural heritage, the environment and the identity of villages and people so that they can acquire cultural exchanges and earnings in certain farming, artisanal and service structures, as well as an improved quality of life. Not surprisingly, therefore, rural tourism has been defined as a specific goal of the European Union Regional Policy, based on an integrated approach to rural development (Commission of the European Communities 1994b). Examples include Lungau, Lesachtal, Bregenzerwald and Eastern Tyrol.

In addition to these five main types, there are many mixed tourism regions such as transit communities, holiday resorts, administrative and economic centres and places of pilgrimage. Nowadays, these mostly overlap with other tourism functions.

8.3.2   Regional trends

This section considers trends in three broad geographical regions: the Alpine West, the Lakes and the East (Figure 8.2b).

8.3.2.1   The Alpine West

A major consequence of the changing structure of tourism demand and supply has been increasing concentration of demand in the west of Austria, together with a strong gradient from west to east. In particular, there has been considerable dynamism in regions with good conditions for winter sports, although this also has diminished over the past few years.

Winter demand has strongly characterised these provinces over the past 10 years and virtually all those regions with appropriate conditions have been affected although with differing degrees of intensity. Consequently, most locations seem to have been involved in tourism developments and, in future, preference should be given to quality improvement rather than to opening up new (winter sports) areas. More immediately, however, an important new trend is that both the Tyrol and Vorarlberg, as well as Salzburg, have experienced large losses of summer demand. This leads to problems in the accommodation sector because the lack of demand in the summer season undermines the profitability of such a high-quality supply. Development seems to be shifting in the direction of single-season, winter utilisation, which has negative consequences for the regional economic structure.

8.3.2.2   The lake regions

The lake regions, which concentrate on the summer season, have been characterised by economic difficulties over many years because the concentration of demand in two high-frequency months yields small net profits. Their situation is that there are heavy losses of summer demand and, therefore, there is little utilisation of tourism establishments and facilities. This leads to an increasing lack of private capital and there is less investment for improving structures, for restructuring and for innovation, even though the present tourist market (with its short cycles of innovation) requires constant adaptation to new conditions. In consequence, the standards of buildings often lag behind modern requirements, there is a low percentage of rooms with *en suite* amenities, and there are low utilisation rates in the accommodation sector. Furthermore, there is a considerable shortage of building sites available at attractive locations and this makes adaptation even more difficult, leading to serious supply gaps and preventing the creation of an adequate marketing mix. This again deters many potential tourists and, as a result, the negative cycle is reinforced.

Tendencies in respect of supply have virtually led to immobility in tourism in these regions. Given the dynamic nature of the competition—in terms of both quantity and quality—this suggests that the future of the single-season lake regions will be fraught with difficulties and they may become increasingly distanced from the international level of tourism supply requirements. Some product improvement measures could be taken, such as enhancing marketing, giving more publicity to the clean bathing waters and the environment, and extending the season by means of short-term tourism. Only in this way will it be possible to realise the innovations and investments that are essential to improve the quality of the industry and of tourism infrastructure.

8.3.2.3   The eastern regions

Stagnation tendencies are particularly conspicuous in eastern Austria, and these emerged as early as the 1960s. They are due to a lack of facilities for winter sport, a low share of foreign guests, the increasing importance of day trips, and the growth of second homes. These developments have mostly affected the former holiday destinations of the Viennese (such as Semmering and Wechsel), and the places which attracted urban residents during the summer (for example Weinviertel). Nowadays, they are experiencing a certain revival as areas for day trips and short holidays. The tendencies to stagnation in eastern Austria have often been accentuated by lack of tourism initiatives, not least because there are a number of alternative sources of income and thus less motivation for the local population to favour tourism development. Nevertheless, there are a number of isolated instances of innovation which have been favourable for small-scale developments in peripheral locations.

One aspect to emphasise is the extremely difficult situation in peripheral regions, which have few alternatives to agriculture as an income source. In these regions tourism development tends to be considered as one possible strategy for reducing disparities. This is often a false assumption as there is frequently a lack of adequate conditions for development and of site prerequisites; the consequences are misdirected investments in those tourism infra- and supra-structures which are supposed to 'improve' the regional structure (see Zimmerman 1985a, 1995).

8.4   The economic importance of the tourism industry

The economic importance of tourism in Austria can be summed up by reference to a number of key features (see Table 8.2). Austria is visited by close to 17 million foreign tourists, who spend 85 million nights there each year. It holds twelfth place among the world's tourism countries and has lost six places since 1991, when it was surpassed only by France, the USA, Spain, the UK and Italy. Receipts from international tourism in Austria are about $15 billion per year. This compares with $64.3 billion in the USA, $28.4 billion in Spain, $28.2 billion in France, $27.3 billion in Italy and $20 billion in the UK (WTO 1997). The negative effects are underlined in Table 8.2, which shows a remarkable decline in overnight figures and a comparable small increase in receipts, compared to the dynamic competition.

Domestic tourism comprises about 5.5 million guests who also make an important contribution to tourism receipts; Austrians account for 31 million overnight stays per year. More significant is the economic importance of the tourism industry when looked at in terms of average tourist receipts per inhabitant. In 1996 Austria was the leader with $1,900 per person, clearly ahead of Switzerland ($1,450), Spain ($730) and Italy ($470).

What is the role of tourism in the labour market? In the accommodation and restaurant sectors there are about 140,000 employees, 63 per cent of whom are female. In winter the level of employment is about 10,000 persons lower than in summer. Foreign workers account for no more than 10 per cent of the workforce. There is less empirical information available on the impact of tourism expenditure on other economic sectors. Based on international comparison of employees (Papadopoulos 1987), total employment in the tourism industries is estimated at about 14 per cent of global employment. On this basis, the share in Austria is approximately 18 per cent, which is equivalent to more than 500,000. In this respect, 'direct' employees seem to account for only a quarter of all employees in tourism–related sectors.

Finally, the role of tourism in regional economies can be noted. Investments by tourism enterprises mainly benefit other firms within the immediate locality. Some 57 per cent of the total capital expenditure is spent within a distance of 20 km, 34 per cent between 20 and 100 km and only 9 per cent is paid to enterprises at a distance of more than 100 km. The multiplier effects of tourism are therefore highly localised.

Table 8.2 Austria and the world's top tourism destinations

Rank 1990	Rank 1996	Country	International tourist arrivals (thousands) 1990	International tourist arrivals (thousands) 1996	Percentage change
1	1	France	52,497	61,500	17.15
2	2	USA	39,363	44,791	13.79
3	3	Spain	34,085	41,295	21.15
4	4	Italy	26,679	35,500	33.06
12	5	China	10,484	26,055	148.52
7	6	UK	18,013	25,800	43.23
8	7	Mexico	17,176	21,732	26.53
5	8	Hungary	20,510	20,670	0.78
28	9	Poland	3,400	19,420	471.18
10	10	Canada	15,209	17,345	14.04
16	11	Czech Republic	7,278	17,205	136.40
6	12	Austria	19,011	16,641	−12.47
9	13	Germany	17,045	15,070	−11.59
19	14	Hong Kong	6,581	11,700	77.78
11	15	Switzerland	13,200	11,097	−15.93

Rank 1990	Rank 1996	Country	International tourism receipts (US $ millions) 1990	International tourism receipts (US $ millions) 1996	Percentage change
1	1	USA	43,007	64,373	49.68
4	2	Spain	18,593	28,428	52.89
2	3	France	20,185	28,241	39.91
3	4	Italy	20,016	27,349	36.64
5	5	UK	14,940	20,415	36.65
6	6	Austria	13,410	15,095	12.57
7	7	Germany	11,471	13,168	14.79
11	8	Hong Kong	5,032	11,200	122.58
25	9	China	2,218	10,500	373.40
8	10	Switzerland	7,411	9,982	33.48
12	11	Singapore	4,596	9,410	104.74
9	12	Canada	6,339	8,727	37.67
13	13	Thailand	4,326	8,600	98.80
14	14	Australia	4,088	8,264	102.15
65	15	Poland	358	7,000	

Sources: WTO, February 1997; http://www.world-tourism.org/esta/highlights.

8.5 The economic organisation of the tourism industry

The organisation of the tourism industry in Austria can be characterised as small- to medium-scale, while capital sources are mostly private with family enterprises being dominant. There have been only limited multinational investments, and venture capital is of little importance within Austrian tourism. The supply of accommodation has developed in response to strong demand pressures dating back to the early 1960s. From an initial 200,000 guest beds in 1950, supply increased to a peak of about

1.25 million by the mid-1980s and then decreased, in line with demand, to about 1.1 million by 1996.

This development is not evenly distributed with respect to either the season or the individual types of establishment. While high-quality establishments (5- and 4-star hotels), with about 165,000 beds in 1995, have developed considerably (+40 per cent since 1985) and 3-star establishments, with 238,000 beds, have also experienced an increase (+18 per cent), 2- and 1-star establishments, which are predominant in Austria's commercial supply with 243,000 beds, have declined sharply in importance since 1985 (−30 per cent). The letting of private rooms is highly significant in Austria, in contrast to Switzerland where this is of little importance (see Chapter 7). Instead, the supply of accommodation in the latter is based more on traditional hotels, and therefore Switzerland has a better image in some respects. In Austria private establishments have contributed to the diffusion of tourism to peripheral regions and function as an important accommodation reserve for peak tourism periods. It is precisely the letting of private rooms which has been most affected by the decline in demand. Development, which had been expansive up to the mid-1970s, reached a peak in the summer of 1976 with a total of 470,000 beds and a 40 per cent share of total bed potential. This compares with a share of 21 per cent in the mid-1990s (240,000 beds) and the decline, of course, is due to greater demand for quality and rapid development of holiday apartments (−45 per cent since 1985). The competitive pressure of apartments has caused an adaptation of the existing structure, with units being created out of several rooms, and quality being improved, but it has caused the elimination of many private rooms from the fierce competitive struggle.

The utilisation rates of the accommodation supply present an interesting pattern, reflecting the rhythmic nature of demand, and the dynamism of the winter season and of supply structures. This has led to shorter cycles of innovation, which the existing structure of the restaurant and accommodation sectors can cope with only to a limited extent. Figure 8.3 shows a tendency towards higher-quality supply, as is inherent in recessions, while at the same time poorly-equipped establishments have suffered losses.

Development in the summer season shows only slight increases in demand, even in the case of high-quality establishments. In contrast, there are large losses in the case of 2- and 1-star establishments, as well as in private rooms. Demand for the latter has changed dramatically: there were 25 million overnight stays in the summer of 1975 compared to 13.5 million spaces in 1985 and 8.5 million overnights in the summer of 1995.

This leads to the question of levels of bed-space utilisation and, thus, the profitability of establishments (Figure 8.4). The major feature is that the utilisation rate in winter, at an average of 52 days, is still lower than during the summer season, at 58 days. Nevertheless there has been a noticeable increase in the winter season, for in 1975 the utilisation rate was, on average, only 37 days. By comparison, in the summer season the utilisation rate was much higher in the mid-1970s, with an average of 64 days of full utilisation. Differentiation according to types of accommodation and quality standards further emphasises the developments outlined so far. In winter, when as a rule only the better-quality rooms are available, most categories, including private rooms, have experienced increasing utilisation rates. However, it should also be noted that in the 1990s, the move to quality, higher prices and oversupply in 3-star establishments has led to an unexpected decrease in utilisation rates.

In summer, only the top categories have experienced increased levels of utilisation. With decreasing quality, utilisation rates have declined, again mostly in 3-star enterprises;

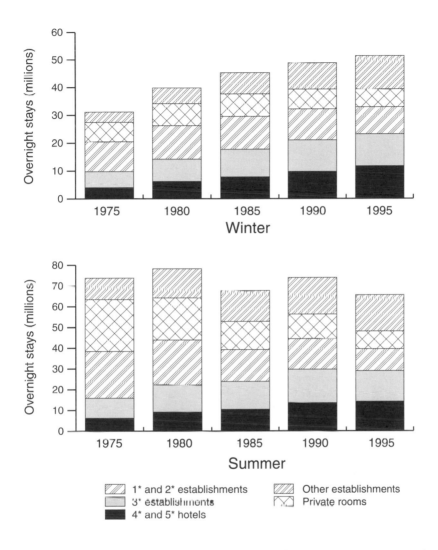

Fig. 8.3 Overnight stays in Austria, by type of establishment, in the summer and winter seasons, 1975–1995

stable conditions for 2- and 1-star hotels and private rooms are a consequence of the quantitative reduction of supply within these categories. These developments show how the present economic structure has evolved. The profitability of establishments has held where quality is adequate and if there is the possibility of two seasons. However, profit margins have decreased elsewhere, and the constant need to innovate to maintain standards requires continual reinvestment. The situation is worse in establishments with lower levels of amenities and in tourist regions which have only one season; here, incomes are too low to maintain or achieve the necessary quality standards. There is a negative spiral, given that only improved quality is able to guarantee an adequate level of

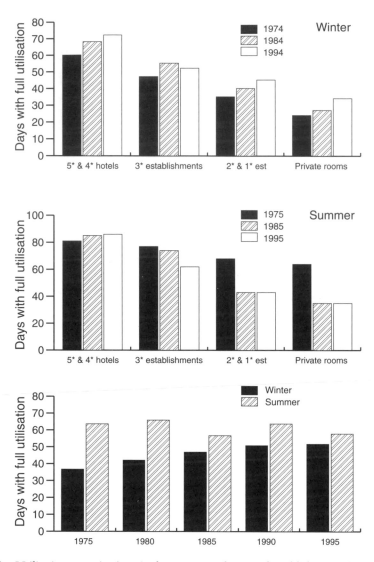

Fig. 8.4 Utilisation rates in Austria, by season and type of establishment, 1974/5–1994/5

demand in modern tourism. As result there are clear tendencies towards qualification, commercialisation and centralisation.

8.6 Impacts on local social structures

In addition to the processes outlined with respect to demand, there have also been important social changes related to the supply structure in recent years. In the Alpine area, the development of modern society, characterised by diverse activities, has overlapped with alpine farming and society (Lichtenberger 1979). As a result, young people, growing up in the context of an assured existence and having frequent contacts with tourists, have become familiar with new ways and styles of life. Consequently, they are no longer prepared to deny themselves leisure time and recreation, and to be tied to traditional family and village ways of life. Extremely high workloads and low net profits have reduced the attraction of taking over a family business in the restaurant or accommodation trade. In some ways, the situation in the tourist industry in the mid-1980s is similar to that of farming some decades earlier. An increasing number of low-quality establishments face the problem of there not being anyone in the next generation willing to take over the business; for this reason, the owners of such businesses are often elderly, and have little initiative to innovate. Loss of quality leads to reduced utilisation rates and net profits and to even less attractive working conditions for tourism. Young people go elsewhere to work, and the local population identifies less and less with tourism and the guests.

There are important consequences for the local housing market, for there are significant connections between quality and the perceived image of a tourism place, and real estate prices. Typically, the average price level of real estate is extremely high; for example, at Kitzbühel, Mayerhofen in the Zillertal, Lech and St Anton am Arlberg the highest price levels were about £250 to £300 per m^2 in 1986. The average price level in leading winter tourism communes is between £60 and £120, whereas the price of real estate in less tourism-orientated communes lies at between £20 and £40. This is the result of the enormous pressure that second homes generate in the local real-estate market and it results in many problems for the young, indigenous populations in tourism regions. In practice they have little realistic opportunity of being able to buy real estate and of remaining in their home areas. As a result, these regions become overwhelmed by foreign influences (the owners of second homes, seasonal employees, etc.) which do not identify with the region and the local culture; there is a real danger that local residents will increasingly lose their regional identity.

8.7   Policies for tourism

8.7.1   *Official tourism policy in Austria*

Under the Austrian Constitution, tourism is the responsibility of the provinces (*Länder*) which, with the Federal government, shape the framework of tourism policy. The main objectives are to:

1. Encourage patriotism and regional identity.
2. Make people more aware of environmental problems.
3. Ensure that tourism provides tourists with positive emotional feelings.
4. Make advantage of old and new segments of the tourist market.
5. Intensify promotional activities.
6. Improve marketing.

In 1981, the Österreichische Raumordnungskonferenz (Austrian Regional Development Conference), an institution founded in the early 1970s by the Federation, the provinces and the communes (Union of Austrian Communes, Union of Austrian Towns), published the *Österreichische Raumordnungskonzept* (Austrian Land-Use Concept). This was to be phased in over a period of 10 years, covering the following aspects of tourism:

1. Further improvements in the quality of accommodation.
2. Development of special packages to prolong the season.
3. Special development strategies for peripheral regions.
4. Conservation of the environment and local culture, and improved presentation of the cultural heritage.
5. Restoration of environmental damage (e.g. re-cultivation of ski slopes).
6. Development of tourism supply without significant changes to the landscape or built infrastructure, the so-called 'gentle tourism', which is more ecologically conscious and pays more attention to the living space and life styles of the local population (Hasslacher 1984; Commission Internationale pour la Protection des Regions Alpines 1985).

Besides this publication, there are further expert opinions on tourist trends, problems and developments which form the basis for tourism-related political decision; for example, Österreichische Raumordnungskonferenz (1985, 1987a,b).

Another institution that establishes tourism policy in Austria is the Österreichische Fremdenverkehrstag (Austrian Tourism Congress), which normally takes place every four years. The discussion forum evidently was cancelled, the last Austrian Tourism Congress took place in 1989! This was organised by the Ministerium für Wirtschaftliche Angelegenheiten (Ministry for Economic Affairs) and Kuratorium des Österreichischen Fremdenverkehrs (the Board of Trustees of Austrian Tourism), an institution which is charged with discussing and coordinating decision-making in respect of Austrian tourism policy. The last meeting was in Baden (1989) and subcommittees discussed the following: tourism and the environment; people and tourism; education, training and information; the tourism economy; tourist infrastructure; tourism supply; traffic and communications; public relations and marketing special offers; future trends; tourism and culture. For the first time a committee discussed future trends in tourism in Austria (see next section).

It is difficult to evaluate the effectiveness of tourism policy in Austria because the influence of the Federal government is very limited compared with the provinces, which have very different frameworks for assisting the industry. Therefore, outcomes depend to a large degree on individual initiative. Nevertheless, in general terms, increased emphasis has been given to policy in recent years, not least because of growing concern about the selective decline in demand. More promoters and entrepreneurs are making an attempt to take into account official tourism policies and plans in their projects—not least to ensure that these receive official sanction.

8.7.2   Future tourism trends in Austria

In order to provide perspectives on future tourism trends, 168 top experts drawn from all parts of Austria were questioned on this topic: 14 per cent had influential positions at either the federal or the provincial level, 25 per cent were hotel-owners or managers of leading tourist centres, while 17 per cent were professionals or others who were active on a freelance basis; the remainder were qualified personnel in travel agencies, principals of Schools of Tourism, etc. The questioning of the experts was carried out in three stages via anonymous written surveys. The results of the previous round were made known at each stage: statistical evaluations, arguments and counter-arguments. The advantage of such iterative group surveys is that the experts can reassess their opinions in the light of the views and arguments of the group as a whole. The results of the third round yielded an optimised estimation of future trends, based on sustained discussion. The results were presented and discussed at the Austrian Tourism Congress in 1989.

8.7.2.1   The weaknesses and strengths of Austrian tourism

The advantages are considered to be:

1.   A central location in Europe (accessible to major markets).
2.   Varied natural features, a countryside that is still intact, and a healthy climate.
3.   Rich in cultural and educational activities.
4.   A general understanding of tourism and of the consequences of rising standards of living.
5.   Organically-evolved structures with long experience and tradition of tourism.
6.   A reasonable size distribution of establishments.
7.   A varied supply, high standards, family-run businesses and a lack of tourist ghettos.
8.   Positive prerequisites for winter tourism.

The disadvantages are considered to be:

1.   A supply side with little free space, and which is over-regulated and over-constrained.
2.   Too many laws which are hostile to tourism such as taxation, labour regulations, social legislation, the opening hours of shops, hard currency policy, etc. These impede the international competitivity of the industry and excessively burden the relationship between price and service.
3.   An antiquated supply side that is too conservative, too imitative, lacking innovation, non-specialised, marketed unprofessionally and has too many substandard rooms and too many establishments that lack self-financing capacity.
4.   Inadequate service for guests and a lack of target-group orientation. Regional and supraregional tourism marketing has little influence on product presentation (packages, price, quality, etc.).
5.   A careless approach to nature with too many scattered buildings, excessive development and too much traffic.
6.   Growing hostility towards tourism due to excessive exploitation of nature and the social environment, the selling-off of the countryside (homeland), land price increases, damage to village communities because of competitive attitudes and cultural overloading.
7.   A negative image due to scandals, political controversy and media treatment.

8. Too little material and non-material support for tourism by public funds, indifference to and even hostility toward tourism by federal and, to an extent, provincial political parties.

8.7.2.2   Major ecological challenges

The main problems of ecology in Austria are seen as:

1. Exploitation of nature by tourism infra- and suprastructures, especially winter sports resorts that are coming to the limits of their carrying capacity. This has already led to a change in the politicians' views on tourism. For example, the province of Vorarlberg ended the development of new cableways in their Alpine regions in 1978. The most important winter province, the Tyrol, ordered a 'meditation phase' of three years to evaluate the ecological and social problems and costs of tourism.
2. Despoliation of the countryside and land speculation are leading to an expansion of settlement into potentially unstable zones, and to the necessity for regulating the channels and flows of streams and rivers.
3. In this way the potentially disastrous consequences of elemental forces (floods, landslides, avalanches, etc.) have increased. Additional factors are the careless exploitation of natural resources, e.g. clearing of woodland, devastation of protective forests, soil damage, opening-up of glaciers for winter sports activities and road-building.
4. The decline of agriculture and, in consequence, a failure to preserve the landscape has impaired the natural scenery that is so important for the summer season. Furthermore, agriculture is losing its function as a stabilising factor in rural social structure, while non-local structures and architectural styles are disrupting the harmonious appearances of villages. Traditional cultures and ways of life are also giving way to an artificial 'Lederhosen-mentality'.
5. The woodlands are threatened by utilisation conflicts and by the increasing space required by tourism. The decline of forests is making improved protective measures essential; otherwise their leisure function will be lost in the future.
6. Waste separation, avoidance and utilisation will be a central problem in the future because there is increasingly fierce resistance from local populations to new landfill sites.
7. Transit traffic is a problem within the Alpine area. In several regions the endurance breaking point has already been reached or passed.
8. Electricity power-supply companies will have to rethink their policies. The rivalry between ecology-orientated tourism and the construction of power-stations, the transfer of water from several Alpine valleys to one huge power-station, and the disfigurement of the landscape by high-tension lines are only a few examples of the negative effects which have to be addressed.

The main ecological problems of Austria will have to be solved through legislation, financial support, training measures, the creation of environmental models and cooperation concepts, and especially by investment in 'human capital' in the form of consultation to find individual solutions to problems. This is essential because in the year 2000 nature and environment will be the main factors in high-quality tourism.

8.7.2.3   Future potential visitors to Austria

Some of the more important new trends in European tourist behaviour are:

- Short-term tourism (resulting from dynamic development of day trips and weekend holidays).
- Spontaneous, immediate decisions as to where to spend holidays (based on increase of single households and senior citizens, which are independent financially, institutionally and timewise; also stronger demand for reasonable last-minute offers and overseas destinations).
- Individual and more flexible holiday planning (with respect to time and content).
- Specialisation and orientation towards particular target groups (new, niche products offer advantages).
- Intensive need for excitement and adventure (preference for exotic destinations).
- Seeking quality and high comfort levels.
- Increased sense of life, escapism and body consciousness.
- Increasing environmental consciousness and significance of ecological quality ('gentle tourism' supply and sustainable developed regions as a counterpart to international mass tourism).

These new trends indicate some of the more important characteristics of the potential 'visitor 2000'. There are three main tourist types:

1. *'Average' guests* who are rather passive and in need of animation and entertainment.
2. *'Educated' tourists* who are initiative- and lifestyle-orientated, conscious of the environment and health, critical and comparative of tourism provision, and conscious of quality.
3. Besides mass-tourism, there is a *small high-income target group*, preferring either small-scale, individual provision in peripheral areas or the exploration of new, exotic, alternative regions.

According to the current situation, the main future potential of guests for Austria should be in the educated and high-income target groups, in order to take advantage of the special high-quality product which Austria is able to provide.

8.7.2.4   The 'new identity of Austria'

The 'visitor 2000', as well as the international competitive set-up, will require new quality-orientated product specifications for Austria. The focal points are outlined below. They are all based on ecological and environmental consciousness, and a holistic approach as the basis of future tourism in Austria:

- *Health*: With an increase in the number of older people in Europe and North America, there will be a new stimulus for health tourism. At the same time, the new health trend will also be boosted by dynamic development due to rising environmental awareness and body consciousness amongst younger people. An intact nature and environment will be of particular importance in this type of tourism provision.

- *Sports*: In the course of the new health–wave, a combination of sports and mental recreation will create new opportunities. The potential market represented by the young and the active elderly suggests growth of 'soft and gentle' activities (cross-country skiing, hiking, bicycle riding, horseback riding, etc.) with an emphasis on the enjoyment of nature.
- *Adventure and attractions*: On the one hand, a policy of filling market gaps by aiming at extreme-sports experiences (mountain climbing, paragliding, rafting, etc.) promises dynamic development. On the other hand, attractions based on good quality and professional know-how (recreation centres, theme parks, themed packages) are definite investments into the future, and can help to protect nature by monitoring the tourism streams.
- *Art and culture*: The cultural heritage in Europe offers good future perspectives on account of increasing demand for non-material products.
- *Nostalgia and tradition*: Based on future markets in overseas areas, the disadvantages of traditional tourism structures could be overcome by combining tradition and culture with high-quality products into a 'nostalgia package tour', for example, by presenting tours covering highlights of culture and history in the former Austrio-Hungarian monarchy.

A consistent orientation towards new products requires a high degree of supply-side specialisation, as well as adaptation to the holiday-styles of segmented target-groups. The tourism products must enable holidays to be as varied as possible, and must be innovative (new leisure technologies) and sociable (individualised provision, personal contacts, possibilities to enjoy culture and/or to study according to individual interests). By using modern information and communications techniques, the tourism supply should be made more consumable in respect of individual preferences. The central message for tourism provision at the end of this century, therefore, is that tourism must present not just a product but also an attractive and individual tourism 'life-style'.

Note

1. The most important and most detailed data available concerning tourism in Austria, based on information covering all types of accommodation, are submitted to the Österreichisches Statistisches Zentralamt (Austrian Statistical Central Office). The first level provides data on the development of accommodation and bed-spaces with respect to both quantity and quality, in both the commercial and private sectors. The second level gives information on tourist flows, that is, number of tourists differentiated by country of origin, and numbers of nights spent in several types of accommodation. Aggregate-level data are published annually for communities and provinces, along with a survey of development as a whole (latest publication: Österreichisches Statistisches Zentralamt 1996). In addition to the published data, it is possible to obtain further, more detailed information from the data bank of the Austrian Statistical Central Office.

    Every three years (since 1969) a micro-census surveys the travel habits of the Austrian population, with respect to the travel intensity of main holidays, day trips, short-term tourism and business trips, differentiated by destination, time (month) and length of stay, and type of accommodation used, etc. (the results of the 1993/94 survey have been published in Österreichisches

Statistisches Zentralamt 1995, 1997). The Austrian Statistical Central Office publishes further detailed information on accommodation establishments (enterprises, employees, etc.) in different surveys as part of the Austrian census of 1991. Beside the official information sources, there are several individual data publications available on particular aspects, mainly collected by regional, provincial, federal and scientific departments.

9 The United Kingdom: market trends and policy responses

Gareth Shaw, Paul Thornton and Allan M. Williams

9.1 Tourism and the UK economy

The significance of tourism to the UK economy is considerable and takes a variety of forms, ranging from its contribution to overseas earnings, through to job creation. In 1997 tourism accounted for 4 per cent of gross domestic product (GDP), compared with 3.1 per cent in 1977. Revenue from international tourism is also a major part of the UK's overseas earnings, and in 1994 spending by overseas visitors accounted for over 8 per cent of invisible exports and almost 4 per cent of total exports. These figures indicate a contribution that surpasses many of the more traditional export industries. In total the tourism industry is estimated to have contributed some £37 billion to the country's economy in 1997. Furthermore, during the 1980s tourism's role as a job provider was clearly recognised and promoted through three key reports: the Confederation of British Industries (1985) report, The Banks Report (1985) and, the most influential, the so-called Young Report (1985) by the Secretary of State for Trade and Industry. All of these reports stressed the growing number of jobs in tourism at a time when other sectors of the UK economy were shedding employment. Thus, between 1974 and 1984 the number of jobs primarily dependent on tourism and leisure rose from 1 million to 1.2 million (Young 1985). In essence these reports highlighted three key elements of the tourist industry; its labour-intensive nature, its strong local economic multiplier effects, and the low capital cost of job creation (less than one-half of that in other economic sectors). More recent studies have suggested that between 1981 and 1989 jobs in tourism-related activities grew by an average of 40,900 per annum, slightly lower than had been predicted at the time but still a very healthy rate (Hudson and Townsend 1992). Significantly, employment in tourism-related industries has continued to increase throughout the 1990s, growing by almost 3 per cent between 1990 and 1996, accounting for a total of 1.5 million jobs in 1995 (British Tourist Authority 1997).

It is against this background of potential wealth and job creation and restructuring elsewhere in the economy that successive UK governments have pursued public policy towards tourism. The early initiatives during the 1960s culminated in the most significant legislation to date, the Development of Tourism Act 1969. This established the British Tourist Authority, together with the three national tourist boards in

Tourism and Economic Development: European Experiences, 3rd Edition. Edited by A.M. Williams and G. Shaw.
© 1998 John Wiley & Sons Ltd.

England, Scotland and Wales. In Northern Ireland a tourist board had been established much earlier through the Development of Tourism Act, 1948 (Smyth 1986).

The economic importance of tourism was reiterated in 1974 when ministerial guidelines were issued that stressed tourism's role, both in the country's balance of payments and as an aid in promoting regional development. At this time emphasis was placed on concentrating financial aid in economically fragile areas with untapped potential (English Tourist Board 1978). This regional dimension of tourism policy was further strengthened in England with the introduction in 1974 of tourism growth projects (Heeley 1981). It was during the 1970s and 1980s that regional tourist boards became important in administering financial aid schemes.

Further reviews of the tourist industry have stressed not only its potential in regional development, but have also given more weight to its role in job creation. In terms of the latter aspect, particular attention was given in the 1980s to the development of tourism to aid in urban regeneration (English Tourist Board 1981, 1989b). Of increased concern more recently has been the plight of more traditional tourism areas, in particular the fate of traditional coastal resorts (Shaw and Williams 1997b). The responsibility for tourism initiatives has, to some extent, shifted away from the national state, reflecting wider processes of 'hollowing out' (Jessop 1995) in the forms of governance. While the EU does not have a separate 'title' for tourism, it does fund a number of significant tourism projects in the UK, especially through the structural funds. Local authorities and various forms of local partnerships have also played an increasingly significant role in tourism development, as is evident in the case of cities such as Manchester, Liverpool, Bradford and Wigan (Law 1994).

Whilst there is considerable enthusiasm to reap the political and economic benefits offered by tourism, any such strategies face numerous problems. Many changes tend to be induced by factors outside the direct control of both the state and the industry, for example, the value of sterling, the cost of oil, political and industrial unrest, and variations in the weather. Government policy is also strongly conditioned by the fact that much of the tourist industry is under the direct control of the private sector. Consequently, the relationship between public concern and the actions of individual tourism capitals is at best one of loose co-operation between the various sub-sectors. Indeed, government policy is somewhat fragmented and uncertain in its detailed aims.

This chapter seeks to explore some of these features by considering a number of broad interrelated themes. We start by presenting an analysis of the changing trends in the tourist industry, by drawing on a wide range of published statistics. This is followed by an examination of market responses to changed levels of demand and competition. Attention is then focused more closely on the nature of these changes in terms of holiday environments. Finally, the chapter concludes by considering the changing nature and role of public policy.

9.2   General trends

9.2.1   Domestic and foreign travel

Historically, domestic tourism received its first real stimulus from the government with the passing of the Holiday Pay Act in 1935, which gave workers one week's paid holiday every year. Its main impact came, however, in the post-war period with the subsequent growth to two, and then three weeks' paid holiday, which saw the annual seaside break become a national institution during the 1950s (British Tourist Authority 1972; Walvin 1978). By 1970, some 20 per cent of workers had four weeks' paid holiday per annum, and by 1980, 80 per cent enjoyed this amount, while 55 per cent of all workers received up to five weeks. By 1995 the average number of paid holiday entitlement had risen to just over five weeks, whilst 10 per cent had six weeks or more (HMSO 1997). Given this clear trend of increasing leisure time and, in many cases, associated disposable income (linked to social polarisation in the 1980s), it can be strongly argued that the British domestic tourist industry has not benefited to the extent that might have been expected from the potential increase in demand.

There is general agreement that a number of factors have led to a complex series of changes in the British holiday market during the last 30 years. Of particular importance has been the growth of foreign package holidays, partly at the increasing expense of traditional domestic seaside holidays, and this has been driven both by cultural changes in the social construction of the tourist gaze and by the economies of inclusive tours. In the critical decade 1978–1988 some 39 million nights were lost at British coastal resorts, which for small resorts represented half of their main market (Cooper 1997).

The domestic market has also increased in complexity because of the development of self-catering holiday accommodation and an increase in the frequency of holiday breaks. This latter trend is related to changes in the duration of breaks and the relative growth in the short-stay market. Another significant change is the increase in business tourism, part of which is related to conference travel. Indeed, business tourism is the third most important reason for domestic trips, accounting for 12 per cent of these and 15 per cent of spend in 1995. In addition, Law (1992) has estimated that in 1990 there were some 700,000 conferences, a figure that includes large international meetings. Such conference tourism accounts for around 13 per cent of all business trips, although it is significant that the big boom in business tourism predicted in the 1980s has not fully materialised. For example, the number of business trips fell from 20 million in 1988 to 12.5 million in 1994, but levels of expenditure rose from £1,925 million to £2,235 million over the same period (British Tourist Authority 1996).

The UK is currently a net sender of international visitors rather than a net recipient, a position that has increasingly prevailed over the last 30 years (Figure 9.1). The year 1977 marks an interesting exception to this trend, partly because it was Silver Jubilee year, which re-emphasised the importance of cultural tourism, and also because the previous summer was one of the hottest on record, with 1977 also being a good summer. This stresses the importance of perceptions of the weather to domestic tourism, a feature confirmed in research conducted in the early 1980s among those who had taken a holiday abroad; significantly, more than half agreed with the statement that 'the main reason I go abroad for holidays is the weather in Britain' (Mintel 1985a, p. 83). As countless studies have shown, there is an increasing trend of holidaying abroad, from 3 per cent of the population in the immediate post-war period to 30 per cent by 1988 and, as Seaton (1992, p. 108) argues, there is 'profound socio-economic bias'. The picture is, however, complex in that whilst a greater proportion of those from social groups 'ABC1' holiday abroad, they are also more likely to take short breaks in the UK. Moreover, those in social groups 'C2DE' are more likely to travel abroad on package tours to mass tourism destinations. As Figure 9.1 shows, the trend for UK residents holidaying abroad continues to increase, and is only slowed down momentarily by economic recessions.

The main motivations for influencing foreign tourists visiting the UK are cultural and historical experiences, and the attractiveness of the British countryside. Foreign

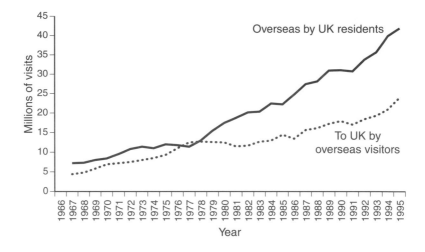

Fig. 9.1   The number of visits to and from the UK, 1966–1995

visitors to the UK have been increasing, although growth rates have fluctuated and slowed down during the 1980s. Figure 9.1 shows that rates have again increased in the 1990s, with just over 24 million overseas visitors in 1995. To holiday in the UK accounts for the main purpose of visit for just under half of all foreign visitors, with business visits and visits to friends and relatives accounting for one-fifth each. Overall, the UK's share of the world tourism market has declined in relative terms, falling by nearly a quarter, from 5.6 per cent to 4.3 per cent between 1980 and 1993. Tourism throughout the world is growing rapidly whilst the UK is failing to keep pace with an annual growth rate of only 6 per cent compared with an EU average of 8 per cent. International receipts from foreign visitors to the UK grew by 9.4 per cent between 1984 and 1994, compared to an 11.9 per cent world-wide average. British Tourist Authority (1997) forecasts suggest an average annual growth at 5.3 per cent in the numbers of overseas visitors to the UK, with spend increasing on average by 9.5 per cent per annum between 1995 and 2000. These forecasts also predict an increase in visits abroad by UK residents by at least an average of 4 per cent per annum over the same time period. National government recognition of these problems has been slow and limited to restoring London to a prime destination for first time visitors to Europe. In the document 'Competing with the Best' (Department of National Heritage 1995), the emphasis was laid on increasing standards in Britain's hotels as well as allocating an extra £4 million to promote London overseas: neither measure is particularly ambitious, and funding remains highly constrained.

As Table 9.1 shows, there are some positive seasonality aspects to foreign visits to the UK, in that they are far less temporally concentrated than visits abroad by UK residents. Furthermore, recent years have witnessed a trend towards a less seasonal pattern of foreign visitors. On the debit side, however, the highest ratios of Britons going abroad to foreign visits to the UK tend to occur in the months of June and September, potentially vital months for the domestic tourist industry. It is also worth noting that overseas visitors in the UK are spatially concentrated in a few sites, such as London and other historic cities, with few visiting traditional coastal resorts. This in

Table 9.1 Seasonality of foreign visits to the UK and visits abroad by UK residents

Month	Foreign visits to UK	Visits abroad by UK residents
January	1230	2055
February	1071	2135
March	1587	2639
April	1684	3015
May	1745	3350
June	1898	4145
July	2366	4183
August	2584	5142
September	2022	4646
October	1822	4066
November	1549	2405
December	1478	2115

Source: International Passenger Survey.

turn raises questions about the need to attract such tourists to a range of destination areas, as well as the failure of the UK tourist industry to appeal to its own domestic market.

9.2.2 *Structural and spatial change in the domestic market*

The domestic tourism market has been in fluctuating decline since the mid-1970s. For example, between 1976 and 1986 the number of domestic holidays fell by 8 per cent, whilst spending declined by 43 per cent (British Tourist Authority 1987). As Figure 9.2 shows, trends in domestic tourism are unclear, since all indicators show signs of fluctuation. This may in part be due to changes in methods of data collection by various surveys, although this would not account for all the variations. It is more likely that the market is extremely volatile and that tourist behaviour is more complex than can be readily identified from simple time-series data. This complexity is bound up with the shift to post-modern forms of consumption, with increased amounts of consumer preferences, market segmentation and what Urry (1995, p. 149) terms 'de-differentiation'. These trends also mask important differential rates of change in terms of holiday type and destination area. Of particular note are the changes in holiday tourism and the changing trends in short (1–3 nights) and long (4 or more nights) stay holidays. Since the 1970s there has been a dramatic fall in the number and value of long-stay holidays. Thus, total domestic spending on traditional, long-stay holidays declined by 48 per cent between 1976 and 1986. Such trends have been continued over the last decade, as in 1986 long holidays still accounted for 78 per cent of the total spend on domestic holidays, but by 1995 the figure was down to 72 per cent (Table 9.2). The nature of the overall decline is also indicated by the fall in the total number of nights between 1986 and 1995; these fell from 360 million to 302 million.

Set against these changes has been a growth in the value of 'short break' holidays and, to a smaller extent, business tourism. In terms of the former, the British Tourist Authority (1987) has sought to highlight the 'short break' market as distinct from

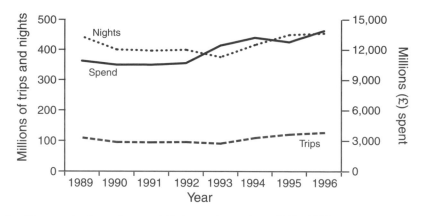

Fig. 9.2   Changes in the volume of all domestic tourism, 1989–1995

Table 9.2   Domestic holiday tourism nights in the UK (percentage, short- and long-stay), 1986–1995

	Trips (%)		Nights (%)		Spend (£)	
	1986	1995	1986	1995	1986	1995
Short-stay	45	67	18	22	22	28
Long-stay	55	23	82	78	78	72
Total (millions)	71	99.1	360	302.1	4250	8920

Sources: British Tourism Survey, 1987; Tourism Intelligence Quarterly 2 1996/7.

short-stay holidays. In their studies, 'short breaks' are defined as 'holidays of 1 to 3 nights by British residents in hotels and guest houses' (British Tourist Authority 1987, p. 1). These differ from the standard short-stay holidays in that they only include tourists who stay in commercial accommodation; in contrast, three-quarters of short-stay holidays are spent in non-commercial accommodation, particularly the homes of friends and relatives. If we accept these differences, and there are problems with them, then it is possible to isolate a strong growth trend. Thus, between 1976 and 1986 spending on short breaks increased by 106 per cent, whilst numbers grew by 60 per cent. Unfortunately, it is difficult to trace this market segment in many of the recent statistics on UK tourism but it is known that the sector is still buoyant. More significantly, it is possible to identify distinct characteristics of the 'short break' tourists and their destinations. As Table 9.3 shows they are heavily drawn from professional and managerial workers and tend to be middle-aged.

The decline in holiday tourism, especially the long-stay holiday market, and the growth of short breaks, and business tourism have had important geographical implications for the distribution of tourism in different parts of the UK (Figure 9.3). Thus, the fall in the numbers of long-stay holidays has greatly impacted on traditional holiday regions such as the West Country (especially Cornwall and Devon) and Wales. One of the most notable trends since the early 1970s has been the decline of trips, nights and spend in the West Country region and also in Wales. Other traditional

Table 9.3   Socio-economic characteristics of the 'short break' market
in the UK

Social groups	Percentage distribution		
	Short breaks	All holidays	Population
AB	33	26	17
C1	28	28	22
C2	29	26	30
DE	11	21	31

Source: BTA/ETB 1987.

resort regions such as Southern England, East Anglia and Yorkshire/Humberside have
also experienced decline, although of a less severe nature (Figure 9.3). The reasons for
this are related to broad changes in holiday and business tourism, as well as
competition from overseas tourism. This latter factor hit the West Country particularly
hard, since its main market for domestic tourists is London and the South-East, which
experienced a 12 per cent increase in people taking foreign holidays. The traditional
holiday regions have also been vulnerable in the economic recessions of the mid-1970s
and early 1980s, which led to further declines in the long-stay holiday market. In
contrast, the growth in the demand for 'short break' holidays has stimulated a wider
range of destination areas, including small towns, rural areas and coastal resorts. Given
the nature of these holidays and the relatively short distances travelled, not all regions
have benefited. Indeed, resorts in the far South-West of England have tended to
receive few of these visitors. This is compounded by the extremely high level of
polarisation of foreign tourists in London and the South-East, so that, overall, tourism
trends have favoured the richer regions in the UK (Williams and Shaw 1995).

9.3   Structural changes in the tourism industry

9.3.1   Changes in tourism employment

As discussed earlier, tourism's role in job creation has become increasingly important
in the post industrial UK economy. Hudson and Townsend (1993, p. 49) argue that
there are definite relationships between 'the changing class structure of the UK
population and the UK's place in the international division of labour, both in general
and more specifically with respect to tourism'. Such ideas are more fully developed by
Urry (1990, 1995), in which the 'tourist gaze can be focused on almost any type or
form of place. In this sense, as Urry (1995, p. 1) suggests, 'places are increasingly being
restructured as centres for consumption'. Such processes are at the heart of the growth
of tourism- and leisure-related jobs, as well as fundamentally reshaping the geography
of tourism employment.

Employment in tourism-related industries has shown strong growth trends during
the 1990s, and in many ways these have been a continuation of the trends recognised
during the 1980s (Hudson and Townsend 1993). As Table 9.4 demonstrates, total
employment in tourism-related activities has grown from a total of 1.502 million jobs
in 1991 to 1.548 million by 1995, with the largest increases being recorded in the
hotel and tourist accommodation sector along with restaurants and cafes. As always,

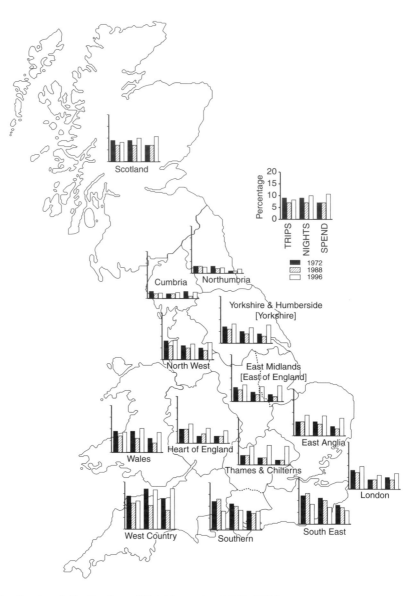

Fig. 9.3   Regional distribution of British tourist, 1972–1996

concern is expressed over the quality of jobs in tourism, in that many may be low-paid, part-time or seasonal (Williams and Shaw 1988). Patterns are changing, especially with the growth of less seasonally-based urban tourism, although it still remained the case in the late 1980s that in seaside resorts seasonality demands accounted for as much as 70 per cent of employment (Ball 1989).

Much of the labour force flexibility has traditionally been provided by female workers who have occupied seasonal and part-time positions. Thus, in 1989, female

Table 9.4   Employment in tourism-related industries in the UK, June 1991–June 1995

	Persons in employment (thousands)					June 1991–June 1995: percentage change
	June 1991	June 1992	June 1993	June 1994	June 1995	
Hotels and other tourist accommodation	307.9	311.0	322.0	322.0	343.9	+12
Restaurants, cafés, etc.	297.7	303.0	298.0	313.1	337.2	+13
Bars, public houses and night clubs	435.0	414.2	370.6	358.2	383.5	−12
Travel agencies and tour operators	69.7	69.2	69.3	71.9	75.2	+8
Libraries, museums and other cultural activities	75.6	74.8	75.6	78.5	83.4	+10
Sport and other recreation activities	316.5	320.8	316.5	316.5	324.8	+3
Total	1,502.4	1,493.0	1,447.6	1,460.2	1,548.0	+3

Source: Central Statistical Office.

part-time workers accounted for the largest part of the workforce, some 36.7 per cent. Overall, by 1995 females made up some 58.9 per cent of the total workforce in tourism-related industries compared with 53.8 per cent in 1989. Such an increase is most probably the product of at least two linked key trends. First, there has been a feminisation of the UK labour force in general and, second, competitive tendencies have led to the growth of part-time rather than full-time jobs.

The growth in tourism-related employment is also reflected at a regional level, although detailed analysis is difficult from published statistics. The London region accounted for the largest proportion of all tourism jobs as Table 9.5 shows. Interestingly, this area has also shown the lowest growth rate in employment between 1984 and 1991. By contrast, over the same time period the Southern and West Country Tourist Board regions have seen the fastest rates of growth, along with Wales. Indeed, the West Country accounted for 22 per cent of spend by domestic tourists, and in counties such as Cornwall and Devon tourism is a major economic activity, contributing an estimated 25 per cent and 14 per cent of GDP respectively (Tourism Research Group 1996). More detailed spatial analysis by Champion and Townsend (1990) for the period 1981–1989 reveals the full extent of employment changes. Their analysis showed that the fastest rates of job growth were to be found in urban areas, especially industrial areas, as well as more remote, rural environments. In resort and seaside areas, whilst all tourism-related jobs did show an increase, those in the accommodation sector declined by 3.1 per cent between 1981 and 1989. This in part is a measure of the decline in many traditional resort areas and the shifting investments taking place within visitor accommodation of all types.

9.3.2   Changes in the tourism accommodation sector

The holiday accommodation sector accounts for well over one-third of all tourist expenditure in the UK. However, as Table 9.6 shows, this sector is extremely diverse and has undergone many demand changes since the early 1970s. Over time the licensed hotel has experienced an increase in its share of the market, whilst the guest

Table 9.5   Employment in tourism-related industries in the UK (by region), 1984 and 1991

Region	Persons in employment (thousands)				1984–1991 percentage change
	1984		1991		
Cumbria	14.2	1.2	18.0	1.2	+27
Northumbria	57.4	4.7	65.1	4.4	+13
North West	154.1	12.7	174.2	11.7	+13
Yorkshire and Humberside	103.0	8.5	128.6	8.7	+25
Heart of England	106.8	8.8	136.9	9.2	+28
East Midlands	67.7	5.6	88.4	6.0	+31
East Anglia[1]					
London	188.5	15.5	203.9	13.8	+8
West Country[1]	79.4	6.5	107.0	7.2	+35
Southern[1]	87.2	7.2	121.8	8.2	+40
South East	74.2	6.1	92.3	6.2	+24
Scotland	131.8	10.9	156.2	10.5	+19
Wales	56.5	4.7	79.3	5.3	+40
Total	1,213.5	100.0	1,482.9	100.00	+22

Source: Central Statistical Office.

Note: Figures exclude Northern Ireland. Figures are rounded, so that component figures may not add up to totals/100%.
[1] West Country excludes Dorset. Southern includes figures for the whole of Dorset. The figures for the former Thames and Chilterns region have been reallocated as appropriate to East Anglia and Southern. In all other respects the regional definitions reflect the boundaries of the Regional Tourist Boards in these years.

Table 9.6   Percentage changes in long-stay holiday accommodation in the UK, 1974, 1984 and 1994

Type	1974	1984	1994
Licensed hotel	14	21	20
Unlicensed hotel and guesthouse	12	8	7
Caravan	21	20	22
Rented	11	10	12
Holiday camp/village	6	7	8
Camping	8	6	5
Paying guest	2	2	2
Friends/relatives	27	24	21

Source: British National Travel Survey.

house has declined in terms of both the proportion of nights and expenditure (Table 9.6). This part of the accommodation sector is highly polarised, a trend that is increasing as the market share of larger hotels is growing. Such a trend is long-established (Stallinbrass 1980); between 1951 and 1971 there was a 5–10 per cent increase in the number of hotel bedrooms in the UK, but also a 40–50 per cent reduction in hotels and guest houses. Stallinbrass (1980) also estimated that by the 1970s, whilst 90 per cent of hotels were still relatively small and independently owned,

Table 9.7   The top twenty largest hotel companies in the UK

Rank	Company	Rooms	Hotels
1	Forte Hotels	26,628	248
2	Mount Charlotte Thistle Hotels	14,126	108
3	Queens Moat Houses	10,430	102
4	Hilton International	7,176	35
5	Swallow Hotels	4,288	34
6	Whitbread Group of Hotels	4,028	83
7	Stakis Hotels	3,742	30
8	Forte Travelodge	3,214	92
9	Rank Hotels	3,202	22
10	Holiday Inn Worldwide	3,152	18
11	Imperial London Hotels	3,031	7
12	De Vere Hotels	3,001	26
13	Scott's Hotels	2,858	15
14	Jarvis Hotels	2,750	33
15	Coast & Country Hotels	2,626	31
16	Novotel	2,499	16
17	Inter-Continental Hotels Group	2,457	6
18	Copthorne Hotels	2,430	11
19	Metropole Hotels	2,280	5
20	Friendly Hotels	2,002	19

Source: Harrison and Johnson 1992/93.

20 per cent of beds were in hotels belonging to larger groups. Estimates by the Hotel and Catering Training Company in 1992 have shown further declines in the number of rooms in affiliated hotels; these fell by 8.5 per cent since 1988 (Harrison and Johnson 1992). These represent the smaller hotels and by contrast the number of bedrooms in larger, corporate hotels grew by 12.5 per cent over the same period. As Harrison and Johnson (1992) argue, the small, unaffiliated hotels have been caught between the expansion of large, corporate hotels and the increasingly harsh, competitive economic climate of the 1980s. It is still the case, however, that the small hotels control the largest share of bedrooms; for example, in 1992 55.5 per cent of all bedrooms were in hotels with fewer than 50 rooms.

Hotel accommodation is not only becoming increasingly dominated by larger hotels, but also by larger organisations that are offering more diversified facilities. Of particular note is the growth in so-called budget hotels as customers have branded down during economic recessions. Furthermore, intense competition has led to many mergers and the creation of larger group organisations. Such competition has also produced a rationalisation of hotels in what some organisations regard as peripheral markets, in favour of major locations. Such trends have tended to be detrimental to many traditional coastal resorts as new hotels have tended to be constructed in larger cities and are mostly absent from centres of mass leisure tourism (Williams 1995). The large hotel organisations shown in Table 9.7 have considerable competitive advantages, with identifiable brand images and the benefits of economies of scale in purchasing and marketing. Surveys in both the British business and pleasure markets have confirmed the importance of recognisable branding and have shown that 60 per cent of guests confirm the influence of branding in their choice of hotel (Tarrant 1989). In addition,

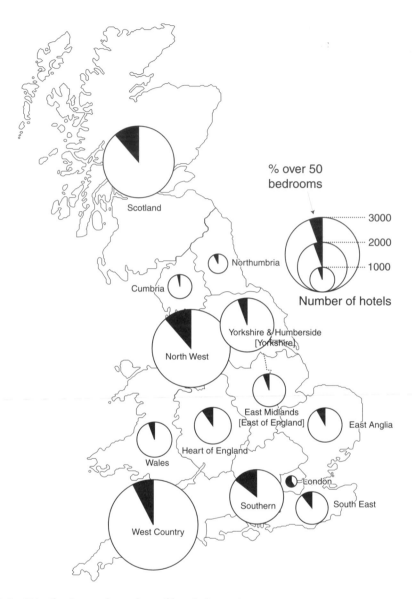

Fig. 9.4   Distribution and number of hotels by region

large hotel organisations are favourably positioned to gain access to capital from bank loans or rights issues.

Obtaining an accurate picture of the number of hotels in the UK is difficult, as there is no compulsory registration scheme and the various tourist board statistics only refer to those that agree to abide by their codes of conduct (British Tourist Authority 1995, p. 89). The hotel data contained in Figure 9.4 is therefore an underestimate of the two numbers, but nevertheless gives some indication of the size distribution of hotels at a regional level. From this we can see that large proportions of small hotels, i.e. less than 10 bedrooms, are concentrated in the main holiday regions such as the West Country.

Other significant changes in accommodation relate to self-catering. This expanded rapidly in the 1970s, and in 1973 camping, caravan holidays and rented accommodation accounted for 27 per cent of tourism spend. Parts of this sector have declined since the 1970s, especially camping, which in 1995 only accounted for 4 per cent of all trips and a mere 3 per cent of spend. Like the hotel sector, self-catering accommodation is experiencing increased trends towards polarisation and internationalisation. Both have become particularly prominent since the mid-1980s, with the English Tourist Board recording 18 new, large self-catering developments, each of which cost over £0.5 million, up to 1989 (English Tourist Board 1989). The earliest significant investments have been the Center Parc holiday villages at Sherwood Forest, Elveden Forest and Longleat Forest. These represent the application of a continental concept and international capital to the building of year-round, environmentally controlled holiday villages. The target market for these developments is the 'ABC1' socio-economic groups, that is, middle-class visitors, usually in family units, between the ages of 25–50. The turnover of the group has increased from £295.1 million in 1991 to £365.5 million in 1995. Since 1992 the group has been controlled by the UK-based brewing, leisure and retail group, Scottish and Newcastle plc (Horner and Swarbrooke 1996). Developments like Center Parc have had two important impacts on the self-catering holiday market. First, they have forced many of the traditional operators to re-examine their products, which has resulted in some major refurbishments taking place amongst the larger organisations. For example, Butlins embarked on a large-scale re-investment programme involving the expenditure of some £130 million on many of their existing holiday centres. The second reaction has been the establishment of new holiday centres directly copying the Center Parc features. One of the largest of these ventures is that by the Granada Group plc and John Laing plc, who announced in 1989 a £500 million joint venture to develop at least five Lakewood holiday villages.

The fragmented nature of the accommodation sector, together with an inadequate system of data collection, make it impossible to gain exact figures on the total number of units. Estimates suggest that in England alone there are some 240,500 self-catering units (Parnell Kerr Forster Associates 1986). In terms of hotels, their regional distribution is highly uneven and London dominates with 20 per cent of bed-spaces, followed by the major holiday region, the West Country, with around 18.6 per cent of bedspaces and up to one-third of all self-catering establishments.

9.3.3   Changing holiday environments

The long-term shifts in the demand for domestic holidays has impacted on holiday areas. In particular, there has been a marked decline in the attractiveness of traditional coastal resorts. Since the mid-1970s these environments have been in decline, and a number of reports have finally given official recognition, at least in terms of the tourist boards, to such problem resorts (see, for example, Association of District Councils 1993; English Tourist Board 1991a; and, for a general overview, Shaw and Williams 1997b). The reasons for decline have been well documented. The traditional long-stay holiday has declined in volume in the face of increased market segmentation, greater competition and higher standards demanded by tourists. Greater competition from newer, overseas destinations has stimulated greater expectations amongst tourists and there has been a shift away from traditional bed and breakfast accommodation and lower-standard hotels, towards better-equipped serviced and self-catering units. Much of the seaside infrastructure is over 100 years old and in need of replacement or renovation. However, the smaller to medium-sized resorts have only limited access to investment capital. There is therefore a shortage of investment that is further hindered by the dominance of small firm economies in those resorts (Shaw and Williams 1997b). The combination of a lack of private and local authority investment has increasingly created a 'down-market' image and poor physical environment in many seaside resorts.

In economic terms the scale of decline is illustrated by levels of average bed-space occupancy in hotels within English resorts, which fell from 37 per cent in 1980 to 33 per cent in 1993. Increasingly, many of the holidaymakers who stay in coastal resorts are drawn from the lower socio-economic groups C2DE, who have less spending power. For example, in 1995 37 per cent of all those in social class DE visited seaside resorts compared with 22 per cent in class AB. There is also an increasing number of day visitors who contribute little to the main parts of the resort economy. The loss of staying visitors has been most strongly felt in the smaller resorts, which are estimated to have lost at least half of their staying market during the last 20 years (English Tourist Board 1991a).

It is still the case, however, that seaside resorts remain the mainstay of the British domestic market. It is estimated that such resorts attracted some 24.5 million overnight visitors in 1994, together with a further 110 million day visitors, and that they accounted for 22 per cent of the UK market, creating between 150,000–300,000 jobs (English Tourist Board 1995). Such demand is uneven and a small number of large resorts account for much of the market. Blackpool in north-west England is the market leader, and it had an estimated 4.2 million staying visitors in 1993.

A major growth point in the domestic market has been short breaks. Such trends, together with a widening of tourist interests, have seen more development in inland centres, either countryside-based, often focused on old spa towns, or established historic centres such as Bath, Edinburgh and York. Added to this group are new tourist environments based around older industrial cities such as Bradford, Glasgow and Manchester (Law 1994). Following on the successes of these places, many other towns and cities have initiated schemes based on attracting visitors. Many of these have been responding to the selective growth of 'short break' holidays, especially out-of-season trips. Older established tourist centres, like Edinburgh, play key roles in attracting visitors. Thus, Edinburgh accounts for almost 20 per cent of all tourism expenditure in Scotland and attracts nearly 50 per cent of the country's overseas visitors. Substantial investment during the 1990s has demonstrated the commitment to the city's tourist industry that directly contributes an estimated £692,000 to the local income (Parlett, Fletcher and Cooper 1995). In contrast, Glasgow, which is making a strong effort to develop as a tourist destination, saw initial success in the late 1980s, culminating in it being the European City of Culture in 1990. Since that time the number of visitor trips has fallen sharply, 44 per cent between 1988 and 1992 (van der Berg *et al.* 1995). Such trends show the potential difficulties in urban tourism within the UK, in that it is a highly competitive market and to remain successful urban centres of all types must continually reinvest in their tourism product.

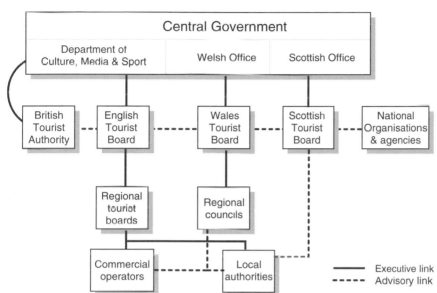

Fig. 9.5   The administrative framework of British tourism planning

9.4   Public policy and governance

9.4.1   *The administrative framework*

It is an often repeated dictum that government policy towards tourism in the UK is at best nebulous, in the sense that little official policy actually exists save to emphasise that tourism is a 'good thing'. On the whole, effective policy-making in UK tourism is left to sub-state agencies which, in other fields of interest, would only be charged with the task of policy implementation. However, given that policy is frequently made during the implementation process, it may well be that policy-making in tourism is really little different from that in other, supposedly rational, policy fields (Ham and Hill 1985).

Mention has already been made of the 1969 Development of Tourism Act, which established the statutory framework of the various tourist boards (Figure 9.5). It was an exercise more incrementalist than innovatory, given that the Northern Ireland Tourist Board had been established some 21 years previously. Given that almost all tourism enterprise is currently in the private sector or (for attracters) the voluntary sector, and that most public sector tourism policy is delegated to sub-state agencies, such as the British Tourist Authority, UK tourism initiatives tend to be distinctly corporatist in nature. Tourism policy analysis, then, is highly amenable to the three-dimensional model of policy analysis suggested by Ham and Hill (1985), in the sense of considering the micro-level of decision-making within organisations, the middle-range analysis of policy formulation, and the macro analysis of political systems.

Table 9.8 Economic considerations leading to public sector involvement in UK tourism

- Improve the balance of payments
- Foster regional development
- Diversification of the national economy
- Increase public revenue
- Improve income levels
- Create new employment

We have argued elsewhere that the relationship between public concern and commercial activity is, at best, one of a loose co-operation between the tourist boards and private operators (Shaw *et al.* 1987). At a local level, often the result is conflict between the demands of private capital accumulation and the contingencies of the requirements of local authorities to discharge their statutory duties in economic, social and environmental terms. In addition, when the policy model is readjusted to interpret the British Tourist Authority as 'the state' for the purposes of public tourism policy, conflict arises out of frustration of the failure of policy outcomes to match the desires of policy initiatives. Much of the frustration is often vented by policy officials towards the small, private sector operator who is the characteristic figure of the UK tourism industry. Such frustration often arises from a failure to consider policy initiatives in terms which take account of the contingencies of these operators; for example, it has long been the policy of national and regional tourist boards to extend the tourist season, especially into the so-called 'shoulder months' of early and late season. In many traditional holiday areas such policy has not been particularly successful, largely because the fragmented nature of the industry militates against co-ordinated initiatives divorced from the interests of other agencies. For example, if accommodation units in a resort close in October, little encouragement exists for the shopkeepers in that resort to remain open throughout the off-season.

Public sector involvement in tourism stems from a variety of economic factors that are listed in Table 9.8. Corporatist elements of tourism policy-making were highlighted during the 1970s by the English Tourist Board and the Trades Union Congress joint initiative to stress the importance of holidays to disadvantaged and low-income groups. In addition, policy initiatives contain environmental motivations in the context of the need to protect and conserve a whole range of environments. Certainly during the early 1990s such environmental issues have become more prominent in policy initiatives to manage tourism developments (English Tourist Board 1991b).

National tourism policy has undergone a series of changes in emphasis and, in part, administration. A 1974 review of tourism by the Department of Trade gave further emphasis to the economic component of the goals that influence tourism policy. It reaffirmed that the development of tourist trade could fulfil two main aims: to ease balance of payment problems and aid regional policy. Incremental initiatives followed with the identification of 'tourism growth points', in an attempt to spread development expenditure away from London into less established areas. Although these attempts were not successful—largely for political reasons (Heeley 1989)—they did help to develop a series of initiatives designed to assist capital accumulation in tourism through the provision of Tourist Development Grants, which formally introduced widespread discretionary measures into the policy process.

Reviews of tourism in the 1980s made further changes in policy emphasis, especially in the review of 1985. This reflected pressures for a more traditional, rationally modelled approach to policy-making for tourism, and it attracted widespread criticism for its limited scope in considering only the burdens and obstacles to the industry. The shift in 1986 in departmental responsibility for tourism, from the Department of Trade and Industry to the Department of Employment, reflected the hopes invested in tourism as one solution to the country's employment needs. Such a move further highlighted the neo-corporatist element of tourism policy, with emphasis being given to public sector strategies joining private sector establishments aimed at creating employment. Further changes in departmental responsibilities came with the establishment of the Department of Heritage to oversee both tourism and cultural developments. In a sense this also reflected the increased emphasis given to the whole notion of heritage in economic development during the early 1990s. The Labour Government of 1997 have made further cosmetic changes by renaming the Department of Heritage, the Department of Culture, Media and Sport. Such constant switching of responsibility for tourism is indicative of the confused nature of government policy.

9.4.2   The role of the tourist boards

The British Tourist Authority (BTA) is mainly concerned with general strategic planning for tourism and as such advises central government directly. It is particularly charged with the role of developing overseas tourism to Britain and as a consequence a considerable amount of its effort goes into overseas marketing. Funding by central government is variable and the British Tourist Authority's overall funding from all sources fell from 1 per cent of overseas visitor spend in 1969 to just 0.6 per cent in 1987, and by 1997 the figure had fallen to a mere 0.4 per cent. This is despite an extra £4 million being given to the BTA in 1995–1996 to promote London overseas. In addition, the British Tourist Authority undertakes a variety of survey work on the activities, numbers and forecasts of overseas visitors. It also provides tourism data via the long-running series of statistical digests, the *Digest of Tourist Statistics*, which incorporates the results of a number of surveys. Finally, the BTA serves as an outlet for central government's economic and regional policy, by promoting particular regions and their attractions to overseas markets.

The various national tourist boards of England, Scotland, Wales and Northern Ireland have the role of focusing the broad strategy of central government's response to tourism within their specific national contexts. For example, the English Tourist Board (ETB), since its creation, has embraced a number of long-term objectives, as shown in Table 9.9. These aims are pursued by the Board through three major strategies: marketing, the provision of information and advice; and, in the past, financial assistance.

Under the first of these the ETB has mounted a number of major marketing campaigns aimed at extending the holiday season. The ETB has also undertaken special national promotions, such as 'The English Garden' between 1979 and 1981, and 'Maritime England' during the period 1982–1985. Apart from the obvious benefits from increased tourism potential created by such schemes, they also serve to stimulate the development of tourism resources. Associated with these aims, there have been more specific marketing campaigns to promote tourism in 'development areas'. For example, in the past efforts have been made to encourage holidaymakers to visit the

Table 9.9   Major long-term objectives of the English Tourist Board[1]

- The encouragement of the general, long term economic performance of England's tourist industry
- To increase public understanding of the social, economic and cultural value of tourism
- To maintain a correct balance between tourism growth and the capacity and types of tourist facilities
- To extend the tourist season and spread the economic benefits of tourism, as appropriate, throughout the country
- To raise the standard of information, accommodation, catering and other services for tourists

[1] Not ranked in any order of priority. At the time of writing, the future of the ETB remained uncertain and it will cease to function in its present form in April 1999. It should also be noted that the Regional Tourist Boards are working more closely with the new Regional Development Agencies.

Cumbria coast, Merseyside and North Devon. More recent emphasis was also given to promoting urban tourism, through the initiatives under ETB's 'Vision for Cities' programme, launched in 1989 for a five-year period (Shaw and Williams 1994). In terms of promotional activity there are differences with Scotland and Wales in that, since 1984, these national tourist boards have been permitted to market overseas and supplement the work of the BTA.

The ETB's information-related strategies cover both the supply and demand sides of the industry. On the demand side, the ETB, together with the regional tourist boards, provide an increasingly well-developed network of tourist information centres. In terms of the provision of facilities, the ETB seeks to improve the situation through its advisory services. These include meetings with potential investors and the identification of investment opportunities in tourism as, for example, in the case of self-catering (English Tourist Board 1981a). In the past it also published a series of development opportunity portfolios in conjunction with the regional tourist boards. More recently it has been promoting the plight of coastal resorts and their needs for renewed investment (Agarwal 1997). Interestingly, one of the main recommendations to aid small seaside resorts was the establishment of a co-operative marketing and research venture between the ETB and BTA, together with support from regional tourist boards (English Tourist Board 1981b). In Scotland and Wales, similar information centres exist. Thus, the Scottish Tourist Board has a 'Visitor Services Division' aimed at enhancing the quality of the tourism product.

It is in the area of financial assistance that the greatest differences between the national tourist boards exist. Under the 1969 Act, the ETB, along with the other national boards, was allowed to give financial help to any project which provides or improves tourist amenities in England (English Tourist Board 1981b). The amounts of money available varied according to the scheme, but in England no project could receive more than 50 per cent of total costs. Between 1971 and 1980, the regional tourist boards in England approved assistance to over 1,250 schemes. Initially, the ETB's activities and overall strategy were limited compared with the increasing demands for support and the costs of major new projects. To compensate for these limitations the ETB acts as an agency for the European Investment Bank Fund for tourism projects and developments within Assisted Areas (which offers some evidence of the 'hollowing out' of the state). During the 1980s the grants scheme, or Section Four grant aid as it became known, had extra money from central government to fund improvements in tourist accommodation and visitor facilities. The result was that many more projects were approved and by 1987 some £45 million of grants had been approved. The abolition of this scheme in England during 1989 was a serious blow to tourism development at a time when competition and segmentation within tourism were increasing in the domestic market. Such burdens have been especially felt by the small to medium-sized operators.

The overall impact of support from the national tourist boards has also been further curtailed by an overall reduction in government funding. This has been particularly the case in terms of the ETB, whose government grant aid declined from £15.7 million in 1991–1992 compared to only £9.7 million for 1997–1998 (Table 9.10). By comparison, the other national tourist boards have been more generously funded and certainly receive aid at a much higher per capita take than in England.

It should also be stressed that the broad aims of the national tourist boards are placed in specific area frameworks by the activities of regional tourist boards. In the case of the ETB, despite relatively strong policy links between the national and regional boards, the latter are, in effect, autonomous administrative organisations. They draw their funds and members from the local authorities and commercial tourism operators within their area. There are 10 such regional boards throughout England and they vary considerably in their area of coverage, constitutions and internal organisations. In Wales and Scotland conditions are somewhat different. Thus, Wales has three regional councils below the national tourist board, whilst in Scotland there are 32 Area Tourist Boards together with the Highlands and Islands Development Board.

One of the most significant roles of the regional tourist boards is to offer advice to both commercial operators and local authorities on tourism planning. It is within this important area of activity that conflict often arises between national aims and local priorities. In order to meet these planning responsibilities, the regional tourist boards in England had a series of regional tourist studies commissioned on their behalf by the ETB during the 1970s. These studies collected detailed information on tourism, and have been used to draw up regional tourist strategies.

9.4.3 Area-based policies for tourism development

During the 1980s the increased importance given to tourism as a form of economic development heralded new policy initiatives by the ETB. These were based on two main ideas: to achieve effective partnerships between public and private funds, and to concentrate such resources on designated areas. The first approach was extremely ambitious and operated throughout the 1980s and early 1990s through a series of Tourism Development Action Programmes (TDAPs). The scale of these initiatives varied but they all showed some common characteristics, as Table 9.11 shows. In general, such schemes proved problematic in that the attempts to bring together a range of interested partners from the public and private sectors often produced considerable conflict. Indeed, the key to success seems to be as much to do with local personalities and their abilities to co-operate than with any problems of funding. It is also the case that some of the early TDAPs gave an over-emphasis to marketing without really exploring the characteristics of the tourist product they were selling. Rates of success also appear to be dependent on the size and scale of the TDAP. In general, as Lavery (1993) suggests, there were five main types of TDAP location, namely:

Table 9.10 Government grants and grant in aid per capita (£ millions) to national tourist boards in the UK

	1991–92	1992–93	1993–94	1994–95	1995–96	1996–97	1997–98
British Tourist Authority	29.2	30.9	32.0	33.2	34.5	35.5	34.4
GIA per capita (£)*	0.64	0.68	0.70	0.73	0.76	0.78	0.75
English Tourist Board	15.7	15.3	13.9	11.3	10.0	10.0	9.7
GIA per capita (£)*	0.41	0.40	0.36	0.29	0.26	0.26	0.25
Scottish Tourist Board	12.7	13.6	13.7	17.3	16.7	15.3	15.3
GIA per capita (£)*	3.34	3.57	3.60	4.54	4.39	4.02	4.02
Wales Tourist Board	11.3	13.7	13.8	14.2	14.2	14.2	14.2
GIA per capita (£)*	4.92	5.97	6.01	6.19	6.19	6.19	6.19
Northern Ireland Tourist Board	7.1	11.7	12.1	12.5	12.7	12.7	12.7
GI per capita (£)*	6.01	9.90	10.24	10.58	10.75	10.75	10.75

Sources: BTA, ETB, STB, NITB, Office of Population Censuses and Surveys and IPS.

Notes: 1. 1991 census of population data used for calculation of GIA per capita.
2. For calculation of grant-in-aid per capita population aged 16+ is used.
3. Scottish Tourist Board's section 4 is expected to be phased out at some time. Its grant-in-aid funding has been boosted in 1994–95 as a result of transfer of £3.3 million from the Highlands and Islands Enterprise.

* GIA per capita (£)—grant-in-aid per resident person.

Table 9.11   Main characteristics of TDAPs

1. Partnerships between public and private sectors
2. Area-based, draw on local expertise to address local needs
3. Action-orientated, emphasis on implementing initiatives rather than research and preparations of strategy
4. Comprehensive and integrated, include information, marketing, and training initiatives
5. Corporate in approach, involve the sharing of objectives and work programmes between organisations
6. Fixed period, usually 3 years
7. Concept based on pump-priming initiatives which can develop sufficient momentum to progress and become self-sustaining

Source: modified from Lavery 1993.

- Traditional seaside resorts; Torquay, Weymouth Weston-super-Mare.
- 'Heritage' towns; Norwich, Lancaster.
- Larger industrial/maritime centres; Bristol, Portsmouth.
- Rural areas; Exmoor.
- Rural resort regions; Cornwall, Isle of Wight.

Since the early 1990s English Tourist Board has given much more emphasis to local area initiatives (LAIs) which, like TDAPs involve partnerships between local expertise and private sector companies. The emphasis is therefore the same but the focus is much more on individual resorts, together with a greater concentration on economic development and employment (Agarwal 1997). Such area based policies have been focused much more on the needs of seaside resorts and between 1991 and 1993 some six resorts were identified for LAIs.

Tourism has also been included as the basis of economic regeneration in strategic programmes funded by both the Urban Challenge and Rural Challenge programmes. These programmes have also attracted EU structural funds (Pearce 1992b). The significant public funding attracted through these channels, which has often generated significant private capital investment, stands in stark contrast to the limited national and EU funding available for tourism *per se*. This seems to underline the continuing 'Cinderella' status of tourism policies in the UK. Tourism and tourism interests are narrowly institutionalised (Greenwood 1993) and so are not strongly embedded into the UK framework of governance. Despite its clear economic significance it too often remains an afterthought rather than being central to national and regional economic strategies.

9.5   Conclusions

The UK tourism scene is one which, in common with many other European countries, has changed considerably in the post-war period. The basic package to the overseas visitor appears an attractive one and despite increased competition there is scope for optimism that, given political backing and a concentration of resources, this sector of the market could continue to do well. In contrast, the domestic market is far more problematic and the future for many small coastal resorts remains uncertain. Structural changes in tourism demand and the competition from foreign destinations have taken a heavy toll on many UK resorts. The rise of specialist holiday centres based on 'short breaks' together with some increases in conference-based trips, has stimulated other parts of the domestic market. However, in many cases such trends have only served to emphasise the plight of the traditional resorts dependent on the declining long-stay holiday. In this sense the geography of UK tourism is undergoing profound changes as demand becomes more segmented and investment reacts to such trends.

In the present rush to cater for the overseas visitor market, the tourist industry would do well not to forget the pressing problems of the domestic market. These are essentially related to an outdated industry geared to historic patterns of holiday-taking based on resorts that lack high-level investment in new facilities. Furthermore, despite creation of a framework for tourism policy and planning, these have been poorly institutionalised, under-funded and generally ineffective in the face of the enormous changes which have occurred in tourism practices.

10 Republic of Ireland: an expanding tourism sector

Desmond A. Gillmor

10.1 Introduction

Tourism had been a significant sector of the economy in the Republic of Ireland for decades but it experienced unprecedented expansion from the late 1980s. The number of visitors increased by an annual average of almost 8 per cent over the period 1986–1996, the highest rate of growth in Western Europe. Associated with this growth, tourism has assumed a greatly enhanced profile in Irish affairs as its expansion has impacted on many aspects of the economy and society. In this chapter, particular attention is given to this growth within the context of a general overview of Irish tourism since 1980.

Against a background of a previous relative dearth of publications on Irish tourism, increased interest has led to a substantial literature on the industry. In addition to academic papers and consultancy and government reports, this includes several books (Feehan 1992; O'Connor and Cronin 1993; Breathnach 1994; Kockel 1994; Convery and Flanagan 1995; Deegan and Dineen 1997). There are numerous publications each year by Bord Fáilte, the national tourism authority, and statistics from this source have been used extensively throughout this chapter. Page (1994) provides a general review of the literature on Irish tourism.

10.2 Tourist attractions and barriers

In assessing the tourism appeal of Ireland, the initial consideration is the main purpose of visit for overseas tourists (Table 10.1). As many as 23 per cent of visitors in 1995 came primarily to visit friends and relatives (VFR), this proportion having declined from 29 per cent in 1990 as tourism in general expanded. This large VFR traffic reflects in part the extent to which Ireland has been a source of emigration. In the twentieth century emigration was mainly to Britain and so the ethnic component is greatest amongst British visitors. Emigration to mainland Europe has been largely a feature of recent decades and, correspondingly, the number of ethnic visitors from that source has increased substantially. Business and conference traffic has grown in line with the general expansion of that type of travel, as well as the development of the

Tourism and Economic Development: European Experiences, 3rd Edition. Edited by A.M. Williams and G. Shaw.
© 1998 John Wiley & Sons Ltd.

Table 10.1   Main purposes for visiting Ireland by overseas tourists, 1995 (%)

Purpose	British	Mainland European	North American	All tourists
Holiday	32	50	63	42
Visiting friends or relatives	30	12	16	23
Business or conference	24	20	13	21
Other reasons	14	18	8	14

Source: based on Bord Fáilte data.

Irish economy in recent decades. The lesser role of this purpose of visit amongst North American travellers reflects greater economic orientation towards Europe, where there has also been a relative shift from Britain towards mainland Europe following increasing diversification of Irish trade. Amongst personal and other motives for visitors from mainland Europe, study predominates, accounting for 11 per cent of all reasons in 1995; this was mainly young people coming to Ireland to learn the English language. While holidaying was the principal purpose for visiting Ireland from all three main markets, the role of this factor was twice as great for North American visitors as for British tourists.

For overseas visitors whose main purpose of visit to Ireland was holiday, apart from those born in Ireland, the motivation for choosing Ireland was explored in a survey in summer 1995 by Bord Fáilte (1996). The scenic appeal of the country was, by far, the reason given most frequently, followed by the wish to experience its culture and history, to visit a new destination, to have a relaxing holiday and to mix with local people (Table 10.2). The dominance of sightseeing was greatest amongst holiday-makers from mainland Europe, while culture and history were most important to Americans and holiday relaxation to British visitors. Interaction with the Irish people is made easy for the British and North American markets by English being the spoken language but it is facilitated also by the increasing extent to which other tourists can speak English, and by some improvement in language ability within Ireland. The opportunity to visit friends and relatives was the third main reason for choosing Ireland (13 per cent), rising to 22 per cent for British holidaymakers. Visiting the country of ancestors was the main reason for 22 per cent of the US tourists, reflecting the earlier importance of emigration to America and the fact that three-quarters of the American respondents claimed Irish ancestry. Thus, even amongst holidaymakers of non-Irish birth, the ethnic factor is important. The Irish diaspora, whereby there are an estimated 70 million people world-wide with distant Irish ancestral links, is an asset in terms of tourist attraction. Lesser but increasingly significant motivational influences were the opportunities for a range of active outdoor pursuits, such as walking, angling, golf and equestrian sports, and for engagement in a hobby or special interest. The five leading factors which respondents assessed as having been very important in considering Ireland for their holiday were: beautiful scenery, 76 per cent; friendly people, 72 per cent; easy pace of life, 58 per cent; nature/wildlife/flora etc., 50 per cent; and freedom from pollution, 43 per cent. Such data provide useful indicators of the perception of Ireland's tourism product but the holiday destination selection process is extremely complex and may not be elucidated fully by such a survey.

It is not only destination appeal but also holiday experience that is important in shaping the tourist attraction of a country. Their Irish holiday was considered to have

Table 10.2 Holidaymakers' reasons for choosing Ireland, 1995 (%)

Reason	Main reason	All reasons
Quality of sightseeing/scenery	29	66
To experience the culture and history	7	43
To discover a new destination	16	41
To have a restful/relaxing holiday	10	38
Opportunity to mix with the local people	4	38
Opportunity to visit friends/relatives	13	26
To visit the country of my/my partner's ancestors	7	18
To engage in active outdoor pursuits	4	14
To pursue a hobby or special interest	4	13
Other reasons	6	10

Source: Bord Fáilte (1996).

exceeded their expectations by 39 per cent of respondents and to have matched expectations by 55 per cent, with 69 per cent of visitors indicating that they were extremely interested or very interested in returning to Ireland for another holiday. The extent to which expectations had been exceeded was greatest with regard to the friendliness, humour and other characteristics of the Irish people (53 per cent) and to the quality of the scenery (48 per cent). These were also the advantages which respondents felt distinguished Ireland most from competing destinations, with the greatest emphasis on the people. Holiday satisfaction leads to positive feedback and the significance of this is indicated by the fact that advice from friends, relatives and business associates was considered to have been important in choosing Ireland as a holiday destination by 53 per cent of respondents, nearly three times greater than the second-ranked influence.

The tourism imagery of a country strongly influences its choice as a holiday destination and, in turn, the expectations and experiences of visitors can be used in fashioning tourism promotion. O'Connor (1993) considered that the predominant tourism imagery of Ireland has been constructed so as to offer residents of the metropolitan centres of Europe and North America an escape from the pressures of modernity to a different world where they can experience the simplicity and authenticity of the pre-modern. She identified people as being an essential ingredient in the publicity package, with emphases on representation of their welcome, friendliness, conversation, wit, quaintness, traditions, leisure and enjoyment, and with stress on the scope for the tourist to interact with them. There is emphasis on the relaxed pace of life and on traditional values (Quinn 1994). The country's historical heritage and culture are also highlighted. Picturesque landscapes, especially of uncrowded countryside, are an essential component of the tourism imagery. Ireland has enjoyed a 'green' image based on the luxuriant colour of the countryside and to this has now been added its relatively unspoilt nature, again contrasting with the home environment of many tourists.

What was claimed to be the most dramatic marketing initiative in the history of Irish tourism, and one of the world's largest tourism marketing ventures, occurred in late 1996 when a new Tourism Brand Ireland was launched. There was a belief in the tourism administration that the basis on which development had taken place could not be expected to continue indefinitely, and that there was a need to project a more accurate representation of the modern Ireland tourism experience. Research had suggested that the essence of an Irish holiday is inextricably linked to the concept of 'emotional experience', so that the overall theme being used in the promotion of the new all-Ireland brand is 'live a different life'. This focuses on the strengths of the country in terms of its people, its warm welcome, its green environment and the range of activities which can be enjoyed by visitors. The quality of an Irish holiday is stressed, including accommodation and food. The project primarily involves the sourcing of a new bank of visual imagery for Irish tourism, extending beyond traditional stereotypical perceptions. The new strategy promotes the whole island of Ireland around the world as a single destination in brand marketing terms, and involves more integrated and focused marketing.

While the attractions of Ireland for tourists indicate the nature of its tourism product, there are also barriers to the numbers of visitors availing themselves of this. The country's island location constrains accessibility and contributes to higher transport costs. The relatively low incidence of sunshine may deter some potential visitors but it means that Ireland can offer freedom from mass beach tourism. The climate contributes also to a problem of seasonality. Ireland has few high-profile tourist attractions, it lacks the widespread appeal of places such as Paris and Rome, and potential tourists may have a bland image of the Irish tourism product. In general the country suffers from an identity problem in that, for instance, some people are unaware of its existence or do not consider it to be separate from Britain or confuse it with Iceland. For many, their clearest image of Ireland since 1969 is a negative one associated with terrorist violence and civil disturbance on their television screens. They do not realise that the Republic of Ireland has been almost free from such violence and that, even within Northern Ireland, tourists have been largely unaffected.

Holidaymakers' rating of their Irish holiday and their identification of any disadvantage of Ireland as a holiday destination focused especially on internal transport, including in particular the cost of car hire and other transport, together with poor road conditions and signposting. Other deficiencies identified were the existence of litter and pollution, unfavourable weather or climate, high costs of living and some deficiencies in food or accommodation. The 4 per cent of respondents whose holiday did not live up to their expectations mentioned a wide range of reasons, with the main disappointments relating to the people, scenery, roads, fishing and litter accounting for only 38 per cent of these. While negative reactions should be addressed, they must be seen within the context of visitors' overall favourable experience of the Irish tourism product.

10.3   Tourism policy: towards increased state interventionism

Overall control of tourism policy in the Republic of Ireland rests with a government department, the name and functions of which have varied considerably over time and the term tourism having appeared first in a departmental title in 1977. The implementation of tourism policy has been the responsibility of a semi-state organisation, Bord Fáilte (Irish Tourist Board), which has played the predominant role in the development of Irish tourism. It has had a broad range of activities, including planning, development, research and regulation, in addition to the primary functions of promotion and marketing. In the early 1990s the government began to bring policy more firmly under its own control than had been the practice previously. It also considered that private interests should play a greater part in tourism administration and development, given that the industry was now sufficiently mature to take more responsibility for its own affairs. Following a consultancy investigation in 1994, Bord Fáilte's activities have become focused more specifically on its core functions of overseas promotion and consumer marketing; various services which it had performed for the industry have been allocated to commercial suppliers and independent bodies. A separate semi-state organisation, CERT, continues to have responsibility for training for tourism, in which it has a unique co-ordinating role (Walsh 1993; Baum 1995). The main private participants in the industry are represented by the Irish Tourist Industry Confederation, which was established in 1984 to provide a more broadly based and effective organisation in this respect. Following the recommendation of the Tourism Task Force (1992), the National Tourism Council was established in 1993 to provide a forum for consultation between the tourist industry, the state tourism agencies and government departments, and to advise the minister on tourism policy.

McEniff (1991) considered the Irish government role in tourism to be relatively interventionist, perhaps in recognition of the organisational and promotional needs of a disparate industry composed almost entirely of small enterprises. Yet the attention given to tourism in government planning and policy had been minimal, particularly in contrast with the focus on agriculture and manufacturing. This changed abruptly in the late 1980s, with a new impetus seemingly coming in response to a combination of several influences. Most important perhaps was the severe economic and employment difficulties experienced by Ireland. There was rising unemployment, ultimately to about 20 per cent, and emigration was at a level which had not been reached since the national depression of the 1950s. As jobs were being lost in agriculture and manufacturing, these sectors were not seen as being able to ameliorate the problems. Tourism, with its high labour intensity and scope for export earnings, seemed to offer an obvious alternative strategy. World tourism was expanding but the Irish industry had been experiencing considerable difficulties in the 1980s and clearly needed assistance. This, and the tourism potential, were emphasised by the Irish Hotels Federation, which exerted pressure on the government prior to an election. There were also vital exogenous influences, in that other governments and the European Union were paying more attention to tourism development and there was the strong prospect of substantial financial support for tourism being available under the Structural Funding of the EU.

A report by the National Economic and Social Council (NESC 1980) had identified deficiencies in the Irish tourist industry but little had been done to address these, and budgetary allocations to the industry were falling in the 1980s. The first indication of increased government interest was the publication of a White Paper in 1985 (Government of Ireland 1985). This recognised the importance of tourism and set broad policy objectives but there was no specific plan or allocation of significant resources to the industry. It was only in 1987, in the Programme for National Recovery, that a strongly positive attitude and specific strategy for tourism were set in a national economic plan. Targets for the next five-year period were formulated which would involve doubling the number of overseas tourists, doubling the revenue from these visitors and creating an additional 25,000 jobs. These ambitious targets were a reiteration of projections made in a report commissioned by the Irish Hotels Federation (Stokes *et al.* 1986). Another influential consultancy report, which had been commissioned by the government, was by Price Waterhouse (1987). The targets set in the national plan were to be achieved through lower access fares, development of inward air charters, improved marketing and substantial investment in the tourism infrastructure and product. Bord Fáilte devised a four-part strategy for growth comprising:

1. A product strategy through stimulating the development of an extended range of tourism projects to provide more attractive holiday options.
2. A competitive strategy to provide a tourism product that would be better value in terms of both price and quality.
3. A market growth strategy through more effective promotion and extension of the range of holiday options, market areas and market segments.
4. A distribution strategy to make the product more readily and attractively available to potential customers through increasing the numbers of tour operators and their Irish holiday offerings and developing a comprehensive tourism information and reservations system.

EU Structural Funding, associated with adjustment to the Single European Market, for which the Republic of Ireland benefits from Objective 1 status, provided essential external funding for tourism development (O'Cinnéide and Walsh 1990–1991; Hurley *et al.* 1994). The national plan for tourism was approved and adopted by the EU in 1989 as The Operational Programme for Tourism 1989–1993, with application of its earlier targets and policies to the programme period (Department of Tourism and Transport 1989). Investment under the programme was IR£380 million, with 73 per cent for product development, 14 per cent for training and 13 per cent for marketing. Almost half of the funding was provided by the EU, one-third by the private sector and one-sixth from the Irish exchequer. Additionally, during the programme period, considerable tax relief on venture capital investment in tourist accommodation enterprises was granted by the Irish government as part of a Business Expansion Scheme. Development in rural areas has been funded under the EU LEADER Programme, with half of total expenditure being on tourism projects. While identifying some criticisms of the implementation of the Operational Programme, Deegan and Dineen (1997) emphasised the enormous enhancement of the Irish tourism product which had been enabled by this access to unprecedented investment funding. Breathnach *et al.* (1994), in view of the high proportion of poor-quality jobs in tourism, queried whether such large sums of EU and state finance might have achieved greater returns if allocated to other forms of development. Based on evidence from tourism managers, Hannigan (1994a) found that half the employment in grant-aided projects would have been created without the assistance, and that proportionately more of these jobs would have been full-time. With reference to the impact of tourism on the environment, Hannigan (1994b) and Meldon (1994) considered that to some extent sustainable tourism objectives were being sacrificed in favour of short-term gains and maximisation of economic benefits.

Building on the achievements of the tourism industry to 1993, a national plan for the next five years was formulated (Bord Fáilte 1994) and a second Operational Programme for Tourism for the period 1994–1999 was approved by the EU (Government of Ireland 1994). This was to be the key plank in achieving government targets of a 50 per cent growth in real terms in foreign tourism earnings, creation of up to 35,000 full-time job equivalents, relative expansion of off-peak business, and service improvement through quality training programmes. The omission of tourist numbers from the targets was in accordance with the Tourism Task Force (1992) recommendation that the primary objective of tourism development should be to maximise the value added from the optimum number of tourists. Despite this shift in emphasis, scant attention was paid to environmental impacts and there was no consideration of carrying capacity. The strategy to achieve the programme targets would concentrate on a major expansion in marketing, further product development to meet specific deficiencies, improvements in the conference, angling and cultural tourism products, and an expansion of training to cater for the anticipated employment growth. Of the projected IR£652 million, 19 per cent would be spent on natural/cultural tourism, 44 per cent on other product development, 19 per cent on marketing and 17 per cent on training. 57 per cent of the funding would be provided by the EU, mainly from the European Regional Development Fund and to a lesser extent the Social Fund, 13 per cent by the national administration and 31 per cent by the private sector. As compared with the first Operational Programme, this represented an increased emphasis on marketing and a greater contribution from the EU. The Operational Programmes underlined that in the Republic of Ireland there is now heavy reliance on public subvention as an instrument in tourism policy.

10.4   Trends in tourism: the renewal of growth

Tourism in the Republic of Ireland in 1980 was recovering gradually from the severe setback arising from the outbreak of terrorist violence in, and associated with, Northern Ireland in the previous decade (Pollard 1989). While not keeping pace with the rapid expansion of world tourism, the Irish industry had been growing steadily during the 1960s but this was brought to an abrupt end in 1969 (Gillmor 1985, 1993a). Between then and 1972 visitor numbers declined by 25 per cent. The revenue in real terms from export tourism, which had increased by half over the period 1960–1969, fell to its 1961 level. Without the ethnic visitor, who was much less affected than other holidaymakers by the fear of violence, the plight of Irish tourism would have been even worse. While violence continued, its deterrent effect on visitors lessened somewhat over time and visitor numbers increased from 1.46 million in 1972 to 2.26 million in 1980.

Despite this partial recovery, tourism in the Republic of Ireland was experiencing considerable difficulties in the early to mid-1980s. The growth in visitor numbers had been interrupted in the early years of the decade (Figure 10.1) and even by 1986 the income in real terms from external tourism was still below that of the late 1960s. An escalation of the terrorist deterrent in 1981 had an effect but other factors were also unfavourable. Economic recession in major market areas, which had retarded recovery in the mid-1970s, again impacted on tourism. As a result of substantial price inflation, the Irish Republic's tourism industry had lost competitiveness. This, combined with a reduction in Bord Fáilte's marketing budget and weaknesses in Ireland's overseas marketing, at a time of greater promotion of other destinations by their state agencies and by tour operators, affected the country's relative attractiveness to potential visitors. Diminished Irish emigration had also resulted in less return visits. These difficulties discouraged capital investment in tourism, the accommodation stock declined and the tourism product deteriorated.

Against this unfavourable background, subsequent developments in Irish tourism were quite dramatic. The number of external tourists increased from 2.47 million in

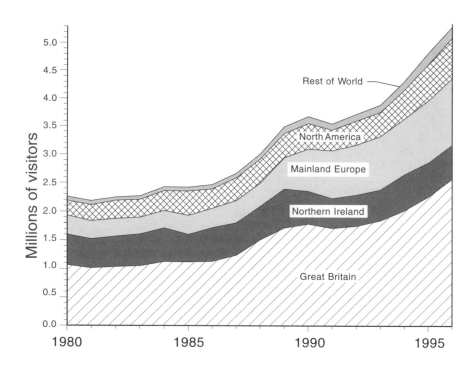

Fig. 10.1   Visitor numbers in the Republic of Ireland, 1980–1995

Source: based on Bord Fáilte data

1986 to an estimated 5.28 million in 1996, a growth of 114 per cent. The number of external visitors first exceeded the population of the Republic of Ireland in 1990. Growth was continuous except for a slight setback in 1991, when the Gulf War discouraged some long-haul travellers. Revenue in real terms doubled but it did not quite keep pace with the increase in visitor numbers.

The individual markets did not contribute equally to the growth in tourist numbers and revenue (Figure 10.1 and Table 10.3). Changes in the relative importance of the different sectors over the period 1980–1995 were, to some extent, a continuation of trends established over the preceding 20 years but at a diminished rate, leading to greater market diversification overall. The number of Northern Ireland visitors fluctuated from year to year but with little overall change, so that their relative contribution to revenue halved. Any increase in holiday-taking there was offset by the trend, shared with the rest of the UK, towards package holidays to sunshine destinations and travel to other places more distant than the Republic of Ireland. If the Northern Irish are excluded from the total numbers of external tourists, leaving only overseas visitors, the growth in the latter over the period 1986–1996 was 149 per cent. The external sector which had been most deterred by the violence was Britain, from where numbers remained static until they more than doubled between 1986 and 1996, from 1.13 million to 2.59 million. As in the period 1960–1980, however, mainland Europe was the major growth market in these years, with numbers of visitors more than trebling, from 0.34 to 1.18 million, and the contribution to external tourism revenue

Table 10.3   Market structure of external tourism revenue in Ireland, 1960–1995 (%)

Market source	1960	1980	1985	1990	1995
Northern Ireland	21	12	8	8	6
UK	58	43	35	39	37
Mainland Europe	3	21	17	29	30
North America	16	19	35	19	20
Rest of world	1	5	5	5	7
Number of tourists (millions)	1.37	2.26	2.42	3.67	4.23

Source: based on Bord Fáilte data.

increasing from 18 per cent to 30 per cent (Gillmor 1993b). Germany, France, Italy and The Netherlands accounted for 70 per cent of the mainland European market in 1996. The North American market was exceptional in that there was growth in the early 1980s, leading to a pronounced peak of 0.42 million visitors in 1985 and a 35 per cent contribution to revenue, equalling that of the UK. This performance was based largely on the strength of the dollar and vigorous marketing of Ireland in the USA to exploit this situation. If the American market had not been so buoyant in the mid-1980s, the difficulties in Irish tourism would have been even greater. Subsequently the number of North American tourists has exceeded the 1985 figure only in 1988–1989, until substantial growth in the mid-1990s. The smaller 'rest of the world' market, which is principally Australia, New Zealand and Japan, grew at a rate not far behind that of mainland Europe.

The unprecedented growth in Irish tourism from 1986 is generally attributed officially to developments in national tourism policy and capital investment under the Operational Programmes for Tourism. Undoubtedly these were important but they are not sufficient to explain the transformation. The annual investment rate increased from IR£25 million in 1987 to IR£200 million in 1992. The accommodation stock, having been declining or static, increased by 42 per cent between 1990 and 1995. The scale and quality of the Irish tourism product have been improved significantly, increasing its capacity and appeal for visitors. Much of this investment, however, would not have had an impact until the 1990s and so does not explain the growth from 1986. More important to the industry in the earlier years may have been the build-up of confidence and enhanced profile given to tourism in government strategies, together with recognition of the development of tourism in other countries.

A very important factor in the development of Irish tourism has been substantial reduction in the problem of the country's accessibility, in terms of both the reduced real cost of transport and a greater range of services. Government contributed to this through promoting deregulation of air transport from 1987 to 1988. The establishment of the private company Ryanair in 1986 provided an alternative to the state airline Aer Lingus. Through these and other companies, the level of air fares declined, especially from the UK, and new scheduled routes were developed. There has also been a major expansion in the number and range of charter flights into Ireland. These extensions have been encouraged by growing demand for holidays in Ireland and facilitated by the development of regional airports in the west of the country. Also significant was the lifting in 1994 of an Irish government requirement that all transatlantic flights on the North American route must land at Shannon Airport, a measure which had been designed primarily to protect that airport but which had discouraged some potential travellers and air companies. Faced with increasing competition from air transport, sea route operators also enhanced their services and fare structures. Improvements in road routes across the UK to ferry ports and the Channel Tunnel made Ireland more accessible to motorists from mainland Europe. An increasing proportion of the expanding tourist numbers travelled by air, rising from 47 per cent in 1983 to 63 per cent in 1995.

Changing fashions and consumer preferences can have a significant effect on tourist movement patterns but are difficult to evaluate. Undoubtedly they have had a major role in the rapid growth of Irish tourism through the extent to which Ireland has become perceived as a desirable and fashionable destination. This is related at least in part to the international popularity of Irishness, including Irish pubs, music and culture in general. Mainly in the 1990s, more than 1200 Irish pubs have been established in 40 countries, spreading the experience and reputation of Irish traditional music and conviviality. The winning and hosting of three Eurovision Song Contests in four years and, arising from that, the Riverdance phenomenon and consequent growth in international interest in Irish dancing, played their part. Rock and other music, through the international reputation of Irish groups and individuals, together with Irish literature and films, also contributed. The good behaviour and the character of Irish football fans at international tournaments and matches were another factor. All this has contributed to an international profile far greater than the country's small size alone would merit, and to widespread perception of Ireland as a desirable 'fun' place to visit. Also of increasing importance, given environmental concerns, is the perception of Ireland as a 'green' tourism destination. This has been reinforced by the health hazards associated with sun holidays and the shifts from sunlust to wanderlust tourism and towards post-modern patterns.

Other influences have contributed to Irish tourism expansion. In part, this is related to factors which account for tourism growth in general, such as greater affluence, mobility, leisure and education. Their influence had been constrained in the early to mid-1980s, so a rebound effect on subsequent release may have contributed to the rapid growth in visitor numbers. One important factor in tourism growth was that competitiveness improved greatly as inflation fell from high to very low rates. This was reflected in a decline in the proportion of visitors who considered their Irish holiday to be poor or very poor value, from highs of 41 per cent in the 1980s to 12 per cent by 1992. Another important factor, although one which has received little recognition, has been the extent of visits home by young emigrants, consequent upon the escalation in Irish emigration in the 1980s. A respite from terrorist violence in Northern Ireland in 1994–1996 encouraged some people to visit Ireland. More focused and effective marketing by Bord Fáilte, and greater involvement in and coordination of marketing by participants in the tourism industry, have also contributed to development. Deegan and Dineen (1997) reported research which suggested that demand factors in the principal overseas markets, chiefly real disposable income and relative prices in origin and destination countries, may have influenced the recent growth of Irish tourism.

10.5 Tourism in national development: the role of market segmentation

The expansion of tourism in the Republic of Ireland has resulted in the industry making a much more significant contribution to national economic and social development. Yet, as elsewhere, it is difficult to assess the contribution of tourism precisely, because of factors such as uncertainty in delimiting tourism, the extent to which its impacts are interlinked with those of other activities, data deficiencies and the different methodologies employed in measurement. Although the benefits of Irish tourism are much publicised, little research has been done relating to costs or negative impacts.

Total tourism revenue of IR£2,294 million in 1995 comprised: out-of-state tourist spending, 59.6 per cent; carrier receipts from access fares paid by visitors to Irish transport companies, 13.2 per cent; and domestic tourism expenditure, 27.3 per cent. The significance of tourism in the national economy is indicated by its 6.4 per cent contribution to gross national product (GNP) in 1995, and this compares to less than 5.0 per cent in the mid-1980s. Foreign tourism's contribution had stabilised at about 3.5 per cent in the early 1980s but from 1987 increased steadily to 4.7 per cent in 1994 (Deegan and Dineen 1997). Domestic tourism's share declined from 1.7 per cent in the early 1980s to 1.0 per cent by 1986 but subsequently recovered to 1.8 per cent. With the difficulty of tracing the direct, indirect and induced effects of international tourists' spending, a range of estimates of the tourism multiplier in Ireland has been made at different times but this is now generally accepted to be about 1.0 (Deane and Henry 1993). Of the spending by overseas tourists in Ireland, 54 per cent is on accommodation, food and drink, 18 per cent on shopping, 12 per cent on transport and 7 per cent on sightseeing and entertainment. There is a substantial yield to the exchequer through tourism tax revenue, estimated to be over 40 per cent of tourist spending and equivalent to approximately 8 per cent of all government tax revenues (Tansey *et al.* 1995).

Foreign exchange earnings from tourism amounted to 5.8 per cent of the total value of exports of goods and services from the Irish Republic in 1995. The beneficial contribution to the national balance of payments is greater than this suggests because the import content of tourist spending, estimated at 10 per cent, is much lower than that of expenditure in the economy as a whole. Moreover, leakage of revenue out of the country is further reduced by the predominantly Irish ownership of tourism facilities. Tourism accounts for over half of service exports.

Employment creation has been the major consideration in promoting the development of the Irish tourist industry. It is estimated that there were about 102,000 full-time job equivalents in tourism in 1995, accounting for 8.3 per cent of total national employment and 12 per cent of service employment. Tourism employment had increased from 56,000 in 1986, contributing nearly one-third of all new jobs created in the country over that period. More than 60 per cent of the jobs are in direct employment in servicing tourists, two-thirds of which are in the catering and transport industries, but many sectors of the economy are affected. It was estimated by CERT that there were 41,900 employed in hotels and guesthouses in 1996. As elsewhere, the benefits of tourism employment are moderated by tendencies to less than full-time jobs and comparatively low wages. The extent of temporary, seasonal and casual employment is partly related to the predominantly small scale of Irish tourism enterprises, which are often family-based. It must be recognised, however, that some of those who work in tourism on a seasonal or part-time basis would not wish for full-time employment in the industry or lack alternative employment opportunities. The bed and breakfast sector is almost exclusively dominated by women and they account for two-thirds of employment in the hotel sector, being disproportionately represented in part-time and unskilled occupations (Breathnach *et al.* 1994). The growth of the industry has led to the development of some labour shortages, especially of certain skills, and recruitment difficulties are reported.

Table 10.4   Characteristics of overseas visitors and holidaymakers in Ireland, 1995

Characteristics	Britain	Mainland Europe	North America	All overseas, 1995	All overseas, 1985
Expenditure per visit (IR£)	219	376	429	304	235
Mean number of nights spent by holidaymakers	9.5	11.6	10.5	10.5	12.4
Visitors arrived in July–August (%)	26	38	30	30	32
On package holiday (%)	19	36	37	28	14
Car hired by tourists (%)	9	21	36	17	19
Socio-economic groups of holidaymakers: managerial/ professional/white-collar (%)	68	85	88	79	74
Age (%) of visitors: <19 years	15	12	4	12	13
19–24 years	7	19	12	11	12
25–34 years	20	28	21	22	17
35–44 years	21	19	15	19	17
45+ years	37	22	48	36	40
Distribution of tourist bednights (%):					
Hotels	12	9	21	12	14
Guesthouses/B&Bs	17	17	21	17	9
Rented	7	21	13	14	8
Caravan/camping	2	5	–	3	5
Hostels	1	6	5	4	2
Friends/relatives	54	16	32	35	49
Other	7	26	8	15	12

Source: based on Bord Fáilte data.

The economic benefits of tourists vary according to their market source, as indicated by the mean expenditure per visitor (Table 10.4). Spending by British residents differs greatly from that of other visitors, being little more than half that of North American tourists. The range is even greater if Northern Ireland and the rest of the world are included, the values being IR£137 and IR£473 per visitor respectively. A significant trend has been a diminishing differential in expenditure levels between North American and mainland European visitors. Expenditure is a function of many different but interrelated characteristics of tourists and their visits, including purpose of visit, length of stay, age and socio-economic status of holidaymaker, accommodation used and the activities in which they engage. The principal influences affecting expenditure, for which comparable data are available, are shown in Table 10.4.

The briefer holidays by UK residents reflect the large ethnic component coming on short visits to friends and relatives, as well as ease of access. These characteristics influence frequency of visit, for only 25 per cent of UK holidaymakers were on their first visit to Ireland as compared with 60 per cent of North Americans and 62 per cent of mainland Europeans. That length of holiday is not solely a function of distance, however, is indicated by the longer stays of Europeans as compared with Americans. One reason for this is that some North Americans spend only part of their holiday in Ireland, combining this with visits to the UK and other European countries. The average length of holiday by overseas visitors lessened by one night between 1991 and 1995, mainly because of growth in holidays of less than six nights. There had also been a decline of one night over the preceding five years, so that the reduced length of stay detracts from the value of tourist numbers as an indicator of the growth and impact of the industry.

The economic benefit of Irish tourism is substantially lessened by its seasonality, so that facilities are under-utilised for much of the year and there is seasonal unemployment and underemployment. The lower concentration of British travel in the peak months of July and August compensates, to some extent, for the smaller expenditure level, especially as compared with the highly peaked mainland European business (Table 10.4). As with length of stay, the lesser seasonality of UK visits reflects ethnic, proximity and business travel factors. The seasonality of Irish tourism has remained relatively constant in recent times, as a result of counterbalancing influences. Tending towards reducing seasonality have been efforts to promote off-season and shoulder period tourism, and growth in activity holidays and short break holidays which are less dependent on summer weather. Their effects have been offset by the growth of the highly seasonal mainland European market and the increased proportion of visitors who are primarily on holiday and thus more seasonal in their travel. One objective of the second Operational Programme is to raise the proportion of tourism outside the peak months of July and August from 70 per cent to 75 per cent by 1999.

The proportion of holidaymakers on an inclusive package arrangement has doubled over a decade, to 28 per cent in 1995. This contributed to the growth in numbers of tourists but it is likely that the expenditure per visitor was less than if the same holiday had been arranged independently. Independent travel is easiest for UK holidaymakers because of proximity and because of familiarity resulting from ethnic connections and more frequent previous visits. The fact that 40 per cent of UK residents brought their cars meant that expenditure on car hire was low compared with other tourists (Table 10.4), thus contributing to the lower expenditure level of UK visitors.

Irish tourism is based largely on holidaymakers of high socio-economic status, four-fifths being in the ABC1 categories, corresponding to managerial, professional and other white-collar occupations (Table 10.4). The lower status of the British market is related mainly to the structure of the ethnic population but it is influenced also by the availability of cheaper travel as compared with more distant markets. The greater prevalence of family groups amongst the UK holidaymakers is indicated by the higher proportion aged under 19 years and this also contributes to their lower spending per capita. Age structure contrasts are greatest between holidaymakers from mainland Europe, half of whom were young adults aged 19–34, and those from North America, half of whom were aged 45 years and over. That the overall age structure of holidaymakers was becoming younger as tourism expanded was indicated by a decline in the proportion aged 45 years and over from 40 per cent in the mid-1980s to 33 per cent by 1993, influenced by the growth of the mainland European market, but a slight reversal has occurred subsequently.

The type of accommodation used by tourists is one of the most important factors affecting expenditure and employment levels (Table 10.4). The significance of the ethnic component is reflected in the one-third of bednights spent with friends and relatives in 1995, though the proportion had declined from half in the mid-1980s. Reflecting the different ethnic compositions, staying with friends and relatives was more than three times greater amongst British visitors as compared with tourists from mainland Europe. Hotel usage was markedly higher by North American visitors, influenced by their older age structure, higher socio-economic status and greater tendency to travel on package arrangements which include hotel accommodation. Other registered serviced accommodation, which includes guesthouses, town houses, country houses and farmhouses—mainly on a bed and breakfast basis—had the most uniform pattern of usage by market source. Mainland Europeans, with a substantial component of young people, were most likely to camp or stay in hostels. The 'other accommodation' sector, which includes unregistered bed and breakfast establishments, second homes and campus accommodation, was also used most by mainland European tourists. There had been some shift in bednight usage towards this sector over the preceding decade, as there also was towards bed and breakfast, rented and hostel accommodation, while the shares of the hotel and camping sectors lessened somewhat (Table 10.4).

10.6   Tourism in regional development: regional convergence and regional redistribution

The spatial distribution of estimated overseas tourist bednights by county is shown in Figure 10.2. The pattern is predominantly coastal but with the main destination zone being along the western seaboard. The attraction of the west is based principally on its coastal and mountain scenery, its cultural character and the scope for varied recreational activities. The west epitomises most closely what many consider to be the essence of Ireland. The two leading counties there are Kerry and Galway that, in Killarney and Galway-Salthill respectively, contain the two most important tourist resorts in the country after Dublin. Coastal areas in the south and south-east are also significant and contain tourist entry points at Cork (air and sea) and Rosslare (sea). Dublin is by far the leading tourist centre, being the capital and largest city with many historical, architectural, cultural, entertainment and shopping attractions, the main place for business, conference and educational travel, and the gateway (air and sea) through which the largest number of visitors enter Ireland. In contrast, the inland counties have the least attraction for foreign tourists. Although 5 per cent of overseas visitors enter the Republic of Ireland from Northern Ireland, proximity to the border seems to be another deterrent factor. This is reinforced in Donegal by isolation, this north-western county having attractions comparable with the most popular western seaboard areas, but far lower levels of foreign tourism.

A different indicator of the spatial pattern of Irish tourism is shown by the data for the seven tourism regions (Figure 10.3), each of which is administered by a regional tourism authority (Pearce 1990). Regional data relating to Northern Irish and domestic tourists are available in addition to overseas visitors, so that the map represents the regional distribution of total tourism in revenue terms. It is evident that the significance of the different market sectors varies substantially by region. Dublin is distinguished by being the region with the lowest proportion of revenue from Irish tourists (19 per cent) and the highest proportion from visitors from outside Ireland and the UK (58 per cent), most notable being the one-third of its revenue which came from mainland Europe. European tourism was next most significant in the south-west, mid-west and west. The UK market was the most evenly distributed sector, ranging from 21 per cent in the west to 32 per cent in the midlands-east. This lower variation is related to the large ethnic component in UK travel, visiting friends and relatives being orientated less towards the usual tourist attractions and more towards the distribution of the resident population, although this would be affected by differential emigration rates between regions. In contrast, one-quarter of the Northern Irish contribution was concentrated in the adjacent north-west, where Donegal is the

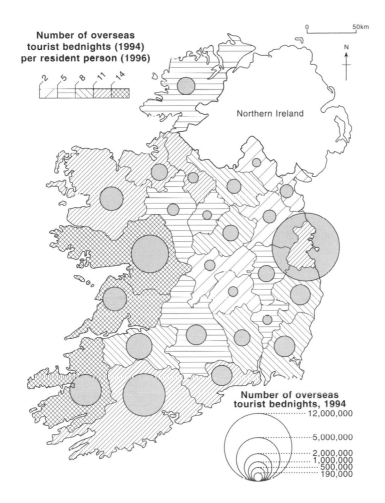

Fig. 10.2 Republic of Ireland: Overseas tourist bednights by county, 1994

Source: based on Bord Fáilte data

favoured destination. Domestic tourism was most important in the south-east, contributing 46 per cent of revenue. This reflects its proximity to Dublin as the major domestic market and the source of over half the trips to the region, together with its sunny climate and beaches, and its stock of second homes and caravan sites.

The contributions of overseas tourists to regional revenue are an outcome in part of their differing propensities to visit the various regions (Table 10.5). British tourists were the most spatially constrained group, reflecting mainly their greater tendency to be staying with friends and relatives and on short stays in one place rather than touring holidays, as compared with other overseas visitors. The most striking feature of the visiting patterns is the strong orientation towards Dublin, with half of all tourists having stayed there for at least one night in 1995, and it was the region favoured most by each market sector. The next strongest sectoral orientation was of North Americans

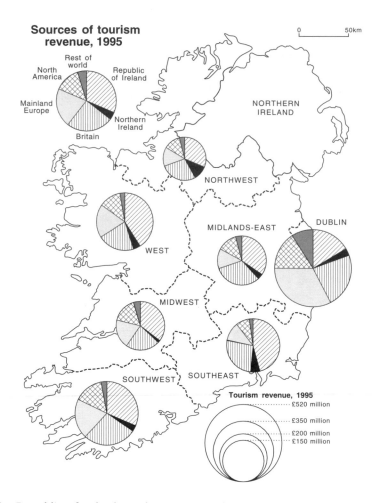

Fig. 10.3   Republic of Ireland: Market structure of regional tourism revenue, 1995

Source: based on Bord Fáilte data

towards the south-west, which reflects in part the attraction of Killarney. The popu-larity of Dublin had increased substantially since 1989. Decline was most evident in the mid-west and west and this may partly reflect the diminished status of Shannon Airport as a gateway. The tendency for overseas tourists to visit more than one region contributes to the dispersal of tourism benefits, as does the fact that Dublin is the major source of domestic holidaymakers who thus travel to other parts of the country.

An indication of the significance of tourism to the regions is given by relating their tourism accommodation and revenue to their resident populations (Table 10.6). Dublin had by far the largest share of national tourism revenue in 1995 (26 per cent) and its dominance was even greater in overseas tourism (33 per cent). It and, to a lesser extent, the midlands-east region seem to have had the highest return relative to accommodation capacity, as suggested by their shares of revenue being greater than

Table 10.5 Regional distribution of overseas visitors staying at least one night in Ireland, 1995 (%)

Region	Britain	Mainland Europe	North America	All overseas, 1995	All overseas, 1989
Dublin	43	58	63	50	42
Midlands-east	18	17	18	17	16
South-east	20	21	26	21	18
South-west	22	36	43	29	32
Mid-west	13	25	36	20	25
West	13	32	37	23	28
North-west	7	14	17	13	12
Mean number of regions stayed in	1.4	2.0	2.4	1.7	1.7

Source: based on Bord Fáilte data.

Table 10.6 Regional distribution of population, rooms and tourism revenue in Ireland, 1995–1996

Region	Population, 1996 (%)	Rooms, 1995 (%)	Rooms per 1000 population	Revenue, 1995 (%)	Revenue per capita
Dublin	29.2	12.3	9.0	26.1	492
Midlands-east	17.0	8.8	11.2	10.6	343
South-east	10.8	12.1	24.1	12.6	640
South-west	13.3	23.4	37.7	17.8	735
Mid-west	11.4	14.8	27.9	10.5	508
West	9.7	17.1	37.8	14.4	814
North-west	8.7	1.4	28.2	8.3	519
All regions	100.0	100.0	21.4	100.0	550

Sources: based on Bord Fáilte and Census of Population data.

those of bedrooms. Dublin's share of income was more than twice that of accommodation. The lesser role of tourism in the overall economy of the midlands-east region, however, is suggested by it having the lowest tourism revenue per capita of all regions, followed by Dublin. Conversely, the south-west and west, being the two regions with the next largest shares of tourism revenue after Dublin, were the regions with the highest amounts of tourism revenue and accommodation relative to population, indicating the comparative importance of the industry in these areas. That the significance of tourism relative to the local population varies within the individual regions is shown on a county basis by Figure 10.2. This indicates the coastal orientation in the importance of tourism within regions.

While comparison of revenue with resident populations gives an indication of the role of tourism in regional development, recent data which would enable measurement of the precise contribution to regional income and employment are not available. Estimates were made by Tansey, Webster and Associates (1991) for the tourism regions prior to changes in their delimitation in 1989, using comparable personal income data. They showed that the contributions of tourism to regional incomes were 7–10 per cent

Table 10.7   Regional distribution of national tourism revenue and numbers in Ireland, 1989 and 1995

Region	Regional share of tourism revenue (%) 1989	Regional share of tourism revenue (%) 1995	Change in share of revenue (%), 1989–1995	Change in number of external tourists (%) 1989–1995
Dublin	21.7	26.1	+20	+75
Midlands–east	10.0	10.6	+6	+57
South–east	9.8	12.6	+28	+77
South–west	17.4	17.8	+2	+44
Mid–west	13.6	10.5	−23	+28
West	18.1	14.4	−21	+18
North–west	9.5	8.3	−13	+15

Source: based on Bord Fáilte data.

in the western regions and 4–6 per cent in the eastern regions, and the respective shares of employment were 8–11 per cent and 5–6 per cent. The lower proportions of income than of employment indicate that incomes in tourism were below the average for other sectors of the economy. This suggests that, as tourism was most important in the lower-income western regions, it may have exacerbated regional personal income disparities, but this is mitigated by its provision of jobs for those who did not have access to or did not want alternative full-time employment. The combined regions of the west and Donegal/Leitrim/Sligo had an estimated 12 per cent of national personal income but 22 per cent of tourism revenue. Regional accounts for 1991 (Central Statistics Office 1996) relate to a set of regions that differs to some extent from the tourism regions but, amongst those for which comparison can be made, tourism revenue expressed as a percentage of gross value added ranged from 4 per cent in Dublin to 12 per cent in the west. The available data indicate that tourism's regional contribution is greatest in the less developed western part of the country, where there are limited non-agricultural job opportunities, although there is likely to be greater leakage of revenue from these peripheral areas. Thus, tourism has a redistributive effect and its important role in Irish regional development is one of the main reasons given for its promotion.

That this role has lessened, however, is indicated by comparisons of regional shares of tourism revenue over time. From the year when regional revenue data first became available until that prior to the change in regional delimitation, that is from 1976 to 1988, the combined share of Dublin and the east increased by 21 per cent, while there were decreases in the shares of the west by 9 per cent, the midlands by 13 per cent and the north-west by 22 per cent. A continuation of much of this trend for the subsequent period is indicated in Table 10.7, the diminishing shares of much of the west contrasting with the expansion of Dublin and the south-east. The west has been disadvantaged relative to the east by an increased concentration of tourists through eastern gateways, a lesser proportion of visitors bringing their cars in recent years and the trend towards shorter visits.

The most unfavourable aspect of the regional shift in demand has been the relative decline of the north-west, reflecting its problems of isolation and proximity to Northern Ireland, and its relatively high dependence on the Northern Irish and UK markets which have been of declining relative significance. Furthermore, the seasonality of tourism is greatest here, with 38 per cent of visitors in 1995 coming in July and

August. The north-west is a region where there had been heavy dependence on tourism and where there is considerable economic need for it. Recognising the need for development in the north-west, tourism projects in border counties can receive grants from the EU's INTERREG programme and the International Fund for Ireland, which was established in association with the effort to bring peace to Northern Ireland. Of the major financial investment assisted by the European Regional Development Fund and the Business Expansion Scheme, however, only 9 per cent was in the north-west in the period 1989–1995 (Tourism and Leisure Partners 1996). In contrast, 50 per cent of this investment was in the Dublin, midlands east and south-east regions.

The increasingly important role of Dublin in Irish tourism reflects the rising general significance of urban tourism. This may seem incongruous in Ireland in that the predominant tourism image of the country is of sparsely populated scenic and green rural landscapes, whilst Quinn (1994) found that only 10 per cent of scenes depicted in brochures were urban settings. Yet, by 1995 Dublin city and county had 26.1 per cent of national tourism revenue, compared with Dublin city's share of 14.6 per cent in 1976. In addition, overflow business from Dublin has benefited adjacent counties in the midlands-east region. Associated with the growth in Dublin and encouraged by tax incentives, there has been a major expansion in its tourist accommodation; the number of registered bedrooms in listed hotels increased by 57 per cent between 1987 and 1997, with a further substantial number of hotels due to open in the late 1990s. Hotels have a uniquely dominant position in Dublin's accommodation stock, accounting for 60 per cent of the total capacity in 1995 as compared with 25–34 per cent in the other regions.

The relative growth of Dublin tourism reflects in part its market structure. The 33 per cent contribution of the expanding mainland European market to Dublin's tourism revenue in 1995 was substantially greater than to any other region, so that 41 per cent of all mainland European expenditure was in Dublin. Conversely, Dublin's shares of the much less favourably performing Irish and UK markets was less than in most regions. In addition, however, within each of the individual market sectors there has been an increased tendency to visit and stay in Dublin relative to the rest of the country. This seems to be the outcome of several influences. It results in part from an increased dominance of Dublin as the main tourist gateway to the Republic of Ireland, so that proportionately more people spend at least one night in the city. This reflects the increased use of air access by visitors to Ireland, contributing to the growth in air traffic through Dublin Airport from 2.3 million passengers in 1985 to 9.1 million in 1996. The lifting of the compulsory Shannon stopover has favoured Dublin Airport, including its use by more North American package tour operators. A major factor in the expansion of Dublin tourism has been the growth in city weekend and other short-break holidays in general and Dublin's increased share of this business in particular. Dublin has become a major European city destination and in the mid-1990s it was the second most favoured venue, after Paris, for British short breaks in cities overseas. This reflects in part the popularity of Ireland as a holiday destination and, within it, Dublin's trendy image. The reputation of Dublin as a 'fun' place is epitomised by the number of pre-wedding parties being held there by young UK people. This business is not favoured by all tourism interests, however, and there are fears that unruly behaviour on such occasions might tarnish the city's image. A very important component in Dublin's tourism is the greatly expanded business and conference traffic and there has also been growth in the education, entertainment and sport event sectors, in all of which Dublin has a dominant role within the Republic of Ireland. Establishment of a separate regional tourism organisation for County Dublin in 1989 aided promotion of the city. Designation of Dublin as European City of Culture for 1991, and its hosting of Eurovision Song Contests, raised the profile of the city. The attraction of Dublin has been increased through urban regeneration, especially in the Temple Bar area, and by improvement in tourism facilities and services. The huge expansion in tourist accommodation, and especially in new hotels, has both facilitated the growth of Dublin's tourism and contributed to it through promotion by these establishments.

Occupancy rates are higher in Dublin than in other regions, in part because Dublin's tourism is less seasonal than most of the holiday market segments. Thus the proportion of visitors arriving in July and August in 1995 was 25 per cent, as compared with 31–38 per cent in the other regions, and one-third came between October and March. Only 18 per cent of UK visitors arrived in July and August, reflecting the importance of off-peak short-break, ethnic and business travel from that adjacent market. Seasonality is higher in the western regions than in the east. Hannigan (1994a) found that only 24 per cent of jobs created in grant-aided projects in the western regions were full-time, as compared with 67 per cent in the eastern regions, reducing the benefit of tourism employment creation to the less developed part of the country.

It is sometimes claimed by some regional tourism interests elsewhere that the growth of Dublin's tourism has been at the expense of the rest of the Republic of Ireland. This is difficult to evaluate but it seems likely that a large proportion of the growth would not have occurred elsewhere and represents a net gain to the country. This applies especially to the substantial business, short-break and event traffic to Dublin. All regions have benefited from the overall expansion of tourism, as indicated by the increase in external tourist numbers over the period 1989–1995 (Table 10.7). The benefits have been unequally distributed, however, with the increase in numbers ranging from 15 per cent in the north-west and 18 per cent in the west to 75 per cent in Dublin and 77 per cent in the south-east. The better performance of the eastern regions as compared with the western ones, indicates development of a tendency towards regional convergence in the role of tourism, thus lessening the regionally redistributive effect of the industry. Indications are that this is being exacerbated on the supply side by the regional distribution of funding under the Operational Programmes for Tourism.

10.7   Conclusion

The major expansion of Irish tourism contributed significantly to national and regional development and constituted a part of the country's economic boom in the 1990s. From an atmosphere of stagnation, there is now almost an expectation of continuous growth into the future. This does not give due recognition to the potential effects on tourism of influences beyond the control of the industry, including exchange rates, inflation and economic circumstances in particular markets. A particularly significant unknown in the Irish situation relates to the conflict in and associated with Northern Ireland. The level of success of the Ireland brand and other marketing initiatives, together with the marketing efforts of alternative destinations and other aspects of competition, will have a bearing on overseas visitor trends. The potentially large Asian market will be one consideration. Trends will be affected too by developments in transport service provision and cost. An important factor in terms of the tourism product will be the investment situation after 1999, when there is likely to be substantially reduced EU funding and less subsidies for tourism; the extent to which the industry will become more self-reliant and innovative will be critical. It is essential that the quality of the Irish tourism product and services should be maintained, improved and extended to meet the increasing expectations of tourists.

Tourism fashions may be quite fickle and so there can be no guarantee that the popularity of Ireland will continue indefinitely. The country is fortunate, however, in that trends in international tourism favour Ireland. Its predominant tourism image of being a green and unspoilt destination accords with the increasing interest in and attraction towards environmentally desirable places. Yet the attributes of a high-quality environment and friendly people are fragile resources which, apart from being susceptible to the effects of other forms of development, as has happened to some extent, would be threatened by continuation of high tourism growth rates. While these rates seem unlikely to be maintained, vigilance with regard to potentially detrimental impacts is necessary and this is in part responsible for the shift in policy emphasis from mere numbers towards economic benefit and an effort to attract more high-spending visitors. Already problems of congestion at the high season have emerged in places, such as Dublin, Killarney, Dingle, Galway and the Aran Islands. Excessive pressures could be alleviated by policies which would endeavour to spread tourists more evenly over time and space, with the consequent reduction in seasonality and extension into areas less affected by tourism having important economic, social and regional benefits. Instruments which could be used would include product development, transport provision and marketing strategy. The benefits would be all the greater from the development of rural tourism and, despite continued growth of urban tourism, Ireland must have considerable further potential in the promotion of sustainable tourism based on the attractions of its rural areas.

11 France: tourism comes of age

John Tuppen

11.1 Introduction: the changing context for tourism

Tourism is now a major sector of economic activity in France, following substantial growth over the post-war period. An ever-increasing number of French people go on holiday each year, with the majority still preferring to remain in France rather than travel abroad. At the same time France attracts annually more than 60 million foreign visitors, making the country the world's leading tourist destination ahead of Spain and the USA (Conseil Economique et Social, 1996). Not surprisingly, France has many advantages for developing tourism, not least the diversity of its landscapes and scenery, and a range of generally favourable climatic conditions. Other assets include an extensive and diverse cultural heritage as well as the country's worldwide reputation for its cuisine, vineyards and wines.

This potential for tourism has been enhanced by various factors. France, like many Western countries, has experienced an extended period of rising incomes, higher living standards, longer paid holidays and generally more leisure time (Py 1996; Cazes 1995; Clary 1993). Simultaneously, substantial public and private investment has provided an ever-greater number and range of tourist facilities and purpose-built attractions. Tourism has also been stimulated by vastly improved accessibility and substantial reductions in the length of journeys and cost of travel. In an international context, France has benefited from cheaper air travel and more frequent services, while within the country itself continuous improvements to road and rail infra-structures have rendered many regions markedly more accessible to tourists. High-speed train services (TGV) now link Paris and northern regions (as well as London and Brussels) with many areas in western, south-western and especially south-eastern France (Thompson 1994). Bourg-St-Maurice, for example, in the heart of the French Alps and at the foot of the major ski resort of Les Arcs, is now within five hours of Paris by TGV.

Road links to the main tourist regions have also been improved dramatically, notably through the extension of the motorway network which now totals nearly 8,000 kilometres (INSEE 1997). Popular tourist regions such as the Mediterranean coast or Brittany have long profited from good motorway access, while this is now increasingly true of many previously isolated areas of the Massif Central. In addition,

Tourism and Economic Development: European Experiences, 3rd Edition. Edited by A.M. Williams and G. Shaw.
© 1998 John Wiley & Sons Ltd.

the region of Rhône-Alpes, with its major winter sports destinations, has one of the densest motorway networks outside the Paris region. Road building in conjunction with the Winter Olympics at Albertville in 1992 brought leading resorts such as Les Arcs, Tignes, La Plagne and the 'Three Valleys' complex within direct reach of the motorway system.

As tourism has expanded, the context in which it takes place, as well as the activity itself, have changed. In the early post-war years the development of tourist activities coincided with a period of unprecedented economic expansion and rising living standards. Over the last two decades this has been far less true and unemployment has become an unfortunate reality for a growing number of people—more than 3 million by 1997. Changed economic conditions might be seen as one factor contributing to the relative stability (over recent years) in the number of French people taking a holiday, as well as to growing price consciousness and selectivity amongst consumers in the choice of their holidays (Mermet 1996a). France has also faced increased competition from other countries as a tourist destination.

The demographic and political backgrounds have also changed. In common with many Western countries, France is characterised by a progressively ageing population and an increasing number of retired people (INSEE 1996), leading to a naturally decreasing potential market for activities such as skiing but also creating new possibilities for tourism. Politically, increasing attention is being paid to the environmental impacts of tourism. Gone are the boom years of the 1960s and 1970s with the launching of large-scale development projects with little concern for their consequences. Greater legislative control of developments has been introduced while, belatedly, the concept of sustainability has become part of the vocabularies of government bodies, local authorities and developers alike.

Tourist behaviour and related patterns of demand have been modified, influencing in turn the nature of tourism products. Patterns of holidaymaking have changed. The French tend to go away more frequently than in the past but for shorter periods (Mermet 1996b). Destinations are becoming more varied. Despite the continued attraction of the Mediterranean coast, the holiday recipe of sun, sea and sand has lost part of its appeal, even for the French (Py 1996). Increasing interest is being shown in localities offering the tourist sports facilities, cultural attractions or opportunities for walking and riding. The desire for a 'change of scenery' has long been a determining factor in the choice of holiday destination, but now this is often allied to an interest in learning about local areas and their customs and traditions (Conseil Economique et Social 1996). A particular appeal exists for areas still possessing their original and natural character, a trait revealed in the growing popularity of holidays featuring a rural setting (Py 1996). The renowned individuality of the French has become more evident in holiday-making, with an increasing preference for new experiences, for holidays that are personalised rather than packaged and for flexibility in their organisation, with bookings increasingly made at the last moment (Mermet 1996b).

The tourist industry has also responded to changing patterns of demand. In a mature and ever more competitive market, increased emphasis has been accorded to quality and efficiency with the principal aim of generating greater customer loyalty. Similarly, in an effort to increase tourist numbers, new services and products have been launched. These range from the creation of centralised reservation systems in resorts to the launching of a series of themed attractions, epitomised by the Disneyland complex at Paris.

11.2   The organisation and management of tourism

11.2.1   *Public sector structures*

In a country with a long history of centralisation, it is of little surprise that the French government should have shown a keen interest in the development of tourism. As early as 1910 a National Tourist Office was created, as part of the Ministry of Public Works, Postal and Telegraph Services, to administer tourist activities. Since then the responsibility for tourism has been regularly transferred between ministries and currently rests with the Ministry of Equipment, Housing, Transport and Tourism. Policy making is the responsibility of the Ministry's civil service, the 'Direction du Tourisme' that is assisted by a series of regional delegations answering to the Prefects of the country's different regions. The part of the national budget devoted to tourism is extremely small, amounting to 398 million francs in 1996 or 0.02 per cent of the total (Py 1996). However, this considerably understates government spending in this field. Other ministries, including agriculture, education, environment and culture also fund tourist-related projects, while the DATAR (Délégation à l'Aménagement du Territoire et à l'Action Régionale: the government's regional planning and development agency) has a long history of investment in this field.

Local authorities (consisting, in ascending order, of the commune, department and region) play an equally active role in the development of tourism. The commune, through its municipal council, is the most directly involved. It grants planning permission for building, is responsible for the local land use plan and may invest in tourism infrastructures. A significant part of a commune's revenue may also derive from tourism, and where local communities depend heavily on tourist activities, they are eligible for supplementary funding from central government; in addition, such communes may impose a special tax on ski-lift operators (where appropriate) and levy a local tourism tax (Py 1996; Conseil Economique et Social 1996). Many councils also control the local tourism office and are thus able to influence its policies directly to attract tourists (Dreyfus–Signoles 1992).

Departments are less concerned with tourism although their general councils can authorise the creation of a Departmental Tourist Committee bringing together local councillors and representatives of the tourist industry to promote the area and carry out related studies (Durand *et al.* 1994). A similar structure exists at a regional level with the creation of Regional Tourist Committees, which have a remit to plan, promote and monitor tourist activities, duplicating in part the tasks of their departmental counterparts. The region has also become increasingly regarded by central government as the most appropriate territorial level at which to define planning and development policies. As a result, a process of contractual planning has been implemented since 1984 (Tuppen 1988). Investment plans (*contrats de plan*), running for five-year periods, are negotiated between the government and the regions, each partner accepting to fund a series of agreed development programmes. Current plans (1994–1998), which form part of the national planning process, envisage a total investment of 1.7 billion francs in tourism over this period (Py 1996). However, the priority accorded to such expenditure varies between regions, although not surprisingly, in view of their tourism potential, Brittany and Provence–Alpes–Côte d'Azur are amongst the highest spenders (Conseil Economique et Social 1996). Programmes supported by such funding are equally diverse, ranging from developing or protecting tourism sites, to assisting in the training of people working in the tourism industry.

11.2.2   Changing roles and policies

Over the post-war period the roles of these various public sector actors have evolved significantly, with central government progressively adopting a lower profile and more selective approach to intervention, and local authorities exerting a greater influence. Traditionally the state's role has been to regulate the tourist industry, a function that it continues to perform and which, in certain cases, has been reinforced. For example, to assist the lowly paid to afford a holiday, the government introduced in 1982 a system of savings vouchers (*chèque-vacances*) for employees, to which the employer makes a further contribution (in return for a tax concession). The government also continues to play a key role in promoting France as a tourism destination, a task currently undertaken by the 'Maison de la France', created in 1987. This organisation operates under the control of the Direction du Tourisme, which is responsible for a further specialised agency (L'Agence Française de l'Ingénierie Touristique), set up in 1993 to improve tourism products and sell French know-how in this field abroad (Conseil Economique et Social 1996).

The development of tourism also became a central feature of the government's economic and regional planning strategies, notably in the context of the 5th National Plan that ran from 1966 to 1970 (Durand *et al.* 1994). At this time two important decisions were taken. First, the creation of three specialist bodies to study the implications of tourism and the most appropriate forms of development in rural, mountainous and coastal regions; and second, the launching of a series of major tourism projects, notably affecting the coastlines of Languedoc-Roussillon, Aquitaine and Corsica, as well as the French Alps (Clary 1993). In all these examples the government played a dominant role, generally failing to consult with the relevant local authorities or the local populations concerned by these developments.

Since this period circumstances have changed, as has the government's approach. In particular there has been an increasing demand to limit rather than encourage major tourism development schemes. At the same time, central government has devolved a number of related decision-making powers to local authorities (following the decentralisation legislation of 1982) and, where development does take place, has preferred to proceed in partnership with other actors rather than act as the sole driving force (Durand *et al.* 1994). In addition, the government has finally gone some way towards recognising the rights of local populations and their representatives to determine how their localities should develop.

By the early 1970s, somewhat paradoxically, as development projects designed to induce economic benefits were under way (such as the building of new resorts along the Languedoc coast), growing pressures were emerging to consider also their potential environmental costs. Progressively the government acknowledged the need to accord greater priority to the protection and conservation of the natural environment (Durand *et al.* 1994). Thus, in 1977, the then President, Valéry Giscard d'Estaing, recognised the need for tighter control of tourism projects in mountainous regions, as well as the desirability of giving local populations a greater say in the form this development should take (Gerbaux 1994). The rapid and often uncontrolled development of tourism in coastal regions was also leading to greater demands for regulation. In 1975 the government created a national agency to help protect 'sensitive' sites along coastlines and lake shores (Conservatoire de L'Espace Littoral at des Rivages Lacustres), although its financial means were limited and subsequent results have been disappointing (Dreyfus-Signoles 1992).

More substantial action was taken a decade later with respect to both mountainous and coastal regions. Government legislation in 1985 (Loi Relative au Développement et Protection de la Montagne) and in 1986 (Loi sur la Mise en Valeur et la Protection du Littoral) aimed to restrict development in these areas and introduce a modified approach to planning (Clary 1993; Becet 1987; Dreyfus-Signoles 1992). In coastal regions this involved trying to extend tourism development inland, away from the congested maritime fringe, while in mountainous areas priority was given to integrating tourism with other forms of activity. Equally, greater attention was to be paid to the social, cultural and environmental impacts of tourism. The legislation also confirmed the importance of the role of the commune in instigating and managing tourism developments.

Since this period, environmental issues have remained at the centre of the political debate on tourism. Opposition to development has emanated particularly from pressure groups and associations. In the case of the Alps, organisations such as the Commission Internationale pour la Protection des Alpes (CIPRA), the Fédération Rhône-Alpes de la Protection de la Nature (FRAPNA), the Club Alpin Français and Mountain Wilderness have all campaigned strongly to limit new investment in tourism and reinforce the protection of the natural environment. In particular they have sought to resist attempts to encroach on the central, protected zones of the country's national parks. Central government has offered a subdued response, seeking to limit the use of heavily visited sites and promote more environmentally-sensitive forms of development (Ministère de l'Environnement: Ministère du Tourisme 1992).

Endowed with increased decision-making powers and faced with changed attitudes to development, the task of local authorities is not always easy. Despite new responsibilities, many small communes lack the expertise to deal with development proposals, leading to the need for advice from external (and often state-run) services. Similarly, they often do not have the financial means to realise their ambitions. Once again the solution is frequently to seek government assistance, although in certain areas funding is also available from the European Union's regional programme, notably for developments agreed within the framework of the regional 'contrats de plan' (Conseil Economique et Social 1996). Many communes find themselves in an equally ambiguous position with respect to the current environmental debate. While aware of the desirability of protecting natural landscapes and historic monuments (or indeed their villages) from the invasion of tourists, they also have a responsibility to help create jobs, a prime consideration for many local electors. Consequently, this frequently implies authorising at least some form of tourism development.

11.2.3   *Tourism businesses*

The tourism sector in France consists of a large and extremely heterogeneous group of businesses. Traditionally the industry has been characterised by a large number of small and medium-sized firms; however, a limited number of large enterprises now play an increasingly major role in determining the provision and organisation of tourism activities, giving a distinct dual character to the sector's structure (Cazes 1995). The importance of small businesses may be illustrated by reference to hotels and restaurants. In total this branch represents nearly 165,000 enterprises, yet less than 200 employ over 100 people; indeed, 85 per cent of these businesses have less than six employees (Py

1996). A similar pattern characterises activities such as travel agents, cafés and coach operators.

The widespread occurrence of small businesses relates to many factors, not least the extreme diversity of tourism products and destinations in France. In many rural areas not only is demand often both limited and seasonal, but the tourism industry itself still has only an embryonic and fragmented form; it remains a family business. The reticence of the French to take package holidays and their continuing preference for organising their own holidays (rather than relying on specialist operators) partly explains the limited development of large tour operator or travel agency groups (Py 1996; Cazes 1995).

Change is taking place, however, through growing concentration and the emergence of a number of large national, and increasingly multinational, companies. This trend is particularly apparent in the hotel sector, epitomised by the Accor group, which is now the clear market leader in this field and one of the five leading hotel chains in the world. It was first formed in 1983 with the merger of the Novotel and Jacques Borel groups. Now Accor controls over 2,450 hotels world-wide, with nearly 900 in France alone (Les Echos 1997a).

Concentration, although on a lesser scale, is also evident in other sectors of activity. The trend is firmly established amongst tour operators (Py 1996). Club Méditerranée and Nouvelles Frontières dominate this activity in France, with a turnover of 8.5 and 7.2 billion francs (1995), respectively (*Le Monde* 1996a; *Les Echos* 1996a), but these companies are still considerably smaller than their British or German counterparts, such as Thomson or TUI (Py 1996). Travel agents are following a similar trend with an increasing proportion of trade conducted by the major companies, such as Havas-Voyages and Sélectour. This movement is partly explained by the competitive nature of the business, a feature which has been intensified recently as large hypermarket chains such as Carrefour and Leclerc have entered this field as part of their own attempts to diversify their product range and increase turnover (*La Tribune Desfossés* 1996a).

Concentration has involved both horizontal and vertical integration. The former has been a particular feature of the hotel industry, exemplified by the expansion of the Accor group and the development of its various chains, such as Novotel and Ibis. It is also characteristic of the transport sector with the formation of large coach companies such as the Verney group and the expansion of Air France; in the early 1990s the state airline acquired UTA and Air Inter to enlarge its operations (Tinard 1994). Vertical integration, involving the development of a complementary range of activities, has also become a common feature of the tourism industry. Club Méditerranée provides a good example. Not only does the company function as a tour operator, but it also owns and manages a series of hotels and holiday villages (Tinard 1994). Frantour, the tour-operating subsidiary of the SNCF (French Railways), provides a similar example through its diversification into station restaurants, travel agents and hotels (*Les Echos* 1997b).

Internationalisation has frequently accompanied concentration, as the need for critical mass and greater market share has intensified. Again the trend varies considerably according to the sector of activity. It is already well established in the hotel industry, with the Accor group present in 70 different countries. There is also growing inward investment, particularly from American and British groups. The hotel sector is once more a prime target (for example, the Holiday Inn chain now controlled by the British Bass group), but there are many other examples including MacDonalds,

American Express and British Airways (through its acquisitions of the French airlines TAT and, more recently, Air Liberté). French tour operators and travel agents have generally proved less expansionist, due partly to their smaller size and lack of experience of the preferences of foreign consumers.

Just as there are considerable differences in the size and structure of tourism businesses, there are also contrasts in ownership characteristics. Most major groups are privately owned (Accor, Club Méditerranée, Nouvelles Frontières), as well as the majority of much smaller, often family businesses. However, there are some notable exceptions. State-owned enterprises are a particular feature of transport industries (Air France, SNCF), while the public sector is also present as a shareholder (via state-owned banks or financial institutions, such as the Crédit Lyonnais or Caisse des Dépôts et Consignations) in a series or tourism-related businesses. The Compagnie des Alpes, for example, which is owned by a subsidiary of the Caisse des Dépôts et Consignations, is a major shareholder in a series of ski-lift companies in the Alps. In France 'mixed economy' companies, which combine both public sector (local authorities in general) and private funding have been used frequently in the development of tourism projects. Prime examples were the development companies set up to provide tourism infrastructure in the Languedoc and Aquitaine coastal regions, whereas more modest and recent illustrations include ski-lift operations in a variety of resorts.

France also stands out due to the importance that associations play in the country's social, cultural and sporting life (Py 1996). As a result, such organisations have come to represent a further important actor in the development and management of tourism facilities, particularly in the field of accommodation. Associations have been strongly linked with the expansion of social tourism, and the creation of holiday villages for families with relatively modest incomes (Lanquar and Raynouard 1995). Villages Vacances Familles (VVF), founded in 1958, is by far the largest organisation, renting accommodation and providing the services of a tour operator. It manages 64,000 beds in France and in 1995 welcomed 650,000 holiday makers (Py 1996). In general, however, such associations have encountered difficulties in remaining competitive in the tourism market. Advertising is limited to their members (restricting the potential market) who, due to successive periods of economic recession, have often been forced to reduce their holiday budgets. At the same time many facilities have not been modernised, lacking the degree of comfort often deemed necessary in the 1990s. Moreover, 'village' is not always synonymous with small chalets or villas; often it means concrete apartment blocks which have aged badly, resembling in this and other respects their urban counterparts in many of the drab post-war suburbs of France's towns and cities. Revitalising this sector's image is therefore fundamental if its role as a major provider of tourist facilities is to be maintained.

11.3   Tourist destinations and holidaymaking

11.3.1   General trends: changing forms of tourism

Regular surveys of holidays carried out each year (until 1994) by the French Statistical Office (INSEE) provide detailed information about domestic tourism in France. (The term 'holiday' refers to stays of at least four consecutive days' absence from a person's normal place of residence for reasons other than business, study or health: INSEE 1996.) Currently, 62 per cent of French people (nearly 35 million) go away on holiday

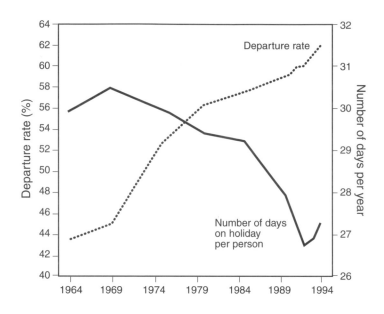

Fig. 11.1   Changes in the departure rate and number of days of holiday of the French, 1964–1994

Source: INSEE (1996)

at least once a year, and of these nearly 83 per cent stay in France (Monteiro 1996). Departure rates have varied little over recent years, contrasting with a period of exceptionally strong growth during the late 1960s and early 1970s; at the same time, people have tended to go away more often but overall for a shorter period (Figure 11.1).

Clearly the propensity to take a holiday varies in relation to a number of socio-economic indicators such as age, job, income and place of residence (Table 11.1). Thus, younger people with well-paid, white-collar jobs living in major towns and cities tend to go on holiday to a greater degree than other social groups. Certain changes have emerged, however, over the last 20 years (Monteiro 1996; Bodier and Crenner 1996). Departure rates for those people with manual and less well-paid jobs have risen progressively, suggesting some success for social tourism policies. Similarly, an increasing proportion of retired people are now taking a holiday. This trend, combined with their relatively high spending propensity (Bodier and Crenner 1996), makes them a privileged target for the tourism industry.

Departure rates also vary in relation to the different seasons, as do the destinations chosen by holiday-makers. Summer is the preferred holiday period when over 58 per cent of the population go away; this compares with a proportion of just under 30 per cent for the winter season. In summer the coast remains the favoured destination, followed by rural and mountainous areas, whereas in winter roles are reversed, with urban centres also being popular (Table 11.2). Despite problems of overcrowding, the Mediterranean coastline still attracts the largest number of summer visitors, representing over 16 per cent of all stays (Table 11.3); the department of Var alone,

Table 11.1   Socio-economic factors influencing holiday departure rates in France

	Winter holidays (1993/94) Departure rate (%)	Summer holidays (1994) Departure rate (%)
Age		
0–13	33.9	68.1
14–24	31.0	59.0
25–29	34.2	59.8
30–39	33.0	63.5
40–49	30.9	59.4
50–64	27.1	55.2
65–69	24.9	48.7
70+	16.7	35.7
Place of residence		
Rural commune	20.5	41.6
Urban centre other than Paris	28.3	59.7
Paris (excluding centre)	45.0	77.0
Paris (centre)	57.6	80.3
Socio-economic category		
Farmers and farm workers	13.0	34.9
Company owners	27.1	59.1
Executives and liberal professions	60.3	82.1
Teachers, government employees, technicians	40.4	79.1
Other white-collar workers	36.0	62.5
Skilled manual workers	18.7	55.1
Unskilled manual workers	11.6	44.5
Retired people	21.9	44.3
Annual household income (francs)		
>100,000	17.5	N/A
100,000–180,000	25.2	62.6
180,000–300,000	45.0	76.8
<300,000	70.2	87.0

Source: Rowenczyk (1994; 1995).

Table 11.2   Major holiday destinations of the French, 1994

	Proportion of stays (%)	
Holiday type/destination	Summer	Winter
Coastal areas	46.7	19.0
Rural areas	25.0	26.4
Mountainous areas	15.7	36.6
Urban areas	7.9	16.1
Touring	4.7	1.9

Source: INSEE, (1996).

Table 11.3   Summer holiday destinations of French
tourists in France, 1994

Region	Proportion of total stays (%)
Mediterranean coast	16.1
Atlantic coast	14.8
Britanny	10.0
Other coastal areas	7.3
Alps	11.4
Pyrenees	5.0
Other upland areas	5.7
Other regions	29.7
Total	100.0

Source: Rowenczyk (1995).

(which stretches from approximately Bandol to St Raphaël), accounts for over 40 million tourist-nights during the summer season (Monteiro and Rowenczyk 1994). The Atlantic and Brittany coasts are also major tourist regions, as are the Alps. However, for those French people going abroad, the most popular destinations are still in countries surrounding the Mediterranean, especially in the Iberian peninsular (Rowenczyk 1995). Relatively few people travel further afield and, for those that do, North America attracts most visitors.

Winter holidays, which in general tend to be shorter than those taken in the summer, are concentrated to a far greater extent in mountainous regions, particularly the Alps, which account for 30 per cent of all stays (Rowenczyk 1994). This spatial concentration appears to have been progressively reinforced over time and clearly reflects the importance of winter sports holidays. However, there are many other motivations for winter holidays, not least the desire to visit friends and relatives during the Christmas break; indeed, the Mediterranean coast, with 9 per cent of stays, represents the second most popular destination. Few French people, however, go abroad during the winter season, and most of those that do so visit a West European country (Rowenczyk 1994).

Patterns of accommodation also vary according to the season. Not surprisingly, hotels are more popular in winter and campsites in summer. Overall, however, irrespective of the time of year, the majority of holiday-makers stay with relatives or friends or in their own, or borrowed second home. This tendency is particularly marked in winter, when relatively few people stay in a hotel or rented accommodation (Rowenczyk 1994).

11.3.2   The short break market: growing domestic and international markets

Defining holidays in terms of four consecutive days away from home not only underestimates the importance of tourism but also fails to take account of fundamental changes affecting the holiday market. The French, like many of their European neighbours, are tending to go away more frequently but on each occasion for a shorter period, and often to a variety of destinations. This is largely explained by the growing importance attached to the 'short break' (Potier and Cockerell 1993). A relatively large number of public holidays, increased mobility and car ownership, the falling cost of travel in real terms, and an increasing number of households with two salaries offering both the financial means to go away more frequently, as well as certain constraints for spending an extended period away (as holiday periods do not coincide), are some of the factors which explain this tendency. However, despite the widespread occurrence of this phenomenon, detailed statistics relating to its growth and importance are not always available (Potier and Chasset 1993). Certain trends are none the less clear. Short breaks, generally including a week-end, have rapidly become more popular since the early 1980s, growing at a faster rate than traditional holidays. It is now estimated that there are more than 170 million such stays a year, representing more than 300 million tourist nights (Potier and Chasset 1993). This compares with approximately 60 million stays of four days or longer (Monteiro 1996). Moreover, it is also estimated that short breaks represent a market worth at least 40 billion francs annually (Potier and Chasset 1993).

In general these visits are confined to France and are intraregional in character, often motivated by a desire to visit friends or relatives. Unlike longer holidays, these visits are spread more evenly throughout the year, while their origins and destinations are frequently represented by towns and cities. As a result, highly urbanised regions such as Ile-de-France, Rhône-Alpes and Provence–Alpes–Côte d'Azur feature a large number of short-break holidays. Given the predominance of the car for such visits, there is also an obvious link with the growth of severe traffic congestion on roads around cities such as Paris, Lyon and Marseille, particularly on Sunday evenings. There is also an international dimension to this activity. While the French show relatively little inclination to spend such breaks abroad, France has become an important destination for other European visitors, notably for the Germans, the Belgians and British (Potier and Cockerell 1993).

11.3.3   Foreign tourists

Foreign tourists also come to France for considerably longer stays. In 1995 nearly 61 million foreigners spent at least one night in France, for the purpose of either holiday or business (Conseil Economique et Social 1996). The majority originate from the countries of the European Union (as well as Switzerland) and in particular from Germany and the UK (Figure 11.2). The only other significant flow is from the USA, although nearly 1 million Japanese tourists now arrive each year. Compared with domestic tourists, foreign visitors make far greater use of hotel accommodation, although the length of their stay is relatively short, averaging approximately eight days (Conseil Economique et Social 1996). Certain contrasts are also apparent concerning the regions that are visited. Paris (Ile-de-France) represents the prime destination for foreign visitors, emphasising the appeal of the capital and its world-famous attractions. A second major concentration covers much of south-eastern France (the Alps and Mediterranean coast), followed by a third, more diffuse grouping amongst the regions of the Atlantic coast (Py 1996). More detailed analysis using data on telephone calls reveals contrasting preferences amongst different national groups (Gillon 1995). Whereas the Germans are particularly attracted to coastal sites, the Dutch and the Belgians favour mountainous regions and areas fringing the southern part of the Rhône valley; the British show a much stronger concentration in areas of western France, such as Brittany, Normandy and Dordogne, as well as along the French Riviera.

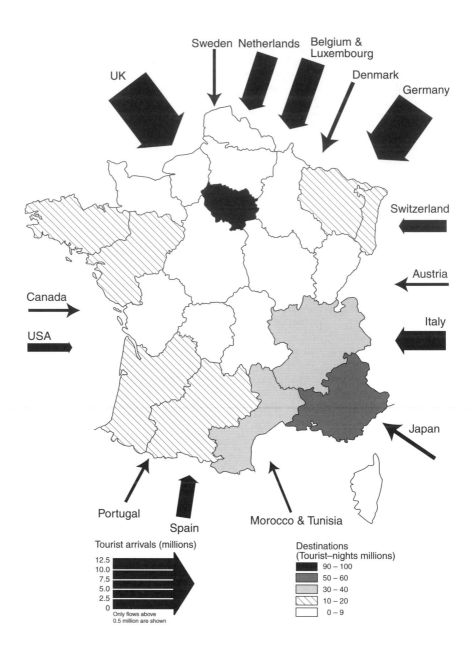

Fig. 11.2 Arrivals and destinations of foreign tourists in France, 1994

Sources: Data from Ministère de l'Equipement, du Logement, des Transports et du Tourisme (1996); Py (1996)

11.3.4   *Concentration in time and space*

Two interrelated organisational problems underlie these various patterns of tourism activity: the excessive concentration of tourism in both time and space (Tuppen 1991; Py 1996). Demand is unequally spread across the country, just as are the major tourist destinations. In more remote rural areas the proportion of the population taking a holiday is relatively low, generating modest flows of traffic; the inverse is true of the Paris region. Similarly, summer holidays are excessively focused on a limited number of coastal regions, while the influx of tourists to winter sports resorts focuses overwhelmingly on the northern Alps, virtually by-passing many other upland areas such as the Vosges, Jura or Massif Central.

This spatial polarisation is matched by a similar concentration within limited periods of the year. In summer, for example, 80 per cent of French holidays take place in July and August, with nearly 30 per cent concentrated in the first two weeks of August alone (Monteiro and Rowenczyk 1994). This pattern is repeated in winter, particularly during the months of December and February (Rowenczyk 1994). Moreover, the adverse effects of these spatial and temporal imbalances are enhanced by the strength of 'north–south' movements in the pattern of holiday-making—in general, northern regions experience a net outflow of tourists (largely due to the large number of people leaving the Paris region) while southern regions, where the major summer and winter holiday destinations are concentrated, feature a net inflow (Figure 11.3). Motorway arteries in particular are increasingly unable to accommodate the resultant flows at peak periods, but many other problems also result: congestion in resorts, inflated prices, under-utilised facilities in off-peak periods, damage to tourism sites and, in many cases, frustrating and stressful experiences for holiday-makers themselves. Tradition, institutional factors and climatic influences partly explain the peaked nature of demand and make it difficult to change tourists' habits. Even repeated attempts to modify the dates of school holidays have so far produced few tangible benefits.

11.4   Tourism resources, products and locations

11.4.1   *The supply of accommodation: diversification and innovation*

France offers the prospective tourist a large and diverse range of accommodation. The commercial sector, representing over 5.2 million beds, has expanded considerably over the post-war period, although more recently this trend has been moderated, reflecting a more depressed economic climate (Conseil Economique et Social 1996). Classified campsites and hotels provide the majority of accommodation, followed by various forms of rented property (Table 11.4).

There are now over 20,000 classified hotels in France, located predominantly in the Paris region and the south-east of the country (Figure 11.4). They provide a range of very different products. The small, independent, family-run hotel still survives, especially in many rural areas, although to facilitate marketing, certain such hotels now form part of voluntary chains such as Logis de France or Relais du Silence. Membership of a chain also often implies an effort to improve the quality of accommodation. Progressively, however, the market has become dominated by the large, increasingly multinational hotel chains such as Novotel or Holiday Inn, offering modern,

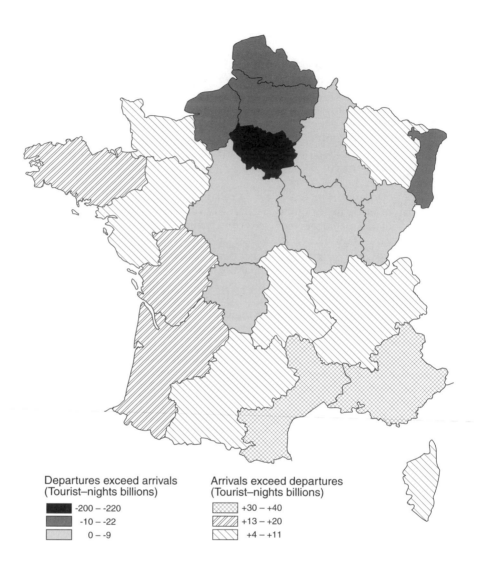

Fig. 11.3 Regional balance of French tourists' movements in France

Source: based on data from Py (1996)

standardised accommodation. These hotels blossomed from the 1960s until the 1980s, in a period of generally rapid economic growth when France was under-equipped in such facilities.

Over the last 20 years the hotel sector as a whole has expanded progressively, with beds increasing by an annual average of 2 per cent. However, not all segments have evolved along the same lines. Recent growth has been concentrated at the bottom end of the market, with the appearance of 'budget' hotels offering basic but comfortable accommodation at a low price. Again such hotels form part of nation-wide chains such

Table 11.4 Tourist accommodation in France, 1995

Type of accommodation	Number of beds
Campsites	2,800,000
Classified hotels	1,200,000
Furnished flats	450,000
Gîtes and bed and breakfast	253,000
Hotel residences	248,000
Holiday villages	242,000
Youth hostels	18,000
Total	5,211,000

Source: Ministère de l'Equipement, du Logement, des Transports et du Tourisme (1996).

as Formule 1, Etap Hotel or Première Classe. Apart from their similarity of appearance, they also share common locations—generally the outskirts of the urban area, including the fringes of industrial estates, where land prices are low. A further recent trend has been the growing development of 'hotel residences'; these are basically comfortable, self-catering flats and studios, built in the form of modern apartment blocks, which also offer common services such as restaurants and sport and entertainment facilities. The concept emerged in the 1970s and has been expanded rapidly since, largely by companies such as Pierre et Vacances and Maeva; currently over 600 residences provide approximately 250,000 beds, located principally in the major winter sports and coastal resorts (Conseil Economique et Social 1996).

Camping and caravanning holidays remain popular with the French, especially for the younger generations and people with comparatively modest incomes (Ministère du Tourisme 1995). Equally, a large number of foreign visitors choose this form of accommodation. As a result, the capacity of French campsites has risen significantly from 1.25 million places in 1971 to over 2.8 million in 1995 (Py 1996). The distribution of sites is unequal, with the largest concentrations in coastal regions (particularly along the Mediterranean and Atlantic coasts) and more generally throughout south-eastern France (Figure 11.4). The departments of the Vendée and the Var each have a capacity of over 50,000 places in their campsites (Béteille 1996). Indeed, in certain coastal regions, notably in the south of France, supply is far exceeded by demand at the peak of the summer season, leading to problems of unauthorised camping and potential health risks (Cazes 1995). Inland the pressures are generally far less, although campsites often represent a modest but significant means for many rural localities to develop a tourism activity. Increasingly there is a demand for better-equipped sites, offering higher levels of comfort. Similarly there has been a growth of sites providing accommodation in caravans or mobile homes which remain permanently on site and which again offer greater luxury.

Second homes have also increased dramatically from approximately 600,000 in 1960 to 2.8 million in 1990 (Béteille 1996). Such residences characterise many locations and take different forms, from the renovated farmhouse or rural dwelling to the modern apartment in a coastal or mountain resort. In total, second homes are estimated to represent a potential of over 12 million beds (Py 1996), although this 'tourist' accommodation is often inefficiently used, being occupied for only a limited number

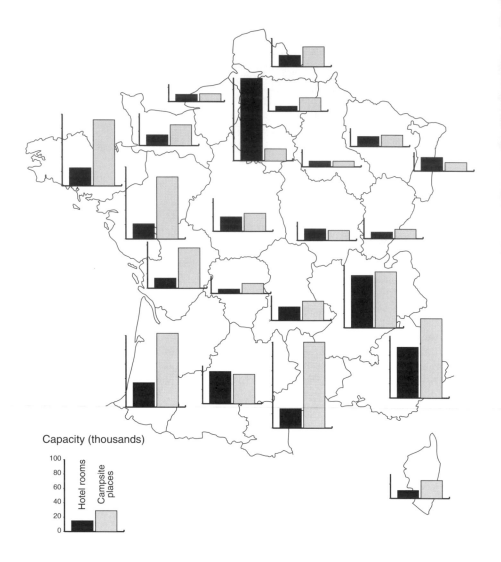

Fig. 11.4   Regional distribution of registered hotels and campsites, 1995

Source: Data from Ministère de L'Equipement, du Logement, des Transports et du Tourisme (1996)

of days per year by the owner, and rarely rented. The presence of second homes is contested for other reasons, notably for potentially inflationary effects on local house prices, the additional costs to the local community (sewage, water and refuse collection services) and the 'invasion' of local communities by newcomers. Indeed, in certain rural areas of the Massif Central, the Pyrenees and the Alps, second homes exceed well over 50 per cent of the total housing stock (Béteille 1996). Yet if this concentration produces problems, it is also often the origin of a vital source of revenue for many small communes.

11.4.2 *Coastal regions: France's prime tourism destination*

With over 5,500 km of coastline, much of it benefiting from sandy beaches, picturesque scenery and high levels of isolation, it is of little surprise that the country's seaboard should represent its prime tourist destination. Not all coastal areas have been developed to an equal extent, in part for purely climatic reasons, as in the case of the relative lack of appeal of Channel coast beaches. While many of the resorts along the Côte d'Azur or the Brittany and Basque coasts are long-established, since the 1960s a new generation of resorts has been added, affecting particularly the Languedoc and Aquitaine coasts. Yet despite such provision, overcrowding is manifest in summer. This is just one of many negative effects that tourism is deemed to have brought to such areas (Clary 1993). However, given the importance of tourism activities to local economies, this has not prevented numerous initiatives to develop the tourism function further. Many resorts have promoted the development of marinas, often as a logical extension or change of use of an existing fishing port. In other cases they have been purpose-built. Port-Camargue, for example, a 'new' resort along the Languedoc coast, now possesses a marina offering over 4,300 berths, one of the largest of its type in Europe (Conseil Economique et Social 1996). Other resorts have sought to extend their range of attractions and season through the provision of conference facilities as in the case of Cannes, Nice, Monaco and Deauville. There are also growing attempts to encourage interest in the cultural or historic background of resorts, enabling visitors to learn more about their destination and its traditions or about the maritime world in general (Clary 1993); Brest, for example, has invested heavily in a maritime museum (Océanopolis), attracting over 300,000 visitors each year (*Les Echos* 1996b).

11.4.3 *Mountainous regions as activity spaces*

Mountainous areas, covering 21 per cent of French territory, provide a further attractive and increasingly over-exploited natural resource for tourism. Although frequently associated with winter sports, tourism flows are far less important in winter than in summer (Cazes 1995); at this time these areas provide ideal surroundings for a wide range of outdoor activities, including walking and fishing or more energetic pursuits such as rock-climbing and rafting. Nevertheless, skiing still represents the primary attraction for tourists. France possesses the largest and most extensively equipped skiing area in Europe. From modest beginnings in the 1920s, when existing summer resorts such as Chamonix, la Clusaz or Megève began to develop a winter season, the provision of skiing facilities exploded in the post-war period, particularly in the northern Alps. This movement culminated in the 1960s and 1970s with the creation of a series of purpose-built, high altitude ski 'stations' such as Les Arcs, La Plagne, Val Thorens and Tignes. As supply increased, so did demand, with a rising proportion of French families taking a skiing holiday each year, and a growing number of foreign skiers choosing France in preference to Switzerland or Austria. By the winter of 1983–1984 over 10 per cent of the French population was going on a skiing holiday each year and the development of winter sports had given rise to a remarkable demographic and economic revival in many mountainous regions.

Since then uninterrupted growth has given way to stagnating, even declining demand, with still only one-tenth of the population taking a skiing holiday. A changed economic climate, heightened concern for the environment, several winters with poor snow cover at the end of the 1980s and the attraction of other winter holiday destinations have contributed to this slow-down in development (Knafou 1991). The ski market, not just in France but elsewhere in Europe, has reached a mature phase with increasing problems of saturation and over-supply of facilities (Tuppen 1988). Consequently, resorts have been forced to invest and innovate to remain competitive; new ski-lifts, snow-making machines, cultural, sports and entertainment facilities and refurbished buildings are all part of the armoury of measures employed to render resorts more attractive. However, not all have benefited to the same degree. The large, internationally renowned and often high-altitude locations, with the resources to invest, have retained their competitiveness, while many smaller, lower-altitude resorts with uncertain snow cover, often encountering financial difficulties, have become more marginalised, presenting problems for local communities that depend on tourism for jobs and incomes.

11.4.4   Rural areas: diversifying from artisanal origins

Just as mountainous areas attract large numbers of summer visitors, so too do many other rural regions in France. Over recent years greater efforts have been made to promote rural tourism, partly to help diversify local economies and also to relieve other more heavily utilised destinations. Similarly, demand has grown for holiday venues offering a 'return to nature' amidst more relaxed surroundings. Yet rural tourism retains a highly diverse character in terms of the regions it concerns, the nature of attractions and the degree to which development has been managed or occurred spontaneously. In general, rural areas offer many advantages for tourism—varied landscapes, unspoilt villages, old churches and chateaux, craft industries, extensive areas of forest and woodland, as well as rivers, ponds, lakes and wetlands offering opportunities for shooting, fishing or wildlife observation. In addition, an existing network of over 8,500 kilometres of inland waterways offers numerous opportunities for cruising and boating (Clary 1993).

   Rural tourism remains essentially artisanal in its organisation. Generally it is not characterised by large-scale development schemes and does not attract major public or private investors. Exceptions do exist, however, as in the case of the Center Parcs complexes in the Sologne and in Normandy. Change is none the less apparent. Attempts are being made to introduce a more professional approach to the management of tourist activities (Vitte 1995); and there are increasing examples of local councils and associations, as well as the more entrepreneurial members of rural communities, contributing to tourism developments (Mamdy 1995). These include 'theme breaks', based on local cuisine or the 'discovery' of the locality, and the provision of new accommodation. Such plans may even extend to whole river basins, as in the case of the Lot in southern France (Béteille 1996).

   A more coherent framework for the development of tourism was provided with the launching of a series of regional parks in 1967. Since that date 32 parks have been created throughout France, covering a variety of areas; certain of these, such as the Montagne de Reims or the Pilat (to the south-west of Lyon), are adjacent to major urban areas, while others such as the Livradois-Forez are more isolated (INSEE 1997). The parks aim to help preserve the local environment (physical and cultural), promote local economic development, particularly through 'quality tourism' and encourage innovative schemes in these fields (Laurens 1995; Dwyer 1991). Certain of these aims might appear contradictory, particularly where parks are close to major towns with strong demands for recreational space. However, this has not prevented innovative developments. In the Livradois-Forez park, for example, funding from the European LEADER project since 1991 has helped launch schemes to develop hiking trails, increase the number of *gîtes* (self-catering accommodation, usually in rural areas), restore local monuments and houses and run a scenic railway line.

11.4.5 *Urban locations: innovations and locational changes*

Just as the countryside has attracted more tourists, urban areas have also become an increasingly popular focus for tourist activities, extending beyond a traditional association with spa towns (such as Aix-les-Bains) and religious centres (Lourdes). In part this trend has been enhanced by a growing number of redevelopment schemes giving priority to tourism and cultural attractions (Cazes and Potier 1996). At the same time, many urban centres have sought to create and promote an image of dynamism and attractiveness (Lille as a 'European business centre' and Lyon as an 'international city') in which their role as tourism centres plays a dominant part. Urban tourism has a number of specific characteristics (Tuppen 1996). Towns and cities as such attract relatively few French holidaymakers, although they are a more popular destination for foreign tourists, particularly in the case of Paris. However, their appeal is much greater for short breaks (Renucci 1991). Large numbers of day visitors are also attracted to towns for leisure, business or recreational purposes, although there are few reliable statistics to attest to their real importance. Motives for visiting towns and cities are varied and often multiple in character, including visits to friends and relatives, to art galleries or museums, to historic monuments, to exhibitions or to concert halls and opera houses (Cazes and Potier 1996). However, in towns of over 100,000 inhabitants it is estimated that the visits of business people, and attendance at conferences or trade fairs and exhibitions, account for the majority of all tourist activity (Renucci 1991).

Municipal authorities and the private sector have not been slow to recognise the potential benefits offered by the development of business tourism. In a market overwhelmingly dominated by Paris (Lahuna 1996), substantial investment has occurred in hotels (including those with conference facilities), conference centres and exhibition halls, leading now to problems of over-supply (Cazes and Potier 1996). Since the early 1980s, the number of conference centres has doubled, with prestigious new facilities recently opened at Lyon, Lille, Reims and Vichy (*Les Echos* 1996c), adding to an already impressive list of venues in cities such as Paris, Nice, Strasbourg, Tours and Deauville. France lies second only to the USA in terms of its provision of conference facilities, while Paris has long been the uncontested world-leader for hosting the largest number of international conferences (332 events in 1995), ahead of Vienna and London (*Les Echos* 1996d).

Such frenzied investment has been motivated by the perceived lucrative character of the conference market. Certainly there are economic advantages, although they are not always easily quantifiable. The activities of the Palais des Congrès at Paris are estimated to create a turnover of 4 billion francs for businesses in the region of Ile-de-France (*Les Echos* 1996d). Similarly, at Nice the Acropolis convention centre employs over 150 people, provides permanent jobs for a further 300 people working for subcontractors and, with other conference centres in the town, is estimated to inject approximately 2 billion francs into the local economy (*Les Echos* 1996c). But there are

Table 11.5   Most visited monuments and
museums in Paris, 1994

Site	Number of visitors (millions)
Centre Georges Pompidou	6.9
Cité des Sciences et Industries	5.6
Tour Eiffel	5.4
Musée du Louvre	4.3
Chateau de Versailles	3.0
Musée d'Orsay	2.2

Source: Ministère de l'Equipement, du Logement, des
Transports et du Tourisme (1996).

also costs, particularly in this highly competitive market. Facilities are often under-utilised, require constant refurbishment to multiply their potential usages and respond to the ever-changing technical requirements of clients, and generate extremely high running costs that are not always covered by income. Many of these comments also apply to exhibition centres, especially those outside the Paris region (Tuppen 1996).

Cities also offer a wide range of opportunities for cultural tourism. Museums, art galleries, ancient monuments, historic buildings and churches, as well as major exhibitions of artists' works, have all become more popular with tourists. France is particularly well-placed to respond to such a demand, given its rich cultural heritage and the diversity of its museums: over the last decade visits to museums are estimated to have increased from 40 to 70 million people (Conseil Economique et Social 1996). As with conferences and exhibitions, much of this activity is heavily concentrated on Paris where, in certain instances, the number of visitors is extremely high (Table 11.5). New attractions have been opened, such as the interactive Cité de Sciences et de l'Industrie at la Villette in 1986, while others have been refurbished, enlarged or modernised, as in the case of the Eiffel Tower and the Louvre (Tuppen 1996). Visitor numbers may certainly be high (although the threat of terrorist attacks led to a fall in numbers in the mid-1990s), but the economic impact of such sites is more difficult to measure, particularly as running and maintenance costs may be important; over 600 million francs is spent each year to run the Louvre (Le Monde 1993).

Although not entirely urban-based, 'industrial' tourism has also grown in popularity over recent years. It is estimated that up to 10 million people each year now visit factories, farming enterprises, power stations and research centres, double the number compared with a decade ago (*Le Monde* 1996b). For firms this is often one means by which to advertise or increase awareness of their products or, in the case of EdF (French Electricity) and visits to nuclear power stations, a way of reassuring the public about issues of safety (*Les Echos* 1996e); for the tourist it provides an increasingly sought-after educational dimension to the visit. Amongst the most popular destinations are the tidal power station at Rance (350,000 visitors per annum), the limestone caverns in the Aveyron, used to ripen Roquefort cheese (200,000 visitors) and the manufacturing site of the liqueur 'Bénédictine' (140,000 visitors) at Fécamp on the Normandy coast (Conseil Economique et Social 1996; *Le Monde* 1996b).

Urban and particularly urban-fringe locations have also been the focus of large-scale investment in a new generation of purpose-built tourist attractions, epitomised by the theme park. Such parks were first developed in France in the 1980s, since when the concept has been widely adopted but not always with success (Potier and Cazes 1996). Mismanagement, over-ambitious investment and poor choice of locations have even resulted in closures (for example, the Mirapolis Park at Cergy-Pontoise, Paris and the Zygofolis Park at Nice). Other sites have proved more successful, such as the Astérix Park to the north of Paris with 1.8 million visitors in 1995 (*Les Echos* 1996f) and the most well-known, Disneyland, on the eastern outskirts of the new town of Marne-la-Vallée in the Paris region. Even this park experienced an uncertain beginning, although in 1995 it attracted 11.3 million visitors and is estimated to have created over 30,000 direct and indirect employment opportunities in the surrounding region (Tuppen 1996; *Les Echos* 1996g). One of the most successful parks has been the Futuroscope, located to the north of Poitiers and opened in 1985. The site is organised around the theme of new technologies and communications and has a distinct educational as well as recreational vocation; it attracted 2.8 million visitors in 1995 and employed over 1200 permanent staff as well as 500 seasonal workers (Conseil Economique et Social 1996).

Other similar attractions have been developed. There are now approximately 40 water parks spread throughout France, following the launching of Aqualand at Cap d'Agde in 1983. The most ambitious scheme opened in Paris in 1989 (the Aquaboulevard), although the most successful water parks are those located in existing resorts, essentially in the south of France, where they benefit from favourable climatic conditions (Cazes and Potier 1996). Large 'sea world' museums such as Océanopolis at Brest and Nausicaa at Boulogne-sur-Mer represent further examples of specialised, themed developments. Yet in many cases high investment costs and over-estimates of the number of visitors have compromised the commercial success of the ventures. It is also questionable whether they contribute greatly to the development of tourism as opposed to satisfying a local or regional demand for leisure activities.

11.5   The impacts of tourism

Many impacts result from tourism, not all of which are easy to assess or quantify. Moreover, whether tourism is adjudged favourably or unfavourably depends on the perspective from which it is viewed. From an economic standpoint tourist activities may bring many advantages in terms of jobs and revenue, but this may be at the expense of environmental damage or an increasing alienation of permanent residents forced to suffer congestion and disruption, not to mention the high prices induced by tourism.

11.5.1   Economic impacts

In 1994 total spending on tourist stays (Tuppen 1996; Py 1996) and related travel exceeded 554 billion francs, representing over 7.5 per cent of French GDP (Conseil Economique et Social 1996). This proportion has varied little over the last decade, attesting to the resilience of the tourism sector to the negative effects of recession which have characterised much of this period. France continues to attract a large number of foreign visitors with the result that tourism makes a significant contribution

Table 11.6   The 'travel' entry in the French balance of
payments (billions of francs)

	Receipts[1]	Expenditure[2]	Balance
1989	104	64	40
1990	110	68	42
1991	121	70	51
1992	133	74	59
1993	133	73	60
1994	137	76	61
1995	137	81	56

Sources: Ministère de l'Equipement, du Logement, des Transports et
du Tourisme (1996); INSEE (1996).

[1] Spending by foreign visitors in France.
[2] Spending by French visitors abroad.

Table 11.7   Employment in the tourism industry, 1992

Activity	Permanent and part-time employees (thousands)
Restaurants	552
Hotels	360
Campsites and youth hostels	35
Other accommodation	129
Cafés	62
Travel agents and tourist offices	56
Hydrotherapy and thalassotherapy	14
Ski-lifts	12
Total	1,220

Source: Conseil Economique et Social (1996).

to the French balance of payments; spending in France by such tourists considerably exceeds expenditure by French people abroad (Table 11.6). This surplus has increased significantly since the late 1960s, so that its contribution to the French economy is now equal to or greater than that of leading export sectors such as agricultural and food products or the car industry (Tuppen 1996).

Direct employment in tourism in France is estimated at up to 1.2 million jobs, of which at least two-thirds are of a seasonal character (Table 11.7). Indirect employment in related activities (manufacturing, services, building and public works) provides approximately a further 600,000 jobs (Py 1996). Indeed, one of the main attractions of the tourism industry has been its ability to create employment, and over the last decade jobs in tourism have increased by an average of 2.7 per cent each year; conversely, employment generally in France rose annually by an average of only 0.5 per cent between 1985 and 1995 (Conseil Economique et Social 1996; INSEE 1996). However, the beneficial effects resulting from the creation of such jobs are limited by the fact that such employment often requires few skills or qualifications and is correspondingly poorly paid. Moreover, in many cases it is seasonal migrants and outsiders rather than the indigenous population that benefit from these jobs, provoking resentment amongst local communities (Debarbieux 1995).

Economic impacts are not spread evenly throughout the country. Only a limited number of regions are affected by mass tourism. In general, southern and western parts of France are far more popular tourist destinations than northern and central regions. However, even within this southern and western arc, not all areas are equally attractive. The three regions of Provence–Alpes–Côtes d'Azur, Languedoc–Roussillon and Rhône–Alpes form a major pole of attraction, while in western France tourism is concentrated in a linear, coastal belt stretching from Brittany through the Pays-de-la Loire and Poitou-Charentes to Aquitaine. The Paris region represents the major exception to this pattern, attracting a large number of French visitors, as well as representing the primary focus of foreign visitors to France; it is a major destination for short-breaks and is the country's undisputed centre of business tourism. At the same time it is by far the most important single origin of tourists within France.

Even within those regions having a clear vocation for tourism, activity is often limited to relatively few areas. This is particularly true along the Mediterranean and Atlantic coasts, with the principal resorts and main tourism activities still confined to a narrow coastal strip. Along the Languedoc coast 80 per cent of tourist nights are confined to this zone (Py 1996). In the department of the Var (with resorts such as St Tropez and St Raphaël) this tendency is even more accentuated with 90 per cent of the 67 million tourist nights recorded in 1994 spent along the coastal fringe (*La Tribune Desfossés* 1996b). Such spatial inequality is also a feature of mountainous regions. The present economic and demographic vitality of the northern Alps owes much to tourism, but not all areas feature a similar dynamism. Certain communities have been by-passed in the process of development, a feature illustrated by comparison of the two almost adjacent cantons of Aime and Aiguebelle which lie to the west of Bourg-St Maurice (Table 11.8). Both were originally dependent on a traditional alpine pastoral economy, but since the 1970s the area of Aime has been revitalised by the development of La Plagne, one of the largest resorts in the French Alps.

11.5.2   *Other impacts: social and environmental*

The growth of tourism can also involve costs and is not always perceived as a welcome form of development. In many areas the influx of tourists has been associated with a growth in drug and alcohol-related problems, as well as a general rise in criminality (Debarbieux 1995). Since the late 1970s the French have also shown an enhanced awareness of the detrimental effects tourism may have on natural habitats and ecosystems, of its intrusive nature in many landscapes, of the environmental damage caused to popular sites and of the costs resulting from tourist-induced congestion and pollution. At the same time there has been an increasing demand by tourists to be able to enjoy areas in their natural state. There have also been sound commercial arguments for adopting a revised approach to development, as it has proved increasingly difficult to dispose of properties in some of the poorly-designed tourism complexes built in the 1960s and 1970s (Knafou 1992).

Progressively, therefore, greater account is being taken of the environmental and social impacts of tourism. In the short term this has resulted primarily in growing action to resolve problems of over-use and determine carrying capacities for sites, as well as to repair damage inflicted by previous ill-conceived developments. Increasing

Table 11.8 Socio–economic contrasts between the cantons of Aime and Aiguebelle in the French Alps

Canton	Population total 1990	Population change, 1982–90 (Annual mean, %)			Proportion of people 60 and over (%)	Employment change 1982–90 (%)	Unemployment rate 1990 (%)	Second homes as proportion of total residences (%)
		Total change	Natural change	Migrational change				
Aiguebelle	4,307	–1.1	–0.5	–0.6	28.3	–2.3	8.7	29.2
Aime	7,753	+1.8	+0.6	+1.2	15.9	+4.3	3.7	78.1

Source: INSEE (1992).

numbers of examples exist of measures to regulate flows of visitors to the most popular historic monuments and museums, such as the Palace of Versailles and the Louvre (Cazes et Potier 1996). Similarly, over the last decade the Ministries of Tourism, Equipment and the Environment have worked in partnership with local authorities to prevent further damage to major tourism sites caused by exceptionally heavy usage, often concentrated over only a few months. The aim is not to prevent access but to manage visitor flows more effectively (Ministère de l'Environnement: Ministère du Tourisme 1992). Sites already treated in this way include the Pyla sand dune on the Aquitaine coast (1.5 million visitors each year) and Ardèche gorges which attract over 170,000 canoeists each year.

Car parking and traffic congestion are widespread problems, not least in many ski resorts. A growing number have responded by limiting traffic in the central area (e.g. Flaine, Val Thorens), although not always with great success. Conversely, in many of the more recent winter sports resorts, such as La Plagne, criticised originally for the unattractiveness of the architecture, the built environment is being slowly refurbished. Moreover, there are growing attempts to remove earlier landscape scars through actions such as the regrassing of slopes. Certainly the preparations for the 1992 Winter Olympics showed a new awareness of environmental issues, even if the destruction of natural habitats and forest areas was not always avoided (May 1995). Similar efforts are also under way to effect qualitative improvements to various coastal resorts, notably in the case of the tourism strategy adopted for Languedoc–Roussillon in 1993 (Conseil Economique et Social 1996; Klemm 1996).

In the longer term, planning frameworks and development strategies themselves need to be rethought to take account of tourism's negative impacts. Already this has occurred through the legislation passed in the mid-1980s to regulate the expansion of tourism activities in coastal and mountainous regions and give local authorities a more active role in the planning of tourism. New organisational structures have also been created to achieve this goal, as illustrated by the 'Espace Mont Blanc'. In this area of exceptional natural beauty the different regional authorities in France, Switzerland and Italy have agreed to a common set of initiatives to promote more sustainable forms of tourism development (Conférence Transfrontalière Mont-Blanc 1994). Similarly, France is a signatory of the 'Alpine Convention' (originally agreed by the six alpine states in 1991), an international charter which advocates strong control over development (Barruet 1995; Knafou 1994). Some encouragement for the future might be drawn, however, from the fact that not all tourist developments have been shown to be environmentally damaging or aesthetically repellent, as demonstrated by the resorts of Valmorel in the French Alps and Port Grimaud on the Mediterranean coast (Knafou 1992).

11.6   Conclusions: continuity and change

France has long prospered from a large and dynamic tourist industry, stimulated to a great extent by the beauty of the country's landscapes and the richness of its cultural heritage, assets that have altered little over time. This should not imply, however, that tourism has remained unchanged. On the contrary, policies and priorities have been modified, often in response to changes in demand, as well as to the constantly evolving economic and political contexts in which tourism activities take place. Further change has been induced by the challenge of responding to increased competition from foreign tourism destinations.

Much of the early post-war period was devoted to developing France's tourism facilities and accommodation in a period of rapidly increasing demand at a time when the country lacked modern resorts capable of accepting large numbers of tourists. These quantitative issues have now been addressed, but less attention has been paid to questions of quality. Currently, therefore, emphasis is being placed on a series of qualitative improvements to tourism products, ranging from raising the standard of welcome and service generally to providing better accommodation at realistic prices. Such transformations also imply a higher level of investment in staff training. Problems remain, however, in many rural regions, where the organisation of tourism activities is still characterised by a lack of professionalism and the persistence of a large number of small and often inefficiently-run firms.

The development of tourism has long formed part of regional planning strategies, as exemplified by past, large-scale investment projects. More recently, priorities and approaches have changed, with the emergence of two key developmental issues: first, the need for more effective management of heavily utilised tourism attractions and destinations; and, second, the necessity to improve the integration of tourism into the economies of the country's more remote rural regions. In the latter case this responds to a growing demand from tourists themselves, as well as to an urgent need to provide additional incomes in areas where farming can no longer provide a full-time activity.

These changes have been accompanied by a partial redistribution of roles amongst the different actors involved in tourism development. In their different ways large multinational groups, local authorities and environmental groups now all intervene to a far greater extent in the provision of tourism facilities and in determining related policy. However, the French planning system remains characterised by a 'top-down' approach and, in a still highly centralised state such as France, the ability of the government to influence development should not be underestimated.

12 Germany: still a growing international deficit?

Peter Schnell

12.1 Introduction

Since the mid-1970s Germans have secured the reputation of being 'the world champions of travelling': this refers not only to the high rates of Germans taking their holidays within the Federal Republic or abroad, but also to the broader economic features of this travel. In 1995 more than two-thirds (69 per cent) of all holidays of five or more days were to foreign destinations, and German tourists spent DM 68.8 billion abroad. Since foreign tourists visiting Germany spent 'only' DM 18.3 billion in the same year, the travel deficit was an enormous DM 50.6 billion in that year.

Germany and its tourist regions also represent a tourist destination. The number of beds offered by commercial accommodation establishments in the Federal Republic increased by 377 per cent between 1954 and 1988 and, during the same period, the number of visitor arrivals and nights grew by more than 200 per cent. After the political reunification of the two Germanys on 3 October 1990, these percentages reached 490, 436 and 427, respectively, in 1995. Although the share of foreign visitors to the Federal Republic has increased, the receipts amounted to 'only' DM 18.3 billion so that tourism is a source of economic deficit for Germany. Furthermore, on a regional basis, tourism development reveals sharp regional differences that cause problems for local and regional tourism organisations and enterprises.

This chapter considers the major features of national tourism trends in terms of the spatial distribution of German tourist flows, the development and regional structure of tourism in the Federal Republic, and the impact of tourism and tourism policies. Particular attention will be given to the changes that have been brought about by the reunification of the two Germanys in October 1990. Data for the period before 1990 pertain to West Germany, unless otherwise stated.

12.2 National tourism trends before and after unification

National tourism trends are summarised in Table 12.1. Travel intensity, that is, the percentage of the German population aged over 14 taking one or more holidays of five or more days per year, has increased rapidly since the mid-1950s. At that time, not

Tourism and Economic Development: European Experiences, 3rd Edition. Edited by A.M. Williams and G. Shaw.
© 1998 John Wiley & Sons Ltd.

Table 12.1 Development and structure of German tourism, 1954–1995 (%)

	1954	1960	1970	1975	1980	1985	1990	1995
Travel intensity (5 days and more)	24	28	42	56	58	57	69	78
Short-term travel intensity (2–4 days)			23	21	26	33	40	37
Travel destinations								
Inland	85	69	47	46	40	34	32	34
Abroad	15	31	53	54	60	66	68	66
Organisation								
Individually organised travel	87[1]		83	82	74	66	65	61
All-inclusive package tour	13[1]		17	18	26	34	35	39
Means of transport								
Car	19	38	61	61	59	60	59	52
Aeroplane	–	1	8	12	16	18	23	28
Train	56	42	24	19	16	11	8	8
Bus	17	16	7	7	8	10	8	10
Other	8	3	–	1	1	1	2	2
Duration								
5–8 days			22	8	9	8	10	11	13
9–15 days			35	35	38	40	43	43	55
16–22 days			27	39	37	35	34	32	22
23 days and longer			16	18	16	17	13	14	9
Travel expenses per person								
up to DM 600			57	72	46	22	22	25	14[3]
DM 600–1,000			26	20	27	26	23	40	21[4]
DM 1,000–1,500			11	8	15	25	23 } 40		29
DM 1,500+			–	–	8	24	26 }		36
No response			6	–	4	3	6	5	–
Type of accommodation								
Hotel/inn/boarding house	29	24[2]	42	46	48	46	46	50
Cottage/bungalow/apartment	–	–	7	9	10	14	20	21
Private room (rented)	17	35[2]	20	16	11	10	8	5
Relatives/friends	43	23[2]	17	13	12	10	11	13
Camping/caravaning	5	9[2]	9	8	10	10	8	8
Other	6	11[2]	5	8	9	10	9	3
Type of holidays								
Rest/pleasure					83	82	71	71	82
Visiting relatives/friends					10	9	9	12	16
Sightseeing/study/education					2	4	7	12	18
Health					3	2	6	11	29
Sporting					2	3	5	5	8

Sources: Studienkreis für Tourismus (1986); von Lassberg and Steinmassl (1991); Koch (1959); Statistisches Bundesamt (1965); Forschungsgemeinschaft Urlaub und Reisen e.V. (1997).

[1] 1958.
[2] 1961–2.
[3] Up to DM 600.
[4] DM 500–1,000.
Note that the Federal Republic of Germany consisted of 11 provinces, including West Berlin, but since 3 October 1990 Germany has comprised 16 provinces.

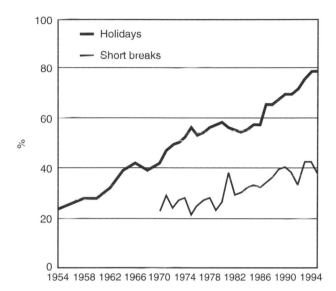

Fig. 12.1   Germany: Tourist intensity, 1954–94

Source: Studienkreis für Tourismus (1986, 1987, 1991); Forschungsgemeinschaft Urlaub und Reisen e.V. (1996)

even one-quarter of the German population undertook holiday travels, although there is no information about shorter holidays in that period. Travel intensity reached a peak of 58 per cent in 1980, then dropped to 54 per cent in 1983. It subsequently increased to a new peak of 78 per cent in 1994 and 1995, so that more than three-quarters of the German population take at least one holiday trip of five or more days per year (Figure 12.1). The recent increase is partly due to the fact that the inhabitants of the former GDR (East Germany) had a strong pent-up demand for travelling, especially to destination countries they could not visit before 1990. Since the early 1970s there has also been a growing trend for short breaks (2–4 days). By 1985 one-third of the population aged over 14 partook in short-break travel, and this rate increased to 42 per cent in 1990, but then dropped to 37 per cent in 1995. The short break curve in Figure 12.1 has a far more uneven shape than the overall holiday curve because demand for this type of holiday is far more sensitive to changes in personal and national economic circumstances.

There has also been a major shift in destinations. While only 15 per cent of all West German holiday travel involved foreign destinations in 1954, this share had increased to 66 per cent in 1985 and since then has been stagnating at around this level. This development not only caused problems for the tourism regions in West Germany, but also meant there was a growing outflow of German currency. In 1960 DM 2.8 billion were spent abroad and DM 2.0 billion were received from foreign visitors to the Federal Republic. However, by 1995, as pointed out above, DM 68.8 billion were spent abroad and only DM 18.3 billion received from foreign tourists, so that the gap between expenditures and receipts is considerable (Statistisches Bundesamt 1965, 1996).

In 1958 only 13 per cent of all holiday travels were booked as package tours, but with the evolution of mass tourism and air transport this share has since increased to 39 per cent. This development and a shift in holiday destinations have led to changes in the type of tourism transport used. In the 1950s and the early 1960s car-ownership levels were relatively low and the railway was the most important mode of transport. Later the car took the lead, accounting for 60 per cent of holiday travels in the mid-1980s; since then there has been a slow but steady decrease in the use of cars. The latest trend—which has to be seen in relation to increased preference for foreign destinations booked as package tours—is the increase in air transport which had reached a share of 28 per cent in 1995.

Most holidays last between 9 and 15 days, but longer holidays are also common. However, shorter (5–8 days) and longer (23 days and longer) holidays are relatively less popular than in 1960. Shorter holidays have obviously been gaining market shares recently. The explanation lies in the trend to shorten main holidays and to divide up the remaining vacation time into additional and shorter trips; this trend is also responsible for the strong increase in short breaks mentioned previously. Although the data seem to indicate an increase in travel duration, and despite the rise of paid holidays, the average duration had fallen from 17.9 days in 1976 to 15.4 days in 1995 (Forschungsgemeinschaft Urlaub und Reisen e.V. 1997, p. 86). This decrease is explained by the growing number of Germans who take a second or third holiday and who participate in short breaks, thereby shortening their main holidays.

The types of accommodation preferred by most German holidaymakers are hotels, inns and boarding houses, and this has changed little since 1970. Staying with relatives or friends has become less popular, dropping from 43 per cent in 1954 to 23 per cent in 1960 and 10 per cent in 1985. Since then this trend seems to have taken a slightly positive change, which may be due to German reunification. Overall, however, this type of accommodation is rather unimportant today. In the 1960s the renting of private rooms—another type of relatively inexpensive accommodation—took the lead, but this has lost prominence since 1970, when foreign destinations became important. A relatively new trend is the growth of self-catering accommodation. The still growing demand for cottages, bungalows and apartments can be explained by the preference for independence, the wish for increased (private) space, and a desire to reduce costs. Camping and caravaning reached their maximum percentages in the 1980s and have been stagnating at around 10 per cent since then. The reasons why this type of accommodation is preferred are partly similar to self-catering, but is also reinforced by the demands of locational independence and opportunities for social mixing. The rapidly growing stock of caravans and mobile homes indicates the strength of this trend: the number of caravans increased from 62,563 in 1966 to 600,229 in 1994, whilst the number of mobile homes increased from 4,839 in 1969 to 311,002 in 1994 (quoted in Deutsche Gesellschaft für Freizeit 1995, p. 41) (Figure. 12.2).

Travel expenses per capita have risen considerably since 1960. There are two reasons for this: first, the general increase in incomes, and second, the growing share of transport costs, given the shift in destination preferences. The average holiday cost DM 365 in 1969 (domestic DM 280 and abroad DM 490), DM 795 in 1979–1980 (domestic DM 553 and abroad DM 977) (Statistisches Bundesamt 1970, pp. 624–25, 1981, p. 869) and DM 1,410 in 1995 (domestic DM 976; abroad DM 1,176) (Forschungsgemeinschaft Urlaub und Reisen e.V. 1997, p. 115). There is a considerable gap between tourists from the former West Germany and the GDR in terms of travel expenses. In 1990, the year of reunification, West German tourists, on average,

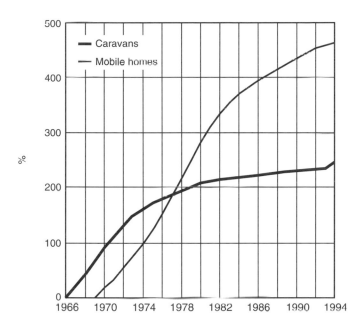

Fig. 12.2 Caravans and mobile homes in Germany, 1966–1994

Source: Deutsche Gesellschaft für Freizeit (1995)

spent 2.6 times more money on holiday travel than tourists from the new eastern provinces (*Bundesländer*), whose holidays lasted 12.6 days compared with 17.3 days in the former West Germany (von Lassberg and Steinmassel 1991, p. 101). Although this ratio has decreased to 1.6 subsequently, there is still a sharp difference related to lower income levels in the eastern provinces. Within the five years period 1991–1995, the average expenditure on main holiday travel rose by 18 per cent; the major increase—104 per cent however, occurred in the eastern provinces, while in the western provinces it was relatively low at only 9.6 per cent. Depending on holiday destinations, travel expenses per capita vary enormously. In 1995 a domestic holiday cost DM 976, holiday travel to Austria DM 1,512, to the Mediterranean countries DM 1,750 and long-distance travel DM 3,612 (Forschungsgemeinschaft Urlaub und Reisen e.V. 1997, p. 115).

Relaxation and pleasure were the predominant aims of holidaymakers in the mid-1980s, but these have decreased in importance since then, while interest in city tourism, snow holidays (winter), medical treatment holidays (*Kururlaub*), holidays in a holiday centre/holiday park, farmhouse holidays, and club holidays has grown considerably (Table 12.2)

According to the Studienkreis für Tourismus (1987), changes in preferred holiday types could be expected to influence the choice of destination. Table 12.3 confirms the general trend towards activity-, adventure- and event-orientated holidays. With short breaks, the two most important forms in 1995 were visiting relatives or friends (51 per cent) and city tourism (36 per cent) (Forschungsgemeinschaft Urlaub und Reisen e.V. 1997, Table 17).

Table 12.2   Participation and interest in different types of holiday in Germany, 1986 and 1995 (%)

Type of holiday	1987	Interest in 1987–1990	1995	Interest in 1995–1998
Health/fitness holidays	18	27	9	23
Urban tourism	15	24	13	29
Snow holidays (winter)	11	20	8	17
Sporting holiday (summer)	10	16	4	9
Camping holidays (tent)	8	12	6	9
Study travel	7	14	6	17
Medical treatment holidays (*Kururlaub*)	7	14	5	15
Caravaning holidays (caravan/mobile home)	6	10	7	13
Further education holidays	4	8	2	7
Farmhouse holidays	3	8	4	11
Club holidays (e.g. Club Méditerranée)	2	6	4	10
Nudist holidays	2	4	1	4
Adventure holidays (e.g. safari)	2	6	3	9
Hobby holidays (e.g. painting, pottering)	1	4	1	3
Cruising holidays	1	5	1	7

Sources: Dundler 1988, p. 49; Forschungsgemeinschaft Urlaub und Reisen e.V. 1997, p. 116.

Note: see Table 12.1 for the definition of Germany and the Federal Republic of Germany.

Aggregating the holiday types shown in Table 12.2 to eight generalised categories reveals some marked changes since the mid-1970s (Table 12.3). Interest in pleasure holidays seems to have decreased dramatically recently; this drop may be partly due, however, to the fact that the 1995 data were collected by a sampling institute which was different to that previously responsible for this task. In addition, the second and third holiday types (rest and summer beach/bathing) do, of course, also contain elements of pleasure. The very high shares of holiday types two and three, and the 'explosive' growth of type three, certainly depend on changes in destination preferences, a subject which is dealt with in the next chapter. Visiting and staying with relatives and friends has undergone a strong increase since the political reunification of the two Germanys. One reason why health-orientated holidays have recently gained importance is connected with changes in the demographic structure of the German population, the so-called 'greying effect'.

Finally, the seasonal aspects of tourism have to be considered. Data concerning the seasonal distribution of travel were deliberately not included in Table 12.1 because there have not been any significant changes during the past 30 years. It is a characteristic feature of German tourist flows that about 50 per cent of all holiday travel takes place in July and August, with about another 30 per cent in May, June and September. This concentration is largely conditioned by the prevailing system of school and works holidays. In 1975 nearly 50 per cent of all holidaymakers adjusted their holiday plans to these kinds of constraints (Fornfeist 1976, p. 15), and there has been little change in this percentage up to 1995. There are of course differences according to family types; 75 per cent of families with children took their holidays in June, July and August, compared to 53 per cent of adults without children. For the latter group, the main holiday season also included the months May (12 per cent) and September (16 per cent). Thus families without children have a longer and much more

Table 12.3 Main types of holidays taken by Germans, 1974–1995 (%)

Type of holiday	1974	1980	1985	1990	1995
Pleasure holidays	12	15	23	35	14
Rest holidays	67	67	28	39	38
Beach/bathing/summer holidays			19	29	39
Visiting relatives/friends	12	9	9	18	23
Health/medical treatment holidays	2	2	6	10	11
Study/sightseeing/educational holidays	4	4	7	12	8
Sporting holidays	3	3	5	5	7
Adventure holidays			1	4	3

Sources: Studienkreis für Tourismus (1986, Table 10); Forschungsgemeinschaft Urlaub und Reisen e.V. (1997, p. 116).

Note: see Table 12.1 for the definition of Germany and the Federal Republic of Germany.

even distributed holiday season than those with children, 39 per cent of whom take their holidays in July alone compared to 20 per cent of those without children (Forschungsgemeinschaft Urlaub und Reisen e.V. 1997, p. 82). The summer season (May–October) is clearly predominant but, since a growing number of Germans take a second and third holiday in winter, the ratio between summer and winter travels has fallen from 89:11 in 1984–85 (Zucker 1986, p. 53) to 82:18 in 1994–95 (Forschungs-gemeinschaft Urlaub und Reisen e.V. 1996, p. 78).

The growth of winter holidays will almost certainly continue because the increase of tourist arrivals and nights in the ski resorts continued undisturbed after the energy crises of the 1970s and the economic depression of the early 1980s, in contrast to the experiences of the summer resorts. This is because of the differences in the socio-economic profile of winter, as compared to summer, tourists.

12.3   The exodus to the sun

12.3.1   *Foreign destinations: the widening international search*

More than 50 per cent of West German holidaymakers travelled abroad as early as 1970 (Table 12.1). By 1995 the destinations of more than 50 per cent of all holidays spent abroad were the Mediterranean countries (Table 12.4 and Figure 12.3). In the early phase of international travel in the 1950s and the 1960s, however, Austria—essentially the Alps—was the country most favoured by West German tourists. At that time more than one-third of all cross-border travel was to Austria, while the combined share of the Mediterranean countries was only 4 per cent greater than this. At the level of individual states, Austria at that time held top position, but by 1970 its share had already declined by about 10 per cent over the previous decade. Since then, this trend has continued, and in 1995 Austria was the destination of only 11.6 per cent of Germans travelling abroad. The Mediterranean countries, on the other hand, were the definite winners in this process until the end of the 1980s. Spain, Yugoslavia, France and Greece had growing market shares; the only exception was Italy, for its share has more or less stagnated and recently reveals a small tendency to decline. Because of the political disturbances in, and the dissolution of the former state of Yugoslavia, German

Table 12.4   Foreign holiday destinations of Germans, 1958–1995 (%)

	1957–1958	1962	1970	1975	1980	1985	1990	1995
Austria	36.0	37.0	27.8	27.9	20.9	14.5	12.2	11.6
Italy	24.0	27.0	22.2	16.2	15.9	18.6	14.5	13.3
Spain	4.0	5.6	9.3	15.7	14.8	17.3	16.7	19.8
Yugoslavia	4.0	2.5	3.7	6.6	6.9	9.1	6.4	0.0
France	8.0	4.3	3.7	6.8	6.9	8.1	8.4	6.9
Greece	0.0	0.9	3.7	2.6	3.5	4.7	4.8	6.1
Scandinavian countries	0.0	4.0	–	5.0	5.8	2.4	4.2	5.2
Other European countries	–	–	25.9	10.2	10.5	12.8	11.9	5.4
Eastern Europe	24.0	18.7	–	4.4	3.4	4.2	9.0	13.6
Non-European countries			1.9	4.4	8.5	7.7	11.9	18.1
Number of holidays (millions)	3.1	5.8	10.0	13.6	16.8	18.3	31.1	40.7
Percentage of all holidays	25.0	38.7	53.0	54.2	60.4	65.9	57.7	63.1

Sources: Koch (1959); Statistisches Bundesamt (1965); Studienkreis für Tourismus (1986); von Lassberg and Steinmassl (1991); Forschungsgemeinschaft Urlaub und Reisen e.V. (1997).

Note: see Table 12.1 for the definition of Germany and the Federal Republic of Germany.

tourism to that destination area has fallen towards zero. The combined share of the Mediterranean countries is, in fact even higher, for Turkey, Malta and the North African countries are not identified in Table 12.4. The greatest increase has been in Spain, which was visited by 8.1 million Germans (over 14 years of age) in 1995 (Forschungsgemeinschaft Urlaub und Reisen e.V. 1997, p. 63).

There are several reasons for changes in destination preferences. There are, of course, climatic differences between Germany and the Mediterranean countries. Unstable weather conditions in Germany have caused many Germans to seek holiday destinations with guaranteed fine weather. Italy became popular at an early stage for this reason and because of its proximity, although cultural tourism also has always been important in this case. A second reason is the preference for a change of 'scenery', and this not only refers to the climate, but also to the physical and cultural landscape. A third reason lies in the nature of mass tourism with innovations such as mass accommodation, charter flights and all–inclusive package tours. The fourth reason is the favourable movement of currency exchange rates, although these differ between destination countries from year to year. This last reason not only caused many (West) Germans to spend their holidays in the Mediterranean countries but also, where possible, to acquire second homes there.

Some of the recent changes in choice of destination depend, of course, on the effects of the political reunification of the two Germanys in 1990. First, the population of the former GDR, who for more than 40 years were highly restricted in their choice of travel and holiday destinations, had a high level of suppressed demand for travel. However, in the early years after reunification they often lacked the economic basis for the kind of tourism practised in West Germany. Thus, in 1990, only 24.8 per cent of the holiday trips of East Germans were to foreign destinations, compared to 68.3 per cent in West Germany (von Lassleben and Steinmassl 1991, p. 55). More than one-quarter (27.3 per cent) of all holidays were spent in eastern European countries which were well-known from the pre-1990 period; if trips to Hungary (12.1 per cent) are added, nearly two-fifths of all holidays had their destination in Eastern European

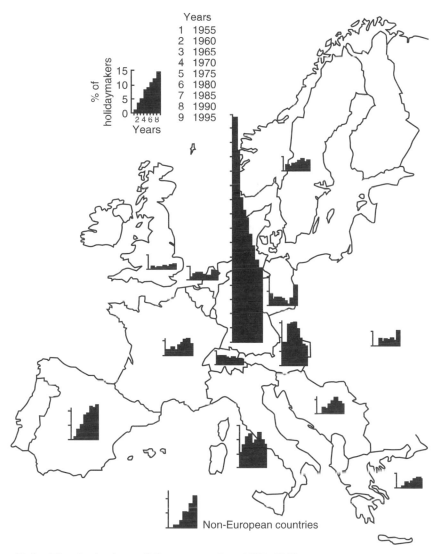

Fig. 12.3 The destinations of German tourists, 1955–1995

Source: Jurczec (1986b, p. 76); von Lassberg and Steinmassl (1991); Forschungsgemeinschaft Urlaub und Reisen e.V. (1997)

countries. Austria (18.2 per cent), Spain (12.1 per cent) and Italy (9.1 per cent) were the top-ranking destination countries in the western hemisphere. Only 3.0 per cent of all holiday trips were to non-European countries.

The process of adjustment in foreign travel has advanced rapidly since then for, in 1995, 59 per cent of all holiday trips from Eastern Germany were already to foreign destinations, compared with 72 per cent in the former West Germany. Tourists from Eastern Germany still have a strong preference for the Eastern European countries, where their share is more than twofold higher than that of West German tourists. There are only two other destinations where their shares exceed those of West Germans: Austria and the Scandinavian countries (excluding Denmark). One reason for this is that East German tourists spend less on their holiday travel than do their counterparts from West Germany: in 1995 54 per cent spent less than DM 1,000 for their holidays (compared to 39 per cent of West German tourists). The process of adjustment is also illustrated by the fact that, in 1990, 82.1 per cent of East Germans spent less than DM 900 on their travel, while the comparable figure for West Germans was only 41.2 per cent (von Lassleben and Steinmassl 1991, p. 100).

Finally, long-distance travel has become increasingly important since the mid-1970s. The reasons for this boom are virtually the same as those for the popularity of the Mediterranean countries. In addition, however, the economic prosperity of a large part of the German population is important since transport costs make up a much larger share of total travel costs than in the case of the latter: the average costs per person for a main holiday to the Mediterranean countries amounted to DM 1,750 in 1995, compared with DM 3,612 for long-distance travel (Forschungsgemeinschaft Urlaub und Reisen e.V. 1997, p. 115).

Long-distance holiday destinations are very much favoured by German tourists. This trend is demonstrated by the fact that, in 1994, 47 per cent of the German population would have liked to have spent a holiday in the Caribbean (compared to 42 per cent in 1991), 35 per cent in Australia (25 per cent), 20 per cent in the Dominican Republic (9 per cent), and 16 per cent in South Africa (10 per cent), to mention only those countries with the highest growth rates. There are another 17 destinations with positive growth rates, the nearest of which is Iceland (Opaschowski 1995, p. 19). This trend corresponds very much with World Tourism Organisation forecasts that, on a global scale, the share of long-distance travels will increase from 24 per cent in 1996 to 32 per cent in 2020.

The negative economic balance of tourism has clearly increased in the past 25 years. In 1970 German tourists spent ECU 2,734 million abroad, and the receipts from incoming tourism amounted to ECU 1,297 million. The comparable figures in 1980 were ECU 14,500 million and ECU 4,501 million; in 1990 ECU 23,222 million and ECU 8,300 million; and in 1994 ECU 35,119 million and ECU 9,257 million (Statistisches Bundesamt 1988, p. 102; 1997, p. 223). By 1995, German tourism expenditure in foreign countries—as mentioned previously—amounted to DM 68.8 billion of which nearly two-thirds were spent in EU countries. On the other hand, since receipts from incoming tourism amounted to only DM 18.3 billion in 1995, there was a net deficit of DM 50.5 billion (Deutsche Gesellschaft für Freizeit 1996, p. 56).

12.3.2   Structural aspects of international tourism

The structural features of German international tourism can best be demonstrated by comparing domestic and cross-border travel (Table 12.5). Unfortunately, this table cannot be completely updated, since tourism has been excluded from the micro-census analyses since the beginning of the 1980s. The results of the surveys of 1962 and 1979–1980 show that, since the early phase of cross-border holiday travel, the car has been the dominant means of transport. Its share subsequently remained stable until the beginning of the 1980s, but then fell to 42 per cent. With domestic tourism, on the

Table 12.5 Structural features of German domestic and cross-border tourism, 1962, 1979–1980 and 1995

	1962, Domestic	1962, Cross-border	1979–1980, Domestic	1979–1980, Cross-border	1995, Domestic	1995, Cross-border
Means of transport (%)						
Car	41.9	59.2	67.1	60.3	73	42
Train	48.1	29.3	23.0	9.2	16	4
Bus	7.7	7.3	7.1	6.9	9	10
Aeroplane	0.3	1.3	0.7	21.0	0	42
Other	2.0	1.9	2.2	2.7	–	–
Type of accommodation (%)						
Hotel/inn/boarding house	15.0	34.0	25.3	43.1		
Cottage/bungalow/apartment	–	–	10.4	14.5		
Private room (without paying)	33.0	8.7	27.9	14.0		
Private room (rented)	34.0	37.0	17.5	12.4		
Camping/caravaning	4.8	15.0	5.8	9.0		
Other	13.2	5.3	13.1	6.9		
Length of stay (%)						
Up to one week	34.0	28.0	19.5	10.8		
Up to two weeks	29.0	32.0	41.5	40.5		
Up to three weeks			13.2	16.7		
Cost per tourist (DM)	125	661	553	977	976	1,176
Number of tourists (thousands)	9,56	5,819	16,482	22,473	22,000	42,500

Sources: Statistisches Bundesamt (1965, p. 41; 1981, p. 869); Forschungsgemeinschaft Urlaub und Reisen e.V. (1997, pp. 92, 115).

Note: see Table 12.1 for the definition of Germany and the Federal Republic of Germany.

other hand, the car has been gaining importance and had a share of 73 per cent in 1995. The use of the car is obviously very distance-related for it is used by 78 per cent of those holidaying in the Alpine region. Transport by train has decreased by 20 per cent since 1979–1980 and is now relatively unimportant, accounting for only 4 per cent of cross-border tourism. To some extent, the importance of the railway in 1962 is explained by the prevalence, at that time, of neighbouring countries as destinations (over 50 per cent of tourists went to Austria, Switzerland and The Netherlands). Moreover, access to private motor vehicles was still limited, while mass tourism had only just begun to develop. When holidays spent in foreign countries are considered, air travel had taken over second place in 1979–1980 and by 1995 had attained the same market share as the car (42 per cent). With the growth in popularity of more distant holiday destinations, air transport is increasing in importance: 67 per cent of all travel to the Mediterranean countries is by air, and with long-distance travels that share reaches nearly 100 per cent (Forschungsgemeinschaft Urlaub und Reisen e.V. 1997, pp. 92–93).

With the rise of mass tourism and the rapid growth of new resorts on, for example, the Spanish and Yugoslavian coasts, these and other countries offering similar accommodation and infrastructure became increasingly popular with West German tourists. Air transport also developed rapidly so that travel time was reduced and, since most holidays in the Mediterranean countries were booked as package tours—in 1986 90 per cent of air passengers to Spain booked all-inclusive packages (Commerzbank 1987, p. 5)—charter flights are of particular importance. In 1995 the share of package tours amounted to 54 per cent of trips to foreign destinations (33 per cent all-inclusive, 21 per cent other bookings with travel agencies) and was only 13 per cent for inland destinations. The proportion of package tours has risen to 74 per cent for destinations in the Mediterranean countries (52 per cent all-inclusive, and 22 per cent other bookings with travel agencies) and to 79 per cent for long-distance destination (38 per cent all-inclusive, 41 per cent other bookings with travel agencies). The role of package tours is obviously strongly associated with distances travelled. Thus, in 1995 only 23 per cent of all holidays in the Alps were booked as package tours (of which only 12 per cent were all-inclusive). The fact that only 38 per cent of long-distance trips are booked as all-inclusive package tours and that more than 60 per cent of all long-distance travellers organise much of their travel on their own, can be explained by the growing experience with this type of travel (Forschungsgemeinschaft Urlaub und Reisen e.V. 1997, p. 101).

German tourists taking holidays abroad are more likely to stay in hotels, inns or boarding houses, or in cottages, bungalows and apartments, as well as on campsites, than are those travelling within Germany, where private rooms—whether rented or provided by relatives of friends—are more popular. Privately rented rooms had accounted for a much higher share of foreign holidays in 1962, reflecting the importance of neighbouring countries as destinations at that time, as these tended to have accommodation structures similar to that of the Federal Republic. Moreover, in 1962 many West Germans spending their holidays abroad could not yet afford to stay in more expensive types of accommodation. Although there are no longer official statistical data available that differentiate between domestic and cross-border tourism, the last detailed travel analysis offers some useful insights.

The choice of accommodation depends very much on the holiday destination country and its accommodation infrastructure. In some of the Mediterranean countries, Spain and Yugoslavia for example, hotels and apartments were often built in the early stages of mass tourism. That is why in these countries 66 per cent of all holidays were spent in hotels and 16 per cent in apartments: in Spain 71 and 19 per cent, and in Italy 47 and 20 per cent, respectively. In the Alps the share of hotels falls to 35 per cent, while that of apartments rises to 23 per cent, and boarding houses and privately rented rooms account for another 30 per cent; in Austria 37, 19 and 34 per cent, respectively. With long-distance travel the preference for hotels is predominant (63 per cent) and apartments are rather unimportant (8 per cent). If the holiday destination is located on the North Sea or the Baltic Sea, apartments take the lead with 42 per cent, followed by boarding houses (17 per cent) and hotels (12 per cent) (Forschungsgemeinschaft Urlaub und Reisen e.V. 1997, pp. 104–7).

Apart from the correlation between distance and type of accommodation, there is also an interrelation with the life cycle of the tourist groups. Apartments and bungalows are the most popular type of accommodation for families with children younger than 14 years (37 per cent), while hotels and similar accommodation are preferred by younger and older tourists without children (Forschungsgemeinschaft Urlaub und Reisen e.V. 1997, p. 107).

Over time there has been a shift to shorter holidays, but in 1979–1980, foreign holidays tended to be longer than domestic ones, and that trend has continued so that, in 1995, domestic holidays on average lasted 13.0 days, compared with 14.7 days for foreign holidays. The mean cost of travel has also increased more for those travelling abroad. This is due to the transport changes mentioned previously and to the fact that the distances travelled are generally longer than in 1962 or 1979–1980. Despite the higher travel costs, a large and increasing number of people are able and willing to meet these, for the growth of cross-border travelling is continuing, although the rate of increase is slackening.

12.4   Tourism in the Federal Republic of Germany

12.4.1   General trends in domestic tourism

Whilst only 34 per cent of German tourists take their main holidays within the Federal Republic, these still number 22 million, although there has been a slight decrease since 1990 (−0.8 per cent). Together with foreign visitors, German tourists spending a short break or a second or third holiday, and those on business, congress and exhibition travel recorded more than 300 million overnights. In reality, however, this figure is an under-estimate because after 1981, as a result of a new tourist registration law, only those enterprises with more than eight beds had to record visitor arrivals and nights. Therefore, there are no data for private rooms which are rented on a cash basis, even though these accounted for 28 per cent of accommodation in 1980 and for 19.3 per cent (47.9 million) of tourist nights in 1979–1980. The consequences of this change in registration procedure are even greater at a disaggregated spatial scale: in the province of Schleswig-Holstein, for instance, there are no data for 51.5 per cent of all beds (1980).

Despite the continuous decline of interest amongst Germans in domestic tourist destinations, domestic accommodation capacity—as well as the number of tourist arrivals and bednights—has increased considerably since the mid-1950s (Table 12.6). At the national level, the accommodation capacity has more than quadrupled between 1954 and 1995, even though private rooms are excluded from the analysis. The

Table 12.6 Development and structure of tourism in Germany, 1954/5–1995 (1954/5 = 100)

	1954–55	1959–60	1969–70	1974–75	1979–80	1984–85	1990	1995
Accommodation capacity (beds)								
Type of accommodation								
Hotels/inns/boarding houses	100	167	236	269	290	337	335	405
Rest centres/holiday centres	100	165	297	366	430	564	648	923
Apartments/bungalows	–	–	–	100	130	222	228	244
Youth hostels and the like		100	92	82	77	88	81	99
Sanatoriums/spa hospitals	100	180	286	369	383	415	436	559
Private rooms	100	195	285	366	382	–	–	–
Total (excluding private rooms)	100	154	224	283	323	395	367	450
Type of tourism resort								
Spas	100	164	238	314	357	354	348	358
Health resorts	100	175	235	259	388	320	310	299
Seaside resorts	100	212	349	425	474	479	591	593
Major cities (> 100,000 inhabitants)	100	156	210	291	325 ⎫	337	430	500
Unclassified resorts	100	150	210	291	325 ⎭			
Total	100	164	239	303	337	395	403	440
Tourist arrivals and nights								
Arrivals	100	147	195	220	267	290	368	436
Germans	100	146	192	224	266	277	347	439
Foreigners	100	166	233	223	297	383	477	421
Foreigners (%)	16.2	18.3	19.3	16.4	18.0	21.4	21.0	15.7
Nights	100	178	260	321	353	301	363	368
Germans	100	179	260	328	353	289	345	420
Foreigners	100	175	252	250	354	429	604	498
Foreigners (%)	9.1	9.0	8.9	7.1	9.1	13.0	15.2	10.7

Length of stay (days)	3.5	4.2	4.6	5.1	4.6	3.6	3.4	3.4
Germans	3.8	4.7	5.2	5.6	4.1	4.0	3.8	3.6
Foreigners	2.0	2.1	2.1	2.2	2.3	2.2	2.5	2.3
Type of tourism resort (nights)								
Spas	100	173	237	308	330	362	304	323
Health resorts	100	156	216	250	269	181	191	172
Seaside resorts	100	216	446	533	561	365	458	533.5
Major cities (> 100,000 inhabitants)	100	148	217	303	341 }	294	370	375
Unclassified resorts	100	131	187	183	219 }			
Percentage of foreigners (nights)								
Spas	4.5	3.4	2.6	2.2	3.1	5.1	7.3	7.7
Health resorts	4.9	6.2	5.3	3.7	6.0	8.1	4.8	4.8
Seaside resorts	3.4	1.8	0.9	0.7	0.7	0.7	8.0	8.0
Major cities (> 100,000 inhabitants)	18.2	27.3	29.0	27.6	30.5 }	21.0 }	2.4	2.4
Unclassified resorts	8.3	9.2	10.4	8.5	10.7 }			
Length of stay (days)								
Spas	11.3	11.5	11.5	9.7	7.9			
Health resorts	7.2	7.4	8.0	6.7	5.3			
Seaside resorts	10.7	11.4	11.1	10.0	8.8			
Major cities (> 100,000 inhabitants)	2.0	2.0	2.0	2.0 }	2.4 }			
Unclassified resorts	2.7	3.1	3.6	3.4 }				
Percentage in winter season	28.8	28.5	28.8	29.6	31.6	34.2		

Sources: Statistisches Bundesamt (Ed.), *Jahrbuch für die Bundesrepublik Deutschland*, 1955, 1956, 1961, 1971, 1976, 1981, 1986; Wiesbaden; Statistisches Bundesamt (Ed.), *Tourismus in Zahlen*, 1951, 199■, Wiesbaden.

Note: see Table 12.1 for the definition of Germany and the Federal Republic of Germany.

reunification of the two Germanys marks a decisive moment in the development of tourism within Germany, for after 1990 the growth rate in most cases accelerated considerably. Nearly two-thirds (65.3 per cent) of all beds are concentrated in hotels/inns/boarding houses, 12.0 per cent are in apartments and bungalows (statistically recorded only since the mid-1970s), 10.2 per cent are in rest and holiday centres which have the highest growth rates, and 7.4 per cent are in sanatoriums and spa hotels. In 1970, the percentage composition looked different because beds in private rooms occupied a 25.9 per cent share, and thus the shares of the other categories were lower: hotels/inns/boarding houses 55.2 per cent; rest and holiday centres 3.7 per cent; youth hostels and the like 10.3 per cent; and sanatoriums and spa hospitals 4.9 per cent. The highest growth rates of commercially and privately provided beds are typical of the seaside resorts which, of course, underline their attractiveness. The extreme increase since 1990 is due to the fact that, with the reunification, large parts of the Baltic Sea coast, a traditional German tourism region since the middle of the last century, were reopened to visitors from the former Federal Republic; in consequence, there was strong demand for construction of new, and renovation of existing, accommodation. Above-average increases are also typical of the spas, which have special tourism characteristics. In most cases the decision to stay in a spa results from illness or a physical disability and, to a large extent, is paid for by the health insurance company sickness fund. Spa tourists usually have a limited influence on the choice of the spa, and cannot even choose the dates of their stay, so that the spas tend to have very high and evenly distributed bed occupancy rates.

Tourist arrivals in accommodation in Germany increased from about 20 million in 1954–1955 to 88 million in 1995. The share of foreign tourists rose from 16.2 per cent in 1954–1955 to 21.4 per cent in 1984–1985, but has since fallen to below the level of 1954–1955. Reasons for this negative development are said to include economic depressions in some of the countries of origin, unfavourable currency exchange rates, the development of new destinations outside of Europe (Bundesministerium für Wirtschaft 1994, p. 13), and, to some extent, publicity for recent discrimination against foreign people in Germany. However, tourist bednights and mean length of stay are better indicators of tourism development. The number of bednights increased from about 70 to nearly 260 million between 1954–1955 and 1995 (+268 per cent). The share of foreign tourists rose from 9.1 in 1954–1955 to 15.2 per cent in 1990, but then dropped to 10.7 per cent because of the reasons mentioned above. These shares are much lower, however, than for arrivals, as most foreign visitors do not holiday in Germany for as long as domestic tourists. The sudden jump in the rate of increase from 354 to 429 per cent between 1979–1980 and 1984–1985 is somewhat misleading, being due to changes in the registration law. This is illustrated by the fact that nearly one-third of tourist nights spent in large cities were accounted for by foreign guests in 1979–1980; since the absolute number of foreign visitors to the major cities has not decreased since then, and tourist arrivals and bednights in private lodgings are no longer recorded, the percentage of the overnights accounted for by foreigners is somewhat exaggerated. The even stronger jump between 1984–1985 and 1990 is due to reunification, because large numbers of foreign tourists were attracted by the political events of the reunification itself and by the opportunities to visit the relatively unknown 'new' provinces.

German tourists normally stay longer at their inland destinations than foreign tourists who, to a very large extent, visit major cities in the course of business, congress and exhibition travel or historical cities such as Heidelberg or Rothenburg ob der Tauber.

The average length of stay in the unclassified resorts, which include the major cities, indicates that it is mostly short-term tourism that, according to German tourism definitions, includes stays of one to three nights. Longer stays are typical of the seaside resorts, where many German families spend their summer holidays, and spas. The data in Table 12.6, and not only those referring to length of stay, show a decreasing tendency with a low mark in 1990; since then, tourism in Germany seems to have recovered, and the problems brought about by the reunification in 1990 have obviously diminished.

Consideration of tourist bednights in terms of types of tourism resorts again shows that the seaside resorts have the highest growth rates, especially after reunification. The reason for this is that, in nearly all the resorts at the Baltic Sea coast in Mecklenburg-Western Pomerania, the accommodation capacities were expanded and qualitatively adjusted to domestic demand soon after reunification, a development that saw positive results. The predominance of foreign visitors is particularly striking with respect to the major cities. Finally, in terms of the seasonal distribution of tourist overnights, the winter season (34.2 per cent of the total in 1984–1985) clearly does not play a very important role in German tourism, although it has gradually been increasing in importance.

12.4.2   Tourism regions and the distribution of tourists in Germany

Current official tourism statistics present data for 148 tourism regions of varying size and attractiveness, 34 more than before reunification. Most popular are the seaside resorts on the islands and coast of the North Sea and the Baltic Sea, and the Alps. Figure 12.4 shows the absolute number of bednights and the percentage of bednights accounted for by foreigners in the tourist year 1979–1980 in the former territory of the Federal Republic. Although this map does not depict the present situation, it represents some of the characteristic trends in the tourist distribution. Germany is clearly divided into three large tourist regions: the coasts and their hinterlands in the north; the midland regions (including the Harz, Eifel, Rhön, Bavarian Forest and Black Forest) which stretch into the far South-West and South-East; and the South, mainly east of Lake Constance, consisting of the Alps and their foothills (Allgäu). On the spatial basis of the former territory of the Federal Republic, the coast increased its share of tourist bednights from 9.5 per cent in 1984 to 11.0 per cent in 1995, while the Alps, on the other hand, suffered a loss of nearly the same dimension (in 1984, 12.4 per cent; in 1995, 12.0 per cent). On the basis of the reunified Germany, the share of the coastal tourist regions rises to 12.2 per cent of all tourist overnights spent in Germany in 1995, and that of the Alps and Allgäu regions of Bavaria and Baden-Württemberg drops to 10.4 per cent. The importance of the Baltic Sea coast region of Mecklenburg-Western Pomerania in terms of tourism is highlighted by the fact that the share of this region amounts to nearly 20 per cent of all tourist bednights in the 'new' provinces in 1995. Table 12.7 illustrates that since German reunification nearly all of the 'old' provinces have suffered losses in their shares of tourist bednights, while the 'new' provinces in eastern Germany have been the winners. This development implies that there has been a shift in destination preferences which is mainly due to the extension of choice, but the charm of novelty does certainly still play an important role, especially for German tourists. Tourism development in the midland areas shows regional differences, and there is a clear shift of demand amongst these regions. The northern part of the

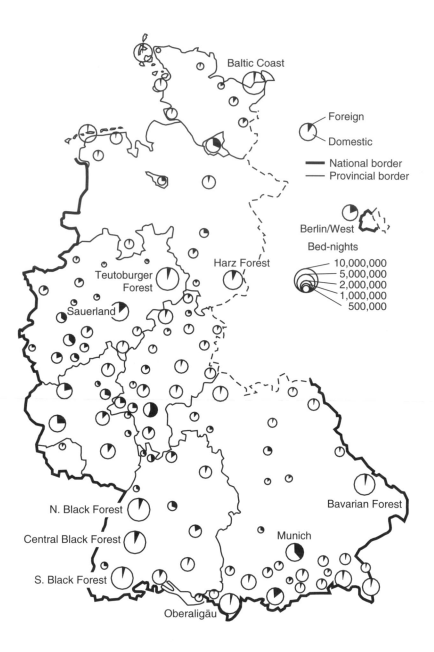

Fig. 12.4   Total number of tourist nights and share of foreign tourists in the Federal Republic of Germany, 1980, for regions and larger cities with over 250,000 nights

Source: Becker (1984a, p. 3); reproduced with permission

Table 12.7   Shares of tourist bednights in the German provinces (*Bundesländer*) 1960–1995 and the percentage of foreign tourist bednights, 1995

	1960	1970	1980	1990	1992	1995	% Foreign in 1995
Bavaria	27.1	26.4	29.3	28.9	24.2	24.2	9.9
Baden-Württemberg	18.4	18.7	18.0	15.2	13.0	13.0	11.3
Berlin[1]	2.6	1.6	1.4	2.8	2.6	2.5	25.0
Bremen	0.5	0.4	0.3	0.4	0.4	0.4	20.9
Hamburg	2.0	1.6	1.2	1.6	1.4	1.4	21.9
Hesse	10.9	11.5	11.0	10.7	9.2	8.8	15.7
Lower Saxony	11.6	11.3	11.0	11.9	11.2	10.9	5.1
North Rhine-Westfalia	13.1	13.0	12.3	13.5	12.3	12.0	14.5
Rhineland-Palatinate	5.9	5.5	5.9	6.9	6.2	5.9	18.9
Saar	0.3	0.3	0.5	0.6	0.6	0.7	8.0
Schleswig-Holstein	7.6	9.8	9.1	7.6	7.5	7.3	3.0
Brandenburg					1.3	2.2	7.4
Mecklenburg-Western Pomerania					2.3	3.3	2.4
Saxony					2.3	3.4	7.2
Saxony-Anhalt					1.0	1.7	8.0
Thuringia					1.8	2.5	4.9
Germany (million) (– 100%)	129.2	184.7	250.0	255.7	293.8	300.6	

Sources: Statistisches Bundesamt (Ed.) (1997); *Tourismus in Zahlen* (1996), Wiesbaden.

[1] *Note*: Until 1990 West Berlin only.
General note: see Table 12.1 for the definition of Germany and the Federal Republic of Germany.

midlands has suffered a relative loss of demand, while the southern midlands have gained from an above-average increase of demand (Uthoff 1982, p. 304).

At the provincial level, there were above-average increases in the number of bednights, between 1954–1955 and 1990, the last year when there were no official tourism data for the 'new' provinces, in Schleswig-Holstein (+250 per cent), Lower Saxony (+419 per cent), North Rhine-Westfalia (+222 per cent), Rhineland-Palatinate (+237 per cent), the Saar (+408 per cent) and West Berlin (+845 per cent). The first official statistical tourist data for the German provinces after reunification are available for 1992. Until that year the increase continued for all of the 'old' provinces, mostly because they were attractive destinations for tourists from the 'new' provinces who made ample use of the new travel possibilities, while the tourism regions of the 'new' provinces were not yet attractive holiday destinations for visitors from the former territory of the Federal Republic because of the poor tourism infrastructure and a lack of information. Since then, however, there has been a remarkable shift, for the 'new' provinces show an increase of 53 per cent from 1993 to 1995, compared with a loss of 3 per cent in the 'old' provinces. The reasons for this are that, on the one hand, many West German tourists have discovered the attractiveness of the 'new' German destinations whilst, on the other hand, many tourists from the 'new' provinces have returned to their old holiday destinations after a period of enjoying new travel freedoms.

Figure 12.5 displays the regional distribution of commercial tourist beds and bednights in 1995 at the provincial level. There is obviously a relatively balanced ratio between bed-capacity (beds offered by commercial accommodation establishments)

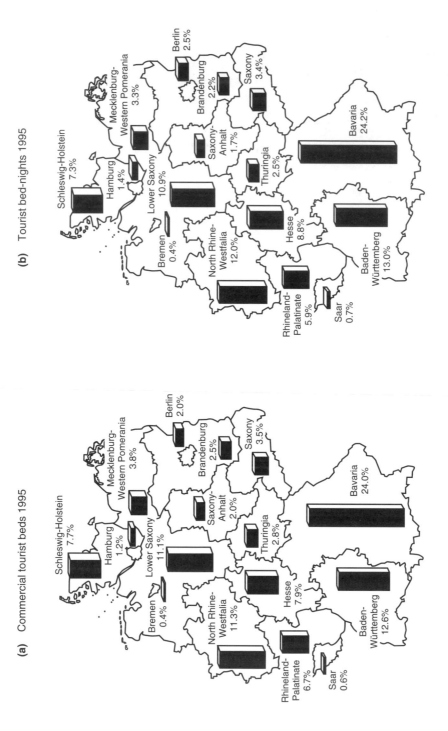

(a) Commercial tourist beds 1995

(b) Tourist bed-nights 1995

Fig. 12.5 Distribution of beds and bednights in Germany, 1995: (a) Beds; (b) Bednights

Source: Statistiches Bundesamt (1997, pp. 82, 104)

Table 12.8 Bed density and tourism intensity in the German provinces (*Länder*), 1995

Provinces (*Länder*)	Bed-density (beds/1,000 inhab.)	Tourism intensity (bed–nights/1,000 inh.)
Baden-Württemberg	27.4	3,781
Bavaria	44.8	6,096
Berlin	12.8	2,170
Bremen	11.9	1,557
Hamburg	15.3	2,440
Hesse	29.5	4,392
Lower Saxony	31.9	4,248
North Rhine-Westfalia	14.1	2,017
Rhineland-Palatinate	37.6	4,439
Saar	13.0	1,934
Schleswig-Holstein	63.1	8,097
Former territory of the Federal Republic	28.9	3,931
Brandenburg	21.7	2,580
Mecklenburg-Western Pomerania	46.4	5,434
Saxony	17.0	2,217
Saxony-Anhalt	15.8	1,821
Thuringia	24.8	3,019
'New' provinces (*Länder*)	30.9	2,649
Federal Republic of Germany	27.3	3,687

Sources: Statistisches Bundesamt (ed.) (1997); *Tourismus in Zahlen*, 1996.

and demand. In contrast to the former West German provinces where, in most cases, the share of bednights is higher than of the beds offered, in the 'new' provinces, the relationship is just the reverse. The bed capacity of the 'new' provinces (without East Berlin) increased from 9.6 per cent in 1991 to 15.4 in 1995; if 1991 stocks are indexed at a value of 100 per cent, then it has expanded by 73 per cent since then, while this rate amounts to only +8 in the 'old' provinces (inclusive of Berlin).

Other indicators of regional differences in the structure of tourism in Germany are provided by bed-density (beds per 1,000 inhabitants) and tourism-intensity (bednights per 1,000 inhabitants). As can be seen from Table 12.8, five of the 'old' provinces and only one of the 'new' ones, Mecklenburg-Western Pomerania which borders the Baltic Sea, attain above-average bed-densities, and it is the 'old' provinces, and again Mecklenburg-Western Pomerania, of the 'new' provinces, as far as tourism-intensity is concerned. Figure 12.6 published in the Federal Government's Report on Regional Planning 1993 illustrates the regional importance of tourism on a spatial basis smaller than that for the federal provinces. The coastal regions of northern Germany and the Alps and their foothills (Allgäu) clearly represent tourist regions with a generally high bed-density, while there is a patchwork of high and low density areas in the midland region. An update of this map would demonstrate the high increase of bed-densities on the Baltic Sea coast region of Mecklenburg-Western Pomerania and in parts of Saxony and Thuringia.

Foreigners visiting Germany concentrate on urban destinations such as Frankfurt, where the share of tourist nights accounted for by this group of tourists reaches a

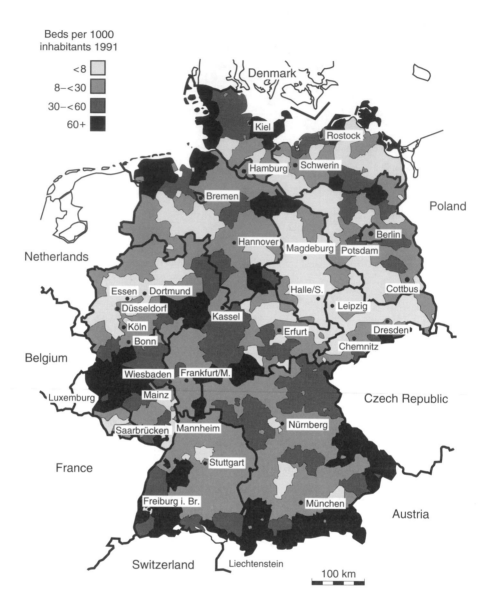

Fig. 12.6 Regional importance of tourism in Germany

Source: Bundesministerium für Ranmordnung, Bauwesen und Städtebau (ed.) (1994), p. 113

maximum, partly because of its international airport (Figure 12.4) (Wolf and Jurczek 1986, p. 101) (57.9 per cent in 1995); Heidelberg (47.1 per cent); Munich (40.3 per cent); Düsseldorf (40.0 per cent); Cologne (37.0 per cent); Stuttgart (26.2 per cent); Hannover (25.4 per cent); Berlin (25.0 per cent); Bonn (23.5 per cent); Hamburg (21.9 per cent); and Bremen (21.2 per cent). Foreign tourism is particularly conspicuous in those cities which have important roles as political (e.g. Bonn and the provincial capitals) and/or fair, exhibition and congress centres (e.g. Frankfurt, Cologne, Hannover, Hamburg, Düsseldorf, Munich, Stuttgart) (Schnell 1996). Cultural and historical motives are especially important in cities like Heidelberg or Rothenburg ob der Tauber. Roth (1984, pp. 160–2) has shown considerable variations in motives for visiting the former Federal Republic and in the spatial travel patterns of foreigners. Accessibility and the attractiveness of the landscape contribute to the popularity of some midland regions for foreign tourists. Thus in the 'Sauerland'— located south of the Ruhr district—there are communities in which more than 90 per cent of all foreign tourist bednights, between 1974–1975 and 1979–1980, were accounted for by visitors from The Netherlands, Belgium and Luxembourg (Schnell 1983, pp. 148–9; 1986, p. 10 and Map 2.3).

West German tourists tended to prefer destinations in southern Germany. According to the micro-census of 1962, the destinations of 14.4 per cent of all domestic travellers were the Alps and their foothills, while 7.4 per cent visited the seaside resorts of the North Sea and the Baltic Sea; in the 1979–1980 survey these percentages had changed to 17.7 and 17.8 per cent, respectively (Koch 1986, p. 11). The same trend emerges from the 'Travel Analysis' surveys of 1990 and 1995 for, in the former year, 25.1 per cent of all domestic holiday travel was to Bavaria and 23.8 per cent to Schleswig-Holstein and Lower Saxony. There has been a slight change in that trend since then for, in 1995, Bavaria's share had increased to 31.4 per cent, but this had been exceeded by Schleswig-Holstein and Lower Saxony (32.6 per cent). These percentages refer to the former territory of the Federal Republic. If the 'new' eastern provinces are included, the three provinces with coastal regions increase their share to 33.6 per cent and Bavaria's share amounts to only 23.2 per cent (Forschungsgemeinschaft Urlaub und Reisen e.V. 1997, p. 66). In 1994, the most attractive Bavarian destination areas and the Black Forest were more attractive for holidaymakers from the eastern provinces than for those from the western provinces, while in the main eastern holiday destination regions there was a clear dominance of tourists from the 'new' provinces (BAT Freizeit-Forschungsinstitut 1995, p. 40).

Despite the decreasing relative interest of German holiday-makers in domestic destinations, the number of holidays spent within Germany increased from 8.5 million in 1970 (main holidays only) to 23.8 million in 1995 (all holidays), mainly because of a rise in travel intensity and the extended choice of inland destinations after the reunification.

12.5   The impact of tourism and tourism policy

12.5.1   Economic impacts

The increasing gap between the expenditures of German tourists abroad and receipts from incoming tourism has already been mentioned. The Federal Government has not considered taking measures to reduce the travel-expenditure deficit; it is argued that the destination countries will, to a large extent, use receipts from German tourists to buy German products so that, ultimately, the German economy does profit from tourism (Deutscher Bundestag 1986b, p. 8).

Until the mid-1980s the economic impact of tourism in the Federal Republic had not been analysed systematically at the national or provincial level. There were, however, several studies of particular regions that gave an indication of the economic impact of tourism. Priebe (1971, p. 27), in a regional study of eastern Bavaria, concluded that tourism could, at most, generate 20 per cent of the regional income. On the basis of several case studies, Becker and Klemm (1978, p. 70) emphasised the three secondary effects of tourism on the local and regional economy: first, the employees of tourism enterprises spend most of their incomes in their respective regions; second, tourists not only pay for accommodation but also have other expenditures; and third, the maintenance and the services required by tourism enterprises create additional jobs in the region. Taking into account these secondary effects, tourism enterprises have a regional multiplier effect of 1.43, which is much lower than was previously assumed (Becker and Klemm 1978, p. 75).

A rule of thumb has been developed by economists to determine the regional income effect of tourism: four tourism nights per inhabitant of a region or a community are considered to represent a contribution of 1 per cent to average per capita incomes (Koch 1986, quoted in Deutsche Gesellschaft für Freizeit 1986, p. 129). The direct job-creating effects can be determined by means of indices, such as the number of full-time employees per bed in the various types of accommodation establishments (Koch 1986, p. 16). The overall economic effects of tourism can thus be estimated from the following formula:

$$\frac{\text{net income per tourism night} \times \text{tourism intensity}}{\text{per-capita income}}$$

If, for instance, there is a tourism intensity of 1,000 (that is, 1,000 tourist bednights per 1,000 inhabitants), the net income per tourist bednight is DM 50, and the per capita income amounts to DM 20,000 per year, then the contribution of tourism to the regional income amounts to 2.5 per cent (Koch 1986, p. 17).

In 1992 and 1993 the results of two empirical surveys carried out by order of the Federal Ministry of Economics and the respective ministries of the federal provinces were published by the German Institute for Tourism Research (Deutsches Wirtschaftswissenschaftliches Institut für Fremdenverkehr—DWIF), in which the economic effect of overnight tourism was analysed on the basis of tourist expenditures. In both studies tourism is understood to comprise holiday as well as business travel and visits to relatives and friends. Moreover, tourism is understood to begin with one overnight stay at the minimum, so that short breaks are also included. Since a large share of bednights is accounted for by private accommodation which, since 1981, has no longer been recorded statistically, the calculation of the overall economic effect of tourism represents a problem. According to the 1993 survey, the number of bednights in commercial accommodation establishments has to be increased by about 45 per cent to allow bednights in private accommodation to be taken into account (Zeiner *et al.* 1993, p. 110). The first survey was carried out in the 11 'old' provinces and the second in the five 'new' ones and in East Berlin. More than 12,000 persons were interviewed in these surveys with identical questionnaires, so that the results are comparable. A variant of tourism with an economic impact that must by no means be underestimated is represented by pleasure and business day trips, the economic effects of which were first analysed in 1986 and then updated and extended to the 'new' provinces in 1993 (Koch *et al.* 1987; Harrer *et al.* 1995). In all of these surveys, the expenditures were split up amongst the following categories: accommodation, food, shopping, entertainment and sports, and local transport; travel costs were not included. Tourists on holiday in Germany on average spend DM 81.10 per day, of which 41.5 per cent is for accommodation, 41.6 per cent to food, and 17.0 per cent to the other expenditure categories listed previously. Because of the spontaneous and often business-based character of short-term stays, daily expenditures are higher and amount to DM 106.60 (33.4 per cent for accommodation, 39.3 per cent for food, and 22.4 per cent for other items). Day-trippers, of course, spend less money: DM 39.90 (36.6 per cent for food and 63.4 per cent for other items). The economic effect of day tourism is illustrated by the fact that in 1993 more than 2.1 billion day trips were undertaken (Harrer *et al.* 1995, p. 27) so that total spending is more than DM 80 billion.

In order to calculate the economic effect of tourism consisting of pleasure and business day trips as well as overnight tourism, the first and second stages of turnover were calculated. On the national level, the contribution of tourism to the national income amounts to 2.81 per cent (excluding transport expenditures). 50.9 per cent of these fall to pleasure day trips, 42.7 per cent to tourism with overnight stays, and 6.4 per cent to business day trips (Harrer *et al.* 1995, p. 182). When the costs of transport to and from the place of destination and/or stay are included in the calculation, the contribution of tourism to national income increases to 4.21 per cent (Harrer *et al.* 1995, p. 191). As can be seen from Figure 12.7, the regional economic effects of tourism vary considerably within Germany. Thus in Mecklenburg-Western Pomerania, for instance, the absolute contribution of tourism to regional income is very low, but the relative contribution is the largest for any region in Germany. In North Rhine-Westphalia, on the other hand, the reverse holds (Harrer *et al.* 1985, p. 184).

It was estimated in 1986 that about 1.5 million jobs depended on tourism, some 6 per cent of all gainfully employed (Commerzbank 1987, p. 1). By 1994 the number of jobs had dropped to 1.1 million (Deutsche Gesellschaft für Freizeit 1995, p. 63). On the basis of the calculation of the economic effect of tourism on the national economy, it is estimated that 1.6 million full-time jobs depend directly and indirectly on tourism. Taking into account the prevalence of part-time jobs and below-average wages, it can be assumed that far more than 1.6 million people earn their living from tourism and tourism-related industries and services.

12.5.2   Social impacts

The impact of tourism on the social structure of tourist communities can be positive, but there are also negative consequences to be taken into account. Among the positive effects are improvements in infrastructure which also benefit the local population, improved income and employment prospects, and provided higher returns for local retailers. The result is improvements in standards of living, which allow people to obtain previously unobtainable goods and services. However, it has also been argued that tourism, especially mass tourism, disturbs or destroys traditional local and/or regional value systems. Moreover, since many tourism places are located in attractive landscape settings, the demand for real estate rises. Thus, in 1978, real estate prices in

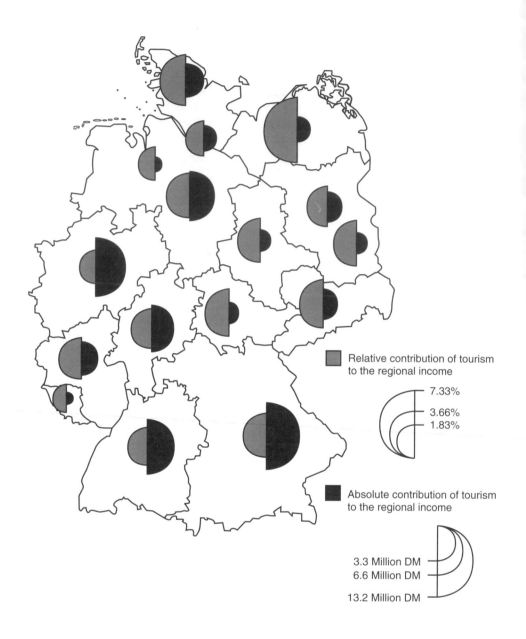

Fig. 12.7 Contribution of tourism to regional income in Germany, 1993: with and without overnight stays

Source: Harrer *et al.* (1995, p. 183)

the Alps and their foothills were as high as those in Munich and its surroundings, while the population had increased at above-average rates between 1974 and 1978 (Bayerisches Staatsministerium für Landesentwicklung und Umweltfragen 1980, Maps 3 and 4). In Mittenwald, a Bavarian tourist resort in the Alps, in 1974 the price per m² of land was five times higher than the Bavarian average, and such prices excluded more than one-third of the local population from owning real estate or from having plans to build their own houses (Alpeninstitut 1978, pp. 31–2).

Other negative impacts involve the physiognomy of the settlements and the landscape. The most attractive parts of the recreation landscape are most favoured as real estate so that, for instance, lake-fronts are no longer accessible to the public. The outward appearance of settlements has also changed under the influence of tourism, because large functional and urban buildings are often superimposed on traditional architectural and building styles. There can also be negative traffic effects. Thus, more than 50 per cent of the inhabitants surveyed in Garmisch-Partenkirchen and Mittenwald (Alps), Meersburg (Lake Constance), Hinterzarten and Titisee (Black Forest) and Heiligenhafen (Baltic Sea) complained about frequent traffic congestion during the main season (Alpeninstitut 1978, p. 41).

Finally, it is to be expected that tourism will have an effect on the demographic structure of tourism resorts, not least because many have attracted large numbers of older people. Initially, they may have become familiar with the resort from a holiday visit, and then may have acquired a second home or an apartment there, to which they have moved after retirement. This tendency to demographic imbalance has been noted in a number of case studies (Alpeninstitut 1978, p. 45).

In the new provinces, where unemployment considerably exceeds the national average, tourism helps to improve the economic situation by providing jobs and earning opportunities.

12.5.3   Tourism policies and tourism innovations

Because of the growing numbers of German tourists who spend their holidays abroad, special efforts have been made to support tourism development in the Federal Republic. There is no national tourism policy, given the federal structure of the Republic but, at the national level, tourism is the responsibility of two ministries, those for Economics and for Regional Planning, Housing and Urban Affairs (Bundesministerium für Raumordnung, Bauwesen und Städtebau). The Ministry for Economics is responsible for a joint task programme developed in 1969 to improve the economic structure of less-developed regions, but the execution of this programme is the responsibility of the federal provinces. In 1975, 12.6 per cent of the programme funds were spent on tourism projects (Becker and Klemm 1978, p. 27; Schnell 1975, p. 78; 1977, pp. 93–98). By 1987 this percentage had dropped to 8 per cent, of which 5 per cent were spent on the creation of new, and the protection of existing, jobs and 3 per cent on public tourism facilities. With reunification, the State programme for the promotion of the economic structure of less developed regions changed considerably because of the far greater need of the 'new' provinces for financial assistance, so that most of the programme funds are now directed to Eastern Germany. In 1991, 500 tourism projects were financially assisted, of which 80 per cent were located in the 'new' provinces. Thus, on the whole, 2,851 new jobs were created and 1,065 existing jobs were protected, of which 87 per cent and 66 per cent respectively, were in the

Table 12.9   Promotion of commercial investments in tourism projects in Germany's joint task programme, Improvement of the Regional Economic Structure, 1989–1993

Year	'Old' provinces (*Bundesländer*)			'New' provinces (*Bundesländer*)		
	Projects	Funds granted (DM 1,000)	Total investments (DM 1,000)	Projects	Funds granted (DM 1,000)	Total investments (DM 1,000)
1989	170	11,102	222,032			
1990	130	20,035	280,280	6	4,710	22,414
1991	101	15,478	180,683	400	141,728	719,018
1992	92	40,800	364,200	732	241,800	1,468,800
1993	83	16,200	205,800	1,183	493,800	2,786,700
Total	578	103,615	1,252,995	2,321	882,038	4,996,952

Source: Bundesminister für Wirtschaft (1994, p. 63).

Note: see Table 12.1 for the definition of Germany and the Federal Republic of Germany.

'new' provinces. The financial support amounted to 17.4 per cent of the total volume of investments in tourism. In addition, this programme supported 437 actions related to improvement of the tourism infrastructure, 84 per cent of which were located in the 'new' provinces (Bundesministerium für Raumordnung, Bauwesen und Städtebau 1994, p. 114). Moreover, in the period 1990–1992 the tourism industry in the 'new' provinces was supported by credits from the European Recovery Program (ERP), which amounted to over 40 per cent of total investments. The ERP assistance resulted in the promotion of 13,000 accommodation establishments with 60,000 beds, so that 35,000 new jobs were created and the existence of 20,000 jobs was secured (Bundes-ministerum für Raumordnung, Bauwesen und Städtebau 1994, p. 115). The shift in the spatial distribution of governmental assistance is demonstrated in Table 12.9.

In addition to the government supports documented in Table 12.9, ERP credits cannot be neglected. Generally speaking, the same development took place, for in the 'old' provinces the number of projects decreased from 920 in 1989 to 576 in 1993, while between March 1990 and February 1994 in the 'new' provinces 3,799 new hotels, inns and boarding houses and 12,773 restaurants were founded, and 6,188 existing establishments were extended and modernised (Bundesmninister für Wirtschaft 1994, p. 64).

In 1975 the Federal Government formulated the following four basic aims of tourism policy (Bundesminister für Wirtschaft 1994, p. 36):

- Guaranteeing the basic conditions necessary for a continuous development of tourism.
- Advancement of the efficiency and competitiveness of the German tourism industry.
- Improving the chances to participate in tourism for large parts of the population.
- Extending international cooperation in tourism.

In 1975 the preservation of the environment was understood to be part of the first aim. Since then, the importance of this aim has been increasing continuously, so that the government decided to add a fifth aim to the 1975 catalogue:

- Preservation of the environment, nature and landscape since they present the basis for tourism.

In 1994, the Federal Government published a report on the development of tourism in which the measures and steps to be taken to achieve these aims were documented (Bundesminister für Wirtschaft 1994).

The new holiday centres and holiday parks in the territory of the former Federal Republic are impressive examples of the application of the joint task programme mentioned previously. Becker (1984b, pp. 164–85) analysed 137 of these centres and parks, which were highly concentrated along the German–German and West-German–Czech borders (Figure 12.8a), where special financial and taxation advantages were available in addition to the tourism programme, and in well-known tourism regions such as the North Sea coast and the Black Forest. The map also reveals that many dwellings—some 31 per cent in 1984—were used as second homes on a private basis (Becker 1984b, p. 170). The construction of holiday centres and parks at that time represented an innovation in West German tourism; the growing domestic demand for self-catering accommodation was taken up by the planners who were able to attract private investors for these schemes because of their taxation advantages, supported by the tourism programme. It emerged later that the level of demand had been overestimated by some investors; therefore, a number of dwellings were sold to private owners or converted to alternative uses so that, for example, in the Baltic region of Schleswig-Holstein, in 1984, only 49 per cent of the 9,355 dwelling units were available for renting to tourists (Becker 1984b, p. 170). After reunification, a large number of plans for the construction of new holiday centres and parks in the 'new' provinces was discussed, because there was a high demand for self-catering accommodations and, again, financial and taxation advantages were available. Figure 12.8b reveals that, in 1994, plans existed for 28 holiday centres, seven of which were to have an accommodation capacity of 500–1,000 beds, 11 of 1,000–2,000 beds and 10 of more than 2,000 beds. The number of planned holiday centres was much larger shortly after reunification, and has now decreased to levels even less than those shown in Figure 12.8b, because it has been realised that the demand for such accommodation, and for privately owned second homes or apartments, had been overestimated.

Farm holidays were advocated in the early 1970s as an alternative to vacation in far-away, noisy and congested places. It was argued that the advantage of holidays in rural areas lay in the contrast they provided to 'normal' tourism centres (Klöpper 1973, p. 5). The share of farm holidays amounted to 4.1 per cent of all domestic holidays in 1972, increased to 5.2 per cent in 1978–1989 (Martin 1986, p. 23), and fell to about 4.5 per cent in 1995 (Bundesministerium für Ernährung, Landwirtschaft und Forsten 1997, p. 103). The people taking farm holidays are mostly younger families with children who live in urban areas. The main attraction for the farmers is the additional income which tourism generates. The federal government supports the 'holiday on a farm' programme and the Deutsche Zentrale für Tourismus (German Centre for Tourism) advertises it abroad (Deutscher Bundestag 1986b, p. 20). The 'holiday on a farm' idea is of particular importance because it is linked to the concept of 'simple', 'soft' or 'sustainable' tourism—that is, a kind of tourism that does not require a sophisticated infrastructure, and which therefore does not substantially alter the landscape and the settlement structure, and does not interfere with the ecological balance. It is argued that this kind of tourism will help to avoid social and ecological conflicts (cf. Bundesforschungsanstalt for Landeskunde und Raumordnung 1983).

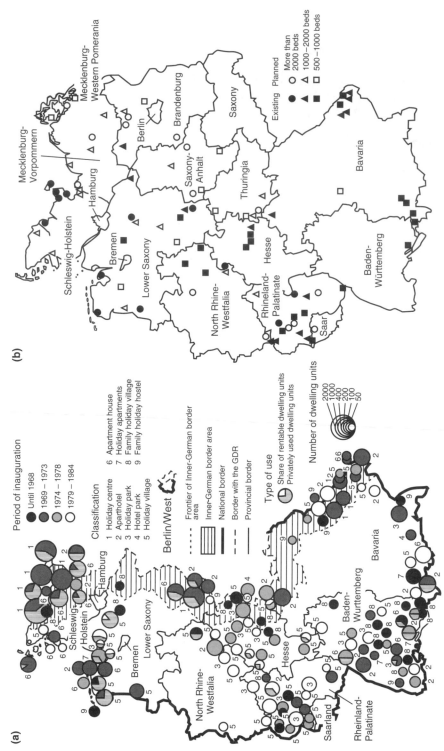

Fig. 12.8 Holiday centres and parks in the Federal Republic of Germany: (a) 1968–1984; (b) 1994

Source: Becker (1984b), reproduced by permission; Bundesminister für Wirtschaft (1994)

City tourism has been promoted in the larger cities, especially in regions that lag behind in terms of economic development. There has been relatively little research on this type of tourism and its variants (day visitors, business visitors, congress and exhibition visitors) but it is important for the urban economy (Becker and Hensel 1982, pp. 174–82; Schnell 1996, pp. 89–113). Cultural and historical motives are also important in urban tourism (Jurczek 1986a), so that many smaller towns and settlements, which have preserved their historical cores, are also interested in developing city tourism.

12.6   Conclusion: tourism in the unified Germany

The situation, problems and prospects of German tourism were summarised in a 1987 sectoral report issued by Commerzebank. The wet summer of 1987 caused a boom in travel agency bookings and for promoters of foreign holidays. Furthermore, as a result of the strength of the Deutschmark, holidays in the classical holiday regions such as the Alps and the Mediterranean, as well as in then 'new' destinations such as the USA and Canada, were considerably cheaper than in the proceeding season. Although there have been some changes since then, the general trend is still the same. The attractiveness of the Austrian Alps and Switzerland has decreased, mainly because of unfavourable currency exchange rates. Increasingly, there is also stagnation in the market for Spain because of the same effect and because many potential German visitors are deterred by the negative consequences of mass tourism. Moreover, and in addition to the arguments just mentioned, the development of travel prices has led to a shift in destination preferences, for more distant destinations can be afforded more easily than in former times, especially due to all-inclusive package tours. The consequences of the German reunification also play an important role in this recent development because there still exists a suppressed demand for this type of holiday travel.

This development is not seen as a cause of grave concern. The federal government takes a sanguine view of the future of tourism. In 1986 the basic economic determinants of tourist demand—increased net income and leisure time—were thought likely to remain unchanged, and there was no apparent reason why the (then West) Germans should cease spending a disproportionate amount of their incomes on travelling (Deutscher Bundestag 1986b, p. 8). However, tourism development has evolved differently, for, although there was an increase in leisure time, the expected increase in net income has not transpired in the same way. Germans nevertheless continued to spend a high proportion of their net income on holidays: the average proportion of household expenditure on holidays was 28.4 per cent in 1991, and 29.1 per cent in 1995 (Deutsche Gesellschaft für Freizeit 1996, p. 87), so that the successful advertising slogan of one travel agent, 'holidays—the most precious weeks of the year' (Touristik Union International, TUI) seems to hold true for most Germans. Many households reacted to the economic recession by reducing expenditure, but that attitude did not apply to main holidays.

The trend to preferring foreign destinations to those within the Federal Republic is likely to continue. Because of his/her travel experiences, the German tourist has become more and more fastidious as far as information and service, the quality of accommodation, destinations and activities are concerned (Steinecke 1996, p. 112); at the same time, however, they pay more attention to travel costs, a development documented by the growing importance of last minute bookings.

There are opportunities to improve domestic tourism because of the 'new' and attractive tourism destinations in the 'new' provinces and the increasing importance of short-term travel, a part of which is city tourism that represents a strongly growing tourism market segment. The differences in the travel attitudes of West and East Germans, which were very conspicuous directly after reunification, and in the early 1990s, have since diminished and are supposed to disappear by 2010 at the latest.

Because of the development of German tourism and tourism in Germany, the tourist location 'Germany' has been severely criticised. It is said that German tourist destinations are, to a growing degree, attractive only for senior citizens, for families with children and for low-income families. The reasons for this are, on the one hand, internal because families with children do not want to travel long distances, and the same goes for older people because of health reasons and travel habits. External reasons, on the other hand, include the fact that Germany is avoided by many foreign tourists because it has a negative image as a high-price destination, where everything is too perfectly or over-organised, and where the quality of tourism services could be better. In addition to that, German tourists profit from the strong competition in the travel market, for a one-week half-board stay in a medium-class hotel on the Mediterranean island of Majorca is offered cheaper than a one-week stay in the Bavarian Forest (Steinecke *et al.* 1996, pp. 260–1). In order to improve the quality of the tourist location Germany, and to attract larger numbers of foreign tourists to German tourist destinations and more German tourists to spend their holidays within Germany, it is recommended that on the one hand, presentation of the tourist location Germany in foreign countries needs to be improved, with the development of more up-to-date provision for new target groups; and, on the other hand, to correct the negative image, the lack of quality of tourism service, and the organisational split-up (Steinecke *et al.* 1996, pp. 260–1).

13

Tourism in The Netherlands: resource development, regional impacts and issues

David Pinder

13.1 Introduction

The basic facts relating to tourism in the Netherlands are straightforward. Despite the growth of foreign opportunities,[1] many Dutch people still take holidays in their own country. In 1995—using the official definition of a holiday as a break of at least four nights—7.7 million did so. In the 1990s this market has expanded by about 1 per cent a year and has been generated by a population of only 15.4 million. As might be expected, almost three-quarters of these holidays are taken in the summer, chiefly in the brief period between late June and the end of August. In addition the Dutch take over 8 million short breaks (up to three nights) each year. These, too, are chiefly summer events, although about one-third are taken in the winter.

Foreign tourism, meanwhile, brings in another 6 million visitors; nearly two-thirds of them are holiday-makers, while most of the remainder are on business. Although there are obviously exceptions, these foreign tourists chiefly expand the short-break market—typical stays in the country are three nights or less. Despite the brevity of their visits, however, on average they spend more than the Dutch. As a result, although less than 30 per cent of all tourists are foreign, they account for 40 per cent of total tourism expenditure. In general this is a reflection of their accommodation preferences. Because of the business tourism market and the role played by package holidays, the typical foreign visitor is hotel-based. In sharp contrast, only 20 per cent of the Dutch take a short break in a hotel, and for longer holidays the proportion is just 6 per cent. Most opt instead for less formal and cheaper accommodation, especially campsites and chalet or bungalow parks (Stoelers and Karssen 1986).

Tourism, therefore, is diverse, by no means restricted to the domestic market, and substantial for a nation of less than 16 million (Bekkers 1995). It has also evolved in the absence of a strong planning framework to guide tourism development (Ashworth and Bergsma 1987) although, as we shall see, numerous reports have expressed concern about the industry's impacts. These observations prompt two related questions. Without a guiding framework, to what extent has the industry's development stimulated the country as a whole, rather than simply the well-known tourism honeypot of Amsterdam? And how has the growth of the tourism resource base supported the expansion of the industry at both the national level and in the regions? This second question is particularly important in The Netherlands because the resource base is normally perceived to be extremely limited: Amsterdam's canals; the bulbfields; windmills, dykes and meadows; and sometimes civil engineering feats such as the reclaimed IJsselmeer Polders. How is it possible for a thriving tourism industry to be supported by such an apparently narrow resource base?

The answer offered by this chapter is that it is not. External perceptions are highly inaccurate, chiefly because recent decades have witnessed impressive resource development that has gone largely unnoticed outside the country. To some extent development has been the consequence of private sector initiatives, spurred on by the upswing in leisure and tourism so common in Western societies. As will be shown, however, any explanation of tourism growth in The Netherlands must incorporate a wide range of other factors. To some extent these also affect many countries: changing tourist perceptions, the influence of cultural attitudes and the commodification of heritage are good examples. Yet it will become evident that even these factors have had a distinctly Dutch flavour to them; and there are some influences that have changed the Dutch tourism resource base in a highly distinctive manner. This is particularly true of the conversion of derelict areas into tourism sites, and of the unintentional effects of some of the leading physical planning policies.

13.2   Tourism beginnings

Until the 1950s tourism's perceived resource base was certainly limited quantitatively, qualitatively and spatially. The best-developed asset was the North Sea coast. Here, from the late nineteenth century onwards, vast beaches close to expanding cities such as Amsterdam, Leiden, The Hague, Rotterdam and Delft witnessed the growth of coastal tourism from Scheveningen northwards to Zandvoort and beyond (Figure 13.1). The most successful resort was Scheveningen, whose pier and *kurhaus* echoed the English Victorian seaside and European spas. Through the link between romanticism and the appeal of uplands, tourism also took root in the southern part of the province of Limburg where, towards the Belgian Ardennes and the Rhine Highlands, heights exceed 300 metres. In a country where to be 20 metres above sea level is unusual, the valleys and rolling hills found here were greatly prized, and in the Geul Valley the small town of Valkenburg became the main resort of The Netherlands' 'Little Switzerland'.

Both the coast and southern Limburg offered rural resources to be enjoyed, but one city in particular—Amsterdam—had also become a significant tourism centre. There, as a legacy of the cultural 'Grand Tour', the canals and seventeenth- and eighteenth-century townscapes of the city core were already attracting a significant flow of foreign tourists. Even so, at that stage tourism was only a minor component of the city economy. Similarly, although the local economic impacts were greater, beach tourism affected only a few accessible points on the North Sea coast, while Little Switzerland covered less than 30 km².

13.3   A country revalued

As prosperity, mobility and leisure time increased in the late 1950s and 1960s, the Dutch attached new value to large parts of the country which had previously been

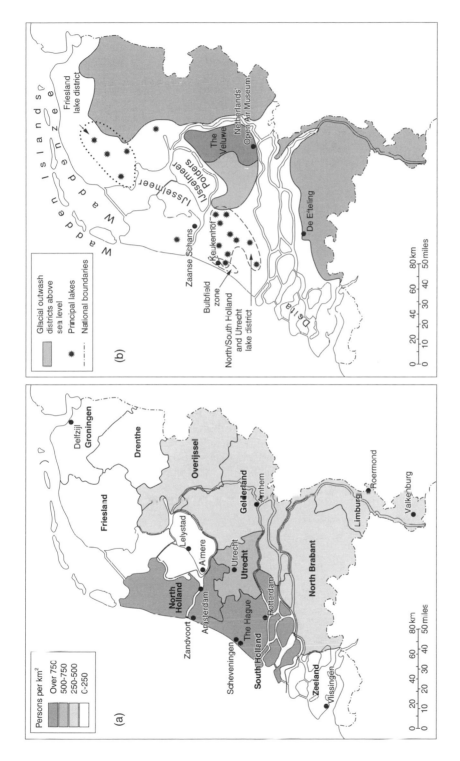

Fig. 13.1 Tourism in The Netherlands: (a) human and (b) physical backgrounds

virtually complete gaps on the tourism map. The most obvious example is provided by the popularity of the Veluwe, an area 45 km by 25 km immediately south of the IJsselmeer (Figure 13.1). The Veluwe is distinctive in that it is an extensive tract of glacial sands forming low hills, rising to 30 metres above sea level and contrasting sharply with the western Netherlands' reclaimed land. Vegetated initially by heathland and natural woodland, the landscape has evolved rapidly since the mid-nineteenth century. Farming has encroached, especially on the periphery, to create a diverse landscape of small farms and woodland. Elsewhere the *Staatsbosbeheer* (State Forestry Service) has established 40,000 ha of coniferous plantations. And, amongst the farming and the forestry, some 60,000 ha of heathland and 1,100 ha of open sand dunes have survived (Hanekamp 1979). Although these heath and sand residuals are now small compared with their mid-nineteenth century extent,[2] together with forestry areas open to the public they are seen as highly attractive for day, short-stay and long-stay recreation. In 1995 almost 2 million Dutch residential tourists based themselves in the Veluwe, more than 10 per cent of the country's long- and short-stay markets (Tables 13.1 and 13.2; Figure 13.2). The area's attractions are also reflected in the presence of two national parks, the *Hoge Veluwe* (High Veluwe) and *Veluwezoom* (Veluwe Edge), although they by no means cover the entire area.[3]

The Veluwe is the outstanding example, but similar factors have led to the social reconstruction of many other areas in the northern, eastern and southern regions as leisure landscapes. Where glacial outwash predominates, the landscape has undergone conversion from heath and woodland. This has generally progressed further than on the Veluwe, yet has still produced what is perceived to be an attractive mixture of small-scale farming landscapes, studded with fragments of heath and wood with good recreational potential. The outcome of this re-evaluation of outwash landscapes away from the marine reclamation areas of the west and north is well documented by the *Atlas van Nederland* (sheet V1-S-5) and the *Atlas van Nederlandse Landschappen*. The latter recognises no less than 23 distinct landscape regions in the country as a whole, half of them in these northern, eastern and southern sandlands. Tables 13.1 and 13.2 provide a flavour of this diversity, and also demonstrate the importance of these landscape resources in spreading Dutch tourism throughout the country. Although more than one-fifth of all breaks are taken in the densely populated western provinces, chiefly because of the continuing popularity of the coastal resorts, most residential tourism is relatively widely spread through the eastern, southern and northern provinces.

Other social reconstructions of landscapes have also occurred. For example, in the north of the country, mobility has added the *Waddenzee* (Wadden Sea) to the mental map of the Dutch in the same manner as the sandlands. Sandwiched between the Wadden Islands and the mainland coast (Figure 13.1), this sea was by tradition a remote periphery to one of the country's poorest regions, the northern Netherlands. It was also inhospitable because of its shallowness, its treacherous tidal currents and its innumerable tortuous, shifting channels. Today, in contrast, it is highly valued by the Dutch for its spacious horizons, its seemingly limitless skies and the biodiversity associated with the twice-daily transition from sea to vast exposed mudflats and back once more to sea (Leroy 1994). As a result, in 1995 the Wadden Islands accounted for 4 per cent of all short breaks and almost 7 per cent of holidays (Tables 13.1 and 13.2).

In a very different vein, the Dutch have also socially reconstructed the historic urban Netherlands. As Lambert (1971) demonstrated in her classic *The Making of the Dutch Landscape*, one result of the country's turbulent political history is that there is a liberal

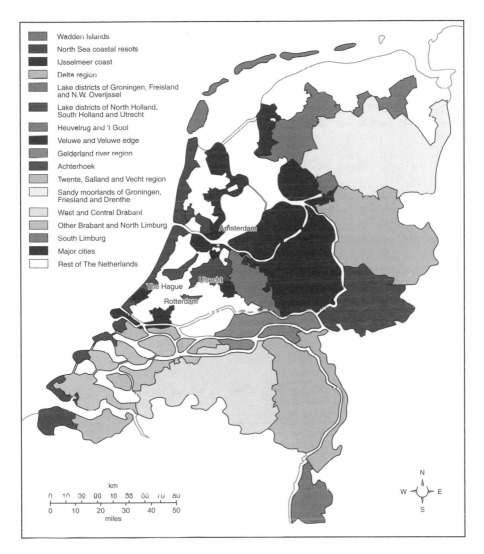

Fig. 13.2   Tourism regions in The Netherlands (cf. Tables 13.1 and 13.2)

sprinkling of what were previously fortified towns and cities (Figure 13.3). In many it is still possible to trace the defended medieval cores and, surrounding them, impressive Renaissance and later fortifications. Within the defences, major civic buildings such as churches and town halls commonly survive, and in regions where the pace of development has been slow it is not unusual for many buildings to date back several centuries. Although almost all these towns were overlooked by tourism for decades, today this is far from true.

One reason for this tourism interest is that their discovery has gone hand in hand with the reappraisal of rural areas in the northern, eastern and southern Netherlands, in which many of them lie. In addition the value now attached to them is the direct

Table 13.1 Regional distribution of Dutch holiday-makers,[1] 1995

	Visitors	
	(thousands)	(%)
West		21.7
North Sea coastal resorts	1,270	16.4
Heuvelrug and 't Gooi	170	2.2
Lake districts[2]	140	1.8
Major cities[3]	100	1.3
North		20.5
Wadden Islands	530	6.9
Lake districts[4]	220	2.8
Sandy moorlands	840	10.8
East		28.1
IJsselmeer coast	360	4.7
Veluwe	1,000	12.9
Gelderland river region	80	1.0
Achterthoek	190	2.5
Twente, Salland and Vecht region	540	7.0
South		26.2
Delta region	380	4.9
West and Central Brabant	680	8.8
Other Brabant and North Limburg	600	7.8
South Limburg	360	4.7
Rest of The Netherlands	270	3.5
Total	7,730	100.0

Source: CBS (1997, p. 457).

[1] Stays of four nights or more.
[2] In the provinces of North Holland, South Holland and Utrecht.
[3] Amsterdam, The Hague, Rotterdam and Utrecht.
[4] In north-west Overijssel and the provinces of Friesland and Groningen.

consequence of the growing appreciation of heritage in Western society generally. Also we may observe here the first signs of the public sector's contribution to fostering tourism resources and spreading the industry's impact throughout the country. Many of these historic centres decayed seriously during the nineteenth and twentieth centuries. More recent restoration is partly an outcome of The Netherlands' prosperity, but townscape preservation would be far less advanced without public subsidies such as those provided by the *Monumentenzorg* (Monument Protection Fund) (Table 13.3).

13.4   Foreign tourism: Amsterdam ascendant

While the Dutch have been exploring neglected parts of their own country, foreign tourists have also been attracted to The Netherlands in increasing numbers. The precise regional impact of the 6 million visitors who currently arrive from abroad each

Table 13.2 Regional distribution of Dutch short-break tourism,[1] 1995

	Visitor numbers	
	(thousands)	(%)
West		23.7
North Sea coastal resorts	1,180	14.5
Heuvelrug and 't Gooi	230	2.8
Lake districts[2]	230	2.8
Major cities[3]	290	3.6
North		16.7
Wadden Islands	340	4.2
Lake districts[4]	260	3.2
Sandy moorlands	750	9.3
East		28.8
IJsselmeer coast	480	5.9
Veluwe	940	11.6
Gelderland river region[5]	50	0.6
Achterhoek	230	2.8
Twente, Salland and Vecht region	640	7.9
South		24.3
Delta region	460	5.7
West and Central Brabant	450	5.6
Other Brabant and North Limburg	590	7.3
South Limburg	460	5.7
Rest of The Netherlands	530	6.5
Total	8,110	100

Source: CBS (1997, p. 456).

[1] Up to three nights.
[2] In the provinces of North Holland, South Holland and Utrecht.
[3] Amsterdam, The Hague, Rotterdam and Utrecht.
[4] In north-west Overijssel and the provinces of Friesland and Groningen.
[5] Severely reduced by spring flooding. 1994 figure, 190,000.

year is difficult to establish because data relating to them are less wide-ranging than those for domestic tourism. However, figures for self-catering accommodation usage strongly suggest that foreign tourism is much more geographically concentrated than Dutch holiday-making (Table 13.4). Although foreign visitors stay in all tourism regions, the western provinces are easily the most popular targets. Here the attractions are partly those of the coast. With its campsites and chalet parks, this is of course strongly reflected in the self-catering data. Beyond this, however, foreign tourists are drawn to the west by the four major cities—Amsterdam, The Hague, Rotterdam and Utrecht—which are underrepresented in the table because their tourism is based chiefly on the hotel sector. And, within this group of cities, Amsterdam is overwhelmingly the dominant target for visitors from abroad. 1.7 million foreigners stayed in the city in 1995, one-third of them from outside Europe (Table 13.5). By contrast, the three other major centres hosted less than 200,000.

Fig. 13.3   Former fortified towns in The Netherlands

To a great extent this reflects the power of the tourism industry to structure behaviour. In collaboration with the international operators, intensive marketing has been the watchword for Amsterdam and, as we shall see later, parts of the surrounding region. This has established the city on the new European Grand Tour for North American, Asian and antipodean tourists, and has also made it the destination of innumerable excursions from neighbouring countries. Much of the city's success, of course, has been based on the cultural resources noted earlier: the world-famous canals and townscapes bequeathed from the era when Amsterdam was a port and trading city of global significance. When the city's private sector visitor attractions are ranked, it is canal trips that head the list—over 2 million passengers are carried each year (Table

Table 13.3 Government expenditure on the restoratation and preservation of architectural monuments in The Netherlands, 1995

	Guilders (millions)	(%)
Houses and mansions	15.055	14.2
Religious buildings	60.551	56.9
Houses of charity	2.115	2.0
Castles and country seats	8.505	8.0
Farm buildings	4.504	4.2
Wind and watermills	6.016	5.7
Other buildings	5.380	5.1
Bridges and other civil engineering	2.030	1.9
Other	2.169	2.0
Total	106.325	100.0

Source: CBS (1997, p. 449).

13.6). Amsterdam also underlines once more the state's role in tourism resource development. The long-established state-owned *Rijksmuseum* and the city-owned *Stedelijkmuseum* remain powerful attractions (with 946,000 and 506,000 visitors, respectively, in 1995); and the cultural infrastructure has also been diversified through state support for initiatives such as the *Rijksmuseum Vincent van Gogh* (838,000 visitors) and the city Opera (137,000 visitors). Public support also plays a key role in other ways. As in historic towns around the country, townscape preservation in Amsterdam owes much to *Monumentenzorg* funds and other public subsidies. And without plentiful cheap public transport, coupled with increasing controls on road traffic, the city would be far less attractive as a visitor experience.

13.4.1 *Cultural attitudes and the resource base: from the hippie trail to sex tourism*

Amsterdam's tourism resources largely serve a major section of the mass market by providing a cultural experience based first and foremost on heritage. But since the 1960s the city's tourism development has also been influenced by the population's relatively liberal cultural attitude. This has not always been a comfortable trend. Bosselman (1978, pp. 99–112), in his essay 'Drifting through Amsterdam', describes how the city's tolerant society became increasingly attractive to young Westerners in the late 1960s. Amsterdam became a mecca for 'hippies' committed to peace and, given a relaxed attitude among the authorities, the pursuit of tranquillity through smoking pot. Many thousands arrived each year, but there were problems. Almost by definition this new type of visitor was a low spender and an indefinite stayer—the opposite of what the tourism industry wanted. Also their focus was Dam Square, one of the highlights of the mainstream tourist scene, where the accumulation of hippies (and their rubbish) was seen as a threat to tourism as a whole. Part of the answer was forcibly to clear the Square, which happened in 1970,[4] but the real solution came through market evolution. Early in the 1970s the hippie fashion waned, to be replaced by 'respectable' youth tourists with more money and no intention of lingering more than a few days.

Table 13.4   Regional distribution of Dutch and foreign
self-catering tourism, 1995

	Dutch (%)	Foreign (%)
West	16.2	39.3
North Sea coastal resorts	13.5	23.8
Heuvelrug and 't Gooi	2.1	0.7
Lake districts[1]	0.2	1.7
Major cities[2]	0.4	13.1
North	19.2	11.8
Wadden Islands	5.4	6.2
Lake districts[3]	2.3	2.2
Sandy moorlands	11.5	3.4
East	29.0	15.8
IJsselmeer coast	5.1	8.8
Veluwe	12.5	2.6
Gelderland river region	0.6	0.2
Achterthoek	3.2	0.9
Twente, Salland and Vecht region	7.6	3.3
South	34.3	28.4
Delta region	3.6	6.5
West and Central Brabant	11.0	6.1
Other Brabant and North Limburg	14.5	14.4
South Limburg	5.2	1.4
Rest of The Netherlands	1.4	4.6
Total	100.0	100.0

Source: CBS (1997, p. 460).

[1] In the provinces of North Holland, South Holland and Utrecht.
[2] Amsterdam, The Hague, Rotterdam and Utrecht.
[3] In north-west Overijssel and the provinces of Friesland and Groningen.

Rejection of the externalities of hippie tourism does not mean that liberal attitudes have ceased to influence Amsterdam's evolution as a tourism resource. The city is renowned for the ready availability of soft drugs, and tolerance has also underpinned the rise of sex tourism as a niche market. Large sections of post-war Dutch society have been progressive in adopting new views on sexuality, particularly in Amsterdam through the same spirit of openness that initially welcomed the hippies. One reflection of this is the *Zeedijk* red light district, which has long been accepted as a legitimate tourism attraction. More recently liberal attitudes to homosexuality have led to the emergence of established gay communities and associated gay tourism, while visitor attractions based more generally on the sex industry have gained a firm foothold. Almost half a million people visited the *Venustempel* sex museum in 1995, and 158,000 the Erotic Gallery. Both figures had risen by one-fifth in just two years. In comparison the 1995 attendance figure for the Heineken Brewery visit—the chief 'alternative' tourism attraction for the 1960s tourist— was a mere 90,000 (Table 13.6). All this is accepted locally much more readily than the incursion of tens of thousands of hippies in the late 1960s.

Table 13.5   Origin of Amsterdam's hotel guests, 1995

	Guests (thousands)	Bednights (thousands)
The Netherlands	156.0	274.9
Belgium/Luxembourg	50.2	89.1
Germany	192.0	414.9
France	126.3	255.6
UK	320.9	720.8
Italy	99.4	258.1
Eastern Europe	45.0	113.0
Scandinavia	86.5	192.9
Spain/Portugal	81.7	203.7
Switzerland	51.7	128.3
Other Europe	58.5	135.8
Total Europe	1,268.2	2,787.1
North America	267.4	598.2
Middle and South America	54.2	116.8
Africa	24.6	55.6
Japan	60.0	123.6
Other Asia (including Turkey)	152.5	287.6
Australia/New Zealand	50.8	115.5
Total	1,877.7	4,084.4

Source: Gemeente Amsterdam (1997, p. 281).

Table 13.6   Attendances at Amsterdam's major private sector visitor attractions

	1993 (thousands)	1995 (thousands)
Canal tours	2,200	2,100
Diamond workshops	753	1,000
Holland Casino	–	812
Venustemel sex museum	411	485
Berlage stock exchange	200	250
De Looier art and antique centre	200	220
Erotic Gallery	129	158
Heineken Brewery visitor centre	85	91

Source: Gemeente Amsterdam (1997, p. 191).

To a great extent, therefore, the wide-ranging impact of tourism is the outcome of complex interactions between many factors: changing tourist perceptions; increased wealth and mobility among consumers; cultural attitudes in society as a whole; the power and sophistication of the tourism industry; and direct and indirect support from the public sector. Powerful though these forces have been, however, it is important to appreciate also the contribution of commodification, both through commercial interests and public initiatives.

13.5   Commodification: towards new tourism experiences

As in the rest of western Europe, the private sector has extended the resource base by creating a burgeoning range of attractions, often to serve niche markets. In The Netherlands this has been a long-established trend, but has accelerated greatly since the early 1980s. Early examples were Madurodam, a model Dutch town built to 1:25 scale near The Hague, and Middelburg's Walcheren in Miniature—again a scale model, in this case of one the delta's largest islands. Today, theme parks are well established, especially those with Disneyesque overtones: *De Efteling* (Tilburg) and Never-Never Land (Drunen-Vlijmen) illustrate the exploitation of this rich vein, as do adventure and fairytale parks at Hellendoorn (Overijssel) and Valkenburg (southern Limburg). As with the landscape attractions noted earlier, the effect of many of these investments has been to encourage the spread of tourism impacts throughout the country.

With its *Thermae 2000*, Valkenburg also exemplifies movement into a quite different market, the modern spa. This is an important reason why southern Limburg now has the least seasonal tourism industry in the entire country. This modern spa strategy has also been pursued in the North Sea resort of Scheveningen, where in fact it has been extended even further. Here the renovated Art Nouveau *kurhaus* offers spa, casino, art gallery, restaurant and hotel facilities, while adjacent redevelopment has added gardens, shops and a fitness centre comprising a wave pool, sauna, solarium and sports hall. Underpinning this development is the perception that, in a highly competitive tourism market, The Netherlands' uncertain climate must be countered by providing diverse, high-quality attractions that are not weather-dependent. This particular example has an urban setting, but the same belief has also spurred some of the larger tourism investments in rural areas. The classic example is provided by the Center Parcs chain of holiday villages, with their carefully devised mix of 'tropical' indoor pools, a wide range of other indoor and outdoor sports facilities, restaurant choice and high-quality bungalow accommodation. Combining diversity with quality and a high degree of independence of the weather has ensured that such developments are highly successful: each year this firm's five developments cater for almost as many tourists as Amsterdam. And, once again, the investment has helped to build the resource base outside the west.

13.5.1   *Heritage commodification*

Although the exploitation of heritage (Ashworth and Tunbridge 1990) is often presented in the literature as a relatively recent phenomenon, in The Netherlands its roots are much longer. The growth of mass cultural tourism in the western Netherlands was, as we have seen, a post-war phenomenon based on Amsterdam's attractions. But, for international tourism especially, growth also reflected the commodification of regional heritage. Cheese markets in Alkmaar, Edam and Gouda; flower markets; clog stalls; traditional dress in farming and fishing villages; all these and much more were seized upon as grist to the tourism industry's (wind)mill. To a great extent this was made possible by packaged coach excursions, offering cheap, comfortable and—very importantly in view of most visitors' brief stays—rapid tours of these cultural experiences.

Commodification has also been central to the marketing of another form of heritage, the horticultural and agricultural industries. Initially the exploitation of

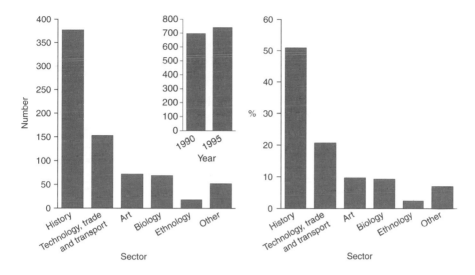

Fig. 13.4   Scale and structure of the museum and art gallery sector in The Netherlands

horticulture by tourism was based simply on the coastal bulbfields of North Holland, between Haarlem and Leiden and some 20 km west of Amsterdam. As tourism developed after World War II, the bulbfields became a spring attraction in their own right—apart from Amsterdam, in fact, they were the only attraction capable of drawing in foreign tourists on any scale. Then, as leisure travel became increasingly package-based, city and bulbfield tourism developed a symbiotic 'Tulips from Amsterdam' relationship. The products began to merge: many visitors to the city would tour the bulbfields, while packages to the latter would commonly include a trip to the city. Commodification fostered this process by means of what is in effect a horticultural theme park, the Keukenhof, in the bulbfield district near Lisse. This is now renowned world-wide for its outdoor and indoor floral displays and is one of the leading tourism attractions in the west. Similarly, on the IJsselmeer Polders the Flevohof celebrates both the horticultural and agricultural industries and, through extensive exhibition space, also supports business tourism in the agricultural sector. An important feature of both these developments is that—through entrance fees, cafés, restaurants and shops—they encourage spending on a scale far greater than simple viewing of horticultural and agricultural landscapes. To cultivate spending is, after all, frequently the name of the commodification game.

Public, as well as commercial, interests have been deeply involved in heritage commodification, especially in the museum sector. In the mid-1990s there are nearly 750 museums and galleries in the country as a whole (Figure 13.4). Some are businesses, an outstanding example being Amsterdam's *Venustempel* sex museum; but the large majority belong either to trusts or to national, provincial or local government—80 per cent of the sector's income is derived from various types of subsidy. Nearly three-quarters of all museums have historical, trading, technological or transport themes, such as the textile museums in Enschede and Tilburg, and the maritime museums of Amsterdam and Rotterdam. The vast majority are small: even when volunteers are included, the average museum creates only 10 full-time jobs, and most are much smaller than this (CBS 1997, p. 449). Generally, therefore, their individual contribution to the tourism resource base, and their influence on the regional distribution of tourism, is not great. They enhance the visitors' range of choices, but they probably do little to attract them to a region or locality in the first place. In some cases, however, heritage has been commodified much more impressively, as two examples from the eastern and western Netherlands demonstrate.

The Netherlands *Openluchtmuseum* (Open Air Museum) lies towards the east of the country on the outskirts of Arnhem. Since 1912 a non-profitmaking Trust responsible for this collection has been moving to the site farmhouses, barns, cottages, windmills and other buildings relating to agriculture and other rural industries from all parts of The Netherlands. Today there are more than 50 exhibits, the large majority of which would almost certainly have been lost if relocation to Arnhem had not been possible. Meanwhile the *Zaanse Schans*, a short distance north of Amsterdam, is in many ways a smaller industrial version of the *Openluchtmuseum*. For centuries the River Zaan was an important industrial centre, where imported commodities ranging from logs to spices were processed using wind power. Hundreds of windmills were employed, and the area developed a highly distinctive appearance because virtually all buildings were constructed from locally sawn planks. Between the late nineteenth century and World War II, however, this distinctive industrial district was threatened by the increasing obsolescence of wind power. Preservation has again only been possible through the activities of a Trust, which since 1949 has assembled the *Zaanse Schans* collection of industrial windmills and domestic buildings from nearby towns and villages. What is particularly relevant about both these examples is that they have arguably made a transition from almost pure preservation to commodification based on conservation. Open-air museums are expensive to create and maintain, even if subsidies are available. Once again, therefore, the marketing of commodified visitor experiences has become central to their continued success.

Heritage commodification has, therefore, significantly extended the resource base in both the western Netherlands and the outlying regions. What may be suggested, however, is that the products created and marketed so effectively are very partial—and often distorted—representations of the original. Perfect preservation, orderliness and the air of tranquillity that are so evident at the *Openluchtmuseum* and the *Zaanse Schans* are far cries from the dilapidation, bustle, noise, poverty and stress which historically characterised the districts from which the exhibits came. Similarly, a coach tour of the tourism honeypots around Amsterdam can create the impression of visiting the dispersed fragments of a theme park, with no hint of the ill-health and short lives which were the lot of most country people. As with a great deal of Western heritage tourism, the sanitisation and romanticisation of experiences has been very much in evidence as the industry has sought to maintain demand growth.

13.6   From land dereliction to tourism resources

A particular feature of tourism resource growth in The Netherlands has been the reclamation of derelict areas. As three examples—the peat industry, gravel extraction and waterfront decline—will demonstrate, this reclamation has made a significant contribution to the tourism industry's resource portfolio in all regions and in both rural and urban localities.

For many centuries the abundant peat supplies available in the low-lying reclaimed areas of the west and parts of the northern, eastern and southern regions were exploited for fuel. This use increased rapidly in the second half of the nineteenth century through population growth and large-scale urbanisation. Peat extraction was essentially open-cast mining, which exhausted and then abandoned areas as it progressed. The result was numerous pockets of land dereliction, and in the lower-lying areas the derelict pits simply flooded as the industry moved on. Clusters of lakes, mainly in north west Overijssel and the provinces of Friesland, Groningen, North Holland, South Holland and Utrecht, were a testament to this process. Before the 1950s these 'lake districts' were socially constructed as derelict sites and virtually no value was attached to them, but since then the rapid growth of watersports has transformed them into a much-prized leisure resource (Figure 13.1). Although their proportional importance for day recreation is unknown, by 1995 their marinas and other facilities were catering for about 5 per cent of all Dutch residential tourism. Most of this benefited the northern lakes in Groningen, Friesland and north west Overijssel (Tables 13.1 and 13.2).

The gravel extraction story differs in detail: large-scale mining only took off after World War II to supply the needs of concrete production, and it has been confined almost entirely to the Maas valley, chiefly in a zone extending 20 km south of Roermond and adjacent to the German border (Voogd, 1988). As with peat, exploitation produced extensive flooded pits, many of which have been seized upon eagerly by watersports interests, planners and tourism entrepreneurs. What is also significant is that this new watersport zone has assumed an international function. Because of its position close to the German border, it provides a strategic filter reducing the pressure of cross-border weekend watersport tourism elsewhere in The Netherlands.

Urban waterfront reclamation has expanded tourism resources in an entirely different manner. Compared with most countries, The Netherlands' extensive waterway network enabled the Dutch to develop over many centuries an elaborate port system. In part this comprised seaports, extending from Vlissingen in the south west to Delfzijl in the north east, with first Amsterdam and then Rotterdam playing a dominant role. But there were also innumerable inland ports served by river or canal, to the extent that a town or city without a working waterfront became something of a rarity. Some of these ports failed in the distant past: in the Dutch delta, for example, silting snuffed out centres such as Zierikzee and Brouwershaven, ushering in nineteenth-century depression and bequeathing to the local townscapes fossilised relics of former prosperity. In the twentieth century the port system as a whole came under pressure. This was partly the result of war: the historic central harbour area of Rotterdam was largely destroyed by bombing in May 1940. Usually, however, the pressures were those common throughout the developed world in the post-war period (Hoyle 1988; Gordon 1997). Old seaport docklands became unsuitable for new types of shipping and new cargo handling technologies, while inland waterfronts were hit by a shift towards road freight. In these ways port restructuring contributed to inner-urban decay, often close to town or city cores.

Since the 1970s there has been a renaissance on many of these waterfronts. As in many other parts of the world, neglected waterfront locations have been rediscovered by local people, visitors and investors, giving them new value. The former port area in the heart of Rotterdam—with its office blocks, hotels, maritime museum and other entertainment facilities mingled with housing—has strong overtones of city waterfront revitalisation around the globe (Pinder and Rosing 1988). Elsewhere, although the spectacular office blocks found in Rotterdam are missing, the market has revalued and revamped waterfronts throughout the country—again helping to spread the regional impact of tourism. Many former quays boast what is by now a predictable mix of cafés, restaurants, shops, museums, housing and—especially where there is no conflict with commercial traffic—pleasure boats and marinas. Much of the time, of course, these revitalised areas depend on local people for their trade, but they are also important for tourism because of their influence on visitors' images. As the Dutch have placed new social constructions on their landscapes, tourism growth has often been inextricably linked with urban image improvement. Van der Knaap and Pinder (1992) have set this trend in the context of city marketing models.

13.7   State policy and resource base spin-offs

Government policies that influence tourism are normally assumed to be tailor-made: tourism is economically significant and therefore justifies the pursuit of tourism strategies. However, any official policy may have unforeseen consequences, and in The Netherlands there are outstanding examples of measures totally unrelated to tourism resulting in important additions to the tourism resource base. This has again influenced the interregional pattern of tourism flows, as is demonstrated by developments in the delta and the IJsselmeer Polders.

As has been implied, the delta has a chequered economic history. Prosperity gave way to depression in the nineteenth century, and the region remained depressed until the 1960s. This partly reflected port decline, noted above, but was chiefly a consequence of isolation. Movement within the delta, and between it and the mainland, relied heavily on elderly ferries, discouraging economic development and causing out-migration in search of work (Pinder, 1983). In the 1950s an opportunity arose to reverse these economic and demographic trends. Widespread flooding in 1953 led to the adoption of a flood protection scheme, the Delta Plan. To gain a dual benefit from this costly investment, the Plan's dams and sluices were used to carry new roads into the heart of the region. Although the project was not completed until the 1980s, by the 1970s the delta's isolation had been broken down. As this occurred the newly accessible region was quickly recognised as a tourism resource. Because of its history of isolation—which had protected landscapes, townscapes and social practices—it was virtually a time capsule compared with most of the country. In addition, within the delta there appeared to be no shortage of space for the watersports that were becoming so popular. While the Delta Plan aimed to prevent one type of flood, therefore, it quickly provoked another. Day and weekend tourism, involving the Germans and Belgians as well as the Dutch, rapidly filled the vacuum. In 1959, 2 million visitor nights were spent in the area, compared with 7 million in 1975 (Bosselman 1978, p. 119). The delta is now the destination for nearly one Dutch tourist in every 20 (Tables 13.1 and 13.2); and—at least so far as self-catering breaks are concerned—the area's importance for foreign visitors is even greater (Table 13.4).

In a country renowned for its commitment to spatial planning (Dutt and Costa, 1985), the most highly publicised public policy of all has been the enclosure of the Zuider Zee to form the freshwater IJsselmeer, and the linked reclamation of the IJsselmeer Polders. Agreed during World War I, and begun during the interwar years, the project had no connection with tourism. Instead its roots lay in the need to control the threat of flooding around the stormy and tidal Zuider Zee. Initially there were deep divisions about the inclusion of expensive land reclamation in the scheme, but a powerful reclamation lobby, combined with wartime food shortages, ultimately swung the debate in favour of creating agricultural land on a large scale. For 40 years up to the 1960s, the IJsselmeer Polders reclamation project proceeded with this as its sole objective, but meanwhile economic and social circumstances changed profoundly. Agriculture became much less important to The Netherlands because of the expansion of the manufacturing and service sectors. Moreover, the growth of European agricultural surpluses made a policy of creating still more highly productive farmland seem extremely questionable in government and planning circles. As a result the policy goalposts were moved. Although much of the reclaimed land was to remain agricultural, it was accepted that large areas should be made available for other purposes. The most dramatic of these was urban overspill from the congested western cities to the new towns of Lelystad and Almere, together with the designation of a large industrial area between the two (Figure 13.5). But the polders were also opened up to the tourism industry, so that campsites, bungalow parks, restaurants, marinas and other watersport centres spread quickly around the polder shoreline (Figure 13.6). Leisure areas were also created by planting woodlands inland, especially on the poorer soils, and the proposed industrial area, which was never properly drained, quietly developed into an important wetland habitat. Today this *Oostvaardersplassen*[5] is one of Europe's largest nature reserves, particularly important for ornithology (Figure 13.5). To a considerable extent, of course, these newly created resources are used for day tourism, especially from the Amsterdam region and the overspill centres of Lelystad and Almere. However, they are also highly popular with short- and long-stay Dutch and European visitors. Here comparison with the delta is appropriate: the IJsselmeer coast and the delta both absorb around 5 per cent of Dutch residential tourism (Tables 13.1 and 13.2), while for foreign tourists the IJsselmeer is even more important (Table 13.4).

13.8   Conclusion: tourism in the 1990s—an issue-free industry?

This chapter has aimed chiefly to explore the tourism industry in terms of its regional impact and the relationship of that impact to the evolving resource base. Three main observations may be made on the basis of the analysis presented. First, as a result of many contributory factors, the resource base supporting tourism is far larger and much more diverse than external observers normally suppose. This diversity is based partly on changing social constructions of the tourism value of environmental and cultural resources, but also reflects extensive commodification, the perception of opportunity in dereliction and the unforeseen consequences of state spatial planning strategies. Second, because the resource base is underestimated, perceptions of tourism's regional importance are also frequently inaccurate. Amsterdam may dominate many mental maps, but tourism today is a genuinely nationwide industry. Key factors behind this extensive impact have been a new appreciation of neglected landscapes and historic centres, a dramatic improvement in the delta's accessibility and the attractions of water. The latter's importance is most evident in the lake districts, the IJsselmeer and the delta's sheltered waters, but in the context of urban tourism it has also been central to the revitalisation of numerous quaysides and harbours. Third, however, the particular interests of Dutch and foreign tourists mean that their regional markets are significantly different. Although both groups have a widespread regional impact, the foreign tourist gaze is turned more to the west—and above all to Amsterdam.

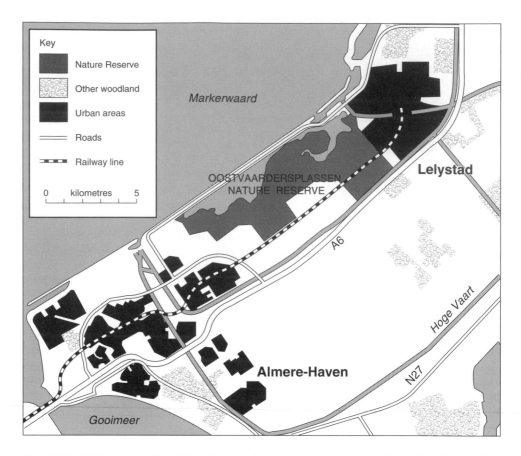

Fig. 13.5   Urban overspill and the Oostvaardersplassen nature reserve, South Flevoland Polder

Because the discussion has focused on the scale of tourism flows and the qualitative development of the resource base, it might well be inferred that the industry's development has been largely problem-free. To end on this note would, however, be misleading. In the 1990s several issues can be clearly identified, and it is therefore appropriate to end this chapter with a brief review of questions currently confronting the industry.

First, it is evident that the indirect support tourism has in the past received through public investment to socialise the costs of service provision is under strong pressure. In the current neo-liberal political and economic climate, the responsibilities of the state have been reduced in The Netherlands as in other European countries, and in the 1990s further constraints have been imposed by government attempts to curtail public expenditure in order to meet the convergence criteria for membership of the single European currency. The consequences are clearly to be seen in tourism-relevant investments such as the restoration and preservation of architectural monuments. Allocations to this programme fell by over 40 per cent between 1985 and 1995, and only one major category of monument—churches—escaped relatively unscathed (Table 13.7). Moreover, because the figures do not take inflation into account, the real

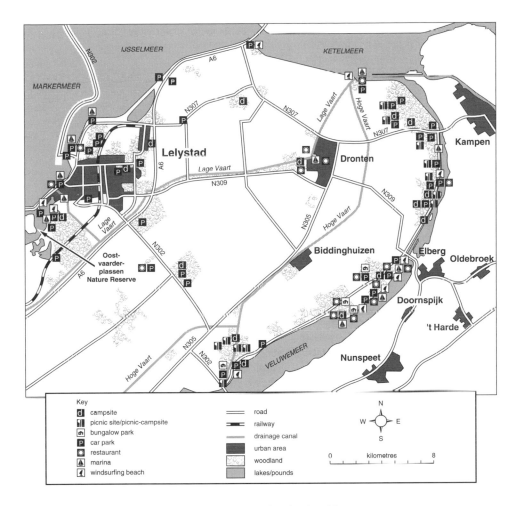

Fig. 13.6 Tourism facilities around the East Flevoland Polder

impact of the economies has been greater than appears at first sight. While tourism has never been highly subsidised, it is clear that funding streams which have in the past done much to improve the range and quality of heritage tourism resources are now under serious threat. Whether the losses can be replaced effectively is highly questionable, given the gap between social and individual costs and benefits.

While public sector cutbacks are a geographically widespread threat, there are also pressing local issues. In economic terms these are most important in Amsterdam where, despite this city's stature as a tourism site, all is not well with the tourism industry. In the 1990s year-round occupancy rates in the hotel sector have been less than 40 per cent, and guest numbers have hovered a little below 2 million a year with no sign of an upward trend. As a result, while some attractions such as the *Venustempel* museum have increased their trade impressively, other more traditional magnets have experienced stagnation. Visitors to the *Rijksmuseum*, for example, have recently

Table 13.7   Government funding changes for the restoration and preservation of architectural monuments in The Netherlands

	Guilders (millions)	
	1985	1995
Houses and mansions	72.932	15.055
Religious buildings	68.845	60.551
Houses of charity	5.202	2.115
Castles and country seats	9.887	8.505
Farm buildings	1.105	4.504
Wind and watermills	7.059	6.016
Other buildings	12.180	5.380
Bridges and other civil engineering works	7.034	2.030
Other	0.894	2.169
Total	185.138	106.325

Source: CBS (1997, p. 462).

fluctuated between less than 950,000 and 1.2 million a year, but not on a rising path. The same is true of the *Rijksmuseum Vincent van Gogh*, although the figures are lower (around 800,000); and in the private sector the number of canal trips taken each year has stabilised at just over 2 million. This may, of course, reflect market saturation and competition from other tourism sites: a cultural centre such as Amsterdam will have relatively inflexible market limits. But it is also probable that price factors are involved. Between 1992 and 1995 the number of visitors staying in 4-star hotels fell by 40 per cent, while business in 3-star establishments increased by half. This strongly suggests that the price elasticity of demand is limited. Foreign tourists—and the tour companies who bring most of them—are now highly sensitive to the cost of quality accommodation in one of Europe's more expensive countries. This is confirmed by Bekkers (1995), who notes that tourism from neighbouring Germany and Belgium is now dominated by middle- and lower-income groups.

This localised economic issue may in turn be set in the broader context of tourism's contribution to the national economy. Bekkers (1995) has provided a relatively upbeat assessment of this contribution. Estimating that tourism and recreation together generate the equivalent of 200,000 full-time jobs, he emphasises, first, that this figure is expected to increase annually by 2.5 per cent until the early years of the next century and, second, that it is already equivalent to employment in the banking sector. However, for a variety of reasons this interpretation must be viewed with considerable caution. For example, total tourism expenditure in The Netherlands by the Dutch and foreign tourists is approximately 6.5 billion guilders a year; this is equivalent to only 0.7 per cent of national consumption (CBS 1997, pp. 387, 453 and 459). Furthermore, while 200,000 tourism-related jobs represent between 3.5 and 4 per cent of the total labour force, depending on the definitions used, the expenditure impacts are seriously weakened because poor pay typifies the sector. In hotels and restaurants, for example, hourly wage rates are little more than 70 per cent of the national average, and per capita annual earnings are less than half the national figure. In contrast, pursuing Bekker's comparison, in the financial services sector hourly remuneration and total annual earnings are, respectively, 17 per cent and 35 per cent above the averages (CBS

1997, pp. 123 and 124). Poor pay in the tourism industry is closely associated with the low levels of skills demanded, and also with seasonality and part-time employment. In 1994, for example, 36 per cent of hotel and restaurant employees worked 12 hours a week or less, almost four times the figure for all activities (10 per cent) (CBS 1997, pp. 119 and 123). Consequently, while tourism demand is certainly strong, it is easy to overestimate the extent to which the industry is a driving force in the economy. In many localities, of course, tourism is more important that the national figures suggest, as much of the discussion throughout this chapter has implied. But everywhere it is difficult to escape the constraints of seasonality, part-time employment and demand for a low-skill, low-pay labour force.

The conclusion that economic benefits are often limited takes on added significance when related to the problems of tourism pressure. As we have seen, the industry has developed extensively in the eastern, southern and northern regions, not least because these offer space and landscape resources that are in short supply in the densely populated western provinces. The drawback, however, is that rising visitor numbers are now highlighting sustainability issues in the most popular areas, issues which will spread as tourism impacts are extended. At present concern is particularly acute with respect to the Veluwe, but trends in the Waddenzee are problematic (Leroy 1994) and it is also recognised that watersport areas are frequently highly vulnerable. The classic example is provided by the delta, where the dramatic improvement of accessibility was already generating problems in the 1970s (Bosselman 1978, pp. 117–129). Today the region is beset by an extensive range of environmental and economic challenges: traffic congestion; the impact of external demand on property prices; pressure from investors—and sometimes local authorities—to permit ever more holiday home and marina developments; water pollution caused by boats; and the impact of watersports on the wildlife of formerly isolated and undisturbed areas.

Since the early 1970s planners have increasingly favoured the adoption of spatial strategies designed to accommodate the pressures generated by a prosperous, leisure-conscious society (Ministerie van Volkshuisvesting en Ruimtelijke Ordening 1977, pp. 39–41; Ministerie van Cultuur, Recreatie en Maatschappelijk Werk 1981a,b; Ministerie van Landbouw en Visserij 1981, pp. 56–65, also 1981b; Rijksplanologische Dienst 1986, pp. 104–13; Ministerie van Volkshuisvesting, Ruimtelijke Ordening en Milieubeheer 1988; Ministerie van Economische Zaken 1994). In recognising over-development problems associated with both land-based and water-based tourism, a common theme of these reports has been to propose various dispersal strategies. It is also possible to ameliorate, or at least displace, some ecological frictions—for example, by creating exclusion zones to protect especially sensitive environments. Thus, parts of the delta are no-go areas for speedboats and waterskiers, and—despite the wilderness image—in especially popular areas of the Veluwe walkers may find themselves constrained by fenced paths installed to protect the surrounding heathland.

Another potentially important planning response has been the revision of the country's *ruilverkaveling* (land consolidation) policy in order to create more recreational facilities in rural areas away from honeypot localities. Originally this nationwide land consolidation policy aimed simply to ensure that farmers' land holdings were as rational, and therefore as profitable, as possible. But in the 1960s and 1970s this policy inflicted considerable damage on environmental and tourism resources by removing coppices, ponds, watercourses, etc., with the result that replacement legislation became necessary to introduce a more sensitive approach. This included environmental protection and the diversion of land into non-agricultural uses such as recreation

Table 13.8   Foreign and Dutch tourists: mid-1990s comparison of main means of transport to destinations in The Netherlands

	Foreign visitors[1] (%)	Dutch visitors[2] (%)
Bicycle	0	3
Car, camper van, etc.	51	89
Train	5	5
Bus, tram, metro	0	0
Coach	11	1
Aircraft	30	0
Other	3	2
Total	100	100

Source: CBS (1997, pp. 452, 456 and 457).

[1] 1993/94.
[2] 1995.

(Ministerie van Landbouw, Natuurbeheer en Visserij 1993). What is not yet clear, however, is the extent to which this revised strategy is relieving tourism pressure by increasing the attractions of less congested areas.

What is also not evident is how effective broad analyses, such as those offered by recent reports quoted above, are in achieving change on the ground. Planning is now a contentious activity in The Netherlands (Faludi and de Ruijter 1985). Much decision-making power rests at the local level, and there is great scope for divergence between national plans and local reality. Moreover, evidence from the Veluwe does not suggest that the powerful market forces are under control. Despite widespread official recognition of pressure problems, between 1985 and 1995 the number of summer holidays taken in this area increased by two-thirds. Similarly, in the delta short breaks grew by almost one-third between in 1993 and 1995. Meanwhile, on the IJsselmeer coast—officially viewed as an area developing to alleviate pressure elsewhere—they fell one-quarter.

Finally, it is necessary to highlight the role of the car in creating challenges for the tourism industry and tourism planners. Over-development is partly a question of too many campsites in a specific location and too many people seeking to experience a limited and perhaps sensitive environment. But it is also a matter of how people travel to their destinations, and how they move around once they are there. Problems in this context are least acute with respect to foreign tourists, many of whom arrive by aircraft, train or coach and then use public transport or excursion coaches during their stay. Even so, half the visitors from abroad arrive by car (Table 13.8) and these car-users account for almost two thirds of the nights which foreign tourists spend in The Netherlands (CBS 1997, p. 452).

Meanwhile the Dutch—despite their legendary use of the bicycle, despite the high quality of their public transport systems, and despite the small size of their country—have moved ever closer to being totally dependent on the car for tourism. In the mid-1980s, nearly one-third of all breaks still relied on other forms of transport; but by 1995 this was true for only 11 per cent of holidays (Table 13.8). Moreover, it appears inevitable that the car will continue to extend its hegemony. In the absence of national policy measures with a reasonable prospect of car-use reduction, this poses major challenges for the most popular tourism regions. Should the car be accommodated as far as possible, for example through road improvements and still more car parks, even though this 'solution' may encourage even greater car use? Should no improvements be made, the assumption being that ultimately this will force motorists towards less congested areas? Could pricing strategies relieve traffic problems? If so, what are the ethical implications of a policy that might exclude the less wealthy tourist from the more attractive environments? If the car is to continue to dominate tourism, as seems certain for the foreseeable future, issues such as these require urgent debate.

Summarising, therefore, tourism in The Netherlands can be seen as an important industry, particularly in terms of its contribution to the quality of life of many Dutch people and the recreational and cultural experiences made available to foreign tourists. Economically its turnover and employment effects are appreciable yet not outstanding, despite the impressive diversification that has occurred in the resource base in recent decades. The fact that tourism is in no sense dominant arguably places it in a relatively vulnerable position, in that it has little leverage to counter government cutbacks in tourism-related programmes. This may threaten some types of resource base development, for example through reduced support for building conservation. There is also evidence of vulnerability in other respects, not least in Amsterdam, the leading foreign tourism magnet. In this case, however, the threats come from a quite different source—an increasingly competitive European and global cultural tourism industry. Elsewhere in The Netherlands, in contrast, tourism appears much stronger, to the extent that in the more popular areas real challenges are posed for the planning system. In this crowded society visitor numbers and overwhelming reliance on the car have been posing serious environmental threats for some time. Ways must be found for the industry to co-exist with other functions in the multiple use of pressurised landscapes, and this need will almost certainly become increasingly urgent as tourism demand continues to be fuelled by social and economic trends in The Netherlands and abroad.

Notes

1. 10.2 Million holidays were taken abroad in 1995, France, Spain, Austria and Germany being the main destinations. In addition 2.1 million short breaks were taken, the leading countries in this case being France, Belgium and Germany.
2. In the mid-1800s there were 600,000 ha of heath and 15,000 ha of sand.
3. National parks must be at least 1000 ha in extent, of interest for their topography and of importance for the preservation of native flora and fauna. The list has been expanded since the 1980s and, in addition to those in the Veluwe, now includes: Schiermonnikoog (one of the Wadden Islands); Het Dwingelderveld (province of Drenthe); De Kennermerduinen (province of North Holland); De Weeribben (province of Overijssel); part of the Biesbosch (provinces of North Brabant and South Holland); and De Groote Peel (province of North Brabant).
4. The hippies were banished to Vondel Park in the city, which at the peak in 1971 was sleeping 85,000 a night.
5. The area is named after the *Oostvaarders*, the ships and crews who sailed from Amsterdam through the Zuider Zee en route to the East and, in particular, to the East Indies. *Plassen* is a reference to the fact that much of what is now the nature reserve is a complex of lakes.

14 Scandinavia: challenging nature

Tommy Andersson and Morten Huse

14.1 Introduction

14.1.1 Tourism at the 'top' of Europe

'New Scandinavia, the top of Europe'. Located at the very top of Europe with a beautiful natural environment, purity, tradition and reliability is the new Scandinavia. This is the way the five Scandinavian countries like to introduce themselves. The Nordic countries consist of Norway, Sweden, Denmark, Finland and Iceland. According to traditional definitions, Scandinavia is composed of Norway, Sweden and Denmark. Efforts are now being made to eliminate the concept of the Nordic countries and to introduce the term 'Scandinavia' for all five. Their nature and beauty have the potential to be marketed to bring inspiration to a stressed world, where population and progress limit the availability of beautiful and untouched natural areas. Fresh air, deep fjords, clean lakes and rivers, the midnight sun and the northern lights are all qualities the Scandinavian countries will be certain to use in their profiling.

Even if there are efforts to market the new Scandinavia collectively, there will be considerable differences between countries in their approaches. The geography of Denmark is very different to that of the other countries. Therefore, in this presentation we focus on the countries of the Scandinavian peninsula, Norway and Sweden. These countries, and Norway in particular, are, probably to a higher degree than the other countries, characterised by the 'Scandinavian' qualities. For most Europeans, this remains an undiscovered tourist destination.

This chapter starts with a general survey of essential demographic, geographic and economic trends, followed by sections on the main features of the tourism product: guest nights in Scandinavia, the tourism industry, tourism and national economic development, tourism and regional economic development, the responsiveness of the tourism industry to stimuli, and finally a presentation of future trends and challenges.

14.1.2 Scandinavia: demography and geography

In order to understand tourism in Scandinavia, it is first necessary to consider some of the particularities of its geography and demography. Compared to continental Europe,

Tourism and Economic Development: European Experiences, 3rd Edition. Edited by A.M. Williams and G. Shaw.

Scandinavia has huge land areas and a relatively small population. There exist relatively few natural environmental problems, and most areas are scenically very attractive. The total area of Denmark, Finland, Iceland, Norway and Sweden is 1,290,000 km². In addition, the area of the Norwegian islands Svalbard (Spitsbergen) and Jan Mayen (situated in the Arctic Ocean between Greenland and Norway) is 62,000 km². Greenland is not included in these figures. Taken together, the area of the five Scandinavian countries is about equal to that of Belgium, France, Germany, UK, Ireland and The Netherlands (1,305,000 km²). The population, however, is only 23 million (1993), which is about 8 per cent of the total for the above-mentioned countries.

The tourism industry has evolved against a background of mostly very low population densities. The population density in Norway (excluding Svalbard and Jan Mayen) is 13 persons per km², while in Sweden it is 19. Nordkalotten, the area north of or intersected by the Arctic Circle, constitutes about one-third of the total area of these countries. The total population north of the Arctic Circle is around 900,000 inhabitants. This implies a population density of about two persons per km².

Figure 14.1 shows a map of Norway, Sweden, Finland and Denmark. The map shows the administrative divisions within the countries and some of the most important tourism destinations. The basic administrative division is the county: Finland has 12 counties, Norway has 19, Sweden has 24 and Denmark has 12. In Norway and Sweden, respectively, about 7 per cent and 5 per cent of the economically active population are in agriculture, forestry and fishing. In mining, manufacturing and electricity production, the figures are about 25 per cent and 22 per cent.

14.2   Main features of the Scandinavian tourism product

14.2.1   Challenging nature

Internationally Scandinavia has been promoted as a single tourist destination, but there are important variations in the particular features of these countries. Many of what are considered the most typical Scandinavian tourist features are, as mentioned above, found in Norway. Norway is characterised by the combination of the sea and mountains, manifested in the famous fjords. In 1996, readers of the British newspaper, the *Observer*, rated Norway as the 'best' vacation country in Europe. The high ratings were mostly due to its wild and unspoiled natural environment. The northern-most parts of the country contain two of the Scandinavian countries' greatest attractions, the North Cape and the Lofoten Islands, which offer fishing holidays in fishermen's shanties, whale watching and other nature-based attractions. The Coastal Line, a coastal steamship service, is also a famous Norwegian attraction, and its combination of local traffic and tourism constitutes a unique part of the local culture. The Coastal Line makes daily calls along the coast from Bergen in the south to Kirkenes in the north.

Sweden and Finland do not have the same nature-based attractions as Norway. These countries, however, compensate for this through having better organisation and coordination of tourism. Their infrastructure is also generally better developed. For example, wildlife tourism has been more developed in Sweden and in Finland than in Norway. These countries also have more liberal regulations concerning motorised

Fig. 14.1 Administrative divisions in Scandinavia

traffic in wilderness areas. Sweden and Finland also have, to a higher degree than Norway, created tourist attractions of their own through marketing initiatives. 'Santa Claus' country, Lappland in Finland, provides an excellent example of such an attraction, and the Finnish national authorities have worked determinedly on incorporating Santa Claus into the national identity.

In addition, Sweden and Finland make use of the famous Norwegian attractions of the Lofoten Islands and the North Cape in their national marketing. Most of the charter traffic to these destinations is organised by Sweden and Finland rather than by Norway. The tourists live, eat, sleep and spend most of their money in Sweden or Finland, while the Lofoten Islands and/or the North Cape are included as a part of the total holiday package. Usually a one-to two-day excursion is arranged during the package in order to visit one of the Norwegian attractions. The Finns have even invested in a large airport in Karigasniemi close to the border with Norway and the entrance to the North Cape.

During the last few years there has been a considerable increase in the variety of activities and experiences provided within Scandinavian tourism. Different kinds of experiences have become essential parts of the tourism industry's product. Market needs seem to be less connected with the quality and range of services offered by hotels and restaurants than was customary in earlier years. Instead, there has been strong demand from tourists for specific activities. In Norway, investment in such activities has resulted in an extensive development of alpine areas for the winter season, and of playgrounds and holiday parks for the summer season. The availability and structure of national public finance arrangements have considerably influenced the speed of development.

Scandinavia is not, of course, an invariable tourism product. There are significant differences according to whether it is a destination for tourists from other Scandinavian countries (the 'home markets'), or a destination for tourists from other countries.

The Scandinavian home market is sun- and sports-orientated. During the winter season, Scandinavian tourists are strongly orientated towards skiing and the mountains, especially the Norwegian mountains. The flow goes the other way during the summer. The coasts of Southern Sweden and of Jutland in Denmark attract the Scandinavian tourists. The coast in Northern Sweden also attracts vacationers from Northern Norway and Northern Finland. In contrast, the capital cities attract visitors all year round, but business travellers dominate this group. At a more disaggregated scale, the most popular counties in Norway and Sweden for Scandinavian tourists, ranked according to guest nights, are Oppland, Buskerud, Stockholm, Gothenburg/Bohuslän, Oslo, Kopparberg, Norrbotten and Västerbotten. Helsinki/Nyland and Åland are the most popular Finnish tourist destinations for Scandinavians.

The really 'international' tourism (understood here as constituting non-Scandinavians) is orientated towards sights and scenery, and it is strongly city-orientated. Business travellers also constitute a major component of this wider international tourism. For vacationers, the capital cities are often the gateways for many foreigners arriving in a country, and these cities usually also have many attractions, related to their histories and cultures. International tourists attracted by the natural environment tend to have different activity patterns and locational preferences than do Scandinavian home market tourists. The scenic fjords in western Norway and the areas at Nordkalotten (north of the Arctic Circle) are most attractive for them. The most popular counties for non-Scandinavians in Norway and Sweden are Stockholm, Oslo, Bergen/Hordaland, Sogn and Fjordane, Gothenburg/Bohuslän, Oppland, Nordland and Malmö/Skåne. Helsinki and Lappland are the most popular counties in Finland.

There are several limitations to tourism in Scandinavia. Among the most important are high prices and costs, as well as long distances to major markets. Wages and salaries are also high, which is particularly important in an industry characterised by personal service.

14.2.2 Guest nights in Scandinavian hotels

None of the Scandinavian countries collects data concerning the total number of foreign visitors at its borders. Furthermore, data are not available for some of the countries (e.g. Finland and Norway) on the total number of nights spent by foreigners in all types of accommodation. Consequently, the best estimate of tourist flows to and between the countries is the statistics provided by hotels and similar establishments. The data for foreigners in all types of accommodation in Denmark and Sweden shows totals of foreign bed-nights, which are around twice those for hotels only. The picture is probably much the same in the other countries, but varies somewhat depending on citizenship of the international tourist. Accommodation in camping sites, cottages, mobile homes and other simple provisions is more common in Scandinavia than it is in most other European countries.

Table 14.1 shows the number of guest nights in hotels in the various Scandinavian countries by nationality in 1994, with some comparisons to earlier years. The table shows that the home markets in the neighbouring countries are important for all five Scandinavian countries. The total number of guest nights in 1994 in Sweden was almost 22 million, while it was 14.6 million in Norway and almost 12 million in Denmark. Denmark has a pattern of international tourists that distinguishes it from the other Scandinavian countries. Denmark is, of course, located between the Scandinavian peninsula with Norway and Sweden, and continental Europe. Compared to Finland, Norway and Sweden, therefore, in Denmark the residents' share of guest nights is only 50 per cent, while it is 81 per cent in Sweden, 72 per cent in Finland, and 65 per cent in Norway. One reason for this is that Denmark is a small country in terms of area, and it is possible for Danes to see or visit most of Denmark without many overnight stays. Copenhagen is a geographical and cultural gateway both to Scandinavia and to continental Europe. Norwegians and Swedes often pass through Copenhagen on their way to continental Europe, and non-Scandinavian tourists often do the same on their way to Norway and Sweden.

Given the strength of the German economy, and the accessibility of Germany to Scandinavia, especially to Denmark, Germans account for the largest numbers of guest nights in hotels in each of the Scandinavian countries. Additionally, German visitors dominate the summer tourism picture on the roads with their mobile homes or caravans. Within Scandinavia, Norway had more French, Dutch, British, US and Japanese visitors in 1994 than any of the other Scandinavian countries.

Over time, there have been some changes in the geographical origins of the tourists. Figure 14.2 shows the changes in Norway and Sweden between 1982 and 1994; before 1991 the figures for Germany related only to the Federal Republic of Germany. The main countries of origin of tourists staying in hotels in Norway are Germany, Denmark, Sweden, USA and UK. The numbers of tourists from France and The Netherlands have, however, been increasing rapidly.

Different regions within Norway have different appeal in terms of particular tourism products: in 'Arctic Norway', Nordland and Finmark are the most popular counties; in 'Mountain-Norway', Buskerud and Oppland are most popular; in 'Fjord-Norway', the main focus is Sogn and Fjordane and Hordaland; and in 'Culture Norway' it is the cities Oslo, Bergen and Trondheim. There are also differences in terms of international markets. In Northern Norway, Germans—tending to use mobile homes to visit the North Cape and the Lofoten Islands—are the largest group, while the Danes par-

Table 14.1   Guest nights in hotels in the Scandinavian countries, 1982–94

	Denmark	Finland	Iceland	Norway	Sweden
Total guest nights					
1994	11,970	11,292	745	14,685	21,974
1988	9,033	9,908	663	11,853	20,981
1982	8,362	7,604	NA	7,159	16,205
Nationality					
Denmark	6,038	76	39	829	510
Finland	84	8099	11	89	289
Iceland			229		
Norway	829	129	43	9,643	513
Sweden	1,356	565	56	680	17,799
Scandinavia total					
1994	8,307	8,868	378	11,241	19,111
1988	6,500	8,366	414	9,821	18,578
1982	5,431	6,436	NA	5,528	14,144
France	85	106	30	283	110
Germany	1,666	591	137	1,160	872
Italy	139	84		128	120
The Netherlands	204	86	17	233	137
UK	367	175	48	381	290
Other Europe	378	709	68	326	366
USA	306	175	35	398	331
Japan	103	93		158	105
Rest of the world	416	405	27	378	531
Non-Scandinavians					
1994	3,664	2,424	367	3,445	2,862
1988	2,533	1,542	249	2,032	2,403
1982	2,931	1,168	NA	1,631	2,061

Source: Yearbook of Nordic Statistics.

Note: Comparisons between the countries should be made with caution on account of differences in degree of coverage of statistics. Denmark excludes hotels with less than 40 beds, night lodgings and youth hostels; Finland excludes accommodation with less than 10 rooms or cottages; Iceland excludes youth hostels; Norway excludes hotels with less than 20 beds and youth hostels; and Sweden includes all of these. In 1982 Iceland is included in non-Scandinavian figures.

ticipating in winter sports constitute the largest group in 'Mountain-Norway', and the Americans are primarily fjord tourists.

Most vacations spent in the mountain counties of Oppland, Buskerud and Telemark are weekend trips, and short holidays in the winter. The tourists are mostly from Oslo, but short holidays/breaks and weekend trips from Denmark and Sweden also have noticeable effects on visitor statistics, especially in winter. Northern Norway, which is distant from the central population areas, has a very different visitor structure. Long-distance summer tourists from Germany, France, Italy and The Netherlands are the most important visitors to Northern Norway. The main cities are attractive the whole year round, with business travellers being the dominant market segment. Visitor patterns in Norway are very seasonal and heavily constrained by climatic factors. An

Guest nights in hotels in Norway

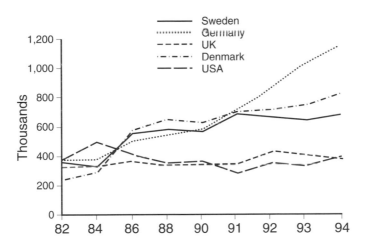

Guest nights in hotels in Sweden

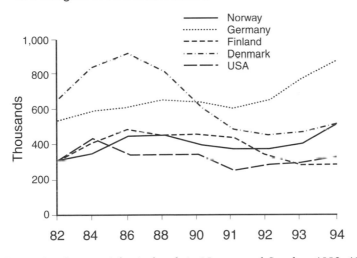

Fig. 14.2 International guest nights in hotels in Norway and Sweden, 1982–1994

important economic consequence is significant seasonal variations in the capacity utilisation of hotels.

Most foreign tourists come to Norway as individual travellers in their own vehicles, and in this sense the country's modern tourism industry has been underpinned by the expansion of car ownership as part of the Fordist boom in mass consumption in the post-war period. Most 'Arctic tourists' on their way to North Cape drive through Sweden and Finland, at least in one direction. These countries, in general, have better road infrastructures than Norway. 'Fjord tourists' often come by cruise ships. Neither of these groups has any major direct economic impact on the Norwegian society, and many of them barely stay overnight in Norway.

As tourists from continental Europe tend to visit Norway by car or mobile homes, and spend nights on camping sites, the actual number of tourists from these countries may be greater than those from the USA and UK. During the years 1982–1994, the number of tourists from the USA and UK was virtually constant, with only temporary and minor variations. The number of US tourists peaked in the mid-1980s, while it was lowest in the beginning of the 1990s, a pattern that broadly reflects the changing economic situation in the USA. The number of tourists from Sweden, Denmark and Germany has been growing constantly, with the largest growth being in the German market. In 1994 German tourists spent three times as many guest nights in hotels as in 1982.

The main countries of origin of tourists spending nights in hotels in Sweden are Germany, Norway, Denmark, the USA and Finland. Sweden also has a large number of business travellers drawn from global markets. In the 1980s the number of Norwegians visiting Sweden peaked, and there were more than 900,000 Norwegian guest nights in hotels in 1986. In the 1990s, there was, on average, only one half this number. A similar pattern is found amongst visitors from Finland. These patterns may relate to changes in the relative price competitiveness of Sweden, Finland and Norway. The numbers of German and Danish tourists have increased, but less so than in Norway. The number of US visitors has remained constant, and follows the patterns of American visitors to Norway.

14.3   The tourism industry

The tourism industry produces a range of services, such as transport and restaurants for tourists, but neither all travellers nor all restaurant guests are tourists and consequently the tourism industry must be regarded as a subset of several industries.

How is the tourism industry to be defined? The World Tourism Organisation (WTO) defines a visitor as, 'any person travelling to a place other than that of his or her usual environment for less than twelve months and whose main purpose for the trip is other than the exercise of an activity remunerated from the place visited'. This definition of a visitor, and implicitly a tourist, makes it relatively easy to define the tourism industry as a demand concept, that is, as the industry that caters to the demands of tourists. A definition in terms of supply, that is as the industry that supplies certain types of services, will be more problematic since these services—in varying degrees—are also consumed by customers other than tourists, as defined by WTO.

This section considers tourism from the perspective of supply as well as of demand. First, the branches of activity that supply services will be considered, and their importance in the national economy will be assessed. Statistics are available for Sweden and these will be used as examples. Secondly, specific customer categories and the patterns of demand emanating from these customers will be considered.

14.3.1   *The tourism industry—a supply side perspective*

In Sweden, there are five main industries that supply services to tourists: the transport industry, which accounts for an estimated 45 per cent of total value added (air transport, 20 per cent; travel agencies, 8 per cent; taxis, 4 per cent; sea transport, 2 per cent; local transport, 1 per cent; and railways, 1 per cent); the hotel and restaurant industry for 28 per cent; retail trade services for 13 per cent (services only, excluding goods); repair services for 8 per cent; and recreation and culture services for 6 per cent.

All these industries supply services not only to tourists, but also to other customers, and are thus to a larger or lesser degree dependent on tourism. Thus, for each industry involved, the concept of 'tourism share' will be used to describe the percentage of total output that is consumed by tourists, defined as visitors by WTO. In Sweden, the tourism share was estimated (in 1993) to range from 56 per cent for hotels and restaurants, to 35 per cent for transport services, 14 per cent for recreational, cultural and sporting services and only 4 per cent for retail services.

The tourism industry produces 2.7 per cent of GDP in Sweden if the use of private houses and the private car are excluded (in line with WTO definitions). These two items, that is the car and the country house, probably account for a major share of the demand for domestic leisure tourism and, if these two items are included, the tourism share of the Swedish GDP would be between 3 per cent and 4 per cent.

During the 1990s major changes have taken place within the structure of hotels and restaurants. According to the *Yearbook of Nordic Statistics*, in 1994 there were 1,133 hotels in Finland (918 in 1987), 1,195 in Norway (1,118 in 1987) and 2,490 in Sweden (2,300 in 1987). The average numbers of beds per hotel were 103 (86 in 1987), 108 (93 in 1987) and 95 (92 in 1987) in Finland, Norway and Sweden respectively, indicating an increase in scale over time. The characteristic company structure of predominantly small and medium-sized units has made it difficult to secure economies of scale. In consequence, there have been attempts to establish voluntary chains of cooperating firms in many sectors. During the 1990s international hotel chains have entered the Scandinavian market; for example, Choice Hotels Scandinavia, which bought Inter-Nor hotels, has obtained control of more than 100 hotels in Norway. There are expectations that, within a few years, the Norwegian hotel market will be dominated by four main actors: Choice, Rica, Radisson SAS, and a fourth actor consisting of Best Western and various smaller chains. While there was a tendency in the 1980s for Swedish hotel chains to gain market share in Norway, Norwegian chains and ownership are gaining influence in the Swedish hotel market in the 1990s.

After the merger of the two main service and interest organisations for the hotel and restaurant industry in Norway, there is now in Norway—as in Sweden—one main service and interest organisation for the industry. In 1994 there were 58,000 employees in hotels and restaurants in Finland, 62,000 employees in Norway, and 89,000 employees in Swedish hotels and restaurants. The relative numbers of female employees were, respectively, 72 per cent, 66 per cent and 56 per cent in Finland, Norway and Sweden (*Yearbook of Nordic Statistics* 1994).

14.3.2 *The tourism industry—the demand side*

The demand for tourism services in Finland, Norway and Sweden can be analysed in terms of three categories: the domestic leisure tourist, who represents 50 per cent of total demand; the domestic business traveller (25 per cent) and the foreign tourist (25 per cent). There is considerable variation amongst these categories in respect of consumption patterns:

- According to statistics in Sweden, the domestic leisure tourist spends 45 per cent on shopping, including fuel (16 per cent) and food. Transport (apart from own vehicles) accounts for 27 per cent, restaurants 10 per cent, recreation/culture 5 per cent, and hotels only 3 per cent. Repair services for private cars or leisure boats account for most of the remaining 10 per cent.
- The domestic business tourist spends 47 per cent on transport (38 per cent on air travel), 21 per cent on hotels, 11 per cent on restaurants and only 1 per cent on recreation/culture. Shopping accounts for 15 per cent (10 per cent on fuel) and repair services for the remaining 5 per cent.
- Foreign visitors spend 40 per cent on shopping (7 per cent on fuel), 23 per cent on restaurants and 24 per cent on transport (10 per cent on domestic air travel). Hotels account for 6 per cent of the total spending, recreation/culture for 5 per cent, and repair services for 2 per cent.

The three profiles are fairly clear and characteristic. Shopping (retail trade) for goods (including fuel) dominates for domestic leisure as well as foreign tourists, and shopping needs to be recognised as a major tourist activity. Compared to recreation/culture, which accounts for less than 5 per cent of total spending, shopping seems to be a much more attractive activity for most tourists. This raises the question of whether those responsible for its marketing have a somewhat distorted image of the average tourist. Destination marketing is very often based on attractions related to cultural heritage and recreation activities, whereas figures from the Swedish tourism industry seem to indicate that tourists spend most of their money (and possibly also time) in shopping areas.

Business tourists have significantly different consumption patterns and are by far the most important tourist category for domestic air travel and for hotels, a fact that these two industries are clearly aware of.

Taking all three categories together, shopping (including fuel) accounts for 28 per cent, transport services for 38 per cent (air travel 20 per cent), restaurants 15 per cent, hotels 9 per cent, repair services 6 per cent and recreation/culture services for 4 per cent of expenditure.

14.4   Tourism and national economic development

Tourism is in many ways an ideal instrument for regional planning. Sparsely populated areas are often attractive as tourist destinations and at the same time require economic activities in order to stabilise and preserve communities. Tourism often offers opportunities to create such economic activity in environments where other types of business fail. Furthermore, economic activity related to tourism is in many ways more productive and creates more employment than other sectors of the economy.

Table 14.2 shows the economic characteristics of the tourism industries in Sweden. The characteristics of the tourism industry differ considerably from agriculture and manufacturing, which have been chosen for comparison since these two industries represent what may be considered 'traditional' economic activities. Tourism services contain a larger portion of value added (51 per cent) than either agriculture (42 per cent) or manufacturing (36 per cent). Furthermore, if the potential for employment generation is considered by investigating the employees/gross turnover ratio—a

Table 14.2 Economic characteristics of four sectors of the tourism industry in Sweden, 1993

	Gross output (GTO) (MSEK)	Share of tourism output (%)	Tourism share of total (%)	Number of employees (EMP)	Value added (VA) MSEK	'Created value' (VA/GTO) (%)	'Labour intensity' (EMP/GTO)	'Labour productivity' (VA/EMP)
Transport services	28,000	45	35	22,500	11,800	42	0.8	0.52
Hotels and restaurants	17,500	28	56	40,700	9,500	54	2.3	0.23
Culture and sport	3,000	5	14	7,100	2,000	67	2.4	0.28
Retail trade	7,200	12	4	19,300	4,900	68	2.7	0.25
Total for the four sectors (equivalent to 90% of 'Tourism')	55,700	90		89,600	28,200	51	1.6	0.31
Agriculture	29,500			115,000	12,500	42	1.2	0.35
Metal manufacturing	308,000			340,000	111,000	36	1.1	0.33

Sources: (Nordström 1995; SCB 1995).

Note: Metal manufacturing includes fabricated metal products, and retail trade includes retail services (not goods sold).
MSEK = million Swedish crowns.

measure of labour intensity—the tourism industry is again superior. It generates 1.6 jobs per one million Swedish crowns in turnover, which is considerably higher than the comparable ratios for agriculture (1.2) and manufacturing (1.1).

A high degree of labour-intensity may be a positive characteristic from a political viewpoint, but may also have a negative economic effect if the cost of labour becomes too high. As the last column in Table 14.2 shows, the productivity of the tourism sector is in fact lower than in the two traditional sectors, but the difference is relatively small and the political advantages of the high labour-intensity in the tourism industry may well outweigh the economic disadvantages. These are, of course, aggregate figures, and they conceal other important sectoral differences, such as comparatively low average salaries and skill standards in the tourism industry.

A comparison among the four tourism industries shows a significant difference between, on one hand, the transport industry and, on the other hand, the hotel and restaurant, retail, and recreation and culture industries. The statistics for the latter three industries reiterate all the points raised above regarding value creation, labour-intensity and labour productivity in the tourism industry, whereas the transport industry is far more capital-intensive. Consequently, the transport industry creates less employment, but has also a much higher labour productivity than all the other industries investigated.

14.4.1   *The tourism industry and external stimuli: three case studies*

The comparative strengths as well as the growth potential of the tourism industry have attracted the attention of politicians and policy makers. There is a belief that the tourism industry is able to contribute significantly to economic development, not only in less industrialised countries but also in those nations experiencing a 'post-industrial' crisis. One reason for this is the comparative labour-intensity of the tourism sector and its ability to absorb skilled as well as unskilled unemployment. Another reason is the potential to decentralise tourism activity to those regions where the need for economic development is greatest.

Interest in the tourism industry as an instrument of economic policy inevitably raises questions about what can be done to stimulate tourism, and this in turn leads to consideration of how tourism may also be affected by exogenous events. In this section we examine three case studies describing different events that can affect tourism. Two of these are expected to have positive effects on tourism and one to have negative effects. Since they occurred some years ago, sufficient time has passed to allow their impacts to be traceable in the tourism statistics. The first case study concerns price sensitivity, which is studied in terms of the effects of the depreciation of the Swedish currency by 16 per cent in 1992. Second, the effects of the Chernobyl disaster and the Gulf War on tourism in Sweden are reviewed. Third, we examine the effects of mega sporting events such as the Olympic Winter Games in Norway and the Athletics World Championships in Sweden.

14.4.2   *The 1992 depreciation of the Swedish currency*

During a dramatic week in the autumn 1992, the Bank of Sweden—as a desperate macro-economic move—set interest rates at 1000 per cent per annum during the last

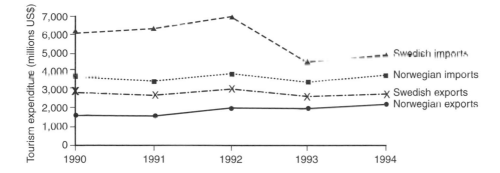

Fig. 14.3 Tourism expenditures and receipts in Norway and Sweden, 1990–1994 (US$ millions)

Source: WTO (1996)

days before they lost the battle with currency speculators, and the Swedish exchange rate dropped 16 per cent. One effect of this was a considerable price reduction in Swedish tourism products for foreign tourists during 1993. Another effect was that going abroad became far more expensive for Swedes. Some of the resultant changes in tourism flows can be seen in Figure 14.3, where Sweden is compared to Norway, which had a strong and stable currency during this period. The effect on foreign tourism to Sweden 1993 seems to be very small and in fact, if anything, negative compared to the development of foreign tourism in Norway. In spite of the 16 per cent 'price cut' in Sweden, Norway seems to have won market shares from Sweden during 1992–1994.

The major effect of the depreciation of the Swedish currency seems to have been on Swedish tourism 'imports' (expenditure abroad). There was a significant drop in the number of Swedish tourists going abroad between 1992 and 1993 and tourism 'imports' seem to have been far more price-sensitive than tourism 'exports' (foreign expenditure in Sweden) in the Swedish case. One reason may be that foreign tourists in Sweden tend to have high levels of spending, while a large share of the market is business tourism, and consequently they may be less sensitive to prices. According to WTO statistics from 1996, Sweden had the world's highest average receipts per tourist arrival in 1994 ($4,182). Swedish tourists going abroad are probably more price-sensitive since this tourism is dominated by inexpensive charter tours to Mediterranean countries.

14.4.3 The effects of Chernobyl and the Gulf War on tourism

War and other disasters may be expected to reduce tourist arrivals since such events increase perceptions of insecurity and uncertainty, so that potential tourists are more likely to stay at home or visit places close to home which are perceived to be safer. In a study of foreign tourism in Sweden, Hultkrantz (1995) used statistics of foreign guest-nights in Swedish hotels, hostels and motels to study the effects of the Chernobyl accident in May 1986 and the Gulf War in January 1991 on international tourist arrivals in Sweden from the USA, Germany, Norway, Denmark and Finland.

The results indicate that there was a short-term negative 'Chernobyl effect' on Swedish tourism 1986 for visitors from the USA, Germany, Norway and Finland. There was also a longer term, four-year, negative effect, but only in the case of US visitors. The Gulf War had a negative effect on American tourism to Sweden but a positive effect on tourism to Sweden from neighbouring Nordic countries, which may indicate that, during periods of instability, there is a preference not to travel too far from home.

14.4.4   The impact of mega events on the tourism industry

The organisation of major sporting events has become attractive to cities and national governments, so that there is now intense competition to host the Olympic Games, World Championships and various football cups. One reason behind this upsurge in interest is that mega events are expected to generate considerable positive economic effects and boost tourism, not only during the event itself, but also before and after it. Norway and Sweden have been successful recently in bidding for major sports events. In 1994 Lillehammer in Norway hosted the Olympic Winter Games, and in 1995 Gothenburg in Sweden was home to the World Athletics Championships.

The effects of these events on guest nights are indicated by the statistics on hotel occupancy rates in Norway and Sweden (Figure 14.4a). A comparison between the Lillehammer region (Oppland and Hedemark) and Norway shows no improvement in Lillehammer during 1994, which is quite surprising. For Gothenburg, however, there seems to have been a significant improvement relative to Sweden as a whole during 1995, the year of the Championships.

Another argument often used in favour of mega events is that they can generate increases in state as well as local tax revenues. After the Gothenburg Championships, the Swedish Ministry of Sports and Social Affairs commissioned an investigation into these effects and a model was developed based on input–output tables to analyse the distribution of value added, for example through taxes (Andersson 1996). The model predicted around £10 million in extra tax income after opportunity costs/taxes had been taken into account.

In 1997, a comparison was made between taxes actually collected in Gothenburg, compared to Sweden as a whole, during July–August 1994, 1995 and 1996 (the Championships took place 4–14 August 1995). Figure 14.4b shows the comparatively higher amounts of taxes that were actually collected in Gothenburg during July–August 1995 compared to Sweden. The analysis shows that the taxes collected in Gothenburg for July–August 1995 (when the Championships took place), increased considerably more than in Sweden as a whole. There may of course be other explanations, but it seems likely that the mega event did have an impact on the amount of taxes collected, especially since much of this increase can be traced to the tourism industry. The actual increase in Gothenburg compared to that which could be expected compared to the average Swedish increase, amounts to £9.5 million, which is surprisingly close to the predictions made by the model developed for the Swedish Ministry for Sports and Social Affairs (Andersson 1996). However, it should be borne in mind that much of the increase in state tax collected in Gothenburg during August 1995 is merely a transfer of taxes (for example, VAT) from other regions in Sweden by domestic tourism, and only the taxes generated by foreign tourists have a real effect on national accounts.

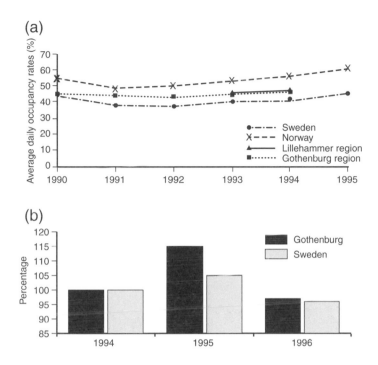

Fig. 14.4   (a) Average daily occupancy rates in Norway, Sweden, Lillehammer and Gothenburg in the 1990s; (b) Changes in local taxes in Gothenburg and Sweden, 1994–1996 (1994 = 100)

14.5   Tourism and local economic development

Tourist expenditure entering an economy not only stimulates it at that time, but has repeated impacts as this represents a multiplier effect. Considerable research has been done into the impact of tourism using multiplier techniques. Huse *et al.* (1998) used multiplier techniques to explore the economic and employment effects of tourism in small sparsely populated towns in Scandinavia by comparing tourism multipliers in nine small Norwegian municipalities. The objectives in using such techniques were to assess impact on sales, output and employment at regional and local levels.

The terminology in Huse *et al.* (1998) identified direct industry effects, direct spin-off effects, indirect effects and induced effects. Direct effects are of two kinds: the primary tourism industry effects and associated or spin-off effects. Direct effects are related to places where the tourists themselves spend their money. The primary tourism industry was defined as hotels, restaurants, campsites, activities and tourism operators, amongst others. Establishments that experienced spin-off effects include firms, institutions and individuals outside the primary tourism industry where the tourists themselves use their money, for example, gas stations, grocery stores and retail outlets. Indirect effects are also generated when tourists spend money locally. There will be several iterations of indirect effects in the local economy when suppliers, employees and the local community use their increased income. The outcome of these

Table 14.3   Coefficient and multiplier comparisons for nine small Norwegian towns

Municipality	Direct industry (%)	Direct spin-off (%)	Secondary (%)	Multiplier 1[a]	Multiplier 2[b]
Economic effects[cd]					
Grong	41	39	20	2.4 (2.7)	1.3 (1.4)
Brønnøy	25	38	37	4.0 (4.2)	1.6 (1.7)
Lenvik/Tranøy	27	49	24	3.7 (3.9)	1.3 (1.4)
Hammerfest	50	25	25	2.0 (2.1)	1.3 (1.4)
Kviteseid	51	16	33	2.0	1.5
Hol	65	9	26	1.5	1.4
Trysil	34	23	43	2.9	1.8
Risør	22	54	24	4.5	1.3
Vinje	59	27	14	1.7	1.2
Mean all	42	31	27	2.7	1.4
Mean Northern Norway	36	38	26	3.0 (3.2)	1.4 (1.5)
Employment effects[cd]					
Grong	65	19	16	1.5 (2.1)	1.2 (1.7)
Brønnøy	41	27	32	2.4 (2.6)	1.5 (1.6)
Lenvik/Tranøy	55	23	21	1.8 (2.3)	1.3 (1.7)
Hammerfest	65	18	17	1.5 (1.9)	1.2 (1.5)
Kviteseid	57	10	33	1.8	1.5
Trysil	45	14	41	2.2	1.7
Risør	42	50	18	2.4	1.2
Vinje	74	13	13	1.4	1.2
Mean all	55	22	24	1.9	1.4
Mean Northern Norway	56	22	22	1.8 (2.3)	1.3 (1.6)

[a] Multiplier 1 = total effect/direct industry effects.
[b] Multiplier 2 = total effect/all direct effects.
[c] Effects for the municipality (effects for the whole region of Northern Norway).
[d] All effects in the denominators are figures from the municipality.

iterations are the induced effects. Indirect and induced effects are sometimes called the secondary effects (Archer 1982). The study of Huse *et al.* (1998) focused on economic and employment effects.

14.5.1   Tourism in small towns—nine case studies from Norway

The nine municipalities studied by Huse *et al.* (1998) (Table 14.3) were Grong, Brønnøy, Lenvik/Tranøy and Hammerfest in Northern Norway, and Kviteseid, Hol, Trysil, Risør and Vinje in Southern Norway. Grong (2,500 inhabitants) is a municipality in a sparsely populated area, located in the interior north of Trondheim. The main industries are agriculture and forestry. There are no towns in the municipality. Because the main road from Oslo to Northern Norway (E6) runs through the municipality, it has a high level of in transit visitors. In addition, there are two attractions in the region that attract some tourists to stop over in Grong: Salmon fishing on the river Namsen and a down-hill ski facility. While the through-traffic runs all the year, the salmon fishing is concentrated in the period June–August and use of the alpine facilities is restricted to the winter season. Brønnøy (7,000 inhabitants) is located on the coast in Nordland county, and its main centre is Brønnøysund. The island, Torghatten, just off Brønnøysund is probably the area's principal tourist attraction. The mountain on the island has a large cave which runs through its centre, and not surprisingly there is a well-known legend connected to this phenomenon. The area also has an interesting history relating to the Vikings and the coastal culture. Tourism in this area is largely based on sightseeing rather than staying to experience the local lore.

Lenvik and Tranøy (12,500 inhabitants) are on Senja, which is Norway's second largest island. It is located in Troms county, and is connected to the mainland via a bridge at Finnsnes. In addition to Lenvik and Tranøy, Senja includes the very small municipalities of Torsken and Berg. In Senja, tourism is based on nature and cultural experiences and staying in traditional accommodation, for example in fishing shanties. Hammerfest (9,500 inhabitants) in Finnmark county is known for being the northern-most located town in the world. Many tourists visit Hammerfest on their way to the North Cape. Hammerfest has around 200,000 visitors every year, most of them during the summer. Grong and Hammerfest have different forms of overnight lodging accommodations compared to Brønnøy and Lenvik/Tranøy. In the two former cases the ratio between inhabitants and guest nights are 14.5 and 6.0 respectively, while for the latter the ratios are 2.4 and 1.3.

Kviteseid (3,000 inhabitants) is located in Telemark county in the inner part of Southern Norway. One of the main roads between Oslo and Bergen passes Kviteseid. The tourism industry is based partly on through-traffic, partly on moderate tourism traffic in the winter (cross-country skiing) and camping in the summer. Hol (4,600 inhabitants) is located in Buskerud in the upper part of one of the large valleys in Southern Norway. For several years it has been one of the most developed winter sports destinations in Norway. Hol, including Geilo, has well-developed alpine sports facilities, and a wide range of hotels, cottages and restaurants. Trysil (7,000 inhabitants) in Hedemark is a newly developed tourism area close to the Swedish border. Tourism is mainly related to winter sports, and recently heavy investments have been made in alpine sports facilities, private cabins and hotels. Risør (7,000 inhabitants) is a small picturesque town located at the south coast. The most important tourist season is the summer, with large numbers of visitors during this period. A major part of the tourism is based on self-provisioning in second homes. A boat festival is arranged in Risør every summer. Vinje (4,000 inhabitants) is located in the same county as Kviteseid, and the same main road between Oslo and Bergen passes through both municipalities. The well-established tourism industry is mainly based on through-traffic, winter sports and private cottages.

14.5.2   Coefficient and multiplier comparisons of the Norwegian case studies

The variables used in the study were: (a) direct industry effects (equivalent to direct primary tourist industry effects); (b) direct spin-off effects; and (c) secondary effects (indirect and induced effects). Together they cover all the tourism effects. Both sales multipliers and employment multipliers are calculated. These are defined according to Archer (1982) as:

$$\text{Sales}_{m1} = \text{Sales}_T/\text{Sales}_{DI}$$
$$\text{Sales}_{m2} = \text{Sales}_T/\text{Sales}_{(DI+DSp)}$$
$$\text{Empl}_{m1} = \text{Empl}_T/\text{Empl}_{DI}$$
$$\text{Empl}_{m2} = \text{Empl}_T/\text{Empl}_{(DI+DSp)}$$

where Sales = sales effects; Empl = employment effects; T = total effects or the sum of all direct and secondary effects; DI = direct primary tourism industry effects; and DSp = direct spin-off effects.

Table 14.3 shows the relative distribution of the total economic effects of tourism in terms of direct industry effects, direct spin-off effects, and secondary effects from all nine studies. Two sales multipliers (Sales$_{m1}$ and Sales$_{m2}$) and two employment multipliers (Empl$_{m1}$ and Empl$_{m2}$) are also reported. Sales$_{m1}$, presenting total sales on direct industry sales, is between 4.5 and 1.5: highest in Risør and Brønnøy, and lowest in Hol and Vinje. Sales$_{m2}$, presenting total sales on all direct sales, is between 1.8 in Trysil and 1.2 in Vinje. In Northern Norway the means of economic direct industry and direct spin-off effects are practically all at the same level, about 36–38 per cent of the total effects. Comparing the means from Northern Norway with the overall sample, the industry effects are 6 per cent less, and the direct spin-off effects are 7 per cent higher. The secondary effects are at the same level, slightly above 25 per cent of the total effects.

The figures from Hol differ from the statistics for the other municipalities. Hol is probably the most developed alpine resort in Norway, and the effects of tourism are largely related to hotels, restaurants and alpine activity facilities. However, the local infrastructure to support tourism is poor. There are few shops, for example, that can receive spin-off effects from the tourists. Consequently, direct industry effects are high and direct spin-off effects are small. Vinje and Kviteseid have similar characteristics, but to a lesser degree. The heavy investments mentioned earlier in Trysil account for the high percentage of secondary effects. Direct spin-off effects in Trysil are higher than in Hol. The large number of cabins and second-homes tourists is the most likely explanation for this difference. Self-provisioning is a primary characteristic of tourism in Risør, and as in Lenvik/Tranøy direct spin-off effects are high.

Sales$_{m2}$, the multiplier showing total sales on all direct sales reported in the studies, are on average far lower than the income multipliers found in studies of, for example, countries like Turkey, UK, Ireland, Egypt and Jamaica, and in US states and counties. They are, however, at the same level as the multipliers found in small UK towns and villages and in small island economies, indicating similarities in tourism impact structures between small towns in the UK and Scandinavia.

Employment effects are also compared in Table 14.3, although data were not available for Hol. The employment multipliers Empl$_{m1}$ and Empl$_{m2}$ are presented. Empl$_{m1}$ showing total effects on direct industry effects, varies from between 1.4 in Vinje and 2.4 in Brønnøy and Risør. Empl$_{m2}$, showing total effects on all direct effects, varies between 1.2 in Grong, Risør and Vinje and 1.5 in Brønnøy. The pattern in the total sample is close to that for the sample from Northern Norway. If Hol figures had been included, more variations would have been expected. Direct industry effects account for about 55 per cent of the total employment effects, whereas the comparable figure was around 40 per cent of the economic effects. The employment direct spin-off effects are considerably lower than the economic spin-off effects. Employment direct spin-off effects are at the same level as employment secondary effects. One deviation relates to direct spin-off effects in Risør. The deviation may be due to the small proportion of direct industry effects, especially those related to hotels.

These data also indicate the relative importance of economic leakages to the region; comparisons are only made for the municipalities in Northern Norway. While leakages to the region had fairly limited economic importance, such leakages were of greater importance when considering employment effects. The comparisons among the nine sparsely populated municipalities indicated that the various kinds of effects (direct industry effects, direct spin-off effects, and secondary effects) are contingent and vary in respect of: (a) the stage of development of the local tourism industry; (b) the size of the local economy; (c) the dominant types of tourism attractions; and (d) the tourism investments taking place in the economy.

It is difficult to give a holistic evaluation of the local or regional effects of tourism based on financial or employment data. An increase in tourism may, for example, have regional and local consequences with respect to local identity, pollution or preservation of the natural environment, or raising international consciousness. Increased tourism, especially in Norway, has resulted in the preservation of jobs in rural areas and in the districts. Tourism-related activities have been combined with traditional jobs in fisheries and farming, and have thus contributed to the preservation of local employment and settlement. Tourism has also contributed to the revitalisation of local identity (Gustavsen and Huse 1994).

14.6   Future trends and challenges

Scandinavia in the 1990s is rather unimportant as a destination area for international tourism. In terms of climate, Scandinavia is in the unfavourable periphery of Europe. European tourism is dominated by a one-way stream from the North to the South. It is very unlikely in the foreseeable future that tourism flows to Scandinavia from non-Scandinavian countries any time will equal the tourist flows from Scandinavia to the Mediterranean countries. The importance of Scandinavia for international tourism will, however, vary depending on a number global trends. Selstad (1993) has presented some interesting scenarios for the future importance of international tourism in Scandinavia, and these are presented below.

Selstad's (1993) three scenarios are based around trends, culture and environment. The continuation of the present trends scenario involves free flows of goods, services and tourists, while economic growth accompanied by an increase in international business and business travel is also expected. The culture emphasis scenario assumes that culture will shape tourism. In this scenario Europe becomes regionalised and 'home-orientated'. The competition in international business leads to reductions in costs and in the travelling expenses for companies. The third scenario emphasises the natural environment. Concern for the natural environment will limit tourism, whilst telecommunications largely substitute for business travel.

The tourism characteristics in the continuation of present trends scenario will be an increase in low quality, large-scale, mass tourism. This scenario will, however, also imply an increase in 'wanderlust' tourism, where tourists visit several destinations. There is a strong preference for the latter kind of tourism in the higher-income market segments, and also for travel by scheduled flights and cars rather than package tours. In this scenario there will also be an increase in the incentive tourism market. The general impact of tourism in this scenario will be a more unified culture across countries, and an increase in pollution. Scandinavia will continue to be an area of tourism origin, even though there will be an increase in winter sports, and growth of special interest elite tourism in Scandinavia. This scenario implies that Scandinavia will remain a relatively unimportant area for international tourism. The 'winning' tourism counties in Sweden and Norway under this scenario will be Stockholm and Malmö/Skåne in Sweden, and Oslo, Bergen/Hordaland, Sogn and Fjordane, Oppland and Nordland in Norway.

The culture emphasis scenario is based on assumptions that culture will shape tourism. Europe will become regionalised and home-orientated. International business competition leads to cost cutting and reduced budgets for business travel. There will be a shift from international charter and 'package' tourism to home-based, domestic tourism. There will, however, also be a growth in 'wanderlust' tourism under this scenario, and a large part of tourism will be town-orientated. The general impact of this scenario will be development of regional town cultures, and the regions will also strengthen their centres. The regions around the Mediterranean will probably lose out under this scenario, while Central Europe may gain somewhat. Scandinavia is in the periphery of Europe and will not be able to compete as a cultural area. Scandinavia, with the exception of the main cities and a limited number of historic cites, will find it difficult to make inroads into the market for international tourism. The 'winning' tourism counties or areas in Norway and Sweden under this scenario will be the main cities such as Stockholm, Oslo, Bergen, Gothenburg, Stavanger and Trondheim.

'Green' tourism or eco-tourism will characterise the third scenario. This scenario may result in a boom for Scandinavian tourism, even though this kind of tourism will be largely based on self-service recreation with little commercial activity. Tourists will come from continental Europe, whilst Scandinavian tourists will avoid long charter flights and instead spend their vacations in their own country. The 'winning' counties in this scenario will be Sogn and Fjordane, Oppland, Nordland, Møre and Romsdal, Finnmark and Buskerud in Norway, and Kopparberg, Värmland and Norrbotten in Sweden.

15 Central and Eastern Europe: tourism, development and transformation

Derek R. Hall

15.1 Introduction: tourism and the new Europe

This chapter discusses some of the major elements of tourism and economic development in Central and Eastern Europe (CEE), and their wider European significance. For current purposes CEE is defined as the former state socialist societies of Albania, Bosnia-Hercegovina, Bulgaria, Croatia, Czech Republic, the Former Yugoslav Republic of Macedonia (FYROM), Hungary, Poland, Romania, Serbia-Montenegro (the current self-styled 'Yugoslavia'), Slovakia, and Slovenia (Table 15.1; Figure 15.1). This definition cuts across the WTO regional classification which includes the former Soviet Union in 'Central/East Europe', but places the former Yugoslavia and Albania in 'Southern Europe'.

The countries under review, several of which are successor states of fragmented federations, are sandwiched between the supranational incrementalism of Western Europe and the instability of the long-term unravelling of the former Soviet Union. They are pursuing economic and political transition within a spatial and structural frame of globalisation superimposed upon local nationalisms, and with aspirations for supranational membership coupled to local and European identity crises. Within this context of diversity, change and uncertainty, the chapter suggests that the relationship between tourism and economic transition is particularly fragile. In trying to unravel a quantitative picture of the region, there are at least three methodological problem areas that exacerbate the general data problems discussed in Chapter 1:

- Uncertain and inconsistent relationships between the actual economic impacts of tourism and the selection, collection and representation of statistical data on receipts and expenditures. There are questions as to:
  (a) The consistency surrounding the definition of tourism receipts and how these are recorded.
  (b) The relationship between tourism receipts and volume of GDP, given the shrinkage of the latter with economic restructuring.
  (c) The relationship between exchange rates and prices, for with consumer prices growing far more rapidly than the prices of foreign currencies, the share of

Tourism and Economic Development: European Experiences, 3rd Edition. Edited by A.M. Williams and G. Shaw.
© 1998 John Wiley & Sons Ltd.

Table 15.1   CEE and selected other European countries: comparative
national data, 1995

	Population (millions)	Area (km^2)	GDP per capita (US $)	GDP real growth (%)
Albania	*3.40*	*27.4*	*600*	*6.0*
Armenia	3.76	30.0	700	5.0
Austria	8.04	83.9	28,980	1.8
Azerbaijan	7.80	86.6	54[1]	−6.5
Belarus	10.30	208.0	900	−10.0
Belgium	10.10	30.5	26,280	1.9
Bosnia-Hercegovina	*3.50*	*51.1*	*524*	–
Bulgaria	*8.91*	*111.0*	*1,400*	*2.8*
Croatia	*4.50*	*56.5*	*3,300*	*4.0*
Czech Republic	*10.30*	*78.9*	*4,300*	*4.8*
Estonia	1.63	45.1	2,340[2]	5.0[2]
France	58.30	544.0	26,200	2.2
FYROM	*1.90*	*25.7*	*700*	*−4.0*
Georgia	4.40	70.0	200	−5.0
Germany	81.80	357.0	25,100[1]	1.9
Greece	10.65	132.0	9,300[1]	1.5
Hungary	*10.23*	*93.0*	*3,882*	*1.5*
Italy	57.31	301.3	17,800[1]	3.4
Latvia	2.53	64.6	1,176[1]	0.4
Lithuania	3.72	65.2	1,078[2]	2.5
Moldova	4.40	34.0	390	−3.0
Poland	*38.60*	*312.7*	*3,050*	*6.5*
Romania	*23.20*	*237.5*	*1,250[2]*	*5.0[2]*
Serbia-Montenegro	*10.00*	*102.1*	*1,550*	*6.0*
Slovakia	*5.40*	*49.0*	*3,244*	*6.4*
Slovenia	*1.99*	*20.2*	*9,100*	*4.8*
Spain	39.20	504.8	12,335[1]	2.9
Turkey	62.30	775.5	2,733	7.1
Ukraine	51.44	603.0	600	−11.8
UK	58.40	244.1	16,304	2.4

Source: Campbell (1997, page v).

Countries defined in this chapter as CEE are *in italics*.
[1] 1994.
[2] Estimate.

international tourism in the region's economies, particularly in the earlier transition phase, has been undervalued.

(d) The relationship between tourism receipts and exports, the latter relating to differences in the industrial structures of the economies and size of domestic markets.

(e) The limited and inconsistent nature of data on tourist expenditures (Baláž 1996a).

• Statistical under-enumeration or even exclusion of self-employed tourism workers and micro-businesses particularly undervalues rural tourism where they are most characteristic.

Fig. 15.1 The countries of CEE, 1995

- Substantial retrospective revision of statistical data by newly independent state authorities, following the fragmentation of former federal states.
- Aggregate international visitor figures' often blurring the distinction between several forms of cross-border movement: (overnight) tourism; excursionism; transiting; petty trading; labour migration; and refugee flight. Substantial cross-border shopping and petty trading activity is carried on as a result of differences in national or local laws, taxes, prices and goods availability, as well as in national attitudes and customs. Of international visitors to Bulgaria in 1995, for example, only 5 per cent of Romanians, 2 per cent of Turks and 32 per cent of CIS visitors were actual tourists, compared to 76 per cent of British, 89 per cent of Germans and 93 per cent of Norwegian visitors (Bachvarov 1997).
- Despite its growing contribution to economic development and recognition by most governments as a priority area, tourism continues to receive scant attention in texts concerned with post-socialist economic and political development. For example, no reference is made to tourism in several works on the Balkans taking a

geographical, economic or international relations perspective (for example, Cviic 1995; Carter and Norris 1996; Jeffries 1996), in Grzegorz Węcławowicz's (1996) social and economic geography of Poland, even though Polish international tourism receipts represented 29.7 per cent of exports in 1994 (Baláž 1996a, p. 9), or in a recent key text on construction of the post-Soviet nations (Bremmer and Taras 1997).

Despite these reservations, an increasing number of analyses of tourism development in the region have been appearing in the accessible English-language literature, albeit with varying emphases and of variable quality. These have included: Harrison (1993) and Bachvarov (1997) on tourism development issues and Koulov (1996) on the tourism development/environment interface in Bulgaria; Johnson (1995) on Czech and Slovak, and Baláž (1994, 1995, 1996b) on Slovakian tourism development; Light and Andone's (1996) geography of tourism development in Romania; Fletcher and Cooper (1996) on developing a tourism strategy in rural Hungary; Kurek's (1996) and Ploaie's (1996) case studies of potential conflicts in rural tourism; Airey (1994) on Poland; Burns (1995) on Romania and Richards (1996) on education and training for tourism; and Karpowicz (1993) on the challenges for ecotourism in the region. Of regional economic appraisals relating to tourism, Baláž (1996a) raises some interesting and important methodological questions in relation to the interpretation of tourism economic impacts on the Visegrád states of Central Europe. Recent appraisals of tourism development in the former Soviet Union include Aun (1966), Jaakson (1996) and Unwin (1996), all on tourism development in Estonia, and Mazaraki and Voronova's (1993) descriptive piece on tourism prospects in Ukraine.

Although international tourism was significant in the region long before 1989 (Hall, 1991b), a symbiotic relationship has developed in the 1990s between tourism development in CEE and processes of economic, political and social restructuring, embracing price liberalisation, encouragement of entrepreneurial activity, programmes of large- and small-scale privatisation, deregulation, divestment, changing circumstances for personal mobility, enhanced and reorientated foreign trade and investment, and varying degrees of currency convertibility. Tourism, therefore, contributes not only to urban and regional economic development in the region, but also to wider processes of economic and political transformation.

15.2   The tourism product in CEE

A substantial range of mass and niche tourism resources reflects CEE's diverse natural and cultural environments (Hall 1990a,c). Inward investment, not least in training programmes, has assisted necessary improvements in customer services and infrastructure (Hall 1992a,b,c). This has enabled realistic market segmentation and product enhancement to be pursued through: (a) the targeting of high-spending groups attracted by activities with minimal adverse social and environmental impacts, and (b) the provision of season-extending activities. Both of these have emphasised the importance of attracting price-inelastic and non-seasonal conference/business tourism. The rise of cultural tourism and heritage has coincided with a heightened awareness of nationality and reinvigoration of a sense of historical perspective in the region. The growing importance of 'nature' and rural tourism has coincided with a period of renewed rural to urban migration, and has important local and regional demographic, economic, cultural and landscape significance. In addition, the restructuring of heavy industry and easier access to border areas have provided opportunities for both environmental improvements and new forms of commodification.

15.2.1 *Coastal tourism and mass markets*

'Postmodern' niche marketing, flexibility and sustainability have not been notable characteristics of CEE coastal tourism. Adriatic and Black Sea coast sun–sand–surf mass tourism was stimulated by the construction of the Adriatic Highway and improved access to Dalmatian islands (e.g. Sredl 1996) in the 1960s, and by regional mass tourism along the Romanian and Bulgarian coasts from the late 1950s. The Polish Baltic littoral, with its short summer season, has tended to cater for domestic needs, although in recent years the Germanic heritage of such cities as Gdánsk/Danzig and the neighbouring Russian enclave of Kaliningrad/Königsberg, has attracted substantial German tourism and inward investment interest.

With Roman and Venetian roots, tourism along the Adriatic coast emerged in the late nineteenth century as a fashionable pastime for well-positioned Austro-Hungarians. The construction of hotels in favoured watering holes such as Opatija (1884), Crkvenica (1894) and Dubrovnik (1896), encouraged development along the Istrian peninsula and later in southern Dalmatia (Rhodes 1955). Latterly, historic Dalmatian coastal cities provided stopping-off points for Italian and Greek cruise liners, with Dubrovnik functioning as a 'model tourist-historic cruise port' (Ashworth and Tunbridge 1990, p. 165), a role which is slowly being re-established in the wake of the Yugoslav wars of succession. With its sheltered bays, harbours and purpose-built moorings, the Adriatic coast is also admirably suited to sailing tourism. In 1990 there were 35 marinas with 9,500 mooring berths and a further 3,500 moorings for wintering purposes (Franzoni 1990). However, this form of tourism is a significant source of marine pollution, which—while also emanating from domestic, agricultural and industrial sources—continues to pose challenges to waterfront and offshore tourism development (Carter and Turnock 1992, Hoyle 1996).

15.2.2 *Urban and heritage tourism*

As metropolitan areas became major European tourism magnets, CEE—with its diverse urban cultures and architecture—needed to reposition itself in order to respond to opportunities. In the face of reduced state intervention and manufacturing decline, many urban and regional economic strategies embraced tourism as an instrument for regeneration (Law 1992, 1994; Shachar 1995; van den Berg *et al.* 1995). Infrastructural investments and the promotion of 'sense of place' through major events and festivals could be bolted onto regional fabric, thereby encouraging a national expression of culture: Poland's 'Warsaw Autumn' contemporary music festival and Chopin piano competition, the Czech Republic's Prague Spring music festival, and the more recent Budafest (sic) summer opera and ballet festival being some of the better-known examples. Dance groups, choirs and folklore ensembles have been maintained by all the countries under review, and in many individual regions (for example, Albturist, nd).

Any cultural interpretation of such events needs to be informed by the view that 'staged authenticity' was an essential element of the ideological apparatus of the state socialist system *per se*, and not only in the realm of tourism.

'Heritage' is clearly not a value-free concept: economic power and politics influence what is preserved and its interpretation (Chance 1994; Lowenthal 1997). Promotion of heritage and recognition of the importance of cultural history was a feature of the communist period in all CEE countries, as exemplified in open-air village museums at Bucharest (Focşa 1970), Szentendre in the Hungarian Danube Bend (Balázs 1984; Kecskés 1987), Prerov nad Labem in Bohemia, and in some 30 locations in Poland (Brykowski, nd). From Albania's 'museum cities' (Riza 1978; Strazimiri 1987; Hall 1994) to large-scale refurbishment of central Kraków (Dawson 1991), such heritage promotion was not primarily for international tourism purposes, but rather to inculcate a sense of identity and achievement amongst each country's citizens: this is symbolised in the priority given to faithful reconstruction of Warsaw's Old Town after World War II.

Many notable religious buildings, such as early Croatian churches on Adriatic islands, and the painted Moldavian Orthodox churches and monasteries of Romania, act as important complements to other tourist attractions. Places of pilgrimage, such as the Roman Catholic shrine to the Black Madonna at Częstochowa in southern Poland (Bajerlajn, nd; Micuła, nd) and the Croatian village of Medjugorje, site of the now somewhat discredited recurrent apparition of the Virgin (Vukonić 1992, 1996), have particular appeal.

While the rapid increase in visitors in Central Europe has placed particular environmental pressures on many heritage sites (Stevenson 1997), the 1990s have seen the region's most advanced tourist economies recognising and responding to niche segmentation, although the lines between heritage and kitsch, and between niche market response and 'staged authenticity' are often thin. For example, Hungarian railways' MAV Nostalgia Ltd was established for operating (often steam) trains for heritage tourism purposes. The marketing leaflet for the 'Trip to the Gypsy village of Solt' (nd) states that:

> During the train ride, enjoy the lunch against the backdrop of line entertainment. The train will be stopped by gypsies. . . . You will join locals at a wedding. An honorary gypsy leader will be chosen from the travellers. He (sic) will help escort the new couple to their wedding bed, while the guests stay behind to enjoy traditional song and dance at the reception.

A notable recent cultural tourism initiative was Hungary's 1996 promotion, '1,100 years in the heart of Europe', which saw a 20 per cent increase in tourist arrivals in the first half of the year. Over 1,000 cultural and sporting events were planned for that year, set in the context of a three-year plan. This envisaged a doubling of hard currency revenues from $1.4 to $3 billion, attraction of $200–300 million investment, and creation of 200,000 new jobs. Developments focused on nature and health tourism, establishing Budapest as a Central European cultural centre, and Hungarian gastronomy and conference/incentive tourism (Roe 1996).

In the context of resurgent nationalism and (re-)creation of new states, the heritage industry has tended to be viewed as an instrument for reinforcing national or particular ethnic identities (King 1996). However, the negative synergy between nationalism and heritage, arising from cultural and economic contradictions, was forcefully illustrated during the wars of Yugoslav succession in relation to the fate of two previous symbols of the tourism industry of a multi-ethnic Yugoslav state: the Turkish bridge over the river Neretva at Mostar, and the medieval walled city of Dubrovnik.

Centuries of oriental domination (Said 1978) of much of the Balkans, and continuing Islamic culture and faith (Norris 1993) were embodied in the cultural and ethnic symbolism of the Mostar bridge. Although physically linking Croat and Muslim communities in the ethnic melting-pot that was Bosnia-Hercegovina, the bridge increasingly had come to symbolise, for some Christian Slavs, a perceived Islamic threat. Its destruction by Bosnian/Hercegovinian Croats graphically confirmed the end of the multi-ethnic dream. By contrast, the bombarding of Dubrovnik by Serbs and Montenegrins was aimed specifically at damaging Croatia's tourism economy (Oberreit 1996). Four-fifths of recorded Yugoslav tourism earnings had been generated previously in Croatia, mostly from the Dalmatian coast and islands: Dubrovnik, as a UNESCO World Heritage Site, alone claimed 3.5 million annual visitors in the late 1980s (Letcher 1989, p. 82). Serbs had long coveted an access corridor to the sea. That the elongated, southward thrusting Croatian territory had become a major source of tourism income generation since the 1960s, contributing to the relative economic development of the northern republics at the expense of land-locked Serbia, had only strengthened the latter's resentment. Dubrovnik, with its Venetian heritage (Beritić and Šuljak 1972), became viewed as anti-Orthodox and anti Serb.

The Western response to the plight of Dubrovnik appeared to place a higher priority on protecting the heritage value of Dubrovnik's *built* environment, rather than on stopping the *human* suffering wrought by the Yugoslav conflicts (Carter *et al.* 1995; Hall and Danta 1996). Moreover, since the ending of hostilities in the former Yugoslavia, there has been the emergence of 'morbid' tourism, whereby visitors follow trails through sites of destruction, as in Sarajevo, to gaze on the physical remnants of human suffering (O'Reilly 1996).

15.2.3   Rural and nature tourism

In a region significantly under-urbanised in 1989, post-socialist structural adjustment has embraced large-scale rural-to-urban population shifts. Under state socialism some rural areas were transformed by major inflows of capital and labour, such as winter sports centres in Slovenia, Bulgaria and Romania, and the holiday complexes along the Black Sea and Adriatic coasts. There is now the potential for leisure-related activities to dominate rural employment growth in CEE, with increasing opportunities for rural attractions to act as a basic resource for tourism organised and sustained through locally-owned small enterprises, and for farm-based tourism—as an element of agrarian pluriactivity—to be a vehicle for integrated rural development (for example, Unwin 1996) to raise incomes, stabilise populations, sustain cultures and redistribute economic roles within rural households.

Attractive landscapes or particular elements of the natural environment can provide important attractions in conjunction with other activities, such as the Plitvice lakes and waterfalls (a UNESCO World Heritage Site) and Slovenia's Postojna caves. In forest and wilderness areas, the attraction of isolation and solitude paradoxically appeals to many visitors. In addition, water bodies can play an important role in enhancing landscapes and in providing arenas for recreational activities. The popularity of Lake Balaton in Hungary and Bled in Slovenia is notable in this respect. The spectacular scenery of the Tatra mountains (Poland/Slovakia) also enhances winter sports resorts and draws summer visitors for walking and climbing.

Horse-riding for pleasure has a pedigree dating from Austro-Hungarian days. In Slovenia, a tourism industry has been built up around the Lipica stud farm, famous for supplying Lippizaner horses to the Spanish Riding School in Vienna since 1580. Horse-riding tours have been available in Hungary since the 1980s, and in Poland in the 1990s (Marciszewska and Wyznikiewicz-Nawracula 1996). Recently, the many footpaths and bridleways which exist across the region have been complemented by improved tourist information systems, and the local provision of bed-and-breakfast/ pension accommodation.

Furthermore, the recognition of 'green-' and 'eco-tourism' as tailor-made high-income generating niche products has shifted emphasis to supporting community-based developments to sustain local economies and culture, as in the work of the ARVI rural development agency in Slovakia (Evans 1996; although see Din 1996). However, even small numbers of tourists can have a disproportionate impact in rural areas, and a range of potential land-use, conservation and economic priority conflicts may ensue (Kurek 1996; Ploaie 1996). But while host communities' responses are variable (Boissevain 1996), the seasonality of tourist movement can be used to advantage if it complements other economic activities, such as aspects of farming or fishing (Neate 1987; Puijk 1996).

Tourism is able to generate employment in accommodation, food, local craft, other service, manufacturing and construction sectors, thereby encouraging population stabilisation or repopulation; more than 600 entries, for example, can be found in the Hungarian Tourist Board's village tourism accommodation guide (Provincia TMT 1996). Previous population losses, and the availability of abandoned buildings, may even be an attraction in providing traditional homes for small-scale tourism purposes, as has been attempted with assistance from WWF and VSO in southern Albania (Fisher *et al.* 1994; Farrow 1995). One consequence of such inward investment can be a marked improvement in local housing quality, along with increased employment opportunities in construction and home maintenance.

Rural and nature tourism have thus received substantial promotion in recent years, with professional marketing being undertaken by local and central government, non-government organisations and the private sector; examples include extolling Budapest's natural heritage (Bognár, 1996), Estonia's protected areas (Ruukel 1996), and even Serbia's 'landscape painted from the heart' (Popesku and Milojević, 1996), the latter with the assistance of Saatchi & Saatchi. Like Spain, Slovenia explicitly reconfigured its tourism emphasis by replacing its 'Sunny Side of the Alps' slogan in 1996 with 'The Green Piece of Europe': its rural–cultural emphasis is encapsulated in promotions for 'wine journeys' (Fujs and Krašovec 1996). Croatia, while still highly dependent on the role of a long coastline, is looking to its interior to promote nature- and culture-based tourism (Stepanic Fabijanic and Klaric 1993). Poland has increasingly moved towards promoting itself as a 'natural' destination, with more niche-orientated tourism literature (Gajewski 1994; Gordon and Wolfram 1995; Witak and Lewandowska 1996). In 1995 the Romanian Ministry of Tourism identified rural tourism as a major growth area (Light and Andone 1996).

However, although Poland/Hungary Assistance for Reconstructing Economies (EU PHARE)- and Trans-European Mobility Programme for University Studies (TEMPUS)-supported schemes for education and training in rural tourism have been developed in the Czech Republic, Hungary, Poland (McMahon 1996) and

Slovakia, there is limited evidence from the region, to date, to indicate the long-term viability of rural tourism small and/or medium-sized enterprises, and their local social impact and multiplier effects: instead, investment and entrepreneurial activity has been concentrated in the larger urban areas.

15.2.4   Health-related tourism and winter tourism

The wider welfare implications of tourism development are only slowly emerging as coherent focal issues for researchers and practitioners (Hall and Brown, 1996). This is not the case for tourists *per se*, one of the roots of tourism having been the pursuit of physical and mental well-being. In Central Europe there is still a heritage of viewing tourism as a benign activity, access to whose health-imparting elements are a human right.

The presence of mineralised water in the region has long encouraged the development of spas to provide treatments for a wide range of ailments (Teleki *et al.* 1985), while curative muds along the Black Sea coast have long acted as a basis for resort development in Romania and Bulgaria. The region's spas thus have long histories: several achieved international fame and many attracted a rich and fashionable clientele, especially during the second half of the nineteenth century, often stimulated through royal patronage. Parks and gardens, concerts, theatrical performances and other recreational attractions were provided to enhance their popularity. Recent diversification of spa activities has taken place alongside upgrading and refurbishment: a number of Czech spas, for example, have diversified into activity and sports holidays, whilst thermal hotels in Budapest record year-round 90 per cent occupancy rates (Roe 1996).

German patronage has long been a sustaining element in the success of these spas, in part reflecting the generous support provided by the German health insurance system; for example, a middle-aged German could take a four-week cure every three years, enjoying full board for a modest price. German health reforms are reducing such support, thereby threatening the viability of some spas (Brierley 1997).

Winter upland tourism, both domestic and international, has been characteristic of a number of countries in the region: Poland, Slovakia, Slovenia, Bulgaria, Romania and, one should not forget, happier times saw Sarajevo host the Winter Olympics. Climatic and topographic conditions for winter sports vary considerably within the region: the best conditions for skiing are in the Romanian Carpathians and the Tatra mountains. Generally, however, facilities and the quality of winter sports have been poorer compared to those of Western Europe. In terms of international appeal, they have tended to attract those less advanced, often young, package groups taking advantage of relatively low costs. In recent years, the international appeal of the Balkan countries, with their relatively shorter season of lying snow, has lessened. The requirement of snow guarantees for winter sports holidays has forced some package companies to pull out of the region, due to a marginal availability of snow at certain times of the season. The region's elite, of course, travel to the more fashionable Alpine resorts of the West. In a market fragmenting into niches in pursuit of 'new sliding pleasures' such as snowboarding (Owen 1996), cross-country skiing appears to be a more appropriate, sustainable recreation form for the region, rather than the more capital intensive and potentially environmentally destructive downhill market.

15.2.5   Business/conference tourism

Business/conference tourism and incentive travel are of increasing importance (Davidson 1993; Shinew and Backman 1995). Unlike other forms of tourism, business tourism tends to be price inelastic and non-seasonal; it usually requires individual organisation involving relatively high costs, and shorter stays than holiday tourism. It also has wider potential long-term commercial benefits in terms of the sectoral development of the particular business activities involved.

Arguably, Hungary led CEE in recognising the higher income, season-extending potential of business and incentive tourism long before the fall of communism in the region. The Budapest convention centre was built in the early 1980s to accommodate over 2,000 delegates. It established Western-standard conference and exhibition facilities, including simultaneous translation in up to 16 languages, at a time when these were in short supply. A recent example of the importance of business tourism has been the development of hotels, a golf course and a retailing centre in what is claimed to be the region's first technology park, a £200 million 120 ha complex at Brno in the Czech Republic (Anon 1996). A significant growth of high-quality accommodation and facilities in cities across the region has complemented these developments, often reflecting a sign of confidence in post-communist and/or post-conflict recovery, as in the case of the Zagreb Sheraton (1995).

Promotion of city breaks, and construction of heritage parks and golf courses, have responded, at least in part, to the incentive travel market, complementing existing tourism employment by generating facilities for all-year leisure pursuits, targeted at high spenders. The resurgence of facilities for gambling and related activities may also be viewed in this context. The casino at Constanţa on the Romanian Black Sea coast was a rarity during the socialist years, but in 1988, a similar venue was set up in Karlovy Vary as a joint venture between Casino Austria and the then Czechoslovak state enterprise Balnex. It was sufficiently successful for the Austrian company to negotiate further casinos with the Čedok state tourism agency for the Forum and Palace hotels in Prague. The Hungarians went one better by establishing a floating casino on the Danube at Budapest.

15.2.6   The challenge of sustainability

The region is vulnerable to tourism fashion changes, which are themselves sensitive to economic, social and political instability. Socio-economic changes are producing rapidly rising crime and accident rates. The nature and extent of tourism's role in the growth in crime is difficult to evaluate, but may not be insignificant (Alejziak 1996). One way of ameliorating such problems is to involve local communities more closely in the tourism development process. Given almost half a century of passive acceptance of centralised *diktat*, however, the region's citizens initially had little experience of bottom-up development (Hall 1991a). Certainly, the paradoxes surrounding concepts of 'sustainable tourism' are amply articulated in CEE (Hall and Kinnaird 1994). Any restriction of personal freedom—in terms of exclusion from environmentally sensitive areas, banning the pursuit of certain activities or discouraging the development of certain types of businesses, and indeed physical and spatial planning generally—might be seen to echo the half century of post-war communist imposition. Certainly the new 'freedoms' are being pursued by an emergent private entrepreneurial sector, not least in the tourism and travel sectors, sharply focused on short-term profit (Koulov 1996).

The impact of tourism activities on the region's environmental biodiversity and fragility requires careful planning and monitoring (Hall and Kinnaird 1994). The sheer weight of visitor numbers, even in pedestrianised areas such as central Prague, has forced planners to think seriously about restricting access to such famous structures as the Charles Bridge and Karlstejn Castle (Stevenson 1997). While official recognition is given to the need for 'sustainable', 'green' and 'eco'-tourism, there may often be conflicting priorities amongst ministries, NGOs, community groups and the private sector. However, opportunities for cross-border cooperation have been opened up both in terms of tourism development and for protecting environments hitherto located in inaccessible borderlands (Karpowicz 1993).

Areas such as Romania's Danube Delta, one of Europe's most important wildlife habitats, which are now subject to conservation and protection, have required considerable efforts to involve the local population in processes of sustainable development and planning. Employment- and income-generating processes, such as the recruitment of park wardens, and encouragement of provision of bed and breakfast type accommodation have been pursued in an attempt to preclude the community perception that its livelihood is threatened by conservation designations, which would, therefore, by definition, not be sustainable (Hall 1993b, 1996a).

Where tourism-related activity is used to stimulate economic development, employment opportunities for the local population are often characterised by a predominance of unskilled, low-paid jobs, such as cleaners, clerks and kitchen staff. The gendered horizontal segregation of occupations is particularly noticeable in semi-skilled, domestic and service-type occupations, such a those in the tourism industry (Kinnaird and Hall 1994, 1996; Norris and Wall 1994; Swain 1995), especially where they mirror the domestic division of labour. While there is a growing reaction against inequities in access to employment and roles in the division of labour within the region, as part of wider processes of gender politics (Funk and Mueller 1993), considerable attention has been focused on the apparent growth of hard currency prostitution and child exploitation. More generally, there has been little attention to gender issues in the emerging debates in CEE concerning sustainable tourism.

15.3 The evolution of CEE tourism

15.3.1 Constrained inbound tourism

Tourism grew in popularity in the region during the first half of this century, especially in upland areas and spa towns. The post-war imposition of a Soviet model of political, economic and social development, however, truncated previous development paths. There appeared to be a number of 'socialist' objectives which appropriate inbound tourism could support: redistributing employment opportunities, promoting positive regional and national images, and legitimisation of the (superiority of the) socialist system (Hall, 1981, 1984). But the structural characteristics of state socialism—centralised bureaucratic organisation, inflexibility and antipathy towards individualism and entrepreneurialism—limited the success of international tourist programmes except within the decentralised Yugoslav system. Yugoslavia was the exception in generating substantial growth in tourist arrivals from the West, and this was preceded by a series of tourism and labour mobility agreements with Western governments in

Table 15.2   CEE: international tourist arrivals, 1988–1994 (millions)

	1988	1989	1990	1991	1992	1993	1994	Percentage change 1988–94	Percentage change 1990–94
Albania	–	–	0.03	0.01	0.03	0.05	0.03	–	0
Bulgaria	4.0	4.3	4.5	4.0	3.8	3.8	4.1	+2.5	−8.9
Czechoslovakia	6.9	8.0	8.1	8.2	11.5	(12.2)	(17.9)	+159	
Czech Republic			(7.3)	(7.6)	(10.9)	11.5	17.0		+133
Slovakia			(0.8)	(0.6)	(0.6)	0.7	0.9		+12.5
Hungary	10.6	14.5	20.5	21.9	20.2	22.8	21.4	+102	+4.4
Poland	2.5	3.3	3.4	11.4	16.2	17.0	18.8	+652	+453
Romania	5.5	4.9	3.0	3.0	3.8	2.9	2.8	−49.1	−6.7
Yugoslavia	9.0	8.6			–	–	(3.3)	−63.3	
Croatia			7.0	1.3	1.3	1.5	2.3		−67.1
FYROM			0.6	0.3	0.2	0.2	0.2		−66.7
Serbia/Monten.			1.2	0.4	0.2	0.1	0.1		−83.3
Slovenia			0.7	0.3	0.6	0.6	0.7		0

Sources: WTO (1994, Vol. 1, p. 106; 1996b, Vol. 1, p. 96); author's additional calculations.

the 1960s. Absolute numbers of international tourists to Yugoslavia were not significantly greater than those to several other countries in the region (and less than Hungary by the late 1980s: Table 15.2). However, the dominance of the Western market did secure a significantly higher level of tourism income, which, by the end of the 1980s, was equivalent to the sum total for the rest of the region (Tables 15.3, 15.4).

Economic barriers, mobility constraints, the low priority given to service industries, coupled with lingering cold war attitudes, rendered Europe behind the 'Iron Curtain' inhospitable to many Western tourists before 1989. Alleged fear of Western ideological contagion and social corruption were early constraints on the region's governments' pursuing international tourism, although the speed of elimination of such perceptions varied considerably (Hall 1990b). As a consequence, the economic impact of international tourism on the region remained relatively limited, certainly by comparison with Western Europe (Hall 1991b). It is unclear, given the range of globalisation processes penetrating the region during the 1980s, and the Gorbachevian catalyst, how far increasing Western tourism and cross-border movement, particularly to Hungary in the later half of the decade, contributed to the political implosions of 1989. Certainly the decision by the Hungarian authorities to remove sections of the border constraints with Austria in the summer of that year was a defining moment in twentieth century European history.

15.3.2   *Domestic tourism: access and underclass*

Under state socialism, domestic recreation was subsidised to provide cheap accommodation and transport for (usually urban industrial) workers and their families to take a holiday at least once every two years. But this trade union and enterprise-supported activity excluded a substantial element of the rural population, rendering them unsubsidised and relatively immobile. Despite the human rights clauses of the 1975

Table 15.3 CEE: international tourist receipts, 1988–1994 (US $ millions)

	1988	1989	1990	1991	1992	1993	1994	Percentage change		Receipts per tourist arrival 1994 ($)
								1988–1994	1990–1994	
Albania		3	7	5	9	8	5	–	–29	167
Bulgaria	484	495	320	44	215	307	358	–26	+12	87
Czechoslovakia	608	581	489	849	1,333	(1,948)	(2,534)	(+317)		
Czech Republic			(419)	(714)	(1,125)	1,558	1,966		+369	116
Slovakia			(70)	(135)	(213)	390	568		+711	631
Hungary	758	798	824	1,002	1,231	1,181	1,428	+88[1]	+73	67
Poland	206	202	358	2,800 (149)	4,100 (183)	4,500	6,150		[1]	327
Romania	171	167	106	145	262	197	414	+142	+291	148
Yugoslavia	2,024	2,230					(2,419)	+20		–
Croatia			1,704	300	543	832	1,427		–16	620
FYROM			45	9	11	13	29		–36	145
Serbia/Monten.			419	134	88	23	31		–93	310
Slovenia			721	275	671	734	932		+29	1,331

Source: WTO (1994, Vol. 1, p. 112; 1995, Vol. 1, p. 102; 1996b, Vol. 1, p. 102); author's additional calculations.

[1] Compensating for the radical change in accounting procedures used as the basis for reporting to WTO as introduced in WTO 1995 and retrospectively adjusted to 1991, the figure would be around +30 for 1988–1994 and around –30 for 1990–1994.

Helsinki agreement, the region's nationals—other than Yugoslavs—were rarely permitted to travel westwards: currency inconvertibility, restricted access to hard currency, and stringent vetting and exit visa policies proscribed most forms of extra-bloc tourism. Cross-border movement tended to be dominated by exchanges of 'friendship groups' between like-minded countries. The political and bureaucratic elite—the *nomenklatura*—with access to convertible currency, was, however, able to travel to the capitalist world. There were clearly several levels of tourist and recreation underclass as a consequence of prevailing social, economic and political relations:

- The rural peasantry, unable to afford or gain access to domestic recreation because of their structural and/or spatial positions within the economy.
- Those workers denied access to overseas vacations within the socialist bloc because of their structural position, lack of access to hard currency or record of non-compliance.
- Most of the population, denied access to non-bloc overseas visits because of their lack of ideological-bureaucratic status and connections.

The subsequent transition has simplified this social and economic order:

- Ability to pay has become the major criterion in access to domestic tourism, severely influenced by national and local inflation, loss of subsidies and the imposition of often high rates of VAT.
- Internationally, the 'Iron Curtain' has been replaced by a 'dollar curtain' lowered by Western host countries in fear of what is portrayed as a possible flood of Eastern European migrants. Although the need to secure exit visas from home countries normally no longer exists, hard currency entry visas, often costing more than a month's income, are required by Western governments for citizens of several of the region's countries.

15.4   The regional structure of tourism in CEE

If distinctive elements can be recognised in European post-war international tourism trends, then in CEE it is possible to discern long-term regional growth, a shorter-term cycle related to the now subsiding curiosity factor of the 'newly-opened' post socialist societies, and the 'erratics' of national upheaval related to the economic and political repositioning of the region's component parts in context of fragmenting state structures, new framework conditions and the impacts of globalisation.

Although international tourist arrivals gained momentum after 1989, this characteristic was not shared by all parts of the region; the Yugoslav tourism industry was most dramatically dismantled by conflict, both directly and indirectly (Tables 15.2, 15.4). This deflation only began to be relieved in 1994 as arrivals in Croatia and Slovenia began to recover.

Overall, the region's share of European arrivals gradually grew from 15–19 per cent in 1985 to 20–24 per cent in 1994. Receipts grew several-fold during this period and, as Baláž (1996a) has suggested, they came at an opportune time, with the loss of former Soviet markets and a rationalisation of manufacturing capacity throughout the region.

However, inconsistencies of accounting aside, the recorded economic performance of international tourism growth has been poor by both European and global standards. Despite attracting more than one-fifth of all Europe's international arrivals in 1994, CEE generated less than one-tenth of the continent's tourism revenues (Tables 15.4, 15.5). A crucial statistic in this respect is shown in Table 15.5, based on WTO's Central/East Europe regional definition and therefore excluding the former Yugoslavia, which reveals that in 1994 the average receipt per tourist arrival was equivalent to just 37 per cent of the European average, and only 31 per cent of the world average. Although these figures represent an improvement on the 1988 levels of 15 and 13 per cent, they underline the need for value added attractions and an infrastructural and regulatory context which permits and encourages visitor expenditure.

Although improved access, changing image projection, penetration of Western inward investment and growth of service industry employment and training have all acted to render the region more attractive to international tourists, it still embraces comparatively low-spending, short-stay visitors. Large numbers of excursionists— cross-border day-trippers and petty traders, both taking advantage of differentials in currency rates—and transit travellers considerably inflate visitor figures. For example, numbers of recorded international visitor arrivals in Poland more than quadrupled between 1990 and 1994, from 18 to 74 million, yet in the latter year only 18.8 million tourist arrivals were recorded (WTO 1996b, Vol. 1, p. 96; Vol. 2, p. 250). Including the former Yugoslavia, in 1994 the region had a recorded 12.6 per cent of all European bed-spaces and 13.7 per cent of rooms, yet average length of stays in accommodation ranged from just 1.9 nights in Bulgaria to 6.9 in Poland, with a regional average of 3.4 nights. Occupancy rates ranged from 16 per cent for Croatia to 47 per cent for Poland, with an overall average rate of just 33 per cent (WTO 1996a).

Table 15.4 indicates a number of key trends in international tourism receipts for the region which, at first glance, appear positive:

- As a proportion of GNP, they overtook the European average between 1993 and 1994, increasing from 1.6 to 2.1 per cent compared to the overall European figures of 1.8 and 1.9 per cent, respectively (Table 15.5). This relationship, perhaps more than any other, suggests the emergence of tourism as an important element of the CEE economy, albeit also reflecting the low levels of economic performance of the CEE countries: the region's highest GDP per capita, for the Czech Republic, is equivalent to just 15 per cent of that for neighbouring Austria (Table 15.1).
- As a proportion of services, they increased from 15.8 per cent in 1990 to 39.1 in 1991, thereby surpassing the European average, which decreased from 28.2 to 27.5 per cent in the same period. To some extent this reflects the low priority given to the service sector under state socialism. The fact that the proportion only slightly increased for 1992 and actually declined in 1993 may reflect the delayed post-socialist growth in service industry development as a whole taking place at that time.
- As a proportion of exports, they overtook the figure for Europe in 1992, increasing from a 1991 figure of 8.3 per cent to 9.8 per cent, compared to all-Europe figures of 8.4 and 8.9 per cent respectively. This reflects a marked downturn in regional exports as the former Soviet market collapsed and medium-term manufacturing decline set in with economic restructuring.

Table 15.4 CEE: comparative international tourism statistics, 1985–1994

		1985	1988	1989	1990	1991	1992	1993	1994	Percentage increase	
										1985–1994	1988–1994
International tourist arrivals (millions)	(a)	31.4	35.4	42.8	46.7	55.3	61.6	69.2	74.3	137	110
	(b)	39.9	44.5	51.4	56.2	57.6	63.9	71.6	77.6	94.5	74.4
	(c)	35.5	38.4	43.6	49.0	50.7	59.1	61.1	68.3	92.4	77.9
Share of European arrivals (%)	(a)	15.0	15.1	16.4	16.3	19.2	20.4	22.1	22.5	50.0	49.0
	(b)	19.0	18.9	19.7	19.6	20.0	21.1	22.9	23.6	24.2	24.9
	(c)	16.9	16.4	16.7	17.1	17.6	19.0	19.5	20.8	23.1	26.8
Share of world arrivals (%)	(a)	9.7	9.3	10.3	11.3	11.9	12.2	13.4	13.6	40.2	46.2
	(b)	12.4	11.6	12.4	13.1	12.4	12.7	13.8	14.2	14.5	22.4
	(c)	11.0	10.1	10.5	11.5	10.9	11.7	11.8	12.5	13.6	23.8
International tourist receipts (US$ millions)	(a)	1,625	2,318	2,360	4,849	7,474	9,517	12,185	14,404	786	521
	(b)	2,686	4,342	4,590	7,745	8,197	10,839	13,795	16,828	527	288
	(c)	n.d.	4,126	4,340	4,993	5,563	8,469	9,743	13,308	–	223
Share of European receipts (%)	(a)	2.8	2.3	2.3	3.4	5.2	5.9	7.7	8.3	196	261
	(b)	4.6	4.2	4.4	5.4	5.7	6.7	8.7	9.7	111	131
	(c)	n.d.	4.0	4.1	3.5	3.9	5.2	6.2	7.7	–	92.5

Sources: Hall (1995, p. 226); WTO (1996b, Vol. 1, pp. 2, 89, 96, 98, 102, 104); author's additional calculations.

Notes:

(a) The region of 'Central/East Europe' as defined by the WTO (which includes the former Soviet Union but excludes Albania and the former Yugoslavia, which are placed in 'Southern Europe').

(b) This comprises the countries of (a) with the addition of Albania and the former Yugoslavia.

(c) This comprises the countries of (b) but with the exclusion of the former Soviet Union.

Table 15.5 CEE:[1] economic dimensions of international tourism, 1988–1994[2]

	1988	1989	1990	1991	1992	1993	1994	Percentage change	
								1988–1994	1990–1994
International tourism receipts: CEE									
Total US $m	2,443	2,493	4,849	7,474	9,517	12,185	14,404	490	197
Percentage of European receipts	2.3	2.3	3.4	5.2	5.9	7.7	8.3	261	144
Receipts per tourist arrival US $									
CEE	64	54	103	135	154	175	193	202	87.4
Europe	425	401	502	497	529	503	525	23.5	4.6
World	495	498	576	583	613	607	632	27.7	9.7
Receipts as percentage of GNP									
CEE	0.2	0.2	0.4	0.7	1.1	1.6	2.1	950	425
Europe	1.5	1.5	1.8	1.7	1.8	1.8	1.9	26.7	5.6
World	1.1	1.1	1.3	1.2	1.3	1.3	1.3	18.2	0
Receipts as percentage of exports									
CEE	1.2	1.3	3.0	8.3	9.8	11.5	10.1	742	21.7
Europe	7.2	7.1	8.0	8.4	8.9	9.4	9.0	25.0	12.5
World	7.1	7.1	7.7	7.9	8.4	8.6	8.3	16.9	7.8
Receipts as percentage of services									
CEE	26.4	23.8	15.8	39.1	41.7	39.5	48.8	84.8	209
Europe	30.2	29.2	28.2	27.5	27.3	27.7	28.6	-5.3	1.4
World	31.1	30.6	29.6	29.2	29.1	29.5	30.4	-2.3	2.7
International tourism expenditures: CEE									
Total US $m	1,404	1,802	1,828	1,250	1,999	2,215	3,424	144	87.3
Percentage of European expenditures	1.4	1.8	1.4	1.0	1.4	1.6	2.2	57.1	57.1

Sources: WTO (1994, Vol. 1, pp. 4, 98–9; 1996b, Vol. 1, pp. 4, 88–9); author's additional calculations.

1 These aggregate figures are based on the WTO region of Central/Eastern Europe which includes the former Soviet Union and excludes Albania and the former Yugoslavia.
2 There are discontinuities in the consistency of these figures between 1989 and 1990, as represented in successive WTO compilations.

15.4.1   *Incoming tourists and visitors*

Although CEE was not in a strong position to respond to the rapid expansion of the West European inclusive-tour holiday industry in the 1960s, there was no inevitability about this. With a relatively few spatial and structural adjustments, the region could have better attuned itself to providing the standardised mass tourism products of sun, sand and surf, or snow and ski-slopes, to hard currency markets. Western mass tourism's lack of interest in the particularities of place, but emphasis upon price sensitivity, was ideally fitted to CEE's anodyne isolated coastal and mountain resorts and relatively low-cost, low-wage economies. Arguably, and with the benefit of hindsight, CEE missed golden opportunities in the 1960s–1980s period of West European mass tourism.

During the 1980s, CEE did experience a doubling of international arrivals, with growth of 20–35 per cent over the 1985–1989 period (Hall 1991b, 1995), particularly notable for land-locked Czechoslovakia (63 per cent) and Hungary (50 per cent) (Hall 1992b, 1993a). During this time the region experienced a slight increase in its share of European arrivals. Niche roles had emerged as a consequence of the artificial division of Europe: Hungary, for example, became a common meeting ground for East and West Germans who could not otherwise easily interact, Lake Balaton being particularly favoured by East Germans. Much intra-bloc movement was now related to cross-border petty trading and shopping. The sun, sand and surf destinations also showed modest growth, but both Yugoslavia and Romania experienced downturns in 1989 (Table 15.2).

In the early transition period, the most spectacular growth in international tourist arrivals was in Hungary, with annual increases of over 40 per cent for 1989 and 1990. Hungary experienced a doubling of tourist arrivals in the 1988–1994 period, but this performance was overtaken by that of (the former) Czechoslovakia (159 per cent). In particular, while substantial growth in tourist numbers took place in the Czech Republic, overall international *visitor* arrivals were some five times higher, exerting inordinate pressures upon the country's major attraction, central Prague. With tourist data accounting changes from 1991, Poland recorded an apparent 652 per cent increase in tourist arrivals between 1988 and 1994 (Table 15.2). By contrast, there was decline in Bulgaria between 1990 and 1993, albeit with subsequent recovery, while Romania continues to display a declining trend. Alongside the particular problems of the fragmenting Yugoslavia and sporadically imploding Albania, the Balkan countries, despite possessing the most favourable climatic and coastal conditions for mass tourism, have experienced stagnation in tourist numbers; this reflects an initial lack of clarity of political change, continuing instability, and generally poorer road transport accessibility from major Western European markets. Furthermore, tourists from the more westerly parts of CEE itself, no longer restricted to Soviet bloc vacation destinations, started to abandon their post-war Black Sea coast holiday playgrounds for more enticing Western venues, to be replaced to some extent by Russians and Ukrainians.

15.4.2   *Tourist markets: challenge and change*

During the state socialist period, the vast majority of international tourists to the countries of CEE were from other socialist states. Even by the end of the 1980s, with the exception of Yugoslavia and Bulgaria, the majority of arrivals were from within the Soviet bloc (Hall 1991b, pp. 91–3).

There has subsequently been a variable increase in the proportion of Western arrivals and a changing complexion of intraregional patterns. At one extreme, Czechoslovakia, a forbidding destination for many Westerners before 1989, saw the number of Austrian visitor arrivals rise from 230,200 (1.2 per cent of total visitors) in 1986 to 9.07 million (10.9 per cent) in 1992, many of whom would be day trippers, while the share of visitors from Hungary declined from 26.0 to 4.3 per cent. At the other extreme, Slovenia, a favoured package holiday destination for Germans (28.5 per cent of all bednights in 1985) and Britons (14.7 per cent), now emphasises high-income niche tourism. As a result, the shares of traditional tourist package markets have fallen compared to those of immediate neighbours Italy and Austria, for whom the proportion of bednights more than doubled to 21.6 per cent and 22.8 per cent, respectively, between 1985 and 1994; the proportion from Germany remained relatively steady at 25.0 per cent (ZRSS 1995, p. 40).

With the lowering, if not elimination, of constraints on east–west, west–east movement in the 1990s, the countries of the region could be expected to draw on a wider range of source markets. However, in practice, a comparison of the proportions of the three most important sources for each country in 1988 and 1994 (Table 15.6), reveals an apparent increased concentration in five cases: Bulgaria and Poland with slight concentrations; Romania more significantly from 51.8 to 62.5 per cent; Poland to a very marked degree, rising to 95.8 per cent with almost two-thirds of visitor arrivals in 1994 being from Germany (compared to one-quarter from the two Germanys in 1988); and each of the Yugoslav successor states compared to the overall figure for Yugoslavia in 1988.

Germany accounts for one-third of the industrialised world's trade with the region (Cook 1996), and it would be expected that German tourist arrivals were significant over much of CEE, as indeed elsewhere in Europe. However, the relative rise in numerical significance of visitors from the former Soviet Union (FSU) between 1988 and 1994 is perhaps less expected. Yet this trend is apparent in all countries except most of the former Yugoslav states and Poland, where FSU nonetheless remained the third most important group. While this phenomenon may largely reflect cross-border petty trading and shopping, high-spending Russian tourists have been a notable feature of European tourism in recent years. In Poland in 1994, for example, Russian tourists spent $225 per head compared to Germans' $178, Austrians' $166, Slovaks' $51 and Americans' $982 (SSTA 1996, p. 9).

While the data do not allow an interpretation which suggests substantial or comprehensive shifts in tourist markets from former Soviet bloc to Western sources, neither do they necessarily suggest the targeting of particular niche groups in the former group, other than high-spenders. At best, patterns are unclear, even paradoxical, and certainly dynamic.

15.4.3   Tourism income and receipts

The second half of the 1980s witnessed changing patterns of tourism receipts: they increased for Bulgaria, Hungary, Yugoslavia and probably Albania, but Romania and Poland showed long-term decline and Czechoslovakia experienced a fall at the end of the decade (Table 15.3). Considerable increases in the 1985–1989 period in particular countries—110 per cent for Yugoslavia and 89 per cent for Czechoslovakia—reflected the role of high-spending tourists from the West: substantial for the former and rapidly

Table 15.6 CEE: major sources of international tourist (visitor*) arrivals, 1988 and 1994 (%) (where more than 1 per cent of total arrivals)

	A	B	BG	CH	CS/ FCS	BRD: DDR/D	F	GR	H	I	NL	PL	R	S	SU/ FSU	TR	UK	USA	YU/ FYU	Percentage of top 3
Albania 1988	–	–	–	–	–	–	–	–	–	–	–	–	–	–	–	–	–	–	–	–
Albania 1994	1.6	1.8	3.2	1.9	–	6.5	6.1	10.9	1.2	23.2	2.7	–	–	–	–	4.0	3.6	8.3	16.5	50.6
Bulgaria 1988*					5.1	3.3:3.7		1.9	3.0			11.1	2.7		5.7	38.9	1.1		17.5	67.5
Bulgaria 1994*						1.6		3.5					18.6		18.2	19.9			31.3	67.8
Czechoslovakia 1988*	1.3					2.5:38.2			26.0			19.4			2.8					83.6
Czechoslovakia 1992*	10.9					41.4			4.3			18.9								71.2
Slovakia 1994	4.7	1.0			22.3	15.3	2.2		7.4	3.5	3.4	16.1			5.4		1.8	2.8		53.6
Hungary 1988	8.7	2.8			21.2	10.7:9.5				1.6	1.2	18.0	1.6		5.5		1.1	1.1	8.8	49.2
Hungary 1994	11.7	1.7			7.5	16.4				1.8	1.2	2.5	18.2		15.9	1.0	1.1	1.1	15.0	50.5
Poland 1988*					22.9	7.9:17.5			9.2					1.1	28.1				3.1	88.5
Poland 1994*					19.0	64.0									12.8					95.8
Romania 1988*		12.7			9.9	2.1:5.9			11.8			14.9			11.4				24.2	51.8
Romania 1994*		17.3			3.1	3.4		1.0	10.6	1.6		2.0			32.5	9.1			12.7	62.5
Yugoslavia 1988	5.1	1.1		2.1	3.0	23.9:–	3.8	5.1	4.6	6.8	3.0	4.6			12.3	3.7	5.7	3.0		43.0
Croatia 1994	15.8				19.0	15.5	1.2		5.6	15.6	1.3			1.5		1.0	1.0		14.8	50.4
FYROM 1994		18.0			20.6	3.9		1.1	2.4		1.1				3.5	3.5	1.1	2.3	44.9	83.5
Serbia/M 1994	5.3	19.8			1.5	3.1	1.7	11.2	6.3	6.3			7.3	1.3	15.6	1.9	1.4	1.6		46.6
Slovenia 1994	17.5	1.5			2.8	17.6	1.8		2.7	23.6	2.6				1.7		1.9	1.8	16.1	58.9

Also: FYROM 1994: Albania 6.3
Yugoslavia 1988: Denmark 1.0, Norway 1.1

Sources: WTO (1994, Vol. 2, pp. 59–60, 167–8, 176, 219–20, 223–6, 341; 1996b, Vol. 2, pp. 69–70, 151–2, 188–9, 250–1, 254–7, 295–6, 371, 391–3, 400); author's additional calculations.

The figures for the three most important sources for each country are *in italics*.

Key to source countries: A, Austria; B, Belgium; BG, Bulgaria; CH, Switzerland; CS (1988), Czechoslovakia; FCS (1994), former Czechoslovakia (Czech Republic and Slovakia); BRD (1988), Federal Republic of Germany (West Germany); DDR (1988), German Democratic Republic (East Germany); D (1994), Germany (Unified); F, France; GR, Greece; H, Hungary; I, Italy; NL, Netherlands; PL, Poland; R, Romania; S, Sweden; SU, Soviet Union; FSU, former Soviet Union; TR, Turkey; UK, United Kingdom; USA, United States; YU (1988), SFR Yugoslavia; FYU (1994), former Yugoslavia.

increasing for the latter. Romania, by contrast, experienced a decrease of some 200 per cent during the 1980s, reflecting the country's unattractive social and economic environment, while Turkey's tourism receipts increased by over 700 per cent in the same period (Hall 1995).

As noted in Table 15.4, the region generated only about 2.3 per cent of total European tourism receipts in the late 1980s, despite attracting 15–20 per cent of all Europe's international tourist arrivals. In 1988, the last full year of state socialism, Bulgaria's tourist income was just 2.2 per cent of that of Spain, while Czechoslovakia earned just 10.3 per cent of that of Switzerland (Hall 1991b).

Growth in receipts was dramatic in the first half of the 1990s, notably in the former Czechoslovakia and Romania, the latter emerging from a low base. Particularly comprehensive growth took place in 1994, as the tourism economies of Central Europe, overcoming the 'shock therapy' stage of transition, began to gain some success in marketing higher-value niche products, and as several Balkan countries began to emerge from the shadow of the Yugoslav conflicts. Indeed, the resurgence of Slovenia's tourism industry was such that, by 1994, it appeared to receive CEE's highest level of receipts per international tourist arrival. At over $1300, this was more than twice the level of the next highest, Croatia and Slovakia, with less than $640, and more than ten times higher than the levels of Bulgaria, the Czech Republic, and Hungary. With near neighbours Italy, Austria and Germany providing almost 60 per cent of the country's tourist arrivals, Slovenia's emphasis on developing a wide range of cultural and natural attractions was clearly successful in attracting tourists from high-spending hard currency markets. Nevertheless, the 1994 level of receipts per tourist appears surprisingly high, particularly when compared to Italy's $870 and Austria's $735 in the same year (author's calculations from WTO, 1996a)

15.4.4   *Patterns of outbound tourism in the context of the new Europe*

Data relating to patterns of outbound travel from CEE tend to be incomplete and inconsistent. None the less, Table 15.7 provides some indications of relative levels of external travel since 1988, although 'total trips' (as with most tourism and travel) data give no indication of the number of actual individuals involved, as the totals may included repeat visitors.

In addition to Yugoslavia's relatively open stance since the mid-1960s, the less austere and more pragmatic social and economic policies pursued in Hungary and Poland were reflected in patterns of outbound travel in the 1980s (Hall 1995). Yet, in both numerical and percentage terms, the number of trips out of more economically advanced but politically hard-line Czechoslovakia exceeded that for Poland by 1988 (Table 15.7). Not surprisingly, there was an outward surge in all countries in 1990, representing a reaction to new freedoms, the expression of pent-up latent demand, and curiosity. Again, in a number of countries, the role of petty cross-border trading, taking advantage of differentials in prices, currency conversion rates and consumer goods availability, and the increasing tolerance of private markets, provided a significant element in the growth of outbound travel (see Gołembski 1990). For Yugoslavs, the significant 1989–1990 increase in outbound trips reflected both growing internal tensions, with Serbs turning away from Croatian Adriatic resorts, and the greater ease and attractiveness of visiting other countries. Just under a quarter of all outbound trips from Yugoslavia were to Italy, where Yugoslavs accounted for

Table 15.7 CEE: travel abroad, 1988–1994

	Number of trips (thousands)							Percentage change		OTR[1]		Expenditure, 1994	
	1988	1989	1990	1991	1992	1993	1994	1988–1994	1990–1994	1988	1994	Total ($m)	Per trip ($)
Albania	nd	nd	nd	nd	nd	3	10	–	–	–	0.3	4	400
Bulgaria	505	922	2,395	2,045	2,610	2,142	4,394	770	83.5	5.6	49.3	242	55
Czechoslovakia	7,258	8,569	20,654	39,613				535		46.5		–	–
Czech Republic			13,380	30,660	32,672	30,981	45,845	–	243		445	832	18
Slovakia					188[2]	159[2]	213[2]		–		3.9[2]	284	–
Hungary	10,797	14,476	13,596	14,317	12,803	12,115	14,374	33.1	5.7	102	141	925	64
Poland	6,923	19,323	22,131	20,754	29,268	31,395	34,296	395	55.0	18.2	88.8	316	9
Romania	948	874	11,247	9,096	10,709	10,757	10,105	966	–10.2	4.1	43.6	449	44
Yugoslavia	21,284	24,923	36,290					–	–	90.3	–	–	–
Croatia				nd	nd	nd	nd	–	–	–	–	552	–
FYROM				nd	nd	nd	nd	–	–	–	–	–	–
Serbia/Monten.				nd	nd	nd	nd	–	–	–	–	–	–
Slovenia				nd	nd	nd	nd	–	–	–	–	312	–

Sources: Hall (1991b, p. 9; 1995, p. 229); WTO (1996a, pp. 3, 29, 46, 50, 80, 137, 143, 160–1, 191); Table 1; author's own calculations.

[1] OTR: outbound travel rate: the number of trips abroad as a % of the source country's total population.

[2] These figures (WTO, 1996a, p. 160) appear highly anomalous and should realistically be increased by a factor of 100.

nd = no data.

80–90 per cent of all inflows from Central and East Europeans during 1989 and 1990 (Hall 1995).

Since 1990, patterns of hesitant growth in the Balkans have contrasted with stronger trends in Central Europe; by 1994 the 'outbound travel rates' for the latter countries ranged between four-fifths and four-and-a-half times the equivalent of the countries' own population sizes, while the equivalent rates for Bulgaria and Romania were just under half (albeit rising significantly from the 1988 position), and that for Albania, officially at least, was minuscule. For Bulgarians, with shopping and visiting friends and relatives (VFR) the most important elements, a 'neighbourhood pattern' has been recognised, reflecting increased transport costs and Western visa requirements (Bachvarov 1997). Indeed, outbound travel rates reflect a complex mix of factors, including a country's area and population size, range of domestic attractions and recreational facilities, levels of economic development and standards of living, and the organisational structure of the outbound transport and tourism industries. For comparison, such rates vary considerably in western Europe: the 1994 figures for small peripheral countries are as varied as 2.3 for Portugal and 66.1 for Ireland, while for larger countries, France had a rate of 30.4 and the UK 68.3 (author's calculations from data in WTO 1996a and Campbell 1997).

Few coherent patterns can be discerned from outward tourism expenditure data (Table 15.7). In 1994, glaring anomalies aside, expenditure ranged from $242 million for Bulgaria to $925 million for Hungary. As might be expected, the Czech Republic returned the second-highest figure at $832 million, yet on an expenditure per trip basis, the $64 figure for Hungary is more than three times greater than the Czech Republic's $18, which in turn is twice the figure for Poland.

Looking ahead, a number of likely trends in CEE outbound travel can be recognised

- Large numbers of low spenders will continue to travel by land transport across Europe, many reinforcing the 'neighbourhood effect' through pursuing cross-border petty trading and shopping trips. Nevertheless, some elements, notably from the former Soviet Union, will be high-level spenders.
- A rejuvenation of the mass tourism product cycle, fuelled by new demands from CEE citizens and those further east, is likely to favour Mediterranean and Alpine locations for some considerable time to come.
- The proportion of high spenders will increase and they are likely to disburse their disposable (convertible) income on tourism and related activities across a wider range of locations in Europe and beyond.
- Within an overall growth trend, numbers of outbound travellers will continue to fluctuate according to particular national circumstances.

15.5 Tourism and economic restructuring

15.5.1 Global shifts and CEE

The shift in demand from standardised, mass package tours in favour of holidays responding to a desire for learning, nostalgia, heritage, make-believe, action, and a closer look at the 'Other' (Boissevain 1996, p. 3), has required smaller-scale specialised niche marketing and more flexible provision. This has created high value added market segmentation and provided opportunities for CEE's new small companies.

Coupled to lower overhead costs and more flexible labour (Williams *et al.* 1989), smaller firms have been able to take advantage of improvements in information technology and so compete in increasingly internationalised markets: in the early 1990s, this was notable in the Visegrád countries. But the still largely inflexible state-dominated tourism structures of the Balkans were less able to respond to such changes in consumption aspirations than they had been to the demand for package tourism in the 1960s. However, there has been no linear or universal shift from modernism to post-modernism in CEE to produce a dominant post-modern tourism. Interwoven with the region's economic and political transition, any emergence of the new tourism (Poon 1993) has been spatially and structurally uneven.

Indeed, an early characteristic of post-communist restructuring and privatisation processes within the tourism industry of the more advanced CEE countries was the rapid growth of travel agents and holiday companies, both responding to Western niche segmentation, but more particularly providing Mediterranean coast packages for the region's consumers (Gibson 1996). In the summer of 1994, for example, some 10,000 Czech tourists took charter flights out of Prague to the reviving Dalmatian coast resorts. Even JAT, the 'Yugoslav' national airline, restarted regular services to Tunisia and Cyprus during 1996. With long-term consolidation of CEE's economic stability and standards of living, there are likely to be increasing levels of individual mobility and access to international travel, although this process will be socially and spatially uneven.

15.5.2   *Regional differences in the restructuring of tourism within CEE*

Privatisation, price liberalisation, reorientation of foreign trade, upgrading and reorientation of infrastructure, adoption of new technology, and skill training programmes (Hall 1995) have provided the regional frame conditions for post-socialist tourism development. Increased visitor activity following political change was stimulated by such factors as the more positive and substantial Western media focus on the region, an overhaul of entry, exit and currency regulations, substantial short-term curiosity value coupled to a longer-term pent-up latent demand, comprehensive Western involvement in aspects of tourism development, and the newly found mobility of many Central and East Europeans.

At the end of the 1980s, the quality of the region's tourist services had been low and very variable by Western standards. Accommodation, catering, utilities, transport and telecommunications had suffered from decades of neglect, although, belatedly, substantial adaptation of existing economic mechanisms had taken place in the last years of state socialism in order to ameliorate the more centralised and inflexible aspects of the Soviet model of political economy. In the accommodation sector, for example, 1988 legislation in Bulgaria permitted private citizens to operate hotels and inns, whilst joint venture investment in high-quality accommodation had been taking place in Hungary and Poland for several years. But in other cases comprehensive political change was required before economic reforms: only from 1989 were private guest-houses permitted in Czechoslovakia.

Foreign investment in the tourism industry has been particularly notable in the hotel sector (Lennon 1995), with international chains supporting new construction and buying into existing capacity. Although initial investment was at the higher end of the market, the extensive gap in middle-range accommodation availability in countries such as Poland has stimulated the French Accor Group and US Holiday Inn chain to plan to develop 120 budget hotels in that country (Simpson 1997). Foreign investment is also upgrading retailing provision, and this is at least partly driven by tourist consumer demand: in late 1996, Budapest's largest department store was opened by the German Tengelmann group at a cost of $160 million in competition with two new North American-style shopping malls.

The requirement for staff training in hotel management, catering, travel agency, and in such areas as computing, telecommunications and foreign languages, has been recognised in a number of multilateral aid projects emphasising training and skills enhancement; one example is an EU PHARE programme project for developing Polish tourism skills through the training of 5,000 industry employees (Airey 1994; also Burns 1995; Richards 1996). The private sector has seen a number of multinational companies training nationals in the region, either *in situ* or in Western institutions. One of the higher profile earlier private ventures involved American Express's $500,000 fund to develop tourism personnel skills in Czechoslovakia, Hungary and Poland (Hamilton 1991).

In the travel agency sector, the privatisation of state sector companies has taken place in tandem with the growth of new competing private enterprises: in both Bulgaria and Poland, for example, there are reported to be over 4,500 travel agencies (Bachvarov 1997). Lack of market experience saw Ibusz, the former Hungarian monopoly travel agent, diversifying too rapidly after privatisation in the earlier 1990s, resulting in the costly liquidation of two key investments and abandonment of its banking operations (Whitford 1993). Following privatisation, Čedok, the former Czechoslovak state tourist agency, had to compete with domestic travel companies, as well as with well-known foreign tour operators such as Fischer Reisen, American Express Travel Service and Thomas Cook; with the latter two able to secure prime office locations in Prague's Wenceslas Square.

Multilateral aid from the major Western institutions has provided an important source of support for infrastructure projects and the encouragement of inward investment. During the four years 1990–1993, international assistance totalled $12.5 billion to CEE and $3.3 billion to the FSU. But with a number of different agencies involved– World Bank, International Monetary Fund (IMF), European Bank for Reconstruction and Development (EBRD) and European Investment Bank (EIB), amongst others—the distribution has been very uneven and the criteria for disbursements are not always obvious. For example, per capita figures for receipt of EBRD financing in 1992–1995 (Table 15.8) range from ECU 17.1 million in Albania to ECU 166.8 million in Slovenia, with Poland (21.2), Romania (25.1), Croatia (41.1), Slovakia (66.9) and Hungary (103.9) representing different positions within those extremes. Further disparities are evident in the sources and distribution of private investment, reckoned at $18 billion for 1990–1993. Hungary, with $7 billion, received approximately $700 per capita; by contrast, only $800 million was invested in Romania, representing just $35 per head (Hall 1995).

Such attractions for Western investors as access to trained labour, relatively low wages, minimum regulatory powers and encouragement from official agencies are very variable across the region. The best trained labour and most sophisticated markets are in Central Europe, where there is often intense competition for qualified labour. Regulatory controls may be least effective in the Balkans and the CIS, where lower levels of disposable income, economic and infrastructural development, and continuing political uncertainty have not inspired confidence in potential investors and visitors.

Table 15.8 CEE: European Bank for Reconstruction and Development financing, 1992–1995

	1995			1992–5			
	Total (ECU millions)	Percentage of regional disbursement	Level per capita (ECU)	Total (ECU millions)	Percentage of regional disbursement	Level per capita (ECU)	Rank for credit risk[1]
Albania	10	0.4	2.9	58	0.7	17.1	–
Bulgaria	66	2.3	7.4	192	2.4	21.5	11
Croatia	95	3.3	21.1	185	2.4	41.1	8
Czech Republic	100	3.5	9.7	452	5.8	43.9	2
FYROM	45	1.6	23.7	120	1.5	63.2	–
Hungary	406	14.2	39.7	1,063	13.5	103.9	5
Poland	107	3.7	2.8	818	10.4	21.2	3
Romania	139	4.9	6.0	582	7.4	25.1	7
Slovakia	7	2.5	13.1	361	4.6	66.9	4
Slovenia	61	2.1	30.7	332	4.2	166.8	1
Total (including FSU)	2,857			7,854			

Sources: Business Europa (1996, **18**, p. 41); author's additional calculations.

[1] Investmentbank Austria's ranking (including FSU) based on economic and political reform, stability and growth: 1 = minimum credit risk.

However, responding to low labour costs, relatively low capital investments and potentially large, unfulfilled markets, the North American fast food and soft drinks industry has targeted the Black Sea countries for rapid expansion. Pizza Hut (a Pepsico subsidiary) opened the first of 15 restaurants in Bulgaria in 1994. Coca-Cola built bottling plants in several Romanian cities, and McDonald's opened its first restaurant in the country in 1995, with plans for no less than 85 in Ukraine by the end of 1999.

Transport and communications have attracted most tourism-related foreign investment in the region, after accommodation (Hall 1993d). That most tourist and transit traffic employs road transport—for example, in 1994, 95 per cent of Hungary's international visitors entered the country by road—has been a major stimulus to foreign investment in upgrading and extending the region's highway system. Hungary and Poland have tendered contracts to domestic and foreign interests for the construction and operation of motorways, on which tolls will be collected to reimburse the contractors. The Czech Republic decided against taking this approach, and is financing motorway construction from the state budget, with a high level of involvement of Czech companies.

Reflecting the need for better and more flexible access to and within the region, several new civil airports have come into operation in the 1990s, often on the sites of previous military operations, such as that in Debrecen, a former Soviet base and now Hungary's second airport. The privatisation of some of the region's airlines (Hall 1993c; Symons 1993) has seen different approaches to partnerships and structural questions, including the purchase or lease of Western aircraft, route rationalisation, internal restructuring and the refashioning of images. When Alitalia took a 30 per cent stake in the privatised Hungarian flag carrier MALÉV, the latter held on to some of its fuel-inefficient Russian-built Tupolevs specifically for charter purposes. Poland's LOT, however, aimed to eliminate all Russian-built aircraft before it was put on the market. In the meantime, such subsidiary services as in-flight catering, duty-free shops and ticketing were franchised out, and a strategic alliance with American Airlines was established. In addition to inward investment and stakeholdings in existing companies, a number of new operators have been established by indigenous entrepreneurs, such as DAC-Air in Romania (Wright 1996), the fortunes of which will be viewed as an interesting barometer of entrepreneurial sustainability in south-eastern Europe.

15.6   Conclusions: trends and challenges

Likely trends and potential challenges within the region present a number of notable paradoxes.

15.6.1   Tourism as an instrument for economic development and conservation

Moving away from the 'shock therapy' phase, Central European countries have been reappraising their tourism strategies. Hungary, Poland and Slovenia have repositioned their marketing and image projection (see Sections 15.2.2 and 15.2.3) to encourage higher-spending season-extending tourists rather than increased numbers. In Slovakia, the tourism industry is seen as an important vehicle for regional development, and has been identified as one of five priority sectors for the encouragement of foreign investment.

Local and regional instability continue to constrain tourism marketing efforts in the Balkans, although paradoxically, hard-pressed governments are likely to turn to tourism as a short cut to employment and income-generation. Both Serbia (Section 15.2.3) and Montenegro (Campbell 1996), currently receiving a significant proportion of international tourists from the politically and culturally sympathetic Bulgaria, Greece and Russia (see Table 15.6), have attempted to shrug off the effects of the wars of Yugoslav succession on international relations by appealing to the global travel industry, although such campaigns do not appear particularly impressive.

Inward investment in the tourism industry will continue to be focused on those countries whose economic and political circumstances are most favourable for entry into the EU, and this in its turn will reinforce their pre-eminence in the region's tourism and, ironically, will further improve access and stimulate increased numbers of low-spending excursionists. This will place increasing environmental pressures on particular urban social and built environments, their often vulnerable attractions and provision of services.

Under these circumstances, and in the context of developing post-modern consumer products, the tourism market for the region needs to become more specialised and niche-orientated but also better integrated with other economic sectors, so as to generate sustainable employment and minimise leakages (Harrison 1994). At present, the ideals of sustainability, in employing tourism income to support wildlife conservation and social and cultural development, often appear far removed from the reality of jostling and trampling tourist hordes in Prague Castle, Buda or Warsaw Old Town. However, the implementation and success of sustainability programmes requires a strategy framework which guides national tourism development in a balanced a coherent way, both in itself and in relation to other components of the national and regional economy.

Small-scale 'sustainable' projects may in the longer term distinguish at least part of CEE's approach and response to tourism's environmental, cultural and other pressures: most particularly in the Balkans and those areas of Central Europe thus far relatively untouched by urban-based excursionism. If the vulnerable natural and cultural environments of the weaker countries of the region can be protected and enhanced through the medium of sustainable rural and ecotourism, then important models will have been established.

15.6.2   *Mass tourism reinvigorated and an expanded tourism underclass*

Two factors confound any simplistic notion of a linear transformation in Europe from mass to niche tourism:

- A substantial growth of the 'tourism underclass' following the privatisation of tourism and travel facilities and loss of former subsidies.
- A resurgence of the mass tourism product cycle, enmeshing the citizens of CEE and helping to reinvigorate some Mediterranean resorts.

Indeed, we can envisage demand waves diffusing eastwards as access to disposable income and leisure time increases in the currently less affluent societies of the Balkans and former Soviet Union.

Until mass market destinations, which include the Black Sea and southern Adriatic coast resorts, develop substantial additional and complementary visitor attractions in their hinterlands (Bachvarov 1997), such resorts will need substantial physical refurbishment and some 'philosophical' reorientation if they are to respond to both continuing mass market requirements and changing global consumer demands.

15.6.3 *Heritage, identity and nationalism*

Tourism and heritage promotion have become important ingredients in national and regional restructuring strategies, including the attraction of inward investment. Yet questions of cultural and ecological sustainability, and the impacts of tourism employment on rural–urban, local–incomer, gender, household and other social relationships have barely begun to be addressed within the framework of such processes (see Delamont 1995). Furthermore, the rise of heritage tourism has also coincided with the resurgence of nationalisms in the region, disastrously so in the Balkans, posing some important questions about their interrelationships.

16 Tourism policies in a changing economic environment

Allan M. Williams and Gareth Shaw

16.1 Introduction: government, governance and tourism

There are a number of reasons why the state does not leave tourism to the actions and decision-making of individual tourism capitals. The most important of these is that individual capitals (tourism companies, financial groups, etc.) are not able to guarantee the conditions for the reproduction of the tourism industry. In addition, tourism has become a focus of state policy—at different levels—because of the opportunities it provides for the pursuit of wider economic goals, such as balancing the current account, employment generation, or improved place imaging. Moreover, with the growing involvement of the state in supporting tourism initiatives across Europe, a minimum level of support for private capital has become a pre-requisite simply to maintain 'a level playing field', and for allowing particular local or national capitals to compete in an increasingly competitive and globalised tourism market. In short, the state is a key agency in the regulation of tourism as a social system, which is understood as 'processes which mitigate contradictions, promote system reproduction and displace crises spatially or temporally' (Goodwin and Painter 1996, p. 638).

The economic logic of state intervention in tourism is reinforced by cultural and environmental considerations. Tourism is a system of global–local interrelationships with significant, and often negative, cultural and environmental consequences for localities. Even though these could, in the longer term, endanger the reproduction of the local tourism economy (with, for example, pollution and development destroying the very resources which attract tourists), the private sector operating in a locality may not be able to respond effectively to such challenges. This is critical in the debate on sustainable tourism and underlies the argument that there is a need for partnership and a holistic approach to address such issues (discussed later in this chapter, but see also Williams and Shaw 1996). The debates on sustainability are particularly apposite here as a reminder that the development and regulation of the tourism industry requires joint action by the principal agencies, and not only state intervention. This in turn leads us to consider the distinction between government and governance.

Governance emphasises that regulation is a continuous process of governing which is, above all, embedded in a wide set of practices (Painter and Goodwin 1995) and so is not subject to easy generalisation. This is an approach which argues against over-

Tourism and Economic Development: European Experiences, 3rd Edition. Edited by A.M. Williams and G. Shaw.
© 1998 John Wiley & Sons Ltd.

concentrating on the state, and the agencies of formally elected local political institutions, for governance is produced by combinations of corporate and non-corporate
institutions. The agents of governance are firms, management, employees, trade
unions, national, regional and local states and non-state institutions. Governance
mechanisms are systems of integration between firms, and of embeddedness beyond
firms. As such, the discourse on governance is influenced by wider debates on the
need to reformulate the traditional dichotomy between states and markets, and to
recognise the increasingly important role of other, often hybrid, forms of socio-
economic cooperation, most notably networks (see Grabher 1993).

How does tourism fit into this picture of governance? The governance agents in
tourism are essentially the same as in other sectors, but are characteristically fragmented
and small-scale. Governance mechanisms are relatively weak, with there being very
low levels of networking and embeddedness (see Chapter 1), poorly developed systems
of interest group representation (Greenwood 1993) and notoriously weak institutionalisation (Pridham 1996). There are exceptions, notably in the complex and
interlinked partnerships engaged in the management of Alpine Tourism (Williams and
Shaw 1996). However, mass tourism areas mostly have relatively weak forms of
governance; this is because tourism has often developed in countries with weak local
government, highly fragmented indigenous firms, and poorly developed workers'
representation. There also tend to be powerful tour companies exercising oligopsonistic powers while having little long-term commitment to any particular local tourism
system. These conditions apply to most Mediterranean tourism destinations, not least
because of the existence of autocratic regimes during the formative decades of tourism
development.

Governance regimes are not invariable in time or space. Instead they stem from the
social relations which are constituted in, and constitute, particular places (Massey
1984). Moreover, local processes influence international processes as well as being
regulated by these. For example, changes in international airline regulation can
influence local tourism economies, just as much as changes in local regulation (such as
a concerted attempt to reposition the place image of a city) can influence the role of
particular localities in world tourism. Such a perspective echoes the views of Held
(1995) on globalisation as a nexus of local–global interconnections.

This brief discussion of governance sets out a future agenda for research rather than
provides a detailed framework for this chapter, or a summary of the policy and
planning discussions presented in the country case studies in this volume. Research on
governance, in respect of tourism, is too little developed to allow such a discourse at
present. Instead, we focus attention on the role of the state, which is often the key
actor in tourism, given the weakness of other agents of governance. The discussion is
structured around three levels—the international (especially the EU), the national and
the local. While we concur with the view of Jessop (1995) that there has been a
'hollowing-out' of the national state to some extent, it remains an important level of
regulation along with the local and the international.

These different levels of the state are not autonomous. However, there are likely to
be different concerns at different scales: for example, the local will be more concerned
with a broader range of community needs, and with employment, environmental and
transport issues. In contrast, the national state will be concerned more with the
economic implications of tourism development for the current account and for its
macro-economic strategy. As Pearce (1981) emphasises, the objectives of the national
state are economic maximisation, including the current account, diversification of

the national economic base, increasing incomes, raising state revenues and creating new jobs.

In this chapter we review some of the issues in the governance of tourism in Europe, and focus the discussion around these three levels. In the final section, we consider one of the most pressing topics relating to governance and tourism, that is sustainability. A critical social perspective is provided on some of the wider social relationships that are often submerged by the emphasis on environmental issues. The current state of tourism research means that the discussion focuses more on government than governance.

16.2   The international regulatory framework for tourism

Tourism is a highly internationalised industry subject to globalisation tendencies, as is evident in respect of the media images which help shape the tourist gaze, and the growth of multinational tourism companies. While most tourism involves activities within national borders, and few tourists have the time and money to engage in a genuinely global scan of tourism destinations, globalisation processes are affecting even the most localised of tourism patterns. Not least, they shape the expectations of tourists, and intensify place competition.

The international regulatory framework for tourism is relatively light. In common with other services, it was largely excluded from the earlier rounds of GATT negotiations. Even the Uruguay round, which finally did encompass international trade in services, was more concerned with financial than consumer services. As a result, there is relatively little supranational regulation of tourism services, except in the air transport sector. The potentially most important supranational regulatory agents in European tourism have been multinational companies (notably hotels in the business tourism sector, and tour companies in the mass tourism sector), and the European Union (EU).

The EU has been a late convert to the need for Europe-wide tourism policies, and there was a gap of 25 years between the Treaty of Rome and the first attempt to draft a comprehensive European tourism policy. There were a number of reasons for this. First, the economic importance of tourism was little appreciated in the first two decades of its existence, when the EU agenda was driven by the aims of liberalising trade in industrial goods, and establishing a framework for agricultural expansion via the Common Agricultural Policy (Williams 1994, pp. 34–56). Second, even when there was greater recognition of the importance of tourism in the 1970s and early 1980s, attempts were made to subsume the industry within other policy initiatives, such as those for regional development, agricultural diversification and the environment; EU tourism policy, therefore, was weak and fragmented. Finally, there was national resistance to EU interventionism as tourism was considered to be a Member States competency; in other words, this was a subsidiarity issue.

1982 witnessed the first significant attempt to promote a specific EU strategy for tourism, when '. . . pressure from public opinion, particularly on the question of the environment, and from the European Parliament on the issue of the protection of Europe's cultural heritage . . . combined with a growing realisation of the scale of tourism's importance . . .' (Robinson, G. 1993, p. 13) led to the 'Initial guidelines on a Community Policy on Tourism'. The Commission of the European Communities (1982, p. 5) established that a basis for such a policy existed in Article 2 of the Treaty of Rome, which assigns to the European Community the task of promoting closer

Table 16.1   The European Community policy framework for tourism

---

(a) Freedom of movement and the protection of EC tourists
  (i)   Easing customs checks
  (ii)   Reduction of police checks at frontiers
  (iii) Social security provisions for tourists
  (iv)   Assistance for tourists and regulation of car insurance
  (v)   Protection of tourists' interests, e.g. in complaints about the shortcomings of tourist
         services

(b) Working conditions for those engaged in tourism
  (i)   Right of establishment and freedom to provide tourist services
  (ii)   Vocational training grants and mutual recognition of qualifications
  (iii) Aid from the European Social Fund
  (iv)   Promotion of staggered holidays
  (v)   Harmonisation of taxation
  (vi)   Promotion of energy efficiency

(c) Common Transport Policy and tourism

(d) Safeguarding the European heritage and tourism
  (i)   Environmental protection
  (ii)   Art heritage

(e) Regional development and tourism
  (i)   ERDF assistance
  (ii)   EAGGF assistance

Source: based on Commission of the European Communities (1985).

relations between the Member States. It was argued that tourism could contribute to this goal by increasing the level of personal contacts amongst the citizens of the Member States, directly providing jobs for 4 million people, and contributing to the development of the poorest regions of the Community. A further measure of the importance of tourism to the Community was the large number of Community policies which, directly or indirectly, had a bearing on the industry. These range from the free movement of persons and the freedom to provide tourist services, to regional development and the protection of the environment.

Five main areas of interest were identified which reflected the Community's broader concerns with internal trade liberalisation and with evolving common policies: freedom of movement of tourists, working conditions in the industry, the impact on transport policy, safeguarding the European heritage, and regional development (see Table 16.1). These represented a combination of a 'wish list' of EU areas of intervention, and an acknowledgement of the areas of current involvement. It certainly could not be claimed that there was a coherent and specifically *tourism* policy in any of these five areas at that time.

In the 1980s and the 1990s, the debate about European tourism policy has become entwined with discussions over the Single Market and the Treaty on European Union. One of the landmarks in this period was the European Tourism Year 1990; although a minuscule programme costing no more than 5 million ECU and achieving a very low level of public awareness (Williams and Shaw 1994, p. 315), it raised the profile of tourism at the European policy-making level (Robinson, G. 1993, pp. 15–16). One tangible effect was the 1991 Action Plan for Tourism, which funded a number of

Table 16.2   The 1991 European Community Action Plan for Tourism

Objectives
- Development of the tourism industry, with a specific emphasis on small and medium-sized businesses
- Improvement of the quality of services supplied by the tourism industry
- Improvement of the competitiveness of the tourism industry at the world level
- Safeguarding the quality of the natural environment, of the cultural heritage and the cultures and traditions of the host population
- Improvement of the (economic) protection of tourists

Summary of actions
1. Improving knowledge of the tourist industry and ensuring greater consistency of community measures
2. Staggering of holidays
3. Transnational measures
4. Tourists as consumers
5. Cultural tourism
6. Tourism and the environment
7. Rural tourism
8. Social tourism
9. Youth tourism
10. Training
11. Promotion in third countries

Source: Commission of the European Communities (1994a).

distinctive tourism initiatives in respect of quality improvements, promoting European tourism to the rest of the world, and policy coordination (see Table 16.2); these initiatives were based on public–private co-funding and constructing international partnerships. The programme yielded few concrete results.

The attempts to reposition tourism in the EU policy framework led to its recognition as a separate entity in the Treaty on European Union, 1992. This ensured continuing activity in the fields of environmental and consumer protection as well as new activities in the areas of education, training, culture and transport. More significantly, Declaration 1 of Article 3 of the Treaty opened the possibility of tourism having its own 'title', allowing the EU to enact specific tourism decrees and acts. This was subject to a consultative Green Paper in 1995, setting out alternative strategies for EU involvement and non-involvement. This was one of the subsidiarity issues which featured at the 1996–1997 intergovernmental conference. Given the difficulties in reaching agreement on even major economic and political issues, not surprisingly tourism failed to obtain its own title.

Irrespective of the lack of a significant revision of the Treaty on European Union in respect of tourism, the EU continues to intervene in the industry through policy initiatives initiated under its other titles. Of the five categories of intervention identified in the 1980s, there has been some progress in respect of freedom of movement (under the Single Market programme and the Schengen agreement) and protection of EU tourists. Working conditions have partly been addressed through some small-firm and training measures. Transport remains the least developed of all the common policy areas, although there has been some progress in respect of liberalising air travel, and there are ambitious plans for a genuinely pan-European transport infrastructure, although this has been stalled by recurrent funding crises. As a result, the European Regional Development Fund (ERDF) and the environment have been the most important areas of common policy impacting upon tourism (Williams and Shaw 1994; Wanhill 1996).

The ERDF has two broad tourism objectives: the use of tourism as an instrument of regional economic development, and diversification to assist those regions which are excessively dependent on tourism or suffer from acute seasonality effects. Tourism has come to occupy an increasingly important role within the ERDF. Between 1975 and 1984 it accounted for only 1.4 per cent of all ERDF expenditure (Pearce 1988) but by 1989–1993 this had risen to 5.5 per cent of all expenditure in Objective 1 regions, 7.5 per cent in Objective 2 regions and 6.8 per cent in Objective 5b regions. A comparison of actual expenditure on tourism projects 1975–1988 (Pearce 1992a) and of planned expenditure within the Community Support Framework 1989–1993 (Wanhill 1996) demonstrates both the increased importance of tourism and changes in the geography of regional aid. Tourism has become particularly important in ERDF programmes in Southern Europe and in the UK.

Tourism is also an important field of activity in respect of environmental initiatives. The Fifth Environmental Action Programme (EAP) states that environmental policy should be based on sustainable development, and recognises tourism as one of its five target sectors (Flemming 1992). The Fifth EAP has seven themes and targets, all of which apply to tourism: climate protection, acidification, nature conservation and protection of biodiversity, water resources management, urban environment, coastal areas and water management. It also identified seven new types of policy instruments: better data, scientific research and technological development, sectoral and spatial planning, economic instruments, information, education and training, and financial support. Again, these all apply to tourism. While there is recognition that the main EU financial support mechanisms for environmental actions are the structural policies and the Cohesion Fund, there is also a separate Community Financial Instrument for the Environment (LIFE).

The environmental programmes have had positive implications for sustainable tourism, as is exemplified by the introduction of the Blue Flag scheme and the funding of sustainability projects within the LIFE programme. However, other common policies, such as the European Regional Development Fund, may have outflanked the Fifth EAP, encouraging tourism developments, and developments which affect tourism, that are not in accord with sustainability principles. The Commission itself has recognised that '. . . the objectives of the Fifth Programme and the measures and the instruments have not yet been implemented thoroughly or on time' (Commission of the European Communities 1996). The 1996 review of the Fifth EAP also set out a number of priority actions in respect of tourism (Table 16.3).

16.3   Tourism and the state

There has been some 'hollowing-out' of the nation state (Jessop 1995) and this has involved a shift in power upwards (especially to the EU), downwards to the local and regional levels, and outwards to organisations in civil society; together these constitute the agents of governance. However, as Anderson (1995) emphasises, pronouncements on the death of the nation state are premature. Hudson (1997, p. 3) argues that:

Table 16.3   EU Review of the Fifth Environmental Action Programme, with respect to tourism

The following priority actions are needed:

A: Integration
- Public authorities in Member States should work together to integrate environmental considerations into their tourism policy at the most appropriate level
- Public authorities in the Member States need to develop integrated land-use planning at local or regional level
- Public authorities in the Member States need to implement stricter control measures on land-use
- At EU level approaches to sustainable development in the tourism sector need to be strengthened, building on suggestions in the Green Paper on Tourism and using principal instruments such as the Structural and Cohesion Funds, to support member States in their efforts to protect the quality of the environment, to change attitudes and approaches and to promote sustainable development

B: Protection of sensitive areas
- Member States need to develop frameworks for the protection of the environment particularly in sensitive areas such as the Mediterranean, the Baltic, the Alps and coastal zones

C: Information to tourists
- Public authorities in the Member States and the tourist industry should make available to the public better information on the state of the environment in order to enable public pressure to act as a driver towards sustainable tourism; the success of the Blue Flag initiative demonstrates the importance of the public's role

D: Management of tourist flow
- Public authorities in Member States and the tourist industry need to examine the carrying capacity of tourist sites and take appropriate measures to manage tourist flows to the lasting benefit of the sector and the environment. The LIFE programme can be used to demonstrate the benefits of more sustainable approaches

Source: Commission of the European Communities (1996).

Nation states remain key sites of power in mediating the relations between processes of globalisation and territorial patterns of socio-economic relationships within national spaces although decentralisation of state power to local and regional levels has altered the forms of this mediation. While there are reciprocal relationships between changes at local and regional and global scales, the impacts of globalisation have been deeply uneven, both between and within national territories.

The particular reasons for state intervention in the regulation of tourism have already been dealt with in the introduction to this chapter. Above all, the private sector cannot guarantee the reproduction of the tourism industry, due to its inability to bridge the gap between individual capitals' short-term interests and the requirements for investments in common goods (particularly infrastructure) which are not in themselves profitable, and for restraint from particular activities which may damage the tourism industry (and other sections of society) as a whole. Tourism also plays a potentially important role in macro-economic policy, especially in contributing to the current account, and in legitimisation. In Spain, for example, the surplus on the balance of travel account helped finance a visible trade deficit and to fund imports of capital and intermediate goods for the modernisation of manufacturing in the 1960s and the 1970s. Since the 1970s, weaker and more volatile economic growth, combined with persistent structural unemployment, have led to increased state interest in tourism as one of the few sectors with consistent employment generating potential.

There has been a long history of collective or social investment by the state to underpin the activities of individual tourism capitals. The examples extend from early municipal investments in piers, promenades and public gardens in British and French coastal resorts in the nineteenth and early twentieth century, through the construction of airports, such as that on Madeira to open up the island to international tourism in the 1960s, to public investment to facilitate such mega events as the Barcelona Olympics or the Millennium Exhibition at Greenwich. In general, the level of state intervention has intensified over time, especially in the post-World War II period.

There have been three distinct phases in the evolution of state tourism policies since 1945 (OECD 1974, p. 3). In the late 1940s and 1950s, '. . . there was a need to dismantle and streamline the many police, currency, health and customs regulations which were the legacy of a war and immediate post-war situation'. In the 1950s the emphasis shifted to promotion as governments became 'aware of the "dollar gap" and hence the need to increase their earning of both dollars and any other hard currency'. Latterly governments have become concerned about the problems of tourism supply and with the link between this and regional development. By the 1970s and early 1980s, broader social and environmental issues had become major interventionist issues, at least in northern Europe.

While there has been a broadening of concern about tourism policies, at the state level they continue to be dominated by economic objectives (Table 16.4). A survey of staff in European tourism organisations revealed that two of the four top-rated policy objectives were to increase the numbers of and expenditures by foreign tourists. Most of the other highly-ranked objectives also related to economic goals such as employment creation, and increasing the size of the industry. These broad objectives are reflected in the relative importance attached to particular policy instruments, with provision of information via international offices being first-ranked, and destination and joint marketing occupying two of the other four top positions. Marketing tends to be the principal role of the national tourism organisations, although tourism is also supported by other sections of national governments concerned, for example, with transport, land use planning, heritage, and education and training. In keeping with the recent political emphasis on rolling back the frontiers of the state, only limited direct state support, in the forms of grants or loans, is available to individual private tourism capitals. In general, national tourism policies are most important in those countries where a relatively large proportion of GDP is accounted for by tourism and where governments have or had an interventionist rather than 'laissez-faire' approach to economic policy; this is reflected in the higher profile of tourism policies in Greece or Portugal than in, say, the UK (Akehurst *et al.* 1993).

By the 1980s, tourism had shed its 'Cinderella' status in the field of economic policy in most European countries, and had moved towards the centre stage in discussions about economic regeneration and international competitiveness. Nevertheless, tourism has achieved a far lower profile in national economic policies than have most other economic sectors. There are a number of reasons for this, including the general neglect of the service sector, and continuing strong growth in tourism, which has belied the need for an effective national strategy. Moreover, the institutional setting for tourism policy has been particularly weak due to fragmentation in

Table 16.4   National tourism policies

Ranking of policy objectives (max. value = 5)		Ranking of policy instruments (max. value = 5)	
Increase foreign expenditure	4.7	Provision of information via international office	3.8
Improve product quality	4.2	Destination marketing	3.6
Reduce seasonality	4.0	Research planning	3.4
Increase number of foreign visits	3.8	Joint marketing	3.3
Redistribute tourism	3.6	Provide printed information to foreign visitors	3.3
Increase industry size	3.5	Environmental improvement	3.1
Create employment	3.3	Training and employment policies	2.5
Provide expert advice	3.2	Disseminating good practice	2.5
Encourage joint initiatives	3.2	Provide printed information to domestic tourists	2.2
Improve training and professionalism	3.2	Capital grants to tourism enterprises	1.9
Promote environmental tourism	3.1	Regulating enterprises	1.7
Increase domestic expenditure	2.4	Development of tourism facilities	1.6
Regulate industry	2.0	Provision of information through local offices	1.5
Increase numbers of domestic tourists	1.8	Subsidies to tourism enterprises	1.2
Assist restructuring	1.7	Provision of soft loans	0.8
Diversification of tourism	1.5		

Source: Akehurst *et al.* (1993, pp. 40, 42).

Note: Scores based on ratings given by staff of national tourism organisations.

the industry and weak interest group representation (Pridham 1996), so that tourism is ill-equipped to compete effectively against other sectors in the contest for state resources.

In addition, there are the general constraints on the role of the state in western European models of social democracy, and the fiscal crises of the states in central and eastern Europe. During the 1990s, the capacity of the state to intervene on behalf of *any* economic sector has been constrained by the rolling back of 'the frontiers of the state', due to both an ideological onslaught from the neo-liberal right and the dictates of international competition and macro-economic strategies (focused on interest rate reductions and public sector borrowing reductions, particularly in the qualifying period for the single currency). This has meant that, in many parts of Europe, the state has tended to withdraw from active intervention in tourism, as is evident, for example, in the proposed sales of *paradores* in Spain, the privatisation of public transport in many countries, and the scaling back of (national) regional policy. As a result, state intervention in tourism has largely been limited to indicative planning, reinforced by negative land use and building controls. While the state may indicate goals, and can invest in public transport and other means to facilitate particular tourism programmes, ultimately the implementation of tourism programmes depends on individual capitals which often have diverse and conflicting goals.

Not all states have the same interest in tourism, for this depends on the capacity for developing tourism, the form of governance, the current state of the industry and the dictates of wider economic considerations such as the need to create jobs in response to recession, or to particular crises in other economic sectors. With respect to the capacity for developing tourism, Wolfson (1964) recognised four main types of countries where tourism:

- Is limited and is likely to remain so.
- Has limited possibilities of being developed.
- Exists and, with proper handling, could become an important component in the national economy.
- Is highly advanced, and the problem is how to maintain the industry.

Wolfson's classification appears dated, at least when applied to Europe, for there are no countries where it would now be predicted that tourism 'is limited and likely to remain so'. Even the most obvious candidates, such as Albania and some of the new states of the former Yugoslavia, are likely to develop significant tourism industries in future, if minimum conditions of political stability can be assured (see Chapter 15). There are also no countries where it could categorically be stated that tourism 'has limited possibilities of being developed'; given the social construction of the tourism gaze (Urry 1990), there is potential for all countries, and perhaps all localities, to become objects of tourism interest. A more useful classification, therefore, would be based on the product cycle, that is between tourism destinations which are in the mature stage and are seeking to restructure in the face of changing conditions of production and consumption, and destinations which are at various stages of development from the early (Albania) to the rapidly expanding and incipient mass tourism of, say, the Aegean and Mediterranean regions of Turkey.

In the regulationist perspective, the state plays a key role in ensuring that production and consumption remain in balance, and there are a number of approaches which can be adopted. Some are broader instruments of state management: examples include macro-economic policies such as income policies, welfare benefits and taxation, and the general regulatory framework for the environment. Others are specific to tourism, such as health and food-hygiene inspections of hotel restaurants, or investment in airports. Here we consider two particular ways in which the state intervenes to support tourism: via marketing, and via state investment/ownership interests in the tourism product.

The promotion of tourism is favoured by virtually every national tourist board. One of the first such ventures was the establishment of the Travel Organisation of Great Britain and Northern Ireland in the 1920s, which was responsible for attracting foreign visitors to the UK. There has been a rapid expansion in the number of tourist boards subsequently and, according to Ascher (1983), more than 170 governments worldwide had foreign travel promotion offices by the early 1980s. There are two main types of promotional strategies, and most authorities tend to adopt these in parallel: encouraging foreign tourism and encouraging nationals to take their holidays in their home countries. While in both cases the early emphasis was on quantitative targets, increasing attention is being given to more refined targets relating to seasonality, expenditure and (sustainable) activity patterns. Marketing strategies are particularly prone to contentious issues of territoriality. For example, the British Tourist Authority is often criticised for over-promoting London to the detriment of other regions. There are clearly difficult issues here of how to reconcile the needs of individual regions with those of the country as a whole, given that country images are usually an amalgam of a small number of place images, with London having a very strong global presence. More generally, this serves to re-emphasise Held's (1995) view of the interdependence between the global and the local.

There are a number of ways in which states may seek to redirect nationals from foreign to domestic tourism destination. The most obvious is to impose restrictions on foreign travel, and this operated widely in Central and Eastern Europe prior to 1989 (Chapter 15). More subtle restrictions were sometimes employed in western Europe, such as exchange controls; for example, limits on the amount of foreign exchange which nationals could take abroad were in operation in the UK in 1966–1970 and in France in 1983. Alternatively the state may seek to promote the attractions of domestic tourism; examples include Belgium's 'Vacances au pays' and Finland's 'Ski cheaply' campaigns (OECD 1986). These tend to emphasise the natural and cultural heritage of the 'undiscovered country' near to home (see also Chapter 14 for the example of The Netherlands). Domestic tourism can also be assisted through social tourism programmes which aim to assist economically disadvantaged groups to take holidays. Such assistance, which may be provided by the state or by voluntary bodies, can involve either social grants (which, being relatively small, will probably be spent on domestic tourism) or provision of free or subsidised accommodation or holiday packages (Chapter 2).

The state may also support the production of tourism services through its investment programmes, either through ownership of tourism attractions or, more indirectly, via provision of infrastructure such as roads, airports and waste treatment and disposal. In this guise, the state frequently acts to fill gaps in market provision and, in effect, the state socialises part of the costs of production; this represents devalorisation of capital (Damette 1980) in support of individual tourism capitals. Such state intervention can involve ownership—usually in the case of heritage features, and occasionally for accommodation as in the case of the Portuguese state-owned luxury hotel chain, the *pousadas*. Alternatively, the state may provide financial subsidies to individual capitals. Examples include the now defunct Section 4 grants offered by the English Tourist Board, or the funding available from Greece's Organisation for the Financing of Economic Development. Support for tourism may also be integrated into wider regional development strategies; for example, Italy's Cassa per il Mezzogiorno spent 7–10 per cent of its budget on tourism in the 1960s (White 1976).

State infrastructural investment is often critical in opening-up localities to tourism. Malaga and Faro airports, in the Costa del Sol and the Algarve, respectively, provide classic examples of such investments in the 1960s. Prior to these investments, international tourists to these areas faced long road journeys from the airports at Seville and Lisbon, which clearly inhibited the development of mass tourism. The state also has a critical role to play in respect of ensuring the delivery of a wide range of other infrastructures, such as roads, electricity and water. With the tendency for tourism development to become more capital-intensive, requiring the construction of marinas, airports, theme parks, leisure pools, etc., there has been growing pressure on the state to intervene to support the industry.

Support for state intervention has, however, been weakened by the tide of neo-liberalism which has swept across Europe since the 1980s. While this is most obviously seen in the transition process in Central and Eastern Europe (see Chapter 15), it is also evident in, for example, the Spanish government's declared intention of privatising part of the state-owned chain of hotels, the *paradores*. However, even where privatisation has rolled back the frontier of the state in areas of utility provision, such as water and energy, it tends to retain an overall regulatory function.

Finally, the state also supports tourism through its regulatory functions; particular cultural and natural heritage sites may be protected by special designations (such as national monuments or national parks) against the actions of individual capitals and tourists. This raises issues related to sustainability, a theme that is considered in the final section of this chapter.

16.4   Tourism and local economic development

The key question for tourism strategies at the local level is how to realise the local ambition to 'pin-down' global processes so that these provide the basis for self-sustaining growth. This is not a passive relationship, for localities are not simply at the mercy of multinational companies which seek to mobilise local resources so as to enhance their competitiveness. Instead, localities can—and increasingly do—play an active role in shaping their own economic trajectories, and therefore contribute to national and global trends.

The precise form of intervention depends on the structure of local governance. Goodwin and Painter (1996, p. 635), commenting specifically on the UK, provide useful guidance on this, stating that:

> The former fairly uniform system of local government has been transformed into a more complex one of local governance, involving agencies drawn from the public, private and voluntary sectors. . . . But behind the alliterative phrase 'from government to governance' lies a series of crucial transformations in the social, political economic and cultural relations which operate in and around the local state.

In the case of tourism, the wider social networks of governance are often poorly developed, which echoes Pridham's (1996) argument that tourism has weak institutional representation. This means that tourism-dominated economies tend to lack 'institutional thickness', which Amin and Thrift (1994) consider to be the key to sustained local economic growth. Institutional thickness is dependent on four factors: strong institutional presence, high levels of interactions amongst the institutions in an area, collective representation by many bodies, and mutual awareness of a common purpose. This thickness '. . . establishes legitimacy and nourishes relations of trust. It is a "thickness" which continues to stimulate entrepreneurship and consolidate the local embeddedness of industry' (p. 15). They contend that institutional thickness produces six outcomes:

> The first is institutional persistence, that is local institutions are reproduced. The second outcome is the construction and deepening of an archive of commonly held knowledge of both the formal and tacit kinds. The third outcome is institutional flexibility, which is the ability of organisations in a region to both learn and change. The fourth outcome is high innovative capacity, which is not just specific to individual organisations, but is the most common property of a region. The fifth outcome is the ability to extend trust and reciprocity. Finally, and least common of all, is the consolidation of a sense of inclusiveness, that is, a widely held common project which serves to mobilise the regions with speed and efficiency (p. 15).

The examples they give of localities with strong institutional thickness are areas such as the City of London and Silicon Valley. In contrast, it is difficult to conceive of most tourism-dominated areas having a strong institutional thickness. However, tourism in some localities, particularly urban areas, may contribute to institutional thickness.

Many of the reasons for the increased interest in tourism development have already been dealt with earlier in this chapter. Essentially there are three interlinked processes: the substitution of local for central government initiatives in response to the scaling down of (nationally organised) regional policies; the need to generate jobs in response to deindustrialisation; and the potential for exploiting the economic value of place differences in response to the growth of new forms of tourism consumption. In addition, tourism may be prioritised at the local and regional level because of the rapidity with which economic growth can be generated, even—or especially—in previously virtually undeveloped regions, such as southern Tenerife or particular Greek Islands. Even mass tourism only requires minimalist provision—an airport, beach and accommodation will suffice, for other facilities will follow in due course. New tourism developments are not the only concern of local governance. There has also been increasing interest in the restructuring of tourism areas which are in the late stages of the tourism resort cycle (Butler 1980) because, as Agarwal (1994) argues, in the current political and economic climate passive acceptance of decline is not possible.

Local tourism development strategies have become commonplace throughout Europe's rural and urban spaces. For example, although the EU's LEADER programme was introduced to facilitate integrated local rural development strategies rather than specifically to promote tourism, this was a leading sector in 71 of the first 271 local programmes (Cavaco 1995, pp. 145–6). Amongst the measures financed by the programme were training, capital grants and advisory services for accommodation and handicrafts ventures, as well as increasing the value added of farm produce.

Tourism has also become a mainstay of many urban development strategies, which have sought to capitalise on the transport links, the existing accommodation and commercial facilities, and the cultural resources of cities (see Chapters 9, 11 and 13). One very specific form of urban tourism promotion is the hosting of mega events. Carreras i Verdaguer (1995, p. 196) writes that, 'The end objective of the organisation of such mega-events is to reinforce local economic activities; so as to mark the position of each locality on the world map, in order to attract foreign capital, foreign investors and foreign visitors'. There are many different types of mega events, including sporting events, notably the Olympics and football's World Cup, and world trade fairs. Europe has hosted a disproportionate share of these world events. At the other end of the scale, there are far more modest strategies to develop tourism as part of local economic strategies in most European cities (Law 1994).

Given that many tourism strategies were established to fill the vacuum caused by the withdrawal of the central state from some forms of economic interventionism, and the geographical diffusion of structural unemployment in Europe, they have largely been informed by economic dictates and have paid scant attention to environmental and cultural issues. The UN's Agenda 21, to which most European states ascribe, seeks to place environmental issues at the forefront of local development strategies, but it is too early as yet to evaluate its effectiveness. The next section addresses some of the wider issues of sustainable tourism.

16.5   Tourism and sustainability

The literature on sustainability is sufficiently well developed to require no more than a brief introduction here (see Becker 1995; Bramwell *et al.* 1996). The Brundtland Report is widely credited as being the catalyst for advancing the debate about sustainability, and provides the classic definition of sustainable development as '. . . development that meets the needs of the present without compromising the ability of future generations to meet their own needs'. Sustainable development is based on four key principles (see Williams and Shaw 1996, p. 50):

Table 16.5   Beyond the Green Horizon: principles for sustainable tourism

- *Using resources sustainably.* The conservation and sustainable use of resources—natural, social and cultural—is crucial and makes long-term business sense
- *Reducing over-consumption and waste.* Reduction of over-consumption and waste avoids the costs of restoring long-term environmental damage and contributes to the quality of tourism
- *Maintaining diversity.* Maintaining and promoting natural, social and cultural diversity is essential for long-term sustainable tourism, and creates a resilient base for the industry
- *Ensuring equity*—both within and between generations
- *Integrating tourism into planning.* Tourism development which is integrated into a national and local strategic planning framework, and which undertakes environmental impact assessments, increases the long-term viability of tourism
- *Supporting local economies.* Tourism that supports a wide range of local economic activities and which takes environmental costs and values into account, both protects those economies and avoids damage to the environment
- *Involving local communities.* The full involvement of local communities in the tourism sector not only benefits them and the environment in general but also improves the quality of the tourism experience
- *Consulting stakeholders and the public.* Consultation between the tourism industry and local communities, organisations and institutions is essential if they are to work alongside each other and resolve potential conflicts of interest
- *Training staff.* Staff training which integrates sustainable tourism into work practices, along with recruitment of local personnel at all levels, improves the quality of the tourism product
- *Marketing tourism responsibility.* Marketing that provides tourists with full and responsible information increases respect for the natural, social and cultural environments of destination areas and enhances customer satisfaction
- *Undertaking research.* On-going research and monitoring by the industry using effective data collection and analysis is essential to help solve problems and to bring benefits to destinations, the industry and consumers

Source: Tourism Concern/World Wildlife Fund (1992).

- Taking into account the true environmental costs of actions.
- Considering the effects of activities on future generation.
- Seeking to ensure greater equity.
- Consulting and empowering all stakeholders.

Echoing the Brundtland Report, Globe 90 defines sustainable tourism as '. . . meeting the needs of present tourists and hosts while protecting and enhancing opportunity for the future'. Tourism Concern/World Wildlife Fund sets out a number of principles for sustainable tourism (Table 16.5) which, it is stressed, should be embraced by all the leading stakeholders in tourism.

There has been an absence of social theory from the debates concerning sustainable development and societal management of the environment, with a few exceptions (Redclift and Benton 1994; Taylor 1995). In particular, there has been a failure to link the debates on sustainability with those on economic restructuring, especially the application of regulation theory to analysing the causes and consequences of the shift from Fordism to what remain contested interpretations of post-Fordism. Gibbs (1996, p. 1) emphasises that '. . . research into economic restructuring has effectively proceeded in parallel with environmental research.'

The reasons for this parallelism are the very different roots of the literatures on sustainability and restructuring. Sustainability is based on advocacy and prescription and is forward-looking. It is a knot of ethics, new organisational ideas and implicit welfare economics (de Kadt 1992), and is strong on morality whilst weak on theory. Notwithstanding this, there have been attempts to provide a framework for sustainable tourism (see de Kadt 1992), but most of this literature focuses on the design and implementation of policy initiatives and case studies of particular projects which provide benchmarks of good practice (Williams and Shaw 1996). In part, this is symptomatic of the effective ghettoisation of tourism as an academic discipline (Shaw and Williams 1994, Chapter 1), so that tourism research has become detached from wider theoretical discourses on, for example, the changing nature of production and governance.

Social considerations have often been overlooked in the wider debates about environmental management, and Hudson (1995, p. 49) argues that there are '. . . grave dangers in examining possible changes to more ecologically sustainable forms of production without full consideration of either the social conditions that this presupposes or the implications for economic and social sustainability'. Wiessman (1994, p. 2) also argues that sustainability '. . . has no meaning in conceptual terms unless it is associated with a definable reference quantity . . . defined in terms of scales of values'. Equity is one of these scales of values, and it involves inter- and intra-generational distributional issues. This is at least acknowledged in the literature on sustainable tourism (see Tourism Concern/World Wildlife Fund 1992). In practice, much of the socio-political debate on, and the practice of, sustainable tourism has focused on intergenerational equity. Not least, this is because of the political difficulties of advancing an agenda for intragenerational equity in the face of a rising tide of neo-liberal, economic and political ideology and practice in Europe.

One of the key questions in the debate about sustainability concerns whether the shift away from mass, to new forms of, tourism (Chapter 1) creates conditions which facilitate sustainable tourism. An initial assessment yields a positive response. Gibbs (1996, p. 5), summarises the relationship between mass production and the environment:

> Industrial mass production not only required mass purchasing power and hence a Fordist system of labour and remuneration, it also demanded massive supplies of raw material and energy from the global economy. The reification of social relations—where people relate to one another with money and commodities on the market—causes natural constraints on production and consumption to disappear from the consciousness of society.

It is not difficult to find parallels with the way that the environment has been perceived, valued and consumed in mass tourism, whether this be in the Alps or the Mediterranean regions. However, it is not possible to extend this argument in any simplistic way to conclude that the demise of mass tourism and its replacement by new forms of tourism will lead inevitably to sustainability, or even to less environmentally damaging forms of tourism activity. There are two major points to be stressed here: first, that the nature of mass tourism needs to be considered, and second, that many of the arguments concerning changing modes of production and consumption are necessarily oversimplified.

First, it can be argued that concentration in mass tourist resorts overwhelms local environmental systems and the capacities of local societies to manage these; as a result, mass tourism resorts can be seen to be the antithesis of sustainable tourism. On the other hand, it can be contested that greater spatial diffusion of tourism would generate more travel and would bring more local systems under threat, while also diluting the economies of scale available in mass tourism resorts in marshalling resources to deal with the environmental, if not the cultural, challenges of mass tourism. This emphasises the need to draw a distinction between the presence of massive numbers of tourists in particular regions and their concentration in mass resorts. Mass tourism has very different environmental implications according to how it is implanted within regions, and the contingencies of space and place.

Secondly, arguments about shifts in the modes of production and consumption of tourism have tended to be oversimplified (see Chapter 1). Mass tourism co-existed with more individualised forms of tourism even in the 1960s and 1970s; in many, and perhaps most, European regions it was not the dominant form of tourism, even if there was spectacular expansion of the Mediterranean mass product. The supposed shift away from mass tourism in the late twentieth century has also been exaggerated, not least because of the focus on short-term fluctuations in demand, particularly in Spain in the early 1990s (Marchena Gómez and Rebollo 1995). Despite the much-vaunted decline of mass tourism, there is at best only evidence of decline *relative* to other forms of tourism. Moreover, the prediction of the early death of mass tourism is based on analyses of northern European markets, and ignores the potential for the growth of mass tourism within the domestic markets of southern Europe, and especially within Central and Eastern Europe (Hall 1995).

The implications of the growing demand for more individualised, flexible and higher-quality tourism may also have been misinterpreted. Not least, there are signs that mass tourism and mass tourism resorts may be able to adapt to such demands by offering greater flexibility within what remains essentially a mass product. This may be facilitated by increased self-provisioning and more individualisation as a result of offering the consumer greater choice in designing his/her holiday package; the latter may be supported by the increased range of choices that can be offered to customers through the use of increasingly sophisticated IT systems in travel agencies, tour operators and hotels. In summary, then, the links between forms of tourism production and sustainability, and many of the wider social relationships inherent in the notion of sustainable tourism, remain areas for investigation.

16.6   Tourism and development: an uneasy relationship

This volume has reviewed a wide range of patterns, processes and practices in European tourism, with a view to disentangling some of the relationships between this sector and economic development. The conclusion, inevitably, is that tourism is not necessarily either a blessing or a blight for this is very much a matter of contingencies. Whether tourism brings net economic benefits or disadvantages to an area depends on the precise form and scale of the tourism demand, the structure of the local economy (including issues of embeddedness) and the nature of governance. Following Held's view (1995), we conclude that the relationship of tourism to development is shaped by the series of interconnections between the global and the local.

Perhaps the most important conclusion to emerge from the case studies in this book is that, as de Kadt (1979, p. 12) argues, '. . . tourism is not a unique devil'. There is a need to consider the impacts of tourism alongside those of other sectors, and to consider the opportunity costs involved. De Kadt (1979, p. 21) spells this out with respect to the need for tourism plans:

tourism projects are often developed without being tested within the framework of a sectoral plan, while their costs and benefits may not even be compared with those of alternative projects in the same sector. Most seriously, although the sectoral plan should establish the place of tourism within the development strategy for the whole economy, in many cases such a plan is non-existent or not decisively implemented.

A second major conclusion is that, in the context of a general internationalisation of tourism activities, there has been a shift in consumption which can be characterised in terms of reduced growth or even stagnation of mass tourism relative to the growth of new forms of tourism. This has meant not only that there is an increasingly complex map of tourism destinations, but that the economic benefits of tourism are more evenly spread. While there are important national and life-style variations to this broad shift, there seem to be two major locational implications: first, production of an increasingly diffuse map of economic impacts; which, second, is overlain by a *relative* shift of tourism destinations away from Europe's poorer and lesser developed regions.

This pattern is likely to be modified by three important developments in the near future. First, the polarisation of incomes in western Europe is likely to lead to disproportionate increases in demand from the more wealthy segments of society; this in turn will probably add to the relative stagnation of mass tourism and to the demand for new tourist activities and destinations both within and outside of Europe. Second, economic convergence within the EU is contributing to the growth of tourism markets in Southern Europe, and this may both reinforce domestic mass tourism destinations in the Mediterranean region, as well as generating new international tourism flows counter to the dominant north–south movements of the post-war period. And third, there is the growing presence of Central and Eastern Europe on the wider European tourism scene, as both a source of and destination for tourists (Hall 1995). This is starkly evident in the opening-up of new, competing destinations, particularly for urban tourism in cities such as Prague and Budapest, and for alpine activities in the Tatra Mountains. In addition, rising and polarising incomes in Central Europe may provide new sources of tourism demand which, at least in the medium-term, may reinforce the increasingly uncertain demand for mass tourism.

Whatever the long-term implications of these trends, it is clear that the European and world tourism industries are in a process of change. Further changes can be expected in consumption, in the industrial organisation of tourism (many sub-sectors remain little internationalised), and in the role of tourism in economic policies. Pressures to expand tourism for economic purposes will have to be counterbalanced by strategies to take into account growing concerns about the cultural and environmental impacts of many different forms of tourism. In the 1990s, possible 'solutions' have tended to focus on the concept of 'sustainable' tourism, but this in not free of contradictions, not least of which is the continuing need to reconcile the public benefits and costs of tourism with an economic sector which is overwhelmingly in fragmented private ownership. One of the key issues for the future is the creation of governance structures for tourism which embrace efficiency and equity interests. This poses major challenges, given the absence of effective global regulatory mechanisms, the weakening of the nation state, and the weak institutionalisation of tourism agents.

Bibliography

nd = undated.

AA.VV. (1993), *Los Caminos de Santiago y el Territorio*. Santiago: Xunta de Galicia.

AECIT (1996), *La Actividad Turística Española en 1994*. Madrid: AECIT.

Agarwal, S. (1994), 'The resort cycle revisited: implications for resorts', in C.P. Cooper and A. Lockwood (eds), *Progress in Tourism, Recreation and Hospitality Management*. Volume 5. Chichester: Wiley.

Agarwal, S.J. (1997), 'The public sector: planning for renewal', in G. Shaw and A. Williams (eds), *The Rise and Fall of British Coastal Resorts*. London: Mansell, pp. 137–158.

Airey, D. (1994), 'Education for tourism in Poland: the PHARE programme', *Tourism Management*, 15: 467–471.

Akehurst, G., Bland, N. and Nevin, M. (1993), 'Tourism policies in the European Community member states', *International Journal of Hospitality Management*, 12: 33–66.

Albturist (nd), *Folk Songs and Dances in Albania*. Tirana: 8 Nëntori.

Alcaide, A. (1984), 'La importancia de nuestra economía turística', *Situación*, 1984/1: 26–49.

Alejziak, W. (1996), 'Tourism and the crime rate in Poland', in G. Richards (ed.), *Tourism in Central and Eastern Europe: Educating for Quality*. Tilburg: Tilburg University Press, pp. 289–99.

Alexandrakis, N.E. (1973), *Tourism as a Leading Sector in Economic Development: a Case Study of Greece*. Ann Arbor, MI: University Microfilms.

Alpeninstitut für Umweltforschung und Entwicklungsplanung (1978), *Belastete Fremdenverkehrsgebiete*. Bonn: Der Bundesminister für Raumordnung, Bauwesen und Städtebau.

Amin, A. and Thrift, N. (1994), 'Living in the global', in A. Amin and N. Thrift (eds), *Globalization, Institutions and Regional Development in Europe*. Oxford: Oxford University Press.

Anderson, J. (1995), 'The exaggerated death of the nation state', in J. Anderson, C. Brook and A. Cochrane (eds), *A Global World*. Oxford: Oxford University Press, pp. 65–112.

Andersson, T. (1996), *En Modell för att Utvärdera Stora Idrottsevenemang med en Fallstudie av VM i Friidrott i Göteborg 1995*. Stockholm: Ministry of Social Affairs in Sweden.

Andronicou, A. (1979), 'Tourism in Cyprus', in E. de Kadt (ed.), *Tourism: Passport to Development?*. Oxford: Oxford University Press.

Anon (1996), 'The Czech Technology Park Brno', *Brno Business*, 4: 8–10.

Apostolopoulos, Y., Leivadi, S. and Yiannakis, A. (eds) (1996), *The Sociology of Tourism: Theoretical and Empirical Investigations*. London: Routledge.

Archer, B.H. (1977), *Tourism Multipliers: the State of the Art*. Cardiff: Occasional Papers in Economics II, University of Wales Press.

Archer, B.H. (1982), 'The value of multipliers and their policy implications', *Tourism Management*, 3: 236–241.

Ascher, B. (1983), 'Obstacles to international travel and tourism', *Journal of Travel Research*, 22: 2–16.

Ashworth, G.J. and Bergsma, J.R. (1987), 'New policies for tourism: opportunities and problems', *Tijdschrift voor Economische en Sociale Geografie*, 78: 151–153.

Ashworth, G.J. and Tunbridge, J.E. (1990), *The Tourist-historic City*. London: Belhaven.

Association of District Councils (1993), *Making the Most of the Coast*. London: Association of District Councils.

Atkinson. J. (1984), *Flexibility, Uncertainty and Manpower Management*. Falmer: University of Sussex, Institute of Manpower Studies, Report 89.

Atlas van Nederland (nd), 's-Gravenhage, Stichting Wetenschappelijke Atlas van Nederland: Staatsuitgeverij.

Aun, C. (1996), 'Economic development and tourism opportunities in Estonia', *Journal of Baltic Studies*, 27: 95–132.

BAT Freizeit-Forschungsinstitut (ed.) (1995), *Tourismus mit Zukunft, Urlaub 94/95*. Hamburg.

Bachvarov, M. (1997), 'End of the model? Tourism in post-communist Bulgaria', *Tourism Management*, 18: 43–50.

Bailly, A., Jensen-Butler, C. and Leontidou, L. (1996), 'Changing cities: restructuring, marginality and policies in urban Europe', *European Urban and Regional Studies*, 3: 161–176.

Bajerlajn, R. (nd), *600 years of the Jasna Góra Monastery, Częstochowa—Poland*. Warsaw: Polish Tourist Information Centre.

Baláž, V. (1994), 'Tourism and regional development problems in the Slovak Republic', *European Urban and Regional Studies*, 1: 171–177.

Baláž, V. (1995), 'Five years of the economic transition in the Slovak tourism, successes and shortcomings', *Tourism Management*, 16: 143–150.

Baláž, V. (1996a), *International Tourism in the Economies of Central European Countries*. Exeter: Tourism Research Group, University of Exeter.

Baláž, V. (1996b), *Regional Tourism Management in the Slovak Republic*. Exeter: Tourism Research Group, University of Exeter.

Balázs, G. (1984), *Szentendre: Szabadtéri Néprajzi Múzeum I*. Budapest: TKM.

Ball, R.M. (1989), 'Some aspects of tourism, seasonality and local labour markets', *Area*, 21: 13–26.

Banco Bilbao-Vizcaya (1993), *Renta Nacional de España y su Distribución Provincial*. Bilbao: Banco Bilbao-Vizcaya.

Banco Español de Crédito (1993), *Annuario del Mercado Español*. Madrid: Banco Español de Crédito.

Banks, R. (1985), *New Jobs from Pleasure—a Strategy for Creating New Jobs in the Tourist Industry*. London: HMSO.

Barbaza, Y. (1966), *Le Paysage Humain de la Costa Brava*. Paris: Librairie Armand Colin.

Barke, M. and Towner, J. (1996) 'Urban tourism in Spain', in M. Barke, J. Towner and M.T. Newton (eds), *Tourism in Spain*. Wallingford: CAB International, pp. 343–375.

Barke, M. and France, L. (1996), 'The Costa del Sol', in M. Barke, J. Towner and M.T. Newton (eds), *Tourism in Spain: Critical Issues*. Wallingford: CAB International, pp. 265–308.

Barker, M.L. (1982), 'Traditional landscape and mass tourism in the Alps', *Geographical Review*, 72: 395–415.

Baron, R.R. (1983), 'The necessity for an international system of tourism statistics', *International Tourism Quarterly*, 4: 39–51.

Barruet, J. (1995), 'Convention alpine: au delà l'effet de catalyse', *Revue de Géographie Alpine*, 83: 113–121.

Barucci, P. (ed.) (1984), *Primo rapporto sul turismo italiano*. Rome: Ministero del Turismo e dello Spettacolo.

Baum, T. (1995), *Managing Human Resources in the European Tourism and Hospitality Industry: a Strategic Approach*. London: Chapman and Hall.

Bayerisches Staatsministerium für Landesentwicklung und Umweltfragen (ed.) (1980), *Landesplanung in Bayern—Erholungslandschaft Alpen*. Munich.

Beattie, R.M. (1991), 'Hospitality internationalisation: an empirical investigation', *International Journal of Contemporary Hospitality Management*, 3: 14–20.

Becet, J.-M. (1987), *L'Aménagement du Littoral*. Paris: Presses Universitaires de France.

Becheri, E. (1993), 'Economia internazionale e turismo: il caso italiano', in *Quinto rapporto sul turismo Italiano*. Milan: Il Sole 24 Ore SEME and Ministero del Turismo e dello Spettacolo, pp. 1–28.

Becheri, E., Manente, M. and Rosati, F. (1995), 'Economia internazionale e turismo: il ruolo dell' Italia', in *Sesto Rapporto sul Turismo Italiano*. Florence: Mercury for the Dipartimento del Turismo, Presidenza del Consiglio dei Ministri, pp. 1–58.

Becheri, E. and Manente, M. (1997), 'Economia internazionale e turismo. Il ruolo dell'Italia', in *Settimo Rapporto sul Turismo Italiano*. Florence: Turistica–Mercury, pp. 3–30.

Becker, Ch. (1984a), 'Der Ausländertourismus und seine räumliche Verteilung in der Bundesrepublik Deutschland', *Zeitschrift für Wirtschaftsgeographie*, 1: 1–10.

Becker, Ch. (1984b), 'Neue Entwicklungen bei den Feriengrossprojekten in der Bundesrepublik Deutschland—Diffusion and Probleme einer noch wachsenden Betriebsform', *Zeitschrift für Wirtschaftsgeographie*, 3–4: 164–185.

Becker, Ch. (1995), 'Tourism and the environment', in A. Montanari and A.M. Williams (eds), *European Tourism: Regions, Spaces and Restructuring*. Chichester: Wiley, pp. 207–220.

Becker, Ch. and Hensel, H. (1982), 'Struktur- und Entwicklungsprobleme des Städtetourismus—analysiert am Beispiel von 19 Städten', in *Städtetourismus: Analysen und Fallstudien aus Hessen, Rheinland-Pflaz und Saarland*. Hannover: Akademie für Raumforschung und Landesplanung, pp. 167–83.

Becker, Ch. and Klemm, K. (1978), *Raumwirksame Instrumente des Bundes im Bereich Freizeit*. Bonn: Der Bundesminister für Raumordnung, Bauwesen und Städtebau.

Bekkers, T. (1995), 'Tourism planning in The Netherlands: back to the future', *Tijdschrift voor Economische en Sociale Geografie*, 86: 93–97.

Bellencin Meneghel, G. (ed.) (1991), *Agriturismo in Italia*. Bologna: Pátron.

Bennett, R.J. (1986), 'Social and economic transition: a case study in Portugal's Western Algarve', *Journal of Rural Studies*, 2: 91–102.

Beritić, D., Šuljak, T. (1972), *Dubrovnik and its Surroundings*. Zagreb: Touristkomerc.

Bernal, A.M., Fourneau, F., Heran, F., Lacroix, J., Lecordier, P., Martín Vicente, A., Menanteau, L., Mignon, C., Roax, B. and Zoilo Naranjo, F. (1979), *Tourisme et Développment Regional en Andalusie*. París: Editions E. De Boccard.

Berry, J. and McGreal, S. (eds) (1994), *European Cities, Planning Systems and Property Markets*. London: E & FN Spon.

Bertrisey, G. (1981), *Valais 2000: Réflexions sur le Devenir Economique d'un Canton*. Sion: Crédit Suisse.

Béteille, R (1996), *Le Tourisme Vert*. Paris: Presses Universitaires de France.

Bodier, M. and E. Crenner (1996), Partir en vacances, in *INSEE, Données Sociales 1996*. Paris: INSEE.

Boesch, M. (1983), 'Raumentwicklung und Fremdenverkehr im Kanton Graubunden', *Geographica Helvetica*, 38: 63–68.

Bognár, A. (1996), *Budapest's Protected Natural Heritage*. Budapest: Municipality of the City of Budapest.

Boissevain, J. (1996), 'Introduction', in Boissevain, J. (ed.), *Coping with Tourists: European Reactions to Mass Tourism*. Providence RI and Oxford: Berghahn Books, pp. 1–26.

Bonapace, U. (1968), 'Il turismo della neve in Italia e i suoi aspetti geografici', *Rivista Geografica Italiana*, 75: 157–86, 322–59.

Bord Fáilte (1994), *Developing Sustainable Tourism: Tourism Development Plan 1994–1999*. Dublin: Bord Fáilte.

Bord Fáilte (1996), *Visitor Attitudes Survey 1995*. Dublin: Bord Fáilte.

Bosch, R. (1987), 'El turismo de masas', in *Turismo: Horizonte 1990*. Barcelona: Editur.

Bosselman, F.P. (1978), *In the Wake of the Tourist: Managing Special Places in Eight Countries*. Washington, DC: The Conservation Foundation.

Bote, V. (1985), 'Plan de acción para la conservación y desarrollo de los recursos turísticos de la Comarca de la Vera (Cáceres)', *Estudios Turísticos*, 88: 51–64.

Bote, V. (ed.) (1995), *La Demanda Turística en Espacio Rural o de Interior: Situación Actual y Potencial*. Madrid: CSIC Instituto de Economía y Geografía (mimeo).

Bote, V. and Marchena, M. (eds) (1995), 'El turismo metropolitano en Europa', *Estudios Turísticos*, 126 (special monograph).

Bouquet, M. (1982), 'Production and reproduction on family farms in South-West England', *Sociologia Ruralis*, 22: 227–249.

Bramwell, B., Henry, I., Jackson, G., Prat, A.G., Richards, G. and van den Straaten. J. (1996), *Sustainable Tourism Management: Principles and Practice*. Tilburg: Tilburg University Press.

Breathnach, P. (ed.) (1994), *Irish Tourism Development*. Maynooth: Geographical Society of Ireland, Special Publications No. 9.

Breathnach, P., Henry, M., Drea, S. and O'Flaherty, M. (1994), 'Gender in Irish tourism employment', in V. Kinnaird and D. Hall (eds), *Tourism: a Gender Analysis*. Chichester: Wiley, pp. 52–73.

Bremmer, I. and Taras, R. (eds) (1997), *New states New Politics: Building the Post-Soviet Nations*. Cambridge: Cambridge University Press.

Brendon, P. (1991) *Thomas Cook: 150 Years of Popular Tourism*. London: Secker & Warburg.

Briassoulis, H. and van der Straaten, J. (eds) (1992), *Tourism and the Environment*. Dordrecht and Boston: Kluwer Academic.

Brierley, D. (1997), 'Bad news for spas as health reforms bite', *The European*, 2 January.

Brinchmann, K.S. and Huse, M. (1991), 'Scandinavia: challenging nature in Norway', in A.M. Williams and G. Shaw (eds), *Tourism and Economic Development: Western European Experiences*. London: Belhaven, pp. 243–262.

British Tourist Authority (1972), *The British on Holiday 1951–1972*. London: British Tourist Authority.

British Tourist Authority (1987), *The Short Break Market*. London: British Tourist Authority/English Tourist Board.

British Tourist Authority (1995), *Digest of Tourist Statistics*. London: British Tourist Authority/English Tourist Board.

British Tourist Authority (1996), *Digest of Tourist Statistics*. London: British Tourist Authority/English Tourist Board Research Services.

British Tourist Authority (1997), *Insights*. London: British Tourist Authority/English Tourist Board.

Britton, S. (1991), 'Tourism, capital and place: towards a critical geography', *Environment and Planning D: Society and Space*, 9: 451–478.

Bryden, J.M. (1973) *Tourism and Development: a case study of the Commonwealth Caribbean*. Cambridge: Cambridge University Press.

Brykowski, R. (nd), *Wooden Architecture and Building in Poland*. Warsaw: Polish Tourist Information Centre.

Buckley, P.J. and Papadopoulos, S.I. (1986), 'Marketing Greek Tourism—the planning process', *Tourism Management*, 7: 86–100.

Bull, P. and Church, A. (1994), 'The hotel and catering industry of Great Britain during the 1980s: sub-regional employment change, specialization and dominance', in C. Cooper and A. Lockwood (eds), *Progress in Tourism, Recreation and Hospitality Management*, Volume 5. Chichester: Wiley.

Bundesforschungsanstalt für Landeskunde und Raumordnung (ed.) (1983), 'Neue Entwicklungen im Fremdenverkehr', *Informationen zur Raumentwicklung*, 1: 1–92.

Bundesminister für Wirtschaft (ed.) (1994), *Bericht der Bundesregierung über die Entwicklung des Tourismus*. Bonn: BMWi Dokumentation, No. 349.

Bundesministerium für Ernährung, Landwirtschaft und Forsten (ed.) (1997), *Agrarbericht der Bundesregierung 1997*. Bonn.

Bundesministerium für Raumordnung, Bauwesen und Städtebau (ed.) (1994), *Raumordnungsbericht 1993*. Bonn.

Burns, P.M. (1995), 'Hotel management training in Eastern Europe: challenges for Romania', *Progress in Tourism and Hospitality Research*, 1: 53–62.

Burton, R.C.J. (1994), 'Geographical patterns of tourism in Europe', *Progress in Tourism, Recreation and Hospitality Management*, 5: 1–22.

Business Europa (1996), 18: 41. Saffron Walden: Walden Publising.

Butler, R.W. (1980), 'The concept of tourist area cycle of evolution: implications for management of resources', *Canadian Geographer*, 14: 5–12.

Bywater, M. (1992), *The European Tour Operator Industry*. London: Economist Intelligence Unit, Special Report 2141.

Cabildo Insular de Tenerife (1983), *Economía y turismo en Tenerife*. Tenerife: Aula de Cultura.

Calatrava, J. (1984), 'Análisis de la potencialidad del turismo rural como elemento generador de rentas complementarias en zonas en depresión socioeconómica: el caso de las Alpujarras granadinas', in *Colequio Hispano-Francés sobre Espacios Rurales*. Madrid: Ministerio de Agricultura, Servicios de Publicaciones, pp. 305–325.

Cals, J. (1974), *Turismo y Política Turística en España: una Aproximación*. Barcelona: Ariel.

Cals, J. (1983), 'El modelo turístico español'. *Estudios Turísticos*, 80: 15–21.

Campbell, R. (1996), 'Am I in paradise or on the moon?', *Business Europa*, 18: 20–21.

Campbell, R. (ed.) (1997), *Europe Review 1997*. Saffron Walden: Walden Publishing.

Canto, C. (1983), 'Presente y futuro de las residencias secundarias en España', *Anales de Geografía de la Universidad Complutense de Madrid*, 3: 83–103.

Carreras i Verdaguer, C. (1995), 'Mega-events, local strategies and global tourist attractions', in A. Montanari and A.M. Williams (eds), *European Tourism: Regions, Spaces and Restructuring*. Chichester: Wiley, pp. 193–206.

Carter, F.W., Hall, D.R., Turnock, D. and Williams, A.M. (1995), *Interpreting the Balkans*. London: Royal Geographical Society.

Carter, F.W. and Norris, H.T. (1996), *The Changing Shape of the Balkans*. London: UCL Press.

Carter, F.W. and Turnock, D. (eds) (1992), *Environmental Problems in Eastern Europe*. London: Routledge.

Castelberg-Koulma, M. (1991), 'Greek women and tourism: women's cooperatives as an alternative form of organisation', in N. Redclift and M.T. Sinclair (eds), *Working Women: International Perspectives on Labour and Gender Ideology*. London: Routledge.

Cavaco, C. (1979), *O turismo em Portugal: aspectos evolutivos e espaciais*. Lisbon: University of Lisbon, Estudos de Geografia Humana e Regional.

Cavaco, C. (1980), *Turismo e demografia no Algarve*. Lisbon: Editorial Progresso Social e Democracia.

Cavaco, C. (1981), *A Costa do Estoril*, Volumes 1 and 2. Lisbon: University of Lisbon, Centro de Estudos Geográficos, Estudos de Geografia Humana e Regional.

Cavaco, C. (1995), 'Rural tourism: the creation of new tourist spaces', in A. Montanari and A.M. Williams (eds), *European Tourism: Regions, Spaces and Restructuring*. Chichester: Wiley, pp. 127–150.

Cavaco, C. (1996), 'Da Quinta de Quarteira à Vila Moura', *in Turismos e Lazeres*. Lisbon: Universidade de Lisboa, Centro de Estudos Geográficos, Estudos para o Planeamento Regional e Urbano 45.

Cazes, G. (1995), *Le Tourisme en France*. Paris: Presses Universitaires de France.

Cazes, G. and F. Potier (1996), *Le Tourisme Urbain*. Paris: Presses Universitaires de France.

CBS (1997), *Statistical Yearbook of The Netherlands*. The Hague: Centraal Bureau voor de Statistiek.

Central Statistics Office (1996), *Regional Accounts 1991*. Dublin: Central Statistics Office.

Champion, T. and Townsend, A. (1990), *Contemporary Britain: a Geographical Perspective*. London: Edward Arnold.

Chance, S. (1994), 'The politics of restoration: the tension between conservation and tourism in Samarkand and Bukhara', *Architectural Review*, 196: 80–83.

Chib, S.N. (1977), 'Measurement of tourism', *Journal of Travel Research*, 16: 22–5.

Clary, D. (1993), *Le Tourisme dans l'Espace Français*. Paris: Masson.

Claval, P. (1995). 'The impact of tourism on the restructuring of European space', in A. Montanari and A.M. Williams (eds), *European Tourism: Regions, Spaces and Restructuring*. Chichester: Wiley, pp. 247–262.

Clement, M.G. (1967), 'The impact of tourism expenditures', *Development Digest*, 5: 70–81.

Cleverdon, R. (1992), 'Global tourism: influences and determinants', in D.E. Hawkins, J.R.B. Ritchie, F. Go and D. Frechtling (eds), *World Travel and Tourism Review Indicators, Trends and Issues*, Volume 2. Wallingford: CAB International.

Cole, J.P. (1968), *Italy*. London: Chatto and Windus.

Commerzbank (1987), *Branchen-Bericht: Hochstimmung in der Touristikbranche*. Frankfurt.

Commission Consultative Fédéral pour le Tourisme (CCFT) (1979), *Conception Suisse du Tourisme*. Berne: Office Central Fédéral des Imprimes.

Commission Internationale pour la Protection des Régions Alpines (CIPRA) (ed.) (1985), '*Sanfter Tourismus: Schlagwort oder Chance füuden Alpenraum?*'. Vaduz.

Commission of the European Communities (1985), *Tourism in Europe*. Brussels: DG XXIII, Commission of the European Communities.

Commission of the European Communities (1987), *Europeans and their Holidays*. Brussels: Commission of the European Communities, VII/165/87–EN.

Commission of the European Communities (1993), *The Evolution in Holiday Travel Facilities and in the Flow of Tourism Inside and Outside the European Community*. Brussels: DG XXIII—Tourism Unit.

Commission of the European Communities (1994a), *Tourism Policy in the EU*. London: European Commission.

Commission of the European Communities (1994b), *Europe 2000+. Cooperation for European territorial development*. Brussels: Commission of the European Communities.

Commission of the European Communities (1996), *Progress Report on Implementation of the European Community Programme of Policy and Action in Relation to the Environment and Sustainable Development*. Brussels: Commission of the European Communities.

Comunidades Europeas (1986), 'Acción comunitaria en el sector del turismo', *Boletín de las Comunidades Europeas*, 4/86: 10–11.

Confederation of British Industries (1985), *The Paying Guest*. London: CBI.

Conférence Transfrontalière Mont-Blanc (1994), *Espace Mont-Blanc: l'Enjeu*. Chamonix: Conférence Transfrontalière Mont-Blanc.

Conseil Economique et Social (1996), *Le Tourisme: un Atout à Développer*. Paris: Conseil Economique et Social.

Conseil Fédéral Suisse (1986), *Message Concernant une Modification de l'Arréte Fédéral sur l'Office National Suises du Tourisme*. Berne.

Conseil Fédéral Suisse (1996), *Rapport sur la Politique du Tourisme de la Confédération*. Berne.

Convery, F. and Flanagan, S. (eds) (1995), *Investing for Tourism in Ireland*. Dublin: Environmental Institute, University College.

Cook, J. (1996), 'Germany survey', *Business Central Europe*, 4: 39–52.

Cooper, C (1997), 'Parameters and indicators of the decline of the British seaside resort', in G. Shaw and A. Williams (eds), *The Rise and Fall of British Coastal Resorts*. London: Mansell, pp. 79–101.

Cooper, G. (1952), *Your Holiday in Spain and Portugal*. London: Alvin Redman.

Coppock, V., Haydon, D. and Richter, I. (1995), *The Illusions of 'Post-feminism': New Women, Old Myths*. London: Taylor and Francis.

da Costa, C.M.M. (1996), Towards the Improvement of the Efficiency and Effectiveness of Tourism Planning and Development at the Regional Level: Planning, Organisations and Networks. The Case of Portugal. Guildford: University of Surrey, unpublished PhD thesis.

CPER (1994), *Preliminary National Economic and Physical Plan for Tourism*. Athens: CPER (in Greek).

CPER (1987), *Reports for the Programme 1983–87: Tourism*. Athens: CPER (in Greek).

CPER (1976), *Programme for Development 1976–80: Tourism*. Athens: CPER (in Greek).

CPER (Centre of Planning and Economic Research) (1972), *Plan for Model Long-term Development of Greece*. Athens: CPER (in Greek).

Croall, J. (1995), *Preserve or Destroy Tourism and the Environment*. London: Calouste Gulbenkian Foundation.

Cuadrado, J.R. and Aurioles, J. (1986), 'Las actividades turísticas dentro de la estructura económica de Andalucía', *Revista de Estudios Regionales*, 6: 41–64.

Cunha, L. (1986), 'Turismo', in M. Silva (ed.), *Portugal Contemporáneo: Problemas e Perspectivas*. Lisbon: Instituto Nacional de Administraçao.

Curry, N. and Stucki, E. (1996), *Swiss Agricultural Policy: the Swiss Agricultural Knowledge Network and the Environment*. Zurich: Institut d'Economie Rurale.

Cviic, C. (1995), *Remaking the Balkans*, 2nd edn. London: The Royal Institute of International Affairs/Pinter.

Damette, F, (1980), 'The regional framework of monopoly exploitation: new problems and trends', in J. Carney, R. Hudson and J. Lewis (eds), *Regions in Crisis*. London: Croom Helm.

Darbellay, C. (1979), 'Peri-urban agriculture of the Crans-Montana region', in Organisation for Economic Cooperation and Development (ed.), *Agriculture in the Planning and Management of Peri-Urban areas*, Volume II. Paris: OECD.

Davidson, R (1993), 'European business tourism—changes and prospects', *Tourism Management*, 14: 167–172.

Davidson, R. (1994), 'European business travel and tourism', in A.V. Seaton (ed.), *Tourism: The State of The Art*. Chichester: Wiley.

Dawson, A.H. (1991), 'Poland', in Hall, D.R. (ed.), *Tourism and Economic Development in Eastern Europe and the Soviet Union*. London: Belhaven, pp. 190–202.

Deane, B. and Henry, E. (1993), 'The economic impact of tourism', *The Irish Banking Review*, Winter: 35–47.

Debarbieux, B. (1995), *Tourisme et Montagne*. Paris: Economica.

Deegan, J. and Dineen, D.A. (1997), *Tourism Policy and Performance; the Irish Experience*. London: International Thomson Business Press.

Delamont, S. (1995), *Appetites and Identities*. London: Routledge.

Dematteis, G. (1979), 'Repeuplement et revalorisation des espaces périphériques: le cas d'Italie', *Revue de Géographie des Pyrénées et du Sud-Ouest*, 53: 129–143.

Denia, A. and Pedreño, A. (1986), 'Problemas de la actividad turística en la Comunidad Valenciana', in *Papeles de Economía Española de las Comunidades Autónomas, Comunidad Valenciana*, 4: 378–405.

Department of National Heritage (1995), *Competing with the Best*. London: HMSO.

Department of Tourism and Transport (1989), *Operational Programme for Tourism*. Dublin: Stationery Office.

Deutsche Gesellschaft für Freizeit (ed.) (1986), *Freizeitlexikon*. Ostildern: Schriftenreihe der Deutschen Gesellschaft für Freizeit, No. 059.

Deutsche Gesellschaft für Freizeit (ed.) (1995), *Freizeit in Deutschland 1994/1995. Akuelle Daten—Fakten—Aufsätze*. Erkrath.

Deutsche Gesellschaft für Freizeit (ed.) (1996), *Freizeit in Deutschland 1996. Akuelle Daten und Fakten und Grundinformation*. Erkrath.

Deutscher Bundestag (ed.) (1986), *Fremdenverkehrspolitik. Antwort der Bundesregierung*, Document Nr. 10/5454, Bonn, 9 May.

Diem, A. (1980), 'Valley renaissance in the High Alps', *Geographical Magazine*, 52: 492–497.

Din, K.H. (1996), 'Tourism development: still in search of a more equitable mode of local involvement', *Progress in Tourism and Hospitality Research*, 2: 273–281.

Diputación Provincial de Valencia (1983), *Urbanismo y Medio Rural: la Vivienda Ilegal de Segunda Residencia*. Valencia: Art. Graf. Soler.

Direcção Geral do Turismo (1986), *O turismo, em 1983/84*. Lisbon: Direcção Geral do Turismo, Gabinete de Estatísticas e Inquéritos.

Direcção Geral do Turismo (1988), *O turismo em 1987*. Lisbon: Direcção Geral do Turismo, Gabinete de Estatísticas e Inquéritos.

Direcção Geral do Turismo (1995), *Férias dos Portugeses em 1994*. Lisbon: Direcção Geral do Turismo.

Direcção Geral do Turismo (1996), *O Turismo em 1994*. Lisbon: Direcção Geral do Turismo.

Doxiadis Association (1974), *National Regional Plan of Greece*. Athens: Ministry of Co-ordination (in Greek).

Drailo, P. (1996), 'Interpreting Croatia', *In Focus*, 22: 9.

Dreyfus-Signoles, C. (1992), *Structures et Organisation du Tourisme en France*. Paris: Bréal.

Duarte, G. de S. (1996), Invnestimento estrangeiro no turismo em Portugal: tendências recentes. Unpublished paper, First International Colloquium on Geografia do lazer e do Turismo, Lisbon.

Dundler, F. (1988), *Urlaubsreisen 1987. Einige Ergebnisse der Reiseanalyse 1987. Kurzfassung*. Starnberg: Studienkreis für Tourismus.

Dunning, J.H. (1977), 'Trade, location of economic activity and the MNE: a search for an eclectic approach', in B. Ohlin, P.O. Hesselborn and P.M. Wijkman (eds), *The International Allocation of Economic Activity*. London: Macmillan.

Dunning, J.H. and McQueen, M. (1982), 'The eclectic theory of the multinational and the international hotel industry', in A.M. Rugman (ed.), *New Theories of the Multinational Enterprise*. London: Croom Helm.

Durand, H., Gouirand, P. and Spindler, J. (1994), *Economie et Politique du Tourisme*. Paris: Librairie Générale de Droit et de Jurisprudence.

Dutt, A.K. and Costa, F.J. (eds) (1985), *Public Planning in The Netherlands*. Oxford: Oxford University Press.

Dwyer, J. (1991), 'Structural and evolutionary effects upon conservation policy performance: comparing a UK national and a French regional park', *Journal of Rural Studies*, 7: 265–275.

Eaton, M. (1995), 'British expatriate service provision in Spain's Costa del Sol', *The Services Industries Journal*, 15: 251–266.

Economist Intelligence Unit (1993), 'The market for cultural tourism in Europe', *Travel and Tourism Analyst*, 6: 30–46.

Economist Intelligence Unit (1994), 'The international ski market in Europe', *Travel and Tourism Analyst*, 3: 34–55.

Edwards, A. (1981), *Leisure Spending in the European Community—Forecasts to 1990*. London: Economist Intelligence Unit.

Edwards, A. (1993), *Price Competitiveness of Holiday Destinations*. London: EIU Research Report R457.

Elsasser, H. and Leibundgut, H. (1982), 'Touristiche Monostrukturen-Probleme in schweizrischen Berggebeit', *Geographische Rundschau*, 34: 228–234.

English Tourist Board (1978), *Bude to Wadebridge: a New Growth Point for Tourism*. London: English Tourist Board.

English Tourist Board (1981a), *Prospects for Self-catering Development*. London: English Tourist Board.

English Tourist Board (1981b), *Planning for Tourism in England: Planning Advisory Note 1*. London: English Tourist Board.

English Tourist Board (1989a), *Major Tourism Investment Projects*. London: English Tourist Board.

English Tourist Board (1989b), *The Inner City Challenge: Tourism Development in Inner City Regeneration*. London: English Tourist Board.

English Tourist Board (1991a), *The Future of England's Smaller Resorts*. London: English Tourist Board.

English Tourist Board (1991b), *Tourism and the Environment: Maintaining the Balance*. London: English Tourist Board.

English Tourist Board (1995), *Revitalising Coastal Resorts*. London: English Tourist Board.

EOT (National Tourist Organization of Greece) (1985), *Tourism 1985*. Athens: EOT, Division A of Research and Development (in Greek).

EOT (National Tourist Organization of Greece) (1979), *Sample Survey of Mobility of Tourists in Greek Space*. Athens: EOT, Division A of Research and Development (in Greek).

Esteban, J. and Pedreño, A. (1985), *Estimación de la Renta Familiar Disponible a Nivel Municipal en la Comunidad Valenciana*. Alicante: Caja de Ahorros de Alicante y Murcia.

Esteve, R. (1986), 'El turismo deportivo en Andalucía', *Revista de Estudios Regionales*, 6: 239–266.

Euromonitor (1994), *European Domestic Tourism and Leisure Trends*. London: Euromonitor.

Euromonitor (1995), *European Marketing Data and Statistics*. London: Euromonitor.

Eurostat (1991), *Le Tourisme en Europe, Tendence 1989*. Luxembourg: Eurostat.

Evans, R.G. (1996), *Support to the Slovak Agency for Rural Development: Inception Report*. Auchincruvie: Department of Leisure and Tourism Management, The Scottish Agricultural College.

Faludi, A. and de Ruiter, P. (1985), 'No match for the present crisis? The theoretical and institutional framework for Dutch planning', in A.K. Dutt and F.J. Costa (eds), *Public Planning in The Netherlands*. Oxford: Oxford University Press, pp. 35–49.

Farrow, C. (1995), 'Qeparo—bringing people together', *In Focus*, 16: 9–10.

Feehan, J. (1992), *Tourism on the Farm: Proceedings of Two Conferences on Farm Tourism in Ireland*. Dublin: Environmental Institute, University College Dublin.

Ferrao, J.M. (1985), 'Regional variations in the rate of profit' in R. Hudson and J.R. Lewis (eds), *Uneven Development in Southern Europe*. London: Methuen.

Figuerola, M. (1983), 'Importancia del turismo en la economía española', *Estudios Turísticos*, 80: 21–31.

Figuerola, M. (1986), 'Tendencias y problemas del turismo actual', *Revista de Estudios Regionales*, 6: 17–40.

Fisher, D., Mati, I. and Whyles, G. (1994), *Ecotourism Development in Albania*. St Albans: Ecotourism Ltd/Aulona Sub Tour/Worldwide Fund for Nature, UK.

Flemming, D. (1992), 'The Fifth EC Environmental Action Programme', *European Environment*, special supplement.

Fletcher, J. and Cooper, C. (1996), 'Tourism strategy planning: Szolnok county, Hungary', *Annals of Tourism Research*, 23: 181–200.

Focşa, G. (1970), *Muzeul Satului din Bucuresti*. Bucharest: Meridiane.

Fornfeist, D. (1976), *Urlaubsreise 1975. Einige Ergebnisse der Reiseanalyse 1975. Kurzfassung*. Starnberg: Studienkreis für Tourismus.

Forschungsgemeinschaft Urlaub und Reisen e.V. (FUR) (ed.) (1996), *Die Reiseanalyse im Westentaschenformat. Ausgewählte Zeitreihen und Hauptergebnisse zu Urlaubsreisen von 1970 bis 1995*. Hamburg.

Forschungsgemeinschaft Urlaub und Reisen e.V. (FUR) (ed.) (1997), *Die Reiseanalyse. Urlaub und Reisen 96. Kurzfassung*. Hamburg.

Fourneau, F. (1979), 'La Costa de la Luz de Huelva', in A.M. Bernal, F. Fourneau, F. Heran, J. Lacroix, P. Lecordier, A. Martín Vicente, L. Menanteau, C. Mignon, B. Roax and F. Zoilo Naranjo (eds), *Tourisme et Développment Régional*. París: Editions F. De Boccard, pp. 135–177.

Fragakis, T. (1987), 'The average length of stay of foreign tourists in Greece is 14 days', *Tourism and Economy*, 2: 127–128 (in Greek).

Franzoni, R. (1990), *Yachting in the Northern Mediterranean*. Basingstoke: Automobile Association.

Fraser, R. (1974), *The Pueblo: a Mountain Village on the Costa del Sol*. London: Allen Lane.

de Freitas, J.A. (1984), *Madeira: Construir o Futuro Hoje*. Lisbon: Editorial Caminho.

Frosch, R. (1992), 'La saturation tourisique à l'exemple du canton des Grisons', *Revue Géographique du L'Est*, 33: 201–215.

Fuentes García, R. (1995), *El Turismo Rural en España. Especial Referencia al Análisis de la Demanda*. Madrid, Instituto de Estudios Turísticos.

Fujs, V. and Krašovec, M. (1996), *Wine Journeys in Slovenia*. Ljubljana: Vas Travel Agency and Republic of Slovenia Ministry of Agriculture, Forestry and Food.

Funk, N. and Mueller, M. (eds) (1993), *Gender Politics and Post-communism*. New York and London: Routledge.

Gajewski, J. (1994), *On the Beskidy Paths*. Warsaw: Urząd Kultury Fisycznej i Turystyki.

Gambino, R. (1978), *Turismo e Sviluppo del Mezzogiorno*. Rome: SVIMEZ.

Gaviria, M. (1974), *España a Go-go: Turismo Charter y Neocolonialismo del Espacio*. Madrid: Ediciones Turner.

Gaviria, M. (1977a), *Benidorm, Ciudad Nueva*. Madrid: Editora Nacional.

Gaviria, M. (1977b), *El Turismo de Invierno y el Asentamiento de Extranjeros en la Provincia de Alicante*. Alicante: Instituto de Estudios Alicantinos.

Gemeente Amsterdam (1997), *Amsterdam in Cijfers 1996*. Amsterdam: Gemeente Amsterdam.

Gerbaux, F. (1994), *La Montagne en Politique*. Paris: L'Harmattan.

Gibbs, D. (1996), 'Integrating sustainable development and economic restructuring: a role for regulation theory', *Geoforum*, 27: 1–10.

Gibson, M. (1996), 'From Russia with years of expertise', *The European*, 17 October.

Gilg, A.W. (1983), 'Settlement design in the Alps: the case of Leysin', *Landscape Research*, 8: 2–12.

Gilg, A.W. (1985), 'Land-use planning in Switzerland', *Town Planning Review*, 56: 315–338.

Gillmor, D.A. (1985), *Economic Activities in the Republic of Ireland: a Geographical Perspective*. Dublin: Gill and Macmillan.

Gillmor, D.A. (1993a), 'Tourism in the Republic of Ireland', in W.Pompe and P. Lavery (eds), *Tourism in Europe: Structures and Developments*. Wallingford: CAB International, pp. 149–166.

Gillmor, D.A. (1993b), 'Geographical patterns of tourism between Ireland and Europe', in R. King (ed.), *Ireland, Europe and the Single Market*. Dublin: Geographical Society of Ireland, Special Publications No. 8, pp. 110–127.

Gillon, P. (1995), 'Les flux téléphoniques révélateurs de l'origine des touristes européens en France', *Annales de Géographie*, 585–86: 475–97.

Go, F.M. and Pine, R. (1995), *Globalization Strategy in the Hotel Industry*. London: Routledge.

Gołembski, G. (1990), 'Tourism in the economy of shortage', *Annals of Tourism Research*, 17: 55–68.

Goodwin, M. and Painter, J. (1996), 'Local governance, the crises of Fordism and the changing geographies of regulation', *Transactions of the Institute of British Geographers*, New Series 21: 635–648.

Gordon, A. and Wolfram, K. (1995), *Wonders of Nature in Poland*. Warsaw: National Tourist Promotion Agency.

Gordon, D. (1997), Managing the changing political environment in waterfront redevelopment, *Urban Studies*, 34: 61–83.

Gordon, I. and Goodall, B. (1992), 'Resorts cycles development processes', *Built Environment*, 18: 41–55.

Government of Ireland (1985), *White Paper on Tourism Policy*. Dublin: Stationery Office.

Government of Ireland (1994), *Operational Programme for Tourism, 1994–1999*. Dublin: Stationery Office.

Grabher, G. (ed.) (1993), *The Embedded Firm*. London: Routledge.

Grabler, K. (ed.) (1997), *International City Tourism*. London: Pinter.

Grafton, D. (1984), 'Small-scale growth centres in remote rural regions: the case of Alpine Switzerland', *Applied Geography*, 4: 29–46.

Gratton, C. (1993), 'A new perspective on European leisure markets', *ILAM Guide to Good Practice in Leisure Management*, 2nd edn. Harlow: Longman.

Gratton, C. and Richards, G. (1995), 'Structural change in the European package tour industry', quoted in Horner, S. and Swarbrooke, J. (1996), *Marketing Tourism Hospitality and Leisure in Europe*. London: Thomson.

Greek Parliament (1984), *The Five-year Plan of Socio-economic Development, 1983–1987*. Athens: National Publishers (in Greek).

Green Globe (1994), *Environmental Management for Your Business: An Introductory Guide*. London: Green Globe.

Greenwood, J. (1993), 'Business interest groups in tourism governance', *Tourism Management*, 14: 335–348.

Gustavsen, T. and Huse, M. (1994), *Reiselivets Samfunnsmessige Betydning*. Bodø: Nordland Research Institute, NF-Report, pp. 1–94.

Gutiérrez, D. (1985), 'El club resort', in *Turismo: Horizonte 1990*. Barcelona: Editur, pp. 157–167.

Hadjimchalis, C. and Vaiou, D. (1986), Changing patterns of uneven regional development and forms of social reproduction. Unpublished paper, Athens.

Haimayer, p. (1984), 'Überlagerungen des Freizeitverkehrs in Österreich', in *Österrieichische Berträge zur Geographie der Ostalopen*, IGU Congress, Wiener Geographische Schriften, pp. 168–176.

Halliburton, C. and Hünerberg, R. (1993), *European Marketing—Reading and Cases*. Wokingham: Addison-Wesley.

Hall, D.R. (1981), 'A geographical approach to propaganda', in A.D. Burnett and P.J. Taylor (eds), *Political Studies from Spatial Perspectives*. Chichester and New York: Wiley, pp. 313–339.

Hall, D.R. (1984), 'Foreign tourism under socialism: the Albanian "Stalinist" model', *Annals of Tourism Research*, 11: 539–555.

Hall, D.R. (1990a), 'Eastern Europe opens its doors', *Geographical Magazine*, 62: 10–15.

Hall, D.R. (1990b), 'Stalinism and tourism: a study of Albania and North Korea', *Annals of Tourism Research*, 17: 36–54.

Hall, D.R. (1990c), 'The changing face of tourism in Eastern Europe', *Town and Country Planning*, 59: 348–351.

Hall, D.R. (1991a), 'New hope for the Danube Delta', *Town and Country Planning*, 60: 251–252.

Hall, D.R. (ed.) (1991b), *Tourism and Economic Development in Eastern Europe and the Soviet Union*. London: Belhaven.

Hall, D.R. (1991c), 'Evolutionary patterns of tourism development in Eastern Europe and the Soviet Union', in D. Hall (ed.), *Tourism and Economic Development in Eastern Europe and the Soviet Union*. London: Belhaven, pp. 79–118.

Hall, D.R. (1992a), 'Skills transfer for appropriate development, *Town and Country Planning*, 61: 87–89.

Hall, D.R. (1992b), 'The challenge of international tourism in Eastern Europe', *Tourism Management*, 13: 41–44.

Hall, D.R. (1992c), 'The changing face of international tourism in Central and Eastern Europe', *Progress in Tourism, Recreation and Hospitality Management*, 4: 252–264.

Hall, D.R. (1993a), 'Eastern Europe', in W. Pompl and P. Lavery (eds), *Tourism in Europe: Structures and Developments*. Wallingford: CAB International, pp. 341–358.

Hall, D.R. (1993b), 'Ecotourism in the Danube Delta', *The Tourist Review*, 3: 11–13.

Hall, D.R. (1993c), 'Impacts of economic and political transition on the transport geography of Central and Eastern Europe', *Journal of Transport Geography*, 1: 20–35.

Hall, D.R. (1993d), *Transport and Economic Development in the New Central and Eastern Europe*. London: Belhaven Press.

Hall, D.R. (1994), *Albania and the Albanians*. London: Frances Pinter.

Hall, D.R. (1995). 'Tourism change in Central and Eastern Europe', in A. Montanari and A.M. Williams (eds), *European Tourism: Regions, Spaces and Restructuring*. Chichester: Wiley, pp. 221–243.

Hall, D.R. (1996a), 'Recovering the Danube Delta', *Environmental Scientist*, 5: 10–11.

Hall, D.R. (1996b), 'Resources for sustainable tourism: cultural landscapes', in D. Turnock (ed.), *Frameworks for Understanding Post-socialist Processes*. Leicester: Leicester University Geography Department, Occasional Paper 36, pp. 17–20.

Hall, D.R. and Brown, F. (1996), 'Towards a welfare focus for tourism research', *Progress in Tourism and Hospitality Research*, 2: 41–57.

Hall, D.R. and Danta, D. (eds) (1996), *Reconstructing the Balkans*. Chichester and New York: Wiley.

Hall, D.R. and Kinnaird, V. (1994), 'Ecotourism in Eastern Europe', in E. Cater and G. Lowman (eds), *Ecotourism: a Sustainable Option?* Chichester and New York: Wiley, pp. 111–136.

Ham, C. and Hill, M. (1985), *The Policy Process in the Modern Capitalist State*. Brighton: Wheatsheaf.

Hamilton, G. (1991), 'Amex sets initiative for EE tourism development', *Business Eastern Europe*, 20: 412.

Hanekamp, G. (1979), 'Het wild en bijster land van Veluwen' in M.F. Morzer Bruins and R.J. Benthem (eds), *Atlas van Nederlandsche Landschappen*. Utrecht: Spectrum, pp. 112–123.

Hannigan, K. (1994a), 'A regional analysis of tourism growth in Ireland', *Regional Studies*, 28: 208–214.

Hannigan, K. (1994b), 'National policy, European Structural Funds and sustainable tourism: the case of Ireland', *Journal of Sustainable Tourism*, 2: 179–192.

Hanns, C. and Schroder, P. (1985), 'Touristische Transportlagen in den Alpen', *Dokumente und Informationen zur Schwiezerischen Orts-, Regional-und Landesplanung*, April: 19–25.

Harrer, B., Zeiner, M., Maschke, J. and Scherr, S. (1995), *Tagesreisen der Deutschen*. Munich: Schriftenreihe des Deutschen Wirtschaftswissenschaftlichen Instituts für Fremdenverkehr 46.

Harrison, D. (1993), 'Bulgarian tourism: a state of uncertainty', *Annals of Tourism Research*, 20: 519–534.

Harrison, D. (1994), 'Learning from the Old South by the New South? The case of tourism', *Third World Quarterly*, 15: 707–721.

Harrison, L. and Johnson, K. (1992), *UK Hotel Groups Directory 1992/93*. London: Cassell.

Hasslacher, P. (1984), '*Sanfter Tourismus-Virgental*'. Innsbruck: Österreichischer Alpenverein.

Haylock, R. (1994), 'Timeshare—the new force in tourism', in A.V. Seaton (ed.), *Tourism The State of The Art*. Chichester: Wiley.

Heeley, J. (1981), 'Planning for Tourism in Britain: an historical perspective', *Town Planning Review*, 52 (1): 61–79.

Heeley, J. (1989), 'Role of national tourist organisations in the United Kingdom', in S.F. Witt and L. Moutinha (eds), *Tourism Marketing and Management Handbook*. Hemel Hempstead: Prentice-Hall.

Held, D. (1995), *Democracy and the Global Order*. Cambridge: Polity Press.

Henriques, E.B. (1993), 'Do turismo urbano: no contexto do espaço turístico', *Inforgeo*, 6: 55–70.

Herrera, J.L. (1984), 'Consideración turística del Camino de Santiago', *Estudios Turísticos*, 84: 17–31.

HMSO (1997), *Social Trends*. London: HMSO.

Holloway, J.C. (1994), *The Business of Tourism*, 4th edn. London: Pitman.

Horner, S. and Swarbrooke, J. (1996), *Marketing Tourism Hospitality and Leisure in Europe*. London: Thomson Business Press.

HOTREC (1995), *The HORECA Sector and the European Union*. Brussels: HOTREC.

Hoyle, B.S. (1988), 'Development dynamics at the port-city interface', in B.S. Hoyle, D.A. Pinder and M.S. Husain (eds), *Revitalizing the Waterfront: International Dimensions of Dockland Redevelopment*. London: Belhaven, pp. 5–19.

Hoyle, B.S. (ed.) (1996), *Cityports, Coastal Zones and Regional Change*. Chichester: Wiley.

Hudson, R. (1995), 'Towards sustainable industrial production: but in what sense sustainable?', in M. Taylor (ed.), *Environmental Change: Industry, Power and Policy*. Aldershot: Avebury.

Hudson, R. (1997), 'Globalisation and the restructuring of the UK space-economy: national state policies and regional differentiation', Mimeo, Department of Geography, University of Durham.

Hudson, R. and Townsend, A. (1992), 'Tourism employment and policy changes for local government' in P. Johnson and B. Thomas (eds), *Perspectives on Tourism Policy*. London: Mansell, pp. 49–68.

Hultkrantz, L. (1995), 'Dynamic price response of inbound tourism guest-nights in Sweden', *Tourism Economics*, 1: 357–374.

Hurley, A., Archer, B. and Fletcher, J. (1994), 'The economic impact of European Community grants for tourism in the Republic of Ireland', *Tourism Management*, 15: 203–211.

Huse, M., Gustavsen, T. and Almedal, S. (1998), Tourism impact comparisons among Norwegian towns', *Annals of Tourism Research*, 25: in press.

Innocenti, P. (1990), *Geografia del Turismo*. Rome: La Nuova Italia Scientifica.

INSEE (1992), 'Profil des cantons—Rhône-Alpes', *Dossiers de l'INSEE Rhône-Alpes*, 44.

INSEE (1996), *Tableaux de l'Économie Française*. Paris: INSEE.

INSEE (1997), *La France et ses Régions*. Paris: INSEE.

Instituto de Estudios Turísticos (1996), *Tabla Intersectorial de la Economía Turística (TIOT 92)*. Madrid: Instituto de Estudios Turísticos.

Instituto de Estudios Turísticos (1997), *Comportamiento Turístico de los Españoles: Verano'96*. Madrid: Familitur: Estadística de Movimientos Turísticos de los Españoles.

Instituto Nacional de Estadística (1960), *Censo de Población 1960*. Madrid: Instituto Nacional de Estadística.

Instituto Nacional de Estadística (1991), *Censo de Población 1991*. Madrid: Instituto Nacional de Estadística.

Instituto Nacional de Estadística (various), *Movimento de Viajeros en Establecimientos Turísticos*. Madrid: Instituto Nacional de Estadística.

Instituto Nacional de Estadística (1985a), *Estatísticas do turismo 1984*. Lisbon: Instituto Nacional de Estadística.

Instituto Nacional de Estadística (1985b), *50 anos, Portugal 1935–1985*. Lisbon: Instituto Nacional de Estadística.

Instituto Nacional de Estatística (1994), *Portugal em Números*. Lisbon: Instituto Nacional de Estatística.

Instituto Nacional de Estatística (1995), *Estatísticas do Turismo*. Lisbon: Instituto Nacional de Estatística.

ISTAT (1996), *Statistiche Ambientali*. Rome: ISTAT.

ISTAT (1997a), *L'offerta e la domanda turistica in Italia*. Rome: ISTAT Informazioni, No. 30.

ISTAT (1997b), *Rapporto sull'Italia*. Bologna: Il Mulino.

ISTAT (various), *Annuario di Statistico Italiano, Annuario di Statistico Italiano*. Rome: ISTAT,

ISTAT (various), *Statistiche del Turismo*. Rome: ISTAT.

Jaakson, R. (1996), 'Tourism in transition in post-Soviet Estonia', *Annals of Tourism Research*, 23: 617–634.

Jansen-Verbeke, M. and Spee, R. (1995), 'A regional analysis of tourist flows within Europe', *Tourism Management*, 14: 73–82.

Jeffries, I. (ed.) (1996), *Problems of Economic and Political Transformation in the Balkans*. London: Pinter.

Jessop, B. (1995), 'The regulation approach, governance and post-fordism', *Economy and Society*, 24: 307–333.

Johnson, M. (1995), 'Czech and Slovak tourism, patterns, problems and prospects', *Tourism Management*, 16: 21–28.

Junta de Castilla y León (1996), *Actas del Congreso de Turismo Rural y Turismo Activo*. Valladolid: Junta de Castilla y León.

Jurczek, P. (1986a), *Städtetourismus in Oberfranken. Stand und Entwicklungsmöglichkeiten des Fremdenverkehrs in Bamberg, Bayreuth, Coburg und Hof*. Munich: Beiträge zur Kommunalwissenschaft 21.

Jurczek, P. (1986b), *Raumbezogene Veränderungen des Urlaubsreiseverkehrs in der Bundesrepublik Deutschland*. Unpublished paper, Bayreuth.

Jurdao, F. (1979), *España en Venta*. Madrid: Ediciones Ayuso.

de Kadt, E. (1979), *Tourism: Passport to Development*. Oxford: Oxford University Press.

de Kadt, E. (1992), 'Making the alternatives sustainable: lessons from development for tourism', in V.L. Smith and W.R. Eadington (eds), *Tourism Alternatives: Potential and Problems in the Development of Tourism*. Chichester: Wiley.

Kahn, H. (1979), 'Leading futurologist traces next half century in travel', *Travel Trade News*, 31st January, pp. 1–8.

Kalligas, A.S., Papageorgiou, A.N., Politis, I.V. and Romanos, A.G. (1972), *Myconos-Delos-Rinia: Regional Study of the Complex of the Three Islands*. Athens: Ministry of State Policy, Division of Regional Planning (in Greek).

Kariel, H.G. and Kariel, P.E. (1982), 'Socio-cultural impacts of tourism: an example from the Austrian Alps', *Geografiska Annaler*, 64B: 1–16.

Karpowicz, Z. (1993), 'The challenge of ecotourism—application and prospects for implementation in the countries of Central and Eastern Europe and Russia', *The Tourist Review*, 3: 28–40.

Kecskés, P. (1987), *Szentendre: Szabadtéri Néprajzi Múzeum II*. Budapest: TKM.

King, R. (1984), 'Population mobility: emigration, return migration and internal migration', in A. Williams (ed.), *Southern Europe Transformed: Political and Economic Change in Greece, Italy, Portual and Spain*. London: Harper and Row, pp. 145–178.

King, R. (1987), 'Italy', in H.D. Clout (ed.), *Regional Development in Western Europe*, 3rd edn. London: David Fulton, pp. 129–163.

King, R. (1989), 'The three Italies: recent changes in the regional economic geography of Italy', *Geographical Viewpoint*, 17: 5–23.

King, R. (1991), 'Italy: multi-faceted tourism', in A.M. Williams and G. Shaw (eds), *Tourism and Economic Development: Western European Experiences*, 2nd edn. London: Belhaven, pp. 61–83.

King, R. (1995). 'Tourism, labour and international migration', in A. Montanari and A.M. Williams (eds), *European Tourism: Regions, Spaces and Restructuring*. Chichester: Wiley, pp. 177–190.

King, R., Mortimer, J. and Strachan, A. (1984), 'Return migration and tertiary development: a Calabrian case-study', *Anthropological Quarterly*, 57: 112–124.

King, S. (1996), 'Montenegro and Slovenia seek new face in tourism', *The European*, 17 October.

Kinnaird, V. and Hall, D. (eds) (1994), *Tourism: a Gender Analysis*. Chichester: Wiley.

Kinnaird, V.H. and Hall, D.R. (1996), 'Understanding tourism processes: a gender-aware framework', *Tourism Management*, 19: 95–102.

Klemm, M. (1996), 'Languedoc-Roussillon: adapting the strategy', *Tourism Management*, 17: 133–147.

Klöpper, R. (1973), *Die räumliche Struktur des Angebotes von 'Urlaub auf dem Bauernhof'—Entwicklungschancen im Rahmen des gesamten Beherbergungsangebotes in Landgemeinden.* Frankfurt: Auswertungs- und Informationsdienst, Volume 179.

Knafou, R. (1991), 'La crise du tourisme dans les montagnes françaises: un système qui a fait ses preuves et son temps', *Dossier de la Revue de Geographie Alpine*, 6: 13–21.

Knafou, R. (1992), 'De quelques rapports souvent contradictoires entre tourisme et environnement', in Ministère de l'Environnement: Ministère du Tourisme, *Tourisme et Environnement*. Paris: Ministère de l'Environnement, pp. 16–23.

Knafou, R. (1994), *Les Alpes*. Paris: Presses Universitaires de France.

Koch, A. (1959), 'Der Urlaubsreiseverkehr. Eine Untersuchung über das Konsumverhalten der Erholungsreisenden 1958', *Jahrbuch für Fremdenverkehr*, pp. 4–70. München: Deutsches Wirtschaftswissenschaftliches Institut für Freudenverkehr.

Koch, A. (1986), 'Wirtschaftliche Bedeutung des Fremdenverkehrs in ländlichen Gebieten', *Entwicklung ländlicher Räume durch den Fremdenverkehr, Forschungsberichte und Seminarergebnisse.* Bonn: Der Bundesminister für Raumordnung, Bauwesen und Städtebau, pp. 9–18.

Koch, A., Zeiner, M. and Feige, M. (1987), *Die ökonomische Bedeutung des Ausflugs- und Geschäftsreiseverkehrs (ohne Übernachtungen) in der Bundesrepublik Deutschland.* Munich: Schriftenreihe des Deutschen Wirtschaftswissenschaftlichen Instituts für Fremdenverkehr 39.

Kockel, U. (ed.) (1994), *Culture, Tourism and Development: the Case of Ireland.* Liverpool: Liverpool University Press.

Komilis, P. (1986), *Spatial Analysis of Tourism.* Athens: CPER (in Greek).

Komilis, P. (1994), 'Tourism and sustainable regional development', in A.V. Seaton (ed.), *Tourism: the State of the Art.* Chichester: Wiley, pp. 65–73.

Komilis, P. (1995), 'Tourism policy and Areas of Integrated Tourist Development (POTA)', *Synchrona Themata*, 18: 55, 77–80 (in Greek).

Koncouris, G.K. and Skouras, I.G. (1991), Tourist Development in Attica during 1970–1990: Problems and Prospects. Diploma thesis, EMP, Athens (in Greek).

Koulov, B. (1996), 'Market reforms and environmental protection in the Bulgarian tourism industry', in D. Hall and D. Danta (eds), *Reconstructing the Balkans.* Chichester and New York: Wiley, pp. 187–196.

Kousis, M. (1989), 'Tourism and the family in a rural Cretan community', *Annals of Tourism Research*, 16: 318–332.

Krebs, P. (ed.) (1995), *Protection des Marais et Tourisme: Rapport de Synthèse du Groupe de Travail.* Berne: Office Fédéral de l'Environment, des Forets et du Paysage.

Krippendorf, J. (1986), 'The new tourist turning-point for leisure and travel', *Tourism Management*, 7: 131–135.

Krippendorf, J. (1987a), *The Holiday Makers.* London: Heinemann.

Krippendorf, J. (1987b), *Là-haut sur la Montagne . . . Pour un Développement du Tourisme en Harmonie avec l'Homme et la Nature.* Berne: Kummerley and Frey.

Kurek, W. (1996), 'Agriculture versus tourism in rural areas of the Polish Carpathians', *GeoJournal*, 38: 191–196.

La Tribune Desfossés (1996a), 15 February, Paris.

La Tribune Desfossés (1996b), 30 May, Paris.

Lahuna, S. (1996), 'Paris—Ile-de-France, capitale mondiale du tourisme d'affaires', *Cahier Espaces*, 45: 52–58.

Lambert, A.M. (1971), *The Making of the Dutch Landscape.* London and New York: Academic Press.

Lanquar, R. and Y. Raynouard (1995), *Le Tourisme Social et Associatif.* Paris: Presses Universitaires de France.

Lash, S. and Urry, J. (1987), *The End of Organized Capitalism.* Cambridge: Polity.

Lash, S. and Urry, J. (1994), *Economies of Signs and Spaces*. London: Sage.

Lassberg, D.V. and Steinmassl, Ch. (1991), *Urlaubsreisen 1990. Kurzfassung der Reiseanalyse 1990*. Starnberg: Studienkreis für Tourismus.

Laurens, L. (1995), 'Les parcs naturels, du concept à la pratique d'une agriculture environnementale', *Annales de Géographie*, 584: 339 359.

Lavery, P. (1993), 'Tourism in the United Kingdom', in W. Pomple and P. Lavery (eds), *Tourism in Europe, Structures and Developments*. Wallingford: CAB International, pp. 129–148.

Law, C.M. (1985), *Urban Tourism: Selected British Case Studies*. Manchester: Salford University Department of Geography, Working Paper 1.

Law, C. (1992), 'Urban tourism and its contribution to economic regeneration', *Urban Studies*, 29: 599–618.

Law, C. (1994), *Urban Tourism*. London: Mansell.

Lawson, F.R. (1982), 'Trends in business tourism management', *Tourism Management*, 3: 298–302.

Lazzaretti, L. (1986), 'Il finanziamento regionale dell' attività turistiche: primi risultati di una indagine condotta in Italia', in *Secondo rapporto sul turismo Italiano*. Rome: Ministero del Turismo e dello Spettacolo, pp. 523–554.

Le Monde (1993), 19 November, Paris.

Le Monde (1996a), 4 June, Paris.

Le Monde (1996b), 18 July, Paris.

Lecordier, P. (1979), 'Tourisme et économie régionale', in A.M. Bernal, F. Fourneau, F. Heran, J. Lacroix, P. Lecordier, A. Martín Vicente, L. Menanteau, C. Mignon, B. Roax and F. Zoilo Naranjo (eds), *Tourisme et Développment Régional*. Paris: Editions E. De Boccard, pp. 41–51.

Lennon, J.J. (1995), 'Hotel privatisation in Central and Eastern Europe: progress and process', in D. Leslie (ed.), *Tourism and Leisure: Culture, Heritage and Participation*. Eastbourne: Leisure Studies Association, pp. 45–58.

Leno Cerro, F. (1997), 'Políticas para la Expansión de las Nuevas Opciones Turísticas', in M. Valenzuela (ed.), *Turismos de Interior*. Madrid: Universidad Autónoma de Madrid, pp 575–601.

Leontidou, E. and Ammer, S (eds) (1992), *The Women's Greece*. Athens: Enallaktikes Ekdoseis (in Greek).

Leontidou, L. (1983), 'Industrial restructuring and the relocation of manufacturing employment in postwar Athens', *City and Region*, 7: 79–109.

Leontidou, L. (1990), *The Mediterranean City in Transition: Social Change and Urban Development*. Cambridge: Cambridge University Press.

Leontidou, L. (1991), 'Greece: prospects and contradictions of tourism in the 1980s', in A.M. Williams and G. Shaw (eds), *Tourism and Economic Development. Western European Experiences*, 2nd edn. London: Belhaven, pp. 84–106.

Leontidou, L. (1993), 'Postmodernism and the city: Mediterranean versions', *Urban Studies*, 30: 949–965.

Leontidou, L. (1994), 'Gender dimensions of tourism in Greece: employment, sub-cultures and restructuring', in V. Kinnaird and D. Hall (eds), *Tourism: a Gender Analysis*. Chichester: Wiley, pp. 74–105.

Leontidou, L. (1995), 'Repolarization in the Mediterranean: Spanish and Greek cities in neoliberal Europe', *European Planning Studies*, 3: 155–172.

Leontidou, L. (1996), 'Alternatives to modernism in (Southern) urban theory: Exploring in-between spaces', *International Journal of Urban and Regional Research*, 20: 180–197.

Leontidou, L. (1997), 'Athens: inter-subjective facets of urban performance', in C. Jensen-Butler, A. Shakhar and J. van Weesep (eds), *European Cities in Competition*. Aldershot: Avebury, pp. 244–273.

Leontidou, L. and Marmaras, M. (1998), 'From tourists to immigrants: international residential tourism and the "littoralisation" of Europe', in Y. Apostdopoulos, L. Leontidou and P. Loukissas (eds), *Mediterranean Tourism: Facets of Socio-economic Development and Cultural Change*. London: Routledge (forthcoming).

Leroy, P. (1994), 'The Wadden Sea: a special area—specially protected?', in J. Deleu (ed.), *The Low Countries*. Rekkem: Stichting ons Erfdeel, pp. 108–113.

Les Echos (1996a), 19 February, Paris.

Les Echos (1996b), 5 November, Paris.

Les Echos (1996c), *L'Atlas des Echos: les Infrastructures et les Villes de Congrès*. Paris: Les Echos, Paris.

Les Echos (1996d), 7 October, Paris.

Les Echos (1996e), 9 July, Paris.

Les Echos (1996f), 11 June, Paris.

Les Echos (1996g), 21 October, Paris.

Les Echos (1997a), 8 January, Paris.

Les Echos (1997b), 9 January, Paris.

Letcher, P. (1989), *Yugoslavia: Mountain Walks and Historical Sites*. Chalfont St Peter: Bradt.

Lewis, J.R. and Williams, A.M. (1981), 'Regional uneven development on the European periphery: the case of Portugal, 1950–1978', *Tijdschrift voor Economische en Sociale Geografie*, 72: 81–98.

Lewis, J.R. and Williams, A.M. (1985), 'Reintigration or rejection? Portugal's retornados', *Iberian Studies*, 14: 11–23.

Lewis, J.R. and Williams, A.M. (1986a), 'The economic impact of return migration in Central Portugal', in R. King (ed.), *Return Migration and Regional Economic Problems*. London: Croom Helm.

Lewis, J.R. and Williams, A.M. (1986b), 'Factories, farms and families: the impacts of industrial growth in rural central Portugal', *Sociologia Ruralis*, 26: 320–344.

Lewis, J.R. and Williams, A.M. (1988), 'No longer Europe's best-kept secret: the Algarve's tourist boom', *Geography*, 74: 170–172.

Lichtenberger, E. (1976), 'Der Massentourismus als dynamisches System: Das österreichische Beispiel', *Tagungsberichte und wissenschaftliche Abhandlungen des 40. Deutschen Geographentages, Innsbruck 1975*. Weisbaden: Franz Steiner, pp. 673–692.

Lichtenberger, E. (1979), 'Die Suksession von der Agrar-zur Freizeitgesellschaft in den Hochgebirgen Europas', *Innsbrucker Geographische Studien*, 5: 401–436.

Light, D. and Andone, D. (1996), 'The changing geography of Romanian tourism', *Geography*, 81: 193–203.

Lockwood, A. and Guerrier, Y. (1989), 'Flexible working in the hospitality industry: current strategies and future potential', *Journal of Contemporary Hospitality Management*, 1: 11–16.

López Cano, D. (1984), *La Inmigración en la Costa del Sol: Análisis de un Desarraigo*. Málaga: Diputación Provincial.

López Ontiveros, A. (1981), 'El desarrollo reciente de la caza en España', in *Supervivencia de la Montaña*. Madrid: Servicio de Publicaciones Agrarias.

López Palomeque, F. (1982), *La Producción del Espacio de Ocio en Cataluña: la Vall d'Aran*. Barcelona: Universidad de Barcelona.

Loukissas, Ph.J. (1977), The Impact of Tourism in Regional Development: A Comparative Analysis of the Greek Islands. Ithaca, NY: Cornell University, PhD thesis.

Loukissas, Ph.J. (1982), 'Tourism's regional development impacts: a comparative analysis of the Greek islands', *Annals of Tourism Research*, 9: 523–541.

Lowenthal, D. (1997), *The Heritage Crusade*. London: Viking.

Lury. C. (1996), *Consumer Culture*. Cambridge: Polity.

Madeira: Plano à Médio Prazo, 1981–1984 (1982). Funchal: Governo Regional.

Mamdy, J.-F. (1995), 'Le développement local par le tourisme rural: enjeux et conditions', *Bulletin de l'Association des Géographes Français*, 72: 24–31.

Manente, M. (1986), 'Il turismo nell' economia italiana', in *Secondo Rapporto sul Turismo Italiano*. Rome: Ministero del Turismo e dello Spettacolo, pp. 321–344.

Marchena, M. (1986), 'Un análisis de los recursos turísticos andaluces', *Revista de Estudios Regionales*, 6: 169–195.

Marchena, M. (1987), *Territorio y Turismo en Andalucía*. Seville: Junta de Andalucía, Dirección General de Turismo.

Marchena, M. (ed.) (1991), *Ocio y Turismo en los Parques Naturales Andaluces*. Seville: Junta de Andalucía.

Marchena Gómez, M.J. and Rebollo, F.V. (1995), 'Coastal areas: processes, typologies and prospects', in A. Montanari and A.M. Williams (eds), *European Tourism: Regions, Spaces and Restructuring*. Chichester: Wiley, pp. 111–126.

Marciszewska, B. and Wyznikicwicz-Nawracula, A. (1996), 'The relationship between tourism products and demand: the example of equestrian tourism', in G. Richards (ed.), *Tourism in Central and Eastern Europe: Educating for Quality*. Tilburg: Tilburg University Press, pp. 275 287.

Marinos, P. (1983), 'Small island tourism—the case of Zakynthos, Greece, *Tourism Management*, 4: 212–215.

Martin, E. (1986), 'Entwicklung der touristischen Nachfrage im ländlichen Raum', in *Entwicklung ländlicher Räume durch den Fremdenverkehr. Forschungsberichte und Seminarergebnisse*. Bonn: Der Bundesminister für Raumordnung, Bauwesen und Städtebau, pp. 19–31.

Massey, D. (1984), *Spatial Divisions of Labour, Social Structure and the Geography of Production*. London: Macmillan.

Mathieson, A. and Wall, G. (1982), *Tourism: Economic, Physical and Social Impacts*. London: Longman.

May, V. (1995), 'Environmental implications of the 1992 Winter Olympic Games', *Tourism Management*, 16: 269–275.

Mazaraki, A. and Voronova, E. (1993), 'Prospects for tourism in Ukraine', *Tourism Management*, 14: 316–317.

Mazenec, J.A. and Zin, A.H. (1994), 'Tourist behaviour and the new European lifestyle typology', in G. Theobold (ed.), *Global Tourism: the Next Decade*. Oxford: Butterworth-Heinemann.

McEniff, J. (1991), 'Republic of Ireland', *EIU International Tourism Reports*, 4: 25–45.

McMahon, F. (1996), 'Rural and agri-tourism in Central and Eastern Europe', in G. Richards (ed.), *Tourism in Central and Eastern Europe: Educating for Quality*. Tilburg: Tilburg University Press, pp. 175–182.

McQueen, M. (1989), 'Multinationals in tourism', in S.F. Witt and L. Moutinho (eds), *Tourism Marketing and Management Handbook*. New York: Prentice Hall.

Meldon, J. (1994). 'Sustainable tourism development and the EC Structural Funds', in P. Breathnach (ed.), *Irish Tourism Development*. Maynooth: Geographical Society of Ireland, Special Publications No. 9, pp. 125–135.

Mendonsa, E.L. (1983a), 'Search for security, migration, modernisation and stratification in Nazaré, Portugal', *International Migration Review*, 6: 635–645.

Mendonsa, E.L. (1983b), 'Tourism and income strategies in Nazaré, Portugal', *Annals of Tourism Research*, 10: 213–238.

Mermet, G (1996a), *Francoscople 1997*. Paris: Larousse.

Mermet, G. (1996b), *Tendances 1996: le Nouveau Consommateur*. Paris: Larousse.

Mesa del Turismo, Servicio de Estudios (1995), 'El turismo en España 1995', *Informe de Coyuntura*, 3: 46 pp. (mimeo).

Micuła, G. (nd), *Pilgrimages to Poland: Sanctuaries*. Warsaw: Polish Tourist Information Centre.

Mignon, C. (1979), 'La Costa del sol et son arriére pays', in *Tourisme et Développment Régional en Andalousie*, 3rd part. Paris: Editions de Boccard, pp. 53–75.

Ministère de l'Equipement, du Logement, des Transports et du Tourisme (1996), *Mémento du Tourisme, 1995–96*. Paris: Ministère de l'Equipement, du Logement, des Transports et du Tourisme.

Ministère de l'Environnement: Ministère du Tourisme (1992), *Tourisme et l'Environnement*. Paris: La Documentation Française.

Ministère du Tourisme (1995), 'Les français et les vacances: des réves à la réalité', *Analyses et Perspectives du Tourisme*, No.43.

Ministerie van Cultuur, Recreatie en Maatschappelijk Werk (1981a), *Structurschema Openlucht Recreatie: beleidsvoornemen*. The Hague: Staatsuitgegerij.

Ministerie van Cultuur, Recreatie en Maatschappelijk Werk (1981b), *Ruimte voor Recreatie*. The Hague: Staatsuitgeverij.

Ministerie van Economische Zaken (1994), *Ruimte voor Economische Activiteit*. The Hague: Staatsuitgeverij.

Ministerie van Landbouw en Visserij (1981), *Structuurschema voor Landinrichting: beleidsvoornemen*. The Hague: Staatsuitgeverij.

Ministerie van Landbouw, Natuurbeheer en Visserij (1993), *Landinrichting in de Jaaren Negentig*. The Hague: Staatsuitgeverij.

Ministerie van Volkshuisvesting en Ruimtelijke Ordening (1977), *Derde Nota over de Ruimtelijke Ordening: nota landelijke gebieden*. The Hague: Staatsuitgeverij.

Ministerie van Volkshuisvesting, Ruimtelijke Ordening en Milieubeheer (1988), *On the Road to 2015: Comprehensive Summary of the Fourth Report on Physical Planning in The Netherlands*. The Hague: Staatsuitgeverij.

Ministry of Coordination (1971), *Study of Employment in Hotel and Other Tourist Enterprises*. Athens (in Greek).

Mintel (1985), *Tourism Special*, Volume 2. London: Mintel.

Miranda, M.T. (1985), *La Segunda Residencia en la Provincia de Valencia*. Valencia: Universidad de Valencia.

Mogendorff, D. (1996), 'The European hospitality industry', in R. Thomas (ed.), *The Hospitality Industry, Tourism and Europe*. London: Cassell.

Montanari, A. (1991), 'For a sustainable tourism in the European Mediterranean countries', *Studies in Locational Analysis*, 3: 21–33.

Montenari, A. (1995), 'The Mediterranean region: Europe's summer leisure space', in A. Montanari and A. M. Williams (eds), *European Tourism: Regions, Spaces and Restructuring*. Chichester: Wiley.

Montanari, A. (1996), 'Tourism: the geography of disequilibrium', in *The Geography of Disequilibrium: Global Issues and Restructuring in Italy*. Rome: Società Geografica Italiana, pp. 189–213.

Montanari, A. and Cortese, A. (1993), 'Third World immigrants in Italy', in R. King (ed.), *Mass Migration in Europe: the Legacy and the Future*. London: Belhaven, pp. 275–292.

Montanari, A. and Williams, A.M. (1995), *European Tourism: Regions, Spaces and Restructuring*. Chichester: Wiley.

Monteiro, S. (1996) *Les Vacances des Français*. Paris: INSEE Résultats: consommation, modes de vie.

Monteiro, S. and C. Rowenczyk (1994), 'Les vacances d'été 1993', *INSEE Première*, No.333.

Morales Folguera, J.M. (1982), *La Arquitectura del Ocio en la Costa del Sol*. Málaga: Universidad de Málaga.

Morzer Bruins, M.F. and Benthem, R.J. (eds) (1979), *Atlas van Nederlandsche Landschappen*. Utrecht: Spectrum.

Mulero Mendigorri, A. (1990), *Espacios y Actividades de Ocio en el Ambito Rural*. Madrid: M° de Agricultura, Pesca y Alimentación.

Muller, H., Rutter, H., Guhl, D. and Stettler, G. (1996), *Tourismus im Kanton Bern*. St Gallen: Institut fur Tourismus, Hochschule St. Gallen.

Murphy, P.E. (1982), 'Perceptions and attitudes of decision-making groups in tourism centres', *Journal of Travel Research*, 21: 8–12.

Navalón, R. (1995), *Planeamiento Urbano y Turismo Residencial en los Municipios Litorales de Alicante*. Alicante: Instituto de Cultura Juan Gil Albert.

Naylon, J. (1967), 'Tourism—Spain's most important industry', *Geography*, 52: 23–40.

Neate, S. (1987), 'The role of tourism in sustaining farm structures and communities on the Isles of Scilly', in M. Bouquet and M. Winter (eds), *Who from Their Labours Rest?* Aldershot: Avebury, pp. 9–21.

Nelson, D.N. (ed.) (1992), *Romania after Tyranny*. Boulder, CO: Westview.

NESC (1980), *Tourism Policy*. Report 52. Dublin: Stationery Office.

Nordström, J. (1995), 'Tourism satellite account for Sweden 1992–1993', *Umeå Economic Studies* No. 385 (Umeå ISSN 0348–1018). University of Ume.

Norris, H.T. (1993), *Islam in the Balkans*. London: Hurst.

Norris, J. and Wall, G. (1994), 'Gender and tourism', *Progress in Tourism, Recreation and Hospitality Management*, 6: 57–78.

NSSG (National Statistical Service of Greece) (1985), *Tourist Statistics: Years 1982 and 1983*. Athens: NSSG.

NSSG (1995), *Tourist Statistics: Years 1991–1993*. Athens: NSSG.

NSSG (various), *Statistical Yearbooks of Greece*. Athens: NSSG.

OAOM & Associates, (1976), *Chalkidiki: Regional Plan*. Athens: Ministry of Coordination (in Greek).

Oberreit, J. (1996), 'Destruction and reconstruction: the case of Dubrovnik', in D.R. Hall and D. Danta (eds), *Reconstructing the Balkans*. Chichester and New York: Wiley, pp. 67–77.

O'Cinnéide, M. and Walsh, J.A. (1990–1991), 'Tourism and regional development in Ireland', *Geographical Viewpoint*, 19: 47–68.

O'Connor, B. (1993), 'Myths and mirrors: tourist images and national identity', in B. O'Connor and M. Cronin (eds), *Tourism in Ireland: a Critical Analysis*. Cork: Cork University Press, pp. 68–85.

O'Connor, B. and Cronin, M. (eds) (1993), *Tourism in Ireland: a Critical Analysis*. Cork: Cork University Press.

OECD (1974), *Government Policy in the Development of Tourism*. Paris: OECD.

OECD (1980–1996), *Tourism Policy and International Tourism in OECD Countries*. Paris: OECD.

Office Fédéral de l'Industrie, des Arts et Métiers et du Travail (1990), *Perspectives d'Avenir du Tourisme Suisse*. Berne.

Office Fédéral de la Statistique Suisse (1986a), *Tourisme en Suisse, 1985*. Berne.

Office Fédéral de la Statistique Suisse (1986b), *Le Balance Touristique de la Suisse*. Berne.

Office Fédéral de la Statistique Suisse (1994), *L'Hôtellerie et la Parahotellerie en Suisse*. Berne.

Office Fédéral de la Statistique Suisse (1996a), *Les Hôtels et les Etablissements de Cure en Suisse en 1995*. Berne.

Office Fédéral de la Statistique Suisse (1996b), *Les Recettes et les Dépenses dans le Domaine du Tourisme International*. Berne.

Office Fédéral de la Statistique Suisse (1997), *Annuaire Statistique de la Suisse 1996*. Berne.

O'Hagan, J. and Mooney, D. (1983), 'Input–output multipliers in a small open economy: an application to tourism', *Economic and Social Review*, 14: 273–280.

Opaschowski, H.W. (1995), *Urlaub 94/95—Tourismus mit Zukunft. 3. Europäische Tourismusanalyse*. Hamburg: BAT Freizeit-Forschungsinstitut.

O'Reilly, D. (1996), 'Massacre trail lures sightseers', *The European*, 14 November.

Ortega Martínez, E. (1986), 'Presente y futuro del turismo de golf en España', *Estudios Turísticos*, 90: 23–47.

Österreichische Raumordnungskonferenz (1985), 'Internationale und nationale Trends im Tourismus. Rahmenbedingungen für die Fremdenverkehrsentwicklung in Österreich', *Gutachten des Österreichischen Instituts für Raumplanung*, 47.

Österreichische Raumordnungskonferenz (1987a), 'Entwicklungsmölichkeiten des Fremdenverkehrs in Problemgebieten', *Gutachten des Österreichischen Instituts für Raumplanung*, 53.

Österreichische Raumordnungskonferenz (1987b), Zweitwohnungen in Österreich. Formen und Verbreitung. Auswirkungen, künftige Entwicklung', *Gutachen des Instituts für Stadtforschung, Kommunalwissenschaftlichen Dokumentationszentrums, Österreichischen Instituts für Raumplanung*, 54.

Österreichisches Statistisches Zentralamt (various years), *Der Fremdenverkehr im Österreich in Jahre*. Vienna: Österreichisches Statistisches Zentralamt.

Owen, D. (1996), 'No lift for skis', *The Financial Times*, 14 December.

Page, S.J. (1994), 'Perspectives on tourism and peripherality: a review of tourism in the Republic of Ireland', in C.P. Cooper and A. Lockwood (eds), *Progress in Tourism, Recreation and Hospitality Management*, Volume 5. Chichester: Wiley, pp. 26–53.

Page, S.J. (1995), *Urban Tourism*. Routledge, London.

Painter, J. and Goodwin, M. (1995), 'Local governance and concrete research: investigating the uneven development of regulation', *Economy and Society*, 24: 334–356.

Papachristou, G. (1987), 'In search of tourist policy', *To Vima*, 19 July, 28–30 (in Greek).

Papadopoulos, S.I. (1987), 'World tourism: an economic analysis', *Revue de Tourisme*, 1: 2–13.

Parlett, G., Fletcher, J. and Cooper, C. (1995), 'The impact of tourism on the Old Town of Edinburgh', *Tourism Management*, 16(5): 355–360.

Parnell Kerr Forster Associates (1986), *Outlook in the Hotel and Tourism Industries*. London: Parnell Kerr Forster Associates.

Pearce, D.G. (1981), *Tourism Development*. London: Longman.

Pearce, D.G. (1987), 'Spatial patterns of package tourism in Europe', *Annals of Tourism Research*, 14: 183–201.

Pearce, D.G. (1988), 'Tourism and regional development in the European Community', *Tourism Management*, 9: 133–151.

Pearce, D.G. (1990), 'Tourism in Ireland: questions of scale and organization', *Tourism Management*, 11: 133–151.

Pearce, D.G. (1992a). 'Tourism and the European Regional Development Fund: the first fourteen years', *Journal of Travel Research*, 30, 44–51.

Pearce, D.G. (1992b), *Tourist Organisations*. Harlow: Longman

Pearce, D.G. (1996), 'Regional tourist organizations in Spain: emergence, policies and consequences', *Tourism Economics*, 2: 119–136.

Pedrini, L. (1984), 'The geography of tourism and leisure in Italy', *GeoJournal*, 9: 55–57.

Peters, M. (1969), *International Tourism: the Economics and Development of the International Tourist Trade*. London: Hutchinson.

Petrin, T. (1996), *Basic facts on Rural Women in Selected Central European Countries*. Rome: Food and Agriculture Organization of the United Nations.

Pina, P. (1988), *Portugal: O Turismo no Século XX*. Lisbon: Lucidus.

Pinder, D.A. (1983), 'Planned port industrialization and the quest for upward economic transition: an examination of development strategies for the Dutch delta', in B.S. Hoyle and D. Hilling (eds), *Seaport Systems and Spatial Change*. Chichester: Wiley, pp. 277–301.

Pinder, D.A. and Rosing, K.E. (1988), 'Public policy and planning of the Rotterdam waterfront: a tale of two cities', in B.S. Hoyle, D.A. Pinder and M.S. Husain (eds), *Revitalizing the Waterfront: International Dimensions of Dockland Redevelopment*. London: Belhaven, pp. 114–128.

Pinto, F.M. (1984), *O Algarve no contexto nacional: Situação regional e estrategia de actuação*. Faro: Comissão de Coordenação da Região do Algarve.

Pizam, A. and Knowles, T. (1994). 'The European hotel industry', in C.P. Cooper and A. Lockwood (eds), *Progress in Tourism, Recreation and Hospitality Management*. Chichester: Wiley, pp. 283–295.

Ploaie, G. (1996), 'The impact of tourism and conservation on agriculture in the mountains of Valcea County, Romania', *GeoJournal*, 38: 219–27.

Pollard, J. (1989), 'Patterns in Irish tourism', in R.W.G. Carter and A.J. Parker (eds), *Ireland: a Contemporary Geographical Perspective*. London: Routledge, pp. 301–330.

Pollard, J. and Rodríguez, R.D. (1993), 'Tourism and Torremolinos', *Tourism Management*, 14: 247–258.

Polychroniadis, A. and Hadjimichalis, C. (1974), 'Lyomena: a solution to the second home problem?', *Architecture in Greece*, 8: 54–61 (in Greek).

Poon, A. (1993), *Tourism, Technology and Competitive Strategies*. Wallingford: CAB International.

Popesku, J. and L. Milojević (1996), *Serbia: Landscape Painted from the Heart*. Belgrade: National Tourism Organization of Serbia.

Potier, F. and C. Chasset (1993), 'Les voyages de courte durée des Français', *Cahier Espaces*, 34: 35–56.

Potier, F. and N. Cockerell (1993), 'Les courts séjours des Européens', *Cahier Espaces*, 34: 19–30.

Poulsen, T.M. (1977), 'Migration on the Adriatic coast; some processes associated with the development of tourism', in H.L. Kostanick (ed.), *Population and Migration Trends in Eastern Europe*. Boulder: Westview, pp. 197–215.

Préau (1970), 'Principe d'analyse des sites en montagne', *Urbanisme*, 116: 21–25.

Price Waterhouse (1987), *Improving the Performance of Irish Tourism*. Dublin: Stationery Office.

Pridham, G. (1996), *Tourism Policy in Mediterranean Europe: Towards Sustainable Development?* Bristol: University of Bristol, Centre for Mediterranean Studies, Occasional Paper 15.

Priebe, H. (1972), *Untersuchungen zur Regionalstruktur unterer Bayerischer Wald. Ergebnisse eines*

Forschungsauftrages des Bundesministers für Wirtschaft und Finanzen. BMWF-Dokumentation Nr. 153, Bonn.

Priestley, G.K. (1995), 'Problems of tourism development in Spain', in H. Coccossis and P. Nijkamp (eds), *Sustainable Tourism Development.* Aldershot: Avebury, pp. 187–198.

Provincia TMT (1996), *Village Tourism.* Budapest: Hungarian Tourist Board.

Puijk, R. (1996), 'Dealing with fish and tourists: a case study from Northern Norway', in J. Boissevain (ed.), *Coping with Tourists.* Providence RI and Oxford: Berghahn, pp. 204–226.

Py, P. (1996), *Le Tourisme: un Phénomène Economique.* Paris: La Documentation Française.

Quilici, F. (1984), 'Invito all' Italia', in *Guida illustrata Italia.* Milan: Touring Club Italiano, pp. 7–10.

Quinn, B. (1994), 'Images of Ireland in Europe: a tourism perspective', in U. Kockel (ed.), *Culture, Tourism and Development: the Case of Ireland.* Liverpool: Liverpool University Press, pp. 61–73.

Racine, J. and Raffestin, C. (1990), *Nouvelle Géographie de la Suisse et des Suisses.* Lausanne: Editions Payot.

Redclift, M. and Benton, T. (1994), *Social Theory and the Global Environment.* London: Routledge.

Redclift, N. and Sinclair, M.T. (eds) (1991), *Working Women: International Perspectives on Labour and Gender Ideology.* London: Routledge.

Renucci, J. (1991), 'Le tourisme urbain français en question: sous-exploitation et efforts d'impulsion', *Dossier de la Revue de Géographie Alpine,* 6: 57–66.

Reynolds-Ball, E. (1914), *Mediterranean Winter Resorts.* London: Kegan Paul, Trench, Tüber and Co.

Rhodes, A. (1955), *The Dalmatian Coast.* London: Evans Brothers.

Richards, G. (1996), *Tourism in Central and Eastern Europe: Educating for Quality.* Tilburg: Tilburg University Press.

Rijksplanologische Dienst (1986), *Notitie Ruimtelijke Perspectieven: op weg naar de 4e nota over de ruimtelijke ordening.* The Hague: Staatsuitgeverij.

Riza, E. (1978), *Gjirokastra: Museum City.* Tirana: 8 Nëntori.

Robinson, G. (1993). 'Tourism and tourism policy in the European Community: an overview', *International Journal of Hospitality Management,* 12: 7–20.

Robinson, M. (1996), 'Sustainable tourism for Spain: principles, prospects and problems', in M. Barke, J. Towner and M.T. Newton (eds), *Tourism in Spain.* Wallingford: CAB International, pp. 401–427.

Robinson, G. (1996), 'Tourism policy', in R. Thomas (ed.), *The Hospitality Industry, Tourism and Europe.* London: Cassell.

Röck, S. (1977), 'Überlagerung von Freizeitformen. Räumliche Auswirkungen der verschiedenen Erholungsformern und ihrer Kombination (Kurz- und Langzeiterholung)', *Raumforschung und Raumordnung,* 35: 224–228.

Rodríguez Marín, J.A. (1985), 'El turismo en la economía canaria: delimitación e impacto económico, in Gobierno de Canarias *et al.* (eds) *El Turismo en Canarias.* Canary Islands: Gobierno de Canarias.

Roe, S. (1996), 'Goulash getaways', *Business Eastern Europe,* 25: 7.

Romanos, A.G. (1975), 'Mykonos: settlement protection as a motive of economic development', *Architecture in Greece,* 9: 197–203 (in Greek).

Roth, P. (1984), 'Der Ausländerreiseverkehr in der Bundesrepublik Deutschland. Eine Darstellung der Struktur ausländischer Gäste in der Bundesrepublik, ihre Nachfragepräferenzen, Reiseziele und Motive. Dargestellt am Beispiel ausländischer Gäste aus den U.S.A., Grossbritannien und der Schweiz', *Zeitschrift für Wirtschaftsgeographie,* 3–4: 157–63.

Rowenczyk, C. (1994), 'Les vacances d'hiver: saison 1993–1994', *INSEE Première,* No. 352.

Rowenczyk, C. (1995), 'Les vacances de l'été 1994: un taux de départ record', *INSEE Première,* No. 396.

Ruppert, K. and Maier, J. (1970), 'Der Naherholungsverkehr der Münchener—ein Beitrag zur Geographie des Freizeitverhaltens', *Mitteilungen der Geographischen Gesellschaft München,* 55.

Ruppert, K. Gräf, P. and Lintner, P. (1986), 'Naherholungsverhalten im Raum München. Persistenz und Wandel freizeitorientierter Regionalstrukturen 1968/80', in *Arbeitsmaterial,* No. 116, Hannover: Akademie für Raumforschung und Landesplanung.

Rumley, P.A. (1983), 'Le tourisme Jurassien', *Geographica Helvetica*, 38: 73–77.

Ruukel, A. (ed.) (1996), *Estonia—the Natural Way*. Pärnu: Kodukant Ecotourism Association of Estonia.

Said, E. (1978), *Orientalism*. London: Routledge & Kegan Paul.

Salvá, P. (1984), 'Las variaciones estructurales y morfológicas en el espacio rural de la isla de Mallorca como consecuencia del impacto del turismo de masas', in *Coloquio Hispano Francés sobre Espacios Rurales*. Madrid: Servicio de Publicaciones Agrarias, pp. 219–231.

Santillana, J. (1984), 'Las migraciones internas en España: necesidad de ordenación', *Información Comercial Española*, 609: 23–37.

Sarmiento, M. (1995), 'El mercado de ferias y exposiciones y otros viajes de negocios', *Estudios Turísticos*, 126: 191–210.

SCB/Statistics Sweden(1995), *Expenditures of GDP: Appendix 1*. Örebro: SCB-tryck.

Schilling, R. *et al.* (1974), 'Tourisme', *Werk*, 8: 908–989.

Schnell, P. (1975), 'Tourism as a means of improving the regional economic structure', in *Tourism as a Factor in National and Regional Development*. Peterborough, Canada: Department of Geography, Trent University, Occasional Paper No. 4, pp. 72–81.

Schnell, P. (1977), 'Die Bedeutung des Fremdenverkehrs im Rahmen der wirtschaftlichen Förderung strukturschwacher Gebiete', in *Tourism—Factor for National and Regional Development*. Sofia: University of Sofia, Kliment Ohridski, Chair of Geography of Tourism/Union of the Scientific Workers in Bulgaria/Bulgarian Geographical Sociecty, pp. 92–110.

Schnell, P. (1983), 'Der Fremdenverkehr in Westfalen', in P. Weber and K.-F. Schreiber (eds), *Westfalen und angrenzende Regionen, Festschrift zum 44. Deutschen Geographentag in Münster*. Part I. Paderborn: F. Schöningh: pp. 129–156 (Münstersche Geographische Arbeiten 15).

Schnell, P. (1986), 'Fremdenverkehr—Nachfragestruktur', *Geographischlandeskundlicher Atlas von Westfalen*. Münster: Geographische Kommission für Westfalen.

Schnell, P. (1996), 'Major city tourism in Germany', in C.M. Law (ed.), *Tourism in Major Cities*. London: International Thomson Business Press, pp. 89–113.

Schwieizerischer Fremdenverkehrsband (1986), *Fremdenverkehr in der Schweiz*. Berne.

Seaton, A.V. (1992) 'Social Stratification in tourism choice and experience since the war, part 1', *Tourism Management*, 13: 106–111.

Secretaria de Estado do Turismo (1986), *Plano Nacional de Turismo 1986–1989*. Lisbon: Grupo Coordenador do Plano Nacional de Turismo.

Secretaría General de Turismo (1990), *Libro Blanco del Turismo Español*. Madrid: Secretaría General de Turismo.

Secretaría General de Turismo (various), *Annuario de Estadísticas de Turismo*. Madrid: Secretaría General de Turismo.

Secretaría General de Turismo (various), *Nota de Cyuntura Turística*. Madrid: Secretaría General de Turismo.

Secretaría General de Turismo (various), *El Empleo en el Sector Turístico*. Madrid: Secretaría General de Turismo.

Selstad, T. (1993), 'Nordic Tourism in Europe and European tourism in Nordic countries: trends and scenarios, NordREFO', *Nord Revy*, No. S: 3/4.

Shachar, A. (1995), 'Metropolitan areas: economic globalisation and urban tourism', in A. Montanari and A.M. Williams (eds), *European Tourism: Regions, Spaces and Restructuring*. Chichester: Wiley, pp. 151–160.

Sharpley, R. (1994), *Tourism, Tourists and Society*. Kings Ripton: Elm Publications.

Shaw, G. and Williams, A.M. (1987), 'Firm formation and operating characteristics in the Cornish tourism industry', *Tourism Management*, 8: 344–348.

Shaw, G. and Williams, A.M. (1994), *Critical Issues in Tourism. A Geographical Perspective*. Oxford: Blackwell.

Shaw, G. and Williams, A.M. (1997a), 'Entrepreneurship, small business culture and tourism development', in D. Ioannides and K.G. Debbage (eds), *Economic Geography of the Tourist Industry: a Supply-Side Analysis*. London: Routledge.

Shaw, G. and Williams, A. (eds) (1997b), *The Rise and Fall of British Coastal Resorts: Cultural and Economic Perspectives*. London: Mansell.

Shaw, G., Williams, A., Greenwood, J. and Hennessy, S. (1987), *Public Policy and Tourism in England: a Review of National and Local Trends*. Exeter: University of Exeter, Tourism Research Group.

Shinew, K.J. and Backman, S.J. (1995), 'Incentive travel—an attractive option', *Tourism Management*, 16: 285–293.

Siiskonen, P. (1996), *Overview of the Socio-economic Position of Rural Women in Selected Central and Eastern European Countries*. Rome: Food and Agriculture Organization of the United Nations.

da Silva, J.A.M. (1986), 'Avaliação do impacto econômico do turismo, em Portugal'. Dissertation for a Master's degree in Economics, Universidade Técnica de Lisboa, Instituto Superior de Econômia.

Simpson, P. (1997), 'Polish hotels: rooms vacant', *Business Central Europe*, 5: 32.

Singh, B.P. (1984), *The Impact of Tourism on the Balance of Payments*. Athens: CPER.

Sinnhuber, K. (1978), Recreation in the mountains, *Weiner Gegraphische Schriften*, 51–52: 59–86.

Sirgado, J.R. (1990), *Turismo e Desenvolvimento Local e Regional: O Caso do Concelho do Lago na Regiao do Algarve e No Pais*. Lisbon: Universidade de Lisboa, Master's Degree dissertation in the Department of Geography.

Slattery, P. and Johnson, S.M. (1993), 'Accommodation: hotel chains in Europe', *Travel and Tourism Analyst*, 1: 65–80.

Smyth, E. (1986), 'Public Policy for tourism in Northern Ireland', *Tourism Management*, 7: 120–126.

Soane, J. (1992), 'The origin, growth and transformation of maritime resorts since 1840', *Built Environment*, 18: 13–26.

Spartidis, A (1969), *Research on the Magnitude and the Characteristics of Employment in Tourist Enterprises*. Athens: EOT (in Greek).

Šredl, V. (1996), *Rab: More than a Game*. Rab: Turistička zajednica grada Raba.

SSTA (State Sports and Tourism Administration) (1996), *Polish Tourism 1995*. Warsaw: SSTA.

Stallinbrass, C. (1980), 'Seaside resorts and the hotel accommodation industry', *Progress in Planning*, 13: 103–174.

Statistisches Bundesamt (ed.) (1965), 'Urlaubs- und Erholungsreisen 1962', *Wirtschaft und Statistik*, 1: 38–41, Wiesbaden.

Statistisches Bundesamt (ed.) (1970), 'Ausgaben für Urlaubs- und Erholungsreisen 1969', *Wirtschaft und Statistik*, 8: 624–626, Wiesbaden.

Statistisches Bundesamt (ed.) (1981), 'Urlaubs- und Erholungsreiseverkehr 1979/80. Ergebnisse des Mikorzensus 1980', *Wirtschaft und Statistik*, 12: 866–870, Wiesbaden.

Statistisches Bundesamt (ed.) (1986), Beherbergung im Reiseverkehr: April und Winterhalbjahr 1986 Oktober und Sommerhalbjahr 1986. *Fachserie 6: Handel, Gastgewerbe, Reiseverkehr*. Wiesbaden.

Statistisches Bundesamt (ed.) (1988), *Tourismus in Zahlen*. Wiesbaden.

Statistisches Bundesamt (ed.) (1991), *Tourismus in Zahlen 1991. Mit gesamtdeutschen Ergebnissen*. Wiesbaden.

Statistisches Bundesamt (ed.) (1996), *Tourismus in Zahlen 1996*. Wiesbaden.

Statistisches Bundesamt (ed.) (various years), *Statistisches Jahrbuch der Bundesrepublik Deutschland*. Wiesbaden.

Steinecke, A. (1996), 'Wohin geht die Reise? Aktuelle Tendenzen im Tourismus', in *Endlich Urlaub! Die Deutschen Reisen*. pp. 112–117, Cologne: Dumont.

Steinecke, A., Brysch, A., Haart, N. and Herrmann, P. (1996), Tourismusstandort Deutschland—Hemmnisse, Chancen, Herausforderungen', *Stadt und Gemeinde*, 7: 260–265.

Stepinac Fabianic, T. and Klaric, Z. (1993), 'Ecotourism in national parks and protected areas—regional park of central Istria: needs and conceptual answers for economic development in a protected area', *The Tourist Review*, 3: 13–17.

Stevenson, G. (1997), 'The good, the bad and the ugly: post-communist tourism in the Czech Republic', *Tourism*, 92: 12–13.

Stoelers, R. and Karssen, A. (1988), *De Vacantie Atlas van Nederland*. Enschede: Intermap.

Stokes, Kennedy and Crowley *et al.* (1986), *Tourism Working for Ireland: a Plan for Growth.* Dublin: Irish Hotels Federation.

Storper, M. (1985), 'Oligopoly and the product cycle: essentialism in economic geography', *Economic Geography*, 61: 260–282.

Strazimiri, G. (1987), *Berati.* Tirana: 8 Nëntori.

Studienkreis für Tourismus (ed.) (1986), *Urlaubsreisen 1954–1985. 30 Jahre Erfassung des touristischen Verhaltens der Deutschen durch soziologische Stichprobenerhebungen.* Starnberg.

Studienkreis für Tourismus (ed.) (1987), *Erste Ergebnisse der Reiseanalyse 1986 des Studienkreises für Tourismus—10. März 1987.* Starnberg.

Swain, M.B. (1995), 'Gender in tourism', *Annals of Tourism Research*, 22: 247–266.

Swiss Tourism Federation (1996), *Swiss Tourism in Figures, 1996.* Berne: The Federation.

Symons, L.J. (1993), 'Restructuring the region's air industry', in D.R. Hall (ed.), *Transport and Economic Development in the New Central and Eastern Europe.* London: Belhaven, pp. 67–81.

Syrett, S. (1997), 'The politics of partnership: the role of social partners in local economic development in Portugal', *European Urban and Regional Studies*, 4: 99–114.

Tansey, Webster and Associates (1991), *Tourism and the Economy.* Dún Laoghaire: Irish Tourism Industry Confederation.

Tansey, Webster and Associates (1995), *The Economic Effects of Tourism in Ireland 1990–1993.* Dún Laoghaire: Irish Tourism Industry Confederation.

Tarrant, C. (1989), 'UK hotel industry—market restructuring and the need to respond to consumer demands', *Tourism Management*, 10: 187–191.

Taylor, M. (1995), *Environmental Change: Industry, Power and Policy.* Avebury: Aldershot.

TCG (1981), *Tourism and Regional Development* (Proceedings of a Meeting in the Context of the TCG Conference on Development. Heraklion (in Greek).

Teleki, N., Munteanu, L., Teodoreanu, E. and Grigore, L. (1985), *Spa Treatment in Romania.* Bucharest: Sport-Turism Publishing House.

Telleschi, A. (1992), *Turismo verde e spazio rurale in Toscano.* Pisa: ETS Editrice.

Teuscher, H. (1983), 'Social tourism for all: the Swiss Travel Saving Fund, *Tourism Management*, 4: 216–219.

Thomas, R. (1996), 'The hospitality industry, tourism and European integration: an overview', in R. Thomas (ed.), *The Hospitality Industry, Tourism and Europe.* London: Cassell.

Thompson, I. (1994), 'The French TGV system—progress and projects', *Geography*, 79: 164–168.

Tinacci, M. (1969), 'Il litorale toscano e il litorale romagnolo: note di geografia comparata dei prezzi e delle strutture alberghiere', *Rivista Geografica Italiana*, 76: 353–390.

Tinard, Y. (1994), *Le Tourisme: Économie et Management.* Paris: Ediscience.

Tourism and Leisure Partners (1996), *Regional Distribution of Tourism in Ireland: Responding to Changing Market Trends.* Dún Laoghaire: Irish Tourism Industry Confederation.

Tourism Concern/World Wildlife Fund (1992), *Beyond the Green Horizon: Principles for Sustainable Tourism.* Godalming: Tourism Concern.

Tourism Research and Marketing (1994), *Theme Parks—UK and International Markets.* London: Tourism Research and Marketing.

Tourism Research Group (1996), *South West Tourist Industry Competitiveness Report.* Exeter: University of Exeter, Tourism Research Group.

Tourism Task Force (1992), *Report of the Tourism Task Force to the Minister for Tourism, Transport and Communications.* Dublin: Stationery Office.

Towner, J. (1985), 'The Grand Tour. A key phase in the history of tourism', *Annals of Tourism Research*, 12: 297–333.

Travis, A.S. (1982), 'Leisure, recreation and tourism in Western Europe', *Tourism Management*, 3: 3–15.

Tuppen, J. (1988), 'Tourism in France: recent trends in winter sports', *Geography*, 73: 359–363.

Tuppen, J. (1988), *France under Recession, 1981–86.* London: Macmillan.

Tuppen, J. (1991), 'France: the changing character of a key industry', in A.M. Williams and G. Shaw (eds), *Tourism and Economic Development: Western European Experiences*. London: Belhaven, pp. 191–206.

Tuppen, J. (1996), 'Tourism in French cities', in C. Law (ed.), *Tourism in Major Cities*. London: International Thomson Business Press, pp. 52–88.

Turespaña. Instituto de Turismo de España (1996), *Análisis de la Oferta de Turismo Rural en España. Documento-resumen*. Madrid: Turespaña. Instituto de Turismo de España.

Turespaña. Instituto de Turismo de España (1997), 'Palacio de Congresos. Balance 96', *Turismo Informa*, 6: 6.

Turner, R.K. (1993), *Sustainable Environmental Economics and Management: Principles and Practice*. Chichester: Wiley.

Turok, I. (1993), 'Inward investment and local linkages: how deeply embedded is "Silicon Glen"', *Regional Studies*, 27: 401–418.

UNCTC (1988), *Transnational corporations in World Development Trends and Prospects*. New York: UNCTC.

UNCTC (1982), *Transnational Corporations in International Tourism*. New York: UNCTC.

Unwin, T. (1996), 'Tourist development in Estonia: images, sustainability, and integrated rural development', *Tourism Management*, 17: 265–276.

Urry, J. (1987), 'Some social and spatial aspects of services', *Environment and Planning D: Society and Space*, 5: 5–26.

Urry, J. (1990), *The Tourist Gaze: Leisure and Travel in Contemporary Societies*. London: Sage.

Urry, J. (1995), *Consuming Places*. London: Routledge.

Urry, J. (1997), 'Cultural change and the seaside resort', in Shaw, G. and Williams, A.M. (eds), *The Rise and Fall of British Coastal Resorts: Cultural and Economic Perspectives*. London: Mansell, pp. 102–115.

Uthoff, D. (1982), 'Die Stellung des Harzes im Rahmen der Fremdenverkehrsentwicklung in deutschen Mittelgebirgen. Eine vergleichende Analyse auf statistischer Grundlage', *Neues Archiv für Niedersachsen*, 3: 290–313.

Vaccaro, G. and Perez, M. (1986), 'La domanda turistica', in *Secondo Rapporto sul Turismo Italiano*. Rome: Ministero del Turismo e dello Spettacolo, pp. 103–226.

Vaiou-Hadjimichalis, D. and Hadjimichalis, C. (1979), *Regional Development and Industrialization (Monopoly Investment in Pylos)*. Athens: Exandas (in Greek).

Valdés Peláez, L. (1996), 'El turismo rural en España', in A. Pedreño and V. Monfort (eds), *Introducción a la Economía del Turismo en España*. Madrid: Edit. Cívitas, pp. 365–403.

Valenzuela, M. (1976), 'La residencia secundaria en la provincia de Madrid. Génesis y estructura espacial', *Ciudad y Territorio*, 2–3: 135–153.

Valenzuela, M. (1982), 'La incidencia de los grandes equipamientos recreativos en la configuración del espacio turístico litoral: la costa de la Málaga', in *Coloquio Hispano-Francés sobre Espacios Litorales*. Madrid: Servicios de Publicaciones Agrarias.

Valenzuela, M. (1985), 'La consommation d'espace par le tourisme sur le littoral andalou: les centres d'interêt touristique national', *Revue Géographique del Pyrénnées et du Sud-Ouest*, 56: 289–312.

Valenzuela, M. (1986a), 'Conflicts spatiaux entre tourisme et agriculture dans les régions méditerranéennes espagnoles', in *Le tourisme contre l'Agriculture*. Paris: ADEF.

Valenzuela, M. (1986b), 'La práctica del esquí en la Sierra de Guadarrama (Madrid)', in B. Barceló (ed.), *Proceedings of the VII Symposium of the IGU Commission on Environmental Problems*. Palma, Majorca, pp. 171–183.

Valenzuela, M. (1988), 'La residencia secundaria. Mito social y conflicto urbanístico en los espacios turísticos-recreativos', *Urbanismo COAM*, 4: 71–83.

Valenzuela, M. (1992), 'Turismo y gran ciudad. Una opción de futuro para las metrópolis postindustriales', *Revista Valenciana d'Estudis Autonomics*, 13: 103–138.

Valenzuela, M. (1993), 'Turismo contra medio natural: las zonas húmedas del litoral turístico español, un espacio acosado', in D. López Bonillo (ed.), *Aportaciones en Homenaje al Profesor Luis Miguel Albentosa*. Tarragona: Diputació de Tarragona, pp. 337–355.

Valenzuela, M. (ed.) (1997), *Los Turismos de Interior*. Madrid: Universidad Autónoma.

van den Berg, L., van der Borg, J. and van der Meer, J. (1995), *Urban Tourism: Performance and Strategies in Eight European Cities*. Aldershot: Avebury.

van der Knaap, G.A. and Pinder, D.A. (1992), 'Revitalising the European waterfront: policy evolution and planning issues', in B.S. Hoyle and D.A. Pinder (eds), *European Port Cities in Transition*. London: Belhaven, pp. 155–175.

Velluti Zatti, S. (1992), 'Edifici rurali: una risorsa culturale, ambientale ed economica da salvaguarde e valorizzare', in A. Montanari (ed.), *Il Turismo nelle Regioni Rurali della CEE: la Tutela del Patrimonio Naturale e Culturale*. Naples: Edizioni Scientifiche Italiane, pp. 57–71.

Venturini, M. (1992), 'Immigration et marché du travail en Italie: données récentes', *Revue Européenne des Migrations Internationales*, 8 (suppl): 145–161.

Vera Rebollo, F. (1985), 'Las condiciones climáticas y marítimas, como factores de localización del turismo histórico y alicantino', *Investigaciones Geográficas*, 3: 161–178.

Vera Rebollo, F. (1987), *Turismo y Urbanismo en el Litoral Alicantino*. Alicante: Institución Cultural 'Gil Albert'.

Vera Rebollo, F. and Dávila Linares, J.M. (1995), 'Turismo y patrimonio histórico y cultural', *Estudios Turísticos*, 126: 161–177.

Viceriat, P. (1993), 'Hotel chains', *European Economy*, 3: 365–379.

Vincent, J.A. (1980), 'The political economy of Alpine development: tourism or agricultural in St Maurice', *Sociologica Ruralis*, 20: 250–271.

Vitte, P. (1995), 'Les problèmes de l'agritourisme en France', *Bulletin de l'Association des Géographes Français*, 72: 14–23.

Voogd, H. (1988), 'Recreational developments in gravel workings: the Limburg experience', in B. Goodall and G.J. Ashworth (eds), *Marketing and the Tourism Industry: the Promotion of Destination Regions*. London: Routledge, pp. 101–110.

Vukonić, B. (1992) 'Medugorje's religion and tourism connection', *Annals of Tourism Research*, 19: 79–91.

Vukonić, B. (1996), *Tourism and Religion*. Oxford: Pergamon.

Węcławowicz, G. (1996), *Contemporary Poland: Space and Society*. London: UCL Press.

Walsh, M.E. (1993), 'Republic of Ireland', in T. Baum (ed.), *Human Resource Issues in International Tourism*. Oxford: Butterworth-Heinemann, pp. 201–216.

Walvin, J (1978), *Beside the Seaside: a Social History of the Popular Seaside Holiday*. London: Mansell.

Wanhill, S. (1996), 'Regional policy', in R. Thomas (ed.), *The Hospitality Industry, Tourism and Europe*. London: Cassell, pp. 93–116.

Waters, S.R. (1967), 'Trends in international tourism', *Development Digest*, 5: 57–62.

Welford, R. (1996), 'Environmental policy', in R. Thomas (ed.), *The Hospitality Industry, Tourism and Europe*. London: Cassell.

White, P. (1987), 'Italy: grand tour to package tour', *Geographical Magazine*, 59: 554–559.

White, P.E. (1976), 'Tourism and economic development in the rural environment', in R. Lee and P. Ogden (eds), *Economy and Society in the EEC: Spatial Perspectives*. Farnborough: Saxon House.

Whitford, R. (1993), 'Will tourism pick up in Hungary?', *Business Eastern Europe*, 22: 1–2.

Wiesmann, U. (1994), *A Concept of Sustainable Resource Use and Its Implications for Research in a Dynamic Regional Context*. Bern: University of Bern, Institute of Geography.

Williams, A.M. (1981), 'Bairros clandestinos: illegal housing in Portugal', *Geografisch Tijdschrift*, 15: 24–34.

Williams, A.M. (1993), 'Tourism and economic transformation in Greece and Portugal', *Inforgeo*, 6: 7–20.

Williams, A.M. (1994), *The European Community: the Contradictions of Integration*, 2nd edn. Oxford: Blackwell.

Williams, A.M. (1995). 'Capital and the transnationalisation of tourism', in A. Montanari and A.M. Williams (eds), *European Tourism: Regions, Spaces and Restructuring*. Chichester: Wiley, pp. 163–176.

Williams, A.M. (1996), 'Mass tourism and the international tour companies', in M. Barke, J. Towner and M.T. Newton (eds), *Tourism in Spain: Critical Issues*. Wallingford: CAB International, pp. 19–36.

Williams, A.M. (1997), 'Tourism and uneven development in the Mediterranean', in L. Proudfoot, B. Smith and R. King (eds), *The Mediterranean: Environment and Society*. London: Edward Arnold.

Williams, A.M., King, R. and Warnes, A.M. (1997a), 'A place in the sun: International retirement migration from northern to southern Europe', *European Urban and Regional Studies*, 4: 115–134.

Williams, A.M. and Montanari, A. (1995). 'Introduction: tourism and restructuring in Europe', in A. Montanari and A.M. Williams (eds), *European Tourism: Regions, Spaces and Restructuring*. Chichester: Wiley, pp. 1–16.

Williams, A.M. and Patterson, G. (1998), 'An empire lost but a province gained: a cohort analysis of British international retirement migration to the Algarve', *International Journal of Population Geography*, 4: in press.

Williams, A.M. and Shaw, G. (1988), 'Tourism: candyfloss industry or job-generator', *Town Planning Review*, 59: 81–104.

Williams, A.M. and Shaw, G. (1991), 'Tourism and development: introduction', in A.M. Willliams and G. Shaw (eds), *Tourism and Economic Development: Western European Experiences*. London: Belhaven, pp. 1–12.

Williams, A.M. and Shaw, G. (1994). 'Tourism: Opportunities, Challenges and Contradictions in the EC', in M. Blacksell and A.M. Williams (eds), *The European Challenge: Geography, Development and the European Community*. Oxford: Oxford University Press, pp. 301–320.

Williams, A.M. and Shaw, G. (1995). 'Tourism and regional development: polarization and new forms of production in the UK', *Tijdschrift voor Economische en Sociale Geografie*, 86: 50–63.

Williams, A.M. and G. Shaw (eds) (1996), *Tourism, Leisure, Nature Protection and Agri-tourism: Principles, Partnerships and Practice*. Exeter/Brussels: the EPE (European Partners for the Environment) Workbook Series for Implementing Sustainability in Europe.

Williams, A.M., Shaw, G., and Greenwood, J. (1989), 'From tourist to tourism entrepreneur, from consumption to production: evidence from Cornwall, England', *Environment and Planning A*, 21: 1639–1653.

Witak, A. and Lewandowska, U. (eds) (1996), *Poland: the Natural Choice*. Warsaw: Sport i Turystyka.

Wolf, K. and Jurczek, P. (1986), *Geographie der Freizeit und des Tourismus*. Stuttgart: Uni-Taschenbücher.

Wolfson, M. (1964), 'Government's role in tourism development', *Development Digest*, 5: 50–56.

World Conference of Tourism Ministers (ed.) (1994), Statements for the World Conference of Tourism Ministers, Osaka.

Wright, R. (1996), 'Living in awe of the Bucharest fixer', *The European*, 22 (August).

WTO (World Tourism Organisation) (1984), *Economic Review of World Tourism*. Madrid: World Tourism Organisation.

WTO (World Tourism Organization) (1994), *Yearbook of Tourism Statistics*, 46th edn, 2 vols. Madrid: WTO.

WTO (World Tourism Organization) (1995), *Yearbook of Tourism Statistics*, 47th edn, 2 vols. Madrid: WTO.

WTO (World Tourism Organization) (1996a), *Compendium of Tourism Statistics 1990–1994*, 16th edn. Madrid: WTO.

WTO (World Tourism Organization) (1996b), *Yearbook of Tourism Statistics*, 48th edn, 2 vols. Madrid: WTO.

WTO (World Tourism Organization) (1996c and 1998), http://www.world-tourism.org/esta/statserv.htm (statistical data 1996).

WTO (World Tourism Organization) (1997), *Yearbook of Tourism Statistics*, 49th edn, 2 vols. Madrid: WTO.

WTTC (World Travel and Tourism Council) (1995), *Travel and Tourism: A New Economic Perspective*. Brussels: WTTC.

Yale, P. (1995), *The Business of Tour Operations*. Harlow: Longman.

Yearbook of Nordic Statistics (various years). Copenhagen: Nordic Council of Ministers.

Young, G. (1973), *Tourism: Blessing or Blight?* Harmondsworth: Penguin.

Young, Lord (1985), *Pleasure, Leisure and Jobs—the Business of Tourism.* London: HMSO.

Zacharatos, G.A. (1986), *Tourist Consumption: the Method of Calculation and Its Use for Research on the Impact of Tourism on the National Economy.* Athens: CPER (in Greek).

Zahn, U. (1973), *Der Fremdenverkehr an der spanischen Mittelmeerküste. Eine verglechende geographische Untersuchung.* Regensburg: Regensburger Geographische Schriften, 2.

Zeiner, M. and Harrer, B. (1992), *Die Ausgabenstruktur im übernachtenden Fremdenverkehr in der Bundesrepublik Deutschland (ohne Beitrittsgebiet).* Munich: Schriftenreihe des Deutschen Wirtschaftswissenschaftlichen Instituts für Fremdenverkehr, 43.

Zeiner, M., Harrer, B. and Scherr, S. (1993), *Die Ausgabenstruktur im übernachtenden Fremdenverkehr in den neuen Bundeländern.* Munich: Schriftenreihe des Deutschen Wirtschaftswissenschaftlichen Instituts für Fremdenverkehr, 45.

Zimmerman, F. (1985a), 'Der Fremdenverkehr in Österreich—Skizze einer praxisorientierten räumlichen Fremdenverkehrsforschung aus geographischer Sicht', *Klagenfurter Geographische Schriften*, 6: 253–284.

Zimmerman, F. (1985b), 'Ausflugsverkehr und Kurzurlaube in Österreich unter Berücksichtigung der Überlagerung mit dem mittel- und längerfristigen Reiseverkehr', *Berichte zur Raumforschung und Raumplanung*, 29: 3–13.

Zimmerman, F. (1986a), 'Day trips and short-term tourism in Austria and their competition with long-term tourism', in *International Geographical Union, Big City Tourism.* Berlin: Commission of Tourism and Leisure, Dietrich Reimer Verlag.

Zimmermann, F.M. (1991), 'Austria: rapid expansion of winter tourism and problems with the summer season', in G. Shaw and A. Williams (eds), *Tourism and Economic Development. The Western European Experience*, 2nd edn. London: Belhaven, pp. 153–172.

Zimmermann, F.M. (1992), 'Issues, problems and future trends in the Austrian Alps: Changes within traditional tourism', in Proceedings of the Vail Conference on 'Recreation Trends and Mountain Resort Development', Burnaby, British Colombia: Simon Fraser University, pp. 160–170.

Zimmermann, F.M. (1995), 'The Alpine region: regional restructuring opportunities and constraints in a fragile environment', in A. Montanari and A.M. Williams (eds), *European Tourism: Regions, Spaces and Restructuring.* Chichester: Wiley, pp. 19–40.

Zimmermann, F.M. (1997), 'Future perspectives of tourism—traditional versus new destinations', in M. Oppermann (ed.), *Pacific Rim Tourism.* Oxon, New York: CAB International, pp. 231–239.

ZRSS (Zavod Republike Slovenije za Statistiko) (1995), *Slovenija v številkah 1995.* Ljubljana: Gospodarska Zbornica Slovenije.

Zucker, W.H. (1986), *Urlaubsreisen 1985. Einige Ergebnisse der Reiseanalyse 1985. Kurzfassung.* Starnberg: Studienkreis für Tourismus.

Zuddas, D. (1997), *Tourism and Economic Development in Sardinia: the Role of Entrepreneurship.* Exeter: University of Exeter, Department of Geography, Tourism Research Group, Discussion Paper No. 10.

Index